THE GOLDEN TALKING-SHOP

The Golden Talking-shop

The Oxford Union Debates Empire, World War, Revolution, and Women

Selected and edited with a historical narrative by
EDWARD PEARCE

OXFORD
UNIVERSITY PRESS

OXFORD

UNIVERSITY PRESS

Great Clarendon Street, Oxford, OX2 6DP,
United Kingdom

Oxford University Press is a department of the University of Oxford.
It furthers the University's objective of excellence in research, scholarship,
and education by publishing worldwide. Oxford is a registered trade mark of
Oxford University Press in the UK and in certain other countries

First Edition published in 2016

Impression: 1

Published in the United States of America by Oxford University Press
198 Madison Avenue, New York, NY 10016, United States of America

British Library Cataloguing in Publication Data
Data available

Library of Congress Control Number: 2016934364

ISBN 978–0–19–871723–2

Printed in Great Britain by
Clays Ltd, St Ives plc

For Deanna

ACKNOWLEDGEMENTS

Essential to the production of this book has been the detailed and pains-taking work of my wife Deanna, and Jackie Pritchard, both wonderfully able to identify muddle and sort it out.

Thanks are also due for their general helpfulness as staff of the Oxford Union Old Library, to its friendly staff:

Su Lockley

Niels Sampath

Diane Hackett

Valerie Beautemps

Thanks also to Jenny Nugee for last-minute searching and finding, and Cecily Pearce for the technical wisdom of her generation.

CONTENTS

PRINTING STYLE

The debates presented here are wearily transcribed from bound volumes of the *Oxford Magazine* (OM) published between 1895–6 and 1956–7. That publication, unsurprisingly, when reporting debates over sixty years, did not follow an identical format or typographical practice. Sometimes, it would give highly compressed accounts, with speakers marginalized. At its worst, OM fell back on snap comments about speaking style only, scorning what speakers had said–a practice not worth reproducing here! The magazine also intermittently, but reliably, ignored the results of voting!

Happily, at other times, particularly over the later period, extra space was found to quote some speakers at 300 words and more, by way of direct speech. Unhelpfully, the magazine also did runs of employing only indirect speech, specifically at the start of my chosen selection, in 1896 and again in 1909. This would be done very thinly to material well worth reproduction. They would mark the practice by shifting from roman to italic typeface and back. To complicate matters further, italics were reliably used for interspersed comments. They are now used only for direct speech. So, to avoid confusion with an original account following this practice, I have used roman type for these OM comments and my own observations. This is also the practice for longer editorial narratives, setting out background events and issues. Readers are asked to concentrate on the living argument irrespective of the changing face in which it appears.

Personally, I would like to see the whole university marching down the High in uniform; nothing would please me more—a great thing for the University.

Col. J. C. B. Eastwood, Officer commanding OUOTC, 3 November 1910

It is impossible to live in Oxford without realising that our civilisation is on the wane ...

Mr Donald, 5 February 1948

PREFACE

First of all, what this book is not: anyone looking for a charming account of personalities, 'characters,' equally charming eccentricities, and institutional gossip, will go hungry. There are a number of such books. Herbert Morrah's celebration (1923) of the society's centenary is amiable and quite useful about developments. Christopher Hollis's account of 1965 sets out how things work and is a good guide book, written with a cool touch. However, in so many studies, there hovers the ambience of 'Dear old Psalmanazar-Smith who, as I recall, later became Archdeacon of Mold...' However, avoiding that sort of thing does not mean blank indifference to individual players, brilliant, absurd, or, as often here, dynastic.

The Mr M. H. Macmillan (Balliol), pronounced opponent of the pre-First War Tories before becoming, as Conservative Prime Minister, one of the truly interesting politicians of the last hundred years, is not to be short-changed. Missing the presidency, to which he had been elected, for the unpleasantness of 1914, Macmillan would say that he 'had been sent down by the Kaiser'. Quick accounts of the careers and general detail of the many speakers, later achieving distinction or disgrace, are interpolated at *their* first appearance, as is background information on notable visitors.

Nevertheless, this is essentially a book about debate, opinion, reaction, and argument. In 2003, I published *Reform: The Fight for the 1832 Reform Act*, a very well-received account of the furious battle for that historic legislation. It differed from previous studies, published in 1914 and 1973, by quoting, deep and wide, courtesy of the London Library, from *Hansards* of the day. As an old sketch-writer, I relied on the vitality of debate, especially old debate. This study follows the same premise. It is concerned to draw evidence from the debaters on public questions: morality, art, manners, religion for sure, but, most of all, politics. The glib and ready mistake of patronizing the Union as some do, for a self-indulgent coterie of privileged persons, sounding off in imitation of elders and supposed betters, is not my option. At its best, the Oxford Union Society is a seriously valuable institution; at its earnest worst, striving light comedy. Students in a great university, taking the world seriously and engaging with its crises, follies, and desperate predicaments, are taking themselves and events seriously—as they should. Oxford students in 1900 were right to have views, for and against, about the South African War and, fifty years later, Apartheid, nuclear weapons, as, going back a bit, they had for the great battle between Free Trade and the Corn Laws. It would be equally right and natural to fret about Welsh Church disestablishment and Keynesian economics.

The famous, but relatively few, larkish debates, their topics staged for light relief, hold up far less well when read decades later. Stars of the Quipping Tendency, greatly admired figures of their day, like Hilaire Belloc, Philip Guedalla, and especially the future Monsignor Ronald Knox, read flat and unfunny, G. K. Chesterton rather better. Ironically, debates about religious and moral questions stand up quite well. The contributions of two successive archbishops of York, William Temple and Cyril Garbett, still carry moral distinction—though interestingly, they spoke briefly here about political rather than doctrinal morality—good Liberals with Socialist sympathies both! Yet this society had been conceived for the first debates in private rooms at Christ Church, opening on 5 April 1823, as a society much given to discussing historical morality and doctrine. Beyond our period and the debating chamber, the intensity of young Gladstone's opinions or indeed those mid-century, of Lord Robert Cecil (future third Marquess of Salisbury and three times Prime Minister), on the 'Nature of Faith' and, sometimes, perhaps more important, ecclesiology—church forms, procedures, and practice—could grow impassioned out of sight.

The politics voiced here pre-First War, can be startlingly brutal, full of social Darwinism: *I see a connexion between Liberalism and degeneracy and watch the sinking birth rate with a rising heart, for it means that we are not perpetuating the dregs of Society.* Uttered by a Mr J. H. Allen visiting from Cambridge, it spoke for a large tranche of Conservative opinion before 1914, reflecting from its day a seam of heroic insensibility. For good, bad, and middling, undergraduate debates distil the age.

In the period covered here, 1890s to 1950s, church doctrine will go down and partisan politics come up, accompanied by all the secular causes awaiting active government policy. Accordingly, fervent Union activists periodically got things wrong by way of violent contradiction of yesterday. Delusion about the Soviet Union through the 1930s and immediately after the Second War, the sort of thinking which drew the hostile focus of Orwell's writings, is here in some force. One honourable member tells us that 'General Stalin is the greatest soldier and statesman of the Century.' Then again, in the mid-1930s, an intelligent and very civil German student, Adolf Schleppegren, makes a defence of Hitler's expansion in terms of Germany's mistreatment at Versailles and vengeful post-war French adventures in the Rhineland. Later, he is understood to have been an associate of the anti-regime Kreisauer Circle. The two contradictory facts about him are instructive far beyond a student debate. There were reports of his having been shot, later corrected.

One speaker in the not too serious 1920s identifies himself happily, as might any lepidopterist or badminton player, as 'President of the University Fascist Association'. Against which, some of the very best, wisest speeches found in these pages come, against prejudice, from future judges—Gerald Gardiner, Herbert du Parcq, Kenneth Diplock, and James Comyn. Many of the worst are delivered, with golden self-assurance, by heirs and younger sons, comic relief with noble particles, uninstructably selfish and ideological about it. Until very late, talk is of 'The Empire' whilst until the late 1940s—Scots, Welsh, and Irish be damned— the United Kingdom of Great Britain and Ireland is always serenely 'England'.

However, though some young men, some of the time, make fools of themselves, many more gravely take on central concerns. They talk unemployment, trade figures, and the League of Nations. The Union would handle, over many decades, the long considered prospect of Indian independence, the Irish Question in succeeding versions, the Welfare State, trade union power, and, with a muffled bang at the end of this coverage, Britain's invasion in 1956 of the Isthmus of Suez. They are all here, or most of them— the issues over which parties and people argued across seven decades.

Many of the young men, passionate in ardent causes, went off to plead in probate disputes, buy and sell advantageously, occupy offices in Whitehall, or indeed, become judges and bishops. And of course, the politics of Oxford produced a steady stream of active, often able, Ministers and MPs. The Union was both finishing school and, as it were, *starting* school. It was serious about the ideas which divide politics. What speakers thought across the period covered here is an excellent reflection of shifting political opinion amongst everyone who, at that time, intensely or casually, held political opinions. The period itself has been selected precisely for its dates—running from the eve of the Second South African War to the invasion of Suez: high rapture of adventurist Empire to its effective end.

The Union is a running, unofficial parliament of prejudice, serious reflection, intense conviction, or long learning curve. As such, it is something else. The actual debates of the Union are, with rare exceptions like 'King and Country', not generally known, nor part of even academic historic coverage of the period. So within the limits of very variable reporting, the reports of the weekly *Oxford Magazine*, a fair idea of those contested opinions has been gathered together. This account is meant as a source book of the moving stream of reasonably intelligent public opinion. It shows what young people, at any rate AB young people, thought and what they changed their minds over, the assumptions and hesitancies of another age, the charm and awfulness of immediate history.

Entertainment, amusing incidents, the great people who visited, are well enough and fully present, but an account of what these young people thought and believed and which prejudices contended, should constitute a modest, but instructive piece of history.

Introduction: Early Days

Before there was an Oxford Union, there were undergraduates meeting to argue about things. They called themselves the United Debating Society. The issues they disputed would be 'the historical, previous to the present century and the philosophical, exclusive of religion'. In rooms at Christ Church, they stirred into argument in April 1823, with the question, 'Was the revolution under Cromwell to be attributed to the tyrannical conduct of Charles or to the democratic spirit of the time?' Anticipating the sensation-creating King and Country debate of 1933, by more than a century, this dispute was picked up by *John Bull*, a rabidly Tory paper, hot against the treason of serious thought. The *Daily Mail* of its day persuaded itself that Mr Wilberforce of Christ Church (a future bishop) more or less approved of beheading King Charles 1.

The Proctors of the same day (and long afterwards) were not liberal nor understanding, though they could be beneficially lazy. The Vice-Chancellor at this date, interim long-stop of Oxford's erratic authority, was Jenkyns of Balliol, averse to the university getting into the papers. The society was saved for the time being by the intervention of an undergraduate, but an undergraduate trembling at the edge of becoming a duke. So Mr Vane of Oriel (soon afterwards Duke of Cleveland), spoke up for Wilberforce and against 'misreporting'. The Debating Society was saved by social deference.

To its credit, the society could not long sustain the tedium of the non-controversial. Early nineteenth-century Oxford was intensely religious or, at any rate, unable to stop talking about it. This was the era of

Tractarianism. Tract No. 90 claimed that the Anglican Church had always been part of the Roman Catholic Church without knowing it. This arose by way of the corkscrew reasoning that apostolic succession had been assured for all future curates and archbishops by the shrewd Anthony Kitchen, Bishop of Llandaff, cheerfully taking the oaths on the accession of Elizabeth and bringing his long since laid-on Catholic validity with him.

Oxford was always more godly than Cambridge. Accordingly, the passionately disputed arguments tended to be pious ones. At the same time, back in Westminster, not very godly Whigs and the Liberal Tory George Canning wanted to give the real Catholics what Americans would later call 'Civil Rights'. This carried implications for Ireland, still reliably misgoverned on grounds, superficially of religion, actually land ownership. An amendment by a Lord Mahon, presumably an Irish Protestant landowner, stating that though intolerance of belief was a bad thing, keeping the people holding the wrong one out of positions of authority was a good one. The society seems to have taken this neat little parcel of self-interest seriously enough to break out in furious controversy and attract the attention of the Proctors.

The prospect of dissolution hovering, a shrewd member, Wrangham of Oriel, counselled pre-emption. Not waiting to be dissolved, the society, on 3 December 1825, shrewdly dissolved itself. Thus, untainted by the chastisement of authority, it could, despite a Proctor's later message instructing members to return to their colleges, coolly take note of it and carry right on.

In 1829, the society, pleasantly pressed for space, moved to the High and a decent property, known as Wyatt's Rooms, plus territory nearby to serve as a reading room, and continued debating and—hopefully—reading. A good deal of both concerned the rights and wrongs of the seventeenth century.

The politics and occasional non-politics debated here reflected the fact that the politics of Oxford were dominated, as any parliament would be, by the presence of William Gladstone. But in those days, Gladstone was as devout a Tory as he was a High Churchman. He would soon deplore the Ultra-Tory Wellington government of the late 1820s for its betrayal of Conservative principles! A motion that 'The administration of the Duke of Wellington is undeserving the confidence of the Country' has provided a formula for descending generations of Union members to assert the same unworthiness of a lengthening list of Prime Ministers. Like so much else in life, it is one of those Oxford things. The real, dangerously liberal, Gladstone, of Turkish outrages and Irish Home Rule, stayed in the wings while his younger incarnation, the son of a family in the slave trade, amended a motion for West Indian emancipation by calling for any emancipation to be gradual and achieved by Christian education.

When it came to reform, *parliamentary* reform, the future Lord Selborne (a reliable reactionary, whose descendant Lord Wolmer is a vivid patch of blue in early twentieth-century debates displayed here), appears as Palmer of Magdalen, sure that reform was principally an attack on Oxford, and that Union funds should help finance its defeat. The Union was always liable to splits: Conservative and Liberal, High Church and Low. It was too, not so much privileged, as socially incestuous. Eton and Winchester, with occasional interlopers from lesser public schools, made up the stars and walking-on parts alike; and their colleges, Christ Church, Trinity, and Balliol, took most of the offices most of the time. Grammar school boys, never mind Ruskin students, were unimaginable. Black balls were ready and available—this was after all, a Gentlemen's club[1] free to exclude any and every applicant to whom they denied that weasel name.

Ruskin himself, a Christ Church man, made a great impact with a speech in 1838, on the contested virtues of the ancient and contemporary, which, at any rate, got the Union away from morality.

It was of course, a society full of aspirant parsons in a university full of aspirant parsons. They would later enjoy a life beyond the university through votes which could be referred to life members. The number was remarked of mildly liberal votes carried on a division in the chamber, then subsequently reversed after the post had carried voting papers to rectories and vicarages from Berwick to Bognor. The same clenched clerical fist

3

would be aimed in 1843, at Anglicans gathered for debate at Convocation, aimed by Tractarians (the High Church party), over the affront to Anglican virtue of the university granting an honorary degree to the US Minister Edward Everett, a Unitarian and thus denier of the Virgin birth!

More usefully, the Union would turn, in the 1840s, to finding better premises than Wyatt's. Dr Bliss, Principal of St Mary's Hall,[2] who identified a site in St Michael Street, and, open-handed as well as trouble-taking, would put in £3,000 of his own money and think up the life membership scheme for steady funding. Sometimes, Oxford, shadowing the immediate politics of Parliament, engages in agreement, then dissent, with Westminster. Over the Reform Bill, Gladstone had moved (and carried) an amendment that 'The Ministry has unwisely introduced and most unscrupulously forwarded, a measure which not only threatens to break up the very formations of the social order as well as materially to forward the views of those who are pursuing this object throughout the civilised world.' This meant France which had just rid itself of Charles X and the royal Ultras.

When it came to Free Trade, the second great liberal cause of the nineteenth century, commanding general controversy, Gladstone had gone to a better place. He stood at the elbow of Robert Peel, a Prime Minister painfully but absolutely convinced that the Corn Laws were an irrational burden on trade and people. In Oxford, the great name was now Robert Cecil, Lord Robert, future Third Marquess and, further into the future, main prime ministerial option to Gladstone. The Cecils descended directly from William, Lord Burghley, Elizabeth's great Minister through his son Robert, Earl of Salisbury, similarly valuable to James 1. They had though lain politically fallow since the first earl's death in 1612, distinguished and inactive, apart from the joint-postmaster-generalship, under Pitt, of the sixth earl which won them a step up to marquess in, of all years, 1789!

Leading the Conservative Party as resentful deputy to Disraeli, outsider, novelist, vivid personality, not serious about God, the third marquess was never happy nor often loyal. He would be, at Oxford and in Westminster, a very intelligent, if often wrong High Tory. His serious interest in science and general intellectual curiosity did not lead him to political innovation. His speech and vote in the Union against admission of Jews to full rights was not anti-Semitic, rather the religious objection of a doctrinaire Anglican to the advance of anyone outside the Church of England to anything. He was an Anglican Clericalist, believing in its pre-eminence and privilege, not something readily understood as a *religious* conviction. While Gladstone is rightly identified as a man moving steadily leftward all his life, Lord Robert at the Oxford Union and the third marquess, as Prime Minister, would share the same fidelities and oppressions.

At Oxford, four years after Protection was abolished in 1846, he formed a society to campaign *for* Protection. In the long debate on the subject of 14 February 1850, his speech might have been a model for the speeches of seventy years later during the Lloyd George Budget/Parliament Bill crises, in which landed gentlemen like the nineteenth Lord Willoughby de Broke complained that the entitlements of land had been diminished to make way for the vulgar middle-class exertions of trade. It was generally agreed that the Oxford version of this lament had been seen off at the Union in 1850 by the evidently detailed, fact-heavy, professional case made by Edward Lomer of Oriel, whose brilliant promise would be frustrated by early death.

Meanwhile the two great men of Oxford Union politics, Cecil and Gladstone, graduated to become, between 1874 and 1894, alternate Prime Ministers of the United Kingdom. Gladstone had been elected Member for the university in 1847 and was turned out in 1865. Although known to be a Peelite (that is a Free Trader within the Tory Party) at the first date, he had still the credit of his earlier High Toryism. Salisbury, doggedly consistent, would *hate* Peel for the rest of his life and bring up his children to think of him as a traitor. By the time of Gladstone's electoral defeat by the historian Gathorne Hardy, the Peelites had coalesced with the Liberals and the university knew its duty.

The Union itself remained essentially Conservative, and would be so when the debates, printed here, began. But there was opposition to it. What were called 'Positivists', essentially radicals rejecting taboos, began to speak and be heard. They argued for divorce, were prepared to talk about birth control, and set the Union, quite often, debating the death penalty. They were tacitly less than orthodox in religious conviction. In our terms, they were Social Liberals and beginning to be less than assured Economic Liberals. Heads of houses worried about them. Prominent in this group was John Morley who, at the end of a long career as Liberal MP and Minister, would, in August 1914, be one of the three members of the Cabinet to vote against a declaration of war.

Such high purpose existed and shone, but it stood at the edge of the crowd, as did the earnest disputants of religion. Serious people of any sort existed in an Oxford University much of which went to the races and threw bottles. The piety and the positivism, also the academic strivers, existed in a territory, most marked in certain colleges, notably Christ Church, very many of whose occupants existed for the pursuit of sport, whores, and practical jokes of a brutal kind, together with contempt for intellectual distinction, serious taste, or opinion, and who constituted in effect, a landed mob. They were not at the heart of the Union, but were always liable to invade it. The ability of the Union to get itself involved with Ruskin or Rossetti and foster Burne-Jones and Morris was impressive. And even if Rossetti's murals in the old debating chamber faded through the chemical incompatibilities of that paint on that plaster, the undertaking was to its credit and against the university norm.[3]

At the Union however, the bloods would for a while find a political version of themselves. For a Conservative group to call itself after Disraeli, or indeed Salisbury, is most natural. To take its name from Strafford is not very good even as a joke—which the Conservative Strafford Club of the early 1890s wasn't. In the text transcribed here, readers will find a young gentleman saying at the height of Parnellist and Irish contention that what Ireland needed was a Strafford. Now serious history can make a case for Lord Strafford, Thomas Wentworth being less harsh and more understanding of the Catholic Irish than his authoritarian measures as Lord Deputy in the 1630s suggest. This however, was not what the bloods of the Strafford Club meant. They thought, after Parnell had made Irish nationalism serious business, that the blackest authoritarianism attributed to Strafford was just what Ireland needed. In the years after 1916, it would be applied—with what consequences we and Ireland know.

The Strafford Club is aptly described by the temperate Union historian Christopher Hollis as bringing 'a not very healthy element into Union politics'.[4] Before the word was coined (I think), they introduced a slate and, in the late 1880s, enjoyed a run of domination across the six presidencies they took. And as Hollis points out, they reliably behaved aggressively, delightedly ready to shout down; the Strafford point of view especially on Ireland made it a welcome venue for defending the indefensible. The Attorney General, Webster, would defend at a Strafford Club meeting the government's ready acceptance of the April 1887 sensational Piggott forgeries which had Parnell approving of the Phoenix Park murders!

It was at about this time that the Union made the important move of occasionally inviting great names, usually from politics, to come as guest speakers. The very first were, incongruously, John Morley, that voter against declaration of the First World War, and Lord Randolph Churchill, a man after the Straffordians' heart, speaking a week apart. Such was the Union's comfortable standing in the political world that *The Times* worried a little—indulgently.

This brings the introduction close to the point where it begins to merge with transcribed text. However, F. E. Smith and Hilaire Belloc,[5] undergraduate performers, stylists, the Fast Eddies of competitive debate, were creating something new—*performance* debate. There could have been a whip-round for the professionals at any of their battles. Smith, the cynic who as Lord Chancellor would restructure English land law, but encouraged a notion of nothing he ardently proclaimed mattering very much, was the antithesis of Hilaire Belloc. Half French and going on about it, Catholic and going on about that, Belloc was truly funny in light verse, but fundamentally poisonous, with anti-Semitism—the real, spitting *Anti-Dreyfusard* thing—still churning in the early 1950s in the senility which Evelyn Waugh, another malignant soul, would record.

Politics itself was changing and the Union with it. Imperialism was shining across Africa, turning young men into flag-silly boasters about national greatness. The irony of all this being proclaimed in the last few years before the long graves called trenches were dug and a multitude of young men put into them, would have been extravagant in fiction. It is where we shall start in recorded speech.

1

Our Empire: Pride Before Fall

30 January 1896–19 October 1899

Topics of debate: A French alliance?/British South Africa Company/Women's degrees/Egypt/American alliance?/Liberal menace/Bimetallism/England at Zenith/ Danger of democracy/Unemployment/the unemployable?/Penrhyn Quarries/ Naval spending/Ireland/Votes for Women/Popular literature/Fashoda Crisis/ International morality/Home Rule/American alliance?/Democracy played out?/A People's University—sapping manhood?/'Dishonourable imperialism'/Anti-ritualism/Financial policy/Lord Rosebery?/Popular education/Dreyfus at Rennes.

This chapter is heavy with Empire and War. The Union discussed other things of course: bimetallism, women's degrees, Egypt, a university education for workers, the eternities of Home Rule, our allegedly sapped manhood, the recent power struggle in a Welsh quarry and in France, the latest mis-trial of Captain Dreyfus. But imperial business—the immediate doings of Cecil Rhodes's British South Africa Company (empire-building by commercial venture), the need for a French alliance or perhaps an American alliance, the Fashoda incident, and in particular, a debate on 'England at its Zenith'—all of them pertain to the febrile mood surrounding a potential colonial war. The Union has people rejoicing in 'our greatness', people fearful that we are about to be tested—tested by war. The cult of 'National Efficiency' does uneasily hint at some sparing sort of welfare provision, but, proclaimed by men like Alfred Milner, such benevolence was part of the business of building a nation of the fit and strong—something requisite for a rather brutal national greatness.

It isn't very pleasant, but the mood is also anxious—jittery about 'Greatness'. Perhaps after all, the English as a nation might soon, in the words of Housman (whose *A Shropshire Lad* had just been published), be making way 'for haler men than they'. The key-note is not reform as a humane virtue, but fraught, snappy scrambling with a heavy hint of threatening catastrophe. There is a lot of near-hysteria set out amid the conceit. It can turn up as shrill bombast on the Conservative side of party debate in the Union. Witness the Honourable Algernon Cecil, two-star gentry, cousin of the current governing family of that name, informing the House that 'The country would be plunged into an ocean of evil under a Liberal administration.' The Honourable Algernon was only an exaggeration. The House reflects a remote society in which class supremacy is cheerfully proclaimed. Witness the Mr Vaughan who impressed the Oxford Magazine commentator with '*his antipathy toward anyone who had not an ancestry of 600 years from father to son. Those who failed in this "necessity," i.e. the Americans, were riff-raff, vulgar, uncultured etc.*' Lord Mauleverer of Charles Hamilton's *Greyfriars* school stories is a steady presence.

We are at the start of the sixty years chosen here to search Union reports. It has been chosen as a period which takes in ambition and nightmare. Beginning in contemplation of imperial expansion in Southern Africa and fearing the rise of Germany, we will, sixty years on, with two world wars fought and the Empire of national greatness brought dramatically down, be talking earnestly about a multi-racial Commonwealth. Meanwhile Oxford debate is taking place at the start of a road ending at Suez 1956—late, last, fraught, and twitching assertion of imperial authority. Half-way through the coming twentieth century, we will be brought, first, to a series of contrived accommodations over an illegally seized but not realistically re-seizable waterway. Soon after will follow invasion of the Canal Zone and in a sort of rattle, less than a week of engagement, expulsion by market forces and American requirement. After which it will be a calling of historic quits by men present in this account like the Union Librarian immediately before the First World War, Mr M. H. Macmillan (Balliol).

In 1896, the government is Conservative and the Prime Minister Lord Salisbury. The essential mood is an odd mixture of comfort and anxiety. Irish Home Rule, great and reliable disturber of the political peace, has been not so much defeated as satisfactorily pushed away. Gladstone, who had started all that up in 1886, making it a great cause of government, is 84 years old and almost gone from the scene. The Natural Party of Government sits comfortably in office. The Opposition is split and the third Marquess of Salisbury, conservative in every sense imaginable, is Prime Minister for the third time.

Ahead of the word being coined to describe a Do-nothing French ministry,[1] Robert Arthur Gascoyne-Cecil is in religion, and economics, an *immobiliste*, a doctrinaire Anglican in very political terms, often seeming to put the Establishment above the Resurrection. Cecil's religion is sectarian, an institutional Anglicanism—ecclesiological rather than spiritual, not a lot loving or caring, and altogether connected with authority. Witness his Commons vote (much earlier, in 1858) against relieving Jewish MPs from taking the (Christian) oath of that House. Told that this would penalize *sincere* Jews, unable to body-swerve their convictions, Cecil said that it was the sincere Jew whom he dreaded,[2] 'someone hostile to all, in a religious sense, that a Christian body swore to uphold'. The Conservative Party occupies for him a similar niche of reverence. The wide streak of obsession in Salisbury had never forgiven the treason of Robert Peel, the rational man whose intellectual conversion to Free Trade had, in 1846, split the party and kept it, barring interludes, for almost thirty years, inexcusably, out of office. His language and behaviour at that time had been reliably virulent. The young Lord Robert had raged like any zealot at a lost argument and cheap bread achieved, and raged quietly on. It was a personal Clause Four and the mood was hereditary. His son, the Bishop Lord William Cecil, would react thirty years later, to the sight of a copy of Guizot's biography of Peel, with the words 'I detest Peel. He's a traitor.'[3]

Salisbury had replaced anger with an uninflected certainty—and he chose the key for his party's overall outlook. Practical and without the clutter of reservation, his thinking was still, even in the mid-1890s, narrowly pessimistic, low on the zeal and passion of the ruthless young men breaking onto the scene over South Africa, but pragmatically accommodating them. He was content to have Joseph Chamberlain in his Cabinet as a commanding figure. Chamberlain had split the Liberals back in 1886 over Irish Home Rule, and would duly split the Tories over Imperial Protection.

Ironically, Chamberlain defended imperialism on the grounds that *internally* the Empire practised Free Trade. 'We in our colonial policy, as fast as we acquire new territory and develop it, develop it as trustees of civilisation for the commerce of the world. We offer in those countries over which our flag floats, the same opportunities, the same field to foreigners that we offer to our own subjects...' The point was that even with internal Free Trade, an empire was a trading territory for exports and South Africa was hard wealth. Diamonds were an economy's best friend; the long-term export trade with such wealthy, developing territory, excellent business for that girl as mother country.

Salisbury's caution did not exclude the accommodation of furiously driving aggrandizement, promoted late in the last decade of the century, by Cecil Rhodes's British South Africa Company, originally based in Mashonaland (later part of Southern Rhodesia, now of Zimbabwe). Already taking rich returns from mining, Rhodes would, in consort with the friends he had found in British politics, wage aggressive war.

The First Boer War—limited conflict with Dutch settlers of the Transvaal, which had been annexed by Lord Carnarvon for Disraeli's government in 1877—ended with defeat by those Boers (1881) at Majuba Hill. Gladstone, by then Prime Minister, pre- and under-imperial, had responded by readily returning effective government of the Transvaal to the Boers. The Second Boer War (1899–1902) derived from the inordinate presence of gold and diamonds in that territory and from Rhodes's inordinate commercial company. The effect suggests a moral fable, perfectly fitting Sunday school or pulpit instruction. But however Christian and cautious, Salisbury had succinctly memorialized his young colleague, Lord Selborne, Under-Secretary for the Colonies, 'to make sure that we, not the Dutch, are the boss of the Transvaal'.[4]

Even so, Salisbury did not do the vision thing. He accepted Imperialism because it was there, serving British interests. The chief Tory impetus for more and better war in South Africa would come (with that party back in power after 1894) from the political friends of Rhodes, men close to, or actually in, the Conservative government, Joseph Chamberlain and Alfred Milner. The idea was to take the Transvaal back from the intruding Dutch and their provoking President, Paul Kruger, by confecting an occasion for armed imperial expansion. Wanting a war, they would make one. From the territory beyond the Zambesi river, those future Rhodesias, named for Rhodes, Prime Minister of Cape Colony who since 1890, had effectively controlled them, would come 'The Jameson Raid'.

It would define a new kind of imperialism, Rhodes's sort, grandiose and unscrupulous in all four suits, but *high-mindedly* unscrupulous. Rhodes was officially a Liberal, but was best described as 'a mystical imperialist and Anglo-Saxon racialist'. He would wave a hand across a map of Africa and say, 'That's my dream—all English.'[5] His key practical step at this time would be the faking of a revolt to be made by the chiefly *British* residents of the Transvaal (freelance chasers of wealth on the Rand, known to the Afrikaners as *Uitlanders*). This was to be achieved by Rhodes's henchman, a Dr Leander Starr Jameson who had run those territories for the company, making enemies, as he did so, of the local Africans, both Mashona and Matabele.

Chamberlain, Colonial Secretary for more than eight years, June 1895–September 1903, knew about it. So did Milner, holding three state premierships and the British High Commissionership in South Africa between 1897 and 1905. The Uitlanders should be given the sign by the raiders and start the popular revolt. Resistance to it by the Boer authorities was intended to spark British military intervention and to take command of the new province. On 29 December 1895, Jameson would lead 500 mounted troops into the Transvaal. The Uitlanders, undirected or unwilling, stood eloquently by, leaving the Raiders to be rounded up, with Rhodes, Chamberlain, and Milner looking like men found out.

Running through what looks oddly like compulsion for power, territory, and wealth was something else—less wholesome than making money or stealing territory. Imperial thinking, which had reached a high, shrill point in the late 1890s, owed much to science. The notion, deriving from Darwin, writing in a far more complex context and sense, was 'the survival of the fittest'. It combined with a supposedly scientifically authenticated racialism, to bring violent aggression deeper into politics and turn older imperatives, very much including Christian ones—care, duty, love?—into futilities defying history.

For the idea of expansionism, new territory and new subject peoples, had also been, despite its arrogance, attended by a panic that as nation and people, Great Britain might *not* be the fittest. Germany, outreaching British industry at a startling rate and now looking around for colonial space, was a threat over-focused by our imperialists into deadly menace. German resentment, British anxiety, and France, internally split open between Republicans and a High Church military, would produce across three decades a degree of international power neurosis, good for nobody's health.

The fashionable notion was to strive for mastery as a race or be destroyed. Lord Rosebery, Liberal Prime Minister (at the time of the Raid) for fifteen months in the mid-1890s, had talked such stuff like a gym instructor with totalitarian leanings. 'An Empire such as ours requires as the first condition of an Imperial Race—a race vigorous and industrious and intrepid. Health of mind and body exalt a nation in the competition of the Universe. The survival of the fittest is an absolute truth in the conditions of the modern world.'[6]

Rosebery was the son-in-law of Sir Hercules Robinson, High Commissioner for South Africa (also a director of Rhodes's main diamond company). Possessed, without notable industrious striving, of enormous wealth, territorial possession, and exalted social connection, Rosebery enjoyed warm Conservative goodwill. After his few months as Prime Minister (March 1894–June 1895), he would manage, through querulous ineptitude, never to hold office again. Milner, a far better mind and most constructive of the Imperialists, had understood that a raggedy, underfed proletariat required a decent diet and good health; and as a leading civil servant, he wished to do something about it. But the point of such fitness was for mastery in a certain and necessary international struggle. What Milner proclaimed, Rosebery and the rest of the political right greedily followed.

There was another fierce objective. Fit or not, so large a population, thought Cecil Rhodes, made for too many people in this island—people likely, he said, to fight each other: in other words, turn to revolution. So, 'In order to save the 40 million inhabitants of the United Kingdom from a bloody civil war, we colonial statesmen must acquire new lands to settle the surplus population to provide new markets for the goods produced by them in the factories and mines...If you want to avoid civil war, you must become Imperialists.'[7] There is boasting, there is panic, and little respect for constitutional nonsense. In the two-decade run-up to the world war, there will be talk (from Milner) of 'That mob at Westminster which should be got rid of for something more efficient.'[8] This motion, the Oxford Union would also, in due course, debate.

The aggressive anxiety of Imperialism would run into the next century, specifically immediate pre-war aggressive anxiety. There would be anticipatory calls from generals for universal compulsory military service. Milner and General Roberts wanted it as a matter of course in peacetime. In a Union debate much nearer the First World War and reproduced in a later chapter, Lt. Colonel Eastwood, commanding the university's OTC, will be loudly cheered for saying, sweetly and prophetically, what joy it would give him 'to see the entire University in uniform and carrying rifles, marching down the High'.

Some of the respectable objectives of the Imperialists—better diet and improved physical fitness—would be achieved by the First World War in an army finally more or less conscripted...together with the disposal of that surplus population in successive pushes at Ypres and the Somme. However the enlightened aspect of Alfred Milner can be overdone. He called himself 'a British Race Patriot', spoke of Africans as 'aboriginals', and approved flogging for recalcitrant, semi-slave coolie labourers in the Rand mines.

Against all which grandiose dreaming and plotting, the defensive, later dangerous, notion of a French alliance—first item debated here—proposal of Mr Seton of Oriel—long pre-dates the Union discussing it. Gladstone had tried without success in the late 1870s to follow a conciliatory foreign policy through such a connection. Salisbury, though more restrained and sceptical than Rosebery, would nevertheless establish the notion of a continuous and activist line. Army and navy would become more professional and administered better, if not necessarily well. An Army Council was set up, creating, together with the Naval Defence Act of 1889, general expansion. They were, in large part, responses to Empire, ours and those of other people.

Alternatively, Germany, looking for a quadrilateral alliance and keen to invite Britain to join, had held out the Zanzibar–Heligoland treaty of 1890 and the status of chief power in eastern Africa. It was the speculative price for delivery of an alliance which would not be delivered. Salisbury, preferring to deal with the French, would postpone it out of sight. The expansion of the British Navy in 1889 reflected his sensible desire not to be saddled with dangerous, see-through bluff. Egypt, recent acquisition, had to be secured, even though Salisbury had no wish to stay there.

No deal with France would be thinkable to the good imperialist Rosebery, for the equally good reason that he was vividly anti-French—and, unlike Salisbury, set upon an imperium in Egypt. France was active in the Sudan, he thought, for the plain purpose of harassing the British in Egypt. At which point of prejudice, the cynical realism of Salisbury resolved matters. Dangerous things were happening in Europe and its colonies. He accepted imperialism because there already was an empire which had to be protected by an empire's resources. A proper Conservative, what he disliked were adventures. At the end of that brush with conflict, we had got by without an alliance and had put together a sounder military/naval machine with the prospect of consolidation—and we had signed up to nothing. Salisbury's cynical pessimism had, for a decent while, sufficed.

Nevertheless beyond that time, the moment for an Entente would come, the cordial one of 1904 with France, as Europe was chopped by diplomats into the febrile alliances which, in 1914, would make war on one another. As Richard Shannon made clear in his 1974 study *The Crisis of Imperialism*, 251, 'The measures adopted by Salisbury to modify this situation in the later 1880s and early 1890s, were essentially of the same degree as those measures which led to the decision to go to war in 1914.' With or without war, that conflict would be a dispute about empires conducted in sight of a war to make the conniving aspiration of all the imperialists an eloquent irony.

As for the Oxford Union, it would, in this term, reject almost impartially both a French *and* an American alliance.

Motion defeated by 33 and 38 votes (French and American respectively!).

<hr>

30 January 1896

Motion not formally given, but clearly calling for an alliance with France.

Mr M. C. Seton (Oriel) *advocated an alliance between France and England. His speech was a splendid rebuke to the admirers of Britain's splendid isolation. The Secretary, Mr Cleland, opposed in one of his most admirable speeches with that fullness of expression and deliberation, to which it is so pleasing to listen as the earnestness of his conviction is beyond dispute.*

Mr P. J. MacDonnell (Brasenose) *spoke third. He was not good; and although his sympathies were evident, he could not give expression to his views with that breathless fluency which is his usual characteristic.*

Mr Belloc[9] *was very much 'at home' with the subject and certainly looked quite 'at home' to judge by his attitude while speaking. He riveted our attention, but the French half of him, we fear, sometimes blinds him to the possibility of any good coming out of Germany; but still he is one of the three orators of the Union; and the excellence of his speech went a long way toward making up for the lack of speakers on his side.*

Mr Page *was extremely patriotic, loves his country and dislikes the French in the old-fashioned way.*

The motion was lost by 88 votes to 65 and the House adjourned at 10.50 p.m.

<hr>

13 February 1896

House holds that the existence of the British South Africa Company is inimical to the best interests of the Empire.

Mr A. S. Ward *is eloquent and at times, startlingly dramatic in his gestures. His speech was an admirable historical résumé of South Africa during the last few years, except in so far as he represented every action of the Chartered Companies, however innocent in itself, as part and parcel of some deep-laid plot. Perhaps his speech would have suffered in effect if he had been a little fairer to Mr Rhodes; as it was, no more powerful attack than his was brought against the Government or Company's[10] lands during the evening.*

Mr C. Eliot (Merton)[11] *defended the company, praised Mr Rhodes and his doings and eagerly upheld chartered companies in general as relieving the country from responsibility.*

Mr Bradbury (Brasenose) *spoke better than he has done, was not so jerky, nor so dictatorial; toward the end of his speech he was eloquent. He was, if possible, even more severe than the opener on Mr Rhodes.*

Mr L. Nightingale (University College) *refused to deal with the Boer question. Being a South African, he was afraid of appearing a partisan, but he devoted his attention to the benefit conferred on South Africa by a company whose charter was in danger. If criticism is permissible, may we suggest a more lively delivery?*

Mr Warschauer (Exeter) *asked how many shares Mr Eliot held in the Company. To him succeeded Mr Struben who should have spoken earlier as his knowledge of South Africa and the Boers might have been useful to succeeding speakers.*

Motion lost 49:109 reversing the verdict of the Cambridge Union.

5 March 1896

House approves the admission of women to degrees.

Mr Blomfield-Jackson *opened with a speech not nearly up to his usual level. Such a subject for debate could only be treated seriously by few people; and Mr Blomfield-Jackson took the topic and himself far too seriously. His manner was dull in the extreme and though his matter may have been good, there was no lightness to relieve the monotony.*

Mr J. S. Bradbury *was evidently nervous, but that did not make his speech any worse.*

On a division there voted for the admission of women to a BA degree 55, against 165.

---

30 April 1896

House views with disapproval the policy of the government in Egypt.

Egypt was territory where Britain was involved for reasons of defensive dithering, not quite deserving the term 'strategy'. It was the living legacy of the dying Ottoman Empire. Russians, French, and the *in situ* British were all involved, more or less honestly, for more or less defensive reasons. In another of those fraught high C warnings in which imperial servants delighted, Salisbury had been told in 1896 by the Director of Naval Intelligence that 'The one way in which Britain could not only maintain herself in the Mediterranean at all, but continue to hold India...is by holding Egypt against all comers and making Alexandria a naval base.'

Holding Egypt against all comers meant staying there and contending with new, remote, and overrated troubles like the Dervishes on the Upper Nile and the French expedition toward it of General Marchand. It meant more imperial acts of war: Kitchener defeating the Khalifa in the much celebrated Battle of Omdurman and, in the process, landing Whitehall with more and deeper commitments in unprofitable parts of the world than Salisbury's rational inertia needed. France, recognizing its own inadequate strength in this theatre, had, with shameless good sense, withdrawn at Fashoda, to indignation in the French press, but leaving toil and overextension to Britain.

Mr A. W. S. Fisher's *speech developed into a general attack on government policy rather than a criticism of its Egyptian action.*

Mr Conacher (Corpus Christi) *opposed. His arguments were cogent and convincing, though one is apt to lose them, owing to a lack of emphasis at the proper moment.*

Mr C. F. Garbett (Keble)[12] *is very fluent and forcible, but very indistinct and difficult to hear. He is one of the few speakers in the Union who happen to have convictions.*

Mr Bailey (Worcester) *if one may criticise him at all, it would be to say that he should not speak in such a high tone and that his right hand should not be jerked forward so frequently and in such a rapid manner.*

Mr Jackson *put fresh life into the debate. He attacked the mover with great vehemence, refusing to stop even when Mr Fisher endeavoured to interpose some remark.*

Mr Meiklejohn (Hertford) *is very rapid in his utterance and was hardly audible.*

Motion lost 29:63.

7 May 1896

An Anglo-American Alliance would be in our interests.

Mr Lenwood (Corpus Christi) *became a fervid exponent of the system, the basis of which was to preside in an Anglo-Saxon hegemony to 'Run the show.'*

Mr Vaughan *opposed in a speech of great vigour. There was no disguising his antipathy toward anyone who had not an ancestry of 600 years from father to son. Those who failed in this 'necessity,' i.e. the Americans, were riff-raff, vulgar, uncultured etc. He afforded some amusement to the House which laughed at him heartily.*

Mr R. A. Johnson *repudiated such a motion as bringing contamination with it. An Anglo-American alliance would bring the unholy thing into the tents of Israel, an eventuality to be avoided for as long as possible.*

Mr F. Soddy[13] *is very good though possibly a trifle too rapid.*

Viscount Suirdale[14] *was earnest in his defence of England and the English against the incoming wave of Americanism.*

Motion lost by 38.

———— ∞∞∞ ————

4 June 1896

House considers the tactics and attitude of the Liberal Party during the past five years to be a standing menace to the welfare of this country.

Mr M. W. Ridley[15] *was amusing and forcible, but not quite intelligible. All that we learnt was that Canning[16] was not quite sound that party government was an evil and that the Radicals were not often respectable. Mr H. E. S. Freemantle pointed out the pernicious methods of the wicked Tories and the inevitable triumph of the good Liberals. His speech was better suited to a more rustic audience.*

Motion carried 66:60.

———— ∞∞∞ ————

29 October 1896

That this House, in view of the American President's[17] lecture and the Bi-metallic movement in England, desires to affirm its conviction that the rehabilitation of silver for monetary purposes is neither practicable nor desirable.

Mr L. C. S. Amery (Balliol)[18] *jeered at the pauper statistics and said 'I am an honest man' as he proceeded to attack the mover's description of the advocates of Bimetallism.*

The President—Mr F. W. Hirst[19] *Moving rapidly over the whole history of mankind, he paused for a moment to characterize our position as* 'Nobler than that advocated by a certain Flaccus'[20] *and denounced the heresies of the bi-metallic party.* 'Bad trade is an entirely faked-up cry' *he declared.*

Mr W. H. Grenfell (Balliol) (Visitor)[21] *dwelt upon the impossibility of persuading the people of India to give up the Rupee and likened the position of the mono-metallists to that of a blind man in a dark room looking for a black cat which wasn't there.*

Mr F. W. Lawrence (President of the Cambridge Union) *pleaded for some deference to the greatest intellects of Lombard Street and Threadneedle Street who strongly opposed the Bi-metallic movement.*

Mr W. Moss (Trinity) *held that the Trades Unions in the North of England had sufficient strength to regulate prices.*

Vote: For the motion 71; against 55.

5 November 1896

That England's fortunes have already reached their zenith and are now on the decline.

Mr G. H. Bloomfield-Jackson (Merton) *proved to his own satisfaction that England was in a very bad way. The Army and Navy, torpedo boats, torpedo-catchers and a new vessel called a 'torpedo catcher-catcher'* [ed.: Like the anti-missile missile?]: *all furnished conclusive arguments.*

The speech of Mr F. Ingle (St John's) was like all his previous efforts, unique.

Mr J. Warschauer (Exeter) *opposed the motion and severely censured the attitude of the Government toward Armenia.*[22]

The Rev. A. B. Beavan M.A. (Pembroke),[23] *an old member, delivered a most vigorous speech. His standpoint was distrust of Democracy; and he solemnly warned the House against the dangers of democratic government. His speech was very effective.*

The President, Mr R. A. Johnson, supported the motion and looked back to the days of Cobden and Bright as the zenith of England's glory.

Mr Willan (Magdalen) *supported the motion, declaiming against the present 'scandalous disproportion in the distribution of wealth' and 'the curse of drink.'*

Motion defeated: For 22, Against 151.

---

26 November 1896

That the policy of the present government is reactionary.

Mr H. D. Reilly (Corpus) *made a capital speech. It was quite surprising how good a speech could be made out of the somewhat commonplace theme of 'Radical Constitution-mongering.'*

Mr A. S. F. Fisher (New College) *supported the motion, dealing at length with foreign policy, and twitted Mr Curzon for his eulogy on Lord Salisbury who had been outwitted by a simple Dutch farmer.*

George, later Marquess Curzon,[24] *supremely assured Conservative politician, lately returned from a term as Viceroy of India, about whom a derisive line ran 'My name is George Nathaniel Curzon. I am a most important person.'*

Salisbury, *at this time, was simply being more cautious about aggressive action for control of the Transvaal, observing, 'We cannot afford to have more than a limited area of heather alight at the same time.'*[25]

Vote: for 49; Against 116.

---

3 December 1896

That the problem of the unemployed is really the problem of the unemployable.

Mr Fisher (Christ Church) *commenced with a classical allusion.* At the present time, England was in a highly prosperous condition, and the question of the unemployed was not one of the first importance. The number of those who were genuinely unemployed was very small.

Mr C. F. Garbett (Keble) received an ovation: *This question of the unemployed constitutes a real danger to the state. It is no good leaving it to private individuals. It must be dealt with by the state and that right speedily.*

Sir John Gorst (St John's Cambridge) (Visitor)[26] *An important survey in districts of a number of large towns shows that out of 109 unemployed, fully 69 are involuntarily out of work…I suggest the establishment of a system of labour bureaux throughout the country which might do good and could not possibly do any harm.*

Motion lost 25:58.

---

4 February 1897

House reaffirms unqualified confidence in Her Majesty's government.

Mr W. K. Stride (Exeter) *defended the attitude of the Conservative press which* 'listens to the beating of the great heart of England'. *He regarded Romford and Walthamstow (Tory by-election defeats) as blessings in disguise.*

Mr F. E. Smith (Ex-President, Merton)[27] *attacked the placards in Walthamstow and proved himself easily the first debater in the Union.*

Mr R. Feetham (New College) *spoke with awe-inspiring vigour. He dealt with Education and seemed to know almost too much about it. We hope to hear from Mr Feetham again, but on a less exciting subject than the Education Bill.*

Vote: For 103; Against 73.

---

11 February 1897

Strongly condemns Lord Penrhyn's[28] recent action with reference to his quarrymen and believes that the action furnishes a strong argument in favour of increasing State control over labour disputes.

Mr Blomfield-Jackson *deplored the* 'tendency of men at Oxford to think they have democratic opinions'. *He held that workmen have no legal right to force their combinations on employers. He presented to the House his sincere objections on the subject of government by political parties.*

Vote: For 63, Against 64.

---

18 February 1897

Increased Naval and not military expenditure should be the first care of HMG.

The Librarian, Mr J. W. Cleland *We stand on the brink of a European war. The insecurity of our position is of the highest moment and should be of the highest moment, something at all costs, to be remedied.*

Mr H. Seymour-Trower Chairman of the executive of the Navy League *It is impossible to summarize his speech. From Thucydides to Drake, from Drake to Mahan; to the Second Punic War to Sluys, to the Armada and everything else he led us in turn.*

Mr E. C. Bentley (Merton)[29] *From the time of Noah, no doubt seen as an alarmist, strong objections have been entertained by many to increased naval expenditure.*

The President, Mr R. A. Johnson (New College) *supported the Army in preference for the Navy, since its needs were greater. It was absolutely necessary to strengthen the Army as, at present, the military power of England was a laughing-stock to continental nations.*

Vote: For 168; Against 26.

---

25 February 1897

That Ireland has a real grievance and a claim to be discussed separately from Great Britain.

Mr Fisher *spoke fifth and emphasized at great length the unanimity of all parties in Ireland on this subject.*

The President *opposed the motion, and adduced Sir Alfred Milner in favour of his position.*

Vote: For 39; Against 29.

No Date

This House approves of Votes on women.*

Mr P. W. Wigan *completely flattened out the few friends of women who showed themselves among the serried ranks of their opponents. At about 11.30,* 'The greatest debate, certainly at our Union—and with all due deference, I suggest also at yours,' *came to a conclusion.* The 'Non placets' were estimated at the outset at 5:1, but the outcome was nearly 9:1.

A postcard ballot on this question recorded 2,200 against and 300 for.

9 June 1897

That the popular literature of today is a sign of national degradation. *The audience was small and apathetic.*

Mr H. G. Fraser (Trinity) *was very severe upon the problem novels of today and upon the wild, would-be-scientific ideas of some latter day novelists. According to Mr Fraser, to read the novels of Sir Walter Scott ought to be the literary consummation of a lifetime.*

Mr R. S. Rait (New College) *Before reading became common, the lower classes knew all the ballad literature of the country, and that state of affairs is certainly preferable to today's.*

---

* Sometimes a debate, barely reported at all (half a sentence!) can, in poignantly illustrating the Union's perceptions, be savagely eloquent.

No vote recorded.

16 June 1897

House Condemns the University of Cambridge with regard to women's degrees.[30]

Mr J. A. Simon (Wadham)[31] *From opposing women's degrees he had come to regard them as a just and moderate demand.*

Mr E. V. Barnes President of the Cambridge Union *proved a worthy exponent (sic) of the vast majority of undergraduates in Cambridge.*

Mr F. Soddy (Merton)[32] *opposed the motion from the standpoint of a Liberal who prefers the old order of things—at least in University matters.*

Vote: For 92; Against 119 *An interesting illustration of modified illiberalism.*

This was followed by the passing nem. con. of a Loyal and dutiful address to the Queen's most excellent Majesty on the 60th anniversary of Her Accession.

Private Business.

Treasurer[33] proposed that the *Clarion*—the Socialist journal edited by Robert Blatchford—be rejected from the list of papers taken.

Vote: To retain 106; to reject 60.

A member demanded a poll. *No result can be found, but polls—of Life-members, a group, heavy with rural clergy not fully reconciled to Galileo,—will almost certainly have succeeded in barring this lively and much admired Socialist journal.*

26 October 1898

House believes the domestic legislation of the government to have been ignorant and ill advised.

Mr H. T. Baker *speaks too fast, not quite loud enough and does not drive in his points; these small faults marred a brilliant and interesting speech by far the most convincing and able of the season.*

Mr S. Armitage Smith (New College) *His aggressive style and forced humour jarred on us most unpleasantly. His witticisms about Lord Salisbury, Lord Curzon and the Senior Proctor were commonplace and trivial.*

Mr P. Wilson (Balliol) *was the exuberant Irishman we knew of old. And as usual, he deluged the House with an irresistible flow of rhetoric and as usual, dared not trust himself on the Irish question.*

Mr MacFadayen (Wadham) *Conservatism, in his view, had no right to exist. He narrated an anecdote about a Liberal and a Conservative frog and a pat of butter. He is too grotesque to be amusing or interesting.*

Mr Pereira (Jesus) *defended the government in a promising speech. His style would be good, but for a tendency to be too clerical and laborious.*

Motion divided the House 50:50. The Treasurer gave his casting vote against the motion.

---

2 November 1898

On Wednesday November 1st the Archbishop of Canterbury[34] *delivered an address of 'Things Indifferent' at 3.45 to a crowded audience. His earnest and strong personality made a deep impression on all present.*

On Thursday 2nd, the Society met in the ordinary way at the ordinary time.

House censures the attitude of a certain section of the English press on the Fashoda Question[35]—

Mr G. Gathorne-Hardy (New College)[36] *The vagueness of the motion and the vagueness of his attack account for the somewhat unconvincing nature of his argument, but his quotations from the press, with side comments, were in the vein most pleasing to the Union audience.*

Mr A. Cecil[37] *must be less languid, must connect his arguments more systematically and must confine himself more closely to the point. He should beware of bits of condescension: 'Notre Dame, a cathedral in Paris' and 'The Emperor Franz Joseph, whose death we shall all deplore.'*

Mr R. C. K. Ensor[38] *His speech was free from his distressing mannerisms, well delivered, forceful and eloquent. His summary of the French position was admirably lucid, his eulogy of France eloquent and dignified and his Zola-esque denunciation of English newspapers powerful.*

Mr A. H. D. Steel *should not resort to witticisms such as 'France is like a pickled walnut.'*

No vote recorded.

---

16 November 1898—Cambridge visit

House does not believe in international morality.

Mr Buchan (Brasenose) Librarian[39] *was fluent and to the point. What does morality mean? He assured us that he was the very embodiment of that quality. For 'a sincere, ardent and puritanical moralist,' Mr Buchan was surprisingly exhilarated and exhilarating.*

Mr Armitage-Smith Treasurer *Such phrases as 'perhaps laudable (sic) and 'certainly admirable' and 'the present time is, in a sense, the beginning of a better order of things' are puzzling to the 'plain man' whom Mr Armitage-Smith represents and on whom he relies.*

Mr R. Asquith (Balliol)[40] *was as usual, clear and good with some good phrases—* 'The bulky anthology of international fraud'.

Mr T. F. R. McDonnell (St John's Cambridge) Vice-President Cambridge Union *Although calm and very much at his ease, his manner hardly seemed to be very effective and his matter rather defective in novelty. Considering his reputation in Cambridge, we were rather disappointed.*

Mr J. P. R. Sclater (Emmanuel Cambridge) *He was more fluent and less lackadaisical than other Cambridge speakers.*

Motion lost 51:122.

∞∞∞

26 January 1899

It is the duty of the Liberal Party to bury Home Rule and offer its leadership to Mr Chamberlain.

Mr A. S. Ward (Balliol) *On the whole, he made a fairly plausible case though the picture which he drew of the reconciliation of Lord Rosebery[41] and Mr Chamberlain can hardly have carried conviction even to the speaker himself. The only defects to the speech were its excessive length and a somewhat artificial and bombastical delivery.*

Mr Wilson *maintains the best traditions of Irish oratory. In a speech of consistent ferocity and intermittent eloquence, he damned England, Liberalism and Mr Chamberlain—all of which things he views with 'disgust, indignation and abhorrence'—denounced the policy of tergiversation and having exhausted all possible*

31

permutations of 'Turpitude,' 'dishonour' and 'unparalleled,' sat down after a lively and provocative contribution to the debate.

Mr R. P. Hill (St John's) *after ten minutes or so of voluble irrelevance, he settled down and made a very sensible speech. Mr Hill always has something to say, but he should say it sooner. As distinguished from Mr Wilson, he believes in tergiversation as a political ideal. But he cannot answer for the intelligence of the Duke of Argyll.*[42]

Motion lost 19:41.

---

2 February 1899

House thinks any formal alliance with America would be both injudicious and impracticable.

Mr Baker *His delivery is excellent and audible, but he should learn to shout in the right places.*

Mr Steel (Balliol)[43] *His contention with regard to America was entirely sentimental and did not carry much weight with the House which happened to be in a utilitarian mood. But when he came to deal with Russia and India, he spoke with real force and feeling.*

Mr Hills *was too fluent, too long, too irrelevant; talked too much about Japan and too little about America.*

Mr A. C. Medd (Balliol) *was a vast relief. He has been to America and knows how to pronounce American names. He was fluent, vigorous, spontaneous and witty; indeed he succeeded in a very short time in raising the spirits of a preternaturally jaded and languid House.*

Mr B. K. Long *is a sound democrat; he spoke in a pleasant voice and style. He is the only man from whom we have ever heard the expression 'Phew'.*

Mr A. J. Jenkinson (Hertford) *reminds us of a phonograph; he spoke as if he had been wound up and we were not sorry when the machinery wound down.*

Mr L. G. Brock (Corpus) *attacked the Treasurer, discussed Japan and used the word 'forsooth.'*

Motion carried 54:38.

⎯⎯⎯ ⚬⦊⦉⚬ ⎯⎯⎯

23 February 1899

House thinks that the Great Joke of democracy is almost played out.

Mr Medd *has a multiplicity of interests, ranging from Genesis to Tammany and said good things about them. At the same time, it shows a dangerous versatility in ex-secretaries of the Palmerston Club, if they think they can deride democracy in such flippant and unmeasured language.*

Mr A. Cecil (New College) *thinks the Duke of Wellington the greatest Englishman that ever was; and after him, as far as we could gather from his speech, all the other dukes in order of seniority. 'Snob' is a hard word to use about anyone, but Mr Cecil's fantastic and indiscriminate contempt for the proletariat comes perilously near to snobbery.*

Mr F. G Williams (Brasenose) *His matter was not always so vigorous as his manner, but the latter proved an invigorating contrast to the invertebrate style so common in the union.*

Baron Von Stumm (Balliol) *upholds the best traditions of Teutonic oratory. He speaks both German and English, but he should make up his mind which it is to be.*

Mr V. S. B. Hoare (Oriel) *was brief but determined. He speaks by accident rather than design.*

Motion lost 33:37.

⊶⊷

9 March 1899

House believes a university for the People is an impossibility.

Mr H. B. Lees-Smith (Queen's)[44] *Opposing, delivered with a spirit of conviction a speech he has already made in every college debating society and political club in Oxford. He identifies entirely with the Ruskin Hall[45] Movement and is obviously very much in earnest, but we are inclined to think that he takes it and himself rather too seriously. But his speech was bright and enthusiastic and he made a number of good points.*

Mr E. S. P. Haynes *attacked the motion on its weak side by showing that even Oxford was to some degree a university for the people.*

Mr B. W. Shepheard-Walwyn (Oriel) *opposed the motion in a somewhat monotonous discourse. He speaks too slowly and said a number of things which were barely worth saying.*

Mr Nelson (St John's) *has an unconventional and picturesque turn of phrase. He made a sound and interesting speech for the motion, pointing out the corrupting influence of Oxford upon morals and economy.*

Mr Gathorne Hardy *quite rightly laid stress upon the Socialist bias of Ruskin Hall.*

Mr Slee (New College) *has been to Ruskin Hall and holds it to be a success. He was serious and businesslike.*

Mr R. Temple (Balliol) *made a speech which would have been distinctly good if it had not been marred by continual references to morality. He must get out of this.*

Motion carried 60:42.

27 April 1899

The present aims and recent objectives of Imperialist policy are neither honourable nor advantageous.

Mr Ensor was thoughtful and epigrammatic: Rosebery posed as a gentleman, Chamberlain as a gentlemanly democrat. The speech abounded in the most courageous condemnations of popular ideals. A Union speaker who quotes Plato and blasphemes Kipling is indeed a hero. It is a great tribute to the truth of what he said that he was well received by the House.

Mr L. J. Fulton (New College) appeared in the character of 'calculating boy.' Accidentally however he was really amusing. His bold assumption that the population of Ireland would remain constant during the next century, the insistent way in which he referred to Mr Ensor as 'the right hon. proposer' drew peals of laughter from his audience.

Motion lost 19:35.

11 May 1899

The present anti-ritualistic movement is unreasonable and dangerous. *There must have been quite 300 people on the floor of the House, many standing crowded together in the gangways, while the gallery too, was full to overflowing. Representatives of many sects, nations and hemispheres; an Elamite and three Parthians being noticeable at the back, their swarthy countenances forming a sharp contrast with the pale ascetic features of the ordinary undergraduate and harmonising with the dusky yellow of Malays, Evangelicals and others.*

The first spark was applied to the gunpowder by the Librarian whose weekly list of books, included Mr Walsh's work on the Oxford movement.—a volume rejected nem.con. by the Society last year. The reading out of the title was greeted by an over-whelming storm of cheers and hisses. Half a dozen members were on their feet, demanding the rejection of the book for various reasons and in various tongues.

An attempt was made to reach public business, but as soon as the paper motion had been read out, Mr Iremonger (Keble) rose to move the adjournment of the debate on the grounds that the rules forbad theological discussion. The House eventually divided on that amendment and by 210 to 180, carried it. The House therefore adjourned.

As by convention, the rather florid Oxford Magazine Union sketches were written by the preceding term's retiring president, this nicely fanciful introduction of the debate (swiftly becoming a takeover) is probably the work of the President for the immediately preceding Easter Term, R. C. K. Ensor (Oxford historian and recurring source for this commentary), being playful!

<hr />

25 May 1899

House condemns the financial policy of the present government.

Mr L. T. Dodd (Merton) *He has no airs and graces and is one of those stern, angular radicals who look suspiciously like Little Englanders and find it necessary to assert their pride in the Empire.*

Mr A. Cecil *seemed to regard the motion as a trivial piece of irrelevant impertinence. The motion however was neither so irrelevant nor so impertinent as Mr Cecil's attack on the Liberal party. To say that the country would be plunged into an ocean of evil under a Liberal administration is almost too confident a prophecy for an amateur politician at the Union. Such a remark is only one instance of Mr Cecil's besetting faults: believing firmly in his own political opinions, he is lacking in the most ordinary and perfunctory respect towards those of other people.*

Mr E. Wright (Balliol) *In matter, his was easily the best of the evening, although he has not so pleasant a manner as Mr Cecil.*

The House was counted out and the motion lost 17:38.

———⊗⊗⊗———

1 June 1899 Cambridge Visit

House thinks that for the Liberals to unite under the leadership of Lord Rosebery[46] and to discard Home Rule would be most advantageous to themselves and to the Country.

Yet for all the heroic attitudes struck, Rosebery, *Roi fainéant*, former short-term Liberal Prime Minister fatally admired by most Tories as their sort of Liberal leader, lacked decision and probably courage. He was always going to make a comeback, a great speech or a challenge, and he never did. Ultimately anyway, Liberal Imperialism, his absolute territory, was a wasting asset ruined by British concentration camps in South Africa. Liberals would be delighted to find in Henry Campbell-Bannerman an actual Liberal to lead them. By the time C-B raised the roof by denouncing (British) 'methods of barbarism' in South Africa, Liberal Imperialism had become a burial club.

Mr E. W. Masterman (St John's Cambridge) *is an ardent imperialist, Secretary of the Cambridge Union and an enthusiastic admirer of Lord Rosebery. He stated his case with great skill in an easy style which gained much from his pleasant voice.*

Mr T. Cuthbertson (Corpus Christi) *was violent and vigorous and attacked the motion with frantic energy.*

Motion carried 69:35.

———⊗⊗⊗———

8 June 1899

Popular education saps the manhood of the race and is pernicious to literature.

Mr F. G. Williams (Brasenose) *opened in a fluent and sensible speech at hurricane pace. He gave the impression of trying to get over as soon as possible.*

Mr Ward *was obviously fresh from Schools. His speech abounded in categories, trichotomies, analyses, fragments from Bosanquet and Aristotle, Isocratean periods, classical puns and all the other useful things people learn in greats.*

Mr A. Lang (Merton)[47]—Visitor *championed barbarism against civilisation in a most convincing and impassioned argument directed against Balliol[48] and the Board Schools.*

Mr Belloc *lashed the age we lived in with all his accustomed eloquence and wit, showing conclusively that all the things we hate and should hate e.g. Americans, Jews, landlords, revision in the Dreyfus case[49] etc. were not due to popular education, whereas all the virtue of England is the direct result of it. True there is hardly any virtue to speak of, but what there is, is confined exclusively to the lower classes i.e. Those who have the advantage of popular education in the proper sense of the term.*

Motion carried 45:43

---

19 October 1899

House believes the recent outcry against the Rennes verdict[50] has been unwarrantable and ridiculous.

Mr Medd *made a plucky defence of an unpopular point of view appearing again as often before, as a martyr to the unpalatable.*

Mr Lees-Smith *cares more about Ruskin Hall than about Captain Dreyfus; but the Union as a whole cares infinitely less. For this reason among others, his speech was not a great success. It is not fair to summon a number of people to hear about Dreyfus and then thrust upon them a lengthy plea for helping the poor to live noble lives on the Banbury Road.*

Mr Wright *had obviously sifted the evidence and could put his finger on weak spots on either side of the case.*

Mr G. I. MacAlister (Merton) *had been to the Rennes trial and spoke with authority.—His speech was quite a good one—earnest, sincere and upto a certain point, eloquent.*

Mr E. S. Tyler *stands in relation to Dreyfus as Kipling to the Empire.* Mr F. M. Spencer *opposed the motion with conviction and spirit.* Mr K. E. Knutsford-Fortescue (BNC) *wound up the debate in a spirit of breezy energy.*

Motion tied 29:29 no casting vote reported.

2

South Africa—Last Late Prize

26 October 1899–29 November 1900

Topics of Debate: South African War.../Joseph Chamberlain/German rapprochement/Theatre censorship/No confidence in (Tory) Government/Temperance movement/Old age pensions/Appeal of War/Annexation of Boer republics/Cecil Rhodes/Modern literature/Morality/Home Rule/Lords Reform/German interests and our own

The Jameson Raid had failed, but the men and the thinking which had made such a primitive adventure thinkable remained and, if anything, grew in general influence. All sorts of talk floated around and, about the issue of Empire, much of it grandly complacent. We stood astonished at our moderation. Edward Dicey, brother of the academic lawyer, Albert, who across three steadily ranting pamphlets had denounced the least atom of Irish Home Rule as a guarantee of England's precipitation down a ravine, had more sweetly expressed a parallel version of English self-congratulation:

> In the strict sense of the word, we have never been a conquering nation. Since the days when the Plantagenets essayed the conquest of France, we have never deliberately undertaken the conquest of any foreign country; we have never made war with the set purpose of annexing any given territory...North and South, East and West, we have planted the British flag in every corner of the globe, but we have done so rather in response to real or fancied exigencies than to any lust of conquest. The definition which Topsy, in *Uncle Tom's Cabin*, gave of the growth of her being, would be about the best that could be given about the growth of our empire.'Spects it growed' is the sum of what one can say about the subject.[1]

Back in 1877, the same Dicey, writing in the Spectator had urged Disraeli 'to do the obvious thing and occupy Egypt'.[2]

Such oceangoing complacency also represents a slightly defensive 'Not me Gov,' kind of Imperial feeling. The reality had been the Elder Pitt, instructing naval commanders to make sure of taking Gorrée in West Africa, which since the sixteenth century had been the Crewe of the slave routes. As plain was that 'Theft from thieves' by which Lord Chesterfield in the 1740s defined British raids on Spanish treasure ships. Dicey had innocently proclaimed what graceless foreigners called 'English hypocrisy'.

The contrasting outlook of a far more complex and highly charged man has already been encountered: Alfred Milner—High Commissioner for South Africa 1897–1905, variously across 1901–5 Governor/administrator of Cape Colony, Governor of Orange River State and the Transvaal, and Fellow of New College, Oxford. Milner, all clear, aggrandizing purpose, everything and anything but complacency, was not at all like Topsy. Half-German, as Kaiser Wilhelm II was half-British, adoring the greatness of England and cherishing what had been coolly taken in our days of healthy aggression, he feared that the truculent inveteracy of our national health was slipping away. German success, economically and in terms of European prominence, was also stirring in Africa. Meanwhile Britain's role in a South Africa necessarily remote had not become the unconditional mastery essential for a man who had candidly anticipated what Orwell would call 'Power Worship'.

Paul Kruger's Transvaal was the immediate problem. Product of Boer trekking earlier in the nineteenth century to escape British command at the Cape, this little nation was Calvinist/reactionary, with bits of the seventeenth century sticking to it. (Kruger allegedly believed in a flat Earth!) Milner would have reformed all that; however, high purpose was incidental, not quite a side-line, but assuredly, a means to more efficient mastery. Milner, with a different sort of irrational conviction, had called himself 'a British Race patriot', seeing the Empire as an extension of the British race and its world standing. Like too many men at the end of the nineteenth century, he viewed 'the survival of the fittest' not in terms of centuries, but as cause for an immediate anxiety to be quelled by ruthless response. Such a taking of age-long developments as immediate crisis might properly be treated very seriously, beyond the usual suspects of incidents and provocations, as a central provoking cause of 'The War to End all Wars'. Milner, who saw aggression as health, is, despite gifts and complexities, a character prefiguring the febrile and remorseless twentieth century. Unsurprisingly, he would go on to back the House of Lords in unconstitutional rejection of the 1909 Budget and subsequent fight to sustain an unelected veto.

Restored to office in the Lloyd George coalition as Minister of War 1916–18, then Colonial Secretary 1918–20, he would flourish again, doing surprising and sometimes useful things, like quietly getting a number of conscientious objectors released and advocating extensive autonomy for Egypt. On the other hand, his mission to Russia (in ironically 1917) persuaded him that even if there were a revolution (which came a few weeks later), Russia could still fight on. Milner, in his own words, believed in 'blood', *English* blood to be recruited in the colonies for the Great Struggle of Life.

To such a virulent apostle of all or nothing, the notion of perhaps falling back a degree, of getting by with difficult neighbours in a reasonable, giving-and-taking, low trader's sort of way, was alien. This was a vivid, absolutist mind. Driving resolutely and to the public danger, it was quite modern enough to anticipate (without sharing its full depravity) the coming worship of a single hero exercising unamended power. Though *that* was something which in due course, the Union would also debate.

In immediate terms, Milner had seen Britain/England's position slipping away and new, upstart powers, perhaps the United States, but immediately and as cause of obsession, Germany, thrusting her aside. The slipping-away had been demonstrated when, back in January 1896, the Kaiser, with his clattering news sense, had dispatched a congratulatory telegram to Kruger, on the defeat of the Jameson Raid. Milner saw that as a wider threat, as he saw so many threats; and for commercial aggrandizement and proof of national virility, he would now seek a declaration of war against the Transvaal republic. He had close ties with Chamberlain, Colonial Secretary in London, alternately plaguing and bossing a Tory cabinet in the latter days of a tired Salisbury, and comparable links with Cecil Rhodes, Rand plutocrat and mystical believer in the supreme destiny of the English race.

Rhodes had wanted Sir John Seeley, historian and apologist for the British Empire—*The Expansion of England* (sic) (1883)—who had anticipated Edward Dicey in the notion of an absent-minded growth of Empire, to head a college, devoted, Jesuit style, to training 'a future secret society of the elect ruling élite'. From this would spring only the generally innocent Rhodes Scholarships of Oxford—something largely financed by the Hamburg-born Randlord, Alfred Beit. Rhodes and Chamberlain had been in on the plot with the more cautious Chamberlain better aware in London of the problems such adventures might afford a British government.[3]

The Transvaal, it was argued, might be a Boer creation, but in Johannesburg, it now had significant numbers of incomers, non-Boers, 'Uitlanders', in pursuit of gold and any other profits—and denied influence. They should, said Rhodes, be roused by a daring act of pure war. The Jameson Raid had been a shot at that. The dynamic activists, Milner, Rhodes, and Chamberlain, had been left with a *fait pas accompli*. These conspirators were left to embarrassment and apologetics. For, on the street, Imperial Britain was not reliably responsive to furtive and bungled decisiveness.

Milner did not give up. Wanting submission or a proper war, he would stick to the rights of the not very interested Uitlanders, making in March 1898, at the historic Afrikaner settlement of Graaf Reinet, a speech demanding internal reforms, ironically including a milder line toward the blacks, but chiefly stressing Uitlander rights. Looking forward to the war, he wanted Chamberlain, as Colonial Secretary, to make concessions to the Germans of South West Africa for cooperation in stopping arms being allowed through Portuguese colonies for Afrikaner defence of the Transvaal. Chamberlain, with a better grasp of the risks and nearer to political sobriety, pressed for a Milner–Kruger meeting in Bloemfontein in May/June 1899. The compromise Chamberlain wanted and Milner, a temperamental gambler, did not.

Kruger's offers—advised by the young J. C. Smuts (Uitlander rights in return for abandonment of British suzerainty)—were rejected, with Milner pressing Chamberlain, pressing Salisbury. Ten thousand men, under General Sir Redvers Buller, late of the Chinese War, the Red River expedition, the Ashanti, Kaffir, and Zulu Wars (winning the VC), sent to back up Milner's meeting with Kruger, had another, altogether harder, war to fight. Chamberlain, would get invasion passed in a queasy Cabinet, and Kruger declined surrender. Accordingly, with the government dragged limping in the wrong direction, the wrong war—to be fought (tactically and morally) the wrong way—would finally be declared on 12 October 1899.

The Second Boer War 1899–1902 would be the sort of success in a bold undertaking to discourage bold undertakings. Milner's military adviser, Sir William Butler, Tipperary Catholic and Home Ruler, also an excellent judge of the military situation, thought the whole thing a discreditable fix whose military prospects were unpromising—and said so, getting himself sent home. The Cape government declared its neutrality. Yet in anticipation of another, later, ill-advised prophecy, it was reckoned that the war would be over by Christmas.

Such confidence did not survive the ill-luck or judgement of Sir Redvers. He would be distracted into Natal by the Boer general, Joubert, meanwhile telling one deputy, Lord Methuen, to move west to relieve besieged Kimberley and drive into the Transvaal. A third group of British forces under Sir William Gatacre was sent into the Orange Free State to drive on Bloemfontein. General Baden-Powell had tried to tie down Boer forces by concentrating a few hundred troops in Mafeking near the Natal border. He did preoccupy about 8,000 of them, but the subsequent investment lasted 217 days—with reports producing shrill demands for relief from the British press. Separate and unnerving reverses, particularly Methuen's bombardment of the wrong target, exposure of his Highland troops to miserable losses, and final defeat at Magersfontein, were suffered by the three commanders in less than a week, 10–15 December 1899, leaving Mafeking still under siege.

The war would be won under a different command: Roberts, assisted by Kitchener. To hysterical rejoicing at home, rejoicing which would turn the place name into a present participle to describe all such subsequent outbursts, Mafeking would ultimately be relieved, on 17 May 1900. But the war didn't end then as, by the rules, it should have. The Boers turned to guerrilla war, raids into Cape Colony, ambushes of convoys and railway track destruction. Kitchener, not an enlightened soldier, practised what he called 'a scorched earth campaign', and the German military called *Schrecklichkeit* (Dreadfulness)—destroying, among other things, the food crops of citizenry likely to support the guerrillas. He would follow that up by establishing 'Concentration Camps' (a merely bureaucratic term, latent with future horror)—where, by Afrikaner reports, 26,000 prisoners, civilians, overwhelmingly women and children, died—of which Kitchener admitted 18,000.[4]

The war itself dragged on. The only point and purpose for Milner, Chamberlain, and Rhodes in this war, absolute victory, with English dominion evident and triumphant, had, in the style of the Jameson Raid, not been achieved. Tagging ardently behind, the Conservative and Unionist Party had suffered, in Kipling's words about the whole country, 'no end of a lesson'.

Whether it had done the war's initiators the 'no end of good' of the verse's next line, is doubtful. Beyond that, the courage of the Boers had won them friends. They had in General Louis Botha and a younger man, Jan Christiaan Smuts, to whom a statue now stands in Whitehall, personable and sophisticated leaders with a touch of chivalry, impressing the British soldiers and the British politicians they would deal with. Milner's war of connivance had proved them skilled, brave, and ingenious. As Richard Shannon puts it in his *Crisis of Imperialism*: 'Increasingly Chamberlain and Milner saw the threat looming before them: that the "great game" was being lost through the combination of Afrikaner guerrilla resistance plus a public weariness of war and inability to share Chamberlain's and Milner's original aggressive motivation.'[5]

The war had provoked furious division between patriots and 'Pro-Boers'. The rightwing Liberals, Milner's actual friends (Grey, Rosebery, Haldane, and a rather shifty Asquith), had rallied round. However, the Liberal Party leader since 1899, Henry Campbell-Bannerman, was proving not to be what Grey and Haldane had patronizingly assumed, a discountable space-filler until Asquith had made enough money at the Bar to afford the leadership. 'CB', as he became to admirers, attracted affection and gave worrying evidence of actual Liberalism. Speaking of 'the vulgar and bastard imperialism of irritation and aggression, of clever tricks...and of grabbing everything, even if we have no use for it ourselves' (quoted Porter, *The Lion's Share*, 204), he spoke to Liberals over the heads of his party's imperialist clique with dynamic effect. 'Methods of barbarism', his phrase about Kitchener's *Schrecklichkeit*, stung, stuck, and enraged the Imperialists. Famously, young Lloyd George, speaking with great effect against the war came very close to being lynched in Joseph Chamberlain's Birmingham.

Events were against Darwinists and Imperialists both. Scandals like those concentration camps (British coining, British creation!) and the subsequent importation of cost-trimming Chinese coolies, might have been dreamt up by an irresponsible left-wing novelist. They had their full effect, making a discreditable adventure look like a discreditable adventure. 'Increasingly, Milner became a man whom fewer and fewer politicians in Britain cared to compromise their political credit by defending.'[6] The military match, the Boers had lost, but what they had fought it for, they essentially kept.

The effects of the South African War were felt in the Conservative Party. The war had been dreamed up by Rhodes, driven by Milner, accepted by Chamberlain, and acquiesced in by Salisbury, but Chamberlain was no longer that sort of imperialist. He had visited South Africa and now discounted the Milner view. Supremacy had cost too much of more than money in the process of not being achieved. Doing deals with the credible Boer spokesmen now available must serve instead. Tariff Reform, his running and dividing struggle inside the Tory Party, now had his full attention.

Although South Africa itself dominates this period, there would be debates on the nature, divine or deranged, of the two towering personalities dominating history under the constitutional reign of Lord Salisbury. The Tory government would finally, in 1902, move to a new official leadership though still rubbing along with the command of Joe Chamberlain. Cecil Rhodes, from the southern hemisphere, had called shots in Westminster beyond all political health and had essentially failed. Very carefully, Arthur Balfour, supposedly fainéant intellectual, would now begin, in consort with George Wyndham and his own, seriously useful, younger brother Gerald, to approach more constructive undertakings, notably in Ireland.

During Balfour's three years as Prime Minister, the Congested Districts Act and a land policy of buying out old ownership to be let or sold advantageously and creating upon it what in Ireland are called 'Strong farmers' had made a serious impact. Such inglorious and far-sighted things would continue. Even so, the Tory Party was in no shape for competitive politics.

This was, though, a period when new and constructive ideas won nervous attention. Old age pensions were *talked* about if thought unthinkable by actual Conservatives. (The Prince of Wales had sat on a commission on the subject—doodling Union Jacks with coloured pencils). But they would, despite much talk of undermining national character, become Liberal policy in 1909, five shillings weekly for those earning £31.10s. or less annually, and with prim moral requirements attached. In the same careful way, women's suffrage began now to be seen as something on the horizon rather bigger than a lace-gloved hand, one later shown to be capable of throwing things. Much talk of that suffrage would be aimed at confining such privilege to middle-/or upper-class women, something resisted by Liberals as a way of recruiting new Tory voters in the name of progress.

At the same time, notions of higher education reaching out and down to what were routinely called 'the lower classes' were finding an outlet in university external courses, by one of which London University had given

H. G. Wells his external degree in General Sciences. Oxford had its own promising redoubt in Ruskin Hall (later College), named after the sympathetic art historian, and with the university (and union members) responding rather more generously than might have been feared. There would be very great earnest about this, with major union leaders like the County Durham miner Jack Lawson speaking on these pages, emerging to major places in the rising trade union movement and Labour Party.

At Oxford, along with Ireland, Women's Suffrage was still patronized, one young gentleman 'prizing the two ounces of brain' which separated him from women. Drink, deserving its capital letter, provoked debates about fighting it at the cost of extensive public house closure. The battle was as dear to Liberals (despite the dangerous indulgence of Asquith), heavily Nonconformist, as abominable to the Tories, reliant as they were upon brewers as contributors, and publicans as getters-in of the vote. The Temperance movement, with leaders like William Booth, was highly relevant and influential in a heavy-drinking (and commonly overworked) nation. It was too serious for easy dismissal, even in the champagne circles of Oxford.

On the side of tolerance, there would be a stirring, encouraged by the likes of Bernard Shaw, for liberalization of the whalebone restraints of theatre censorship. Such thinking would stir rather elderly young men of good family to lament in the Oxford Union the dangerous liberality of the Lord Chamberlain. In the foreign sphere, contrary and virulent anxieties were proclaimed which, in the name of vigilance, would prove a stimulant to the war that duly came. Such anxieties were, certainly in Oxford, a jittery and masochistic hobby, not least the talk of compulsory military service, suggesting the long-after (and wiser) view that a measure of complacency might have been a good idea.

---

26 October 1899

House believes that war in the Transvaal could and should have been avoided.

The benches were full, the gallery was packed, and many members (and not a few non-members) were content to sit on the floor.

Mr Asquith *launched into an unsparing diatribe against Mr Chamberlain and his diplomatic methods. His speech was clear and he spoke with more conviction than usual. The House gave him a better reception than might have been expected from the nature of his views.*

Mr J. G. Jameson (Balliol) *was in fighting mood; he obviously felt very deeply on the subject. He began very well, but later on, his speech was somewhat encumbered with blue-book quotations. Mr Jameson has inaugurated a new epoch in Union oratory by adopting to great effect a number of Dantonesque mannerisms; his device of pacing up and down the floor of the House like a caged tiger while wrestling with his thoughts is an excellent one.*

Mr Ensor *had strong views about a nation's personality which he found incompatible with Mr Beit.*[7] *He dwelt largely on the Capitalistic basis of the war, and compared the Uitlander grievances to those forming the grounds for the Jameson raid.*

Hon A. M. Herbert (Balliol) *preferred personalities to technicalities. There was a good deal too about archangels and cannibalism.*

Mr A. Cecil *spoke, as he always does, as a high Tory. He made an able defence of Mr Chamberlain and attacked Mr Gladstone's policy after Majuba* [Concessionary policy of Gladstone, after that defeat in 1881, toward Transvaal Boers see Commentary above], *welcomed on both sides of the House.*

Mr J. H. Morgan (Balliol) *made a bitter attack on the South African League, taking the same line as Mr Ensor. He has considerable command of language and his speech showed no lack of point or energy.*

Debate adjourned till next week

2 November 1899

Transvaal war debate resumed.

Mr Cecil[8] *moved an amendment to the effect that responsibility for the war rested with the Liberal Party. He had one good point—Mr Gladstone's policy in 1880, but after that, was vague and unsatisfactory. A settled gloom came over him when he reflected upon the unpatriotic conduct of certain Liberals, and after that he never quite recovered his vivacity.*

Mr G. F. Tomlinson *took Mr Chamberlain under his wing and kept him there in the kindest possible way. He spoke in the tone of one reluctantly compelled to talk to an audience of babies.*

Mr S. A. Gillon (New College)—Librarian *dislikes the Boers but dislikes Mr Chamberlain more. The outcome of that was some very passionate invective—vastly and justly appreciated by the House.*

Mr B. K Long *allowed himself to be carried away in an artificial frenzy into a vituperation of Mr Kruger which was neither relevant nor well expressed. Eventually the President had to interpose.*

Mr E. T. Nelson *is a real African and he thinks Mr Chamberlain has committed heavy crimes against his country. He dwelt on the chivalry of the Boers and made a sturdy attack on government policy.*

Both motion and amendment were lost, the motion 46:59, the amendment 55:73.

---

16 November 1899

House believes that, apart from his management of South African affairs, House has no confidence in Mr Chamberlain.

Mr Steel Opposing: *We have heard him in better form. Anyone who sets out to depict Mr Chamberlain as a deep thinker, holding the balance between collectivism on the one hand and individualism on the other, gives himself a hard task. And surely it was hardly worthwhile justifying the Transvaal war by the plea that it bound our colonies closer together.*

Mr Knotteford-Fortescue *was interesting inasmuch as he criticised Mr Chamberlain from a Conservative point of view—the point of view of a sparrow finding a cuckoo's egg in its nest.*

Mr C. Waley-Cohen *made a very fair defence of Mr Chamberlain whom he appears to worship with an ardour which is almost profane.*

Motion lost 29:112.

———— ◈ ————

23 November 1899

House would welcome some further rapprochement with Germany.

Considerable interest might have been expected to attach to the debate. But we have rarely seen a more lethargic and indifferent audience.

Mr Gillon *has a charming individuality but was at his least persuasive where he tried to be logical and most pleasing when he condescended to being frankly Gillonesque, as for instance, in his vivid description of 'the bounding Slav.'*

Mr Ensor *concerned himself mainly with the moral contagion which would accrue to us from any union with the untempered militarism of Prussia.*

Mr Waley-Cohen *made another good debating speech but has not quite mastered the technique of speaking and at present, wavers between hesitancy and hysteria.*

Motion lost 35:45.

———— ◈ ————

30 November 1899

House believes that the drama in this country should be liberated from censorship.

Mr Waley-Cohen *was very much too long, but otherwise good. Parts of his speech might have been omitted, including an irrelevant attack on the Fabian Society and some rather crude strictures upon Mr Bernard Shaw who, by the way, was roughly treated by the mover as well. We are sorry to see that so brilliant a writer is so little appreciated by the Society.*

Mr G. J. F. Tomlinson (Univ.) *made quite an amusing speech. We sympathise with his strictures on the Oxford Theatre, though he seemed to us to exaggerate the moral influence of the drama. Mr Tomlinson is much better on general rather than political subjects.*

Mr R. F. Sawyer (Ch.Ch.) *defended the state censorship with somewhat inadequate arguments.*

Mr V. R. Aronson (Merton) *made a serious and careful speech in defence of the censorship. His account of the defects of modern drama was true and well expressed, though we doubt if the Lord Chamberlain does much to remedy them.*

Viscount Tiverton[9] (New College) *thought that the censor usually erred on the side of leniency. His speech was not very good in delivery and—to our thinking— execrable in substance. It is hard to say any good thing of a man who thinks 'Little Eyolf' should have been*[10]*suppressed.*

Mr R. A. Scott-James (BNC) *made quite a good little speech. His ideas are excellent and he has plenty of them in his head, though at present, they are not arranged in the best possible way.*

Mr A. Chalker-Pearse *was cut short by the absence of a quorum.*

Motion lost 19:48.

25 January 1900

That the present Cabinet have been guilty of such negligence as to forfeit the confidence of the country.

The attendance was exceedingly large, the hall being quite full.

Mr R. Asquith *confined himself to Mr Balfour's*[11] *indiscreet words at Manchester and within that rather narrow area, succeeded in making out a very convincing case, but the fact that parts of his speech were exaggerated and over-coloured, detracted to some extent from the effectiveness of the rest.*

Mr Cecil—Treasurer *Many of his points, though persuasive at the time, were easily picked to pieces by subsequent speakers; but on the whole, the speech was a very good one—particularly in the sobriety and moderation by which it was characterized, but he should speak rather louder: at times he was almost inaudible at the back of the hall.*

Mr Macfadyn *also has a weak voice; and the somewhat querulous tone in which his speeches are delivered, is apt to obscure their very real merits.*

Mr E. T. Nelson (St John's) *has a stentorian voice, a considerable command of language and an inexhaustible fund of conviction.*

Mr Long *is always a pleasant speaker, but also a disappointing one… the substance of his speeches is usually mediocre, his arguments are apt to be dull and unoriginal; he lacks new ideas and new ways of expressing them. For this reason he seems to us to be a very fair speaker, but no more.*

Mr M. L. Gwyer (Ch.Ch.), *apt at times to be a little prosy and long drawn-out, made a great point of the terrible alternative which would confront the country if the present government were ejected.*

Mr W. Pulling (Keble) *delivered himself of a somewhat feeble piece of invective about 'Little Englanders';*[12] *these men of straw have been set up and knocked down so often that the exhibition has ceased to be very amusing.*

Motion lost 50:126.

8 February 1900

House debated Temperance—the form of the motion being omitted.

Mr A. D. Lindsay (Univ.)[13] *He obviously knew his subject and consequently abstained austerely from the hysterics of the amateur reformer. He seemed shy of his own points and spoiled them by a too rapid and indistinct delivery.*

Mr F. Roscoe (Balliol) *His speaking is not of the flashy and elaborate type. He grips the facts hard and sets forth his conclusions in perfectly simple and lucid language.*

Mr J. B. Holborn (Merton) *bears an unfortunate resemblance to St Sebastian— especially when he casts his eyes upward toward the Gallery. Which make him less effective before a secular audience than he might otherwise be.*

Mr Maxwell (Ch.Ch.) *Discouraged by the emptiness of the House, stopped almost before he had begun. If he had spoken the speech he had meant to speak, it might have been a very good one; and again it might not. One never knows.*

The unidentified motion was carried 43:4.

15 February 1900

House discussed Old age pensions—again no motion stated.

Mr H. du Parcq[14] *said some wise things about the nature of Imperial obligations in Home Policy.*

Mr Dunbar *was very strongly against the motion; he took a somewhat stern and inhumanly economic view of the position. He does not seem to have any particular talent for speaking, either in construction, vocabulary or delivery, but he is certainly above the average.*

Mr Shepheard-Walwyn *made a fair debating speech from the point of view of a philanthropist who loves the poor, but does not think the Pension scheme the right way of remedying their condition.*

Motion carried 22:21.

---

22 February 1900

House thinks the trend of modern civilisation is against the abolition of war.

The main interest naturally centred on the speech of Mr Keir Hardie which was in every way worthy of his reputation and rose at times to real eloquence.

Mr Long *delivered a carefully worded panegyric upon war in the abstract, interspersed with topical allusions to the present state of affairs in South Africa. But heroics are dangerous ground for a young orator: a single slip and your eloquence becomes bombast, your tragedy a farce. Mr Long unfortunately made more than one such slip.*

Mr Keir Hardie[15] *was received with tremendous applause. He confined himself to attacking War in the abstract; within those limits his speech was really admirable; it was moderate in tone; it was cogent in argument and excellently delivered. His speech was a great success; we only hope he enjoyed his visit to Oxford as much as the House did.*

Motion lost 55:60.

---

1 March 1900

House approves the annexation of both South African republics. Cambridge visit.

Mr Raymond Asquith *dwelt on the impossibility of establishing a satisfactory government by force, on the dangers of militarism and on the fact that the declared object of the war was to secure political equality for the white races. The prospect in any case was not very hopeful, but much less desperate if we conciliated than if we annexed.*

Mr Cecil *thought Dutch feeling had made friendly relations impossible; our soldiers were brave; the Queen's reign had been long and distinguished; Let us annex.*

Mr A. C. Pigou (King's College Cambridge)[16] *made an uncommonly good speech. He took a more hopeful view of the situation than the opener.*

Mr C. S Montagu (Trinity Cambridge) *We are in a difficult place; justice must go to the wall; in this case, force is our only hope, and as a matter of fact, our Empire is originally founded on force; affection was a result, not a cause. Debate adjourned till next meeting* Vote carried over.

<hr>

8 March

Debate resumed.

Mr Morgan *delivered exceedingly bitter and splenetic invective against the Cape plutocrats and the Rhodesian Press.*[17]

Mr Tomlinson *is never at his best on a subject which requires hard reasoning. His arguments were of the most trite and trivial nature and the whole speech was lacking in logical coherence; it carried no conviction.*

Mr Steel *made a very good speech, though few people will agree with his suggestion that the South African problem can be settled by the institution of a civil service on the model of that of India.*

Mr Ensor *made the best speech we have yet heard on the anti-capitalist theory of the war. By neglecting all the other factors in a situation, it is usually possible to say something striking. Socialists usually seem to labour under a kind of apostleship; every question for them centres on their King Charles's head.*

Mr Boyd-Carpenter (Balliol)[18] ex-president *There is a large class of people who think that they know everything because they have been round the world. They are usually very stupid. Mr Boyd-Carpenter is not stupid, but he makes a very great mistake if he thinks that three years residence at the Cape has made him the ultimate authority on South African politics. He said many things which seemed to us grossly unfair and it was not surprising that Mr Ensor was constantly on his feet making personal explanations and corrections. Altogether the speech seemed a most hysterical and ill-balanced performance quite unworthy of the ex-president's reputation.*

Motion lost 29:94.

---

10 May 1900

House regrets the popularity and influence enjoyed at the present moment by the Rt. Hon. Cecil Rhodes.

Mr A. Cecil (Against) *The first part of his speech was better than the second which was full of detailed irrelevancies about Mr Kruger, Clive and other heroes of Mr Cecil who seems to have been dabbling in Indian History of late.*

Mr Lewisohn (Trinity) *was the only speaker who realized the demands of the motion. He proceeded to emphasize the Raid and discussed the general policy of imperial expansion, of which he took Mr Rhodes to be the embodiment and high priest; it takes a brave man in these times to abuse imperialism, but Mr Lewisohn has the courage of his convictions. And he did abuse it without fear or stint.*

Mr Shepheard-Walwyn (Oriel) *asked the House to repudiate a motion which regretted the popularity of an Oriel man;[19] at Oriel only champagne is drunk; why then complain of Rhodes drinking it at Kimberly when most people could hardly afford ditch water. Rhodes was certainly right to keep back luxuries for himself; it was his duty to the empire.*

Motion lost 53:56.

14 June 1900

House deplores the decadence of Modern literature

Mr Waley-Cohen *showed more humour and rapidity and incisiveness of delivery. The defect of his speech was its excessive length, the defect of the speaker, his inability to appreciate Thomas Hardy.*

Mr Pereira *As a defence of modern literature, his instances were hardly happy. Kipling's poem about the 'Ten league canvas' is a case of meaningless, megalomaniac nonsense which is one of the chief dangers of contemporary poetry.*

Mr R. Farer (Balliol) *made perhaps the best speech of the evening; his defence of Hardy and Meredith was particularly good and much needed after the ignorant diatribes of other members, apparently unacquainted with the work of either author. Mr Farrer deserved a better audience.*

Motion carried 22:19.

18 October 1900

House views with regret the return to power of the Government of Lord Salisbury.

Mr Cecil *The best part of a good speech was undoubtedly the peroration, a fine vindication of the sublime and unselfish Imperialism of Mr Chamberlain based on that principle which has led us into war and which in turn, has led us to annex the Transvaal.*

Mr Cadogan (Balliol) *The policies of Majuba, Home Rule and Abolition of the House of Lords, he described as dead, and he went on to define Lord Salisbury as the 'Great Peace Minister.'*

Mr Farrar *pictured Mr Chamberlain wallowing in disgrace like a duck in the mire, now seizing the reins of state in bloodstained hands. He is dramatic and melodramatic, his model, Burke rather than O'Connell. But he should perhaps be careful of the pathetic octave.*

Vote not given.

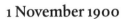

1 November 1900

House deplores the decline of morality in British politics.

Mr A. Herbert (Balliol)[20] *The remarkable good fortune has been given to Mr Chamberlain to sail close to the wind in a dead calm.*

Mr Nelson *complimented the proposer on his petty vindictiveness and drew a pathetic picture of the Colonial Secretary seeking peace in the fortress of Gibraltar.*

Mr Farrer *depicted Mr Chamberlain crying to the ages for mercy while concealment preyed upon his damask cheek and ended with an appeal to keep pure and spotless this England we know and love and live in.*

Mr R. E. Young (St John's) *was reminiscent and mythological. He recalled the days of Pericles and made a quiet protest against reverence for the white flag.*

Motion lost 40:68.

15 November 1900

House believes the present is a fitting opportunity to grant Home Rule to Ireland.

Mr Lewisohn *pointed to the fact of continuous evictions and emigrations leading to the survival of the least fit and urged that the divorce of sentiment from politics was the most dangerous form of cant. The most valuable part of his speech related Ireland to the whole question of Imperial Federation.*

Mr Long *said that Home Rule was a political ghost, but did not succeed in laying it. While showing an actual belief in Home Rule, he forcibly reiterated the old objections and claimed that the grievance, if any existed, was a sentimental one, having its origin in the unfortunate temperament of the Irish people.*

Mr Maclaren (Balliol) *claimed that the vileness of the Irish MPs was a reason for their immediate withdrawal from Westminster. The real disunion he found was in the present so-called Unionist party.*

Mr W. H. Buchan (BNC) *argued that the unanimous voice of England on the Irish question could not be disregarded.*

Mr Scott-James *would only concede Home Rule to a united Ireland.*

Motion lost 35:59.

---

22 November 1900

House believes drastic reform of the House of Lords indispensable to national progress.

Mr Cuthbertson (Corpus) *gave historical proof of the political blindness of the House of Lords and showed the hereditary principle to be untenable.*

Mr Grigg[21] *described Home Rule as the only option between coercion and violence.*

Mr Cecil *described the present as a time of ceaseless attempts at revolution. He claimed that the Lords had seldom made any selfish use of their great power, instancing Lord Rosebery and Mr Chamberlain as typical Members of the two Houses. Finally, he declared himself in favour of gilded rather than brazen nonentity.*

Mr G. Rankin (Trinity Cambridge) *defined their Lordships' House as a historical parasite living on its past because no one will lend money on its future. The most opportune time was now for a measure which would long leave the passing of a game law as a matter of astonishment. This was a sectional house needing to be reformed until it was not.*

Mr F. Armstrong (St John's Cambridge) *spoke as an Irishman and a Unionist and consequently a defender of the peers' privileges. It should be preserved as an Olympian home for elder statesmen.*

Motion lost 54:93.

29 November 1900

House believes that the interests of Germany and Italy are compatible with our own.

Mr Grigg *claimed Italy as our sole friend and urged that Germany, the nouveau riche among the powers, was rapidly assuming a similar position.*

Mr J. Crabb Watt (Balliol) *thought the Anglo-German agreement one-sided and directly intended to increase the stress of commercial competition. In every quarter, the Germans opposed us and behind her was a conspiracy of the European powers to oust us from our markets.*

Mr Scott-James *came forward as a partisan of France, denouncing the purblind who would not see that we were already at war with Germany. Citing in one breath, Charles Lamb, the Wars of the Roses, Mazzini and Morocco, his speech was a strange mixture of good and bad, combining the comprehensiveness of an All Souls general paper with the Oxford Review.*

Mr Zimmern (New College) *protested against insularity, showed that Germany had no genius for colonisation and said that if commercial rivalry meant a state of warfare, Europe was already the scene of universal war.*

Motion carried 27:14.

3

Chamberlain and Milner
Go to War

17 October 1901–18 May 1905

Liberal Failure?/Chamberlain as leader/General Buller/fewer Irish MPs?/Press freedom/Russian alliance?/Rosebery at Chesterfield/Kipling on sport/theatre finance/Ritchie's tax changes/Russia 1905/Balfour's education bill/French decline?/ Trade Unions/'Social Reform'/No Confidence motion/Ireland/Licensing Act/ Disestablishment/South African forced labour/Payment of MPs/Prize ring/ French politics/Pub Compensation/Degenerate England?/Universities out of touch/A French alliance?/Imperial preference/Macedonia/Socialism/Boer War enquiry/Russia & Japan/Protection taxes/Passive resistance/Tariff commission/ Chinese labour/Russia/Government methods/Licensing/Labour Party/Women's suffrage/Anglo-French pact?/the Government/Defence programme/Aliens?/ Milner/Home Rule/Redistribution/(Chamberlain's empire/The Church of England/ Abolition of the Lords?/Russia/School meals/Tibet/Compulsory Greek/French Revolution/Aliens/Sir Anthony MacDonnell.

The second South African conflict, begun on 12 October 1899, had gone badly. Redvers Buller, protégé of the Commander in Chief, Wolseley, was an outstandingly brave and popular soldier (holder of the VC), who had played a vital part in the Zulu War. However, anticipating, with most British opinion, the larger fallacy of 1914, that the war would be over by Christmas, he had sent one general, Methuen, westward to relieve Kimberley. A second, Gatacre, was directed to drive back Afrikaner forces from the Orange Free State and attack Bloemfontein. He himself would lead a drive into Natal. It didn't happen. Across what was understandably called 'Black Week', actually not so long—10–15 December, all three had suffered defeats. Each of the assaults had failed against superior weaponry and generals with better knowledge of the territory. The garrison at Mafeking was surrounded. This was a lesser humiliation than it seemed—and the eventual raising of it a lesser triumph.

Something would indeed be concluded before Christmas—in Black Week, December 1899—but it was not British victory; rather relief in both senses of the word. Victory, when it came under the command of the replacements, Roberts and Kitchener, was marked in London by the crowd hysteria of Mafeking Night (May 1903). The very word, often converted into a present participle, would come to mean any kind of large-scale, irrational, exalted, and commonly drunken behaviour.

The implications were profound. Milner and Chamberlain had wanted a war of clear-cut triumph and British Imperial assertion. Instead, after marching triumphantly into a hole, they had scrambled out of it. Those Liberals who detested the war, the original 'Little Englanders'—Campbell Bannerman, the young Lloyd George, and again, Edmund Morel—had argued with effect that the Boer War was a shoddy piece of power-grabbing. It would be won, but only after a fearful scare and irretrievable loss of political face for the seekers of territory and maintainers of national greatness.

Despite the imperialism of Asquith, Rosebery, and the inveterate Liberal Leaguer Grey, the next, and Liberal, government would come to office and *then* election (1905–6), bent on undoing the great aggrandisement of Milner and Chamberlain. Meanwhile the Conservative government inherited here and now the immediate consequences. If Buller had been a luckier general, winning a quick triumph, front-foot imperialism would have been the theme. As it was, that soldier was the object of Tory hostility expressed naturally through *The Times*. Having been savagely attacked there by Leopold Amery, Buller made a speech on 10 October 1901 defending himself. The Tory War Minister, St John Broderick, demanded his resignation for breach of regulations and, on Buller's refusal, sacked him.

The fact of the general also being, in his own words, 'a Whig and a Liberal Unionist' helped.

Amery's virulence had demanded a speech by the hero in self-defence. Convention—that generals do not make speeches—provided the War Office with a pretext for sacking the man and concentrating the blame. Buller's past successes, notably in the Zulu War, and his great personal courage—a snatching up from horseback of otherwise doomed individual junior officers—were brushed aside by a War Minister, St John Broderick, with his own questions to answer. These concerned supply, equipment, and a declared personal programme of army reform clearly not providing the numbers for war overseas. He would now replace Buller with Roberts, hero of the oversold relief of Mafeking.

Buller had been the innocent instigator of doubt in the very premises of imperialism, its function in a game of pure power and military assertion. The war party in Britain had to be placated. Meanwhile political debate centred on the civilian originators of the Boer War, in inevitable particular, the Colonial Secretary, Joseph Chamberlain. Oxford, for all its Conservatism, would, by a small majority in the debate of 24 October 1901—a week ahead of approving that dismissal—go on record as regretting the notion of his ever leading the Conservative Party.

The South African War, now ending in titular victory after a struggle and reverses which marked it as a historical defeat, had been the doing of new men, Rhodes and Milner, and a former new man, Chamberlain: ex-radical, ex-future leader of the Liberal Party, and, for too many years, the dominant personality of the Tory Party. He had now split them as he had split the Liberals. *They* in the late 1880s had divided into Liberal Unionists (readily become an annexe of Conservatism) and a not yet properly cohering Liberal Party of sound Free Traders, ready for Irish Home Rule. Meanwhile the other Chamberlain effect, his dismissal of Free Trade for Imperial Protection, had split Tories into Protectionists, ascendant but unfulfilled, and Free Traders, resentful and fighting back...witness that vote at the Union.

As for Salisbury, he had lingered too long in the highest place, past the best of his health and energy, too tired perhaps to have exercised his natural caution when Milner and Rhodes had set out on that last grand act of imperial piracy. In 1902 he made way for Arthur Balfour, serious academic philosopher and former Irish Secretary, known to the Irish Press as 'Bloody Balfour'. That sobriquet, thrown at him back in 1887, concerned 'The Mitchelstown massacre'—after-the-event and inevitable action of outnumbered and badly knocked-about policemen, fifty-seven of them injured, finally opening fire with three fatalities.

In practice, Balfour, in depth rather than by incident, had as Commons leader, with his brother Gerald as Chief Secretary, done essential things in Ireland, notably the Land Act of 1896, legislation to establish agricultural and technical training, and, supremely, the Local Government Act of 1898. This had really mattered. It put Irishmen into actual, if limited, local government of other Irishmen—a promise and perhaps a precedent. Ironically, that act derived from Chamberlain (at his best): the Ireland-wide local government scheme which he had planned back in 1885/6, before colliding with Gladstone's grand, but blurred vision of full-dress Home Rule.

Even so, the Ireland which the Union would debate at this time was full of grief—Augustine Birrell, Liberal Irish Secretary from 1907, would speak of the sheer horror of the poverty he had seen in country districts. 'The melancholy of it was overwhelming...Galway and the workhouse at Clifden will never quit my memory.'[1] Nevertheless, Balfour's 'Killing rebellion with kindness' had represented a modest but recognizable amelioration. The land reforms meant extensive, 'strong farmer' Irish ownership. An agricultural rate Act of 1896 halved the tax burden on landholders, so many of them new and Catholic, while the British Exchequer picked up the tab. In May 1897, an Irish Local Government Bill had been passed. It 'stripped the Grand Juries of their administrative and fiscal powers and vested these in county councils, borough councils elected with a wide franchise...'[2]

So many of the Balfours' doings in Ireland as members of Salisbury's Cabinet had shown a marked Meliorist or even Socialist cast of mind. Beyond Ireland, there had been, in 1896, a Conciliation Act for industrial disputes. The new Prime Minister would give serious thought to old age pensions, though this cue would be missed, leaving the next Liberal government to make that step and be abused, not least at the Oxford Union, by hard-edged Tories shocked at such coddling of the undeserving poor. Actually, the core of governmental policy at this time was, despite a floor-show of party political animus, calmer and more constructive than it had been, certainly more so than in the recent days of seeking national great-ness. The many loose ends of the Balfours' and Birrell's policies, plus the establishment by Birrell of Catholic universities, would have their due benign effect—all to be lost by the War to End Wars and the grotesque mishandling by the War Coalition caught up in it during an initially derided Irish rising—by 1916 and 1920–2.

At the turn of the century, violence had faded in Ireland, though debate, parliamentary and Oxford Union, maintained, especially on the Unionist side, much of the comfortable ill-will of earlier years. Even so the reforms of the Balfours were taking, and they would be followed through and expanded by their long-term successor from 1907, Birrell, Liberal and Nonconformist. Outside Ulster, the Protestant Ascendancy was being dismantled, and per-haps for this reason, Ulster would grow ever more destructively 'loyal'. But Oxford was noticing. Despite individual outbursts—'The bulk of the Irish population is not fit to exercise the power of voting'—(a Mr Cadogan of Balliol), Oxford got the message. A debate of 13 November 1901 deplored by 79 votes to 43 any reduction in Irish representation at Westminster.

None of this tempering of injustice had affected the House's enthusi-asm for conflict, conflict of any kind. They debated manliness and fitness, and in one debate, they looked back admiringly eighty and more years to the great days of bare-knuckle boxing, the sixty and more rounds fought to the quite literal crunch by the *Game Chicken* and the *Lancashire Giant*. The current cerebral tendency was scorned. Real men, said one brisk gentle-man, didn't linger about discussing fine points in tea-rooms.

However, every subject touched upon had its heroes and villains readily swapped by partisan undergraduates. France, at this time, fascinated Oxford. The aftermath of the *Affaire Dreyfus*, which had split secular, liberal France from the aristocratic/clerical elements and its pious, aristocratically officered army, had put into solid power a Radical government. The moving spirits of Reform, as mentioned, were René Waldeck Rousseau, a constitutional reformer objecting to the intrusive power of highly political religious orders like the Assumptionists. His successor, Dr Émile Combes, was not a socialist, but a man who at this time was stripping out every social privilege, precedent, or entitlement enjoyed by Church, army, and gentry.

Oxford High Tories, automatically hostile to long-discriminated-against Irish Catholics, deplored his short way with the over-privileged and politically meddling clergy of *French* Catholicism. It was in the university blood. Oxford, with its loyalty to Charles 1 and non-resistance to James II, had men ready to proclaim the *fleur de lys* and Christian reaction. The Combes package was, said one of them, 'an assault on all that was best in France'.

France would also figure in a different role as the Union cheerfully anticipated war against *somebody* and the variety of alliances for fighting them, available to what they would invariably call 'England'. Advocates of one or more of these—with France, Germany, Russia, or even, with some surprise, a new and rather fearsome player, Japan—spoke up for their choices.

The mood was not pacific, let alone inclined to appeasement. We might have managed a narrow win across three years fighting Cape farmers, but an assumption of invincibility dies hard. Out of the mouths of babes and undergraduates came fearful proposals. Mr Thorp of Wadham believed that an alliance of England, Germany, and Japan would prove invincible. Mr Thorp was worried about Afghanistan—Can't trust Russia there! So, for this undergraduate strategist, 'The Emperor William of Germany is our staunchest ally.' Of the international bumptiousness of Oxford undergraduates there was no end. So on 12 July 1902, we got back to the doing-down of France. Mr Maxwell of Christ Church lamented 'failures, not caused by a bad system of individual weakness, but by degeneration of the oldest people in Europe. A century of Revolution has been too much for France.'

Kipling's sinister call for compulsory National Service (on the *German* model) would be sinisterly applauded. However, in the very Oxonian way of setting fires and putting them out with lemonade, this approved Prussianization would be compared to 'the old Anglo-Saxon *Fyrd*'! In Ireland though, it was a period of relative calm, quiet and Conservative reform, but one that had no hope of diverting St Michael Street prejudice from its happy contempt. 'Is Ireland worth keeping?' asked one undergraduate. It was a question to be subsequently put in reverse.

Anxious debate ran however well beyond Ireland and France. The mood was recurringly pre-war in the literal sense, that fear of prospective enemies, demonstrated by debates about the best partners in alliance with whom we should dispel the mood of war. A Mr Noble put together all the elements about the unsuitability of candidate-allies, before settling in this not altogether hypothetical prospect, upon the negative virtues of France. It was all very grand: 'For 100 years we have not waged war without an ally, and we must find out who the best might be if the situation becomes a crisis. Germany is impossible. Her colonial interests clash with ours. *Russia* would not suit. Her consistent objective is India...'

When the House talked anxiously about alliances in terms of who could be trusted with our empire, it largely reflected territories taken by force in the past and now treasured as sweetening self-interest with decent British concern for their welfare. Sometimes the mask slipped: Mr Heath of Corpus spoke for the decencies: 'When the Chinese' (indentured labourers in Rand gold mines) 'are sent back to China, they will be destitute. They would be slaves. Though free to come, they will not be free, having come.' To which Mr Samuel, of the same College, responded, 'I object to idealism. We have to face the facts.' So of course, did Chinese indentured labourers.

That labour, something cheaply employed in the gold-bearing territory dominated by Cecil Rhodes, was the immediate responsibility of Alfred Milner, 'English blood-patriot' rather pushing his ruthless coherence. The Tories had been uneasy. Most of the Liberals now gaining electoral traction were clear-cut opponents. Balfour was left defending it while Chamberlain, jointly responsible for the whole South African adventure, and devouring and assertive as ever, now urged him to drop everything for a campaign on behalf of Joe's own alternative obsession, Imperial Protection...

Balfour had an open mind on the pure economics of it, but was too well aware of the strength of the Tory Free Traders. As a nailed-up Prime Minister, he had lost blood to one of these, Charles Ritchie, who, as noted, had in May 1903, with Treasury backing, abolished a corn duty imposed originally for revenue, and done so as a Free Trader's political duty. Balfour, a man in a weak position, looked upon as a weak man (essentially untrue), would shortly fire Ritchie only to provoke the resignation of other Ministers, Balfour of Burleigh and Lord George Hamilton, while Chamberlain, for freedom of crusading action, also resigned. Winston Churchill, another Free Trader—given to quoting Disraeli on the subject—now left the Tories for the Liberals. The objective had been, a grand national campaign (with further divisions among the Tories) for Protection, but Chamberlain, clever, imperious, expert, though probably wrong on the question, even in the terms of the day, would call no more shots. A stroke silenced him in 1906, though he would not die until 1914.

Home of lost causes, Oxford was full of Imperialists and Protectionists who turned to motions damning the Liberal Opposition. 'Was there a man among them?' asked one self-assured boy. There are worse things to be than underrated. That assessment did after all get Henry Campbell-Bannerman chosen. Asquith needed to clean up financially at the Bar, while Rosebery, formerly Foreign Secretary, given credit for negotiating an end to the Fashoda incident and briefly Premier in 1894, admired by Imperial Liberals and most Tories, was turning slowly into monumental masonry. At Chesterfield in December 1901, he had made a speech calling on his party essentially to chuck Gladstone and what he stood for—Free Trade, Home Rule, and the old man's cool view of Imperialism. The Chesterfield speech showed sovereign contempt for the people who belonged to his party. With that, seven years after his incidental premiership, facing a Tory Party in toils over its central purpose and the new Liberal leadership happy for a fight in which he would have been on the other side, Rosebery walked off the stage—into the orchestra pit.

Sir Henry Campbell-Bannerman, universally known as CB, but at that moment identified only for a muddle about cordite at the War Office way back, was Rosebery's antithesis. In the Liberal Party, he was a Liberal. He had been talked about as only a stand-in: for Asquith certainly, perhaps for a risen Rosebery. His lordship, one cartoonist thought, might suddenly, like the effigy of Queen Hermione in *A Winter's Tale*, be 'stone no more' and step down from the plinth. The statue stayed put, but it spoke and spoke disastrously. Deference to Chamberlain, assent to the Milner/ Chamberlain line in South Africa (and for that matter a bland discounting of the Kitchener's concentration camps part of it), these, plus bored impatience with Home Rule, defined him. Rosebery's view was to embrace, late but plainly, the Conservative consensus, a consensus now fading.

CB, on the other hand, said, without calculation, everything that younger and more radical Liberals thought. He had contemplated the camps and the dead women and children and asked out loud, 'When is a war not a war? When it is carried on by methods of barbarism.' Abused in the Tory press, he came out fighting against 'the insane policy of subjugation and obliteration...it will not be enough to say that Lord Kitchener ought not to be interrupted by inquiries...the character of our nation is at stake.' There was no reason to doubt Campbell-Bannerman's straightforward revulsion, but the words took on even more force from the Conservative reaction.

They offered a public dinner to Asquith for having criticized the speech. CB called a meeting of Liberal MPs, asked for a vote of confidence, and got it. Rosebery's response was a defence of Kitchener characteristically five months later—7 December 1901—and included the observation that 'As to the methods of barbarity, the refugee camps were a result of the necessity of clearing the country.' He also went public on precisely those private convictions, the de-Gladstoning of Free Trade economics and a quiet dropping of Home Rule. At a speech, CB was free.

It was now open for him to define the party he led. No longer a stand-in, he looked to the radical side, something readily harnessed with renewed for support for the Gladstonian priorities, Home Rule and Free Trade, in all of which, Asquith, however busy in the courts, shrewdly joined. Slowly and sympathetically, he led the Liberals who responded with deeply felt affection. For disregarding the fissured contemporary Liberalisms, all needing a prefix, he was on happy terms with the main, unapologetic stream. Liberals now knew again where they were, and liked it.

This was good front-line politics directed at the next election, but Gilbert's little Liber-al and little Conserv-ative were not quite alone. Back in 1900, a committee had been formed to get the trade union voice into the Commons to match the 'Parliamentary Council' already formed by employers to offset the perceived menace of trade unions. The 'Labour Representation Committee' Secretary, Ramsay MacDonald, mindful of a big lock-out of engineers, would go beyond the lobby function and started running candidates in suitable towns. The Taff Vale Case of 1900 where obstinate judges treated a strike as actionable and awarded damages, gave the unions further and urgent cause for a parliamentary presence. Three by-election victories close together in 1903 indicated both rebellion against the received social and economic order and, more immediately, a long-term challenge to the Liberal Party, hinting that, not too remotely, the subject of political conversation might be changed.

The other Union had been debating Socialism for some time with the remote but nervous edge that might have applied to a debate on sex. 'Socialism must mean', thought a Mr Devas, 'a nation of slaves who periodically elect their absolute masters. The real solution for present difficulties is the spiritualization of the masses.' Instead they were stuck with three Labour MPs, something that hadn't happened before. It was a new and startling development, still politics, nothing spiritual about it, something to make speeches about.

Soon, undergraduates of a university lately given over to issues like Women's Suffrage, (soon to get rough), or questions about 'Our Empire' and the need to see off all the rival colonizers, might mutate. Labour men, members of ancient foundations, would be addressing Mr President about disgraceful working conditions and the need for something exciting called 'industrial action'. The Oxford Union would never quite give up the urge for spiritualization, but even the two future (and outstanding) archbishops, the undergraduates Cyril Garbett and William Temple, would take the point of these strange, new and quite different unions. The argument was widening alarmingly.

17 October 1901

House believes the Liberal party has failed and has no ideas.

The first debate of the term…was singularly lacking in interest. The traditions of the Liberal party demand that its members should abstain from imperial questions and confine themselves to social domestic reform.

Mr E. M. W. Grigg (New College)[3] *There has been a diplomatic success over Fashoda[4] and Uganda consequent upon the policies of Lord Rosebery. If Liberalism is to recover its former prestige, it must learn to reconcile Imperialism with a due regard for domestic reform.*

Mr J. R. Brook (Corpus) *We hear too much about Empire and should remember that charity begins at home.*

Mr W. A. Moore *What would become of the Empire if the Liberals discovered Imperialism?*

Mr W. Temple (Balliol)[5] *Liberals should free themselves from traditions. In the Empire, they have the best opportunity of disseminating pure Liberalism.* [An extremely fluent delivery, but should learn to vary the pitch of his voice occasionally.]

Mr H. Thorp *The motion is a recommendation to the Liberals to commit suicide.*

Motion lost 27:17.

24 October 1901

House would regret to see Mr Chamberlain as leader of the Conservative Party.

L. S. Flet *There is not the usual friendliness which can exist between leaders of opposing parties. We should recognise the universal hatred with which Mr Chamberlain is regarded by the Opposition. The Union alliance only exists in order to prevent Home Rule.*[6]

E. MacFadyan *Mr Chamberlain has that touch of the heroic which makes a leader of men, something abundantly shown by the way he has commandeered the whole Conservative Party. The standard by which to judge that party is its policy in South Africa; and that policy is solely due to Mr Chamberlain. There is another side to grasp, namely the necessity of ensuring a race fit for Empire.*

W. Temple *Mr Chamberlain has been spoiled by his connexion with the Conservatives and he has done more than anyone to bring them to their present condition.*

E. Zeitlyn (Jesus) *Mr Chamberlain is hated on both sides of the House of Commons. He is destitute of the sensitivity and magnanimity marking a true leader.*

J. Oppe (New College) *Men with great personalities are not necessarily the best leaders. Moreover Mr Chamberlain's ideal is that of the capitalist; and in home legislation and political economy, he is equally unsound.*

C. P. Blackwall (Wadham) *Statesmen must, above all things, be moral, but Mr Chamberlain is only fit to be a bottle-washer.*

Motion carried 54:49.

———— ⌒⌒⌒ ————

31 October 1901

House approves the act of the War Office in dismissing Sir Redvers Buller.

R. W. Livingstone (New College) *King's regulations forbid on the part of officers, anything in the nature of political utterance or appeal to the public against decisions of the Secretary of State.*

A. Herbert (Balliol) *Buller has been, on more than one occasion, a thorn in the side of the Government which has eagerly embraced an opportunity of getting rid of him.*

Lord Haddo *The policy of dismissing generals for making indiscrete speeches might usefully be applied to HM Ministers.* [Spoke better than usual.]

Motion carried 136:57.

———— ✺ ————

13 November 1901

House views with disapproval a reduction in parliamentary representation of Ireland.

Hon. E. C. Cadogan (Balliol) *The bulk of the Irish population is not fit to exercise the power of voting.*

L. S. Brock (Corpus) *I beg the House to take Ireland seriously for once and deprecate any slight on its people. The discontent of Ireland is due solely to English misgovernment. Rather than reduce representation, it would be better to end it altogether.*

F. W. Curran (Lincoln) *Obstruction can be just as well practiced by 20 Irish members as 100.*[7] *The government will be better advised to turn its attention to the financial and agrarian problems of Ireland.*

L. E. Buchan (Merton) *The proposed measure would be an enforcement of the Act of Union which has already been violated by the disestablishment of the Irish Church.*

Mr Sacher *Inequality of representation is not a valid argument. Ireland is like a picture by Burne-Jones. In both cases the canon of mathematical accuracy is inapplicable.*

D. L. Savory (St John's) *Irish legislation has substituted an oligarchy of priests for an oligarchy of landlords. We should respond by introducing the secularizing methods of the French.*

H. Thorp (Wadham) *I deprecate Mr Chamberlain's attitude to the Irish Party and wish we might go back to the conciliatory policy of Mr Balfour. The right response to Irish grievances is to give them a share in the responsibilities of Empire.*

Motion carried 79:43.

The early twentieth century, like the early twenty-first, was one of right-wing preponderance in the media—what were then happily called 'newspapers'. But they had only just, through technology and malign ambition, become *mass* newspapers, incidentally far less reliant upon advertising than any contemporary paper. Although Asquith *fils* here talks far beyond Lord Justice Leverson, the Union would follow parliamentarians in deploring them and being helpless before them.

---

20 November 1901

Any interference in the liberty of the press would be inexpedient and dangerous.

H. du Parcq (Exeter)[8] *There is no serious demand for restriction. On the whole, there is very little perversion of fact. If the first offenders are punished, they will acquire a fictitious notoriety. The condition of the Russian press ought to be a warning.*

H. Asquith (Balliol)[9] *The plea of liberty is a most dangerous weapon in the hands of unscrupulous men. We should distinguish liberty and license. The press should be licensed like public houses.*

A. D. Lindsay (Univ.) *Look at the evils of press censorship in India.*

Aubrey Herbert (Balliol)[10] *Consider the evils of the pro-Volscian party in Ancient Rome. Note the parallel of war correspondents during Kitchener's campaign in the Sudan. The individual, the nation and the government suffer equally from the calumnies of the press. The only answer is a rigorous censorship.*

Professor Lee (Visitor—Cornell) *I wasn't sure if this should be taken seriously, but I was surprised at the aspersion cast at the English press. To interfere with the press would alienate the people and the empire.*

Mr Savory *shook a rhetorical fist at Professor Lee.*

D. L. Savory (St John's) *I know your American papers.*

Motion carried 86:32.

4 December 1901

House would welcome a rapprochement with Russia.

H. D. Maclaren *The growing unfriendliness of the continental powers has proved the futility of splendid isolation. It is useless to seek an alliance with our continental rivals. But the antagonism between this country and Russia is nothing more than a superstition. We have never been able to check her claims in that direction. It would be wiser to recognise them.*

H. Thorp (Wadham) *The whole sentiment of this country is opposed to Russian methods and ideas. Numerous assurances have been given over Afghanistan and never fulfilled. If we need an alliance, we should look to Germany. And in the Emperor William, we should look to our staunchest friend on the continent. An alliance of England, Germany and Japan would be invincible in Europe and the East.*

Mr L. C. Jane (Wadham) *We ought to let Russia advance, if only to bring her within convenient striking distance. I am prepared to see Russia obtain possession of Manchuria and the Dardanelles, provided that our interests in the Yangtze Valley and the Suez Canal are uninjured. I am sceptical about the Kaiser as friend—look at his telegram to President Kruger.*

Mr Fletcher (New College) *Interest, not sentiment, is the usual bond of unity between countries; and Russia is the one great country whose continental interests do not conflict directly with our own in the struggle for open markets.*

Lord Haddo *I see no reason why we should not return to our old friendship with Russia. An alliance with that country will have the further advantage of securing the goodwill of France.*[11]

Mr E. Walls (Corpus) *Russia is greatly maligned in England. As for the Nihilists, they are not a whit less desirable than the Independent Labour Party.*

Mr M. H. Woods (Trinity) *A rapprochement with Russia will alienate Germany. Meanwhile Germany will throw us over when it suits her purpose.*

Motion lost by 28 votes.

---

23 January 1902

House believes that Lord Rosebery's Chesterfield speech points the way.

Rosebery, at odds with the Liberal Party of Campbell-Bannerman, was working, as ever ineptly, for a coalescence of Liberal Unionists and Conservatives hostile to Balfour. Hence that Chesterfield speech of December 1901 against Free Trade, and in favour of 'National Efficiency' and another renouncing Irish Home Rule. He had also been at this time like Milner, listening to the Webbs, source for the 'Efficiency' bit. Having no head for ideas, he was, as here, widely praised for principle.

Hon. E. Macfadyan (Balliol) *It is no mean platitude to say that at the present moment, the country is passing through a very real crisis. It has suffered for three years from ignorant and casual advice. Everyone from Sir William Harcourt,*[12] *a revered Oxford head and Rudyard Kipling, has contributed; and the result is formidable confusion. The Chesterfield policy is the policy of a statesman and not a mere politician.*

Hon E. Cadogan (Balliol) *Rosebery is only a vague theoriser on politics.*

A. J. Costain (Lincoln) *Rosebery has no constructive policies and no suggestions on, say Army reform. His idea of consulting foreign countries about the justice of our cause is futile. His peace policy is logically impracticable and useless—equally impracticable and useless.*

Motion lost 52:55.

---

6 February 1902

House agrees with Kipling about sport occupying too large a place in English life.

Mr D. L. Savory (St John's) *It is just as bad in the army. In the dear old town of Norwich, soldiers waste their afternoons playing polo, so only rich men can enter the Army. Kipling has pointed at the only remedy—compulsory military service. This would after all, be only the revival of the old Anglo-Saxon* fyrd.

Mr W. H. Buchan (BNC) *It is only by our athleticism that we can be as prepared for war as Germany and yet escape the militarism which is Germany's curse.*

Mr G. C. Upcott (Corpus) *Let Mr Kipling read Aristotle, in particular, the* Nichomachean Ethics *and he may yet be of some service to his country.*

Mr H. Maxwell (Ch.Ch.) *Kipling*[13] *has already been letting off steam in poetry and should not be taken too seriously.*

Mr E. Zeitlyn *I believe that before long, war will be replaced by international competition in sport.*

No vote recorded.

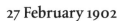

27 February 1902

House believes that the stage should be supported by the state.

H. du Parcq *The result of the present state of things is the production of insipid things which pay because they please the sort of people who go to the theatre every night. The state should support one or two theatres for other than commercial reasons.*

C. Wertheimer (Balliol) *I object to putting the stage on the same level as the Church or the vaccination question.*

Motion carried 65:40.

15 May 1902

House believes that the Chancellor's proposals violate the principles of sound finance.

The Chancellor, Hicks Beech had not so much put on a new tax, as a 'registration on corn', intended to please colonial producers. It did not cause an increase in bread prices. As stated above, a year later, his successor, Charles Ritchie, took it off in harmony with his 4*d.* reduction in income tax. Not at all harmoniously, this reversal was a statement of Free Trade principle and defiance of Joseph Chamberlain which went public by way of the endemic Tory split of Free Traders against Imperial Protectionists. Straddling it all, Balfour sacked Ritchie and provoked the Free Trade resignations mentioned above.

Mr J. R. Brooke (Corpus) *The corn duty: surely there are other subjects for taxation than the food of the people. I appeal to the Tories in the name of the economic laws to which they are attached. And I appeal to Liberals in terms of conscience and common sense.*

Mr L. S. Fletcher (New College) *The government have raised £73 million by dint of direct taxation against the £225 million spent on the war. The price of bread was no higher this year than last. It should be remembered that in the last generation, we have given the lower classes the franchise. If they have votes, they should pay their share towards the expense they approved. Some way must be found for preventing the masses from plunging into expensive wars without a thought for the morrow.*

F. Evelyn (Balliol) *I fear the Union is almost as low as the House of Commons. I find it lower. Stale party cries on the government side are met by staler ones from the Opposition. What is there so horrible about modern protection?*

E. T. Kighie (Balliol—a Canadian) *Beware the struggle between American money and Imperial sentiment.*

E. Zeitlyn (Jesus) *The tax will affect Ireland adversely, and Ireland is poverty-stricken. The life of the nation is affected by the price of food, and our Army will have to do its recruiting from among those most affected by this tax.*

Motion carried 46:43.

---

29 May 1902

House believes that a revolution in Russia is both probable and desirable. It attracted the smallest House of the term.

Mr W. Temple *Winter society in St Petersburg is very like Mayfair. It gets up very late, over-eats itself and talks scandal. The real life in Russia is in the country. By emancipation, the serfs have merely been impoverished. As for the Church, the parish priest is the necessary magician. The government does everything to alienate educated opinion. All is ready for the spark which will produce the revolution. This, I expect, will come from outside when the Austrian Empire breaks up. The accession of Slavonic parts to Russia must set up a fermentation. No proof is needed of a revolution being desirable. It will make a flash? And a democratic dictator will make the ancient dynasties set their houses in order. To Russia it will mean rejuvenation.* Apart from the tragic assumption of a Russian revolution ending happily, the future Archbishop spoke like a prophet.

Mr A. J. Costain[14] *I am surprised to find the mover in an ordinary waistcoat and not in the red ensign of revolution. If the seeds of revolution were planted in 1861,[15] they were a long time in sprouting. Revolutions will likely do more than is meant. Tractor engines are not the means to move drawing room chairs. It is not impossible to reform by steps.*

R. S. H. Noble (Non-collegiate) *Russians seem to be disagreeable people who smoke pipes in cathedrals. Even Tolstoy has taken care to dissociate himself from Mr Temple's revolution.*

F. Lewisohn (Trinity) *Russia is too large and too sparsely populated for a revolution to be possible. Again, the lofty ideas whose spread has compensated the world for the French Revolution, have no equivalent in Russia today. The peasants suffer but do not think. Even the French Revolution cost more than it was worth. Russia can gain but little and Europe nothing.*

Mr E. L. Buncher (Merton) *I consider an Irish revolution as likely as a Russian one.*

Motion carried 28:13.

---

5 June 1902

House warmly approves of the Education Bill.

Essentially Balfour's 1902 Education Bill had performed a major service by bringing elementary education under a single authority. But to do this, he abolished the School Boards cherished by Nonconformists and brought the denominational schools, chiefly Anglican, all of them desperate for money, under the roof of public subsidy. This gave a religious/political colour to what Balfour very seriously intended as state provision to a degree approaching continental standards. The cost of the war also played a part, giving a reason for not extending public funding to the Nonconformist schools which Chamberlain, in particular, a Nonconformist himself, wanted. The cost of Chamberlain's war in South Africa would provide the argument against. Meanwhile the Conservative Party, very sectarian in its identification with a reciprocally loyal state church, registered a cheap but historically irrelevant triumph.

Hon. E. Cadogan *It is proof of the government's interest in reforms at home.*

H. du Parcq *No one can deny the excellence of the principle of one authority only. But where is it? A catchword, nothing more. County council? The management? 3 or 4 other committees?—which is that authority? Nonconformist convictions should be respected and the government bill has been a surrender to the Church party.*

C. Wertheimer *I want to see established a uniform system of board schools.*

At this time, Churchill was officially a Tory, but he was also a Free Trader at odds with Chamberlain's Empire Preference/Tariff Reform project which hoped to erect protection beyond colonial borders. In 1904, a group of virulent Tariff Reformers, following Chamberlain's own imperious approach to his purposes, set about trying to drive Free Traders out of the Conservative Party. Churchill was one of a group of them who would simply wash their hands of a party whose persecuted Prime Minister, Arthur Balfour, had lost control of it. Declining to be pushed, they jumped.

Winston Churchill MP (Visitor) *The citizen has a right to claim that a child be brought up in his belief or even in his disbelief. The object of the bill is to co-ordinate education. That is the reason to vote for it.*

D. L. Savory (St John's) *Popular control is a good thing, but at present, it doesn't really exist.*

Motion carried 106:62.

12 June 1902

House believes that France is in a state of decline.[16]

Mr A. Maxwell (Ch.Ch.) *I deprecate the charge of British bumptiousness. I criticise France as an admirer. But anyone can see that the Third Republic is nothing like the First. The failure is not caused by a bad system of individual weakness but by degeneration of the character of the oldest people in Europe. A century of revolution has been too much for France.*

E. Zeitlyn *In taking care of her population, France is far ahead of England. Compare London and Paris in the management and training of children. As for agriculture, we don't compete with French peasant proprietorship.*

Lord Haddo *The decrease in French population would be even worse if you discounted the influx of aliens. Compare 1871 with 1814 and observe the decline in the position of the French language.*

Lost on a small poll by 11 votes.

---

23 October 1902

House believes that the present opposition to trade unionism is likely to endanger the prosperity of the country.

Mr J. St G. H. Heath (Corpus) *The Times has promoted a number of fallacies and unnecessary prejudices against the TUs which may make it necessary for them to flood the Commons with Labour members.*

W. H. Buchan (BNC) Not quoted. Oxford Magazine reporter writes, 'It needs some hardihood to oppose a motion without even an elementary knowledge of the question involved.'

Lost 20:27.

---

13 November 1902

House deplores the increasing apathy, manifest in politics, with regard to Social Reform.

C. Wertheimer (Balliol) *I am disappointed in the presence of the Liberal League and the activities of Lord Rosebery. There is surely room for both Imperialism*[17] *and Social Reform. The existence of the Labour Party shows that the Liberal Party is not doing its duty, but I perceive a sort of silence in the House.*

W. A. Moore *I need to speak about Imperialism and our relations with the United States.*

N. A. J. Primrose[18] *The nation is inert. As for social reform, the public has shown its view by electing a government with no social reform in its programme.*

T. Bouch (Magd.) *All such interference is wrong, and in Germany it has ground proprietors down flat.*

G. K. McBean (New College) *My concern is with the interests of common justice for the poor of this country. I look with scorn upon an imperialism which would exclude Social Reform.*

Motion carried 75:31.

20 November 1902

House thinks the present government has proved itself unworthy of the confidence of the Nation.

H. Asquith* *This is a worked-out one. Mr Broderick† is served by paper soldiers rather than real ones. The Education Bill is a subtle joke and the government has used closure to force through the unburied fragment of a defective measure.*

J. G. Gordon (Trinity Cambridge) *The Workman's Compensation Bill shows the eagerness of the government to improve social conditions. The Opposition frankly opposed the war and cannot be relied upon to effect a lasting settlement. Meanwhile Home Rule continues a danger. As for Mr Balfour, where are the men to whom Liberals would give the loyal support he receives from his party?* In spite of which mechanical devotion, few leading figures have ever been as thoroughly campaigned

---

* Still Asquith *fils.*
† St John Broderick, War Secretary.

against by party colleagues or abused by party newspapers as Arthur Balfour, one of the most merely intelligent men to be Prime Minister.

E. S. Montague (Trinity Cambridge) *Let me speak as an honest Conservative. Such a Conservative puts aside all desire for Reform and, as Lord George Hamilton has put it, 'he helps his friends' with pensions and . . .* [19] The mention of the noble recipient of the bounty of the Government convulsed the House.

T. R. Brackly (Corpus) *The War Office has been shown to be admirably designed for peace. As for international relations, what subsists between the Prime Minister and Mr Chamberlain resembles those between Seneca and Nero. We are told about the government's concern for the working man. Lord Salisbury made it quite clear that the Employer's Liability Act was not intended to help working men.*

Motion lost by 103:115.

---

27 November 1902

House condemns the Government's Irish Policy. [20]

F. W. Carson (Lincoln) *The present condition of Ireland after the resolute government of Lord Salisbury is a drag on the Empire.*

E. Cadogan *I want to warn the House against the resolution. Coercion is necessary in order to prevent anything savouring of treason.*

R. H. S. Noble *Ireland is said to be full of crime. Is Ireland worth keeping? What are Irish troops doing in South Africa then? If so, let us try do something to deserve the loyalty of Ireland.*

G. W. Crystal (Balliol) *Is the government to wait until awful crime exists before applying coercion? The Government's Irish policy has been consistent and unwavering and when necessary, patient and considerate.*

G. R. Day *Behind my childlike and bland exterior I conceal the ruthlessness of a staunch Conservative.*

Motion lost 65:57.

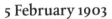

5 February 1903

House believes that the new licensing act is an unwarrantable encroachment on the liberty of the subject.

Mr Shaw (Trinity) *A vital first principle of English law holds the accused innocent until proved guilty. It does not require the accused to prove his innocence.*

Motion defeated 60:62.

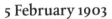

12 February 1903

House would welcome Disestablishment and Dis-endowment of the Church of England.

H. Thorp (Wadham—Treasurer) *When the Church was younger, she represented the national religion and she does so no longer. Scotland is the only country where a state church is logical or feasible. In Ireland disestablishment has benefitted Church and people.*

W. Temple (Balliol—Secretary) *Our church is the most democratic institution in existence. Endowments are the property of the Church and must remain so.*

E. Cadogan *I regard clergymen as the sole civilising influence in the country districts. Disraeli argued that Disestablishment spelt revolution. If we want to try the experiment, we should do so on some uninhabited volcanic island.*

F. W. Curran (Lincoln) *The Church is neither hated, representative nor uniform. The Church may have signed Magna Carta, but within the last century, she had opposed the Great Reform Bill and the abolition of the Slave Trade.*

Lord Hugh Cecil *I have proposed that the five oldest bishoprics should carry seats in the Lords, the others to be represented by life peerages. Disestablishment is a precedent—what the state has given, the state may take away. Disendowment might not injure the Church, but would certainly injure the people.*

Lord Hugh was in turn humorous, ingenious and a little fanatical.

Motion lost 87:91.

---

19 February 1903

House strongly objects to the proposal to subject the native races of South Africa to compulsory labour.

E. L. Buncher (Merton) *What is proposed, compulsory black labour in the Rand mines),—is 'a degrading helotage' and is slavery in everything but the letter.*

E. G. Kilsoe (St John's) *Mr Chamberlain is coming round to the proposal, and the Bishop and clergy of Mashonaland are entirely in favour.*

H. Thorp (Wadham) *Compulsory labour may be synonymous with slavery, but it is by no means confined to the nigger. England is the educator of all parts of the globe with which she comes into contact. If she leaves them 'better though poorer,' it is not for them to complain.*

H. D. Roome (Merton)[21]—His diatribe against the Jews was not very good, either in conception or execution. He mentioned 'our bitterest enemies at home and abroad.'

Motion lost 21:37.

---

4 March 1903

House considers that payment of Members would promote the efficiency of Parliament.

C. Wertheimer *I pray that the House of Commons never becomes democratic. Cobden refused office because he thought that by taking pay he would fetter his freedom of action.*

W. Sibley (Lincoln) *Consider the plump rich woman coming out of the theatre and the poor woman selling matches at the door.* This kind of thing must be done very delicately if it is to be done at all; Dickens often failed at it and so we fear did Mr Sibley.

Motion carried 49:37.

---

30 April 1903

House would approve of the revival of the Prize ring in England.

Mr Woods (Trinity) *In this sedentary age, this motion is a truly progressive one. Fortitude is what is chiefly needed at present, and it is wrong to stigmatise as brutality that which is really hardihood.* Mr Wood seemed to suffer from a nervousness which was a great drawback.

Mr Walls (Corpus) *In the days of Young Jem and Mr Pitt[22] (Standing Jack and Shelley), men spent their afternoons at the ring, not the tea house, and learned the science in the open air, not the tea tables. The only ones who box today are niggers, young men who learn physical culture from one-and- sixpenny handbooks and members of the Irish Party.[23]*

Motion carried 25:17.

---

7 May 1903

House considers the attitude of the French government against religious congregations[24] as a flagrant branch of individual liberty.

B. W. Devas (Corpus) *4,000 schools have been suppressed* en masse. *The charge that the French Church is anti-Republican is untenable. Since 1892 no act of disloyalty can be proved against it. The banishment was caused by opposition, not to the Republic, but to a government openly irreligious and anti-Christian.*

E. G. Kilsoe (St John's) *Five orders have been suppressed. The Clerical party has misused its powers and made the aggrandisement of papal power in France its sole object.*

C. F. Silver (Wadham) *These orders make profit from morality. The Assumptionists have amassed large sums from questionable proceedings. Their acts during the Dreyfus case are sufficient warrant for the government's action.*

Motion carried 43:35.

---

14 May 1903

House disapproves of the Compensation Bill[25] now before Parliament.

Compensation is too small and goes to the Brewer, not the publican. This is an attempt to visit a permanent endowment on a single class out of privileges granted for one year. Nine tenths of public houses are tied.

Mr F. Evelyn *I protest against the attack on Mr Balfour.* He then made a violent attack on rabid teetotallers, allied with habitual drunkards, in opposing all temperance legislation.

Motion carried 26:16.

---

21 May 1903

House believes that modern England is degenerate.

H. Thorpe (Wadham—Librarian) *Despite the great discovery of science and the improvement in material comfort, our moral character is not as good as that of our forefathers. We have the slums and we have the sweated labour—we are a party to showering honours on the likes of Sir Thomas Lipton.*[26] *There is material progress a plenty but moral earnestness is lacking. Yet it was to this quality that the age of Elizabeth and Cromwell owed such greatness.*

E. S. Tyler M.A. (Balliol) *While grit and determination are still shown, there is everywhere a spirit of muddle.*

Motion lost 77:93.

Sometimes the self-assurance of undergraduate speakers, accommodated across a hundred years becomes a social scorn—witness Mr T. R. Strachan visiting from Clare College Cambridge—and perfectly unendurable.

———— ∞ ————

4 June 1903 (Cambridge Visit)

House believes that the Universities are out of touch with the hopes and aspiration of the British people.

W. Temple (Ex Secretary) *The most important part of the Education Act created a ladder for the clever youth of the lower classes to ascend to the Universities. And it has been vitiated by the universities refusing to provide a sum for its proper execution. A fifth of our scholarships should be appropriate for the purpose. Oxford is out of touch with the county because the county is Conservative while Oxford, looking at our officers, is Liberal.*

T. R. Strachan (Clare Cambridge—President C.U.) *I congratulate the universities .They are out of touch with the people and the chief characteristic of the people is a rotted distaste for knowledge.*

A. S. Carr (Trinity) An excellent jest about the *'opes and haspirations of the nation.'*

H. G. Wood (Jesus Cambridge) *I observe the deplorable apathy of the Universities in the matter of Social Reform.*

No vote recorded.

---

11 June 1903

House would welcome an alliance with France.

R. H. S. Noble (New College) *For 100 years we have not waged war without an ally and we must find out who the best might be if the situation becomes a crisis. Germany is impossible. Her colonial interests clash with ours. Russia would not suit. Her consistent objective is India. French colonial interests do not clash. She is a democracy. She has had respectable governments for 30 years. Combes and Waldeck-Rousseau are really a single one. However France is not likely to give up the Russian alliance for a platonic friendship with England. Something is needed more substantial and ready to make advances.*

H. L. Stewart (Lincoln) *Our position is insular, and that fact makes all foreign alliances undesirable. Anyway with the Egyptian question remaining as it does, real concord between us is impossible. This is the country which drove out Zola and condemned Dreyfus, which prosecutes the Jews and is rotten with militarism; an alliance is not to be thought of.*

W. A. Ferguson (BNC) *England is gradually freeing herself of many antiquated and injurious ideas like Free Trade and splendid isolation. Moreover the realization of the imperial Idea is in the future; and for this, England must be at peace and in safety. This necessitates an alliance. The German Empire is not the Prussia of 50 years ago, and through its ideas of Weltpolitik, it has become a great danger. The Kruger tele-gram, the Kaiser's speech in England before Queen Victoria's funeral, show what German feeling toward England is... Yangtze, Venezuela, Belgium, naval supremacy show that she is intriguing against England. How better to balk this idea than by allying with France?*

T. W. Daynes (Magd.) *The history of the dual alliance of France and England shows that such an alliance is unworkable. A French alliance would make the Colonies less willing for federation. Are we going to weaken Germany by making Colonial consolidation*[27] *more difficult. The dual alliance (Russia and France) is sufficient check on Germany. France has the largest debt of any country in Europe and the like-lihood of a plunge into war to stave off criticism of her finances would be increased by having a wealthy ally. The only safe course for England is to keep clear of alliances until war either breaks out or is resolved.*

Mr Woodville-Sherwood (Magd.)[28] *The King's visit was only a quasi-success. France is split into many hostile groups, and her population is going down. Our true ally is Russia.*

Mr C. P. Blackwell (Lincoln) *Since 1870, France has been labouring to recover from that downfall. The fact is that in peacetime, that makes her a most desirable ally.*

Mr N. Hey (Balliol) *We can be of no use from a military point of view while Germany is neutralized by her attempt to be at once a military and naval power and by the Austro-Hungarian problem.*

Motion carried 19:15.

<hr>

22 October 1903

Macedonia was the subject latest episode in the highly episodic Near Eastern Question, and inevitably perhaps, produced a rather dull debate.

House desires the active intervention of England in the Macedonian crisis.

Mr R. H. S. Noble *The Turks who committed terrible atrocities, are an Asiatic nation in Europe, an anomaly and quite unfitted to govern any Christian people. A Christian governor is needed and England is the only nation in Europe who could supply it.*

Mr H. D. Roome (Merton) *The atrocities are not committed by the Turks alone. The Bulgarians are guilty across years and were the first to engage in extreme measures. The manifold claims of a great empire forbid England to intervene.*

A. A. Pallis (Balliol) *Intervention will bring us no advantage. The argument rests on moral grounds. Action in 1878[29] brought us to action now. We sacrificed a nation for a hollow epigram;[30] and what a mockery it is to speak of honour today. In Macedonia, intervention will be quite easy. We have done it before and can do it again.*

Rev. K. Lake *Ill-judged intervention will only increase the misery of the Macedonians. The state of affairs there is doubtless the result of Beaconsfield's cynical attitude in foreign politics.*

H. M. Paul (New College) dwelt on the history of English policy in the Near East...

B. de B. Davidson (Balliol) made a typically dull and unnecessary speech.

Hon. H. Lygon (Magd.) (One of the Worcestershire Lygons, friends of Elgar. A Lady Mary is Number 13 in The Enigma Variations) has plenty to say and a charming manner...His immediate disappearance immediately after he had spoken was a rather unnecessary slight on subsequent speakers.

Mr P. S. Meiklejohn (Merton) cynically advocated an attack on Russia now, when she is unprepared. He was interesting, but has an unfortunate suggestion of clericalism in his manner.

Mr J. H. N. Taylor (Hertford) pointed out that principle is, after all, the proper guide in foreign politics.

Motion carried 88:5.

29 October 1903

House welcomes the tendency to socialism and believes it to be inevitable.

E. G. Kilroe (St John's) *The idea of socialism is not a mere division of prosperity, but a united nation where all individuals should work together for the common good. Socialist mutations already existed and worked—the Post Office and municipalities. The great trusts, dangerous in themselves, are the first steps toward socialism, preparing the way for it.*

B. W. Devas *Socialism implied the nationalisation of all means of production. That can be done for land, but not for capital. Capital can emigrate. There is no stopping place between moderate and extreme socialism. That must mean a nation of slaves who periodically elect their absolute masters. The real solution for our present difficulties is the spiritualization of the masses.*

Hon. H. Lygon *Consider the state of the municipalities today. If the working classes are notoriously incompetent and indifferent in local affairs, what reason is there to expect them to control the complicated mechanism of the socialistic state?*

S. G. Vesey Fitzgerald (Keble) *Capitalists are doing their fair share of work, and a leisured class is essential to a country. What will happen to family life under socialism?*

W. Temple (Librarian) *A leisured class is no use unless it ceases to be leisured.*

R. H. Charles (Ch.Ch.) *I distinguish between Christian Socialism and the political socialism before us.* Mr Charles talks rather than speaks.

Motion defeated 37:82.

12 November 1903

The report of the War Commission[31] directly incriminates the present cabinet.

T. N. Daynes (Magd.) *What I want to know is, who in the Cabinet was responsible. The blunders are notorious and for those who, on the analogy of other officers, the Secretary of State is responsible.*

Hon. H. Lygon *During his time in office, Lord Lansdowne[32] effected many non-striking reforms. The war has been on a far larger scale than expected; in each case of alleged negligence perfectly adequate explanations are given. The system was thoroughly bad, but the government was not to blame.*

H. M. Paul (New College) *The Army was in an absurd state at the start of the war. Sir William Butler had prophesied the exact course the war would take, repeatedly warning the government that it needed more troops. Sir William Butler was recalled.*

R. H. Charles *Any open preparations for war would have warned the Dutch. The questions of events and of medical failures have not been really shown to involve the failure of the government.*

E. M. C. Denny (Jesus) *Mr Chamberlain knew all about Boer dispositions and strength. He ought to have communicated this to the War Office. The blame for the War must rest with him.*

H. M. Woods (Trinity) *The real responsibility lies with the Opposition, with Sir Henry Campbell-Bannerman and with the public, because the general public could, if it had wished, have insisted on adequate preparation.*

F. W. Challis (Oriel) *The transfer of Mr Broderick to the India Office showed that responsibility had been misused.*

T. G. Dehn (Balliol) *The faults in the case of the remounts lay not with Mr Broderick, but with the horses which were quite contemptible. The lack of maps for the Transvaal was inevitable for it is not possible to map a foreign country.*

Vote not given.

19 November 1903

House believes the recent action of Russia shows the folly of the Anglo-Japanese alliance.

W. A. Ferguson *This is a matter of the utmost importance to England. The foreign policy of a world-wide empire should be a matter of importance to every citizen. The Eastern Question is extremely complicated. For many years, Russia has been maturing deep-laid schemes of policy with such success that to move her from Manchuria today is a practical impossibility. Her next object is Korea…The interests of Great Britain do not coincide with those of Japan[33] who constantly endangers the peace. For this reason the alliance is foolish.*

E. H. Strong (St John's) *The real danger of Russia's aggression is to the trade of other countries. Here we and the Japanese coincide. We both want freedom of trade. Neither of us is bent on aggression.*

J. H. N. Taylor (Hertford) *By this treaty we have put our commercial relations in the Far East entirely in the hands of Japan. Is Japan trustworthy? It is a very dangerous policy to strengthen the position of the Yellow races. The treaty tends to prevent the proper organisation of our own Empire.*

C. P. Blackwell (Wadham) *From the British point of view the continual aggression of Russia is most dangerous. The foreign policy of England has always been directed, and rightly directed, against Russia…The Anglo-Japanese alliance…would be the prelude to a lasting peace.*

C. M Fry (Ch.Ch.) *Our antagonism with Russia is inevitable. Peace is most important for us, but Russia is bent on breaking the peace.*

J. St G. C. Heath (Corpus) *Let me examine the opposers of this motion. According to them, France and Russia are possible allies. Yet they think that a European war is inevitable in the immediate future. The real danger is the youthful ambition of Japan.*

T. G. Hubbard (Ch.Ch.) *The idea of an invasion of India is ridiculous, so are the horrors invoked earlier of a Yellow Peril.*

Motion defeated 21:55.

26 November 1903

House condemns the protection taxes involved in the proposals of Mr Balfour and Mr Chamberlain.[34]

Unidentified Speaker *This is Mr Chamberlain's thing, and it is with Mr Chamberlain's help that the Prime Minister hopes to carry it. What Mr Chamberlain says varies according to where he says it. The arguments for London are quite different to those used in Liverpool. The pearl button industry is dying because ladies have abandoned pearl buttons.*

E. J. Kylie (Balliol) *Imperial politics which alone are concerned with tariffs, are quite pure. The only possible future for England is a union with the colonies, in which a starving population might find a better hope of life.*

J. St. G. C. Heath *I divide protectionists into two camps, those who believe in it because Mr Chamberlain does and those who do so in spite of that disadvantageous advocacy. The former are beyond argument. The latter have forgotten the meaning of figures.*

Mr Temple *I was a protectionist long before the present government thought of it.*

Mr D. Lloyd George MP (Visitor) *Who would benefit? Not the farmer, not the industries suffering from dumping—iron and steel are flourishing. Not the workmen. In Germany, unemployment is 30 per cent—here 3.5 per cent. The idea that German shipping is a danger is absurd. After protection, US shipping has ceased to exist. Mr Balfour has been tricked into helping Mr Chamberlain. He is sitting on a cuckoo's egg. The well-to-do should be very careful about increasing the burden on the poor.*

Mr E. L. Bowes (Balliol) *English capital, hampered with trade regulations, will emigrate unless we protect it.*

Hon. H. Lygon *As 12 million of our population subsist on casual employment, only a scheme to make it more certain is to be welcomed.*

Mr G. S. Rentoul (Ch.Ch.) *It is cheaper to print an English book in the US and send it to England to be published.*

Motion carried 158:129.

---

3 December 1903

House condemns the principle of passive resistance.[35]

Mr H. M Steinhart *The Nonconformists have been paying rates to sectarian schools for 30 years. Either they were so thick-headed as not to have seen this as fraud or illogical in objecting now.*

Mr C. S. Buxton (Balliol) *Society has nothing to do with a man's religion, and in making society the supporter of a sect, we are wrong and passive resistance is justified.*

Mr J. S. B. Reed *In most cases, the martyrdom of the passive resister has been a farce.* Mr Reed chatted to the House in a familiar, annoying manner. He has no notion of speaking.

Motion carried 63:74.

---

28 January 1904

House regards the appointment of a Tariff Commissioner with alarm.

Mr H. M. Paul (New College) *'Protection' is an academic term, but we have got past that stage. I am no longer astonished at Mr Chamberlain. Who will pay for the tariff—the colonies? Mr Chamberlain is completing the policies of Lord North.*[36]

Motion lost 58:62.

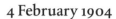

4 February 1904

House is opposed to importation of Chinese labour into South Africa.

Mr J. N. Daynes (Magd.) *The Chinese will be slaves in all but name. Why should the mines be allowed this help? There is labour in plenty.*

Hon. H. Lygon *There is not an ample supply of labour. The capitalists have been much abused. Natal has Chinese labour. Why shouldn't the Transvaal? The white man will not work with the black. The miners have made Johannesburg the London of South Africa.*

Mr J. H. N. Taylor *That was a blatant defence of a corrupt oligarchy. South Africa does not exist for the mines and ought to be a white man's country. Have we fought the South African War to find a home for superfluous Chinese?*

Hon. H. G. Hubbard (Ch.Ch.) *Ideas of equality and fraternity will not work in South Africa. The Kaffirs[37] prefer the farms to the mines. It is nonsense to call the Chinese 'slaves' as they are not compelled to come.*

Mr W. Temple *We should not introduce demoralisation into a country for whose welfare we are responsible.*

Mr F. Streatfield *I doubt if this high moral line is feasible.*

Mr L. J. Swallow (Lincoln) *There are too many races in South Africa already, and the Chinese will only complicate the business of Government.*

Mr D. du B. Davidson (Balliol) *Modified slavery is already established. If the Chinese labour is refused, the war debt will be repudiated.*

Mr W. Bancroft *South Africa is a good field for English emigrants. China ought to find her own outlet.*

Mr J. H. Morrell (Magda.) *The mines are generally unfit for white men to work in.*

Mr T. S. C. Heath (Corpus) *When the Chinese are sent back to China, they will be destitute. They would be slaves. Though free to come, they will not be free, having come.*

Mr H. B. Samuel (Corpus) *I object to idealism. We have to face the facts.*

Mr G. P. Blackwell *The Importation of Chinese labour is a fitting conclusion to a war fought to free helots. It will make South Africa un-English and useless to us.*

Motion carried 67:23.

11 February 1904

House considers that the policy of Russia in the Far-East is justified.

Mr H. M. Steinhart (Ch.Ch.) *Russia seriously needs a warm water seaport. The China–Japanese war should change awareness; and this is Russia's opportunity. Russia cannot allow an open door or she will lose her only remaining market.*

Mr W. A. Ferguson (BNC) *Would he approve Russian policy in Poland and Thibet?* [sic]

Mr A. A. Pallis (Balliol) *I ask the house to put aside its natural anti-Russian prejudice. Manchuria is only nominally subject to China. Russia's policy in China is the counterpart of ours in Egypt.*

Mr H. T. Silcock (Oriel) *Russia's Eastern policy is of a piece with her policy everywhere else, a piece of cast-iron imperialism to crush all smaller states.*

Mr H. Lygon *How can an Englishman possibly blame cast-iron Imperialism?*

Mr E. G. Southam *Would the Opposer suggest that England ought to have stayed quietly at home when the new world was open to her?*

Mr U. Wolff (Wadham) *In international affairs, any means are sound which lead to good results.*

Mr W. H. Moberly (New College) *Our past should make us lenient, but even so we shouldn't justify Russia.*

Mr M. S. Thompson (Corpus) *It is mere hypocrisy to claim the right for England to bully as she pleases and then sympathize with the smaller power in the one struggle not affecting us.*

Mr W. A. Moore (St John's) *I'm not waiting for results. Russia has acted wrongly and that is enough.*

Mr H. B. Wallis (Balliol) *Russia must expand East or Westwards. Either would be justified and it is to our advantage that it should be Eastwards.*

C. J. Swallow (Lincoln) *Russia has quite enough to do at home and should not neglect this in order to expand.*

Mr G. White (Univ.) *Diplomacy consists in duping, and Russia is no worse than the rest. Russia is a barrier against the Yellow Peril.*

Mr E. S. Kirk *Russia's policy isn't just morally unjustifiable, but from her own point of view, reckless and suicidal.*

Mr J. R. Brooke (Corpus) *We shouldn't be applying the canon of morality to states.*

Mr C. L. Rae (Balliol) *If Russia is to be secure in Manchuria, she must possess Korea.*

Mr H. C. Lakach *If Russia's policy is like ours, that only means that we are as bad as Russia.*

Mr A. L. Kennedy (Magd.) *Russia's policy is necessitated by her country and resources.*

Motion defeated 31:100.

18 February 1904

House believes the methods adopted by the Government during the past year are unworthy of the traditions of British Statesmanship.[38]

Mr W. A. Moore *The government has acted bailiff for Germany in Venezuela and her banker in Mesopotamia. Then over the fiscal question, as Lord Lansdowne pointed a revolver at the German Emperor, Mr Balfour was the friend of Publicans and deceiver of the nation.*

Mr M. J. F. McDonnell (St John's) *The fiscal question has been asked, the Irish question has not. The University question seems to have been permanently shelved.*

Motion carried 90:83.

As noted above, in all her imperial glory, Britain was mightily afflicted with drink. Liberalism, heavily Nonconformist, wished to fight it. Champagne consequently reached out understandingly to strong beer; and public houses notoriously fitted into Conservative election plans. Even so, slowly, stronger licensing and closing powers became more detailed and effective. The argument about compensation for growing numbers of withdrawn licences was a contingent part of a long contemporary conflict running in happy parallel with the one about Disestablishment and Church Schools.

25 February 1904

The licensing authorities should have full discretion to refuse the renewal of licenses, no compensation being granted from public funds.

Mr R. H. S. Noble (Lincoln) *On two questions, Mr Balfour seems to have two settled convictions—Chinese labour, and drink! Drink makes a man shoot at his landlord and drink makes him miss.*

Mr E. S. Tore (Hertford) *The reduction of licenses is no remedy. For where there are fewest licenses, there are most offences. Insecurity after reduction will put the trade in the hands of inferior men. Crime will increase. The Whisky money should go for compensation.*

R. C. Bonnerjee *A licence is a privilege, so removal of a licence is in no sense, entitlement to compensation. Do Brewers give compensation when they dismiss managers? The value of licences would increase.*

Mr F. C. Bovenschenen (Corpus) *There are many dear old friends in this argument. As to compensation, both sides are right. Reduction is required. The smaller the number of public houses, the greater the facility for the police to watch them.*

Mr J. G. S. Heath *I look forward to the application of a scientific method of handling the question—such as the Gothenberg system.*[39]

Mr S. G. Vesey Fitzgerald *As for the benefits of closing down public houses, why not shut up half the colleges in Oxford?*

Motion carried 45:34.

The new Labour Party, standing in by-elections, had recently won three of them.

⸻⸺∞∞∞⸺⸻

3 March 1904

House is opposed to the principle of Labour representation.

Mr M. H. Woods (Trinity) *The Labour Members represent a class and not the community. Liberals and Conservatives should unite against the common enemy. A bitter struggle will ensue. Working men should be admitted to the House, but not as representatives of working men only.* Mr Woods achieved the difficult task of combining real passion with thorough Conservatism.

Mr Heath *Labour representatives follow from the Taff Vale decision.*[40] *Class representation is as much the case with other parties, especially the Conservatives. The Labour programme is not sectarian.*

E. H. Strong (St John's) *I have experienced the evil effects of labour representation in the colonies. It always involved corruption. The representative must not be either the odious 'Friend of the People' or the Working Man. The latter involves payment which leads to corruption and bureaucracy.*

Mr A. S. Carr (Trinity) *Labour Members would strengthen the Liberals, even if some of them were socialists, why shouldn't that idea be represented in parliament as well as others?*

Mr J. R. Brooke *The truth is that there is no halfway house on the way to socialism at which we can stop.*

Mr Moore *No socialism can go too far for me. Power is the means to education.*

Hon. H. Lygon *Labour representatives should abstain from voting on Labour questions.*

Mr W. H. Moberly *I don't wish for a dominant Labour Party, but think the presence of a few working men in the House of Commons quite welcome.*

Motion lost 31:56.

10 March 1904

Listening to the dominant opinions proclaimed over this subversive motion by 19- to 20-year-old public school boys graciously proclaiming what in black youths from tower blocks is called 'attitude' makes one wonder at the restraint of Suffragettes.

House would welcome household suffrage for women.

A. A. Pattison (Univ.) *It is hard to persuade people to take this idea seriously. If women are calling for political power, it is because they have always been deprived of it. Consider their interests. The wages of working women are going down. They would be less reckless than the men in declaring war.*

Mr G. C. S. Rentoul (Ch.Ch.) *To keep women out of political life is to increase, not diminish their dignity. The case of Peers is really parallel. They pay taxes, but no talent is displayed in that—it might be displayed in avoiding paying them. It is unreasonable to claim more for them. A love of peace: Medea? Marie Antoinette? Women cause wars and men conduct them. They lack interest in politics; also they are profoundly ignorant of the issues at stake. Household suffrage will lead to women having suffrage and in itself, is an insult to marriage.*

Mr R. G. Burn (Balliol) *Ignorance is not regarded as a fatal obstacle in the case of men.*

Mr J. H. N. Taylor *I have the interests of women at heart and for that reason I wish to crush out the political woman.*

Mr E. S. Tore[?] (Hertford) *I hope that the type of English womanhood will be preserved; and political life will not permit this.*

Mr R. H. Charles *I think this motion is subversive. The judgment of the world should be accepted.*

Mr M. Thompson *Women's suffrage would produce a parliamentary majority that did not represent a majority of real power.*

Motion lost 41:48.

---

28 April 1904

House approves the Anglo-French agreement.

Lord Lansdowne, Foreign Secretary 1900–5, advised that the local regime in Morocco was breaking down and that France could not be stopped from taking over. Accordingly, given guarantees for Gibraltar and obtaining Spanish compliance, he did a deal which would make possible the achievement of the Triple Entente which he had favoured since 1888 as a defence against Germany.

E. S. Tore *I oppose it as a Conservative because Germany has improved its position lately and because the Liberals support it. We should have insisted on greater freedom in Egypt. We have enabled a French protectorate in Morocco and gained nothing but Free Trade. We have given territory and received none.*

H. M. Steinhart (Ch.Ch.) *England and France are the pioneers of civilisation in North Africa and it is their duty to open the commercial development of the country.*

Mr L. J. Swallow *Egypt gives to us the barren glory of the pyramids and the inferior kind of cotton*[41] *while Morocco is rich in minerals.*

Hon. H. Lygon *No good can come of Lord Lansdowne and I would be pleased to have his head on a charger. He has given prestige to a French government which is loathed by all that is best in the French people.*[42]

M. H. Woods (Trinity) *We have got what we wanted and it is idle to object to prestige for the French government. Hindrances to our expansion have been removed and the shadowy possibilities abandoned in Morocco. As much could only have been realized through a European war.*

C. A. Chavasse (Ch.Ch.)[43] *We have deprived Spain of all hope of attaining her objects in Morocco.*

Motion lost 22:58.

---

2 June 1904

House believes the government deserves the confidence of the country and that its defeat would be a national misfortune.

Hon. H. Lygon *Let me list its virtues, including the introduction of Chinese labour, all its South African policy and the Licensing Bill.*

A. Shaw (Trinity) *The government has many virtues, but lacks the virtue of resignation. It mistakes expenditure for profit and bustling delirium for efficiency.*

R. H. Charles *All attacks on the government resolve themselves into argumentation* ad hominem *and the homo is always Mr Chamberlain.*

Motion lost 87:89.

20 October 1904

House considers that until the Liberal Party has a definite programme, its return to office would be a national misfortune. *New method of voting introduced—by tellers taking the votes of earlier departures and producing proper, larger, full record of attendance.*

Mr Bovenschen *The Liberal Party is a hydra-headed mass of slippery units.*

Hon. H. Lygon *The Liberals have sold themselves to the Nonconformists. Does the sum of Liberal leaders amount to one man?*

Mr C. P. Blackwell *Disillusion is in the air and ministers try to stave it off by saying 'What's in your programme?'*

Hon. R. H. O'Neill (New College) *I fear a lethargic and laissez-faire attitude to the Navy.*

Motion carried 150:146.

Despite which rejection by political Oxford, the Liberal Party would take office by default following Balfour's despairing resignation in November 1905, and before the election which, in January 1906, gave them more than 500 seats in the Commons.

3 November 1904

House believes immediate steps should be taken to restrict the immigration of aliens.[44]

Hon. J. G. H. Hubbard *Three kinds should be excluded: the criminal, the pauper and the cheap wage worker. It is the most undesirable of aliens who come here to England. English working men are crowded out because their places are taken by the refuse of Europe.*

A. H. Pattison (Univ.) *The alien does more work and does it better and that's the simple truth. We are too insiderish. We must look across the Channel and see that there are other men there as worthy of the name of men. England must keep her reputation of being a country where freedom is worshipped.*

Mr E. H. Strong *Every alien admitted should be sound of body and limb; and I would go so far as to impose a high poll tax.*

Mr J. St. G. C. Heath *I smell in this motion a disguised form of protection.*

Mr H. H. Woods *I object to England being made a cosmopolitan dumping ground.*

Motion carried 122:89.

---

10 November 1904

House believes the aims and policy of Lord Milner are essential to the maintenance of British supremacy in South Africa.

Mr J. W. Hely-Hutchinson *Milner had nothing to do with the management of the war; with the cause of it he has, but it could only have been avoided at the cost of British supremacy. The agitation against Chinese labour has been used to develop the worst side of the British character, the nation truckling to humanitarian blather.*

Mr C. P. B. Sacheverell (Wadham) *We should tell the Boers that though they have lost their independence, they have not lost their freedom. And that we shall give them self-government as soon as possible. Lord Milner's management of the Chinese labour question shows that he was in alliance with the mining magnates. The Dutch hate Lord Milner; it is not wise to leave him there.*

Mr N. S. Talbot (Ch.Ch.) *Johannesburg cannot be set free from the mine-owners until the gold is got out of the country and prosperity raised.*

Mr H. du Parcq (Exeter) *I suggest chivalry toward a fallen foe. The object of Chinese labour was to create an oligarchy, if not a limited monarchy. When the Liberals come to power, Lord Milner must inevitably be recalled.*

H. M. Steinhart (Ch.Ch.) *The real question at issue over Chinese labour is whether it was the best way to secure British supremacy in South Africa.*

Mr J. H. N. Taylor (Secretary) deserted his party to oppose the motion. *Lord Milner's policy assisted extravagance in Park Lane and Monte Carlo...*

Mr E. H. Strong *Is Lord Milner to be welcomed in his hour of critical need?*

W. G. C. Gladstone *If supremacy means the supremacy of the mine owner, I agree with the motion. While the Colonial Secretary's[45] wife brings out a play to discourage sweating in England, he is bringing in a measure to encourage it in South Africa.*

Motion carried 108:85.

---

17 November

House would regard with distrust any measure of Home Rule in Ireland. Cambridge Visit

Mr J. H. N. Taylor *Under the sort of Home Rule which leaves Irish members in an Irish parliament, Ireland will have Home Rule and England only a spurious kind; absolute Home Rule puts Irish Members in their own country.*

Mr J. H. Sheppard (King's Cambridge—President Cambridge Union) *I am not afraid of total legislature, nor partition, for it would not be as bad as the moral separation that exists now.*

F. E. Storrs (Jesus Cambridge) *Compromise is impossible. It must be either Unionism or separation. Ireland is divided against itself and Home Rule will not cure its difficulties.*

Mr G. S. Rentoul (Ch.Ch.) *Has Ireland a right to a separate parliament? Is it possible to give it to her? And would it benefit her? Ireland needs the gentle firmness of the government.*

Mr J. M. Keynes (King's Cambridge—Secretary)[46] *Because one Home Rule scheme was objectionable, it does not follow that all schemes will be. Home Rule will not discontent the Empire. Clemency and kindness are found the best system of governing ever discovered.*

Mr R. H. S. Noble *Irishmen are best qualified to say what Ireland wants. England judges Ireland from her own point of view.*

Mr E. S. G. Sternberg (Hertford) *The problems are Ireland's own fault. Land leagues, political acrobats and agitators are the country's scourge.*

Mr W. S. Armour[?] (Jesus) *They call us agitators, but what have we ever got without agitating?*

Motion lost 65:166.

25 November 1904—a Friday

House approves Mr Chamberlain's conception of empire.

Mr M. H. Woods *The preferential proposals are a part only of a misconception of Empire which, in its final form, would be a definite Imperial Federation.*

Hon. H. Lygon *Preference is a means to an end. If England is offering the Colonies little or nothing, their earnestness to obtain it would be remarkable.*

Mr A. Short (Trinity) *The sort of Empire I want would not forget in the midst of its material power that its higher calling was to proclaim peace on earth and 'build with the mind of man* an empire that abides.'

Motion carried 148:111.

1 December

House desires to maintain the Establishment of the Church of England.

Mr W. Temple *Old institutions should not be moved about without very strong arguments, and those in favour of the Establishment cannot answer without massive and cogent argument. The Established church is responsible for Magna Charta [sic]. Secular authority reinforces the authoritativeness of the Church. The 'Sectarian inequality' argument is sound, but not enough for the whole case. The Church asserts a national ideal, a witness to national usefulness, a great immemorial symbol.*—A very great speech.

Mr R. H. O'Neill *The doctrine of the Church in bondage to the state is erroneous and unfounded. Parliament can come to hasty legislation of ecclesiastical questions. The experience of Disestablishment had not been altogether good.*

Mr E. H. C. Denny (Jesus) *The Church of England is devoid of government and unable to make its own laws. Disestablishment is sure to come. I regret the representation in the House of Lords. Disestablishment would free the Church from outside power.*

Mr H. du Parcq *When Disestablishment comes—and it may come from within—it will be the freeing of the Church from the fetters which bind her.*

Rev. H. A. Meade (St John's) *Disestablishment might make for peace but not for justice. It would entail Disendowment.*

Motion carried 118:100.

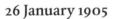

26 January 1905

House would welcome abolition of the House of Lords.

Mr L. J. Swallow (Lincoln) *The House of Lords is only Conservative on some points. It would probably pass protection and conscription without a blush.*

W. M. Eagar (Exeter) *Peers are able in the House of Lords to enjoy a good training in politics. Furthermore I support it as a barrier against plutocracy.*

H. M. Paul (New College) *The House of Lords is the most democratic institution of modern times. And I would plead for its really important element. It is the great fortress against demagoguery and prevents people being carried away by the impulse of the moment.*[47]

Motion lost 80:156.

2 February 1905

House believes the granting of full representative government to Russia is imperative.[48]

Mr M. Woods *What is wanted in Russia is a gradual and not a sudden and violent extension of the franchise. At present, autocracy is the only hope of Russia.*

H. H. Symonds (Oriel) *Russia accepts that the present depends on the reverence of the people for the Czar. This label of the Czar as 'Little Father' has been rudely shattered and nothing remains except democracy.*

B. W. Devas (Ch.Ch.) *India is well governed under a bureaucracy and would be badly governed by a democracy. This is also true of Russia, for democracy only fits for a highly educated people.*

Mr W. Temple *The other side have left out human nature. The Russians have become conscious that they are a nation and must be given control of their own destinies. Nothing could satisfy them but representative government and a franchise given, not as a privilege but of right.*

Motion carried 85:82.

---

9 February 1905

House believes the state should undertake the feeding of destitute children attending our public elementary schools.

Mr A. H. Pattison (Univ.) *In one London school, no fewer than 90 per cent of children were certified as unfit to do any work. Why spend money on education, if we are not able to spend a few thousand on making that education really useful? Look at the recruiting figures.*[49] *In some towns, 80 per cent of the men who volunteered could not pass the standard. What a pity a fine spirit is not carried in finer bodies. The whole thing could be done on a three-farthing rate. It would only cost a penny a day to give a child two meals—this and the legal corollary of compulsory education.*

J. V. Davies (Ch.Ch.) *The quality not the quantity of food provided is what needs to be reformed. The State should provide real food in the Board Schools, making the parents pay the cost, rather than embark on this perilous experiment. The Physical Deterioration Committee has declared against it and the cost would be between 15 and 20 million a year.*

Councillor Dodd (Ch.Ch.) *Instead of supporting a child of a few years in a workhouse away from the parents, it is better to make sure that it has at least two good meals a day.*

Mr T. H. Dehn (Balliol) *You cannot condemn the motion by calling it socialism. The word requires careful definition.*

Mr R. Henry *Too long—and he seemed to have great difficulty in keeping to the point— and not dealing with the arguments of preceding speakers. Otherwise he was good.*

E. S. Schoenberg (Hertford) *I deprecate the Conservative Party touching this question. It is too difficult and everything which is difficult* is bad.

Motion carried 98:6.

———— ✺ ————

16th February 1905

The House holds that the conduct of the Irish Party is not conducive to the best interests of Ireland—Visit of Trinity College Dublin.

Mr Noble *The curse of Ireland is politics. The Nationalists[50] do not represent the best of the nation.*

Mr H. L Murphy Treasurer, College History Society, Dublin (founded 1770) *I apologise for any lack of sweet reasonableness in what I have to say. By the rules of the Hibernian Society no questions of party politics are allowed to be debated. So I shall be releasing the pent-up ardour of a century. No one can say that the Nationalists are not a united party; and if they do not represent the gentry, why then it is the gentry who are to blame. Led by Isaac Butt,[51] they were moderation itself. As a result, they achieved nothing. Then comes Mr Parnell who declares that a revolution is needed, a revolution Ireland must have. His tactics gained Ireland most of her claims, something which quite justifies our present policy in the Nationalist Party.* It is impossible not to observe that in this single speech, there is a wit and good humour and want of self-importance, for which in most debates, the representatives of Oxford (and Cambridge) barely start looking.

Carried by 22 votes.

———— ✺ ————

2 March 1905

House believes that the present Unionist government is no longer deserving of the confidence of the country.

Mr H. M. Paul was scornful of members of the Cabinet.

Hon. H. Lygon (Secretary) *Mr Balfour's policy is clear to all sensible men; and the Aliens Bill and Licensing Bill are models of perfection. I stand only to uphold the Anglo-French alliance and the Anglo-Japanese alliance.*

Mr H. du Parcq *The Thibetan policy is wrong.*[52] *Tariff Reform is dead, not just in Oxford, but all over England.*

Mr G. S. C. Rentoul *Fiscal Reform is imperially demanded by the state of our trade. The Conservatives have never wished to be better.*

Mr M. H. Woods *Mr Chamberlain says 'The Conservatives are bad. The Liberals are worse.' So let the Liberals come into power and the country will soon be rid of them.*

Motion lost 102:133.

9 March 1905

House approves the retention of Greek as a compulsory subject in Responsions.

Mr N. S. Talbot *I can't argue with people who say that Greek is nonsense. I want to argue only with those who argue that Greek is a good, but an unattainable good. That is due to the way it is taught, and that method ought to be reformed. The end of Oxford is to supply professions with brains and not professional men.*

Mr R. V. H. Burn (Keble) *Greek is now residually a mental gymnastic, put to ignoble use. By retaining it, we shut the doors on people educated in Grammar Schools and continental schools.*

R. P. B. Davis (New College) *Once leave Greek as an extra and, as we know from the experience of American and Colonial schools, it will go altogether.*

H. du Parcq *I am for it, because directly it is made optional, it will cease to be taught in the public schools.*

Motion carried 44:23.

———— ∞∞∞ ————

4 May 1905

The French Revolution is a disappointment to the friends of Democracy.

Hon. H. Lygon *I deplore the French government's attitude to state employees, to the religious orders, to the Catholic Church and to religion itself.*[53]

A. H. Villiers (Magd.) *The Pope interfered with President Loubet's visit to the King of Italy. In France there is no national Church. A church which cannot live without the support of the state is already dead.*

H. M. Steinhart *There has never been anything in the French system to keep the military forces in check except a disgusting system of espionage.*

H. M. Paul *It is irrational to condemn the French government on the grounds of Disestablishment. That bill was carried in a free parliament by an enormous majority.*

Motion carried 69:68.

———— ∞∞∞ ————

11 May 1905

House condemns as unsound the Aliens Bill, at present before parliament, and regards it as a menace to the right of asylum in this country.

T. N. Dayns (Magd.) *This bill is like a remnant in a shop window at sale time. The government would admit the ne'erdowell, if he had scraped together a little money. However a penurious, but eminently desirable political refugee will be excluded. I can give the House a list of trades in which the alien has made us supreme. The political refugee requires a certificate of character from the police hunting him down.*

T. H. Hubbard *The goods made by aliens are bad. Why harbour the men who made them? We receive aliens who were not good enough to go to America and come here to work off their undesirability.*

E. M. C. Denny (Jesus) *In the US, the proportion of aliens to the total population is 13 per cent. Here it is a mere fraction of one per cent. The real response to the evils complained of is not the exclusion of aliens, but the introduction of Social Reform. The present bill outrages the principle of English law that until a man is proved guilty, he should be presumed to be innocent.*

H. E. Cummings (Trinity) *Every nation has the right to decide whom to consider fit and whom unfit to be its citizens. There is competition with British labour, forcing our citizens to accept a lower standard of living.*

H. du Parcq *The Descendants of aliens have fought for us in the South African War. I recall the impressive service in the London Synagogues in memory of those who fell. Every Jew who goes to work in East London has his eye on a house in Park Lane.* The speech of the evening.

Motion carried by 29 votes.

---

8 May 1905

House views with satisfaction the discovery of HM Ministers that the present system of government in India is indefensible, but regrets that their policy was constructed in secret and that it involved an unmerited censure upon a distinguished servant of the Crown.

R. H. S. Noble *Sir Anthony MacDonnell*[54] *has been appointed (permanent under-secretary for Ireland) on special terms. The government has yielded to the outcry in the Unionist press.*

W. M. McEwen *I oppose the present government as a Conservative Home Ruler. The trouble with the Government is that it is cemented together by Unionism. Devolution is an Imperial necessity. We are by the way, sending thousands of disloyal Irish peasants to the Colonies—a most dangerous proceeding.*

Motion carried 69:29.

4

Enter the Liberals

26 October 1905–21 May 1908

Fewer Irish MPs/Compulsory National service/Isolating Germany/Welcoming a Liberal Government/Education Bill/Transvaal/Plural Voting/No confidence/ Milner/Welsh disestablishment/Women's Suffrage/Home Rule/German elections/ Land nationalisation/the government/Women's suffrage/Haldane's Army plans/ The point of Oxford?/House of Lords/Colonial Conference/Ireland—Redmond's visit/Avoiding World War/Indian self-government/Railway dispute/Disestablishment of CE/Russian agreement/Liquor laws/Irish administrations/Confidence in Government/Spirit of Party/Compulsory Military training/Growth of Labour Party/Middle-East/By-election/Licensing bill/Tory return?

A difficult time this had been for the Conservatives—Arthur Balfour, for all his intelligence and general quality, had, from the start, been caught between a pre-imperialist body of Tory Free Traders and the independent creation of Joseph Chamberlain and his highly concentrated party (only word for it), the Liberal Unionists. They might be mocked by Lady Bracknell—'Oh they count as Tories and dine with us—or, at any rate come in the evening.'[1] But allied with the Tories from a position of strength, they came all right—and to the dinners they chose, occasionally declined the invitation, and virtually commanded the Tory protectionists. Balfour, open to and interested in ideas—and successful with them in a much quieter, better governed Ireland—was a more interesting politician than his uncle Salisbury and had none of his authority!

His serious and useful Irish policy, not being Home Rule, passed Joe Chamberlain's test. The Liberal Unionists had begun like Joe himself, baulking at Gladstone's Home Rule before following him into Imperial Protection and the *coup d'état* in the Transvaal. A cohort of Conservatism, the Liberal Unionists might seem to Lady Bracknell, but even after 1906, with Joe *hors concours* after a stroke which left him sentient but silenced, they knew independently what they wanted. The central belief of this adored middle-class intruder was a gigantic trading group of Britain and its colonies (as Canada and New Zealand were still called), to delight Tory instincts—old land and new territory—and make a mere Conservative government happily conform. Chamberlain never led the Conservative Party, but tended to command it.

Even so by 1911, and the second of two Colonial conferences, Imperial Protection (splendid politics, dubious economics), involving dearer food from the Colonies than could be had from world markets, wasn't going to happen. Those higher prices hit hardest those for whom food was the biggest item on the bill, poor people; and historically, it wouldn't happen, as Free Trade Tories kept pointing out, though Lord Beaverbrook would rant on about the notion in his newspapers into the late 1950s. But the emotional mood persisted. Colonies were part of the Empire and British, damn it. Something perhaps showing today in the contemporary sullen Tory response to the European Union.

It is important to define the man who by way of screw-manufacture in un*chic* Birmingham, had come to deny and promote across the political field. His quarrel over Home Rule, before our time, in 1886, was both rational good judgement and towering temperament. He objected to Gladstone's belief that the entirety of Ireland would welcome Home Rule as assuredly, the Catholic greater part would. Gladstone on his North Sea holiday cruise in 1885, had read up Irish history from a standing start. That start was unfortunately, the brief and only moment of coalescence between the sects—1798. Unfortunately, northern participation in the '98, occasion of the execution of an exemplary Protestant radical leader, was misleading. The fact that Henry Joy McCracken had been hanged for his part in the rising—leader of the rebels of incontestably Protestant County Antrim, had convinced Gladstone that in 1886, a similar identity of purpose remained.

In fact, Ulster's economic resentments having been met and satisfied, religion, backed by the good luck or virtue of Ulster in escaping the main nineteenth-century miseries, had cast fellow-feeling away for revulsion at the rural, impoverished, priest-ridden, and bidden 'Rest of Ireland'. Chamberlain as usual, well informed, understood this; and, junior but rising Minister, had taken on the Prime Minister. On top of which, typically of his whole career, he had then a plan of his own, devolution through local government. It was actually a better plan. Salisbury and the Tories might have grumbled at expensive innovation and indeed at doing anything for the Irish. But Ulstermen, marvellously self-assured about their own ability to make a great show of such new local powers, would not have rejected such authority for the likes of Lord Randolph and his ranting crusade talk which, against Home Rule, had taken the issue so far from reason.

Given reflection, Gladstone would have seen Chamberlain's point and Salisbury remained low key on it. A shift, limited but major, in the whole state of Ireland might have been achieved with successful and enhanceable local powers and the effective statehood of 1922, pushed long term into the future conditional tense. In sad reality, Gladstone did not see the point, and Chamberlain's reaction would be the model for the rest of his career, absolutely certain of his purpose and imperious about getting it. His approach to colleagues was, to quote Harold Macmillan about a tiresome colleague,[2] thoroughly *cassant*, also overbearing and assured, but it won him devotion and, as it were, faith.

This extended to his immediate family. His son Austen would be prominent after the Great War as a wholly decent, earnest and highly intelligent man, talking peace, meaning it, and, in the circumstances of the age, not getting it. Yet the view of Alfred Gardiner, Editor of the *Daily News* and brilliant commentator, that Austen showed his father not so much filial devotion as filial servitude, touched the truth. Joe expected and got devotion.

Austen and so many rank and file Liberal Unionists gave it. Chamberlain was never the creature of the Tories, nor reliably of Right or Left. More thoughtful and imaginative than most of them, knowing more about city life and pressures, he functioned as consultant and/or equal coalition partner. Negotiating the next informal co-habitation, he would offer them the liberal, the practical, and the downright shameful. As a Nonconformist, he would cheerfully vote with the Liberals for Disestablishment in Wales (just as Gladstone, the old Puseyite, had to be held down from voting against this business of his own government). In radical mode, Chamberlain pressed improved Employers' Liability legislation, also pursuing an intelligent approach to the poor.

Knowing that hard-driven working class of Birmingham very well, strengths and weaknesses, he knew what should be done about drink. He proposed the Swedish model of municipalization of the pubs, taking profit out of the business and spending the receipts on city housing projects, something to be debated, not very expertly, by the Oxford Union. Knowing Birmingham as Salisbury probably never knew the urban parts of Wiltshire, it was natural for him to advocate the old age pension which debaters, caught here, would think far too good for them. So had too many members of the Commission, like the Prince of Wales, thinking it likely to demoralize an insufficiently thrifty (or punished) working class. Chamberlain, who had fought for the pension throughout, walked out, leaving a stinging memorandum about its failure. The idea would be taken up and enacted in 1908, by Campbell-Bannerman.

For all the ferocious partisanship, disagreeably caught by Oxford's high and unhandsome Tories, as with pensions, the more practical thinking of one side of the party debate could be picked up by the other half. In the same useful way, witness the radical notion of death duties! Harcourt, Chancellor in the last Gladstone government of the mid-1890s, pre-Transvaal, had taken advice from Alfred Milner (then blamelessly of the Inland Revenue), on the idea as a single graduated tax, to provide a redistributive impetus in tax policy. This would naturally be deplored as 'class legislation' by Rosebery, at the Foreign Office, itself rather a class occupation.

Advice given by Chamberlain to the Tories was not all humane and sensible. He understood dirty tricks well enough to point out to them the increasing (actually tiny) influx of Russian and other East European Jews—future retailers, government Ministers, and violinists—and how this could be turned to electoral account. At a very little distance, Oxford undergraduates squeakily complaining of an influx of the 'scum' (alternatively 'dregs') of Europe had picked up this cheap trick and miserable idea from the same Mr Chamberlain.

Meanwhile the actual Conservative leader, Balfour, a serious man doing rational things, not least in Ireland, would endure far greater trouble from his party than Rosebery or any other Liberal leader. Influential Tories would, echoing the proprietor and editor of the viperous *Morning Post*, grow personal about Balfour and set to drumming the slogan, BMG—Balfour Must Go. Whoever, in the light of this and several other crises, coined the phrase about the Conservative Party's secret weapon being loyalty spoke invincible faith. Balfour had been caricatured by *Toby*, sketch writer of *Punch*, as 'Prince Arthur' catching his odd mix of intellectual assurance and personal shyness. Actually there are most affinities with the tribulations of John Major leading a perfectly sensible Conservative government through stupid Conservative hostility in the mid-1990s.

Constitutional royalty surrounded by sniping courtiers, Balfour had embraced at any rate the principle of Imperial preference—Protection. Unfortunately for retreat there is often somebody waiting up a back defile with trouble. There were still serious Free Traders in the Cabinet. It was on this occasion that, as noted earlier, the Chancellor, Charles Ritchie, celebrating both a nice surplus and Chamberlain's absence on a colonial tour, had cut the duty on corn, making it cheaper and competition of the colonies more difficult for those colonies' already more expensive grain. In sacking him, Balfour demonstrated his retreat before Chamberlain and, in the process, lost three free-trading Cabinet ministers and the pushy junior, Winston Churchill, already threatened by Protectionist Tories in Oldham, who went further—straight over to the Liberals! The ministry talked 'Social Reform' and 'Efficiency' as if it were Soft and Hard.

Then, at a time when the immigrant percentage of the national population was under 1 per cent, Balfour, against character and judgement,
pitched forlornly at popularity and with Joe's briefing, offered an Aliens
Act, balancing it, with contrasting good sense, with a Licensing Act, socially
essential, but outraging the loyal, organizing, and contributing brewers.

The Aliens were not just aliens, they were Jews. They were not just
seeking to come to Britain, they were trying to escape violent persecution
in Russia and Russian-dominated territory in Poland, a persecution which
had the warm and cretinous approval of Tsar Nicholas II, as earlier that of
his father Alexander III. English anti-Semitism was of course not murderous; it was a case of trade union self-interest directed against people (like
so many other subsequent people!) 'coming here after our jobs', one also
of quiet ill-nature and slumped ignorance. The notion of such excluding
legislation had been kicking about for a decade before Chamberlain took
it up, driven by a clutch of Unionist backbenchers known as *Restrictionists*.

The whole shabby thing was quite alien to Arthur Balfour. He had been
a partisan of Captain Dreyfus and he would of course put his name to the
Balfour Declaration. In the Commons, he would condemn 'the bigotry, the
oppression, the hatred the Jewish race has too often met with in foreign
countries'.[3] Yet the Aliens Act of 1905 (employing a euphemism which
gathered its own harsh colour, 'Undesirable Aliens') was put through
Parliament by his government. The same self-contradictory Balfour
would set up a commission into the brutal Poor Law established by
Melbourne sixty years earlier.

The licensed trade (universally 'the Trade'), hardly ever a political topic
in the twenty-first century, apart from concern at the thinning-out and
decline of the pub, something generally liked and enjoyed, was heavy politics at the end of the nineteenth. It was cherished by Tories, Anglicans,
and people without political bias, but detested by Liberals, Nonconformists,
and social reformers who knew the drinking poor and saw in that jolly
solace a deeper enmiring to further impoverish the poor. The trade lived
in mutually advantageous sin with the Tory Party, whose ground organ-
izers were commonly the licensees and among whose contributors the

actual brewers stood high. The power to limit the licensed selling of alcoholic drink dated from no earlier than 1891. The setting of minimum standards of fitness to be 'Licensed to sell beer, ale, porter and spirituous liquors', as it says over pub lintels, was the doing of legislation in 1902.

Acknowledging that the licensed trade was, if not quite so chaotic as it had been, heavily over-subscribed, Balfour looked for compensation of landlords leaving or removed from their premises. He set about the work pretty much on his own, ignoring the recommendations of a cabinet committee.[4] Its key point was that when licensees jumped or were pushed, the trade itself should provide the compensation by way of a state tax, exacted, against customary Treasury practice, from the trade itself. This, unlike the Aliens Act, was necessary and sensible legislation, but the Ministry promoting it would not escape the political unpopularity of so many things necessary and sensible.

This had been a government which stumbled, and now it was falling. Stepping over it came the Liberals; and with some panache, came Sir Henry Campbell-Bannerman, not so far much noticed, but forthright, down-the-line Liberal, recognizable as such by delighted Liberal voters, and indeed Members. By what Soviet terminology would call 'The Group of Rights', he was at once scorned and underrated. Liberal Imperialism embodied in the *Liberal League* (Rosebery, Grey, Haldane, and Asquith) had however lost caste. The last three would meet in September 1905 (two months ahead of Balfour's eventual resignation), for a supposed fishing trip, at Grey's cottage in Relugas, a Scottish village.[5] There, on the initiative of Haldane, ablest and most arrogant, they agreed to tell the surely not quite serious Sir Henry that, given his defects as older man and taker of radical positions, they—quite indispensable—could not possibly serve while he outstayed their tolerance in the Commons.

The conspiracy had several strands, a gross underestimate of CB's abilities, concern to advance Asquith to command in the Commons, and, possibly, a desire to bring back that ghost-ship, Rosebery. It was made clear, however, that if the current leader accepted their, very slightly presumptuous, offer of the Lords, he might function as Premier there—ceremonially as it were. The King, as a reliable Tory, approved it. However, sustained by his valiant, dying wife, Sir Henry sweetly declined the invitation, offered Asquith the Treasury brief in return for loyal support, watched him take it and the challenge fall.

Observers of this episode have wondered at, first, the presumption of the threat, then the passivity of its abandonment. The cause of such urgency among the conspirators soon became apparent. With his government out on its feet, Balfour was about to turn referee and stop the fight. He resigned on 5 December 1905, advising the King to call on the Leader of the Opposition. Campbell Bannerman, so lately so dispensable, formed a government and as Prime Minister (the first head of government to be formally known by this title), called an election. The Liberals, already a minority government in the Commons by default, would win it with one of this country's rare landslides, and Sir Henry, dying in 1908, would spend his short remaining life outraging Court, Conservatives, and Lord Rosebery. Liberals generally rejoiced and a period of genuinely radical and constructive legislation began, material at which undergraduate debate took delight, umbrage, and sides.

One major factor had been removed. In July of the same year, Joseph Chamberlain collapsed with a stroke. It didn't kill him—he lived until the summer of 1914—or damage his brain, but effective speech deserted him, together with normal mobility. Recognizing an authority stronger than that of Joe Chamberlain, he left politics altogether. It is an irony, however, that, in foreign policy, he strongly supported making peace secure through a cool alliance with Germany, something he would have argued for across the floor. This would have kept us out of the lethal company of Russia—meddling in the Balkans—and her ally in France, the revanchist Lorrainer, Raymond Poincaré.

One moment the Conservatives are briefly still in office and, like their supporters in the Oxford Union, keen to reduce the number of Irish MPs. Then suddenly, without an election, they are out, telling the brand new government overnight that it promises a great deal, but has delivered nothing. Out of office, the Tories continue quarrelling with Irish Members, but the Liberals, after calling an election and winning seats by a landslide, presume to legislate. Their first affront is a monstrously un-Anglican Education Bill which diminishes Church of England hegemony, a little puffed up by the Tory Education Bill. This new legislation will be snuffed out by a House of Lords now entering a phase of terminal presumption. Their Lordships will flutter their feathers and the Bill will fail. With that, in the spring of 1906, everyone—Parliament and the Oxford Union—settles down to enjoy the old confessional fissure of Established Church and unestablished chapel, a miserable/delightful row going back at least 200 years to Dr Sacheverell and Daniel Defoe.

Some political themes run to any music, none more sadly and entertainingly than Ireland. About trying to solve which question, one might say that the Conservatives, after the Balfour brothers' achievements, were against trying to, and even more surely, that the Lords would reject any bill that did. Outrageously, the idea begins to achieve authority that the House of Lords is a presumptuous, single-party, over-mighty body which ought to be, at least, diminished.

In practice, the Lords, under the leadership of Lansdowne, did have the wit to pick and choose. They were not going to pick a fight with a new and fancied player. The trade unions had recently more or less created the Labour Party which would then proceed to win fifty seats at the election as the Liberals achieved their landslide. When the same trade unions objected to a union-hostile High Court decision, Campbell-Bannerman, faced in 1906 with Labour and its fifty or so seats, seeking redress and authority in its own sphere, proved a natural radical.

The new government would have to find some legislative reply to the Lords' legal judgment that trade unions should be liable in tort for industrial action, as the unions like to call strikes. CB surprised cautious men in his Cabinet by avoiding any compromise and, in a Trade Disputes Act he had personally strengthened, going straightforwardly with the unions' aspiration. This would *not* be voted down in the Lords. In a famous *Punch* cartoon, Lansdowne, halbard-in-hand, is shown standing at the top of a flight of Upper House steps beside the dying body of the Education Bill and saying to the Trades Disputes Bill, 'Bar your way, my dear fellow? You've got a mandate.'

The disposition of the Lords to destroy by a vote, to veto legislation which displeased them, was not a recent practice. Conservative ennoblements had long since made the Upper House a sort of Supreme Soviet, unreservedly devoted to the party. William Pitt, with George III behind him and the French Revolution as horror-show, had created 140 new peers in seventeen years. That veto, directed in the 1830s at corporation bills, Irish and English, eased for a while and was then directed at a Ballot Act, thought to grant voters an 'unmanly' freedom from retributive dismissal or eviction for voting wrong.

It was, though, dispatch of a second Home Rule Bill in 1893 which had changed the game long term. Even Rosebery would be moved to talk about 'ending an intolerable situation'. Campbell-Bannerman, a member of that short-lived Cabinet, had civilly sent the Queen a memorandum pointing out that a democratic franchise had changed the balance between Lords and Commons. He would be told of the need to restrain 'the subversive measures of the so-called Liberals but better called destructives'.[6] The confirmation by democratic election of the caretaker Ministry of 1905 into the smashingly elected one of 1906 would put CB's memo to the Queen to the issue.

Ireland, at this stage, was a country getting better, essentially making peaceful economic progress and with a rational leadership in its National Party under John Redmond. The government's social policy: school meals, the miners' eight-hour day, medical inspections, and old age pensions were real and substantial social betterment, hard for the Tories to oppose when it stood square with their own Milnerite talk of 'National Efficiency'. But significantly, Asquith, as Chancellor, put some social measures to the Lords as finance bills, thus protecting them from rejection or weakening. To do either would be a breach of a convention going back to Queen Anne and Robert Harley. Should they challenge a Finance Bill, the Lords would be acting against received constitutional practice, a breach to be made by their Lordships very soon—with dire consequences.

The new Trades Disputes Act of 1906 Act gave the unions powers, valid enough for a very long time until abused from the late 1960s by unions with Upper House delusions of their own. The idea of Imperial Protection as the all-preoccupying issue had faded a year or so before Mr Chamberlain. The new government did not introduce what was oddly called 'Woman Suffrage', not least because of Herbert Asquith's inveterate horror of the notion. (He was married to an exceptionally silly woman who insisted on calling him 'Henry'.) Asquith had achieved the leadership unopposed after CB's dying resignation—and would now enjoy it or otherwise.

———— ∞∞∞ ————

26 October 1905

The House would approve the reduction of Irish representation.

The Hon. H. Lygon[7] *The special interest plea is of no avail. If ever Ireland had special interests, Free Trade has destroyed them. As to the Act of Union, that has already been broken by the disestablishment of the Irish Church [Church of Ireland]. Even the illegitimate over-representation of Ireland might have been passed over if it had not been taken advantage of to reduce the mother of parliaments to an impotent condition.*[8] [For the rest of his speech, Mr Lygon pointed out that Efficiency was the real justification of the motion and attacked the Irish obstructionists with tremendous vigour. Mr Lygon was obviously not quite himself and this produced a certain lack of grip on the subject] ...

Mr H. E. Cummings (Trinity) *Opponents' adherence to the letter of the Union is an attitude of mental cant, joined to a cynical opportunism. The real issue in all constitutional questions is not the validity of an arrangement made centuries ago*[9] *but the immediate good of the Empire of today.*

Mr H. A. Smith (St John's) *The fall in the population in Ireland is directly due to English misgovernment and we should not visit our own blunders on the Irish people. The Act of Union is sacred until such time as both parties agree to break it.*

No vote recorded.

---☙☙☙---

2 November 1905

This House is in favour of some form of compulsory national service.

Mr H. F. Wyatt (Visitor)* *It is a high honour to plead the case of England tonight. A few days ago I visited the scene in Trafalgar Square and the crowds assembled there to do honour to Nelson. The qualities which gave us the victory over Napoleon were energy, courage and self-sacrifice; and we could not hope to repeat those triumphs if we shrank from the idea of national service . . . it is not so much an ideal as a neces-sity . . . Russia is a greater danger than ever because, as the French Revolution showed, an upheaval of national spirit was always a source of danger to a neighbouring power. I deny that national training is the same thing as continental conscription . . . It is not opposed to English traditions;*[10] *it has been the groundwork of our whole national history.*

For the motion 134 against 92.

---☙☙☙---

9 November 1905

That the diplomatic isolation of Germany is essential to the peace of Europe.

* Subsequently author of *England's Imminent Danger* (1912).

Mr R. P. B. Davis (New College) *The end of German expansion is the absorption of the dependencies of this Empire.*

Mr C. S. Buxton (Balliol) *That speech smacked of the dangerous dogmatism of the illustrated magazine... Germany's great commercial organisation is too great a thing to risk. We are in danger of taking the Kaiser too seriously. Socialism is the force of the future in Germany and its growth would hinder warlike designs.*

Mr Rentoul (Christ Church) *We should not mix ourselves up with European politics by isolating Germany.*

For the motion 74 against 70.

---

1 February 1906

House welcomes the return to power of a Liberal Government.

R. M. Barrington-Ward (Balliol)[11] *The Radicals are for peace at any price; they have no foreign politics; British interests are endangered in the Persian Gulf. At home, radical policy is a vast attack on property.* Mr Barrington-Ward has a quiet and charming manner and really wished to persuade the House. His speech would have been even better if he had omitted a few personalities at the end.

Mr R. Bevir (Hertford)[12] *The Liberals are making a direct attack upon the Union Jack.*

Mr D. B. Somervell *The Tories are merely an opposition... Apart from Tariff Reform, they would do nothing. Mr Redmond*[13] *is not a dictator; he would never turn the Liberals out.*

Mr R. B. Whyte (Balliol) *Tories are responsible for class hatred.*

Motion carried 132:120.

26 April 1906

This House condemns the Education Bill.

N. S. Talbot (Christ Church) *Mr Birrell*[14] *reminds me of the recent eruption of Vesuvius. Before 1870 Education was in the hands of the denominations in that year the Cowper-Temple agreement*[15] *had been directed at religion… The 1902 bill had aimed at unification, definitely inflicted grievances upon Nonconformists. The present bill aimed at establishing one form of religious teaching and that a bad one. The state should give absolute fair play to the denominations for whose purposes the schools were built. The 'facilities' offered by this government are a sham.*

Mr A. H. Villiers (Magdalen) *The state has an undoubted right to take over schools now. It is part-proprietor of those schools.*

Mr W. Temple (Queen's ex-president)—Impartial tumult of applause[16] *I do not regard the present bill as perfect, but I do accept it as the only means of averting that crowning disaster, secularism. I have no patience with the idea of imposing religious tests upon religious teachers and say to the High Church party that this is suicidal. It could only end in a government saying 'You all have to go' and in the Church, incurring the reproach of not having suffered the little children to come. The Church of England to me means not merely the Anglican Church, but the whole body of religious feeling in the country.* [To praise Mr Temple would be superfluous if not impertinent].

Mr E. M. C. Denny (Jesus) *Undenominationalism is a violation of religious equality and liberty of conscience and pure secularism is preferable to Birreligion.*

Motion carried 255:163.

3 May 1906

House finds the policy of the government in the Transvaal contrary to the interests of the Empire.

Lord Wolmer[17] *Members of the Government have slandered our fellow countrymen in the Transvaal. The British outnumbered the Boers there and provided all the prosperity. However the Liberal Government is going to abandon their sacred principle of one vote, one value,[18] simply for the sake of the Boers who very naturally and very properly hate us. Self-governing Transvaal will be receiving lectures on morality from Mr Winston Churchill.*

Mr R. B. P. Davis (New College) *I would ask for moderation and sanity in discussing Colonial quotations. They shouldn't be dragged at the wheel of party politics. To have one party exclusively fluttering the Union Jack and the frame of minds by which one party tries to sow suspicion about the other in the minds of our fellow citizens in the Colonies helps nobody.*

Mr V. D. Harris (Corpus) *The government is sowing perplexity and unrest throughout the Empire. The business of making an issue over Chinese slavery is deplorable.*

Mr C. T. Le Quesne (Exeter)[19] *He speaks of deplorable publicity about Chinese slavery. How then was it the monthly wages of Kaffir labourers went from 47 shillings to 30 before the cry went up for Chinese Labour. The capitalists are deliberately holding back from any attempt to improve the pay and conditions of labour.*

Mr H. M. Steinhart *The Liberals have systematically tried to convert South African discussions into personal attacks on Mr Chamberlain and Lord Milner.*

Motion carried 75:55.

10 May 1906

House welcomes the Government's proposals for the abolition of plural voting.

Mr A. G. Harris *Plural voting is forbidden in municipal elections. Why allow it in Parliamentary ones?*[20] *University voting is a sham. I know of a number of cases where individuals, some of them clergymen, make a hobby of collecting votes—and see how many they can record in a day.*

Mr H. I. P. Hallett (Christ Church) *If a man had a substantial interest in a locality, he had a right to vote in that locality, whether he had a vote in another locality or not. Plural voting is one of the fundamental principles. The Bill makes no provision for the principle of 'One vote, one value.' Universities attract intelligence and provide education. To disfranchise the Universities will be to disfranchise intelligence and education.*

Mr E. R. Mackie *It all rests on a fundamental fallacy that all men are equal. I doubt if the government will ever bring in a redistribution bill. An expert in manipulation like Mr Birrell would never consent. This government is made up of political pedlars who buy their party in the cheapest market and sell it in the dearest.*

Mr H. E. Sturge *There is no connection between property on the one hand and morality and intelligence on the other. It is no more an insult to question a voter in a poll booth than to ask a train traveller for his ticket.*

Mr G. C. S. Rentoul (Christ Church) *Mr Gladstone always believed in plural voting for qualified people. Plural voters were generally men of intelligence. The owners of shares in a company vote when called to according to the number of shares they hold.*

Mr M. H. Richmond supporting the motion was noisily interrupted by a small band of unmannerly opponents.

Mr T. G. R. Dehn *The question really amounts to an argument between aristocracy and democracy. If all men were equal, why is Sir Henry Campbell-Bannerman only a member of the Oxford Union?*

Mr Ridley *I support this motion as a Tory. Parliament exists to represent men, not land. One man, one vote is the only sensible principle.*

Mr U. Wolff (Wadham) *This bill has been rushed in and it is directed at abolishing the representation of local interest which is a barrier against violent democracy.*

Mr A. N. C. Shelley (Worcester) *Although Mr Disraeli sinned against the light in* 1867,[21] *that was no reason why we should do so now.* He was a little lachrymose.

Mr H. H. Symonds (Oriel)[22]—(Teller for the ayes) had not appeared in the customary glory of evening dress. *A man has a vote* qua *human being, not* qua *owner of property.*

Mr G. B. Allen A capital speech. *This bill represents another fulfilment of the Liberal motto* vae victis.

Motion lost 54:70.

———∞∞∞———

Eights Week—17 May 1906[23]

The present government neither possesses nor deserves the confidence of the country.

Mr Rentoul *The Liberals perpetrated a confidence trick. The election was really won by log-rolling. If they possessed the confidence of the country, how was it that no Liberal dared to stand for the University?*

Mr Denny *The confidence of the people of this country had communicated itself to the people of the Empire.*

Vote for 239; against 127.

———⊗∞⊗———

24 May 1906

That the services rendered by Lord Milner in South Africa are in the highest degree deserving of the gratitude of the country.

Mr W. McG. Eagar (Exeter)[24] *I would as a Liberal, rather give up politics for the rest of my life than propose this motion.*

Mr Armour *Lord Milner stood for a policy typified by that Imperialism which denied a smaller nationality even the right to exist. We might have had peace at an equitable price, but Lord Milner was for war at any price. He treated the Dutch with contempt; and, with great abilities, he followed a policy which was wrong and fraught with incalculable disasters for England's fair fame.*

Mr Allen *Mr Armour has blamed Lord Milner for facing facts and stating them.*

Mr F. J. L. Day (St Edmund Hall) *Lord Milner utterly failed to allay racial animosities or treat the Dutch fairly. After the war, he made not the slightest attempt to soothe the natural bitterness. If his proposal to suspend the Cape constitution had been carried out, we would have lost South Africa.* [We would like Mr Day ever so much more if he would bestir himself and shake off his dreadfully ecclesiastical delivery.]

Lord Wolmer *Mr Armour is actively opposed to the British community in South Africa.* He then paid a tribute to Lord Milner's vast labours which would have been more effective by far if it had been quietly delivered.

Motion carried 79:44.

———⊗∞⊗———

31 May 1906

The time has come for the disestablishment of the Anglican Church in Wales.

Mr H. A. Smith (St John's) *Most of us suppose a National Church to mean a Church supported by national money. The Welsh one had been endowed in Roman Catholic times and when it was indeed 'National.' Now it is neither. Disestablishment has been entirely satisfactory to the Irish Church as even Colonel Saunderson concedes.*[25]

Mr Ridley *The cases of England and Wales are really one and I will ask whether there ought to be an establishment at all. The notion comes from the New Testament and the Fathers. Disestablishment would involve dis-endowment; yet religious use is the highest and best to which property can be put. Churchmen will after disestablishment, have to support priests and churches.*

Mr R. V. Leonard (New College) *I support establishment in England but in Wales, the Anglican Church is the alien church of a rich minority and it has failed to win the sympathies of the Welsh people. Disendowment does not mean confiscation as the endowment was mostly given by men who would have liked to see the present Welsh clergy burned at the stake for heresy.*

Mr Wolff *The Nonconformists are the noisiest of the Welsh people, but not necessarily the best.*

Mr Harris *If we disestablish the Church in Wales, the next thing we shall be made to do is to disestablish them in Westbourne Park and Mansfield Road or anywhere else where two or three Nonconformists are gathered together.*

Motion lost 54:65.

7 June 1906

This House believes that the parliamentary suffrage should be extended to women.

Mr Symonds [We much regretted that lack of time compelled the mover to pass over the arguments of St Paul] *Not Quoted*.

Mr G. R. Wykeham-Fiennes (New College) *The power of Government lies in force. I find it easy to sympathise with those men who murder their wives with broken beer bottles.*

Mr F. E. Smith MP (Merton) ex-president, made an impassioned speech for the motion and concluded by voting against it. The House was and always will be delighted to welcome so brilliant an ex-president.

Mr S. F. S. Johnson *There are 500,000 women who have bound themselves not to rest until those rights have been obtained.*

Mr P. Barter (Jesus) *Queen Elizabeth would have been nowhere without Raleigh, Frobisher and—Lord Balfour of Burleigh.*[26]

Motion lost 56:64.

---

18 October 1906

That the time is now ripe for Home Rule to be accorded to Ireland.

Mr W. C. G. Gladstone (New College)[27] *It will not be 'Home Rule on the instalment system,' as Mr Chamberlain has dared to call it, but 'Home Rule on the deferred payment system.'*

Motion lost 123:134.

---

14 February 1907

House regards the defeat of the Socialists at the recent German election with great satisfaction.

Mr G. B. Allen (Wadham) *As a champion of sane individualism, I am very satisfied at the check given to one of the wings of International Socialism in Germany. 'You may socialize means, but you cannot socialize men.'*

Mr Hallett *We should be worrying about the people who won. This country has most to fear from a triumphant Imperialist party in Germany.*

Mr W. T. S. Sonnenschein (Christ Church) *The defeat is to be approved because it is a victory for Free Trade. One country's prosperity is the prosperity of all countries. The Kaiser has been criticised. I see the victory of his forces as the victory of 'Spirit over Matter.'*

Mr C. T. Le Quesne (Exeter) *I lament the result in Germany. The Socialists are the opponents of the Kaiser and represent democracy. They have been defeated today and the Kaiser laughs at them today, but they will trample him underfoot tomorrow.*

Mr R. G. Laffan (Balliol) *As an Irishman, I am a nationalist. As a Socialist I am an internationalist.*

Mr L. Cohen (New College) *Socialism is the curse of modern politics.*

Mr R. A. Knox (Balliol)[28] *I would like to see Germany experiment with Socialism as an* Experimentum *in her* corpus vile.

Mr E. C. Bentley (Christ Church) *It is very late Mr President, but I hope you will give me leave to poke about a bit on a worn pitch.* [He made one run in good style].

No vote recorded.

21 February 1907

This House opposes the Nationalisation of Land.

Mr Richmond *What has Lord Wolmer done to deserve his being robbed of his thousands of acres?* [Prolonged cheers]

Mr J. Blades (Ruskin) *What has he done to* deserve *his thousands of acres?* [Prolonged laughter] *My scheme for land reform is simple. It would provide that after a certain time, all land would revert to the state. I don't want either to rob the living or respect the rights of the unborn. So there is no question of compensation.*

Mr P. T. Fletcher (Ruskin) *It is all about practicability. Land nationalization is 'wild cat' thinking compared to simply taxing land values and making provision for small-holdings.*

Mr A. G. R. Hickes (Wadham) is an unblushing lover of squires. *What would a village be without its squire?*

Mr M. H. Goodby (Christ Church) *I doubt if the land would support many people.*

Motion lost 58:111.

----- ⌾ -----

28 February 1907

The present government is unworthy of the support of the country.

Lord Wolmer *A few months in office of this government has shaken the Empire to its very foundations.*

Mr Steinhart *The Prime Minister has mistaken the females of London for the Women of England.*

Mr F. E. Smith MP (Wadham) *The Liberals have come to power through Chinese labour* [Thunder—at times almost portentous]. *Their attitude to the House of Lords is represented by 'an attack from Mr Churchill upon hereditary ability.'* Mr Smith is a master of cumulative rhetoric but, except at one point, hardly aroused the enthusiasm of which the numbers in his favour were capable.

Mr Winston Churchill MP (Colonial under-Secretary) A great appeal to the House on behalf of the poorest classes who remain to a great extent unbenefited by the advance of civilisation, will remain long in the minds of many who heard him.

Motion carried 486:274.

---

7 March 1907

House regrets that the King's speech contains no proposal for the extension of the franchise to women.

T. H. T. Case (Queen's) *I would be satisfied with an extension of the Franchise to women on a property qualification.* Mr Case holds that women are of two kinds and that it is the sterner kind who deserve the franchise.

Mr L. J. Stein (Balliol) *The true ground for granting women the vote is that they share the labour market with men. 'Women's rights are due to women's wrongs.'*

Mr C. S. T. Watkins (Lincoln) [Lugubriousness itself] *The Franchise would degrade women. The idea invokes the nightmare of the cycle of evolution, bringing round the identical stages of degradation and restriction from which they have emerged.*

Mr W. J. Rose (Magd.) *Motherhood is too sacred for party politics.*

Mr A. W. Keith-Falconer (New College) *I have 1,001 objections to urge against the grant of votes to brainless women.*

Mr Brinsley-Richards *I object to the arrogance of such socialists and their pretended monopoly of soft-heartedness.*

Motion lost 52:57.

⸎

2 May 1907

This House believes that Mr Haldane's Army Scheme will render a compulsory Military System completely unnecessary.

Mr G. R. C. Fiennes *We don't need Mr Haldane's scheme to make conscription unnecessary. I find the fear of invasion ridiculous. We had a tradition of the Militia; and Mr Haldane's scheme improves on that.*

Mr E. P. Swain (St John's) *The Haldane scheme is neither adequate nor workable. The defence of kingdom is not the business of the Government but of the people themselves.*

Mr F. W. Leith-Ross (Balliol) *There are many better ways of improving national physique than by conscription. That is something out of sympathy with the country.*

Mr Rose *Conscription has not improved national physique in France and probably not in Germany either. If we need conscription on account of India, conscript India.*

Mr Hallett *Mr Haldane is not a free agent. The disarmament party is behind him and must be guarded against.*

Motion lost 66:102.

⸎

16 May 1907

What is the point of Oxford?

Mr Brinsley-Richards *Oxford exists to stimulate thought in the nation; and Oxford overflows into all channels of useful and honourable occupations. Pious* founders would be shocked to hear of two theatres, a volunteer corps and devotion to athletics.

Councillor Dodd (Ch.Ch.) *Today Oxford is too much the handmaid of one party in politics.*

Mr Allen *I reject the idea that Oxford should only produce lackeys in the train of democracy.*

Motion lost 94:101.

---

23 May 1907

The House of Lords at present constituted fulfils no useful function.

Mr Villiers *The last election has proved that Mr Balfour was not to direct the affairs of this country. The House of Lords extended protection to three classes—the Bishop, the plural voter and the blackleg. It has sold itself to one party.*

Mr Davis *Abolition, not reform is essential.*

Motion carried 212:196.

---

30 May 1907

This House regrets the attitude taken at the recent Colonial Conference toward establishing a system of preferential tariffs within the Empire.

Mr Allen *The attitude of the present government toward Preferential Tariffs is not reasonable, contrary to expectation and reached the lowest ebb of political pedantry.*

Mr Cohen *Though a Tory, I don't see the fun of always sneering at Winston Churchill.*[29]

Mr Richmond *It was not the Colonial Premiers who had been badly treated over the conference, but the government. Look at the role, sometimes libellous, of the press.*

Motion carried 86:50.

6 June 1907

Ireland should have the right to manage her own affairs.

Visit of Mr John Redmond.[30]

Lord Wolmer *I have come straight from my militia training to oppose this motion. I would deny that Ireland is a separate country and the Irish a separate people. I think that the two countries are working together toward an end vastly higher than that of parochialism.*

Mr C. T. Le Quesne *It is said that Ireland manages her own affairs already. She doesn't even control her own constabulary. Our Empire was built up on freedom. How then can we deny one part of the Empire what we give to others?*

Mr Redmond *I deny absolutely the idea that nationality and Empire are antagonistic.* He stood at the table unable to continue through the storm of applause. *However Ireland is separate in race and largely in religion. Ireland is no more the sort of English county that she was years ago. England has failed miserably to govern Ireland. The administration of Ireland has been carried out through blood, the scaffold and the prison cell. Ireland's population has decreased by half across the last fifty years.*

Home Rule would mean that we would never be so foolish as to reject an extension of self-government on liberal and democratic lines. However, the present bill has 'Suspicion of the People' written all over it. It is said that Ireland is disloyal, but loyalty would be a result of Home Rule. Look at Canada. At Queen Victoria's accession, she had been in open revolt. At the Jubilee, she was loyalty itself—because of the Durham Report![31] A majority of Ulstermen are in favour of Home Rule. It is only in a corner of Ulster that an opposition exists.

Motion carried 359:133.

The Oxford Magazine observed: When the result was announced, the enthusiasm was such as we have never seen before. Oxford is full of converts to Home Rule.

---

13 June 1907

A motion (omitted in printing) but clearly advocating the avoidance by civil means of the War which naturally followed.

Mr Rose *War cannot last much longer. In the long run, arbitration must take its place. Great Britain in her prominent position, should be in the van of the great humanitarian movement. I believe that the better judgment of humanity must prevail in the end.*

Mr Mackie *One: Germany will not co-operate; Two: the position that the armaments of every nation are its own concern, not that of a conference. Three: That we have done so already to the endangering of our safety. Four: History shows that peaceful relations were only too liable to be upset very suddenly and just when thought to be most secure.*

Mr R. G. Laffan *The Army keeps too many men from acting in a productive capacity. But what attracts me is the ideal side of the question. In India, we have to keep troops, but fear [in Europe] is overestimated because due allowance is not made for the growing power of the Socialists in Germany.*

Mr F. W. Baggalay (Exeter) *There are occasions when War is not only justified, but the lesser of two evils. The object of armaments was not to provoke wars, but to preserve peace. Arms expenditure is only a form of insurance. Human natures are so little to be trusted that for England to lead the way in reduction of arms would be an act of criminal folly.*

Mr Watkins *Luxury and ease are the worst things for a nation, witness Rome and Carthage.*

Mr Cohen was lucid and laid great stress on the Navy.

R. T. Weeton (New College) *Prince Von Bulow has called for the German navy to become equal to that of England. So we should beware of relaxing our efforts until the German Socialists had effected an actual reduction.*

Mr A. W. Cockburn (New College) *The Crimean and the Franco-Prussian wars followed a period of false security.*

Motion lost 51:60.

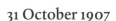

31 October 1907

While sympathising with India's needs, House believes that the establishment of self-government would be fatal to her best interests.

Mr Brinsley-Richards *I must stress the vast difference between earlier, western conceptions of liberty and the criminal folly of imagining India to be a nation.* Words like 'Native' and 'criminal tribes' he might have avoided.

Mr H. Aronson (Lincoln) *There has been from England a crushing influence on India. Does this university really fit men for training up a new India? The coalition of the Native States is proof surely that we are not indispensible.*

Mr S. V. MacFadyan (Exeter) *I must confront the colossal ignorance of gentlemen opposite. Foreign rule brings material gain, but what profit is it if India ceases to be herself?*

Mr Cockburn *Government by agitators would be intolerable.*

Mr S. Mirshahn (Worcester) Somewhat indistinct, but there was about him more of that strange, indefinable pathos of the East than about any of his predecessors.

Motion carried 172:87.

7 November 1907

Mr Lloyd George's unexpectedly speedy settlement of the Railway dispute robbed the debate of Thursday November 7th of some of the interest which would have attached to it, had it not been held in the very middle of final negotiations. We regretted very much the absence of speakers to defend the Railway directors, and incidentally, we might point out the paucity of really capable Conservative speakers at present—despite the preponderance of underdog graduate opinion upon that side.

Mr F. S. Johnson (Trinity) *The case for the men who had barely a living wage under the present paternal regime, is incontrovertible.*

Mr L. L. Cohen *Why should the Railway companies recognise as all-powerful a body which only represents 12 per cent of the total of employees? To say that the companies are hostile to trade unions in themselves is nonsense in view of the facilities they gave their men in allowing them to attend union meetings.*

Mr L. T. Stein [Opening with unusual vigour] *Gentlemen opposite are troglodytes, cave-dwellers utterly out of touch with the conditions of modern industry. I have no patience with the Seven Sleepers of Euston Road.**

Mr L. J. Fox (Queen's) *Competition is the great evil we have to face. Nationalisation will prove the great salvation.*

Mr A. H. Clarke (Hertford) *There is not much individuality to grow on at 12 shillings per week.*

Mr R. N. Flew (Merton) *I wonder if Labour should not be organised just as powerfully as capital.*

Mr K. McCartney (Queen's) *It is high time for somebody to speak for the directors. Trades Unions are socialistic in their tendency and therefore should be watched.*

* Railway company offices.

Mr A. H. M. Lunn (Balliol)[32] *The directors are utterly beyond salvation.*

Mr F. J. Romanes (St John's) *The directors are not fools, but sound businessmen.*

Motion tied 88:88. The President gave his casting vote for 'the men.'

Wednesday 20 November 1907

House believes that Disestablishment would be disastrous for the Church and to the Nation. Despite the rival attractions of The Mikado, a full house assembled on Wednesday November 26th. There must have been fully 600 'on the floor'.

Lord Wolmer *Parliament has absolutely no right to confiscate Church property.*

Mr Le Quesne *The idea of it being a clean sweep of the Church's property is absurd. It will make the Church a more coherent whole—and one enjoying greater freedom.*

Mr Hallett *Disestablishment will not bring liberty to the Church. As far as the nation is concerned, it will do away with religion altogether. Nor indeed should the Church exist on her prerogative. Mr Gladstone came to repent of disestablishment of the Irish Church*—Strongly contested.

Mr Richmond (Secretary) *Do we really think that alliance with the powers responsible for our present social conditions is the one they need? When Disestablishment does come, it will remove one of the many misunderstandings about 'The Church's One Foundation.'*

Lord Robert Cecil MP (Visitor ex-President)[33] *I am still an old Tory and have great fears of the effect on the public mind if the state should be severed from religion. Do we use our churches for political meetings? I believe that only the Anglican and Roman churches have a hold on the poorest or at any rate, have it in London. The Church as handmaid to the State is disgusting.*

Mr Hallett *Someone had referred to Scotch bishops not having seats in the Lords. Since when has the Church of Scotland had Bishops? Lord Robert says that the Church was the Church of the Poor. For my part, it sanctifies by its services and its ministry, the public acts taking place in the country.*

Mr C. F. G. Masterman MP (Christ's Cambridge)[34] *Living outside Hatfield (Home of the Cecils), I have never met a farm labourer who was not a Primitive Methodist. The Catholics and Anglicans are doing good work in crowded slums, but that is precisely where there is no endowment. I differ from Lord Robert in regarding Liberty not as a means to an end, but an end in itself. Do we want the Church to care more for her material position than her liberty?*

Motion lost 260:270.

---

28 November 1907

House condemns the agreement with Russian Autocracy by which British interests have been compromised and Persia's national claims completely ignored.[35]

Mr N. Micklam (New College) *The agreement is rotten to the core. We have alienated the Russian people. We don't know if Russia will keep her word. We have isolated Germany and sacrificed Persia and Tibet. And in Afghanistan, we have nothing to boast about.*

Mr R. N. Flew (Merton) *To refuse to treat with Russia is sentimentality. Is it an evil to isolate Germany? Above all, we have secured India.*

Mr Lunn quoted Antigone, then compared Russia to the Devil. *Most serious after the abandonment of Persia, is the effect of this treaty on the Mohammedan[36] world.*

Mr J. Hunter (Balliol) *Persia is dying. Why not leave Thibet (sic) to China which ever slumbers and sleeps?*

Mr MacFadyan *I have a profound distrust of anything calculated to weaken our hold on India.*

Mr Watkins *Though I am not afraid of the Russian army bogey, I am concerned about India.*

Mr P. R. Diggle (Univ.) *Just how can India be invaded from the north and what possibility in markets is offered by Thibet?*

Motion carried 65:61.

---

5 December 1907

Recognising that Oxford is not sufficiently in touch with the Nation, House would welcome some measures of reform.

Mr H. Symonds (Oriel) *I regret the fact that Oxfordians come from the educated classes. It is impossible for poor men to be educated here. Our Pass schools are irredeemably bad; our scholarships had been meant for the poor, not the rich.*

Mr A. W. Cockburn (New College) *The notion of poverty as a barrier is absolutely untrue.* He astounded us with pictures of the zeal of the country parson for Reform. *The Passman is someone after my own heart.*

Mr B. W. Livingstone M.A. (Corpus) *I want no mechanical university. Oxford should be like a drama. We want the working man. Still more do we want to be representatives of the lower middle classes. We need to be in touch with the secondary schools of the country. Compulsory Greek is surely not a guarantee of the higher culture.*

Mr T. H. H. Case (Queens) *The country is at the cross-roads. Oxford must wait.*

Mr Rose *Surely it is for Oxford to lead, not to follow. The approbation of the* Daily Mail *is surely ominous. The non-resident M.A.s[37] should lay down their imperium. Here in most matters of University government involving change, a vote of graduates could be called.*

Mr Shaw-Stevens (Balliol) *I wonder why the nation should be educated at Oxford. How far is it regrettable that we are not in touch with the nation?*

Mr W. M. Ogilvy (Univ.) *Country parsons are admirable in their own sphere, but we must not be a class university.*

Mr E. W. M. Balfour *We cannot get over the antagonism between the world of trade and our world.*

Mr H. B. Bingham (Univ.) *I do protest against the fallacy that Oxford should be a poor man's university. It must be for the leisured classes.*

Mr J. A. Dale (Jesus) *Surely it is for Oxford to leaven the nation.* Mr Dale has improved incredibly and his earnest speech was warmly applauded.

No vote recorded.

⚬⚬⚬

23 January 1908

House would welcome the imposition of severe restriction on the liquor traffic.
   The Attendance was not very large and the question evoked no great enthusiasm.

Mr Ogilvy *A heavy expenditure on alcohol and a high standard of national prosperity cannot go together. The liquor trade naturally fights for its own hand and blocks the path to social reform.*

Mr Brinsley-Richards *True reform must begin with the individual consumer.*

Mr Stein *The true extent of the evil has not been emphasized. Even the liquor traffic has been forced to acknowledge its enormity. No trade pays lower wages in proportion to its profit and benefits the working class less.*

Mr E. P. Swain *It is absurd to say that the trade is being persecuted. It would be truer to say that it is being abused.*

Lord Wolmer *I see no better things in the reduction of licenses. It would be wise not to check the facilities for getting a drink. Have not men been known to walk half a mile or more for a drink? And after all, sin must be forgiven.*

Mr A. J. Macmillan *I don't think that a connection of the upper classes with insobriety should be represented as a law possessing the force of absolute necessity.*

Motion carried 74:50.

30 January 1908

House deplores the weakness of the present Irish administration.

Mr F. C. McDermot *The anti-grazing agitation is a bogus movement based on no economic ground. Mr Birrell failed to check the disturbances when they began.*

Mr Laffan *The Land League rule Ireland as much under the last government as under this. As for law, it isn't verdicts that are difficult to secure, so much as evidence. The new spirit which is arising in Ireland is so valuable and promising that it would be asinine to risk destroying it by over-hasty attempts to remedy the present trouble.*

Mr Cohen *Ireland needs the protection of the police. Evidence may be had in abundance. The sole reason for the disturbances has always been political.*

Mr Micklam *No mention has been made of the sweeping away of all coercive measures; and the evictions and cattle-driving apart, there is hardly any agrarian crime in Ireland.*

Mr Hallett *To call enforcement of the law 'repression' is true only in the sense that all law is repression. Judges in Ireland do the work juries do not.*

Mr Richmond *Ireland is suffering from the old complaint, an unsympathetic government.*

Mr Diggle *Weakness in a government is always a sin. Ireland needs a modern Strafford.*[38]

Mr Fox (Queen's) *As a socialist. I would uphold cattle-driving and insist that the starving man has a right to steal.*

Mr H. A. Smith (St John's) *Cattle-driving sprang from the failure to meet the needs of the Irish people. The law is associated in Ireland with persecution and so naturally, meets with little support.*

Mr W. Goodchild (Lincoln) *You must remember the low level of civilisation which prevails amongst the peasantry of Ireland.* He was good.

Motion carried 92:60.

---

6 February 1908

HM Government is deserving of the confidence of the country.

Mr Rose *They are hardworking. The old valuable principle of Free Trade is secure in their hands. Liberal Imperialism in which the ideal of a federation of nations is sought is the only sound Imperialism.*

Lord Wolmer *This attack on the Lords evokes no sympathy, for with the closure system in the Commons, the House of Lords now remains as a last safeguard against the autocracy of the cabinet. Ireland has been reduced in two years from peace to chaos. The whole Colonial Conference supported a system of preferential tariffs, yet the Government slammed the door in the face of the Colonies, forgetting that only colonial prosperity can relieve the evils of overcrowding and unemployment at home. Capital is going abroad and still the government adhere to the antiquated system of Free Trade.*

Mr Aronson *There is more unemployment in Germany, a protectionist country than here. In 124 Acts, the government have loaded up a plethora of benefits. Above all, the House of Lords has been obstructive and is justifiably attacked.*

Mr Shaw Why did the King's speech contain no reference to an attack on the House of Lords? Is Sir Henry Campbell-Bannerman to go there and join the very peers he has created in 20 months?

Mr Stein The Government are trying to govern Ireland sympathetically. They are pledged to Free Trade, have given equality to Boer and British and settled the state of the Trade Unions. Their financial ability is not disputed. They are sane and sincere. Mr Stein made the best defence of the government.

Mr Swain I find the government inconsistent in their attitude toward the House of Lords. It would be better to deal with low wages and unemployment than to dabble in Old Age Pensions. The Opposition at least have Tariff Reform[39] *to meet the evil.* Mr Swain was as vehement and fierce as ever.

Mr Watkins I am angered at the Imperialist sentiments proposed by Liberals and deplore the underhand ascent of the House of Lords.

Mr Case Old Age pensions will not encourage thrift.

The Hon. R. S. A. Palmer I condemn the insane partiality of the government for petty class legislation which benefits few people and annoys many. They have furnished the Trade Unions with a weapon against capitalism.

Mr A. V. Harding (Wadham) Sweated labour exists in protectionist countries.

Motion lost 88:115.

---

13 February 1908 (Cambridge Visit)

House deplores the current exaggeration of party spirit in contemporary politics.

Mr Baggalay The watchwords remain, but have lost their meaning. There must be something wrong with a system in which Lord Rosebery and Lord Hugh Cecil[40] *can find no party to include them.*

Lord Wolmer *The government no longer hold it a moral duty to enforce the laws still unrepealed. Honest deliberation is at an end when ministers tour the country when they should be engrossed in their official duties.*

Mr E. Evans (Trinity Hall Cambridge) *The mover engages in fantastic imaginings. The uprising of new parties threatens the existence of the two-party system. Parties feel less bitter toward one another than has been the case. Party feelings no longer destroy or weaken private friendships. The party system is essential to stability, to maintain a healthy criticism and public interest in politics.*

Mr R. E. H. Somerset (Queen's) *It is a defence of a thing to say that it is engrained in the custom of a country. When leaders meet, like the ancient Augurs, they exchange a wink. Only the young politician is serious and adheres to an idea with 'the desperate tenacity of one who never knows when he may get another.'*

Mr R. M. Patton-Muir (Caius Cambridge—President) *Extremists in both camps consider their creed eternal virtue and that of their opponents an everlasting lie. If anyone in a municipality wishes to substitute electric trams for horse trams or treacle for butter in a workhouse, the scheme is supported or opposed on party lines. Men struggle in oblivion of the fact that no set of political principles can last for ever.*

Mr MacFadyan (Univ.) *The other side has exaggerated. Party feeling never excludes decency and good order,*[41] *at any rate in the House of Lords and runs too high in the country.*

Mr Ogilvy (Univ.) *The last speaker is a bigoted libertarian. In other times, bitterness was rife in politics and is so still. Expediency and compromise are the rule of life for the modern cabinet. The present government is only surpassed as a political menagerie by the present opposition.*

Mr Richmond *No sufficient cause has been shown why we should doubt the goodness of the present system and desire to change it by sweeping it all away. It is difficult to account satisfactorily for all the actions of political life, but it is illiberal to doubt entirely the sincerity of their motives.*

Motion carried 145 against 39.

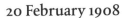

20 February 1908

House would welcome a system of compulsory and universal military training.

Mr T. S. Wilding (Lincoln) *I would use military training to check physical degeneration.*[42] *The need for a home army in addition to the regular army is obvious since the Navy can only be effective if it is free to act at once on the offensive.*

Mr Case *I see a nation moving to war; even babies in perambulators and women in pain believe it. Why restrict the proposal to men? The real question of vital moment is our national character and its preservation from demoralising and corruptive influences. As to the unemployed, it is no solution to put them into barracks and then say they are at work. Teach men to fight and they will soon look for an antagonist.*

Mr R. A. Weston (New College) *Normal military training differs as much from conscription as a spoon does from a spade. We do not wish the destruction of Germany. A scheme essential for national security can never be too expensive. All foreigners think an invasion of England quite feasible. And we have India to defend as well. In taking such measures we are not becoming mere militarists.*

Motion carried 90:58.

Friday 6 March 1908

In view of the rapid growth of the Labour movement, the existing connection between Oxford and the industrial class is dangerously inadequate.

Mr Lennard *The governing classes are still uneducated. Is Oxford to cease trying to educate these classes?*

Mr R. S. A. Palmer (Univ.)[43] *Nothing could be more democratic than Oxford, at least than the Union Society.*

Mr J. Lawson (Ruskin)[44] *As things are, no miner, no railway worker ever presumes to hope that he may become a member of a university.* Mr Lawson spoke with feeling and, eloquence and conviction. He struck a note of genuine sympathy and his speech was proof of his statement that Oxford would lose nothing by welcoming the working class.

Mr J. H. Thorpe (Trinity) *A close connection between Oxford and the working classes, if it means bringing them to Oxford, would destroy the University and coherence of University life.*

Mr Baggalay (Exeter) *Oxford has an ideal which the education of England cannot afford to lose . . . To alter her system to suit the motion would create irreparable loss.*

Mr Cohen *To bring working men to Oxford to live in the colleges would have to be a severe drain on the national exchequer.*

Mr Watkins *I have no desire to see a return to the Oxford of Wycliffe.*

Mr J. Fox (Queen's) *I object to the use of the words 'lower classes'—the so-called lower classes.*

Mr J. Hunter *I am unwilling to substitute a grade for classes. Oxford cannot contain everyone.*

Baron W. von Ow-Wachendorf *Give thought to the use made in Germany of universities in order to mitigate social differences.*

Mr G. St J. Jones *Children who win scholarships from primary to secondary schools are rarely successes.*

Mr S. R. Plimsoll *Education can do no harm.*

Mr MacFadyan (Wadham) *Surely children of the working classes already have splendid opportunities of education.*

Motion carried 73:59.

30 April 1908

A hearty note of congratulation to the new Prime Minister [H. H. Asquith] was unanimously carried.*

House desires, in the light of affairs in the Middle-East, a more vigorous policy from HM Government.

Mr Micklam *The Turk must go. The Macedonians, once free, will be capable of self-government. The role of liberation is England's historic role.*

Mr Brinsley-Richards *Has military action in the Mediterranean always proved effective? . . . In concert with other powers we have done our best.*

C. A. Gunner (Oriel) *England's role in international displays cannot be guided by sentimental considerations.*

A. H. Clarke (Hertford) *If 'The Turks must go,' where are they to go to?*

Mr V. D. Harris (Corpus)[45] *The Christian races fight so murderously among themselves that they do not deserve intervention.*

Mr M. C. Perks (Oriel) *I am in favour of the Turks. The Turks are teetotallers and the Christians are not.*

Motion lost 46:87.

7 May 1908

* Sir Henry Campbell-Bannerman had resigned as Prime Minister during the university vacation on 4 April—and would die on the 22nd.

This House welcomes the result of the N.W. Manchester by-election.[46]

Mr Richmond *The government cannot be blamed for passing evils in delayed business when the Lords obstruct them.*

Lord Wolmer *It is hypocrisy to suppose that public houses, believed to be Tory strongholds, should be suppressed and leave clubs alone because radical clubs are numerous. The [by-election] result condemns cheese-paring in the Navy. We welcome the result as a sign of the rising Tory flood.*

Motion carried 98:62.

———— ⊗⊗⊗ ————

14 May 1908

This House believes that the Government's Licensing Bill is both just and necessary.

Mr Stein *We are spending enormous amounts on drink, and licenses are too numerous. A reduction in licenses means a reduction in drunkenness.*

Mr MacFadyan (Univ.) *The 1904 Bill (Tory), recognised the principle of propriety in licenses. Can the Clubs? Local police stations show how much drunkenness they cause.*

Mr Cockton *The Church (as represented by the established Church) has condemned the bill.*

Mr William Temple M.A. (Balliol) *The provision for children under a Unionist Government welcomed by nearly everyone in the House, has been mutilated by a committee on which they had a large majority.*

Lord Wolmer *I doubt whether the Bill could diminish thirst. Working men would resent an improper supervision of clubs and the point of clubs is quite manifest. The financial burden on the Trade will be crushing. The Bill is a scandalous attack, notably on the widow and the orphan, but on every investor. Even if much drink is consumed, the brewers will suffer through the loss of profits.*

Motion carried 123:65.

———— ✺ ————

21 May 1908

House would deplore the immediate return of a Tory government.

Mr Ogilvy *Education and Scottish land reform has been blocked by the Tory House of Lords and the clerical landlords. Promises of Tariff Reform are unscrupulous and cannot be fulfilled.*

Mr R. A. Knox *Tariff Reform should not be a party question. The only way to effect it is to put the Unionists into power. A Tory government will not wreck the licensing settlement. It will not know how to do it. The Government's Old Age pension scheme is a sham. The Tory opposition is so bad in opposition that it ought to come to power.*

Mr Laffan *Consider this in the light of a) the present government, b) a possible Unionist Government. The present one is progressive in industrial matters— Merchant Shipping, Land and the Housing Bill. Best of all, the Budget[47] and the expected reform of the Poor Law. Mr Birrell's University Bill[48] was an effort to concili- ate Ireland. The Licensing Bill, if defeated, would mean vast numbers of public house licenses. The Tory nostrum, Tariff Reform, is only possible under Socialism. The House has lately been supporting measures reassuringly. But it must support the sum of those measures preferable before the government.*

Motion lost 66:177.

5

'The Whole University Marching Down the High'

28 January 1909—17 November 1910

No confidence in government/Budget in prospect/Alternatives to Socialism/Naval spending/Lloyd George's Budget/a Parliament for Ireland/Discarding democracy/House of Lords as menace to the state—G. K. Chesterton visit/Osborne Judgment/No confidence again/Nationalist movements in the East/Home Rule/Revolution in Portugal/Compulsory OTC/Case for Puritanism.

Conflict between the two Houses of Parliament had been coming precisely as British politics began to involve major reform. It was, as many Conservatives would say, Gladstone's fault. He had made the shocking move of establishing Irish Home Rule as a principle. His first Reform Bill of 1886 had been defeated in the Commons in 1886 after Chamberlain's defection, with tumultuous Ulster Members chairing Salisbury round the lobby. The Second Bill of 1893, after passing the Commons securely, had been killed by the unelected chamber.

In 1906, with the Liberals newly elected, Alfred Milner, the English blood patriot, now in the House of Lords, made a characteristically virulent speech there, saying that the Liberal conciliation policy in South Africa was something which 'the public should have spat out of their mouths'. The Commons replied with a motion specifically condemning the former Master of the Veldt for defending the flogging of labourers. Winston Churchill, new and rising Liberal, was dismissive. 'The public know him no more. Having exercised great authority...he now exercises no authority...Lord Milner has ceased to be a factor in public life.' Conservative peers responded with a motion of grateful thanks to this strange man. Passing by 170 to 35, it thumbed the noble nose and measured the Conservative majority handy for use against reforming legislation.

The Lords next killed that Education bill directed at the Nonconformist interest as Tories served the Church of England. It is made little of in godless today, but at that moment, it was an affront to both the party in power, with a grand public majority, and its supporters nationally. Balfour underlined the mood by another affront—to the cross-party discussion on the compromise. The Minister, Birrell, had wanted the conciliatory Duke of Devonshire present. Instead, Balfour sent Lord Cawdor, his fag at Eton. For although the Lords would readily bridle at government policy, they did so at Balfour's signal. Lloyd George's famous observation at this time was that 'The House of Lords is not as it claims, the Watchdog of the Constitution. It is Mr Balfour's poodle.'

Then it came in 1908 to pass a Licensing Bill affecting Tory interests in contributing brewers and sub-agent publicans. It would be killed in the Lords. Ironically, the sheer effrontery was best spelt out by a cheerful young rural Warwickshire ultra, Willoughby de Broke.[1] In his memoirs, he speaks of a whip sent out and the subsequent convergence of country peers upon Lansdowne House.'... a great nobleman living at the heart of Mayfair causes a few letters to be written to his brother noblemen in the country, summoning them to take private council with him under his own roof where, after a desultory conversation lasting less than an hour, it is agreed to turn down a proposal that has occupied the Liberal party for something like a quarter century. The thing could not have taken place anywhere except in England.'

Willoughby's good humoured recollection of the total erasure of an elected ministry's proposal, part of it a publicly known and proclaimed programme, at the suggestion of 'a great nobleman in a Mayfair drawing room' describes constitutional crisis, nothing less. When the actual Finance Bill for the coming year was thrown out, the road was open to more than driving through that specific legislation. Their Lordships had indicated an unfitness for the great reserve powers they held and had abused. There were two fights ahead. That Finance Bill established, the House of Lords must now be disestablished, must become a picturesque leftover, a plain clothes Yeomen of the Guard.

The Finance Bill of 1909 was to pay for useful things to be done. The two years, 1909 and 1910, would see the passage into law of the foundations of what would later be called the Welfare State. It saw the old age pension. Conservatives had talked a little about social concerns and asserted their slogan of National Efficiency. Though their hectoring style implied a sort of army corporal's task of making slackers and weaklings fitter than the current, fearful evidence of their flat-chested, underfed debility, which demonstrated their real need of the school meals and free milk which would come later. Such concern usually came in military wrapping, devoted to readiness for a war endlessly and lightly contemplated.

The Liberal government had produced the old age pension, something discouraging thrift, militarily irrelevant, and subject to snappish abuse in Westminster and Oxford. It had shocked Rosebery who considered payment of 5 shillings a week, otherwise 13 pounds a year, 'so prodigal of expenditure as is likely to undermine the whole fabric of the Empire'. That legislation had been announced in Asquith's 1908 Budget making the full Bill, when it came to the Lords, as noted, unequivocally a Finance Bill, incapable, under convention dating from Queen Anne, of amendment, never mind rejection. By the end of 1908 600,000 pensions had been approved.

The Budget of 1909, delivered by Lloyd George, Chancellor since Asquith's succession to the Premiership, and with Asquith himself fully involved in the drafting, was assuredly a Finance Bill. Its tax provisions—charges put onto tobacco, alcohol, and petrol—did indeed have a busy, remunerative career ahead of them. Interestingly though, Sir George Murray, Permanent Secretary at the Treasury, would do Civil Service imperception on a heroic scale in an anxious letter to Asquith,[2] describing this tax on motoring as something 'which I believe will be quite unworkable'.

No motorist would, then or later, make the fuss which now came from the House of Peers. The response to the land charges, most of them on urban land, developable and frequently to be developed, was, they thought, a great cry of assault on the custodians of England's green and pleasant private domain. In reality, it was a tax, like all taxes, not popular with those paying it, generally useful, and hardly ruinous. As Lady Gwendolen Cecil, clever sister to the current and fourth Marquess of Salisbury, James (*not* particularly clever, but very decent), remarked, 'It will cost Jem another £3,000 a year, but, as he observes, he is very rich; and I don't think it need make any catastrophic change in his life.'³ What would trouble the fourth Marquess twenty-five years later, when that resistance, against the 1909 Budget, had long since brought on the retributory Parliament Act, was the sad condition of the Upper House 'Out on its feet in the Thirties,' another Cecil recalls him saying.

Rosebery, so much better as a moderate Conservative than a cavilling Liberal, wasn't going to 'stake all my hopes on the tumultuous hazards of a general election'. However the response among Tory lords, though it contained any amount of financial resentment, was most interesting as reflecting their wider and fearful imaginings. So it seems appropriate in commenting on the debates of undergraduates, to set another debate out here—debate as narrative—a section of that Lords reading, a scatter of that other debate, the affair opening on 22 November 1909, in the House of Lords.

It starts with Lansdowne as leader, asking, 'Shall we stand better or shall we stand worse when the struggle comes if we shirk our responsibility now?'⁴ Lansdowne, not an extremist, was the prisoner of his loyalty to Balfour who had made retreat a guiding error—retreat to Protection, to Chamberlain, and now to a mood in party and Upper House, bent on doing the *Boys' Own*, gallant, thick-headed, and doomed thing. They should, he meekly said, disregard convention and reject the Budget.

Loreburn, Liberal Lord Chancellor, observed that the Lords had killed that Licensing Bill of the same year after a private gathering at Lansdowne's London house—It was, he said, 'a case of perishing by the stiletto in

Berkeley Square'.[5] It had become 'impossible that any Liberal government should ever again bear the heavy burden of office unless it is secured against a repletion of such as our measures have had to undergo for the last four years'. 'This would be war.' The Trollopian Bishop of Bristol stressed episcopal antiquity and Christian loving-kindness, one toward the other; and damned Lloyd George. Willoughby de Broke, nineteenth baron, that younger peer just met above, was still burdened by abolition, in 1846, of the Corn Laws. By contrast, Lord Cromer was scared and practically said so. Throwing out the Bill would create 'a ceaseless hesitation to secure a material alteration, in not merely the composition, but the functions of the second chamber'.[6]

Lord Hardinge thought the Budget 'cunningly devised as a vehicle for socialistic revolution. It adopted the doctrines of the extreme Socialistic Party whilst at the same time providing all the machinery which is necessary for carrying these doctrines into effect at any time hereafter.'[7] Taking that view, their Lordships were going to be up for the unthinkable. Rejection of this Finance Bill, most unconservative of measures and a blow against the healing and binding effect of not being taxed, would demonstrate contempt for an unwritten, long-standing fingertip constitution, one binding practice. This could be foreseen as simple calamity. A coterie elect, but not elected, dependent on unspoken rules, and now breaking them, would scatter all assumptions. It would reliably destroy the great powers of restraint still available to an Upper House which accepted a reversal the way Jem Cecil had accepted a loss of income.

Interestingly, Rosebery, so often over the wrong top, would, in the Lords, go hard-headed and sensible, spelling out to the assembled ermine the consequences of a heroic noble tantrum. 'My Lords, I think you are playing for too high a stake.' He recognized 'a considerable body of opinion which is hostile to this House. We must all be aware...that the hereditary constitution of this House does lend itself to effective, even if it be unjust, satire.' It was not something that most of them had noticed.

Then with real insight, Rosebery defined the subtle strength of the Lords in 1910. It was a power of latency—it exercised enormous power as to what it *might* do. Witness Home Rule. *That* would be coming up again. John Redmond, leader of the Irish National Party and Catholic Ireland, had said that 'The only obstacle to Home Rule is the House of Lords. Are you going to weaken that barrier?' Rosebery understood what was good for the Upper House and, three years into a seven-year term, it wasn't a lightly picked fight with an elected government. They did sometimes have to pull back from what they wanted to do. They wanted to stop Home Rule and they had already, with their massive adverse vote of 1893, done precisely that to Gladstone's second and Commons-approved Home Rule Bill.

This was one of the great parliamentary debates, calling up a centrally important issue and running it through liberal and illiberal, rational and irrational opinion. Milner, the returned Pro-Consul, soon to be encouraging sedition among armed Ulstermen, observed that 'we cannot shrink from the conflict which is now forced upon us'.[8] At Glasgow, a week later, crediting the Liberals with his own contempt for law, he would speculate that a Commons free of Lords' restraint might give itself perpetual power by abolishing the term of Parliament.

Milner thought other people thought like him. Asquith did not. For in the Parliament Act of 1911 which rejection of this Budget would precipitate, that term would actually be *reduced* from seven to five years. Milner was a fearfully twentieth-century man, the sort for whom direct action beckoned, one who preached the other side's reforms as revolutionary so as to validate the delightful option of counter-revolution.

Balfour of Burleigh, Liberal Tory and remote cousin of Arthur, sacked by him as a Free Trader, said that it was no good proclaiming a Lords' right to reject the Budget, since 200 years of usage had made it clear that the Lords didn't challenge budgets or governments, and that both commodities were settled in the Commons. Stopping a budget meant readiness 'to spoil and destroy the control of the other House of Parliament over the government'.[9] Showing great prescience, Burleigh pointed out the current increased management of parliamentary politics, also that, in the affronted teeth of Edmund Burke, MPs increasingly *were* delegates. As a Free Trade Conservative, he had experienced the bullying instituted by

Chamberlain, herald of machine politics, and saw that system, rightly, as the future.

Lord Stanmore, despite the suburban title, a former colonial governor, compared Asquith's administration with 'a tropical bee which deposits a spider for its grub to eat when it comes out of the egg...it injects a fluid into the spider, paralysing every faculty, but at the same time keeping it alive'.[10] Their Lordships' heirs would be similarly paralysed against stopping the coming Socialist generation. Lord Cawdor, Macbethian-titled Balfour fag, also a friend of Edward VII, anticipated single chamber government, 'a suspension of the Septennial act and the establishment of the Rump Parliament again...I do not know how you would get rid of it without a revolution'.[11] Perhaps counter-revolution?

A Liberal peer, Lord Courtney, now reminded the do-or-die faction that an opinion poll—rare and unnerving thing half a century before the exercise's pre-eminence as constitutional warning system!—had shown interesting figures. Liberals and Tories were all square with solid numbers for the Irish Nationalists and Labour. How did the Tories think these two groups would vote on any harsh measures against the Lords? It was a strong, notably modern point, but no warning that Conservative Lords would stroll into marginality whenever an angry Commons with a majority made up of their enemies should next frame a parliament bill would be grasped on that last and voting day of debate.

Their Lordships divided on the Finance Bill—Contents 75, Not Contents 350.

As the Oxford Union debated in the same zone as the Lords: Budget, Upper House power, and, uneasily, 'Women', it shared a general mood certainly to the right of politics, about readiness for war. Admiral Fisher had wanted eight dreadnoughts—in an overwhelmingly land-bound war. The 1914–18 reality was of one drawn battle at sea! Oxford also inclined to the option of compulsory military service. The British tended to damn the Prussian tendency within the then German Empire for fitting young men for life with weapon-proficiency plus dumb and uniform obedience; and, having damned them, asking for lots of all that (and compulsory) here!

A speech to the Union, set out here and heard with apparent rapture, from a Colonel Eastwood—in charge of the University Officers' Training Corps, a body (as might be expected in theologically obsessed Oxford) heavy with unarmed curates, yearns in a perfectly amiable way, for the splendour of seeing 'The entire university in uniform and with rifle, marching down the High'.

This wonderful utterance has not passed into general record, like the white feather handed out to men *not* in uniform—initiated by middle-class ladies in Eastbourne before 1914 was out. It does though, add something to debate about the origins of the impulse that would send men happily on their way to their long graves. Christopher Clark's superb account of miscalculating nations getting into the First War is shrewdly called *The Sleepwalkers*. 'The whole University marching down the High' suggests that that is how they would march.

—⊗⊗⊗—

28 January 1909[*]

House believes that it is high time the government resigned.

Mr A. W. Cockburn (New College) *Ireland and the Licensing Bill were his chief points. On Old Age pensions, he refused to pronounce.*

Mr P. Marsden (St John's) *There was, he urged, work still to do in chastening the Upper House and educating the electorate with another Free Trade budget.*

Mr F. J. Romanes (St John's) *had no sympathy with anyone who ran down everything English. He rated the Territorial Force, scouted Navy policy and pointed the imperative need of many things.*

Mr Swain—Librarian *saw Tariff Reform as the only way to cement commercial union with our colonies and, as he had said before, he believed in the British Empire.*

* *Oxford Magazine eccentrically goes into reported speech—and then out of it.*

Mr L. J. Stein (Balliol) *warned that associating the colonies with dearer food would be the worst thing imperialists could do to imperialists. As for promises, the Tories had delayed fifteen years until the Liberals had created pensions.*

Mr T. D. Robb *said the old age pension would have happened anyway, but it was the fault of the government that we didn't have the German contributory ones.*

Mr R. Bevir (Hertford) *asked what right the government had to murmur against peers when they had created so many of them.*

Mr A. V. Hocking (Wadham) *thought Imperial Preference exploited the English artisan in the interests of affluent artisans in the Colonies.*

Motion carried 111:81.

---

4 February 1909

House hopes the budget will make further advances in the taxation of land and capital.

Mr F. K. Griffith (Balliol) *began with the prevailing cry 'Where is the Money going to come from?'*[12] *He referred to the Penrhyn Quarries. See below.*[13]

Mr E. Hancock (Lincoln) *saw this motion as the thin end of the wedge and made some rather crude anti-socialist arguments. We personally would have no objection to the genteel poverty of £5,000 which he puts on a level with destitution.*

Mr Hocking *alleged that the poor already pay three or four times as much, collectively, as the rich. The inhabited house duty put a premium on insanitary dwellings and overcrowding. Capital was especially capable of bearing strain.*

Mr A. D. C. Russell *was full of a fine fury. Was landowning a sin? Why should we hate landowners more than railway shareholders or clothiers? Lord Penrhyn turned out his workmen because he had a rooted objection to trade unions. Land needed attention, it was not an unearned increment. But the financiers of the Liberal Party happened to be rich manufacturers.*

Mr S. Herbert *reckoned Mr Lloyd George positively simian, swinging by the tail of vulgarity from any branch on the tree of democracy. Would Old Age Pensions make up for the people turned out of work by over-taxed landlords?*

Hon. L. U. Shuttleworth *Mr Chamberlain admitted that tariff reform would not tax the foreigner. So if you broaden the basis of taxation you must put burdens on the poor.*

Mr E. Close (Keble) *renewed the protest against landlord-baiting. But there were bad land-lords. He had no sympathy with putting down smallholdings in the middle of deer forests.*

Motion carried 109:71.

———— ✖ ————

25 February 1909[14]

House does not see in Socialism the only remedy for modern economic problems.

Hon. R. S. A. Palmer *Can a man be called a parasite whose business it is to watch the markets of the world; who has to take all the risks of commercial ventures? An investor owns money as another man owns sheep. What will be the result if the state has to give employment for all? Bumbledom and bureaucracy will be the predominant power. Let us take warning from the treatment accorded Socrates and Galileo. Organised and systematic intolerance must follow.*—Query can we call the Vatican of the Renaissance the tyranny of a democracy?

Mr W. M. Ogilvy (Univ.) *Our system produces distress, not as an abuse, but as a normal result. Property has no inviolable rights to assert, that is to deny, the progress of civilisation. Socialism does not involve the abolition of property altogether.*

No vote recorded.

———— ✖ ————

29 April 1909

House considers the government's naval programme entirely inadequate.

Mr Bevir *Germany means to fight and we must have, not superiority, but supremacy. Extra dreadnoughts have been postponed till next year because then the government will not have to pay for them. Four more dreadnoughts now will cost seven millions, and save a hundred millions in time of war. So Eight Dreadnoughts now and at once please.*[15]

Apart from the drawn, semi-immobiliste Battle of Jutland, where David Beatty, British Admiral commanding, observed 'Something seems to be wrong with our ships today,' 'the 1914 war would be a dull, not to say dry, time for navies'.

Mr P. W. Dodd (Jesus) *There is a lot to be said for the* via media. *The economist will starve the Navy for social reform while the Big Navy man will drive it up out of all reason. Fanatics preach that war between England and Germany is inevitable, and of course demand more dreadnoughts to make it so.*

Mr A. P. Herbert[16] *Austria is also building three dreadnoughts! The Liberals got themselves into office by promising economy and have found the only way to get it was by decreasing the naval programme. The future of our Empire depends upon policy across the next twenty years. I think Mr Asquith's intentions are good, but let him beware Messrs Lloyd George and Churchill. The poor man is quite ready to make sacrifices for his country. The rich have got used to it. The nation which does not strive is decadent and so we must expect and prepare to fight. The fact that we might have allies does not alter the position, for without a supreme navy, we shall soon have no friends.*

Mr Hocking *The Tories try to claim a monopoly of patriotism, but if the jingoism displayed by the Opposition is patriotism, I am glad we Liberals don't have it.* Mr Hocking was very uncomplimentary to the National Review.[17]

Motion carried 135:58.

---

6 May 1909

House gives its cordial support to the Budget proposals.[18]

Mr Marsden *the Budget ought to bring together all sections of the Liberal Party. It should unite Big Navy-ites, Social Reformers and Free Traders.*

Mr L. L. Cohen *Mr Lloyd George has produced a wartime budget in time of peace. If they continue to pile taxes on the rich, the financial prosperity of the country will be seriously impaired. I do not object to the supertax, but the death duties will have the ultimate result of driving capital out of the country. As a Unionist free trader, I suggest as an alternative: taxes on sugar and tea.*

Mr E. D. Basden (Lincoln) *Two sets of people will be disappointed: Tariff Reformers startled to find that this was not to be the last Free Trade budget and those who have read, not the reports but the newspapers. Protection means heavy taxes on all necessaries. As for License duties, well, Ministers have no more reason to love the brewers than scripture suggests.*

Mr W. Goodchild *Liberals make monotonous coo-ings about loving their enemies and the 'blessings of peace,' and then proceed to rob their friends. The working class cannot afford to pay more for tobacco which to them, is not a luxury, but a necessity. Anyway who decides when an increment is earned or not?*

Mr Ogilvy *How can tax on undeveloped land be an attack on agriculture? How could a Tariff reformer like Mr Goodchild object to the tobacco tax on the ground that it was a necessity? Tariff Reform, if imposed, would raise the price of food!*

Motion carried 80:79.

3 June 1909

House believes that the establishment in Ireland of a separate legislature with an executive responsible to it is urgently needed.

Mr Ogilvy *The old questions remain unanswered. Catholic emancipation and a Catholic university have failed as panaceas. Ireland must be treated as a nation.*

Motion carried 135:58.

---

21 October 1909

House thinks democracy a discarded ideal.

Mr Goodchild *Tory democracy once had attractions to me. But the sight of fellow men among the poorer class has disillusioned me. Tory Democracy is a contradiction in terms. Democracy is founded on fallacies—equal ability to use a vote and the confusion of liberty and democracy. 'The people have no will and cannot express it, and if they could, it would be wrong.' Is government to be beneficial or representative? The day is past when it can be both.* Mr Goodchild was very refreshing in his consistent and reactionary position, so seldom to be met in the Union.

Mr L. N. G. Montefiore (Balliol) *Democracy does not demand equality of ability, but opportunity for all to use a varying degree of power. Every extension of democracy has been justified by experience, and the aim of democracy is the service of individuals. Efficiency is not the end of all politics. Democracy is a school of character. Does he propose temperance or morality only for the few as with participation in government?*

Mr R. W. G. Cecil[19] began to dance around democracy, pointing a mocking finger and scoffing. *Today only the Irish Nationalists and Labour can be said to be Democrats.* Mr Cecil would do well to speak louder and remove his hands from his pockets.

Mr A. J. Penston (Non-Collegiate) *The question is not whether democracy is ideal in its present form, but whether it is discredited as an ideal for the future.* In his best and most convincing manner, he pleaded for higher education for the working classes and declared Democracy to be the fulfilment of fraternity.

Mr Russell (New College) *I will not take England as a typical democracy. The political machines of France and America greatly discredit the concept. Historically, democracy has always fallen before other states; and for me, Sparta has more attraction than Athens.*

Mr R. Barrington-Ward *There are no democracies. The search for them has been, and will be, in vain.* He spoke at too great length, especially as regards his long survey of ecclesiastical history.

Mr W. F. Phillips (Jesus) *in a very telling manner and the accent of Gwynedd, declared Democracy to be national self-realisation.*

Motion lost 127:137.

---

18 November 1909

House considers the House of Lords as at present constituted, to be a standing menace to the state.

Mr L. J. Stein—Librarian *This is not a question of government by one House or another, but as to whether we should be governed by three chambers: Upper House, Lower House or Lansdowne House?*[20] *Before the Reform Act of 1832 there was very little faction. For then, it was not a matter of one vote but of one peer and three boroughs. But since then, all the parties, not least the Conservatives, have pledged themselves to democracy. Under which, an upper house should inspire public confidence above party warfare. Yet now we have to submit legislation to a House of Landlords, the licensing problem, appropriate to a tied house.*[21]

As a debater, Mr Stein has been unequalled in the Union for some time. It is impossible adequately to report so able an opening speech.

Mr R. S. A. Palmer (Univ.) *A pamphlet published by the* Daily News[22] *is concerned to show the Lords opposed as large landowners, bishops, enemies of women, or dischargers of their under-gardeners. The Lords exist to keep a check on controversial legislation, mostly emanating from the Liberal Party.* [No, No].

Mr R. H. Brinsley-Richards (Hertford) *The House of Lords is no more a 'fortuitous concourse of atoms'[23] as alleged, than is the Universe. The new members, by their eminence would be out of touch with the national feeling, while the House of Commons would become a talking shop. Leaving serious business to the house of experts.*

Mr G. K. Chesterton (Visitor)[24] *This isn't a party question. All the great issues of the day—Imperialism, Socialism, Woman Suffrage cut across party lines. Let us admit that all politicians are inconsistent and that every cabinet breaks its pledges. But what is the House of Lords? They are a hustling, breathless body. Today they exist solely to kick out with violence all bills that touch their own interests and kick on with violence all that do not. Today it is the function of a small ring of rich people to dictate what should be an important and controversial matter. England needs great change. Venice? Carthage? No one knew the hour of their decay. It is said of England that she has no people. The people must be free to vote; and as to what they vote upon, untrammelled by the incubus of the present house.*

Motion lost 308:316.

House strongly opposes the agitation for the reversal of the Osborne Judgment (21 December 1909).[25] Debate held early 1910, no date given.

A. D. C. Russell (New College) ... *Their (the unions') political character is a recent development. Their proper object of mutual benefit and support among the members of particular trades is in danger of being sacrificed to gross political tyranny. We seem to be getting back to the guilds of medieval days.*

A. J. Penston (Non-Collegiate) *I do not question the legality of the Law Lords' decision. But I strongly deny its equity ... the law as it stands, hampers the natural and proper development of the Trade Unions and deals a grave blow at the working classes. I am willing to concede some measure of freedom to the non-socialistic unionist. But at all costs, a great capitalist victory must be avoided.* [A very welcome re-appearance.]

Mr G. W. L. Talbot (Christ Church) *The whole point is that the Labour Party does not represent the views of thousands of Trade Unionists, and it is intolerable that they should be able to compel men to subscribe for the furtherance of even national and imperial questions, which are radically opposed to their own. Honest men are to take their choice between a livelihood and conscience—that is the monstrous sacrifice of liberty proposed by the champions of progress and freedom.* Mr Talbot has the ugly habit of beginning nearly every sentence with 'I think' or 'I do believe.'

Mr J. Gilbert (Exeter) *I insist that labour requires representatives in Parliament... Neither of the other two parties adequately reflects the views of Trade Unionism. It is wrong to say that Unionism is to be permanently identified with Socialism; the alliance is purely temporary as, in my view, it is bad tactics.*

Mr R. M. Barrington-Ward (Balliol) *We must recognise the attempt made by the Labour Party to suppress anyone who disclaims belief in Socialism and yet supports the Socialists.* He is full of pleasing common sense.

Mr R. B. Beckett (Lincoln) *Lord Lansdowne's having to pay taxes to finance Old Age Pensions is just as unjust as the alleged injustice of a compulsory levy in Trade Unions.*

J. H. Blaksley (New College) *The idea of there being one law for the rich and another for the poor is absurd. The reversal of the Judgement would have a disastrous moral effect on the working men themselves.*

Mr W. T. Monckton (Balliol)[26] *I cannot stress too strongly the importance of having large-minded, independent men in politics.*

Result not given.

---

17 February 1910

House has no confidence in the Government.

Mr R. Cecil *This debate is memorable. It occurs on the threshold of a Parliament pledged to pass the budget and Home Rule, and cripple the Lords. The budget hits the poor harder than the rich. The liquor taxes are dishonest and do nothing to check drunkenness. Home Rule will disintegrate the empire and we should remember cattle driving*[27] *and the interests of the [Protestant] minority. The Lords are right to have rejected the budget; we should reform the Commons first.*

Mr P. Guedella (Balliol) *The government has, with the Nationalists, a majority of 124. Reform of the Lords is a Unionist deathbed repentance. Tory democrats unite the arrogance of the oligarchs with the blatancy of demagogues. The government can proclaim Free Trade, Social Reform, No Veto and Peace in Europe.*

Mr S. Herbert (Balliol) *Unemployment, the Poor Law, child labour and the rest are to be shelved, the House of Lords reduced to a mere sham.* He quoted Burke and the Daily News. *The Budget has grazed the Lords and killed the Law Guarantee Society.*

Mr G. S. Woodhouse (Lincoln) *The European situation is critical and the government is not strong enough to deal with it.*

Motion carried 131:117.

---

5 May 1910

House deplores the hostility of British statesmanship toward Nationalist movements in the East.

Mr A. H. Lunn *We must either conciliate the nationalist movements or be prepared to lose our Empire in the East. Our ideal should be a free federation of autonomous states. Beware the example of the partition of Bengal. Lord Curzon's attitude*[28] *is an antithesis of the Queen's Speech. The result is a policy of repression opposed to British tradition. England's need has been called Ireland's opportunity. I am inclined to say the same about India.*

Mr Barrington-Ward *British statesmen have shown no hostility to legitimate native aspirations. Still, events like the recent murder of the Prime Minister*[29] *have shown the necessity of our presence in Egypt. As for India, it is not a nation, but a* continent; premature self-government would produce chaos. The agitation is confined to a small clique of short-sighted sentimentalists.

Mr F. N. Broome (Oriel) *If we leave India, some other nation will step into our place. Religious strife must inevitably ensue on the withdrawal of British control. What India requires is firm government.*

Mr R. E. Snow *Many concessions have been made. The National movement is anarchism in disguise.*

Mr S. T. van den Bergh (Balliol) *If we evacuate India, Russia will step in.*

Motion lost 87:113.

<hr />

26 May 1910

House believes the Irish Question can only be solved by Home Rule.

Mr Griffith *Ireland demands Home Rule as a national right. She fulfils all the tests of nationality and one cannot ignore national sentiment. Home Rule will not mean Rome Rule. It will strengthen the Empire by allowing India to revert her national attitudes of devoted loyalty.* [A model of what Union oratory should be.]

Mr Woodhouse *We cannot afford rashly to experiment with a country so close to our shores.*

Mr Portman (New College) *Let us not forget how much Ireland has contributed to British supremacy in the acts of war and peace alike.*

Mr Bevir *Irish interference in English politics is one of the evils inherent in representative government.*

Mr A. T. Macmillan *I am afraid of what might happen under Home Rule to Irish Land Lords.*

In 1800, middle date of the War with France, Irish membership of the British Army has been put at one third.

Motion lost by 3 votes.

———— ⚬⚬⚬ ————

27 October 1910

House deplores the recent revolution in Portugal.

Mr H. E. Stewart (New College) *The 1822 constitution of Portugal introduced the characteristic vice of democracies, the professional politician. In endeavouring to get rid of that vice, King Carlos was murdered.*[30] *Senhor Braga*[31] *is a mere philosopher, unfitted for his new profession. The expulsion of the religious orders is a pretty comment on this liberty loving republic.*

Mr Jessel (Balliol) *The combination of the Roman Church and a feeble throne has produced disorder, of which the events of 1821, 1847 and this Republic, are symptomatic. Senhor Braga is a University don, ardent in the cause of education,*

Mr Cooper *Was Portugal corruptly administered under the monarchy? Then consider France and the US under republican regimes. When in this world, has a republic successfully administered an empire?*

Mr Lewis (Ch.Ch.) *The Portuguese navy is ridiculous. An appalling percentage of the population are illiterate and the whole country dreadfully priest-ridden. There are laws by which people can be banished without trial.*

Mr F. C. Davidson (Univ.) *With the expulsion of the monarchy has gone the only visible tie between Portugal and her colonial empire. A similar event against England is threatened now that the ancient throne has been overturned.*

Motion carried 145:133.

———— ⚬⚬⚬ ————

3 November 1910

House would welcome a scheme by which membership of the OTC would be compulsory for resident undergraduates.

Mr Cecil *We cannot afford to run any risks by inefficiency. Yet the upper classes are slack in the matter of national defence. A man who is not keen on his college is condemned by public opinion. Those who are not patriotic deserve the same condemnation.*

Mr D. Davies *Mr Haldane's territorial scheme[32] is superior to any compulsory one; it must not be looked upon as a stepping stone to conscription. Our first line of defence is the Navy. My experience is that those who belonged to the school corps, had had enough of soldiering before they left school. The notion is rotten to the core and must be deprecated.*

Col. J. C. B. Eastwood, Officer commanding OUOTC *Personally, I would like to see the whole university marching down the High in uniform; nothing would please me more—a great thing for the University. I have never known a man who had not been improved, morally and physically, by serving with the colours. The OTC is going very well and numbers 1,168, but many of those are going to take Holy Orders and could not accept commissions. Not but that it isn't very important that the clergy should be able to drill Boy Scouts and the Boys Brigade. None of this is because we are going to fight the Germans, but because the position and responsibilities of the Empire demand a greater guarantee of security than the voluntary system can ever provide.*

Motion lost 117:130.

17 November 1910

House would welcome a larger element of Puritanism in English social life.

Mr N. Birkett (Emmanuel Cambridge)[33] *The old Puritanism was too rigid and inelastic, but the spirit and soul of Puritanism is sufficient for all things. Our life is marred today by a kind of mad, vulgar competition for social supremacy: everywhere a kind of speeding-up is proceeding. I would prefer that the English Sabbath was preserved intact from continental influences.*

Mr Montefiore *Puritanism blighted England after the Elizabethan age. The old fire is out and hypocrisy and narrowness are all that are left. English life deserves no such censure as the mover suggests.*

Mr Barrington-Ward *Puritanism is not to be identified with cant. What it really fights against is decadence. It keeps the spirit of the Nation healthy and pays a country best in the end.*

Mr G. E. Davies *I oppose the cant of anti-cant. Oh for the Puritans in this frivolous age.*

Motion carried 158:93.

6

Mourning their Lordships, Worrying about Women

2 February 1911–30 November 1911

Alien immigration/Russo-German understanding/Navel overspending/Two-keel superiority?/Parliament bill—end of the veto—end of the Lords?/Imperial preference/Women's Suffrage—Conciliation bill/Licensing bill/National Degeneration!/ Compulsory Military Training/More naval spending/Pestilential heresy—Liberalism/ excessive intervention by HMG/Triple Alliance condemned/Insurance Act/Home rule for Ulster/national support for the Government/franchise extension.

This was a parliamentary session running late in a summer turning tropical. The Tories would spend six days from 28 June proposing and passing amendments to be certain of rejection: a Committee of both Houses to decide if it was a money Bill or not; no bill denied the rank of money Bill to enjoy the protective word 'Finance'.

It was a waste of time. The weather got hotter. Asquith stayed firm. There would be no parley. The Cabinet minuted George V that these amendments would be rejected *en bloc* by the Commons. The ministers must then advise the Crown to use its prerogative to end the deadlock. Although the Oxford Union managed also to talk about a roll-call of pet themes and cherished anxieties, this short, vivid period was dominated by the Parliament Bill. Brought about by the presumption of the Opposition and the failure of authority in its leader, rejection of a Finance Bill (the Budget of 1909) in the teeth of a binding, two-centuries-old convention, established by a Tory Minister, Robert Harley, and as such, something to be revered by coherent Conservatives, the House of Lords would now demonstrate itself unfit for a serious role and suffer legislative demotion at the hands of the lower and stronger House. It was characteristic of Arthur Balfour's leadership. He flinched from giving a realistic lead to his party, still following Joseph Chamberlain through the stroke-bound and silent last eight years of his life. (He would die six weeks before the outbreak of war—on 2 July 1914.) Which war, Chamberlain, an opponent of the fatal French and Russian commitments of Sir Edward Grey and the Foreign Office, would never have declared.

The impracticality of Imperial Preference had, as noted above, been established by two conferences at which the 'Colonies', as the likes of Australia and Canada were called, denied the concession sought. Expensive, imported colonial foodstuffs and a bias against European trade, had been recognized as such during the two elections of 1910, notably by working-class voters, selfishly preferring lower prices. The rejection of the Budget spoke the same gallant doggedness. Supply could be maintained by an emergency motion, but the principle of a government being able to pass its Finance Bill with the authority of a majority chosen by the voters was clear enough.

The next requirement would be an election. That could not be denied even by the new and anxious George V, but the other requirement, approving guarantees that further rejection would be met by creation of enough new peers to do the job, confused him. It took the good sense of Sir Francis Knollys, royal secretary and rational man at Court, to extract them. The election, as expected, showed a swing to the Tories if only as still-outs doing better. Though that swing felt the drag of northern working-class seats going the other way, their votes probably directed against prospective high colonial food prices under Imperial Preference! Parity between the major parties was discounted by the two Liberal-tolerant blocks of Labour and Irish Nationals. A second election produced no change from a tired electorate.

Accordingly, the Parliament Bill of 1910 would become the Parliament Act of 1911. It would end any Lords interference with Finance Bills and put a two-year limit on interference with the others. Tories dragged their feet. Lord Hugh Cecil offered an amendment establishing an institutionalized secret vote at third reading to frustrate the government caucus. That binding caucus had been invented in his Birmingham Council days by Joe Chamberlain, but no matter. It was a scoundrel thing in the hands of Asquith. Willoughby de Broke, charming extremist, prophetic of later right-wing tactics, wanted a referendum. Only seventeen Tory peers voted in favour. It would require the creation of enough peers to pass the Parliament Bill. If the Lords maintained their undoubted right to reject the Parliament Bill, the government spoke of coming 'contingencies'. This was a nicer way of saying 'wholesale creation of peers', a debasing of the blood of noble descent with commerce, local government, even literature: Sir Thomas Lipton, a job-lot choice of mayors, and Thomas Hardy? What about royal consent? What Knollys had earlier told the fazed new King he must do, he must then do.

As Lansdowne's friend and biographer, Lord Newton, put it in his biography,[1] 'On July 18th, Mr Lloyd George met Mr Balfour and Lord Lansdowne and stated that a pledge to create peers had been already obtained from the King as far back as November: that nothing would induce the Government to run the risk of losing the Parliament Bill in the House of Peers.' What followed was a war of nerves. Chiefly, with the replacement Budget passing its third reading, they were Conservative nerves. Lansdowne was joined by the grand, but rational person of Lord Curzon, whilst mortal conflict was proclaimed by the likes of Lord Selborne. (His heir, the junior ultra, Wolmer, was providing good, absurdist copy here in Union debates.) Increasingly, these days irreconcilables listened to elder unwisdom in the person of Hardinge Giffard, Lord Halsbury—once, remotely, Lord Chancellor—born 1823, early George IV. In similar fashion to the party, the shadow cabinet was split; Joe's son Austen, F. E. Smith, and the current Salisbury joining Halsbury and Selborne in their ditch while Bonar Law, Walter Long, and Middleton faced the arithmetic.

The government, however embarrassed by the whole absurd (and unconstitutional) crisis, was going to win. Not much remained for diehard

Tories, noble and elected, to do except scream. This, as mentioned above, in the person of Lord Hugh Cecil on 24 July, they did. It was an exceptionally hot day, cricketers wilting and ice cream melting; whilst Mr Asquith, career model of reasoned civility, was to make a statement about the government's response to the Lords' amendments—rejection.

To quote *Toby* (Henry Lucy), sketch-writer of *Punch*: '…Cries of "Traitor! Traitor!" Shout taken up by front benches below gangway. Cousin Hugh [Cecil] in corner seat, pale to the lips with blazing eyes and frail form shaken by tempestuous passion, led the rally…Despite the Speaker making his "earnest appeal for preservation of order," it was impossible for Asquith to get a hearing…All the while in a corner seat, sat Cousin Hugh, like the bird of evil omen perched on the bust of Pallas, above the door, forlornly croaking "vide, vide vide…" *Divide*—call for a vote and end of business.'[2] A young Violet Asquith would say in a letter that 'they looked like mad baboons'.[3] By contrast, Birrell a few days later, told a Liberal meeting in Northampton that 'They had not even had the excuse of losing their tempers; it was a carefully planned, cold-blooded orgy of stupidity and ruffianism.'[4] Continuing forty minutes until suspension, it could best be seen, this incident, quite seriously, as the nervous breakdown of a social class.

The government was embarrassed, but not displeased. Their Chief Whip, Elibank, moved among the backbenches, urging perfect silence and courteous attention for Balfour's reply. *Toby* again: 'Effect marvellous. Prince Arthur was listened to in silence, an unexpected reception he gratefully acknowledged.'[5] As anyone might have told the rioters, while the government was being confirmed in a common tough line, Conservatism would, far from imperceptibly, split. The far right press—*National Review, Morning Post, Standard,* and *Globe*—turned on Balfour—he was 'A. J. Foozle', his supporters, 'white flaggers'. Also damned was Lord Curzon, who could out-aristo any of them, 'who has played perhaps the worst part of anybody in this crisis'. Curzon was indeed thoroughly disabused of the degrading mess his party had got itself into and ready to do serious politics. As for Asquith, the *National Review*, in psychotic style, said that he had 'hounded one king into the grave and betrayed another by traitorous advice...he has smashed the British Constitution to oblige the enemies of Britain; he is preparing to install another Transvaal at our doors.'[6] This of course would be Home Rule for Ireland, something its opponents should have thought about sooner.

Ignoring all this, Curzon stiffened up Balfour to do clearly what he now had to do, acknowledge and have his party acknowledge, as had Lansdowne (also encouraged by Curzon), 'that we are no longer free agents'. Balfour would now circulate a letter to Newton, his friend and biographer of Lansdowne. It began, 'I agree with the advice Lord Lansdowne has given to his friends.' It would, he added, 'be a misfortune if the present crisis left the House of Lords weaker than the Parliament Bill by itself will make it, but it would be an irretrievable tragedy if it left us a divided party'.

It had. The people with bit-parts in the Lords Riot proceeded to identify themselves and would do so around a political dinner given on 26 July 1911 in honour of Lord Halsbury.[7] For this 87-year-old, gambolling about, citing fourteenth-century precedents, law was to be measured by antiquity. The Halsbury banquet would be attended by the curdled cream of the high, snapping, and intractable Tories, four dukes among them, F. E. Smith cynically available for the lark and mischief of impossibilist politics, also Austen Chamberlain, who would be greeted with cries of 'The next leader of the Tory Party', present apostolically for his still living father, Joe, then Edward Carson and Milner—respectively prospective seditionist in Ulster and former putschist in the Transvaal. The most typical representatives though would be the Earl of Selborne and his Oxford Union son, Wolmer, Tories not so much high as obdurate and dull.

The meal, held aptly at the Hotel Cecil, was attended by an estimated 600 men. The guest of honour lived up to expectations by musing about the possibility of impeaching Asquith. Matching the dramatically awful weather, Halsbury would turn upon the absent Balfour and the calamity he had failed to stop. 'The Crown is not safe,' he said, 'the constitution is not safe, the union is not safe, the Church is not safe.' He would turn next to the possibilities offered by H. H. Asquith. 'Such things as impeachment

have been known.' But the act deserving impeachment—accepting ultimate passage of the Budget—ought to have been resisted. 'Did you vote
against it? You knew it was wrong, you denounced it as wrong, you said it
was an outrage to the constitution.'[8] At Lansdowne and Balfour he snarled,
'You had the power to vote and had not the manliness to do so.' It was
antiquarian thinking and old man's malevolence.[9]

The House of Lords was in the pickle where it found itself precisely
because it had disregarded a constitutional convention, dating from 1711
and a Tory first Minister, Robert Harley, a rule itself quite old enough for
observation by peers revering constitutions. Lansdowne and Balfour, by
acknowledging that they could not stop the extreme measure of peer creation they had triggered by throwing out a Finance Bill, were now damned
by their irrational wing for recognizing as much.

Milner, not a man anxious about constitutions, observed that 'the
spectacle of men in full retreat turning to hurl defiance at those upon
whom they have turned their backs is not an inspiring spectacle'.[10] Austen
Chamberlain defied the threatened and fearful numbers, of academic,
retail, and fine arts products of peer creation. The government 'talked of
100 to 200 incomers. I say that is bluff and fraudulent bluff'.[11] Edward
Carson, ready for the real impeachable offence of raising an armed force
and violent resistance to a Home Rule created by parliament, told the
Lords, in his familiar snarling way, to tell Asquith, 'We shall walk out and
leave you to create your harlot peers.'[12]

Asquith was bent on 'destroying a constitution which has stood for
700 years and couldn't do it without creating peers and then doing it by
adding men who are willing to sell their honour for a coronet'.[13] Back in
the quiet days of 1909 and its Budget, Lloyd George had playfully described
the House of Lords as 'not the watchdog of the constitution, but Mr
Balfour's poodle'. At the Halsbury banquet, it better resembled either a
disturbed Alsatian or yapping Yorkie.

Though ironically, we are served (rather well) today with a House of
(overwhelmingly created) single life-term peers, August 1911 was a
supremely difficult time when, through all the barking, mass creation was

avoided by threatening it. What, after all that fuss, must inexorably be done, was the supreme humiliation, the passing of the Parliament Bill by the House of Lords. To avoid the lowering of tone represented by a tide of useful commoners, their Lordships had to acknowledge that they would no longer have power to stop *any* legislation approved by the Commons. They must admit to having spent two years losing a battle against a Finance Bill, now law. They were to assert, in place of the 1711 convention, the effective and wide-reaching Statute of Demotion before them. The weather stood at 97 in the shade. The diehards put down amendments and were met by the succinct this-worldliness of an archbishop—Lang of York. 'It is unreal at the present time to discuss either the bill, however deplorable, or the amendments, however admirable, because we know perfectly well that the bill must, and the amendments cannot, become law.'

It was a simple question: damn the consequences or accept them? The Lords had overplayed their hand for two years, had had their bluff called, lost the leverage of threatening Finance Bills and seriously intruding upon non-finance ones. A little bureaucratic delay was all that remained to it. The choice was between shrivelling to powerlessness by submitting or being swamped by bourgeois as jumped-up as meritorious. It was to be, as they say, a damn close-run thing. Pointless for Lord Ampthill (from the right wing of the Russell family) to compare the distress of the Lords to the cries of a woman whose house was being burgled, or for Milner to claim that resistance to the very end would 'be better for the country, for the wholesomeness of our political life and for the honour and character of all those concerned in this transaction'.

The Duke of Northumberland, observing the note of armigerous self-pity present throughout, proclaimed the country to have been on the edge of revolution in 1832, but that as for this bill and the House of Lords, nobody cared a brass farthing. Finally, Curzon, whose rallying to the rational side and support for Lansdowne as leader may have done most to pull their Lordships from the fire, pointed out that the alternative grand-scale New Creation would be a degradation of their House, so they should vote against. It was directed, like most successful arguments, at self-interest and seems to have worked, achieving the gentler descent—slow, irrecoverable diminution of their Lordships' House. The government motion had 131 votes and the diehards 114. Thirteen bishops had voted for, and eight dukes against.

'We were beaten by the bishops and the rats who are selling the Crown and the Church to men who despise them,' said George Wyndham, a former and quite constructive Chief Secretary for Ireland who had subsequently descended into automatic reaction (anti-Semitism included).[14] At the Carlton Club, a little later, there were cries of 'Traitor' and 'Judas' aimed at those following the leaders of the Conservative Party. It was over. The political power of inheriting men, the limit set upon reforming legislation, never imposed on the Conservative sort, was reduced to a maximum delay of two years—at this date; reduced by the Attlee government to one in 1949. The lesson learned by the cadet politicians of the Oxford Union was of an immutable heroic resistance turning sullenly mutable. Though its full effect would be delayed by the vastly bigger things about to happen.

If the Budget plus Parliament Act *affaire* of this time was a great crisis of government and constitution, the future status of Ireland was something quite as weighty, later to be swept into resolution by tragedy. Notoriously, Gladstone's first draft of a Home Rule Ireland had been for the whole island. He had come to the subject suddenly without contemporary detail and had assumed that because Ulster had rebelled in 1798, along with the rest of Ireland, it would share a wish for Home Rule. The quarrels of '98 had been about tax and trade and roughly in step with radicalism in the main island. They preceded all the political differences of the nineteenth century. Protestant Ulster would be economically successful, contemptuous of Catholic Ireland's equivalent weakness, had been hard-faced about the Famine, and was determined to be brutally the master in own territory. Any amount of *British* patriotism now asserted in the North cloaked the narrowest provincial self-preoccupation.

The Conservatives had, with Salisbury, in the late 1880s, closed their minds to the whole notion of devolution. The disturbed mind of Lord Randolph Churchill had put across three ranting speeches to confirm

Conservative identity with Ulster in violently resisting any treasonable thought of accommodation. 'Ulster will fight and Ulster will be right.' In office, they had been more constructive. The Balfour brothers would do excellent work on the land question; whilst a Catholic university, work which Birrell for the Liberals had been happy to create, was of a piece with general good sense about Ireland.

Actual Home Rule remained unattended, quiet, but with a pained expression on its face, waiting patiently for the seeing off of noble martyrs, self-impaled. The great point in favour of the Parliament Bill contest was that it provided a wholly credible reason for not rushing into Home Rule. However that fight about the Lords' parliamentary powers, Tory management, and strategy had left a goal undefended to Liberal government and Irish national Members voting together. The Lords had lost their veto in *non*-financial legislation and deprived reforming Ministers of an alibi for not trying in Ireland to do something horribly difficult. Thoughtful Tories might, more wisely, have kept out of ditches good only for dying in, and on the first murmur of a consequent Parliament Act, have retreated on the Budget.

The Balfour brothers had done excellent work in Ireland, but knives were now out for Prince Arthur. 'BMG', screamed Leopold Maxse in the *National*–Balfour Must Go.[15] Walter Long, eyeing the post, resigned pointedly from the Front Bench.

On 11 November 1911 Balfour, beaten down, withdrew from the leadership. He would be replaced by Andrew Bonar Law, narrow Scots/Irish Canadian, teetotal, two years in mourning for his wife, contemptuous of literature, music and theatre, agreeable to Asquith and Balfour, and son of a minister from Coleraine, a Wee Free minister, the Stalinest end of Presbyterianism. Leopold Amery would admiringly describe his debating style as that of a man expertly hitting a rivet ever and again with a hammer.

Conservative opposition was placed for perfect negativity. Back in Opposition, the old bogeys leapt out of the same cupboards. Home Rule was treason in spite of the fact that mainstream Irish nationalism had lately become sensible, patient, almost pedestrian. So far from murdering Chief Secretaries as the *Invincibles* had done in 1882, they talked constructively with him, working for rational consensus. The element of violence had always been recognized by the Nationalist leadership as a calamitous negative. The spokesman for Ireland was John Redmond, serious Catholic—and the more moderate because serious—lawyer, and constitutionalist.

It was all too sensible for the Protestants of East Belfast and perhaps three and three-bits counties.[16] Edward Carson, southern accent, former hurley player, leading northern Presbyterians, a man professionally grim and unaccommodating out of sight, did the early violence-threatening big meetings of the twentieth century. One of these, on the lawns of the great house of Craigavon, heard him say, 'We must be prepared, the morning Home Rule passes, ourselves to become responsible for the government of the Protestant province of Ulster.' Several menacing twentieth-century vulgarities followed; a 90-foot flag-post supporting a Union Jack 48 foot by 25 duly marched past, eyes alerted by 100,000 prospective volunteers.

The Tory Party, so recently sensible over Irish land and Catholic education, saw all this and responded to Asquith's acceptance of Home Rule as the necessary, dangerous thing with a mixture of calculation and unreason. Kipling at his sick, malignant worst, applauded in the voice of Ulster—inciting open, armed rebellion at any change in the status of Ireland:

> Before an Empire's eyes
> The traitor claims his price
> What need of further lies
> We are the sacrifice...
> We know the Hells declared
> For such as love not Rome...
> One Law, one Land, one Throne.
> If England drive us forth
> We shall not stand alone.

All these were preliminaries. It would take two years for a Home Rule Bill, after its limited holdings-up in the Lords, to emerge as law and a Home Rule Ireland with extensive devolved powers to be established. The Bill would be introduced in the spring and be good law in ironically 1914—and would also be the business of the Oxford Union. See 'Unions, Women, and Unionists'.

⎯⎯⎯ ⨯⨯⨯ ⎯⎯⎯

2 February 1911

House deems necessary further restrictions on alien immigration.[17]

Mr E. H. G. Roberts (Trinity) *The present act is inadequate. Why for example should only third class passengers be examined, and of them, only 2 per cent? British labour should be protected from alien competition in this country. England must rid itself of the riff-raff of Europe, of whom some came under the impression that the streets of London are paved with gold.*

Mr O. Lewis (Christ Church) *Less than 1 per cent of the population is alien. As to convictions, only one and a quarter per cent of them concern aliens.*

Mr J. Jessel (Balliol) *I do not mind how many aliens there are in the country, not 10,000 organ-grinders, provided only that they grind organs. The country does not want murderous aliens, however rich.*

Mr G. S. Woodhouse (Lincoln) *I protest at and deplore the sentiment which is taking the place of justice.*

Mr J. H. Blaksley *It is disgusting that this country should harbour criminals who are a danger to all countries, but our own. Any alien coming into the country should be made to prove that he might be of some use.* [Sound and forcible.]

Mr L. N. G. Montefiore *A British workman would turn up his nose at some of the work the alien does. England is the only refuge of the persecuted: let the door not be closed.* Interesting, serious, and short.

Mr N. King (Keble) *Aliens depress the social standard, do no good to the working man and do not mix in society. I strongly disapprove of the floating masses of aliens.* Lively and cheerful but a trifle jerky.

Mr H. Thompson (Balliol) *Pray note the foreign aspect of the question! Europe is overcrowded, the scum comes over here…With regard to the undesirable alien, should England or should she not, try to keep them out?*

Mr A. R. Herbert (New College) *Keep in mind the ability of the Jews. The East End outrage*[18] *is distorted and offers no basis for new legislation.* Fluent and deserving a better house.

Mr P. G. Bestall (Lincoln) *Why is Russia allowed to say whom we should admit.*

Motion carried 86:69.

---

9 February 1911

House views with concern the understanding between Germany and Russia in the Near East;

Mr Montefiore *proposing: The British supremacy of a hundred years is being threatened. Britain is being supplanted by Germany, and British interests are vital. Russia has promised Germany support in a railway dangerously near to India. Russia has never been the friend of liberty, as Finland and Poland bear witness.* A reasoned and interesting speech and commendably brief, made to a house somewhat apathetic.

Mr S. H. Wall (Lincoln) *I do not believe in the pacific intentions of Germany. War with her is imminent and inevitable for us. It is true that Baghdad might be a pretext for war. But Germany always has a pretext for war at hand. The Triple Entente is of the greatest importance to Britain; that should on no account be weakened*—[Fluent to torrential, learned and a trifle too long].

Mr Cox (New College) *The interests of Russia and Germany rarely clash and the Triple Entente is the only obstacle to this agreement; if it should be broken, Germany would be able to take away a good deal of British Trade.*

Mr Monckton *The agreement is still pending; it is neither prudent nor dignified to be afraid of it yet. We have allowed an open door to any nation in the south; why be afraid if Russia opens the door to Germany in the north? An Anglo-Turkish agreement is pending. Let the House temper hysteria with common sense and investigate before it fears.* [Excellent and refreshing—short and pointed.]

Mr A. Ghaffar (St John's) *The Liberals have ruined the cause of Persia even more than the Conservatives had. England should not make the same mistake as in Egypt.* [The speech of a keen Nationalist, fluent and impassioned and welcomed by the House.]

Mr Guedella* *I deny that Berlin is on the Euphrates. Who could invade India along that line? In this matter, England must gain the confidence of Turkey. Russia is not leaving the Entente.*[19] [We have rarely heard an abler speech in the House.]

Mr J. G. Lockhart (Trinity) *Why should the confidence of Turkey in this matter be sought if there is no danger? Germany is gradually dealing blows at the British Imperial system. Germany only has commercial interests in the East, not territorial ones.* [Very pleasant and effective.]

Mr F. Schenck (Balliol) *I rejoice whenever Germany finds a harmless outlet for her vigour. All the money Germany puts into the Baghdad railway is security for her good conduct.* [Calm, clear and forcible.]

Mr Hartog (Balliol) *Germany's policy is directed against Egypt.*

Mr E. A. Bigsby (Lincoln) *Germany is looked upon with great suspicion by Russia whose autocracy is waning.* [A new point of view, listened to with interest.]

Mr Dodds (Wadham) [Gave the House the inner workings of the Kaiser's mind. Very much at his ease.]

Mr Cannon (New College) *In my view, it would be good for Britain to be rid of the Triple Entente.*

Vote: Motion lost 48:78.

---

* Philip Guedella—witty, elegant, melancholy popular historian and commentator, a name which has naturally faded.

The Liberal government in office since 1905 and in power since the vast victory of 1906 had been cool about naval expenditure, and for 1908/9 had sought to freeze it, but a new Naval minister, Reginald McKenna, had been nagged by Fisher into paying up. At the same time, Fisher was keen to scrap serviceable older ships and entered into bitter controversy with Admiral Beresford. Remarks about a German naval threat by a third party, the ubiquitous Lloyd George, provoked Kaiser Wilhelm into public objection to British politicians telling Germany what size of navy it should have. It was the sort of two-sided folly along the way which created a mood acquiescent to world war.

—∞∞—

16 February 1911

House believes our present scale of expenditure on the Navy futile and unnecessary.

Mr Phillips (Jesus) *The limit of possible expenditure has almost been reached... the present level of expenditure on the navy and social reform cannot go on together, and it is on the Navy that retrenchment is possible. When is this expenditure without public control going to stop?* [An experienced speaker and a sound radical.]

Mr Gilbert (Exeter)... *England's existence depends upon naval superiority. A superiority of two keels to one must be maintained*[20]... [Knew his case well, inclined to be dull—too long.]

Mr Beckett (Lincoln) [Suffering from a bad cold and a pile of notes.] *A comfortable margin is often the resource of cowards... The country is becoming hysterical.* [Serious and carefully prepared but rather funereal.]

Mr H. E. Stewart (New College) after a prolonged dialogue with the proposers of the motion *War may crop up at any moment, and the proposers of the motion are not the only ones who care for social reform.*

Mr N. Micklam (New College—President) *Even from the material point of view, war simply doesn't pay. Is it credible when only a few people in each country want a war, that war is inevitable?*

Mr Griffith (Balliol) *The question is whether or not England would maintain her superiority? If England disarms, the rest of the nations may follow suit, but we dare not take so great a risk. No government could survive the resignation of two war lords.*

Mr Penston (Non-Collegiate) *England should surrender her claim to rights at sea so that some agreement as to disarmament might be accepted by Germany* [A very good speech.]

Mr Roberts (Trinity) *England cannot surrender her colonies.*

Mr Finnemore (Pembroke) *The Admiralty has confessed that its programme is based on a mistake.* [Much his best speech.]

Mr Lewis (Christ Church) *Disarmament in this country would drive the nations of Europe at one another's throats.*

Mr L. F. Urwick (New College) *There is no need for a two-keel standard. Mr Norman Angell's[21] economic argument was not seriously questioned...*

Mr J. T. Thorson (New College) *I believe in the necessity of British naval supremacy, yet I support this motion.* [The House always welcomes speeches from Colonials. Why are there not more?]

Mr C. F. Purcell *argued pleasantly for the motion on the ground of the discoveries of aviation.*

Mr E. F. W. Besly (Balliol) looked upon the schemes of the proposal as Utopian...

...Mr C. E. S. Dodd (Balliol) made a good speech but should not lie on the box.

Motion lost 48:105.

2 March 1911

That in the opinion of this House the time has come when the control of Irish affairs can safely be entrusted to an Irish Parliament subordinate to the Imperial Parliament.

Mr Guedella *The visit of the Irish Secretary (Augustine Birrell), is like the visit of an angel. He is one of Nature's Oxford men. The Irish problem is a European one, not an Imperial One. Emigration is not the sincerest form of flattery. Why should Ireland be given twelve million pounds to play in the next street? That is the alternative policy, Ulster feeling is very serious. But Home Rule would weaken the influence of the Roman Church. Catholic Irishmen had not shown themselves intolerant in local government.*

Mr R. Bevir (Hertford) *The time will not come for Home Rule until there is a direct and clear mandate for the subject. I am a Democrat and as such, protest against depriving democracy of the opportunity to express its opinion. Again there is the 'All for Ireland' movement, whose aim is peace. Premature Home Rule would crush that movement. Difficulties in the way of Home Rule are insuperable. Part of Ireland but not Ireland, demands Home Rule. The Home Rule now proposed is a parliamentary farce. The parallel of the Colonies would not hold.*

Mr K. G. Griffith (Balliol) *I beg the House not to harden its heart against Pharaoh's Chief Taskmaster. Let the Irish govern the Irish (as they wish) and let them not mis-govern England and congest business. Government against a nation's wish will always be futile. Ireland was filled with a vague discontent which no English Government can put to right. Ireland would be happy under her own administration. The whole case for Home Rule is that Ireland wanted it; the case against Home Rule was that Ulster did not want it. It is the Tory Party which gives the mandate for Home Rule by saying that every vote given to the Liberals would be a vote cast for Home Rule.*

Mr G. S. Woodhouse (Lincoln) *I am content with the arguments which persuaded an earlier generation. Ireland is not in so bad a state as it was thirty years ago. Home*

Rule is not the only remedy. Home Rule cannot be supported without a knowledge of the details. Every argument applied by proposers to Ireland might equally be applied to Ulster. Who can allow a new country to spring up, with a separate foreign policy, under the very eyes of Britain?

The Rt. Hon Augustine Birrell (Chief Secretary for Ireland) *I still detect in Ireland the mystic, haunting, all-pervading sense of nationality which can never be destroyed. The Union has always been, and still is the great failure: it is to us as Sicily to old Rome. Sir Walter Scott's prophecy of Ireland's future was not fulfilled. What is the cause of depopulation? Not the climate, not the smallness of families, not emigration. The Irish marriage rate is far lower than in Scotland or England. The figures I have show that the real cause of suffering in Ireland is poverty. The back of Irish Landlordism is broken. In thirty years, an entirely new Ireland has arisen. Twenty three per cent of Irish soil is unproductive. There is a larger population in Ireland than could be employed.*

The problem of Old Age Pensions is made difficult in Ireland because until recent times, births were rarely registered. But the figures showed poverty staring us in the face. The Union is no sort of success. Yet Ireland is charged with an army of occupation and the Royal Irish Constabulary. The Lord Chancellor of Ireland costs as much as the whole judiciary of Denmark. The cost of Ireland is five times that of Scotland. The Union is a failure and a mess. 'Banish Home Rule from the hearts of the Irish?' That is impossible. Buy off Ireland with money, scraps and doles—and more—and more to the end of the chapter?—intolerable! Ireland must above all, regain her self-respect.

The economy in Ireland has not been affected in the last forty years in the Imperial parliament; yet it must be done; only a National Assembly can do it. Home Rule cannot be put into a bill. Specified powers have been given in different parts of the Empire. The difficulty is, what is to be done with Irish members in the Imperial parliament? Remove them? Leave them unrepresented in the Imperial Parliament? In which case they should not be taxed. If they remain present, what are they to do? What then of religion? Is no Roman Catholic community under any circumstances, to be entrusted with any control over a Protestant minority?

True, there are strong forces in the cry 'No Popery!' The bitterness is not gone out—no, not even in the House of Lords. No wonder Protestants feared—especially outside Ireland. These superstitions will be allayed. In Ireland, except in a few places, religious bigotry has greatly died down. Ireland is not full of bitterness and perpetual dispute.

But the suspicions are not unreasonable. The new Ireland has no hankerings after Dreadnoughts and a private Foreign Policy. The financial situation is the crux. Let them find out what justice demanded, and add what political expediency may justify. Finally, about Ulster, half of 'Protestant Ulster' is Roman Catholic.[22] What is arising in Belfast is not the problem of the Battle of the Boyne, but a labour problem. It is everyone's duty to wait until he is actually oppressed; it is a majority under any circumstances whatever. It is useless to say one could never tolerate the idea of living under a Roman Catholic majority under any circumstances whatever. The new bill will be like Mr Gladstone's in main outline.[23]

[The Rt. Hon. Gentleman, having addressed the House, his words were received at the end of the debate with general enthusiasm.]

[When the House divided, there voted—for the motion 385; against 304; the motion was therefore carried by 81 votes. The result was received with loud cheers.]

In 1909, their Lordships outraged at a finance bill mildly affecting land interests, while, in noble eyes, weakening the morale of the lower classes with a five shilling old age pension, broke a 300-year-old convention not to block Finance Bills and blocked this one. The outcome in 1911 was a Parliament bill, removing by statute any possibility of their Lordships rejecting any certified finance bill. As the fifth Marquess of Salisbury would tell his family long after, the House of Lords became when he knew it in the thirties, an embarrassed shadow which the current, overwhelmingly nominated, House is not.

9 March 1911

House would welcome the passing of the Parliament Bill.

Mr Finnemore *We cannot afford to postpone. We must have a strong and efficient chamber. The referendum is rubbish: away with it! The parliament bill does not mean single chamber government.*

Mr A. G. Morkill (New College) *The Liberals have made more peers than the Tories. We must have the* status quo …

Mr J. H. Martin (Brasenose) *This is a deliberate attempt to destroy our Constitution. How about the Irish members! We want a referendum.* [His perorations are gems …]

Mr G. F. Urwick (New College) [An awkward simile was forced upon us, but we like Mr Urwick's manner immensely.]

Mr R. B. Whyte (Balliol) … [is Scotch and sound.]

Mr T. F. Merriman (St John's) [does not like written constitutions.—Rather dull!]

Mr King (Keble) [believed in the Lords and was quite convincing …]

Motion lost 63: 71.

However the final stage of the Parliament bill sent up by the Commons, would pass the House of Lords 131:114.

11 May 1911

This House would welcome a system of Imperial Preference at the forth-coming Dominion conference.[24]

Mr Lewis *I dislike Preference because it necessarily involves protection. A tax on wheat must be supported by a Protective tax for millers. The avowed object of Tariff Reformers* is to reduce foreign trade and give the balance to the Colonies. That in itself, would weaken the cause of peace for which our foreign trade is a great guarantee...Even with our preference, American exports into Canada are increasing faster than our own.

Mr Lockhart sneered at the Liberal-Free-Trade-Imperialist—his misinterpretations and delirious hallucinations...He regretted the proposed Reciprocity Agreement as tending to loosen the bonds of Empire. 'We want our Imperial trade for ourselves.' [Much the best speech we have heard from Mr Lockhart...But he should take care not to descend to mere abuse.]

Mr Timpson...The Tories are always talking about 'binding the Empire together,' but they don't know what it means. And if they did, it would only mean dissolution. Colonial preference would breed jealousy and would probably lead to an Anti-Colonial party. [Fluent, but a little apt to dogmatize.]

Mr Blaksley Forget about an anti-colonial party. We have one already. The solution of our industrial problems lies in our Imperial ideals...

Mr Dodds What hurts Germany hurts us too. What are the Tariff Reformers going to do with India? The revenue obtained would be hopelessly insufficient if the pledges about reducing tea taxes for bread taxes were fulfilled...

Mr Roberts The objection of India is invalid. The revenue derived would be ample...

Mr G. P. Dennis (Exeter) [Emphatic in his treatment of Imperialism. Preference will mean war.]

Mr W. M. Codrington (New College) [wound up the debate by discussing Universal Peace.]

Vote not given.

18 May 1911

House would welcome the passing of the Conciliation bill into law.

It was no longer possible for Conservative males to speak as George Romanes did in the May 1887 issue of *The Nineteenth Century* that 'Even under the most favourable conditions as to culture…it must take many centuries for heredity to replace the missing five ounces of the female brain.' This was the second of three successive bills, 1910/11 and 12, by which Asquith (a strangely dedicated suffrage denier) offered as 'Conciliation' a vote to upper and upper-middle-class women, an evasion readily detected as an irrelevance. Objection even to this came not only from Cambridge male-supremacists, but from a barely acknowledged, but reasonable fear of unmerited new Conservative votes at subsequent elections.

Mr Urwick *On the question of woman suffrage, most opponents refuse to take it seriously. Women have tried serious methods for fifty years and have been treated as children for doing so…they would now have a majority in the Commons. It is disgraceful that the bill had not been passed…*

Mr Monckton[25] *I take Woman's suffrage very seriously, but the Conciliation Bill is a joke. It would not please the wives, only the sisters. It places a disability upon married women and if it passes, its primary result would be an increased mortality among husbands…It is a hesitant step, either wrong altogether or leading inevitably to adult suffrage…This is not the time to start tinkering with the suffrage…*

Mr Schenk *What is wrong with taxation without representation? I pay taxes in Oxford but have no vote. The vote depends upon citizenship as taxation does not. The franchise is not an inherent right. In return for his privileges, man is called upon to fight. Can women do equivalent duty?*

Mr Griffith *I do not like the Bill because it is undemocratic, but we must start with something, to get ourselves used to the idea of women voting! Politics are not the sphere of man; they are no one's sphere. Legislation affects the home more than the office.* [Mr Griffith at his best.]

Mr Talbot *If women should come into politics, they must keep to the rules of the game. And not appeal to man's pity…*

Mr Bevir (President) *There is too much unfair inequality between the sexes which the franchise could remedy…Nothing in these days is pushed to its extreme logical conclusion…*

Mr H. R. Raikes (Balliol) [gave quite an effective discourse upon women in war.]

Mr King [Condemned the suffragette as unfit to be trusted with government.]

Mr Dennis *Mr Asquith is endangering the liberties of the people much more than the House of Lords by denying facilities for the bill.*

Motion lost 35: 56.

---

25 May 1911

This House would support the Government in opposing further restrictions upon the Licensing Trade.

Mr Smith-Gordon *I had thought this notion was 'dust and ashes, dead and done with.' If the government take further steps,*[26] *it will be in order to destroy the trade altogether and, as a Liberal, I would find it hard to follow them. Are the aims of the government financial, moral or political? The real object is political—revenge for defeat in 1904.* [Quite irresponsible and inconsequent, but that doesn't matter with Mr Smith-Gordon.]

Mr Finnemore *I resent the charge of political rancour. It is a moral question. And the last has not been heard of the bill of 1908—and next time there will be no Lansdowne House.*[27]

Mr Martin *The decrease in alcoholic consumption is already greater in England than in anywhere else in Europe. A great Temperance advocate, Sir T. P. Whitaker, has suggested an improvement in the quality and price of beer. Liberals are not a temperance Party. They are too fond of meddling with trade.* [Mr Martin hits hard and straight.]

Mr Lockhart *It is the fault of the Radicals that this has become a party question. The bill of 1908 is dead…when will they realise that if they want unpopularity, they have only to re-introduce that bill…?*

Mr J. Holmes (Corpus) *The greatest evil comes from Grocers' licenses.*

Mr R. S. Elkin (Trinity) [tried to avoid party points.]

Mr W. H.Moore (New College) [did not want to avoid party politics at all.]

Mr Morkill *The way to check intemperance is to make it an offence.*

Mr C. W. B. Marsh [wound the debate up sedately.]

Motion carried 64:50.

1 June 1911 Cambridge visit

House believes the British nation is degenerating.

Mr Dodds *Wealth is the only passport to a large proportion of society. The power of the great financiers, more especially in the press, is enormous. The position of both Mr Cadbury[28] and Lord Northcliffe must be detrimental to the large numbers of people who read the press. I am alarmed by the physical condition of the working classes. It has to be significant that the standards of the Army have had to be reduced. The progress of the last century has been in scientific inventions and is not one of real intellectual social and moral progress.*

Mr D. H. Robertson (Trinity Cambridge)[29] *We cannot blame the present age for having no poets any more than we can blame the apostolic age for having none of our mechanical instruments…We are trying to improve the environment of the race without improving the race itself.*

Mr J. H. Allen (Jesus Cambridge) *I see a connexion between Liberalism and degeneracy. I watch the sinking birth rate with a rising heart, for it meant that we were not perpetuating the dregs of Society. There has been an unfavourable comment on Lord Northcliffe,*[30] *but if that member had read Wilkes,*[31] *he would not complain of degeneracy. I deplore the condition of clerks, but they only replaced far worse classes...* [He concluded with a fine defence of Imperialism...]

Mr L. P. Napier (King's College Cambridge) *Degeneracy could be defined as loss of virility... Physical stature is greater than it was in the old days; intemperance is on the decrease and, as for intellect, the average city man had none at all until the progress of modern science gave him one.*

The Rev. J. A. V. Magee (Merton) *The birth rate is an evil which cannot be denied or overlooked—a manifest sign of national degeneracy. The Fall of Rome was caused by this, not the invasion of barbarian hordes... Everyone nowadays has nerves; even our public schools are becoming tainted with effeminacy.*

Mr R. W. H. Brinsley-Richards *The tragedy of recent years has been the spoiling of great men. The Chancellor has admitted the degeneration of statesmen. Did it not necessarily follow that they must have sprung from a degenerate people?*

No vote given.

8 June 1911

This House would welcome a system of compulsory military training.

Mr Griffith *I want England to guard against little more than a hundredth chance. Mr Haldane*[32] *has called the Navy 'the first line of Defence', but in judging the efficiency of the second line, one always assumes that the Navy is still fighting. The first burst of territorial enthusiasm is dying out. The economic pressure from employers will become harder and harder to overcome.*

Mr Talbot *...The desire to serve as regulars goes out of those who are forced to serve. The whole spirit of service changes... There is in England today a spirit of service arising, but there is no patriotism in being compelled to fight for one's country.* [Mr Talbot is getting the Cecilian habit of choking with indignation while he speaks. It is effective.]

Mr J. W. Bland (Lincoln) *The Navy is still up to the two-power standard which is all that is required. Volunteers are always necessary for the outposts of Empire.*

Mr J. G. Lockhart (Trinity) *With the increase of fighting machinery, there has been a decrease in the need for the fighting spirit. The army that can shoot straight wins the battle.*

Mr Guedella *We are safe under the present system. The two main schemes put forward are inconsistent.*

Mr Smith-Gordon *I question the power of the state over the citizen. Money has too much influence on international policy.*

Mr Blaksley *Citizens should look upon defence as a duty in return for their rights.*

Motion carried 64:46.

---

15 June 1911

House holds That Liberalism is in theory a pestilential heresy and in practice a pitiful illusion.

Mr Blaksley *I object to the mild wording of the motion. I would never have moved even this one against the old Liberalism, but today!—is anything safe? If Liberalism is heresy, what is orthodoxy?*

Mr P. S. Cannon (New College) *What could be more ridiculous than to take the Miners' Eight Hours Bill as an example of liberty? It is the negation of liberty. For me Liberalism is all talk. I believe in Tory Democracy…*

Mr A. E. K. Slingsby (Exeter) *There was no satisfactory definition of Liberalism than the sum total of its acts. Judge it by that and vote for Tariff Reform…*

Mr F. C. Davison (University) *The Government rules the Empire like a parish council.*

Mr S. L. Marwood *Liberalism is like a strong and healthy youth throwing down the gauntlet.*

No vote given.

---

19 October 1911

House deplores the excessive intervention of HMG in recent labour disputes.

Mr L. F. Urwick *The government has no right to safeguard anything beyond the food supply; instead it kept open the paths of general commerce.* [Mr Urwick is such a good speaker that we always expect him to make a better speech.]

Mr G. W. L. Talbot (Ch.Ch.) [debated rapidly on relevant matters: Government impartiality, syndicalism, the consequences of non-intervention and the milk supply.]

Mr W. A. Keen (Balliol) [discussed the heroism of strikes and the 'incredible bumptiousness' of the government. He spoke like some solemn and irresponsible magistrate in an insane court of Justice.]

Mr L. E. P. Smith-Gordon (Trinity) [thought some pleasant things aloud about the Leviathan, the French Revolution and the British Soldier.]

Mr H. W. Wilson (New College)[33] [struck the personal note rather too hard but was quite interesting. He knows Manchester.]

Mr T. K. H. Rae (Balliol) [kept to the point and spoke sincerely. He knows Liverpool.]

Motion lost 92:160.

---

26 October 1911

House condemns emphatically the recent foreign policy of the Triple Alliance.[34]

Mr W. J. Bland *The annexation of Bosnia*[35] *is merely the completion of an earlier process. German policy over naval matters in Morocco and Asia Minor was necessitated by Germany's need of expansion.* [A vastly genial speech well expressed and interesting. When Mr Bland informed us of his nationality, earlier suspicions were confirmed.]

Mr W. H. Moore *Why has England remained silent throughout the Moorish question? She needs Mohammedan* [sic] *support everywhere.* [Quite serious and careful.]

Mr F. McCance (Queen's) [denied the existence of the Triplice...] *England has not asked leave to annexe her empire.*

Mr Guedella [debated briefly on the fatuity of the motion, Germany's need of expansion...the uselessness of Tripoli as an outlet for surplus population and German] *'methods of doing well in an unconventional way.'*

Mr A. C. von Grunelius (Univ.) [In a speech for which all were grateful, put the German case in admirable English.]

Mr A. H. Ghaffar (St John's) [put the Turkish position and gave some sound advice to England.]

Mr V. A. C. Mallet (Balliol) [made the best maiden speech of the evening. His cheerfulness with a somnolent House was heroic and attractive.]

Motion carried 161: 114.

2 November 1911

House would welcome the passage into law of the Insurance Bill.

Mr D. Davies (New College) *With sickness and unemployment always threatening, it would meet a real need.*

Mr E. H. G. Roberts (Trinity) *Liberalism has deserted individualism to undermine the character of the workers...The worker would pay ultimately the contributions of state and employer.*

Mr F. C. Davidson (Univ.) [hardly compensated for his reiterated 'ipse dixit' by some interesting points. It is not funny to say (of Lloyd George) 'Mr George.']

Mr G. E. Dodds (New College—Librarian) [uttered good party sentiments as to Unionist depravity—a fighting speech.]

Mr Barrington-Ward [uttered good party sentiments at the depravity of Mr Dodds. Like him, he was passionate, effective and irrelevant.]

Motion carried 146: 118.

---

16 November 1911

House believes that special provision should be made in any scheme of Home Rule for the government of Ulster.

Mr W. T. Moncton[36] *Ireland has found self-expression under English rule. Separation would be the consequence if Ulster was part of Ireland and of the Empire. It must protest against an anti-imperial policy. Separation would be the consequence under Home Rule. Ulster has the spirit, if not the letter of loyalty.*

Mr Smith-Gordon *Ulster will not be right to fight because its fears on the religious side are groundless. Neither will Ulster fight, Sir Edward Carson's loyalty is treason.* [This was received with enthusiasm, showing how susceptible the house is to sincere sentiment.]

Mr J. G. Lockhart (Trinity) *Ulster is as different from the South of Ireland as Ireland is from England. Separation will be the dividing issue in the Dublin parliament. The supposed fanaticism of the Ulstermen deserves only praise.*

Motion lost 91:141.

⋘⋙

23 November 1911

House believes the present government better deserves the support of the nation than the Opposition.

Mr F. K. Griffith (Balliol) *Socialists must support the government for fear of finding something worse. In the matter of democracy, Tory opinion is thoroughly disunited. On poverty, Tariff Reform is the only plank in Tory policy and, at the next election, they will have to walk it. Liberal social policy may be inspired opportunism, but it is far better than anything the Tories have to offer.* [Sincere, forceful and fanatical with good fanaticism.]

Mr G. S. Woodhouse (Lincoln) *The Conservatives are the only united party. The government always wished to interfere between communities in Ireland and the Empire. Home Rule was supported by oratory but opposed by the facts.* [He suffered from 'damnable iteration' and heart-burnings among the grammarians.]

Mr Barrington-Ward *The attack on the Lords is the Government's central point. It will rush a number of contentious issues into law before 1915. Lords reform is a constructive Tory policy. The case of the domestic servant is one of grave concern.*

Mr Herbert Samuel (Postmaster General—Visitor)[37] *The Conservative Party is no longer conservative; it contains such revolutionary proposals as the referendum, Women's Suffrage, Protection and Conscription. It is not stick-in-the-mud. It is flibbertigibbet. Its sole principles are the preservation of one church against all others. On Home Rule, the attitude is 'Those who are peaceful don't want. Those who aren't peaceful shan't have.'* [Mr Samuel's maiden speech was an unqualified success; the House was delighted with him. We were grateful.]

Motion carried 261:225.

30 November 1911

House welcomes the Prime Minister's proposals for an extension of the franchise.

Mr J. Holmes (Corpus) *A democratic franchise means individual self-reliance and guards against legislation by class.*

Mr H. F. Stewart (New College) *There is no actual bill yet, and it has been talked about in the obscurest terms. What is meant by 'men of competent understanding'?* [A number of good points, but his staccato delivery is disquieting.]

Mr S. S. G. Leeson (New College) *The adoption of the referendum by the Conservatives has removed the need for any improvement in the present system. I object to the argument that having the vote is an educative process. It is like saying that giving a man a degree gives him an education. It is unwise to set uneducated power free without fitting it for the responsibilities which a vote implies.*[38]

Motion lost 65:89.

7

Unions, Women, and Unionists

25 January 1912–22 May 1913

Trade union power/Two-keel advantage?/Disregard for property/the Home Rule
bill—Belloc rant/Party system/No Anglo-German deal/Coal strike—minimum
wage/Changing the second Chamber/Welsh disestablishment/the Home Rule
Bill—Carson speech/duty to be in Egypt/No confidence/First Balkan War
(Turkey)/party spirit exaggerated/Insurance Act carried with indecent haste/
Woman's suffrage/Disestablishment/Universal Military Service/Public schools
as menace.

Ireland would continue to be trouble, the biggest, most exhausting trouble, chronic in the sense of naggingly continuous, but chronic with crisis
eruptions. The Liberal government had, overall, a record of constructive,
humane, and simply sensible legislation. A later Oxford debater at the
Union, R. B. McCallum, future head of an Oxford house and holder of a
chair here, would argue that it was the best government ever to run this
country. It was, however, also the most plagued, overburdened, and crisis-
ridden government, all the more strikingly so for working through a time
of peace. Wartime governments quickly become coalitions, and in those
times, an often excessive sense of responsibility falls upon MPs *not* in the
government. Newspapers grow altogether responsible about the matters
such a Ministry gets wrong, not to mention little, wartime illegalities.
Such coalitions, sustained by a sense of responsibility and over-observed
special powers, are accordingly rather boring affairs.

The last word to describe the Liberal Ministry of 1905–14 is boring. Treating the hysteria over Ulster and its semi-treasonable native generals, public drilling, and arms brought in from Germany by an Ulster Protestant patriot, then an all-Ireland Catholic alternative patriot, are pleasures in store. We might first consider what is primly called 'Labour Unrest'. The Osborne judgment, requiring union contributions for political activities to be positively approved by union members, had reduced their available reserves to the disadvantage of Labour Party funds, but had left militancy, in the new form of syndicalism, free and provoked to make a vivid impact.

Syndicalists despised Labour politics and believed in unions' own ability to make the political and economic weather by 'Direct action'. Such action was taken, not without provocation, by the historically meek Lancashire cotton workers, initially over treatment of a single worker, but eventually getting a general settlement from the Board of Trade. Syndicalism wasn't thought fair, very much Rugby League with its own ungentlemanly rules—lightning strikes and stay-in strikes—the gentilities of preliminary talks and action only after their breakdown. The boxing maxim of 'fustest with the mostest' faced the employers' own rough play—the lockout. *That* was a bosses' strike, one to hit a strike before it was struck, the card which had been played, not too successfully, by the cotton masters.

In the late summer and autumn of 1910, the cotton conflict would be followed by a fourteen-month lock-out of boilermakers in the north-eastern shipyards, in response to unofficial strikes. In such affairs militancy *tout court* was less the underlying cause than distrust of certain union leaderships, notably the Seamen's, too cautious, conservative, and 'close to the bosses'—bribed! In the South Wales pits, a dispute over rates on a single seam produced a side-riot and the sending-in of troops.

Discontent of a sudden, eruptive sort continued in the next year after a lull. They were not all to be dismissed as irrational. There were some very low wages patiently endured by employees grown accustomed to that sort of thing. In June 1911, one of these, those miserably paid seamen neglected by a company union, did their own thing and won. The government, in the persons of Lloyd George and Churchill, were sent in to respond sympathetically. In the most important dispute, a strike involving in August almost the whole railway system, a good result would be achieved: reinstatement for men sacked, trains running, and arbitration undertaken for dull, final settlement.

Negotiating with unions was something for which Lloyd George had near genius. He might be a lawyer, but a Welsh country solicitor lacks the cool distance of an establishment silk. He was a radical who had blasted the hereditary aristocracy as 'Five hundred men chosen at random from among the ranks of the unemployed,' in the famous East End speech. The charm of a busy, working seducer also had its other, useful applications. It was to Lloyd George that the general business of handling what were (still are) called 'industrial disputes' fell. In consequence, the Asquith government came better out of the current burst of class bitterness—occasional riots—from time to time, a fatal casualty—all now tempered by intelligent talk and the priority of making a passably fair award, as well or better than over other griefs blowing about its head at this time.

High among these, not least for sheer theatre, was what was, originally and oddly, called 'Woman Suffrage'. It was, in itself, entirely reasonable and, if one dare use the word deplored by all Oxford philosophy, 'right'. Of course, women getting more education, and seeking to get it for the first time to enjoy the vote, deserved the attention of MPs and of this government in particular. Votes for Women had had since the 1870s, a long, perhaps too respectable, history of arguing reasonably and being ignored. Beatrice Webb, of whom most other Fabians were rightly afraid, now stood before the political world, advising male politicians, Balfour among them, indicating in detail how to act on Poor Law reform. That point would be lost on the maker of one quotation in the Oxford debates recorded here who congratulates himself on his additional two male ounces of brain!

Sadly, as noted elsewhere, Asquith, for all his grace, good manners, and quick, business-dispatching mind, couldn't see it. His predecessor could. Henry Campbell-Bannerman, born in 1836, responded generously as the older CB generally did. In 1907, witness his open-hearted welcome to the Woman's Enfranchisement, set out in the Liberal MP Willoughby Dickenson's

Private Member's Bill! He was committed to voting for the bill, but it was, inevitably, talked out, with some Liberals involved in that undertaking.[1] 'I am' he said 'in favour of the general principle of the inclusion of women in the Franchise...a woman pays taxes. She has to obey the laws, in shaping which she has no share...I think the time is long past when it can be urged that woman by her position in society, is sheltered in some mysterious way from the rough and tumble of life and is precluded from exercising a share in public affairs.'

Edward VII, who knew women as a consumer, wrote to his son, the future and incurious George V,[2] 'Thank heaven those dreadful women have not been enfranchised. It would have been better if the PM had not spoken on the Bill ...' Asquith, devotedly married first time, had, later as a widower, been caught in the chattering company of Margot Tennant, then finally plunged into chaste but researcher-friendly correspondence with Venetia Stanley, a bright, and level-headed girl due to marry someone else, and never really got the point.

Meanwhile his 1912 encounter in the company of his eminently vote-worthy daughter, Violet, at the hands of two militant suffragettes flourishing horsewhips, was not persuasive. Respectable Women's Suffrage had always been liable to turn into Suffrage for Respectable Women. Asquith had contemplated that niminy-piminy little Bill which in practice, would have given votes to a clutch of well-to-do ladies, Conservative voters to the last glove-button. Provocatively inoffensive, it was painlessly put aside.

The trouble was that the rational, respectable case for suffrage having been shrugged off, moved down the paper as something considered inappropriate at this moment, unremarkably, *disrespectful* suffrage took its place: physical affront, damaged property, every act winning attention and getting the cause nowhere. And few people have been as communicative (and crazily communicative) as Christabel Pankhurst. With her, in 1909, had begun the wider and directed violence, self-conscious, attention-seeking violence—window-breaking, a little arson, getting yourself locked up then going on hunger strike. Though Christabel, a model of the non-playing activist, never risked forcible feeding.

A virulent, quarrelling power-hugger, she had first driven out of the organization, Woman's Suffrage Political Union, the amiably leftish Pethick-Lawrences, who had been among its earliest activists. Her instincts, remote from their mild idealism, were intensely authoritarian, and snobbish with it, something which split her from her incomparably more attractive sister Sylvia, an idealistic Socialist without power crazes. Christabel was the impresario of events—physical attacks on chosen men, the picture-slashing, most famously of the too sexy *Rokeby Venus*, something done by Mary Richardson (later a declared Fascist), acid on the fourteenth tee, private homes burned down, also valuable places like the Orchid House at Kew Gardens. Unfortunately for her considered historical reputation, throughout the key period of violent, imprisonable activity, Christabel lived abroad, characteristically encouraging from Paris offences carrying a prison tariff. Having done her stint as a remote-control rebel, she greeted the First War like a sister, came back to Britain, changing the name of her news-sheet to *Britannia*, ordered distribution of white feathers, and urged the drafting of *men* into the trenches.

The response to violence had been a clumsy use of the criminal law perfectly calculated to create a long-running public scene! The subordinate authorities, Chief Constables and prison governors, had, with ministerial assent, begun prosecutions and imprisonments for acts done during demonstrations. And when the women went on hunger strike, they had applied the brutal and politically suicidal process of force feeding. Strong government, well short of the South American Field Marshal model, demonstrates the terrible publicity involved in 'firm measures'. Force feeding was, however often denied by the Home Office, severely painful and dangerous. Someone might be killed. Eventually, Reginald McKenna, a new Home Secretary, introduced the 'Cat and Mouse Act'. Kinder than it sounds (or than cats are), it let a self-starving woman out to make a recovery and then offered her the chance of surrender away from publicity or going back.

Effectively though, the splendid theatre/good copy of violence and destruction of direct action had lost women's suffrage support, while non-violent organizations would come together as the National Union of

Suffrage Societies and begin to talk seriously with Ministers. With the war came swift postponement and a fairly secure promise kept in an attenuated and gradual way. Votes for women would come then for those aged 30 and be shrewdly brought by Stanley Baldwin into male parity ahead of the 1929 election. 'Getting the Flapper vote', it was called—and it may well have done so. Good sense equality had been nervously delayed, but, in the hands of rational, adult, conventional politics, would finally come through.

In parallel with all this, the Irish issue had ticked over quietly enough on the assumption that the Liberal government, committed to Home Rule, would deliver on the issue. The problem was semantic. What did the word 'Irish' exactly mean? For even quite moderate Irish nationalists and very much for their leader, John Redmond, it meant the island of Ireland—and it couldn't be. Religion (with a dash of ethnicity—two lots of mutually self-defining Celts) said so. As to the two versions of the Christian religion flourishing to excess all round, both stood at base. For most Catholics it was still Ten Hail Marys and 'Bless me, Father.' For the Calvinist equivalent, two jobs better off in the shipyard, it would be 'Can you show me where it says *that* in Leviticus' and other fine points of his essentially Old Testament religion.

The English, especially the Liberals, couldn't understand how this could matter so much. Even the sincere Christians among them assumed tolerance and reasonable good will. Periods of quiet made them assume it even more. Reasonable men in Westminster were doomed to totally misread the mind-set of specifically Ulster patriotism. Ironically, the leadership of Irish nationalism had contained its share of Protestants. Charles Parnell, supreme figure in modern Irish history, among them. A modest minority in the south, they were mostly Church of Ireland, disestablished, uppish-market, and quiet with it.

Ulster, as it kept saying, was different. Birrell who spent a lot of time in quiet conversation with all sorts of people in his territory, described the Ulster Protestant outlook unflinchingly in a memo to Asquith. 'At the bottom, the moving passion is hatred and contempt for the papist: at the top it is contempt and fear for the papist as a man of business.'[3] Conflict was something which the Tories were perfectly certain both to cynically exploit and earnestly believe. They had the ideal new leader for both. Andrew Bonar Law, was as remarked, a son of Coleraine and the Manse, Wee Free at that. Though since his wife's death, he was not really a believer at all, but someone in whom ingrained prejudice, 'hatred and contempt for the papist', flourished. Under him, the Tories would be fighting a battle they had won twice before in 1886 and 1889. But on the second occasion, they had won in the House of Lords where they would never win anything that mattered ever again. The fight must be in the Commons and the country.

The hysteria was as marked as in those Budget and Parliament Act debates. Whibley of *Blackwood's*, a fat little man in a permanent state of shrilling and poisonous affront, announced that 'Not one word has been said to allay our just fears for the future defence of the Empire...the granting of Mr Asquith's Home Rule to Ireland can make nothing except civil war.' Far too many people in the normally sane world of politics sometimes seemed to cherish a crazy hope for that civil war, and that Ulster particularism might bring it. The problem was that a religious division more bitter than racial hatred existed at the same time in six counties, whereas the most moderate men in the twenty-six, Redmond very much among them, earnestly believed in a single, thirty-two-county, Ireland.

For all the clamour from both sides, the notion of a solvent, coherent state, whatever its boundaries, was generally appreciated. Perhaps precisely for this reason, the compromise of Home Rule as against a nation state was generally accepted, if not loudly proclaimed, by serious Nationalists. The doctrinaire Tories and Ulster demonstrators refused to acknowledge this practical underpinning of Home Rule Ireland. Fixed angry purpose grew greater as they followed up the monster-meeting, giant-flag salute and march-past at Craigavon with actual drilling. They were wooden rifles indeed, but real ones would be purchased in Germany before this malign pantomime was through. Protestant JPs stood ready to exercise Protestant counsel's opinion that they could authorize military exercises if 'consonant with constitutional intent', whatever that is, which might seem constitutional in Ulster Protestant eyes!

The government was trying to do something entirely reasonable, given the clean hands of both Asquith and Redmond, but Ulster zealotry could not believe it. Meanwhile hysteria and opportunism ruled jointly in a Tory Party unfit, at this time, for rational purpose. On the Irish side, a responsible, dissenting view would be put by William O'Brien, an interesting, intelligent man who had stood closest to Parnell and had run the nationalist newspaper. Redmond was happy at Home Rule; Ireland's place in an Empire he admired. O'Brien wasn't and would have preferred 'fiscal independence full and at once'.[4] What O'Brien's perceptions illustrate is that at some later time along the line, Home Rule would not suffice. But the point lay in the 'at some time'. In a pretty fair interim, Home Rule could work. Though, for brute money reasons in a very poor country, it wouldn't come quickly. Ironically the Irish counties would be better bound to the UK with hoops of redistribution—fiscal hoops; and following the growth of welfarism in the UK, Ireland would be a steady beneficiary.

Here and now, the Conservatives were doing what Randolph Churchill had acknowledged doing cynically in the early 1890s, 'Playing the Orange card and hoping it is the ace and not the deuce.' Secondary syphilis had induced the wild candour of that remark. Bonar Law was in his right mind, but temperamentally a bitter, quarrelsome man and he had at his ear the endlessly machinating Maxwell Aitken. Canadian, Presbyterian of a widely sinning sort, lifelong Imperial protectionist, and ruler of the coming four million readers Express group, no one was better disposed than the future Lord Beaverbrook to manage the opinions of mass markets or crowds.

The next step in Ulster would be the Covenant, a very Protestant thing reaching back to another very creditable thing, the Covenant of 1638, signed in Greyfriars Churchyard Edinburgh by Scottish citizens resisting the imposition of prelacy upon them by the sensationally ill-advised Archbishop Laud. The second-time-round Covenant was good theatre—*touring* theatre, the document appearing at a succession of public meetings—from Portora Hill to Enniskillen, then Lisburn which housed lots of 'Papishes'. It would be accompanied by the bullying Ulster Protestant nonsense of drums, fifes, and the tune 'Protestant Boys', attracting solemn, multiple signings and straight faces, with British Tory politicians in bit parts.

There was too, a yellow banner, supposedly carried before King William at the Battle of the Boyne. It would be placed, together with a silver key, into the hands of Carson KC while a leading figure of the Ulster gentry, Captain Craig, loosed the banner and proclaimed its right 'to fly over a people that can boast of civil and religious liberty'. The ability of supposedly dour men, who had banished all show and tinsel from their worship, to out-Italian and out-opera Italian opera impressed all hands. It was excellent publicity and would raise a fevered temperature to clinical concern.

The next quarrelling step of this choreographed tantrum would be a paramilitary affair, inviting General Roberts, principal surviving military reputation of the South African War, centre-stage, to review troops assembled to resist the British government—Ulster civilians pretending to be soldiers. Roberts ducked the offer of this, but recommended a General Richardson, distinguished in Waziri campaigns and appreciative of Ulster soldiery. All this turning of ordinary civilian clerks, tradesmen, and other useful people into marching men in uniform looks to the eye familiar with other street armies, like an unpleasant intimation of forces to be raised for real elsewhere within a decade...Interestingly, F. E. Smith KC, who had acted as galloper to the general, fell flat with a speech rightly perceived by these earnest men as, ironically, blarney!

Given the trouble being made and able to be made, the sheer unreason of it all, Asquith, too reasonable himself to be a good judge of mania, would have been wise at this point or earlier to think and talk partition, even thought it would be partition involving two non-states. Partition, when he came to it in 1913, and before world war sent Antrim Calvinists and men from Kerry, carrying rosaries, to the same mortal midden, was *technically* difficult, rising impossible. There were too many scatterings of the denominations, especially in the west, for the most inspirational wiggly line quite to master.

A Commons motion, that of a Tory, Agar-Robartes, sensible among the usual Tory rage, had proposed simply an exclusion of four Protestant Ulster counties from Home Rule. It could have become the basis for dealing. But here Redmond's combination of general reasonableness, sheer inexpertise on Ulster, and doctrinaire inability to make concessions on territory encouraged a ministerial rejection. Meanwhile an Ulster zealot, Frederick Crawford, would sail to Germany and return with a cargo of newly purchased arms for the marchers, as he put it, 'to hold Ulster for the Empire'. In due course, Eoin MacNeill, a southern academic with a sense of humour, would do as much, smuggling past Dublin customs other German weapons intended for the parallel force building in the south, saying lightly that 'they would hold Ireland for the Empire'.

Things had got horribly out of hand and it would with hindsight have been better for Asquith and Birrell to have taken up the partition option earlier. But the Conservatives and, in particular, Bonar Law, not to mention the Tory press, had chosen a non-conciliatory line of the most bitter kind from the start. Law had no half-tones. A Northern Irish Canadian with those Ulster roots, in Parliament for only twelve years, he had been made leader with no ministerial experience, as an uncompromising Imperial Protectionist, and precisely, as a man with neither inclination nor flair for compromise or consultation. His language in the main debate had been primitive and snarling.

> Mr Law *The bill is nothing better than the latest move in a conspiracy as treacherous as has ever been, formed against the life of a great nation...the present government turned the Commons into a marketplace where everything is bought and sold.*
> Mr Asquith *We have sold ourselves? This, Mr Speaker, is the new style...Let us see exactly what it is: it is that I and my colleagues are selling our convictions.*
> Mr Bonar Law *You have not got any.*

Prominent front bench figures like Smith had gone to drum-rolling meetings/cum paramilitary displays and endorsed them. They were not quite innocents in the matter of improper pressure. The Ulster Unionist council with which they worked had its origins in furious reaction to a floating of some form of Irish devolution, and by Curzon's appointment of the Catholic (and Liberal) Sir Antony MacDonnell as Under-Secretary to the Lord Lieutenant of Ireland at a time of Conservative government in Westminster. The Conservatives had now embraced a savage conflict for its savagery. They could hardly complain if the good idea of partition, snarled out by them, received less sympathy than it inherently deserved. Conservatives, and in particular Law, had shouted down dialogue when they actually had something useful to say.

---

25 January 1912

House regards the power and policies of the Trade Unions with apprehension.

Mr P. R. S. Nichols (Balliol) *The whole community must suffer from the exercise of unlimited power by a minority which can laugh at the government.*

Mr A. H. M. Wedderburn (Balliol) *What I object to is using a strike as the normal remedy for an industrial grievance.*

Mr F. McCance *Rising wages will benefit the whole nation. I look forward to an expansion of Union power.*

Mr G. R. McGusty *The trade unions have now performed all the useful work they could hope to do.*

Motion carried 115:100.

---

1 February 1912

House supports the principle of adult suffrage.

Mr S. G. Leeson *What we risk doing by following the terms of the motion is placing the critical problems of the present day in the hands of fools.*

Mr Smith-Gordon *What is actually wrong with fools?*

Mr Dodds *One thing is clear: women must not have the vote.*

Mr Griffith *If we believe in government by consent and the people do the consenting, which is what democracy means, how should we be against it?*

Mr D. L. Finnemore (Pembroke) *People agree that they believe in social betterment. It does gradually come, and does so in the train of an extending franchise. What this country needs is an oligarchy of educated men. I would recommend the model of Professor Dicey.*[5]

Mr F. J. T. Baines (Balliol) *The vote does not give education and the best women do not want it.*

Motion lost 90:127.

8 February 1912

House considers that the standard naval power to maintain the security of the British Empire must be on the basis of two keels to one against the next strongest European nation.

Mr Gilbert *The two-keel standard is too great and too expensive.*[6] *It is an extravagance and such overspending is a fatal threat to Social Reform.*

Mr C. F. Purcell (Balliol) *Threats of invasion exist but we should try to measure the probability rationally. Simply saying 'Two keels superiority' is completely arbitrary.*

Mr R. A. Yerburgh (President of the Navy League) *The standard of naval power must be definite. The peace of Europe rests upon a strong British Navy. At the moment, we are probably strong enough. But look to 1920 and what may happen when the Japanese alliance expires. We have nothing to gain by war, but for that very reason, the other side will have the first move, a very great advantage.*

Lieut. Dewar (New College) *Two-keel superiority as a standard is indefinite and illusory. No admiral wants an advantage of more than two or three ships.* Prolonged applause.

Mr Moncton *Only the strong man armed can put his house in order.*

Mr P. R. S. Nichols had nothing new to say, but was quite pleasant to listen to.

Motion carried 145:111.

———— ∞ ————

15 February 1912

House considers the acts and policy of the present government to have shown a reckless disregard for property.

Mr E. H. G. Roberts (Trinity) passed quickly to his special subject, Welsh Dis-endowment (sic)... It was the finest we have heard in the Union since Mr Smith-Gordon's Ulster oration.

Mr Davidson *Capital is a sensitive thing which responds to attacks in one obvious way. The vindictive attacks now being made on a single class must mean ruin for the whole country.*

Mr G. S. Woodhouse spoke of the lowness of Consols, general insecurity and other gloomy topics with the utmost cheerfulness.

Motion carried 80:79.

About to take place at this time, was the third bite at the Irish cherry, after the Commons rejection of 1886 and that by the Lords in 1893, something brought about by the loss of an overall majority by the Liberal Ministry, leaving it reliant, though comfortably, upon Irish Nationalist support. It was a preoccupying issue, one which would, by mid-July 1913, involve a gathering at Buckingham Palace, including King George V, to look at maps for a way of dividing nine-county Ulster. The object would be to create a homeland territory for the disaffected Calvinists of Antrim, Down, North Armagh, parts of Londonderry, East Belfast, and assorted smaller territories.

---

22 February 1912 (Cambridge visit)

House welcomes prospective passing of a Bill granting Home Rule to Ireland.

Mr Bland *Irishmen do not want complete separation and the settlement of Home Rule carries for the future the steady commercial advantages of something resolved.*

Mr K. F. Callaghan (Gonville and Caius) *The proposals are being brought forward in a way to make great hazards. As to business, there is no settled agreement where the lines and authority of Customs and Excise will lie.*

Mr Barrington-Ward complained that Home Rule distracted government from practical grievances. He is wonderfully reasonable for an Ulsterman.— Arguably the slightest compliment ever made.

Motion carried 134:118.

---

29 February 1912

House considers the party system inherited by the modern political system in this country, to be useless, false and a peril to the conduct of the state.

Mr Woodhouse *A better idea than our hard-and-fast party division would be a variant of the French group system, but not pushed to extremes.*

Mr Dodds *The things complained of in politics—honours sold, secret funds and so on, are simply accretions and not essential to the system itself.*

Mr Moncton *I would like to see a moderate party to look at questions like insurance and workmen's compensation simply on their merits.* The Treasurer could not be dull if he tried and when he has a grievance, he is irresistible.

Mr Barrington-Ward *Party Loyalty means loyalty, not to a career, but to principles. It is pointless railing against financial support. You couldn't run politics without it. Our guest, Mr Hilaire Belloc, would find himself fighting his non-party causes wanting non-party money to do it.*

Mr Hilaire Belloc (Visitor)[7] *A small knot of politicians and financiers stage-manage the issues on which politicians divide. This clique dominates the House of Commons and controls the enormous powers and patronage of the Executive.*

There is no call for tariff reform, insurance, or the referendum until the ruling clique chooses to put them forward; and where, as with Chinese Labour, the Licensing Bill or the Insurance Act, there is a burning popular feeling, it is the ruling clique and not the People that decides the result. Members who resist are driven out of politics. Consider the treatment of the House of Lords, which has stood in the way of both front benches by acting in a minor matter as a jury of Englishmen. The result is that in spite of the opposition of the Die-hards, a group that really cared for their principles, the House of Lords has lost its veto. Neither party has any intention of reforming it now that their object has been achieved. In the same way, the Insurance Act which the whole country loathes, is being forced upon it because it suits the financiers upon whom the Front benches depend...The only cure for the disease is exposure. The speech left a strong impression of the personal sincerity of the speaker and the reality of the evils which he is trying to expose.

Motion carried 311:181.

———⌾———

7 March 1912

House believes that in view of the existing European situation, a rapprochement between England and Germany is an unrealizable ideal.

Mr S. S. H. Wall (Lincoln) *Beware treaties generally. Beware especially the pro-German party in France and above all, of the two gentlemen from University College opposite. The two leading members of the two great European confederacies could not possibly draw together.*

Mr Urwick *War as well as peace, can be obtained by press agitation. Public opinion in both countries desired peace.*

Mr O. Nield (Keble) claimed that he was not anti-German, and proceeded to denounce German statesmen, German policy and the German Emperor in the bitterest terms.

Mr von Grunelius (Univ.) certainly made everyone in the House wish to vote on his side...'claiming that both nations must make sacrifices if they wished to achieve this ideal'. He richly deserved the very enthusiastic reception which he received.

Mr Guedella *We are an ally of France and as an ally, we have responsibilities. The Agadir Crisis*[8] *and its resolution do show that this alliance is the right one.*

Mr K. K. R. Hahn (Ch.Ch.)[9] *England must avoid Guildhall orations and keep to the usual channels of diplomacy. She must resign the role of Policeman of Europe and she must make Mr Guedella live for at least four years in Germany.*

Mr W. G. von M. Pendlebury (Keble)[10] *England has abandoned her 'Policeman of Europe' role by becoming the ally of France.*

Mr P. S. Cannon (New College) *I protest against the introduction into this debate of facts!* Loud applause.

Motion lost 64:82.

2 May 1912

House condemns conduct of the government in the recent coal strike.[11]

Mr Wedderburn *After much vacillation, the government has introduced the Minimum Wage Bill, a comfortless remedy by which we must judge them. No provision has been made for making contracts valid. It is though useless to ask the Opposition for an alternative. They will only introduce fancy bills which have no chance of passing.*

Mr D. M. Hartog (Balliol) *First, the strike was legal. Notices were duly printed and handed out, and in a large number of places, peace was kept. Time had been needed for a cooler atmosphere, and the government has rightly bided its time before bringing in the Minimum Wage Bill. Tory tactics responding to it, are merely destructive. Excluding a fixed rate of wages is wise, firm and courageous.*

Mr Moore *The government has made no attempt whatever to deal with industrial unrest. Its conduct would have been criminal for any government, but especially for this one.*

Mr M. K. Jackson (Magd.) *The last speaker must have been on strike for a minimum contract with the subject under debate. State interference is right from every point of view. Beneath all the troubles lie the real reasons—the terrible conditions of life and labour among the miners. I have figures here on mortality to prove it.* Mr Jackson was convinced and convincing.

Motion lost 81:102.

9 May 1912

House thinks it the duty of the government to carry out the promised re-constitution of the Second Chamber.

Mr J. G. Lockhart (Trinity) *Failure to carry out government pledges has left us with one half of the legislature suspended. Was there then any mandate for the [Welsh Church] Dis-establishment Bill?*

Mr F. W. Wilson Speaking as a member of the Labour Party. *A reconstituted upper house will simply mean another Tory second chamber. There is more pressing business on hand.*

Mr G. C. Allsebrook (Trinity) *I am for a second chamber, but not yet. As it is, this House of Lords is an improvement on the last one.*

Mr A. W. Bland (Ruskin College) thanked the president for his standing invitation to Ruskin students to attend debates. *Frankly, I want a single chamber. The country made its institutions not the institutions the country.* [First ever Ruskin contributor.]

Motion lost 70:87.

23 May 1912

House would welcome the passing of the [Welsh] Disestablishment (*sic*) bill.

Mr F. E. Smith (Wadham ex-President)[12] *'There is money in it' says Mr Ellis Griffiths 'and if only we had the church dis-endowed, we could lower the pension-*

able age in Anglesey from 70 to 60.' The proposal of the government was to take money, which was being well and piously used, away from an impoverished Church and devoted it to secular purposes. And this House and this University, whether they belonged to this Church or not, had always revered it, an appeal should not be made in vain which asked only that money originally consecrated to the service of God, should be maintained for that service and should not be diverted in a Christian community to purposes, admitted by every apologist for the bill as secular in their character.

Motion lost 206:352.

———— ◦◦◦◦ ————

6 June 1912

House finds the Home Rule bill at present before the Commons, unworthy of support.

Rt. Hon. Sir Edward Carson[13] had a magnificent reception. *My crime, if it is a crime, is that I want to stay in the bond of Union into which Pitt invited Ireland.[14] I believe that Pitt was as great a man as Asquith. The desire for Home Rule in Ireland exists because it was widely supposed that it would give everybody something for nothing. I recall the tale of the Irishman who said that he longed for Home Rule, but he would rather have a bullock. What about the position of Scotland? Why should not Ireland be in the same position and work in co-partnership for the benefit of the whole of the British Empire? Nobody would grudge that Mr John Redmond should be Chief Secretary of State for Ireland and that other Irishmen who show themselves capable, should take their proper part in work for the benefit of the whole British Empire.*

Motion carried 348:262.

———— ◦◦◦◦ ————

13 June 1912

House considers British occupation of Egypt necessary for the peace and prosperity of that country.

Mr Nichols *England has permanent interests in Egypt, and no adequate cause has arisen yet for her to relinquish her hold on that country.*

Mr M. S. Loutfy (Lincoln)[15] *Honesty is the best policy in the long run. I do not hate England, but I love Egypt better. England went to Egypt originally to annoy France. That is no longer necessary. Nationalism is strong in Egypt, and the twentieth century should be a century of national liberties.*

Mr L. F. Adams (Keble) *Western people have shown the greater capacity for self-government. England has lent Egypt the benefit of this governing capacity. England must stay in Egypt for Egypt's benefit.*

Mr Bland (Ruskin) *England has no legal status in Egypt. The real reason why we are there is that we have interests there. There is no proper system of interests between Englishman and native. Otherwise why don't Egyptians have the right of free speech in their own country?*

Mr Keen (Balliol) moved an amendment adding to the end of the official motion the words '*but dishonourable to the reputation of the British Empire.*' Mr Wedderburn opposed and the amendment was lost by acclamation.

M. le Comte d'Albon defended French dealings with Egypt. It is not often that we have the privilege of hearing the French point of view.

Motion carried 100:96.

17 October 1912

House has no confidence in the present administration.

Mr G. P. Dennis (Exeter) *The Insurance Act is mistaken in detail and in method, but is a fair attempt to deal with an acute problem. Tariff Reform, the Tories' only plank, is a fraud and an election loser of first merit. The Tories of today are opportunists without principle or creed.*

Mr Lockhart *I do not wish to attack Sir Edward Grey, the right man in the right place. Where is the mandate for Home Rule? Welsh disestablishment is simply a form of legalised robbery: all for such a paltry sum. The guillotine*[16] *has been used to stifle discussion. The government has made the representative system as nothing.*

Mr Talbot *The land policy is prompted by revenge and spite.*

Lord Spencer Compton (Balliol) is not very bright, but he improves.

Motion carried 302:164.

---

24 October 1912

House holds that the sympathy of the House is with Turkey.[17]

Mr F. J. P. Richter (New College) *I want Turkey to win in order that the Young Turks may be able to carry out their reforms; if they were to lose, vital interests would be affected and a European war not an entire impossibility.*

Mr Mallett *The Balkan States are awakening from medieval slumber and are seeking a new life of commercial enterprise and of liberty of religion and politics.*

Mr El Ghaffar *King Peter of Servia's*[18] *only claim to humanitarianism was that he had assassinated his predecessor and his wife; and King Nicholas*[19] *had sent his parliamentary opposition to life-long imprisonment.*

Motion defeated 212:210.

---

21 November 1912

This House believes that party spirit has become exaggerated to absurdity.

Mr A. H. M. Wedderburn *A party system of some sort was inevitable. The disgraceful scene in the Commons last Wednesday is a revelation of what the party spirit had produced. There is now on one side a ministry determined to break down long-standing traditions to recover a temporary party disadvantage. On the other, there is a party trying to make parliamentary legislation possible.*

Mr D. H. Hartog *No one now cares for the serious in politics… We have come to such a pass that they scorn the prejudices of party spirit.*

Mr H. A. Secretan (Balliol) *The party system has made itself necessary through the weakening of party spirit.*

Motion carried 368: 344 majority.

———✦———

5 December 1912

House believes that the Insurance Act was carried with such indecent haste and with such manifest anomalies as render it a dangerous rather than valuable reform.

Mr Wiggin *What I object to is the coercion of the medical service. This bill was hurried through, a hastily devised imitation of the German scheme. It is an anomaly to place the healthy and unhealthy under the same footing.*

Mr V. A. L. Mallet (Balliol) *Nobody likes being compelled; nobody liked paying. The act enforces both; hence its unpopularity.*

Mr E. B. Turner FRCS (Visitor) *It is absurd to imagine that doctors would have time to manage private practice as well as service under the Act. They would be working at insurance patients nine hours a day.*

Mr H. G. Strauss (Christ Church) *Let us see the BMA for what it is, a Trade Union.*

His charges against those who professed to have nothing to do with party politics and at the same time roused their supporters to frenzied enthusiasm about the 'rollicking Irish Party' were entirely justifiable.

Mr M. H. Macmillan twitted an opponent gently and the Tory Party almost fiercely; he has a pleasant voice. He might make more use of it.

No vote recorded.

---

6 February 1913

House thinks the Women's Suffrage amendments to the Franchise bill were just and expedient.

Mr Allsebrook *Every argument for democracy is a vote for women's suffrage. It is wrong to say that women with a vote would not support a strong military/naval policy. New Zealand, which has women's suffrage, sent men to South Africa and gave us a dreadnought.*

Mr L. L. H. Thompson (Exeter) *I am in apostasy and revel in the fact. Women's labour was forced into the market and, from a variety of causes, has been used to drive down wages. Meanwhile unemployment among men has increased.*

Lord Spencer Compton (Balliol) *Women object to being governed by their more virile sisters. It is foolish to talk of the disadvantages under which women labour without remembering the compensating advantages e.g. for married women after divorce. The idea has never been before the electorate. Our opponents are trying to foist the vote on the women of the country when the majority of them do not want it.*

Mr Urwick *Chivalry is neither sufficiently strong nor universal to support the contention that women's interests were safe in men's hands.*

Mr E. H. G. Roberts (Trinity) attacked militancy and made several points forcibly.

Mr H. J. Laski (New College)[20] was a wholehearted champion of the militants.

Motion lost 89: 108.

———∞∞———

13 February 1913

House views Disestablishment and Disendowment of the Church of England in Wales with emphatic disapproval.

Mr Wedderburn *I am an extremist on this issue. It is a disgraceful thing to divert Church money into secular uses.*

Mr Urwick *The Church of England in Wales is in no sense adapted to Wales, as a nation; until this is passed, the sense of national grievance against an alien church will remain.*

Mr V. Gollancz (New College)[21] defended the bill in an able speech marred by an obvious determination to make up for time lost in previous efforts to catch the speaker's eye.

Mr M. H. Macmillan (Balliol) defended the bill on its merits, not on its popularity. He should go far.

Motion carried 124: 57.

———∞∞———

20 February 1913

House believes that the exigencies of the situation demand the adaptation by this country of universal military service.

Mr Lockhart *The territorial forces are inefficient in numbers and energy. I accept the need for a policy of 'A strong man strong-armed.'*

Mr Nicholls *We have become a continental power and in order to be of any strength or value in European politics, we need a vastly more powerful army; at present to be a patriot means voluntary submission to a handicap.*

Mr Guedella *In the East, men die of inaction, in the West, of overstrain: we cannot afford a conscript army.*

Motion lost 107:150.

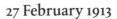

27 February 1913

House believes that a Public School education provides an adequate education for active citizenship.

Mr M. H. Macmillan (Balliol) *Religion is taught in school to make it as little, if at all, superior in interest to Demosthenes. So many Public School men go into the Church, the Services and Governorships of dependencies that they cannot be called citizens. They succeed in producing gentlemen, but these gentlemen are lethargic and cannot be termed active citizens.*

Mr F. J. Bechmann *Public school men are deficient in intellectual curiosity.*

Lord Spencer Compton *In my opinion, girls' public schools are producing far too active citizens.*

Mr J. Sykes (Worcester) made a strong case, especially for fagging.

Motion carried 71:45.

22 May 1913 [Cambridge visit]

House believes that modern Trades Unionism is a menace to industry.

Mr G. W. Theobald (Emmanuel Cantab.) *I start by insisting that this is a worry about the future rather than something dangerous now. When a minority tries to force something upon a majority, there is danger and what currently get forced are the narrow ideas of the working man.*

Mr L. E. Wharton (Oriel) *The present system relies necessarily upon collective agreements. If there are dangers, then we must change that system. The way to make Trade Unionism dangerous is to take up a reactionary attitude to it.*

Mr A. C. C. Willway (Oriel) does not have a happy manner, but he stated the case against Trade Unionism logically and fairly. *Let us do our best to encourage that section within Trade Unionism which wants peace.*

Motion carried 151:131.

8

On the Eve

16 October 1913 to 11 June 1914

Home Rule Bill/Trade Union growth/Eugenics/Land policy/Theatre Censorship/
'Worn-out Democracy'/Imperial federation/Opposition policy/Despair at Irish
crisis/Reform of public schools/Home Rule—Federation?/Triple Entente/Single
vote only/Liberals and Labour distancing themselves?

In a fit of bathos, Thomas Gray produced the lines 'Alas regardless of their
fate, the little victims play'—something observed of Etonians! It could
have applied far better (even to the men of Christ Church) across the three
terms of 1913—so many of whom would, soon enough endure their fate
from the random firing squad of World War. Winners and losers at that
table spent a good part of this Michaelmas term discussing cheerful or
irrelevant subjects, throwing in Eugenics (which is neither), theatre censorship, the public schools, and Opposition policy. Eugenics was modish.
The logical next, small step, the elimination of the unfit, the handicapped,
nothing to do in this limited area, with race, would be a small, but assured
part of the mass slaughter of Nazi social policy, a quarter of a century
later. The House approved Eugenics by a majority of 39 as it disapproved
of 'The modern developments of Trade Unionism' by nine.

Censorship was topical. Bernard Shaw had made it so in early, not funny,
plays like *Widowers' Houses* and *Mrs Warren's Profession* discussing slum
landlords and socially mobile prostitutes. Censorship, a thing devised by
the government, in the person of Robert Walpole driving Fielding out of
the theatre to write novels, was, by this time, mostly prim and peremptory,

worried about innuendo and generally in the hands of men wonderfully uncreative. If the example of George Colman the Younger who, in the later eighteenth century, wrote his own plays, while as official censor cutting and amending those of the competition, was too cheerful for the turn of the late nineteenth/early twentieth century, new, equally entertaining ideas were about. William Archer's productions took on the censorship—with private productions. As in the 1950s, Clubs, formed to run plays sure of banning, put them on until, very eventually, in a fit of Labour majority broad-mindedness, the suppressing authorities would limp off the field fifty-five years later.

Doing down democracy was another and instructive topic: a reaction in part to all the reversals which the established classes had suffered, that same rise of trade unionism, stronger, new, plebeian, and worrying. Such a motion was a defiance of a historical trend rather than a perception of the non-democracy to come—Italy, celebrated by so many Liberals, upper or lower case as 'Italia Unita!' was, by this date, accelerating the run to war. Less than ten years before Mussolini, Italy played at empire by invading Libya. Oxford was simply nostalgic for the squire.

It is appropriate that, in the debate of 28 May 1913, two undergraduate speakers stated succinctly the entire argument, contemporary and historical, for and against, also wrong and right about Sir Edward Grey's Triple Entente. Mr J. H. B. Nihill of Emmanuel College Cambridge did not believe that the Triple Entente could balance the Triple Alliance—its ostensible object. Britain's current misguided policy was making a rapprochement with Germany impossible. However Mr H. Barnard of Jesus College Cambridge thought the Entente very different from the Alliance and believed that the time was ideal. As for the benefit of the Entente to European peace, that was ample justification.

The balance of retrospective judgement on involvement with war-primed continental alliances comes down on the side of Cambridge in the person of the visiting Mr Nihill. Professor Clark's *The Sleepwalkers* gives a detailed account of the group of over-mighty British civil servants like Sir Eyre Crove, senior adviser in the FO and Sir Arthur Nicholson, Permanent

Under Secretary for Foreign Affairs 1910–16, weighing heavily with Grey himself, old Liberal Leaguer, with secretive tendencies toward Cabinet colleagues. They were all anti-German by conviction and insufficiently open to the dangers of a Russian Ministry. This body had shifted from the domestic preoccupation of Stolypin and Kokovtsev—small 'c' conservatives, preoccupied with economic advance and needing peace to get it—to the adventurists Sazonov and Krivoshein. Both men were well connected with militant Balkan contacts, friends to Pan-Slavism, whom the great event in Sarajevo 1914 would find ardent for the war they would get. Stolypin had spoken of any war at that time as taking bread out of the mouths of peasants, a remark given resonance in 1917.

Meanwhile the recurring Balkan wars, fought in these ironically *pre-war years*, followed their petty, destructive ways. It began with Serbs, Bulgarians, and Greeks against the Turks and winning. Then after the peace-making conference in London, war would continue with under-rewarded and resentful Bulgarians against the Serbs—and losing. *Those* Serbs emerged from all of them as winners, looking for another fight against Austria, something to help create a greatly enlarged nation of all the Southern Slavs, a country of the South Slavs—a Yugoslavia. Austrian pressure had made Serbia retreat from Albania which they had invaded, leaving a still greatly enlarged, but resentful small nation looking for another fight over Bosnia—mixed race and mixed religion, not unlike Ireland. A previous Austrian Minister, Aehrenthal, had silly-cleverly converted this territory in 1908 from its 1878 Treaty of Berlin protectorate status into an involuntary Imperial Province. Involving, as it now did, territory belonging to the Austrian (Habsburg) Empire, the contingencies, starting with another war, were fearful and seen as fearful.

A member of the Habsburg family had remarked that if a great European war did come about, it would be over some damn-fool business in the Balkans. The Archduke Franz Ferdinand, following his prophetic judgement, had settled in his own circle of advisers long-term plans to bring the smaller states in Austria's imperial orbit—Croatia, Bosnia, and the like—into a confederation—a Danubian Confederation, a toned-down name for a toned-down empire and good sense if it could be got. Austria had long since settled differences with Hungary on generous terms of rational self-interest, trading as Austria-Hungary on terms too favourable to Hungary to warrant her splitting, but highly provocative to the other Habsburg nationalities. What Franz Ferdinand would have been talking animatedly about to his friend Leopold Berchtold, the Foreign Minister, a day before his murder, would have been the prospect of Austria-Hungary-Several-Smaller-Countries. Even though Hungarian opinion, sitting pretty anyway, was unsympathetic to sharing autonomy with Slavs, this had a better chance of success than anything else.

Unhappily, such conflicts before the First World War were those of patrons following uneasily on the barking of their respective fighting dogs. In Ireland, the steady, trusting, and thus compelling faith of the southern partner anticipating thirty-two Home Rule counties, set against the all-night barking of the northern province, had made it embarrassing for Westminster to grant any partial concession of say twenty-eight. The Archduke's plans for acknowledging the Empire's weakness by treating territories as, at the very least, Home Rule states in that loose 'Danubian Confederation' was an ironic parallel to Westminster's problems with the two Irelands.

Ulster Partition, when parties would eventually come round to it in 1914, would prove, under a first examination at the Buckingham Palace conference, horribly tricky. It was the contemplation of maps laid out on a table there which provoked Winston Churchill to make his remark about 'The dreary steeples of Fermanagh'. It was, though, every kind of sense to make Ulster both smaller and more securely Protestant. A Home Rule Ireland of twenty-eight and several half- or quarter-counties, had the inspired wiggly line been traced, would have left an ironically coherent and much calmer Ulster. Such an arrangement would be denounced internationally in the later twentieth century when applied by the Turks in Cyprus and it has worked.

All this might have been dismissed as pantomime, but for the fact that general officers, a great many of them Ulster-bred, had begun to forget the universal military obligation of obedience. The idea of wooden rifles turning steel and pointed at a British obstacle was crazy, but in 1914 Ulster, crazy didn't show. In the same exalted condition, Bonar Law had made dark, unconstitutional threats at a monster meeting in the grounds of Blenheim Palace. Very soon the murder of Franz Ferdinand by a Balkan gang known to the Russian government, failure of European diplomacy to grasp the suicidal Pan-Slavism of Tsar and Imperial ministers, Austrian rash/despairing declaration of war against Serbia, and British over-commitment via France to Russia, would between them put rational argument out of bounds.

In Westminster, it had been put out of reliable practice already. A Home Rule Bill had been put to the Commons in January 1913 with riotous effect. A bound, and thus injurious copy of the rules of parliamentary conduct had been thrown in the Commons, at the head of Winston Churchill, by an Ulster member, Ronald McNeil, later Lord Cushenden. In the background, Tories were lobbying George V for a dissolution over the Premier's head, even his dismissal, any of which that anxious King had to be told plainly was flat unconstitutional. Bearing in mind George's later flinching from a grant of asylum to his own cousin, Nicholas II (left with his family to face a Soviet firing squad), telling George everything very plainly was a necessity.

War was coming, but before it came, the arrival in Dublin of German military equipment, purchased for the recently formed Volunteer Force, would be met by enthusiastic crowds, crowds which on Bachelors' Walk would encounter British—actually Scottish—troops whom they pelted and by whom they would, by return of service, be fired upon, leaving three people dead and thirty-nine wounded. This, in 1916, proved a perfect foundation in rhetoric for Irish people, lacking John Redmond's affection for the British Empire, people who would rise at Easter that year in a short, bloody battle for the Post Office and a flour-mill amid street killings prettified by the florid imagination of W. B. Yeats. They would seize buildings, conduct a shoot-out—and be spat on by a Dublin crowd. After which, nineteen of them would suffer politically calamitous executions, and their cause would be given enormous impetus by the further martyr-making follies of successive Irish Secretaries: notably H. C. Duke and Hamar Greenwood. The unresolved crisis of 1913–14 had delayed a solution. The martyr-making gave armed revolt impetus and credibility. British, mainland commitment for the fight was turning to weary indifference while nine-county Ulster had too many Catholics for mutual tolerance.

Greenwood, another ill-informed Canadian, followed an uncomprehending 'strong line', the counter-terror of Black and Tan irregulars from 1919. He found a retainable Irish good will—and dispelled it. Ultimately, this vicious little running war compelled a British government, of which both F. E. Smith and Bonar Law were members, to concede in 1922 an Irish Free State, an independent nation in all but name. The six counties, under a clause agreed in the settlement to establish what is never called Ulster Home Rule although it plainly was; its rulers able, by constructive manipulation, to leave the Catholic population as under-represented as discriminated against.

Beyond which, Ulster men and women of both Christian persuasions have suffered miserably across recent years at the hands of a criminalized IRA, exploiting, intimidating, and reliably killing Protestant officials on the one hand and quite enough people in the cross-fire among the long-subordinated Catholic population. Such acts, including the murder of women, seem now to be immune from prosecution for any crime. Home Rule, in whatever imperfect alignment of counties, supported by a calmer Tory opposition before the First War, does look like the better option which didn't happen.

16 October 1913[1]

House believes that a reference to the electors is the urgent and immediate duty of HMG.[*]

A. P. Herbert (New College)[2] *Moving a motion does not suit Mr Herbert as it does not give scope to his brilliant gifts of debate and reportage.*

[*] The *Oxford Magazine* strays back briefly into italics and running commentary.

Mr Macmillan *An exceedingly brilliant speech—He is not afraid of making the most of a grandiloquent and melodramatic style. But ... does he or anybody think that to say Ulster is bluffing is an argument worth anything except cheap laughter and applause of the moment?*

Mr Gollancz *is quite a good speaker. If he tried to appreciate the view of his opponents, he would be better.*

Mr H. R. B. Grey-Edwards *He would speak quite well if he (a) addressed the audience and (b) did not regard all his hearers as beyond contempt.*

Mr A. F. Harrison (Queen's) *must not read his speech and must learn that his manner is grotesque.*

Motion carried 164:143.

———— ∞∞∞ ————

23 October 1913

House disapproves the modern development of Trade Unionism.[3]

Mr E. H Davenport (Queen's) *He has a considerable gift and also a certain verbose wit. But he has everything to learn in the way of (1) drastic self-restraint (2) control of ugly gestures and (3) intelligent political thinking.*

Mr C. E. M. Joad[4] *was entirely delightful. It was not argument but it was amusing, and vigorous. It also displayed considerable power of invective.*

Mr H. J. Laski (New College) *said some very odd things in quite a sincere way.*

Mr J. K. Spencer (BNC) *had nothing very new for us but might have been worse.*

An enormous house.

Motion carried by 9 votes.

———— ∞∞∞ ————

13 November 1913

House approves the principles of Eugenics.

Mr L. L. H. Thompson *showed that he had clear opinions on the subject. An amusing, unconventional and good-humoured speech which held everyone's attention.*

Mr E. F. Porter *If he were a tithe more cheerful, he might be distinctly good.*

Mr J. L. Hore-Belisha (St John's)[5] *delivered a very carefully prepared speech, not at all a bad one either, but impromptu speaking is better at this hour of the evening.*

Motion carried by 39 votes.

---

20 November 1913

Visit of the Chancellor of the Exchequer—House has no confidence in the Land policy of HMG.

Mr Roberts *His speeches are excellent, full of polemic, vigorously delivered, which expressed the strong objection which so many feel toward the policy and methods of Mr Lloyd George without being at any point discourteous.*

Mr Dennis *In many ways, the speech had great merits. But he has still to learn the art of attracting the audience to his own personality and consequently to the policy he advocates, instead of leaving behind him a great feeling of irritation.*

Mr Lloyd George *He triumphed in spite of his speech. No one who heard it will ever forget the magnetic personality of the man, the winning quality in his manner, the adroitness, the good humour and the unlimited capacity to deal with interruption… When all is said, it was a speech which no other man could have delivered.*

Motion lost. Vote not given.

4 December 1913

House would welcome the abolition of censorship.

Lord Spencer Compton *Managers use it as a two-way generous insurance policy. The rules cannot be enforced: witness Carlyle, Ruskin and [Herbert] Spencer, all of whom were, at different times, banned.*

Mr J. S. Lithiby (Wadham) *People who support a censorship are called Puritans. Puritanism spells hypocrisy. The motion demands a root and branch abolition, not a re-examination of the detail. Indecency pays and police interference is ludicrously impossible. At present however, a play will not be a financial success unless it has the censor's hall-mark.*

Mr J. B. Clearihue (Jesus) *The Censor is an extraordinary person, above appeal, the victim of his own caprice. If censorship is to exist, why not universalise it, introducing it into the domain of Rag Time (sic) or the National Gallery?* He triumphed in spite of his speech.

Mr C. T. Chevallier (Worcester) *This is a time to stand against the popular condemnation of old institutions. As a general rule, theatres provide a wholesome treat. The public does not see countless small expurgations which the censor orders.*

Mr Gollancz *The censorship was founded in 1737 against political satire; it is now misused as a moral safeguard. Ibsen's 'Ghosts' was censored for attacking two social evils. The censorship bans reform and blocks one of the avenues of progress.*

Mr Devonport *The fall of the censor would see the rise of cranks to regulate the public's conscience.*

Mr K. E. Bonnerjee (New College) *was original at 11.10, though we personally do not go to the theatre, another way of getting round the Censor.*

Motion carried 89:83.

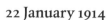

22 January 1914

House believes Democracy is a warn-out creed.

Mr Lithiby *The people do not really govern; neither is legislation honestly carried out on their behalf.*

Mr F. Haldenstein (Ch.Ch.) *Democracy should be given a chance.*

Mr J. D. O. Coorts (Balliol) had carefully thought out his remarks but Rousseau at 10.40 has a soporific effect.

Mr L. Lascelles *was proud of being a Conservative.*

Motion lost 110:125.

29 January 1914

House would welcome some scheme of Imperial Federation.

Mr J. B. Ragiv (New College) *There are imperial responsibilities. And we are awakening to their existence. Continuing with the present system is no longer warranted.*

Mr D. F. Jerrold[6] *A man is called a patriot when he is proud of nothing, but his country. Empire is the oldest fallacy in history.*

Mr Lockhart *I deplore the Little Englander spirit.*

No vote recorded.

A very thin house assembled for this; and after the opening speakers, the debate was lamentably dull. This was probably due to the fact that a larger number of members were attending the Bishop of Oxford's mission.

———— ✺ ————

19 February 1914

House would welcome the passage of the Welsh Chapel Bill.

Mr Macmillan—Secretary *The great majority of Welsh MPs favour this. Disendowment follows, a sort of justice for the people, for is this not the tithe, a hated property. Further, the Act takes the Church outside secular control. The Church is in danger from the state. Is she going to sacrifice her faith to her privileges?* A strong case against Erastianism deservedly winning the applause of the House.

Mr Wedderburn—Librarian *The money to be taken means so little to the state and is so large a share of the Church's income.*

Dr Selbie President of Mansfield College (A Methodist and Congregationalist foundation) *I support the bill because it will help the church, and for no other reason.*

Motion lost 215:227.

———— ✺ ————

5 March 1914

House believes the constructive policy of HM Opposition deserves the support of the House.

Mr Wiggin did so—not very well.

Mr H. C. Strauss (Ch.Ch.) *Peasant proprietorship is economically impossible under Free Trade. Tariff Reform does not mean work for all. On the contrary, it means higher prices and an increased cost of living.*

Mr Joad *delivered a speech not in the best of taste. At the conclusion of which, his noisy little band of supporters left the House in a body.*

Mr W. G. Sargeaunt (Trinity) *is inclined to preach in a hearty way; but if he can correct his faults of manner, should become quite good.*

Motion lost 48:75.

7 May 1914

House regards with despair the management of this Irish Crisis by HM Ministers.

Mr Moncton Moderate but telling…in that attractive style of which Mr Moncton is the master.

Mr Jerrold *The real plot is between the rebels and the Unionist Party.* The rather commonplace material was enlivened by a running fire of epigrams and jokes, all of which we enjoyed.

Mr Lockhart managed with considerable skill born of long practice, to make imperialism relevant to the question.

Mr T. R. Butler was so violent a nationalist as to be out of sympathy with the coalition—a good speech ill-delivered.

Motion carried 137: 94.

14 May 1914

House is convinced of the need for drastic change in the Public Schools system.

Mr Haldenstein *The method of teaching the subjects taught and the masters who taught them were all chosen on a wrong basis, long since out of date. Public School men are always given all the credit and all the rewards in life. But those brought up in a less stereotyped world are more useful to humanity.*

Lord Spencer Compton *Destructive criticism is useless without an alternative being suggested. The motion derives its force from class antipathy, but I willingly admit the necessity of opening the Public Schools to all classes.*

Mr P. H. Lyon *This system only turns out the useless good fellows.*

Mr Gollancz *The period of education is far too long and the system's scope far too narrow. Schools should contain all classes and both sexes.*

Mr G. A. Edinger *For the admittedly excellent quality of the public schools, the rest of the community pays a heavy price in the loss of material among the uneducated masses.*

Mr J. W. Wrangham (Balliol) *Any such scheme would lead to the crushing out of all human variety. Confusion is the socialist language for freedom of thought.*

---

21 May 1914 Eights Week Visit of Mr Austen Chamberlain.[7]

House supports the Home Rule Bill as a step toward the ultimate federal organisation of the UK.

Mr Strauss (Treasurer) *I congratulate Mr Chamberlain on preferring to discuss, not Tariff Reform, but a subject of living interest to the present generation. Local government is everywhere taking the place of the system of central administration.*

Mr Wiggins *This is inconsistent with the usual Home Rule attitudes. The claim that Home Rule could be a good nucleus for a federal scheme is often enough made, but can never be substituted.*

Mr M. H. Macmillan *The Treasurer gave us an excellent epigram and good rhetoric, but not too much close reasoning. Even relevance was wanting. Taken as a whole, this speech consisted of a most moving appeal to support the Liberal policy and fulfil long-held ambitions for unhappy Ireland.*

Mr Austen Chamberlain *Even if a case for the Federal solution could be made out, the connexion with it of the current Irish Bill is obscure. That bill puts it in the power of a Dublin parliament to get to its professed goal which is not federation, but separation. I would fight Ireland's claim to separation to the end. That claim could be put forward by Ulster against Dublin. Against the dangers of that bigotry, the Imperial Parliament provides a safeguard which no parliament can break.*

Motion lost 219:234.

---

28 May 1914—Cambridge visit.

House condemns the Triple Entente as embodying both an unnecessary and an unnatural policy.

Mr J. H. B. Nihill (Emmanuel Cantab.) *I do not believe that the Triple Entente can balance the Triple Alliance—its ostensible object. Our present misguided policy is making a rapprochement with Germany impossible.*

Mr H. Barnard (Jesus Cantab.) *The Entente is very different from the Alliance and the time is ideal. As for the benefit of the Entente to European peace, that is ample justification.*

Mr Wedderburn *I dislike a policy which divides Europe into two armed camps encouraging competition in armaments.*

Mr Mallet *Ten years ago when an understanding with Germany was out of the question, the Entente was created. It is the welcome end of our traditional enmity with France for which nation I have an intense admiration.* His eulogy left us cold, but the speech was backed by sound knowledge.

Mr Lithiby *Why is the Entente so secret? If it isn't an alliance, it proposes no useful function; if it is, then it is highly dangerous. The crux of foreign policy is Germany's attitude toward us, and the Entente is a challenge well calculated to provoke her and so to produce a European conflagration.* An effective speech.

Mr W. G. Woodroffe (Pembroke Cantab.) *A true insight into the character and aims of the European powers gives full justification for the Entente. For Germany, the one necessary policy is expansion. To meet it, the Entente is essential, and without it, war will be inevitable.*

Mr C. T. Chevallier (Worcester) *I expect startling changes in European history. I greet both Alliance and Entente. They will duly come together in a second Holy Alliance.*[8] Mr Chevallier's godfatherly approach towards Europe in general provided his speech some unconscious humour.

Baron von Richthofen *gave to those who could follow him an interesting defence of German policy.*

Motion carried 96:60.

4 June 1914

House believes existence and sanity qualify every adult man for the possession of one vote and one vote only.

Mr B. L. Strauss *Political incapacity and mental atrophy are not confined to one class only. Stupidity and even insanity are commonly attributed to political opponents.*

Mr Davenport *I deprecate the claim to a monopoly in benevolence by the Liberal party. Possession of a vote does not make a man qualified to use it. The larger the electorate, the greater the influence of a corrupt press. Universal suffrage is not essential to the democratic axiom of popular control.*

Mr J. L. Hore-Belisha *Manhood suffrage is seriously opposed by no party in parliament; and exclusion of the remaining 20 per cent of the male population is capable of no logical defence.*

Mr Chevallier *I would justify plural voting by the varying interests of various constituencies and the restriction of the franchise of the undesirable character of those whom it now excludes. Of the slander of sanity I will be no judge.*

Mr Strauss *What other test than sanity is possible for insanity? If votes are to be given as a reward rather than right, no system is even plausible.*

Mr Barnard *The ludicrous farce of modern elections is not an argument for a low voting qualification. It is difficult enough for the educated to make themselves fit for a vote. And it is no argument that the unfit shall be added to the fit.*

Mr Gollancz *Real popular government tends against corruption. Social equality can only be obtained by political equality.*

Motion carried 79:51.

---

11 June 1914

House believes that the course of modern politics is tending to increase the difference between the Liberal and Labour Parties.

Mr F. J. Baines (Balliol) *For this motion, the Liberal Party must be taken as a whole which is clearly impossible.[9] Triangular contests at by-elections prove as much. Modern Liberalism is of the Lloyd George type. So some shifting may be expected. True Liberalism is more likely to form an alliance with Unionism than to draw near to the Labour Party.*

Mr Prescott (New College) *Parties should be taken as a whole, Labour is confessedly drawn to every form of nationalisation and ultimately to Socialism. It is startling how far the Liberals have gone to adapt it. The choice for Liberals in the future will be between extinction and junction with the Labour Party.*

Mr W. T. Sargeaunt (Trinity) A lengthy discourse on the Army and a quotation from Shelley concluded a speech of conspicuous irrelevance.

Mr R. B. Graham (Magd.) *Labour has the right ends in view; and Liberals will come to see that they themselves are merely a step behind them on the same road.*

Mr J. A. Pugh *I regret the fact that previous speakers have made the mistake of taking the Labour Party seriously. In the fundamental principles of government, the real gulf is between the traditional parties and Labour.*

Mr H. C. Harwood *The Labour Party is not the one caricatured in the Daily Herald; and Mr Keir Hardie is an anachronism.*

Mr E. S. Brown *I am convinced of the unreality of party politics and the probability of fusion in the future against the forces of Labour.*

Motion lost 29:39.

The last debate of the term was held on 11 June.

Union debates now ceased for the period of the First World War.

9

The Threshold of the New

16 October 1919–26 May 1921

Coalition domestic policy/League of Nations/Direct Action/Liberal return?/ Replacing the Lords/End of operations in Russia/Labour as national disaster/ Ending compulsory Greek/Wider divorce/Montague's Indian policy/Dissolve the coalition?/Policy toward Russia/Armaments cut?/Debate invitation to women?/Inadequate peace treaty/Modern press/Coercion in Ireland.

Members, like the government, found the post-war scene heavily preoccupied with industrial disputes and Ireland, but, over the second question, were nearing the end of a policy of intervention. While the Union and the Nation had been away, changes had ocurred. Asquith had resigned, after much conspiracy against him, on 5 December 5 1916. Following some hesitation by the contending groups and refusal of the Premiership by Bonar Law, Lloyd George took over as head of that Coalition government created in May 1915. It had replaced the Liberal government and brought in leading Conservatives, but Lloyd George would remain in power, worshipped, admired, distrusted, and loathed, for almost six years until 18 October 1922. Immediately however, he would be preoccupied by two issues: Ireland (continued) and industrial conflict—the trade unions on the Home Front.

The other, quite notable, shift of power was the seizing of authority in Russia by Lenin and the Bolshevik[1] faction of Russian Marxism. Lloyd George had approved the sending of an expeditionary force of about 40,000 men to link up with assorted other non-Russians into Russia. This, at a later stage, would involve giving support to the Tsarist Generals

Kolchak and Denikin who had raised a counter-revolutionary force against the Soviet government.

In terms of civilized standards, there was very little to choose between the ruthless effectiveness of Soviet commanders and the two Tsarist soldiers. But the British trade unions were responding to the intimation that the Coalition planned full intervention against the Soviet government. This was to be effected on the side of a major player in the conflict, the forces of what had effectively become Poland. British trade unions declared themselves, with clear rank and file approval, against any intervention—notably on 10 May 1919, when they denied the dispatch of supplies to the Tsarist forces to be carried on the *Jolly George*. This was something energetically done under the direction of Ernest Bevin of the Transport Workers, later, as union leader and Foreign Secretary (1945–51), the Soviets' clear, illusionless enemy. However that intervention turned into widespread and effective protest, involving major unions and their leaders. A general strike was threatened and Lloyd George quietly dropped the idea of full-dress intervention.

His government was, anyway, quite sufficiently preoccupied with a far narrower, but comparably vicious war—in Ireland. After the nineteen executions, eighteen by firing squad, one, Roger Casement, by hanging, as a supposed traitor. Casement had arrived seasick in a German submarine carrying arms. Quite what would have been the alternative future if all the accused had been kept under house arrest, pending all round amnesty at the war's end, can be reasonably worked out as better.

The Dublin Rising of Easter 1916 had not been popular—not popular with the usual Dublin people in the Dublin streets. They had *not* risen and had actually spat on the rounded-up temporary seizers of the GPO and Boland's Mill. Ireland, though excluded from the call-up, served in the war in large numbers as cause or employment—soldiers with families to feel betrayed by the silliest of failed coups. An astute, proper politician in Dublin Castle would have held the ringleaders prisoner under wartime regulations and quietly used a general amnesty of some sort to let them later and ingloriously out. Henry Duke, risen backbencher, would, as the new Chief Secretary, do the obvious wrong thing, with all England behind him, turning romantic bunglers into high and ennobled patriots, just what the secure British government of Ireland needed.

The people who did finally come out of prison—in the case of Eamon De Valera, held in Lincoln, escaping from it—would find, when they started a new shooting war, quite enough new general support and a new, heightened Irish patriotism to fight the sort of unwinnable, unlosable, and unendurable war of which the home support base of the Imperial authority grows sick and tired. What was ready and waiting all around southern Ireland at the end of the 1914–18 war was the Irish Republican Army. They wasted no more time on flour mills, but at the height of the fighting, in April 1922, took over the Four Courts, the principal and historic centre of Irish justice. In the spirit of carefree destruction which the years of street fighting had created, they also blew up half of it,[2] taking 800 years of Irish documentary legal history with it.

Good and quite friendly government plus an improving economy, since Gerald Balfour's major shifting of Westminster policy as chief secretary between 1895 and 1900, had made rational self-interest an increasingly superior bet to the best terrible beauty anywhere to be had. Duke and his final successor, the insensible colonial Hamer Greenwood, were backed by Lloyd George in assured and fallible mode—'We have murder by the throat.' They hadn't. And enough murder had been done by the free-range British irregulars to intensify all the cruelties all the way round, most famously the firing at random into a football crowd in retaliation for the massacre earlier in the day of a group of irregulars known as the 'Cadets'. Known, some of them, as the 'Black and Tans', others as the 'Auxies', they were unofficial soldiery on the spree, good for freelance violence up to murder and capable of a credible attempt to burn down the second city of the twenty-six counties, Cork.

The entire conflict was scattered with instant grievance, product of an imagination-free administration and wild or calculated atrocity, also a thing, at once very Catholic and Irish, the act of suicide (mortal sin according to the Church's correct line), undertaken by men mindful of posthumous acclaim, or its clerical equivalent alternative, sainthood. The deaths of the forcibly fed youngster, Thomas Ashe, or the elder victims, Thomas MacCurtain and Terence MacSwiney, successive Lord Mayors of Cork, respectively shot dead by 'men with blackened faces' and dying on the 76th day of a hunger strike, said everything. It didn't ultimately matter that MacCurtain was generally reckoned a member of the IRA. What did and has mattered to a long posterity, was that they died as sure and certain 'victims of British oppression' with the inverted commas dubious even to English ears. The Black and Tans tended to get worse. As noted, the outstanding event in their career came on 11 December 1920 with that burning down, fire hoses cut, citizens driven indoors, fires set at several places well apart, of a great part of Cork.

There was a great deal of criminality on the part of the IRA—that 'Murder' which Lloyd George thought he had by the throat. However the response, a long short-cut finding its way round the military and civilian authorities in Ireland, was not only dishonest in all four suits, it was incredible. The Prime Minister would be reproached by Sir Henry Wilson, fanatical Ulsterman, for its want of candour. '...It was the government's business to govern. If these men ought to be murdered, then the government ought to murder them.'[3] Lloyd George danced at all this, said no government could possibly take this responsibility. In due course, Wilson himself, a long-term major meddler far from his official duties, against British policy as it affected Ulster, would be shot dead on his own doorstep.

Peace would eventually be made, not least because mainland British public opinion, influenced by the very credible findings of a commission set up by the Labour Party, had turned against the ferocity of a war manifestly not being won, and by the constructive intervention of Jan Christiaan Smuts, Boer general and enemy almost a quarter of a century earlier. Smuts advised De Valera that Ireland should take Dominion status. The term, recently dreamt up, meant simply that Ireland, governed, taxed, policed, armed, and represented by itself diplomatically, wasn't—or rather didn't call itself—a republic! Acceptance of this form would collide with the Jesuitical personality of Eamon De Valera who took, or decided to take, republican status as grounds for civil war against Irishmen not following him. There would be more grief in Ireland as De Valera obscurely reasoned himself into a war with the Irishmen accepting that effective independence did come with the vapid British flourish of Dominion. Given the new state's effective independence on signature, it hardly belongs here.

The problems of the coalition with organized labour and its reverse overlap with the 'Troubles' of Ireland were arduous. They did however reflect very much better on Lloyd George. The end of war led to the end of controls, meaning an end of the quasi-Socialist web of business and supply regulation which occurs in world wars. This was also occasion for the return, personal and economic, of great numbers of men out of uniform onto the economic market. It began well immediately, with the four millions released. However, this practical business coincided with the cruel side-symptom of a sweeping, fast-killing outbreak of influenza.[4] This, across June 1918, with a dip in November, resuming to peak in March 1919, would kill 150,000 people in England and Wales. During the worst week in early November, London and ninety-six other big population centres witnessed 3,889 deaths from influenza.

Demobilization, coming after the discipline of the 'war effort' and the temporarily shining example of the Soviet Revolution, would produce militancy, especially and unsurprisingly in Scotland, specifically Glasgow, hard-hit and hard bitten, its core, the shipyards, where a general strike was called by the shop stewards' committee to get a forty-hour week. These were the Clydesiders, men who would be names in the unions and left-wing politics for another forty years: Emmanuel Shinwell, a future Labour MP and Minister after 1945; David Kirkwood, also a future MP by way of the ILP (Independent Labour Party) and the most impressive of them, Willie Gallacher, puritan and total abstainer, who would join, and through everything, stay faithful to the new Communist Party of Great Britain. Shinwell, a man immoderately sour, would by contrast become famous for a supposed wrong, purely personal. A Minister of Fuel moved sideways in 1947 because of the poorly handled fuel crisis, he cherished the affront for life.

The Clydesiders as men behind the strike—though the war was over—would be arrested and held in prison. The dockers, who had marched across the city to George Square, were threatened with troops and machine guns and would suffer a brutal police baton charge, beating men and women alike. It all repellently echoed the Irish pattern, something from which Lloyd George's coalition would be saved by a boom, swift and effective in an erratic economy, one creating jobs and circulating money.

Lloyd George's response had been liberal—in the economic sense. The extensive system of controls, the war-Socialism of 1914–18, had the potential to be turned into a similar pattern of nationalization, not necessarily always a bad thing. Lloyd George's response was to abolish controls and sell off the many factories created for war supplies since 1914. Meanwhile, the badly run railways had been effectively nationalized during the war and would now be returned by the Railway Act of 1921—not to the many ownerships of 1914 but to four *groupings* of companies, none of them much good.

Above all argument about ownership and production lay the political apprehension aroused by events in Russia, fear of industrial unrest gathering the political velocity of a General Strike, and the martyrdoms creatable by sent-in military firing ill-considered volleys into people making up 'a dangerous crowd'. It was fear of 'Something' followed by a break in officer control of the military and of troops, enough of them, 'going over'. A variant of this would be the Metropolitan Police strike (actually the *two* strikes of August 1919 and August 1920). The Prime Minister's response was a succinct paying-up and the installation of that intelligent soldier, Nevil Macready. The return required was the closing of the police union. When Macready announced this, tactful as he was by military standards, the response—close to the anniversary of the first police strike—was the second police strike! The response was instructively weak, police thinking being very much economic rather than political. A swift Police Act would turn Macready's office decision into law; and sustained by that still effective union substitute, the new Police Federation—also a tradition continuing to the present day, of flattery ('Our Policemen are wonderful'—Margaret Thatcher) and constructive over-payment.

By September 1920, another risk had to be run. Unions combining together have very great political power. So the 'Triple Alliance' (railwaymen, other transport workers, and miners), might, given a rising cost of living, make more than fraught headlines. The government came on, as it were, heavy, by way of an imperious, offence-giving man, Sir Auckland Geddes, a professor of anatomy turned Conservative MP, who offered terms which in practice at some levels made actual reductions of more than a fifth. This was seen by many trade unionists as a government scheme to take on workers, beat them, and force down wages generally. When the railway strike came at the end of 26 September 1919, the government talked conspiracy and reacted as if it were one: troops called out and talk in *The Times* of 'a fight to the finish'. The unions replied very effectively with their own *Daily Herald* and big advertisements elsewhere. The government duly backed down.

There would be a coda to all this. An initial settlement in the railway dispute had been vague about the point at which output would be judged to warrant the new wage level. A date was set by the union on the coming of which, the increase was not paid. A second round over a pit strike, followed by resumption on the detail of the railway settlement, would be met by express legislation, the Emergency Powers Act, giving a government the right to invoke summary courts, something thinkable by excitable people at that point, but over the top in times not contemporaneous with a Russian revolution. As it was, the railwaymen got the 2s. a shift they had originally sought, and that crisis passed. The government had played an unnecessarily risky game against unions whose leaders outside the Clyde region thought essentially in terms of wages and conditions.

The losers were those in the unions who thought otherwise—in terms of a great spilling into the streets and the fearful possibilities beyond. Lloyd George in Labour matters, on which he had made a great reputation before the War, had got by rather well in the long term. In Ireland, facing armed revolt, he took the worst sort of murderous advice and, in effect, lost a small war which ended in disgust, a brutish course which Campbell-Bannerman would never have countenanced.

16 October 1919 The first debate of Michaelmas term.*

Motion That the Peace terms met with the approval of the House—carried 167:132.

House supports the domestic policy of the Coalition Government.[5]

Mr C. R. N. Routh (Ch.Ch.) *led off but did not quite keep up the high level of his beginning.*

Mr E. J. Lassen *maintained his last term's reputation as a clear and insistent speaker.*

Mr Hopkinson (Exeter) *was persuasive but unnecessarily quotational.*

Mr A. Gray-Jones (St John's) *spoke fluently, if rather monotonously. He scored a strong point against the agent provocateur.*

No vote given.

23 October 1919

House desires the immediate and actual establishment of a League of Nations.

Mr J. B. Nicholls *A League would be the best means of preventing the recrudescence of war.* His appeal reached great eloquence and was assisted by an excellent delivery.

Mr H. M. Andrews (New College) *I do not want a via media. Foreign Affairs would establish a vicious dualism with FOs and the League overlapping.*

---

* *Oxford Magazine*, reporting this debate, carries a routine lecture notice. It is 'to be given at All Souls by Spenser Wilkinson, Chichele Professor of Military History, on The Theory of War'.

Lord Robert Cecil (Univ. ex-President) (Visitor) *What we must do firstly is to organize public opinion against war. We must also show that the League of Nations will give time for deliberation on questions at issue before a declaration of hostilities. The Balance of Power is a Council of Despair; and the same nationalism would assist the League rather than selfishly oppose. The tradition of this country, which had always led the world on the path of justice, now has its noblest opportunity.* A magnificent speech which was enthusiastically received by a crowded house.

Motion carried 924:99.

---

6 November 1919

House considers Direct Action an unjustifiable attack on the rights of the community.

Mr J. W. Russell *Labour leaders would themselves be occupying the green benches were they to be present this evening. The tyranny of the proletariat is well illustrated by the Leninists. I cannot see any case against the present constitution. The government's policy in Russia demonstrates the fatal ignorance of the masses and the impotence of men faced by popular hysteria.*

Mr J. L. Hore-Belisha[6] *The mover has delivered a panegyric on the British constitution. I have the deepest admiration for this time-honoured institution; and my anger is directed against the forces which made it what it is. How are grievances to be redressed? Religion, the press, free institutions generally are the outcome of direct action. [Sensation. Cries of 'Question' from the cross-benches.] Out of forty million inhabitants, thirty seven million are workers. The strike weapon is not positively indecent; it is a universal, constitutional weapon placed in the hands of the 37 million by a Tory government.*

Where is the difference between a meeting of Lancashire magnates intriguing to raise the price of cotton wheels and an assembly of railwaymen endeavouring to heighten their own wages: the ceremonial dinner of the former and the strike of the latter? The price of labour should rise with the price of boots: the blame should be laid, if on anybody, at the door of the employers who decided that the price of boots should go up.

The Russian affairs are a betrayal of its election pledge by the government. The poster was intended to lure the unsuspecting recruit and an insult to intelligent people. No one but a gentleman could pick up the government's statement that 'We must redeem our pledge to Russia;' no one but a greengrocer that 'We must retain the fruits of victory.' The expedition is a foolish one; direct action is the deus ex machina which prevented it. I am voicing a widespread desire for revolution and direct action is a symptom of that, not a cause. [The speech, correlated with an allusion to the War which was not well received.]

Mr J. S. Collis (Balliol)[7] impugned the irrelevancy and insincerity of the last speaker *When an attempt is made by one section of the community to coerce the government, the result must be starvation and misery or broken promises. How can the men who set up the government and for whom it works, be justified in conspiring to thwart it? It was not voted for. The Railwaymen have been coerced. And in any case, the ignorance of Mr Hore-Belisha's 37 million as to production and the economic factors renders their opinions worthless. The heroism which animates the working man in time of war itself is eclipsed in peace by more self-centred considerations; the employee cannot comprehend the possibility of co-operation between himself and his employer. As well might Socrates work with Mr Charles Chaplin. Thus he does not understand the devastating effect of direct action, nor the criminality of paralysing vital industries. Direct action may only be described as 'blood and fire,'* with which observation, Mr Collis subsided.

Mr C. Sunthorne (Balliol) *Democracy is frustrated by the stubborn overlooking of the conventions of the constitution. Representative institutions have failed to bring this factor into play.*

Motion carried 318:117.

13 November 1919

House would welcome a return to power by the Liberal Party in preference to the coalition.

Mr T. B. Ashford (Ch.Ch.) *Perhaps the Liberals failed before the war, but the cause of that failure was the illiberal attitude of the rest of the world. Secession from the party is no symptom of weakness, but one of independence, of unwillingness to submit to the arbitrary authority of the PM.*[8] *As to the strike, I suspect that the government deliberately provoked it to demonstrate its own strength.*

Mr H. J. Hope (Ch.Ch.) *Party government is far from desirable. The PM is not an autocrat, but a zealous statesman too busy to become a parliamentary Aunt Sally. The Liberals led the country into war, unconscious, unprepared. Mr Asquith, attacking profiteers, suggested only the unconstitutional device of a capital levy and confiscation of property. With the war upon them, they had toyed with conscription, shrinking from the firm action demanded by circumstances. Ireland they had found a happy country; they left it a hotbed of discontent. The Liberal Party is already a thing of the past, the remotest of back numbers.*

Mr J. H. Patten (Oriel) *We shall beware of Mr Asquith and the Old Gang. Labour cannot rely on Liberal support for state socialism—or nationalisation.*

Mr Chevallier *Mr Lloyd George will return to the wing of his former chief in time.*

Mr C. A. Edinger (Balliol) *The Tories represent corruption. The Liberals stand for the League of Nations abroad and for talent at home. They can prove that they foresaw and forestalled the war, having established the first dreadnought, the OTC and the Territorials. The coalition had launched us into 23 petty wars and been hustled by the oppressors.*

Motion carried 189:169.

20 November

The House of Lords should be replaced by a non-hereditary chamber.

Mr C. Gallop (Balliol) *The Parliament Act 1911, though prompted by party strife, advanced from faction in its operation. The House of Lords is essentially Conservative. So under a Tory government, it is passive and superfluous and under a Liberal one, antagonistic and reactionary. Enlightened statesmen have long ago abandoned heredity as a criterion of administrative worth. The House of Lords is emblematic in the sons of peers, peculiarly in touch with officers of state through environment and education. It isn't even representative of the Old Nobility. So many peers are now created for services rendered.*

Mr G. Howard (Balliol) *The abolition of heredity would be nothing short of revolutionary. The House of Lords, free from party spirit, affords a relief for eminent patriots; introduce an elective element and the refuge will be gone. The hereditary principle has been the mainstay of imperialism. For the colonies look for the permanent and not the ephemeral.*

Mr C. T. Chevallier *The chances of a noble peer acquiring an intelligent grandson are 66:1 against.*

Mr V. A. L. Raeburn (Ch.Ch.) *If the Upper House is to be nominated, who will do the nominating?*

Motion carried by a majority of 39.

---

27 November 1919

House welcomes the abandonment of operations in Russia.

Mr J. Victor Evans (St John's) *This is to be supported, not out of sympathy for Bolshevism, but from common sense. I want to see a true peace following the prin-*

ciple of the League of Nations. The object of the Russian expedition was to smash Bolshevism (applause). And to discharge the debt of honour to General Kolchak.[9] In both objects it failed. That is a harbinger for the future. The Russian peasantry have found in Bolshevism a gleam of liberty never before perceived. Bolshevism can only be destroyed from within through intrinsic rottenness. It is useless to attack it with external violence. However I believe that a bleeding Russia and a fragile Europe may be restored by a peace radiant with the idealism of the League of Nations.

Mr G. H. Baxter (New College) *Why does Britain intervene in Russia? Partly for selfish reasons, but also because obligations have to be contracted and authority imposed on this chaotic farrago of parties and cabals. Debts of honour cannot be ignored mainly because their discharge is difficult.*

Mr A. M. Harris *Intervention is immoral. It is not justified on the merits the principles it supports—both Kolchak and Denikin have records of great discredit (Excitement)—nor by popular demand in Russia. Mr Lloyd George admits that the presence of the British expeditionary force is distasteful to the Russian peasantry as a whole. The Bolsheviks must be left to work out their own ruin—and pose as martyrs owing to the Atlantic blockade. The only need of Europe and Russia in particular, is for peace. Our intervention could not have a pacific effect.*

Mr E. Marjoribanks (Ch.Ch.)[10] *Bolshevism is non-representative, destructive of education, subversive of justice over property, anarchical in legislation, a check upon industry, a scandal in food-distribution and the epitome of arbitrary cruelty. The necessity for force inculcating the Bolshevik creed proves its unpopularity.* Here the speaker grew extremely excited, almost we had said, incoherent. *The Bolshevik movement is widespread; it is already rampant in India, might afflict Italy, menaces France—what of England? Every Britisher has a duty to realize that the Russian cause is our cause.*

Mr A. C. Graham *The original purpose of intervention was to thwart Germany; and until the War evicted the policy, it was not to be abandoned. The Intelligentsia can also claim to represent Russian thought; and they are anti-Bolshevik. We must remain alert to the Yellow Peril and not to stray into that as it talks reform.*

Mr M. I. Machin (Wadham) *I am not ready to condemn Bolshevism until I am in possession of the facts. As far as I can see, they mean well and are doing well [Sensation]. The Russian expedition is an involuntary band of Scarlet Pimpernels* More sensation, cries of 'Withdraw.'

Motion lost 101:176.

---

4 December 1919

House believes that the return to power of the Labour Party would be a national disaster.

Mr E. L. O. Sachs (Ch.Ch.) *The attractive exteriors of Mr Henderson*[11] *and Mr Clynes* (applause and laughter) *are being used to shield the extremist policy of the real leaders, Messrs Smillie,*[12] *and Tom Mann.*[13] *I object to class government. The Labour Party will have to rely on the Civil Service to make up their deficiencies or call in its intellectual Fabians like Mr H. G. Wells, to guide the destiny of the Board of Trade or Mr Bernard Shaw to control the Ministry of Health. The attempt to carry out the Labour Party programme will result in trade paralysis and finally chaos.*

Mr C. B. Ramage (Pembroke) *Having Labour in power will be the acme of representative government. Labour would remedy the ferocious treaty of peace, but would be too late to avert the resulting famine. The party has widened its ranks to include some of the most brilliant thinkers of the day and is the only party with an ideal. The claim that Labour is unfit to govern is caused by a superb egotism bordering on megalomania.* (laughter).

Mr K. M. Lindsay (Worcester) *The ossifying orthodoxy of the previous speaker is pathetic. No party is really fit to govern, but I object to a coalition.*

Mr Russell *A vote for Labour will be a vote for nationalisation. The prosperity of the country will vanish if Labour comes into power before it has persuaded businessmen to approve of their [sic] theories.*

Mr J. Beverley Nichols (Balliol)[14] *I am not a member of the Labour Party, but I am inclined to become one after the last speech. We are currently governed by an invertebrate monstrosity which introduced the Wages Bill during the pantomime season—and the attitude of the* Morning Post[15] *is fatal.*

Mr D. F. Brundit (Wadham) *It is impossible to lead an ethically sound life under existing economic conditions. Labour stands for doing that. It involves nationalisation which I believe in.*

Mr E. Beddington-Behrens[16] *I think that the experiment will be worth trying for the sake of improving the Labour Party.*

Mr S. Sidebotham (Ch.Ch.) *Labour will disappoint their support and lose the Empire through their ignorance of colonial and foreign policy.*

Motion carried 211:171.

---

5 February 1920

House believes that a levy on capital should be introduced forthwith.

Mr Nicholls—Librarian *There is nothing intrinsically comic about finance. Mr Austen Chamberlain realizes that he is in a financial morass and needing to take extraordinarily drastic measures. Eighty per cent of capital in the country can be subjected to some levy. Evasion there would be, as there is evasion of income tax returns.*

Mr A. J. Hopkinson (Exeter) *I know a demobilized officer who has saved £1 000. Are you going to put a levy on that? The answer to our problems is to work harder and produce more, not impose a revolutionary levy.*

Mr Chevallier *If members opposite don't like the name 'Capital levy,' let them call it by another name such as Capitalized Anticipation of Income Tax.*

Mr C. A. Petrie (Corpus)[17] *If the government is prepared to live on its capital, it sets a bad example to individuals to do the same.*

Mr D. M. Morrah (New College) had hardly spoken long enough to afford material for criticism. He is quite confident in manner.

Motion lost 163:193.

---⊗⊗⊗---

19 February 1920—At Cambridge

House would welcome the nationalisation of the mines.

Mr Victor Evans *The miners wish to exercise their functions as men, not mere cogs in a wheel. I speak as someone who has lived his whole life in a mining community.* People were overheard saying that Victor Evans was quite good.

Mr Sidebotham must avoid phrases of the 'Old bean' type—also 'I don't think it matters frightfully.'

Mr J. L. Rees (Ruskin College) *An earlier speaker said that miners struck during the war. The commission on Labour Unrest has exonerated them. The same miners volunteered to work seven days a week and had done so.*

Motion lost 83:176.

---⊗⊗⊗---

26 February 1920

House believes the Peace Treaty is an economic disaster for Europe.

Mr Nichols *Attacking the treaty is not a defence of Germany, but a recognition of its utter inexpediency. Germany's power to trade—at home and abroad is ruined—her ships, coal and iron ore. Austria is crippled too.*

Mr J. W. Russell *The Reparation Commission has sweeping powers on a unanimous vote to modify the treaty.*

Mr N. A. Beechman (Balliol) In the Spen Valley and elsewhere, Mr Beechman has learned the art of oratory. *The opener has explained the treaty, not condoned it. Our politicians have treated the peoples of Europe as keepers treat wild beasts, pampering some and starving others.*

Mr G. H. Baxter (New College) *The allies must be established before their enemies. If a man was wounded by the roadside, the finder would not hasten down the road because his assailant had met with an accident there.*

Mr Chevallier gave the House some impressions he had gathered during 31 months in the front-line trenches. This Member seems always to appeal to the heart rather than the head.

Motion carried 176:123.

⧔⧕

6 May 1920

House condemns the action of Convocation in abolishing compulsory Greek.

Mr Routh *I am a whole-hogger and I lament the deficiencies of Engineering and the like from an educational point of view. Convocation has done what may be irreparable harm—to the university, to Greek and to education. Classical education will suffer and the name of the university be tarnished.*

Mr P. T. Homen (Lincoln) *I am an American, but want to approach this from an English point of view. In fact, I feel that am present at the disinterring of the corpse of a deceased criminal against whom I am to give evidence. Greek no more deserves special treatment than science or modern languages. Its presence shuts the door against some of the best brains in England.*

Motion lost 165:189.

⧔⧕

3 June 1920

House approves extension of access to divorce.

Mr A. G. Willway (Oriel) skated on thin ice on matters theological.

Mr Chevallier made a logical case for divorce that marriage was simply a contract.

Mr G. K. Chesterton (Visitor)[18] His quips were innumerable, but his very earnest appeal to the sanctity of marriage vow made an impression.

Motion carried 340:271.

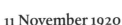

11 November 1920

House expresses confidence in the Indian policy of Mr Montague.

Mr Mahmoud (Non-Collegiate)[19] *I speak as an Imperialist, an idealist, but first and foremost, as an Indian. England deserves full credit for the work she has done in India. But India is a nation and Mr Montague's policy, though not perfect, is one step in the right direction.*

Mr P. C. Lyon M.A. (Oriel) *From my own experience in the Indian Civil Service, I can tell you that Mr Montague was not the originator of his own policy, also that Indian Civil Servants who know the facts, could not do other than support the motion. Indian nationality is a reality and the tendency toward self-government is not only inevitable but right and just.*

Motion carried 144:121.

18 November 1920

House would welcome the dissolution of the Coalition.

Mr W. S. Churchill (Visitor) *In Ireland one sees the moonlight and the footpad and gang of assassins, liars, blackguards and thieves. I am a Liberal supporting the enfranchisement of women, the abolition of conscription, the minimum wage, measures great in scope, most domestic in character more searching in intention than any other administration, Radical or Conservative during the last 100 years.*[20]

Motion lost 359:663.

———— ⟨∞⟩ ————

25 November 1920

House approves the Government's policy toward Russia.

Mr V. A. Cazalet (Ch.Ch.)[21] *That policy has of course been striving to cope with changing circumstances. The Government must steer a middle course between a war on Bolshevism involving us in large expenditure, and shaking hands with those who deserted us in the war and aimed at overthrowing our empire.*

Motion lost by 48 votes.

———— ⟨∞⟩ ————

20 January 1921

House calls on HMG to effect an immediate and drastic reduction in armaments to meet the urgent necessity for economy and to give a lead in disarmament.

Motion carried by casting vote.

———— ⟨∞⟩ ————

3 February 1921

That women be invited to a joint debate at the Union given the prominent and valuable part taken by women in public life.

Mr Charles L. Morgan (BNC)[22] *We are standing at the beginning of an new era. I want Oxford to set an example of courage and show imagination. For as things are, 'The rivers of imagination are choked with the wrecks of old men's illusions.'*

Mr L. E. Wharton For pointed humour and what he calls the 'sentimental point of view,' Mr L. E. Wharton has no equal in the Union.

Mr Routh *I go so far as to doubt the advisability of having ladies in the gallery. As for them becoming members of the Society, I am alarmed.*

Motion lost 123: 136 amongst the cheers of the winning side.

———∞———

24 February 1921

House believes the government failed to secure a peace worth the sacrifice or adequate to the purposes of the war.

Mr H. M. Andrews (New College) *The Prime Minister and his government have imposed upon the enemy, terms of peace grossly inconsistent with the solemn undertakings given at the time of the armistice* ... He is still far too transcendental to grip a large audience, but this was the most thoughtful speech of the evening.

Once again loud cheers greeted Mr Asquith as he rose to join in the debate.

Mr Asquith Speaking in those somewhat polished sentences for which he is so famous, he began in a reminiscent vein explaining what should have been recognized at the outset as the essence of a sound Peace and how these principles had been ignored.

Motion carried 476:343.

12 May 1921

House considers the influence of the modern press is excessive and pernicious.

Mr Victor Evans *The press is guilty of both suppression and falsification of truth. Worse, it gives more space to the sordid than to the beautiful and makes sensation the master of us all.*

Mr R. G. S. Bankes (Magd.) *The influence of the press is not pernicious. One lie contradicts another and truth slips out between them. The harm lies not in publicity, but the ignorance of the reader.*

Mr W. A. L. Raeburn *I can see the case for establishing reform of the press along state socialist lines.*

Mr D. M. Morrah dislikes democracy very well.

Mr E. J. Strachey[23] *It is public demand which regulates type of news which editors, not the editors themselves, govern public taste.*

Motion carried 98:72.

26 May 1921

House condemns the Coercion policy* as repugnant to the first principles of democracy.

---

* In Ireland—where else?

J. B. Herbert *There has been a chance to conciliate Ireland; and in 1919, the government threw it away. The present regime in Ireland is a military domination of one nation by another, a gross tyranny against which the Irish nation is fighting by any methods however discreditable.*

Mr E. J. Marjoribanks *There have been many brutal crimes committed by the Irish in the name of freedom and those criticising Government policy have no satisfactory solution themselves.*

Mr J. S. Collis *The spirit of Ireland is not something which the soul of a manufacturing country like England can recognise. I would urge the youth of England to meet the spirit of liberty and poetry which is at the heart of Sinn Fein, by a policy of faith and reconciliation. It is not then surprising that England should meet it with Sir Hamer Greenwood,*[24] *with Prussianism and by the casting out of Beelzebub by Beelzebub. But for all that, England is wrong.* Mr Collis sat down to loud applause.

Effectively he was sent to meet IRA brutalities with British brutalities, which he did. Committed by the Black and Tans, irregular troops, they were irregular brutalities, a distance but nothing like an adequate one, from total Ministerial culpability. The firing at will into the crowd at that football match, offsetting an IRA group-killing, hours before, is regularly quoted as the low point, as well it might be. The use of retaliatory killing—a return-of-service criminality, sickened public, parliament and the will to go on. The 1922 Treaty and virtual independence for 26 counties followed. Collis's nonsense about the Spirit of Ireland notwithstanding, his conclusion was true. England *was* wrong—had been, certainly since 1886.

Mr W. M. McGovern (Ch.Ch.) *I applaud the idealism for which many of my countrymen have died. However because of the cowardly methods by which they fought, any coercion by the government, even the most brutal, is amply justified. By terror, Ireland must be freed of the gang of terrorists or the Empire must go down in ruin. He* is evidently a present day follower of Caesar and admiring blood and iron government.

Rt. Hon. Sir John Simon (Visitor)[25] *The terror is driving the youth of Ireland into the Republican Army: that is not quelling Irish disorder but rather increasing it. There are no prisoners being taken. Can this possibly be justified?*

No vote recorded.

10

The Consequences of the Peace

10 November 1921—15 June 1922

Unemployment and the War/the old party division/Curse of Victorianism/Ulster should join Irish state?/Franco-German alliance/Indian disorder/Principles of Conservatism/Russo-German agreement/Deploring democracy/US foreign policy/Irish Republic!

One assured concern by this time was 'The Peace', by which was meant the Treaty of Versailles, an accomplished but destructive fact. Outside of France, and sometimes in that country itself, there is very little dispute that the Peace which had been imposed was of the kind which starts wars.

The recovery of Alsace Lorraine, unwisely taken from France by Prussia after the 1870 war, was a perfectly inevitable recoup, though the resentment created throughout France for two generations since Bismarck's initial annexation carried its own warning. The loss in the East of Danzig, Memel, and a section of Posen and, in the west, of the Saar coalfield were moves certain to arouse German nationalism and humiliate moderate German politicians trying to live with treaty terms. The assured instability of a defeated and now humiliated country sowed a poison which should have been obvious.

Insistence on supreme German war guilt, treated as effectively sole responsibility, is not now the view of modern, long researched historical studies culminating in *The Sleepwalkers*, which argues a ring of contesting national anxieties primed for pre-emption. It was also expressed in money terms by a bill for reparations which placed an impossible burden on the German nation and citizen. It had been fixed in April 1921 by an international commission at £6,600 million and the payment schedule of £100 million annually, plus just over a quarter (26 per cent) of the value of German exports. If it were not agreed in six days, France undertook to invade the Ruhr. Payment was maintained until December 1921 when unsurprisingly, a beaten-down Germany defaulted.

At this time, the Prime Minister of France was Aristide Briand, a humane and rational man who could see the limits of rage and revenge in diplomacy. One very different British overview had been summed up by Eric Geddes's left-wing cartoon notion of a grinding British businessman, who advised that 'I have personally no doubt that we will get everything out of her (Germany) that you can squeeze out of a lemon and a bit more.'[1] Lloyd George, Prime Minister of a coalition since December 1916, short-term enough in the early days, to have gone along with all this, was discerning enough to know what the inexorable line would do. He and Briand, meeting at Cannes, were ready to work both for Anglo-French entente and a wiser, more conciliatory approach to Germany.

It can happen that a man with a reputation for short cuts and stunts can be engaged on a piece of enlightened, thought-out policy when the first reputation comes up and hits him. The conferences of those days were marked by side-meetings of greater importance. Representatives of Germany and Russia would slip away from the big meeting at Genoa 10 April–19 May 1922 and go off to Rapallo for a trade and general accommodation deal, outraging everyone still in school at Genoa. So it might have been with the round of golf Lloyd George organized for Briand and a prospective ally, Ivanoe Bonomi, pre-Mussolini Prime Minister of Italy, to create wider trust and good will.

The story got out. Offence was taken in France and vented upon a Briand clearly about to be seduced into betraying his country. He was out of office two days later, 11 January 1922. Hoping to handle the dire consequences of a Germany unable to pay, Lloyd George would find this assuredly conciliatory French statesman suddenly replaced by the narrow-visioned, immobile, and literalist Raymond Poincaré, demanding the last centime and standing ready to extract it by military action and territorial occupation, ultimately of the Rhineland, with what consequences the France of 1940 would discover.

Immediately, Germany would haltingly start paying, then pay less and less. Poincaré had created a policy which inflicted immediate and unknowable future injury, but whose stipulated terms would not be met, terms which were destined to end a year on with French troops in Germany and all the remembered injury that the future would inherit. This period is littered with place names made famous by meetings and speeches. Bar-le-Duc, a little town best known for its currant jelly, but significantly situated in Lorraine (Bismarck had annexed it in 1871), achieved grim eminence from the speech Poincaré made there. It was in the sullen spirit of Eric Geddes, demanding exaction from Germany of the full terms of Versailles. Lloyd George twice attempted talking to the new Premier, got nowhere, and would see the ditch deepened when Poincaré threatened unilateral French enforcement.

Long term, the new approach encouraged British informal disengagement, a writing-off of the French as impossible and providing, a dozen or so years later, a false validation for the early days of appeasement. Genoa, of which so much had been expected, not least with Russia present, had, as its only clear outcome, the Russo-German deal quoted above. The spirit of goodwill among nations, sincerely enough hoped for and proclaimed, had evaporated, leaving the narrowest of self-interested 'Home's best' populism dominant. To paraphrase an old American theatre term, the question had become 'Will it play in Bar-le-Duc?' Whatever blame for the Second World War may easily go to the passive role in the mid-1930s of Stanley Baldwin and Neville Chamberlain, that war owed as much or more to the swaggering virulence of men proclaiming a mined and toxic peace a decade and more earlier.

There was though, an immediate foreign policy issue with political consequences. One of the causes of the first war had been its immediate predecessors, those lesser Balkan wars in which the Balkan states, Serbia,

Bulgaria, and Greece in quick succession defeated and drove back Turkey, then fought each other for the spoils. It happened that with the Great War over, the new, modernizing regime in Turkey fought and won a war begun by the deluded (German) King Constantine of Greece. At the hands of the modern Turk, Mustapha Kemal, he lost. Kemal pushed on towards Chanak, a town whose name would reverberate beyond the straits.

Those straits were still obsessional to the Imperial streak of the British as a waterway which must always be kept from Russian control, hence endless alliances complained about in radical British newspapers, with old style sultans given to reliable atrocities. Lloyd George sought Dominion support, normally so reliably forthcoming—and except from kindly New Zealand, didn't get it. The others felt themselves taken for granted; and the new term, Dominion, replacing the below-stairs colony, they saw his request as devaluing that status and declined. This was the Chanak episode which would a few months later be quoted as the last straw of Lloyd George's way of governing.

In rough sync with a sterile record in foreign policy, good purposes frustrated by allies, no longer accurately allies, would come brutal depression in the economy and a perfectly understandable revolt among workers and their Unions. Across 1921–2 overseas trade had crashed with exports and imports both down by nearly half (47.9 per cent and 43.7 per cent).[2] The monthly pig-iron statistics (later so sweetly familiar in Soviet propaganda) fell and fell again with production in stumbling stride with steel. Wage rates overall fell from an index rating peak of 260 in 1920 to 170 by 1922. These were falls from wartime highs. But with dividends also falling, there was little sign of coming recovery. And there was fearful unemployment, with certain towns in the historically industrialized north and Wales hitting new grim lows: among the most stricken being Barrow with 49 per cent followed by Hartlepool 60 per cent, Brynmawr 47 per cent, and Handsworth (Birmingham) 44 per cent.

There followed the extreme poverty such figures bring, accompanied by levels of relief, some of it produced by recent legislation like the Unemployed Workers Relief Act of 1921, the passing of whose harsh terms had made Labour MPs walk out of the Chamber. Beyond such dab-on measures lay the old Poor Law which some working-class boroughs interpreted with improvisatory generosity as when George Lansbury and fellow councillors at Poplar broke the legal limits for borrowing and were jailed for it—so embarrassing an act as to prompt legislation to spread the costs over London.

The circumstances of victory, followed by slump, were quite bad enough without the re-entry, like a pantomime Demon King, of Sir Eric Geddes, bidden to cut expenditure which—in respect of Army, Navy, Airforce, Education, Public Health (including tuberculosis care and child welfare), also war pensions, he did. A proposal from Sir Eric to abolish the recently created Labour Exchanges, helping men into work at this moment of rocketing unemployment, was declined. The 'Geddes Axe', as it was quite reasonably called, was a programme of cool immiseration. All this was pre-Keynes, that is to say pre-Demand theory, and calculated simply to limit expenditure with whatever crashing effect—and in so doing, to reduce demand, production, and employment.

Neither had any favours been done during the war by a return to another branch of Cro-Magnon Conservative thinking—not Imperial Protection, just Protection: tariffs—protecting British jobs by keeping out foreign goods to be seen as hostile, a policy supplemented by one-third charges on a variety of luxury articles—like bicycles. Now, in 1921, came the Safeguarding of Industries Act, covering 6,500 articles. The sale of foreign articles at lower prices would be termed 'dumping' as if those goods were inferior stuff breaking a binding norm of quality. This was 1922 and the thinking behind it, acquiesced in by the modern man and interim thinker Lloyd George, shrugged off Cobden and Bright, Adam Smith and Robert Peel. It was a return to the thinking of the third Marquess of Salisbury, for whom Free Trade was a defilement.

A decade later, the Lloyd George who, as Prime Minister, accommo-dated all this economic recidivism, would campaign in detail and with fer-vour for a full Keynesian programme. As it was, he sat in a Cabinet where the sort of clever/adaptable Conservative he could count on, someone like F. E. Smith/Lord Birkenhead, was nearly as distrusted by regulation Tories as Lloyd George himself. The move to be rid of him was not reached just at this juncture, but the forces of inertia to which he was currently deferring, with wrong policies, were not appeased.

⁃⊶⊷⁃

10 November 1921

House thinks that the present unemployment is an unavoidable result of the Great War.

Mr J. G. Morgan (St John's) *Look at what happened in a very similar way after the Napoleonic wars when, as now, trade depression and adverse exchanges did the damage, but did it from outside. Then, as now, there was nothing you could do about them.*

Mr M. J. MacDonald (Queen's)[3] *The peace is very much to blame. It didn't recognise that trade is international. It imposed a vast indemnity upon Germany which is the chief cause of unemployment. On top of which, we refuse to trade with Russia.* An able speech well delivered, but lacking colour. He has in this respect much to learn from his father.

Mr W. M. McGovern (Ch.Ch.) *We lack the capital and we need a place where we can sell our goods—those are the causes of unemployment and war and the labour disputes aggravate them. The ship of state has returned from the wars very much mangled.*

Mr T. W. Harris (Balliol) was vivacious, at times brilliant but, at other times, a little acrid. *We have divided the world into black and white and lost a great deal of trade. We need rigid controls and the sort of effort and sacrifice we put into the war.*

Lieut. Col. Worrall DSO, MC (Keble) strongly deprecated 'the cheap references' to the Peace Treaty. *It was the only possible end to the war. From long experience as a regular soldier, I also object to the association of militarism and the British Army.*

Mr R. H. Bernays (Worcester) *The real source of all these afflictions is the 1918 election. The only involvement into economics which the politicians made was reparation.*

Mr MacKeown (Worcester) *What really needs to be done and something which would have the best effect, is cancellation of inter-allied war debts.*

Mr Marjoribanks (Secretary) and Mr Collis (Treasurer) were fit representatives, the former boldly defending Mr Lloyd George and the latter heroically upholding President Wilson.

Motion carried 135:93.

24 November 1921

House prefers the old division between the parties to the new split between the Coalition and Labour.

Mr Victor Evans *Fear and social status are not sufficient bases for a party. Temperament is the vital thing. It naturally separates Conservatives and Progressives.*

Mr J. S. Collis *Communism is like Conservatism to me, things I can sympathise with, but never agree to. As to the parties, they have thinkers behind them and for my part, the guide is not Mill but Tawney.*[4]

Mr R. M. Carson *Only an Englishman can tell you the difference between a Liberal and a Conservative. In fact, I would regard the ability to do just that as the definition of an Englishman. But domestic issues are what now dominate everything; and on that, Liberals and Conservatives find themselves united—against Labour. It is the Labour Party which is making democracy effective.*

Mr J. L. Stocks (Fellow of St John's) *Party is a device for obtaining political consistency, and a coalition is created to make it possible. The Labour Party has emerged because it is nearer to life and facts. Two things need to be done, the realisation of democracy and the re-organisation of industry. The Labour Party is there to see that they are done.*

Rejected by small majority.

---

1 December 1921

House regards Victorianism as the curse of the age.

Mr Gerald Gardiner[5] *Today we are reacting against repression, a good thing to do. Each man does what is right in his own eyes.*

Mr W. Gaunt (Worcester) *The present age is full of idleness, cynicism, immorality and irreligion. Sensationalism dominates the modern press and hysterical scurrility has replaced the desire for truth. Cynicism is a barren and withering thing and it epitomises the age.*

Mr C. H. O. Scaife (St John's) *Consider antitheses: Faith, love and hope against riches and dominion. We should break the Victorian mould of stability and security and give the new age a chance.*

Mr R. de C. Matthews (New College) *The new age will involve not a condemning, but an accepting of life. Its god will be Dionysius and its prophet Blake.*

Mr A. M. Clark (Oriel) *The Georgians created an age of pigmies and a cloud of hornets. The only fruit are Dead Sea apples and sour grapes.*

Motion lost 78: 114.

---

26 January 1922

House thinks it essential to the Security of the Empire that Ulster immediately takes her place under the provisional government in Ireland.

Mr Collis *We have a new era in Ireland. The days of Dublin Castle are gone forever.*

Mr Marjoribanks *I do not believe that Ulster can cohere in independent Ireland. She played a magnificent part during the Great War and by accepting the Home Rule Acts, has assured peace. But the time isn't right for North and South to come together.*

Mr H. A. Newnham (Balliol) *Religious differences have ceased to be the main cause of dissension. Business and finance are the question. The hand of the South is outstretched, and Ulster should take it.*

Mr J. P. O'Reilley *Partition means separation and separation is indefensible.*

Mr J. D. E. Firth (Ch.Ch.) *Ulster can only come in as a minority. That guarantees a struggle and one which would demonstrate that Ulster is much better apart.*

Motion carried 128:100.

---

9 February 1922

House believes that the future of Europe depends upon an alliance between France and Great Britain.

Mr Heathcote Williams (BNC) *The future of Europe must be the peace of Europe. And that requires us to have some regard for the French view of reparations. Seeking equity is not enough. It should be done. An alliance with France will help her to a more comprehensive and international outlook.*

Mr Morgan *France doesn't behave altogether well. At Washington she made excessive demands, amounting very much to a threat. France is as militaristic now as she was in 1870. An alliance means a balance of power; and like last time, that will mean war.*

Mr S. Tetley (Keble) *The trouble with France is that she will have the Treaty of Versailles and nothing but the Treaty. Behind the Treaty lies international capitalism. The present French attitude to Germany is pernicious.*

The Hon. Henry Lygon (ex-President Magd.) *France is not a menace and England is in no position to moralise against her.*

Mr Cazalet *France is the only country which is dangerously armed. The demand for submarines speaks her spirit.*

Mr J. R. Bolton (Non-Coll.) *We would do best to concentrate upon the value and mission of the Empire. It is a better thing to lead than any alliance.*

Mr D. D. A. Lockhart (Trinity) *What France wants is her own peace, not Europe's.*

R. H. Bernays (Worcester) *I fear a great danger in the East. There is a dangerous awakening of Islam. England and France are the hope of civilisation.*

Mr C. B. Farrar (St John's) *France is disillusioned. She has been deceived in every way. England has done well out of the war and France knows it.*

Motion lost 90:129.

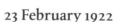

23 February 1922

House believes that the present disorders in India are due to the policy of HMG.

Mr Wedderburn *The government supported Mr Ghandi with the result that the whole authority of the Indian civil Service has been destroyed and all British authority shaken.*

Mr S. W. R. D. Bandaranaika (Ch.Ch.)[6] held the house with delightful fluency and a big capacity for debate. *Even now, vacillation of policy has destroyed India's faith in British Justice. Ireland responded by rebellion. India has been more moderate. She has adopted non-co-operation as a means of attaining the freedom within the Empire to which she aspires.*

Mr M. C. Hollis (Balliol)[7] *The prime reason for unrest in India is the 'Morning Post'[8] and the Tory Die-hards.*

Mr Gwynne (Visitor)[9] *It will be generations before India deserves self-government. England has done more for India in the last hundred years than India had over a thousand. Mr Ghandi is largely culpable. He is free, his duped followers are punished. Law and order must be maintained and the Secretary of State[10] must go.*

Mr Marjoribanks *I want the house to appreciate the point of view of a 'Die-hard'. It means great belief in principles. India has a debt of gratitude to England.*

Mr Carson *We have made a wilderness and called it peace.*

Mr Heathcote Williams *I am proud of empire, but prouder of civilisation.*

Mr M. C. Chogla (Lincoln) *Law to the movers of this motion means martial law.*

Motion lost 142:151. A great debate, remarkable in every way.

---

9 March 1922

House believes that in the present state of affairs the principles of Conservatism are of vital importance.

Mr Marjoribanks (Librarian) *Conservatism wishes to preserve the Empire because upon that, depend the unity and solidarity of the English people. The days of the Coalition are over. It has not the respect, honour and the hope of friends which usually accompany old age. We must revert to the principles which made England great. Conservatism means stability and immobility. It pays more attention to form than to life. A Conservative is a man who worships the bones of a dead radical. Agitation is not an evil thing. It is the forerunner of all reform.*

Mr Ramage *There is a narrow Conservatism as there is a narrow radicalism. The Conservative Part does not stand for such narrowness. It seeks to change gradually our ancient institutions and preserve the flexibility of our constitution.*

The Earl of Middleton[11] *Heredity and tradition go a very long way in public life. Free Trade cannot be maintained in 1922 as in 1846. The power of trade unionism is the greatest tyranny in this country. Meanwhile Liberals shrink from telling home truths to Labour. The coalition has been weak in dealing with Ireland and Egypt.*

Motion lost 170:273.

<hr />

4 May 1922

House believes that the Russo-German treaty[12] is a menace to the peace of Europe.

Mr Morgan *The vice of the treaty is its singular untimeliness; it comes just as Genoa promises a pooling of European interests. It will give France an excuse for breaking the peace of Europe.*

Mr Gardiner *All I see in this treaty is an economic agreement whereby two bankrupt countries agree not to bankrupt each other further. It does not infringe the Treaty of Versailles. France would have found somewhere else the excuse for taking the measures they wish to take.*

Mr Cazalet *France distrusts England because of the shifting policy of our coalition and has declared that Russia is as despotically ruled and as militaristic as ever.*

Mr Matthews *The treaty is merely a commercial document. The real anger lies in the cultivation of a* revanche *spirit; the old saying* daemon est deus inversus *applies to the German also.*

Mr Scaife *This treaty is a rapprochement of two powers toward an event which France has long feared.*

Mr Bandaranaike *To my mind, the spirit of France is opposed to the welfare of Europe.*

Motion lost 88:103.

——— ∞∞ ———

1 June 1922

House deplores the tendencies of modern democracy.

Mr R. Pares (Balliol)[13] making his first appearance *Democracy is a thing in which I believe, but what we actually have today is a parody of it, something deflected by capitalism into ways of impotence and injustice. At present, the common interest of bread-winners is a better bond than the political interest of members of a special kind of state. Democracy at present, produces an over-educated upper-class like most of this House, whose intelligence divorces them from reality.*

Mr C. H. O. Scaife (St John's)[14] *Democracy is the spirit which went into war. Foreign democracies, though not in the proposition, are involved in that spirit. Democracy justifies one's faith in human nature as people learn to express themselves through concrete measures. Democracy lets the proper man rise from any walk of life.*

Mr M. Lipton (Merton) *Democracy is an assertion of class-consciousness based on an erroneous notion of equality. The people are put at the mercy of demagogues. Witness Mr Bottomley.*[15] *It has not solved a single problem and has not advanced over two centuries.*

Earl of Longford (Ch.Ch.)[16] *Ireland suffers from an entire absence of democracy and lots of demagoguery. Aristocracy is a dead principle.*

Mr A. M. Clark *We are all living in decrepitude and that is our order. Under our sort of government the fool and the malcontent are allowed to prey on the earnest and the hard-working. Democracy is a well- meaning cannibalism, a benevolent fratricide, a government of fools by fools for the benefit of the knaves.*

Motion carried 62:60.

⦿⦿⦿

8 June

House thinks the present conduct of foreign policy of the United States is not in accord with her position as a World Power.

Mr Marjoribanks (Ch.Ch.) *The Monroe Doctrine is an outworn principle. The general denial of credit is paralyzing Europe and doing real harm to American business. The current presidency* thinks nothing of universal isola-tion. Yet President Wilson's universal brotherhood of nations is the only notion to fit the aspirations of the time. Isolationism is simply absurd. It would logically*

---

* Harding's—not the best. Rather over-mocked Republican who kept USA out of a League of Nations, inoperable then with or without the USA, signed separate treaties with First War adversaries, and showed decent purpose toward blacks, but tolerated the corruption of a lethal circle of acquaintance.

involve pinning to the Statue of Liberty a familiar message, 'Trespassers will be prosecuted.' America does not seem to be properly grateful for having been discovered.

Mr James M. Beck US Solicitor General[17] *In the first place, the so-called US doctrine of isolation never existed. George Washington wanted to keep out of ordinary European disputes, leaving emergencies for separate decision. This has proved wise. Because of the mixed blood of her population, America would find that any steady intermeddling in European matters would produce domestic discord so great as to destroy the unity of the Republic. On the League of Nations itself, the council gives a perpetual authority to five nations, a voting trust in the bankruptcy of civilisation.*

Mr D. M. Fyfe (Balliol) *The plain and simple difference over policy toward Russia is that America is self-supporting and England is dependent upon foreign trade.*

Viscount Birkenhead[18] *As an Englishman, I do not very much mind what another country does. America must judge her own foreign policy. The point of the motion seems to be that when one is well-off, one doesn't care for co-operation and that when one is badly off, one does care. The ever present tendency to interfere must be subordinated to the healthy spirit of self-reliance.*

Motion lost 179:187.

———— ⊶✖⊷ ————

15 June 1922

House should not accept an Irish Republic involving severance from the Empire.

Mr R. J. G. Boothby (Magd.)[19] *If the Irish really wanted separation, De Valera[20] would not have used methods of terrorism. He has reminded us that force is the true and only sanction of law. The peace of the world depends upon the Empire because the*

Empire alone can impose peace. Things like Amritsar and Moplah are not to be tolerated,[21] *but brute force without sympathy has not been a tradition of British imperialism. Of course, self-government must be offered to Ireland, but Irish autonomy must not be carried so far as to make the military position of England intolerable, and to set a precedent of exit from Empire whose noblest task is just beginning.*

Mr A. C. Collingridge (BNC) *This motion is akin to the Prime Minister saying 'I notice there is an adverse vote; I cannot accept it.' The British people simply must accept the deliberate sentiment of the Irish... the alternative of coercion is simply is unthinkable.*

Mr J. W. Parkes *I would not urge the motion if I thought the Irish really wanted a republic. But I am not convinced of that. An Irish republic would be the gravest disaster for Ireland... and exploitation by Germany would inevitably follow. In conceding Dominion status to Ireland, public opinion has gone as far as it will go.*

Mr Scaife *The common good is now the motive of Imperial domination. England's right to force Ireland is involved in the fact that we cannot divorce the interests of the two countries.*

Mr D. C. Thompson *That speech was the reductio ad imperium. So many Irishmen would rather be dead Irishmen than living members of the Empire: so Great Britain had best accept her answer now.*

Mr R. de C. Matthews (Ch.Ch.) *If a country wishes to do what isn't good for it, it should be free to do the thing because it wishes to.*

Lord Longford *'No man has a right to put a boundary to the march of a nation.'*

Mr J. P. O'Reilley opening in the Irish language *The Irish people recognise that the Free State should be accepted for the present, but the republic offers no real dangers to Britain.*

Motion lost 64:74.

11

A Rather Circumspect New World

26 October 1922–3 December 1925

Party lines again/British Sovereignty in India/A Tory Government?/Prohibition/ French errors/International friendship/population fears—eugenics?/German defeat regretted/Mussolini/Baldwin/Labour government/Rhineland separatism/Liberal retreat/Civilisation/Russian and French??/Public schools/Doubtful reputation/ Soviet treaty/'Socialist threat'/PR/Cinema—a degradation/1924 election-result/ Geneva/easier divorce/Capital punishment/Oxford has no purpose/contributory insurance/Recognising Soviet Russia/Politics as a career/LG's Land policy/ Representative democracy a failure/Compulsory vaccination/No future for Indo-European race/Cruisers.

The Conservative Parliamentary Party of today, meeting off-stage, calls itself the 1922 Committee, and does so because a meeting was called in October 1922 to ask for a vote of confidence in the Coalition government ruling since 1916. It was provoked by the risks of a conflict with Turkey, that Chanak Affair, from which, given Lloyd George's high stakes negotiation style, actual war was feared. There was, too, underlying dislike of the Prime Minister from Tory die-hards, hating a Liberal, and a Welsh Liberal at that, and from others, resenting his distinctly personal rule, also a specific and immediate anxiety about Lloyd George calling and winning a snap election.

It was a speech by Stanley Baldwin, no die-hard, only in the Cabinet since 1921 and in opposition to the party leader, Austen Chamberlain, which upset expectations. Denouncing Lloyd George, master of the Coalition, as 'a dynamic force; and a dynamic force is a terrible thing', Baldwin swung the meeting. Lloyd George's close Coalition followers among the Tories—most of their ablest men—lost that vote and the Conservative Party left the Coalition. Stanley Baldwin himself, flat cocktail of shrewdness and inertia, would soon be elected at the head of the Conservative Party (and most governments) until 1937.

The immediate succession to Party leadership and Downing Street was Andrew Bonar Law. The ferocious Canadian Ulsterman who had talked so much fire and catastrophe during the pre-war Irish crisis was calmer. He was now a cancer case, undiagnosed but with months to live. However as leader of his party, he would be invited to form a Conservative government, one from which much of the Tory talent of the Coalition, Balfour, Lord Birkenhead (F. E. Smith), Robert Horne, and Worthington-Evans excluded themselves.

It was a government for all that; and Stanley Baldwin, lifted by his leadership of the Lloyd George-destroying coup and with bigger Conservative names missing, became Chancellor. Curzon remained, grandee and Foreign Secretary, in deluded expectation of the Premiership. King George, very properly, asked Balfour, last leader of a plain Conservative government, for advice, took it, and sent for Baldwin, highest placed Minister in the Commons. It hadn't been calculated, but it had happened. A new precedent would also be established—peers might not in practice become Prime Ministers, a rule which in 1940 would helpfully exclude Lord Halifax.

Baldwin's particular quality was to be Lloyd George's opposite, comfortable, non-dynamic, non-adventurist, a sentimental but sincere ruralist, always looking back and talking about his beautiful home town of Bewdley on the Worcestershire/Shropshire borders. He was not hostile to foreign countries in the old bristling Tory/Imperialist way, but, apart from long holidays in France (Aix-en-Provence), oddly indifferent to them. Still, with him setting the tone, the snarling, arrogant style of the Tories retreated, if readily on hand in other men. He liked, and was liked by, Labour members. Conservative rather than Tory, he was, in the way of a certain sort of Englishness, inactive, sceptical of initiatives making any difference, but not above deft slips into opportunism.

His dislike of Lloyd George, something which had prompted the move against him, was deep and sincere enough. 'The Man Who Won the War' took corners fast, kept brilliant company, yet had the quality of a word not then in use, a 'chancer'. while also being, by way of another tiring neologism, 'pro-active'. Baldwin disliked them both—deviousness and dynamism. It was not merely as neighbour that he returned to the poems of A. E. Housman who had summed up his world view in the lines: 'The troubles of our proud and angry dust | Are from eternity and shall not fail.' Whatever the cosmic truth of that, at the low, useful level of party politics, Baldwin would avoid troubles better than most men, though neither immediately nor ultimately. He was working in a three-party parliament, with the Labour Party a clearly rising force, but not one currently threatening the Tories.

An election looked a reasonable and hopeful step. Baldwin called it, and in a shrewdly humble opening speech, suggested partial return to Protection, not a good idea, but in a country becoming worryingly less competitive, with unemployment standing at 1,350,000, promising politics. A tempting response suggested this regression as an unacknowledged option. Protection, the restriction of trade by surcharging imported foreign goods and taking a chance on retaliation, was in the blood of a whole line of Conservatives, a sort of recidivism. It tied in with gentry revulsion at low, unlanded commerce's preference, Free Trade. Lord Salisbury had looked back in the 1880s to Peel's rational judgement of 1846 as plain treason. Chamberlain's campaign for imperial tariffs had been embraced as a cause by so many Tories precisely because they were a form of Protection.

For so long as the economy had flourished, sold abroad, and grown, Free Trade had been an unavoidable and serviceable treason. But British trade figures had been declining for some time. Protection, with its invitation of reprisal, was no answer, but it was an 'auld sang', in which a powerful fraction of Baldwin's party could join like so many Burns nighters. A reluctant King was persuaded to grant a dissolution; and with Chamberlain's son Austen at the campaign front, the imposition of tariffs to protect jobs, profits, and statistics was proclaimed. All that remained was a triumph in the election of 6 December 1923—one which signally failed to materialize. The Tories at 258, had lost 88 seats; there were 158 Liberals, whilst Labour, under Ramsay MacDonald, had 191.

In popular terms, the Conservatives led with 5.3 million votes and 258 seats (88 down). Labour leapt from 142 to 192 on the back of a popular increase of only 100,000 votes. The Liberals had 158 seats. What was clear though was the absolute rejection of Protection. This cheered Asquith, whose faction of Liberalism had done significantly better than Lloyd George's. Asquith disliked Protection far more than he ever would Labour. A Labour coalition with the Asquithians could have made a secure progressive government, but only at the expense of Labour being, as it needed to be, a party with a clear identity.

A Labour government with non-playing Liberal support, the next best thing, was, despite an outburst of *Daily Mail*-type hysteria, a rational choice. Ramsay MacDonald, farm worker turned Board school teacher— also a pacifist who had opposed First War service as a conscientious objector—would be Prime Minister. Philip Snowden, excise clerk crippled in a cycling accident and as ardent a Free Trader as Cobden, was to be Chancellor. Johnny Clynes, the Oldham textile hand and at 10, so much child labour in a mill, would be Leader of the House with the title of Lord Privy Seal, all amid a set of men come from skilled labour or clerking. They would combine with an admixture of lawyers, academics, and other middle-class Socialists and the former star of the ready-for-war Liberal League who had tried to block Campbell-Bannerman's Premiership, R. B. Haldane, who emerged as Lord Chancellor.

The government would last for eight months, entering a world of formal court dress and general flummery which George V, with great good sense, waved away, as he showed his new Ministers open and friendly treatment. The new Ministers were, though, horribly preoccupied with looking like a government, no one more so than MacDonald, though he knew well enough how to look like a Prime Minister. As his own Foreign Minister, he set himself to get relations with France down from the just-below-ceiling level at which we and they had been screaming at each other. Raymond Poincaré, demander of impossible reparation who had since invaded the Ruhr, had been injured by a falling franc, and went within a month. Édouard Herriot, perpetual Mayor of Lyon, broad-brush and decent-purposed social reformer, a sort of better-equipped, more confident version of MacDonald, came in.

The two men hit it off. Both lit upon the just published Dawes Plan which put German reparation onto a manageable basis with a fixed reparation schedule in place of the territorial assaults of Poincaré.[1] It sought, in the all-round interest of peaceful relations and reducing hardship, to temper the terms of German repayment. Both got and deserved credit for a London conference over July/August 1924 to which Gustav Streseman, one of the (very) good Germans who died before 1933, came and contributed. The withdrawal of France from the Ruhr made that conference something like a triumph.

Labour was naturally at home with the League of Nations, high purposed, but dependent on a wider and deeper measure of all round trust than generally happens. The Protocol for settling disputes peacefully accepted by the Geneva session of 1924 required ratification, shortly after which the Labour government would fall over a nonsense. Foreign policy, which happens more quickly than anything economic, remained centre stage. MacDonald, a man of the categorical Labour Right, nevertheless and rightly regarded non-recognition of a Soviet Union after seven years in power, and the presence since 1921 of a trade pact, as simply irrational, and set up negotiations with a Soviet representative.

They led to a commercial treaty of the orthodox sort as arranged with any other country, and a general treaty, coupling a commercial loan to the USSR with the opening up of enquiry into private British claims from holders of Tsarist financial paper with the government willing to guarantee a loan to the Soviet government.[2] It was something done which, after seven years' establishment of a state not at war with this country, a sensible Conservative government could have done, and done safely. Labour, however cautious, could always be damned and Lloyd George, eternal snapper-up of unconsidered trifles, withdrew his diminished sub-party's share of support from the government.

On 26 October 1924 the Attorney General's office announced the intended prosecution, for an article in *Workers' Weekly* urging soldiers not to fire on strikers, of J. R. Campbell, a prominent member of the British Communist Party, actually one of its few likeable leading figures. The Attorney General, Patrick Hastings, not attuned to the scale of risk in politics (or the laws of consequence), laid charges of treason which were sensibly withdrawn, but set the tone. Conservative and Liberal motions were debated. Hastings took all responsibility, but Baldwin, seeing the opportunity and unable to resist temptation, supported the Liberal amendment of no confidence, endorsed by the Conservatives. After a bitter factitious debate in the Commons, on 8 October, unwisely treated as one of confidence, MacDonald, as nervous a man as a touchy one, in whom the cool indifference of political armour was wanting, responded with resignation. The election which followed was a model of Daily Mailism, much of it conducted by *The Times*. To all of this was added toward the end of the election, the 'Zinoviev Letter', a document allegedly written by the head of the Third Communist International, proclaiming, amid any amount of ranting Sovietese, the great advantage to the world revolutionary cause of such dealings with the Labour government.

The letter is now generally agreed, after much later investigation, to be a fake, denounced by Grigory Zinoviev himself as 'typical white-guardist forgery', but an effective and successful forgery which carried shrilling Conservatives to a hysterical result worthy of a hysterical campaign. Baldwin, receiving a swing of 8.8 per cent, now had, in round figures, 7.4 million votes and 412 seats to MacDonald's 5.3 million and 151 seats. Meanwhile the combined Liberal factions enjoyed 2.28 million votes and 40 seats; as observed by an early speaker here, the end of Lloyd George as a force in politics. We are today far enough away from 1924 to acknowledge dispassionately a chapter in which MacDonald's clumsy responses were overwhelmed by a Tory press-led campaign of shrill, consistent falsity, worthy not least of the Soviet Union—and an extreme version of a British tradition.

At this point the *Oxford Magazine* briefly experimented with interpolated comment in reported speech and italics. These have been retained but are no part of this editing of Union debates.

--- ⚬⚬⚬ ---

26 October 1922

House welcomes the return to government on Party lines.

Mr R. G. A. Elwes He is certainly a charming speaker. *The coalition is dead and rightly dead. It has served its purpose in winning the war. Failures in Foreign policy—India, Ireland and France, may have been the result of our lacking an effective opposition. Mr Lloyd George simply shares the characteristics of all other Prime Ministers. They all changed their minds and they all made promises. Though he has brought about a permanent solution in Ireland.*

Mr Pares *The first effect of a return to party politics has been to eject Mr Lloyd George. He had been so great a menace to the whole of the world that a return to party government is justified by his removal alone.*

Mr Gardiner *The old divisions are meaningless. Mr Lloyd George did not promise to make Germany pay the full cost of the war; he did settle Ireland and there is abundant evidence of the Coalition's achievements.*

Mr J. G. Morgan (St John's) *All politics adds up to today, is moderation on one side and Labour on the other.*

Mr Godfrey Nicholson[3] *Party government is government by halves. One party alone has only half the talent in politics.*

Mr Llewellyn Smith (New College) *The Coalition wasn't a coalition at all. It was the despotism of one man's will.*

Motion carried 202:104.

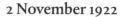

2 November 1922

House believes indefinite continuance of British sovereignty in India is a violation of British political ideals.

Mr Collingridge *True loyalty to the Empire can only come through loyalty between the various parts of the Empire.*

Mr A. A. Hope (Trinity) *I can put no term to British sovereignty in India. 'Democracy' in our sense has no meaning in India. The demand for independence was made in English as a result of English education. But it is in the interests of the vast majority of uneducated Indians that British government should continue.*

Mr Bandaranaike *I am in favour of India remaining inside the British Empire. The whole of the British political ideal was inspired by freedom. I think of the British Empire as a true League of Nations.*

Mr Nicholson *India is only a geographical expression; there can be no national demand for independence. Britain saved India from the worst of tyrannies, the injustice of petty tyrants, and hopeless anarchy.*

Mr Wedderburn *To support the motion is to be fantastic. England has given all the freedom that India possesses.*

Mr A. N. Emanuel (Trinity) *Speaking with the authority of twenty five years in the Indian Civil Service, I judge the Indians who have spoken here as by no means typical of India as a whole.*

Motion carried 165:139.

16 November 1922

House believes that in the present crisis of National and International affairs, a Conservative Policy will serve the best interests of the country.

Mr G. Bankes (Magd.) *The Liberals, more the pity, are not upon the scene at all; and in power, their policy has led this country to disaster. Labour is on the scene talking about a capital levy and war on private enterprise.*

A. G. Bagnall (St John's) *Treasurer A future Conservative government must pursue a Liberal policy in order to survive. Since Conservatism means stagnation, I think that will work. Meanwhile, the Tories and Labour must increase the level of class warfare.*

The Marquess of Londonderry[4] *The Labour Party is no party at all: it threatens to introduce class government which is entirely alien to British political philosophy. As for the Coalition, freedom of opinion and expression have been destroyed and suppressed by just such an insincere Coalition government. As for Ireland, the Conservative government has hardly been unsuccessful. The Act of Union was one of the most beneficent acts in Irish History. Conservative policy is the negation of class politics, it aims at government from the convictions of all sections of the community.*

Motion carried 202:195.

---

23 November 1922

House believes that the introduction of Prohibition would benefit this country.

Mr E. S. Griffiths (Merton) *Personal liberty is a great thing, but personal sacrifice is a greater.*

Mr M. C. Hollis (Balliol) *To stop drinking is to shed an element of humility. To prohibit the use of things because they are occasionally misused is to abolish human life altogether. Prohibition is unworkable, intolerable and also wicked.*

Mr R. B. McCallum[5] *Vast sums of money spent on drink could be spent productively. Alcohol does terrible harm to mind and body. Government is far stronger here than in America, so prohibition can be enforced here far more easily.*

Mr Nicholson *It is not the existence of drink, but bad working conditions which cause excess. Prohibition will strike at the root of law. Leonardo da Vinci has written 'Heaven save the world from short cuts.' Prohibition is one of them.*

Mr Evelyn Waugh (Hertford)[6] was gruff and businesslike speaking as a Conservative in support of the motion.

Mr R. S. Mundy (Queen's) *An international point of view should be adopted in this matter.*

Mr Maier (Balliol) *An American Prohibition law is being satisfactorily enforced and is purifying American life.*

Mr Stanley Little (Keble) *Such brilliance as I possess may be attributed to the influence of liquor. The American Law [Prohibition] is spreading corruption and exploitation.*

Mr Pares *At worst, drink does away with an inglorious old age—and would prevent me from having children I don't desire.*

Motion lost 98:145.

A shift of government in France had, as noted above, replaced sympathetic, responsive Aristide Briand with narrowly legalistic Raymond Poincaré, who would take advantage of German war debts and general chaos to seize the Ruhr and its industrial resources in early January 1923, over default in deliveries of timber. Bonar Law for Britain dissented, proposing a moratorium. The seizure, an act of blazing folly, would contribute through inflation to German misery and longer-term political extremism. By November, the Mark had reached 22,300 million to the pound. Britain's attitude was mixed, opposing the seizure, but allowing French enforcement troops to pass through British-held territory and seeing British pits benefit from the crisis. But Grey's always dubious Anglo-French Entente was effectively over.

25 January 1923

House deplores present policy of France as a grave menace to the welfare of Europe.

Mr Pares *If the present French approach continues, there are two possible outcomes. There will be war or Germany will be crushed and her already enfeebled cultural life destroyed.* Mr Pares is always effective as an advocate by reason of the most appealing impression of honesty. No Buzfuz he.

Mr A. A. Hope (Trinity) *How can steps which weaken Germany, but strengthen France be regarded as a menace to Europe? It will not matter if Germany goes bankrupt. The salaried classes will suffer, but goods will still be produced.* Mr Hope would win more support if he could appear a little less contemptuous of those who oppose him. But he is a real debater and a tower of strength to Union Conservatism.

Mr Nicholson *I am reminded of the man who says to a goose 'Lay me a golden egg or I will wring your neck.' France has refused the German offer to restore the devastated areas. Now she has aroused a hatred which was unknown four years ago and has united all classes in Germany. British trade will be ruined and unemployment doubled as German credit is destroyed ... and then French.*

Mr T. B. Causton *As somebody who is opposed on all points, to extreme Tories, I am speaking on their side because France's policy is their surest undoing.*

Mr Bandaranaike *It is a bad thing for Europe if France can think only in terms of French advantage. The French have killed the Entente, a disaster not only for France but for Europe.*

Motion carried 192: 72.

22 February 1923

House believes that enmities engendered by the war should give way to a friendly attitude to all the peoples who fought under the Central Powers.

Mr R. H. Bernays *In 1914, I was surveying life from the perambulator. Everything that the other side will say about the Germans is true, but remember they cannot help having been raised in the doctrines of Nietzsche.*

Lord Longford[7] *Think what the Germans would have done if they had won. I never expected to agree with the* Morning Post, *but that slightly murky flag must be invoked against the Hosts of Darkness.*

Mr Scaife *It is the way of opponents to talk about Germany and the Germans as a definite person of evil record and doubtful repentance. Enmity is the product of propaganda. Nothing has been said about Germany which was not at one time urged against France.*

Mr Evelyn Waugh (Hertford) unfolded a strong doctrine of patriotic hate claiming that he was the only man in the street amidst all the precocious intellectuals of Oxford.

Mr McCallum had a depressing effect, his speech reminiscent of a provincial University debate, full of abstract generalisation.

Mr Nicholson *Speaking as a Tory, I find hatred of Germany to be a luxury which a really patriotic man cannot afford himself.*

Mr Causton *Let's not forget the issue of Russian guilt for the war.*

Motion carried 177:74.

1 March 1923

House recognises the dangers of a population rising in numbers and deteriorating in quality.[8]

Mr Gardiner *The indisputable increase since 1890 cannot continue without grave consequences. It is the root of all our political problems. The opponents of birth control say it is immoral, but don't say what they would put in its place.*

Mr Carrigan (Trinity) *There is no fixed number of people who can survive. A hundred million Americans live in peace where a hundred thousand Red Indians could not live without war.*

Mr R. O. Raphael (Queens) *It is madness to employ science in the breeding of dogs and horses and leave the human races to Haphazard.*

Mr Hughes stressed the spiritual degradation involved in securing material gain.

Motion carried 137:93.

---

8 March 1923

In view of the present state of affairs in Europe, House considers the overwhelming defeat of Germany a misfortune.

Mr Victor Evans ex-President (Visitor) *A recuperative and creative peace treaty is needed if we are not to sow the seeds of a future war. The completeness of victory was dominated by the vindictive spirit of M. Clemenceau. Let us throw ourselves on the side of moderation.*

Mr Wedderburn *France has been in error, but Germany has been sly. We entered the War with the idea of destroying Prussianism; and to destroy it, we had to win.*

Mr Hollis *Politically, we have, since the time of Henry VIII, sought to prevent Europe being dominated by one military power. In the four years of 'peace,' there have* been twenty three wars. And more people killed, according to the League of Nations than in the years of war.

Mr W. M. R. Pringle MP (Visitor)[9] It is no use talking about Prussianism. Prussianism exists in every country, stronger than before the war: more conscription, stronger armaments, more protective measures. Force is dominant everywhere in Europe. It is arrant hypocrisy to blame France for a treaty for which we are as responsible as they. It is humiliating not to be able to lift a finger while France pursues a policy which, in a thousand ways, hurts the people of this country.

Motion carried 154:123.

17 October 1923

House considers the government of Signor Mussolini has proved itself a menace to the wellbeing of Europe

Mr H. A. McClure-Smith (Balliol)[10] Peace is essential for Europe and peace depends upon the scrupulous keeping of contracts and such has not been the practice of Signor Mussolini's government.[11]

Mr McClure-Smith is living too much in a world of convention—of wicked Communist, of noble Royalist. He left the House to choose between Signor Mussolini and chaos.

Mr Gordon (BNC) dealt with the philosophy of fascism. Mr Gordon probably thinks more than most people in the Union, but he should be careful in letting it be known.

Mr Stanley Little loathed chaos and could not exist there. He stood for efficiency.

Mr Dennison condemned the self-righteousness which blamed Mussolini and was blind to its own faults.

Mr Broadbent (Merton) distinguished between a Mussolini who was obnoxious and a Mussolini who was a menace.

Motion carried 208:98.

——— oeeo———

29 November 1923

House approves Mr Baldwin's government.

Mr A. H. E. Molson (New College) *We sometimes rather doubt whether Mr Molson realises how funny it is for undergraduates to talk about politics at all and he is therefore liable to lose the attention of his audience.*

Mr P. J. Monkhouse (Trinity) *What has the election done? The Tories can't bring in Imperial Preference. But we haven't got a Labour government and a capital levy.*

Mr F. W. Hugo (Ex-President, Wadham) *Developments in the US and Germany reinforce the case for Free Trade not Tariff Reform.*

Motion carried 113: 109.

On 23 December Baldwin, in office with a minority government in a three-party chamber, took the risk of going to the country, only to give Labour as third party in another three-way house, able with Liberal support to form its first government.

———oeeo———

24 January 1924

House welcomes the advent of a Labour government.

Mr R. J. Woodward *Labour is the only party which can carry on the King's government. For as the party of the workers, it is the only one fitted to deal with unemployment.*

Mr F. M. Bebb (New College) *The new Prime Minister, Mr MacDonald, deserves credit as an idealist, but his ideals are perverted. Neither Labour nor the Conservatives has the claim of right to form a government. As for the Liberal Party, it combines knavery with foolery.*

Mr M. J. MacDonald *Labour have a right to govern because they are the Constitutional Opposition. We have never been controlled by extremists. Neither Free Trade nor protection will lie at the front of policy as they are mechanical devices. Labour puts first and foremost the living issues of working men and women. There is a greater proportion of working people living in slums today than was true 60 years ago. The older parties are only able to respond to it as something outside their experience. What we look to and appeal for is the democratization of politics as people, never part of it, finally come in.*

The Junior Treasurer—Mr R. de C. Matthews *I speak as Secretary of the Oxford Fascist Society. Though Labour cannot cure unemployment, they can palliate it. The Conservatives at their Plymouth conference have shown themselves unsympathetic toward it.*

Mr K. F. Wynne Jones *Labour may well spoil its chances by taking office dependent on the support of Liberals.* He was quiet and self-possessed, these attributes are rare and valuable.

Motion carried 248:161.

---

31 January 1924

House approves of the support given by France to the separatists of the Rhineland.

Mr Carrigan *The strength of Germany is a forced strength; the armistice has shown the German people anxious to escape from Prussian domination. Silesia is now prosperous. France, by this policy, is striving to complete the destruction of Prussianism.*

Mr M. A. Thompson *Are the French to leave the inhabitants of the Palatinate to fight amongst themselves, even though the majority of them are neutral? The German empire was vicious. It had produced no good art.*

Mr C. R. De Gruchy (Jesus) *Germany is not homogenous. The Junkerism, so much complained of, is not even particularly Prussian, only prevalent among their upper classes. Germany, across the time of its empire, has contributed in distinguished degree to philosophy, science and music.*

Mr J. L. Parker (New College) *French policy is a new menace to peace. The antagonism which follows from mistakes made after the armistice is a permanent factor in European politics. People who refuse generosity toward a defeated antagonist, are now committed to crushing their enemies.*

Mr J. S. Done (Non-Collegiate) *France has a right to take steps for her own security.*—Much questioning.

Mr L. H. Nye *If Germany is dismembered, the chances of any indemnity actually being paid will vanish.*

Mr W. F. K. Wynne-Jones (Balliol)[12] *We go on about Prussianism. Has the history of England toward her neighbours been so very pure?*

Mr H. V. Lloyd-Jones *Prussianism is a frame of mind possible in any country. We are not talking about German disintegration but whether France should have a hand in it.*

Motion lost 32:143.

---

21 February 1924

House would welcome the disappearance of the Liberal Party—Cambridge visit.

Mr G. M. Lloyd (Trinity) *It is dead. It is an obstructing albatross round the neck of Parliament. Never mind its traditions. Always it has been a vote-catching party. Richard Cobden was quite happy, in a letter to John Bright, to contemplate extending the franchise simply to win Radical support. It has no fundamental principle, unlike the Conservative Party which has.*

Mr R. C. Matthews *Compromise as a tool is useful. Compromise as a principle is absurd. There is far greater risk of a traditional party becoming lethargic than of a progressive party becoming extreme.*

Mr E. C. Barrett *If the Liberals disappear, the division remaining would not be those only of party difference. They would amount to class war. The old parties divided us vertically, the new pair would do it horizontally.*

Mr Bandaranaike (Ex-Secretary visiting) *The issue today is which of two parties, Liberal or Conservative, should disappear to present a united front to socialism. The Tories have lost their character and are becoming Liberals. The only true Conservatives are the Die-hards.*[13] *The recent acts of the Tories were Liberal—Reforms in India, the Irish treaty, Home rule in Egypt.*

Motion lost 120:133—21 February 1924 and Liberal Party saved.

---

28 February 1924

Centenary debate—House believes that Civilisation has advanced since this house first met—many (historic) guests.

Dr Gilbert Murray (Ch.Ch.)[14] *The House long ago deplored the state of Ireland, since when it got worse and worse.*

Mr John Buchan (BNC) *Civilisation has definitely declined, at least within living memory. The real test was on our souls; youth should have an adventurous spirit, a wide world in which to travel and security of soul. These have gone. Science lays bare the secret places of speculation...where is the unconquerable dogmatism and assurance of the founders of the Society? They have disappeared and we are none the better for it.*

Father Ronald Knox (Balliol ex-president) *Mechanical contrivances do not constitute an advance of civilisation and I want to say over and over again that we are getting, not only worse, but more barbarous. We eat and drink less than they did—witness young men who were now vegetarians or teetotallers. Let the younger generation boast of its kinematograph and its wireless, but let it not say that these are the marks of an advancing civilisation.*

Rev. Dr Carlyle (Univ.) *I contest the point of the opposer that the field of knowledge is now exhausted. Also the manners of the best society under the Regency showed a degree of vulgarity with which no Bolshevist can vie.*

Mr Gerald Gardiner *Surely it cannot be said that that civilisation has made no progress since the Society last met. We have electoral reform, extension of the franchise, the League of Nations, the freedom of Greece from Turkey, the freedom of Ireland from England.*

Dr H. A. James (St John's) *it is nearly sixty years since I spoke as an undergraduate in the Union ... I think that the present generation has not gained more of the spirit of brotherhood than was possessed a hundred years ago, nor the love of beauty which characterised the great Victorians.*

Motion carried 576: 279.

———∞———

1 May 1924

House believes that, between them, Russia and France were as responsible as Germany for the World war.

Mr Molson *Since the secret alliance of Russia and France, in 1891, Germany has been suspicious of the armaments accruing to her neighbours. In the ten years before the war, those two have spent between them £842 million on armaments and the central kingdoms only 682 million. Russia and France also have nearly a million more men under arms.*

Mr Carrigan *That alliance was entirely defensive and formed only in response to German aggression. In the days immediately prior to the war, every country, except Germany, was seeking a peaceful solution.*

Mr Wedderburn *Germany desired and planned the war.* This is the sort of speech the House likes. It contained less matter than the previous speeches, but was undoubtedly the best of the evening.

Mr Gyles Isham[15] It was refreshing to hear such an admirable maiden speech delivered without a note of any kind. However when Mr Isham speaks again, he will have learnt not to speak so loudly that the emptying hall sets up an echo.

Motion lost 78:108.

⚬⚬⚬

15 May 1924

House considers that immediate and very drastic reforms are needed in our so-called Public schools.

Mr I. B. Lloyd (Exeter) *They are of course private schools reserved for the members of one class. These may have been good in previous centuries when there was one distinct ruling class. They are now pleasant but useless. All education should be under state control.*

Mr P. J. Monkhouse (Trinity) *What we need are more schools of the public school type so that everyone can attend them.*

Mr Matthews *What kind of men do we want to turn out from our schools, intellectually, morally and physically? The god of sport was a bad god for a monarchy. All schools should be co-educational.*

Mr McClure-Smith *My opponents are in their persons a complete vindication of the Public Schools. Those schools were productive of character rather than trained scholarship. And this is more important for the upper classes. It is for this and the Public School code of honour, that an Englishman is honoured throughout the world.*

Mr Wylie thought that Civics should be taught instead of Classics. Mr Scott said that public Schools fostered prejudice.

Mr E. Waugh was sorry that all the speeches so far were no good. His was certainly no better.

Motion carried 115: 108.

29 May 1924

This House deserves its doubtful reputation.

If the Union is unpopular in some quarters, that is probably because it is more an institution than a club. It is catholic and unexclusive, but not catholic and unexclusive enough. Women and dogs are still barred. The debates are dull and the competition for the presidency are responsible for an atmosphere of restraint.

Mr Pares *The debates are mere irresponsible talking. Members come to debates with their minds made up. Statistics are invented and ambition, the worst of all evils in a state, is encouraged.*

Mr Wedderburn *The Union is a great source of political experience and a great school of oratory.*

Mr Wynne-Jones *The working man has never heard of the Union and the Union has no reputation.*

Mr M. A. Thompson *I joined the Union because, unlike any other club in Oxford, no one was worried here to actually do anything. Politically, the Union is always opposed to the established order.*

Motion lost by 14 votes.

15 October 1924

House believes that to give effect to the proposals contained in the draft Treaty with the Soviet government would be an act of supreme folly.

Mr A. L. P. Gordon (BNC) was rather unfairly attacked by interrupters.

Mr Wynne-Jones (Balliol) *The treaty is necessary for European peace and British trade and was only opposed out of prejudice, ignorance and mistaken principles.*

Mr Isham *The conditions for a treaty are satisfaction of claims and cessation of propaganda in the British Empire. The Bolshevists have proved themselves untrustworthy in both requirements. Our trade with Russia has never been very great in the best of times.*

Mr Parker was too serious; Mr Kulken said that holders of Russian bonds were wanton gamblers who deserved to lose their money. Mr Fenby thought it was dangerous to displease the Russians.

Mr Fulford[16] was rather vague but he has a good voice.

Motion carried 194:136.

---

22 October 1924

House believes the prospects of social improvement in this country are being gravely damaged by the activities and growth of the Socialist Party.

Mr Maclehose (New College) *The Socialists are engaged in telling the workers to concentrate their brains on their grievances.*

Mr Lloyd-Jones (Jesus) *The socialist idea of the state is very like a prison where men were provided with food, clothing and regular employment. The socialist measures of the pre-war Liberal government are the result of the growth of socialist ideas which are doing great harm to people. They represent an anti-democratic approach from an academic basis. If there is ever another revolution in England, it will be against the tyranny of the socialist movement, the last and most obnoxious of England's oppressors.*

Mr Matthews (New College) thought it absurd that political control should be democratic while industrial control is not.

Motion carried 180:119.

The election forced by a factious issue saw Labour's share fall to 151, the Tories rise to 412 and the Liberals quite collapse historically to 40. Though there was on percentages of votes cast a swing to Labour of 2.8 per cent since the recent election, the Liberal percentage fall was much smaller than the fall in seats; and Labour and the Liberals could on that basis have formed a government. Talk of proportionate representation began here, not that it got anywhere.

———— ❦ ————

30 October 1924

House regrets that yesterday's elections were not conducted by proportional representation.

Mr Llewellyn-Smith (New College) *It is possible under the present system to elect 615 members with only slightly more than one third of the total poll. Labour is over-represented in this parliament, but under-represented in this House.*

Mr Thompson (Exeter) *PR will encourage the faddists and cranks who desire to be more clever than their creator meant them to be. I don't want a system which might return 318 1/2 Liberals and 50 Prohibitionists.*

Mr Fraser (Balliol) *The wrong people are being elected. In many cases two good men who both should be in parliament are set up against each other. The Liberal party was not eliminated, but every 70,000 Liberals were represented by one member as against 19,000 Tories.*

Mr Buck (Wadham) *Parliamentary groups must not only represent. They must govern.*

Motion lost 103:111.

———— ❦ ————

6 November 1924

House thinks that the Cinema has done more to degrade than brighten the public mind.

Mr Dannreuther (Balliol) *The few good films are weighed down by the inevitable hours of appalling boredom, occasioned by false sentimentalism.*

Mr Asquith[17] *If our sisters run about the house like little sunbeams, whom have we to thank but the films which portrayed them so beautifully? There are many bad films, but no theatre of art is without bad art.*

Mr Sutro (Trinity) went on to talk about the effect of films on the retina. *The film is an excrescence in a world already too full of activities.*

Mr Grundy (BNC) *People should provide their own amusements. Those provided for them are degrading.*

Mr Thomson *We do not see light there, but only stars.*

Mr Herbert (Univ.) *The emotionalism taught by the films is not in accordance with the tradition of the English character.*

Motion lost 143: 178.

13 November 1924

House approves the verdict of the country as expressed in the polls.

Mr R. J. Hill (St Edmund Hall) *I rather gathered the impression that he was reading an essay on Conservatism, but it was a very good essay.*

Mr A. P. Grundy *The 'overwhelming majority' for the Conservatives consists of seven and a half million for them while eight and a half million had polled elsewhere.*

Mr Marjoribanks *The Labour government has failed to do anything in domestic policy and its housing scheme has been a fraud on the electorate.*

Mr Molson (New College) *There is a justifiable impression of the Labour govern-ment being not only incompetent, but corrupt.*

Mr Dawson exposed the detestable attributes of 'The Red Flag.'

Motion lost 99: 139.

---

21 November

House disapproves of the recent proceedings at Geneva[18] and doubts the capacity of the League to maintain the peace of the world.

Mr McClure-Smith *Disarmament in the cause of peace is like destroying umbrellas in the hope of obtaining fine weather.*

Mr R. H. Scott *The Geneva protocol is the only practicable way of changing the status quo. Opposition to it arises from ignorance of its provisions.*

Mr A. T. Lennox-Boyd (Ch.Ch.)[19] *The League is trying to impose peace by force without having the power to do so. It must not be assumed that the League will always win. The Protocol is essentially a continental document to which a maritime nation ought not to subscribe.*

Motion defeated 71:94.

---

29 January 1925

House condemns further extension of the facilities for divorce.

Mr D. M. Foot[20] *Although the Liberal peers disagree with me, I have the support of the whole bench of Bishops. The whole of morality will be shaken by such a move. For one per cent of the population, it is not worthwhile outraging the sensibilities of vast numbers who still maintain biblical standards.*

Mr Lennox-Boyd *The Royal Commission of 1909 is the foundation of my argument. I would allow divorce for cruelty, insanity, and drunkenness. The principle of Church opposition crashes to the ground the moment they sanction a single kind of divorce.*

Mr H. V. Lloyd-Jones *Divorce is not a philosophy, but the absence of one. Liberty, apart from the institution with which it is concerned, is impossible.*

Mr Molson *Bad laws make hard cases. Judicial separation is cruel and pernicious.*

Mr McClure-Smith *This is a debate between Hobbes and Rousseau.*

Mr C. Fenby was clear and short. He must speak again.

Motion lost 87: 111.

---

5 February 1925

The House would end capital punishment.

Mr Fulford (Worcester) *Penal servitude is more equitable and more effective.*

Mr R. L Hurst (New College) *If a man was in the act of committing murder, only the shadow of the gallows would deter him from murder.*

Commander Kenworthy (Visitor) *It is time that the hangman's rope was kept in a museum with the rack, the thumbscrew and the executioner's axe.*

Mr E. F. M Durbin (New College)[21] was clear and convincing but must avoid addressing the house as if he were lecturing a WEA audience.

Mr L. A. Nye (Pembroke) *The thought of death prevents me from committing murder.*

Motion carried 175:90.

---

26 February 1925

In Private Business a proposal to increase the subscription by 5s after next March was approved.

House believes that the activities of Trades Unions should be confined to the economic sphere.

Mr P. W. Buck (Wadham) *The development of the Trade Union movement should not be endangered by harnessing it to politics.*

Mr J. P. Hennessy *Trade Unions are not monsters. Don't persecute them by bringing up motions like this.*

Mr Hill *The alliance between a trade union and a political party is antagonistic to the whole theory of democratic government.*

Mr Isham—Librarian *The Trade Unions have every right to interfere in foreign politics. It is their absolute duty to see that similar conditions of industry are obtained in other countries.*

Mr E. H. Birley *The Conservatives have no intention of depriving the working classes of the right to express their views.*

Mr C. Fenby defended the paid agitator in a promising speech.

Motion carried 57:53.

---

7 May 1925

House believes that this University serves no useful purpose.

Mr Fulford *Such are the bewildering activities to be found in university life that they induce a terrible indecision. But at the same time, may I put in a word for an institution, now frowned upon: the old-fashioned hard-drinking Don?*

Mr E. L. Malalieu (Trinity)[22] was cheerfully complacent about Oxford.

Mr Maclehose argued that Oxford was useful but not useful enough.

Mr R. C. Matthews closed the debate with fragments of a Socratic dispute.

Motion lost by 13 votes.

14 May 1925

House approves of the principle of contributory insurance as expressed in the bill now before parliament.

Mr Durbin *It is tantamount to theft to do this. Such are the evils and inequalities of life, giving rise to such schemes, that only a redistribution of wealth will put it right.*

Mr Grundy *Unless the individual contributes to such an insurance scheme, it will be a servile one. Accordingly, contributions should be compulsory for all.*

Motion carried 52:49.

28 May Visit of Bates College USA

House believes that the Government of Russia should be recognised.

Mr Buck (Wadham—himself an American) *The government of Russia satisfies the people, is functioning, and is hardly likely to be replaced.*

Mr Edwin Canham (Bates College) *Russia wants to be admitted to the family of nations without meeting the tests such as good faith and acceptance of international law. She refuses to pay her debts and has confiscated the property of foreign nationals. You cannot recognise her without doing violence to the principles of international law. Also I see no advantages to either the US or your country in giving such recognition.*

Mr Fred T. Coggins (Bates College) *The quarrel is not with the internal economy of Russia, but with her attitude to the international law of our faith. It is in the interest of these things that she should not be recognised.*

It is perhaps not surprising that the representatives of a nation founded on such a doctrinaire and dogmatic basis, should reveal a legalistic tendency which is much nearer to continental ways of thought than to England.

Motion lost 127:179.

11 June 1925

House believes that politics do not offer any scope for a career.

Mr Maclehose *Politics is pursued primarily for remuneration—official and unofficial.*

Mr T. M. Marten (Corpus) *On the contrary, politics in the modern world is the very reverse of self-seeking. There can be something close to a religious quality in the pursuit of a cause and in a materialistic society.*

Mr T. P. Price (New College) *Even party politics should not be scorned. They are signs of vitality.*

Mr Buck *To put it shortly, a man going into politics is going to the dogs.*

Mr Ayerst (Ch.Ch.) *The growth of trade unions is robbing political life of its significance.*

Mr Nobbs (Wadham) *Politics presumes parliamentary sovereignty, but parliament, in practical terms, doesn't have sovereignty.*

Mr Bonagee (Jesus) *What I find missing in politics is enough men with independent standpoints.*

Mr Durbin *Present conditions, especially the ignorance of the masses, make politics unreal.*

Motion lost 36:57—at 12.27 in the morning!

———— ∞ ————

29 October 1925

House condemns Mr Lloyd George's Land policy.

Mr Acland *I am one of a small class of Union speakers who knows his subject. There are many evils in respect of land at present and the Lloyd George plan would go some way to remedy them.*

Mr F. Murthwaite-How (Balliol) *The scheme is planned as a vote-catching addition to the Liberal platform. And nothing in Mr Lloyd George's agricultural past inspires confidence in his new offspring.*

Mr F. S. Bailey *Two things would really improve matters on the land, co-operation between farmers in production and co-operation in selling.*

Mr R. H. Scott (New College) *If the state becomes an owner of agricultural land, it will find itself as landlord, caught up during the bad times with quantities of tenantless land on its hands.*

Mr S. Stopford Brooke[23] *The main trouble with the land industry is the existence of a class which is landless.*

Mr R. M. M. Stewart (St John's)[24] *In terms of usefulness there is an affinity between the Georgics of Virgil and the Lloyd Georgics of the Twentieth Century.*

Mr Isham *I have the experience of being a landlord, and the experience has convinced me that landlordism is now indefensible.*

Motion carried 149:143.

———— ∞ ————

5 November 1925

House holds that representative democracy is proving a failure.

Mr Hill *I made a remark about liberty under fascism which the House found hard to believe, then observed that representative government, far from being an ancient and immutable principle of government among Teutonic peoples from the earliest times, was a Nineteenth Century invention of the middle classes in certain states. So if J. S. Mill has not succeeded in giving democracy immortality, it is no more certain that Signor Mussolini has succeeded in killing it.*

Sir Edward Holton (BNC)[25] *English ideas were imported at a time when they were thought to have universal application. Recent history in France, Italy, Spain and South America shows that this is a fallacy.*

Mr Murthwaite-How (Balliol) has drunk deeply of the National Review[26] and not unnaturally, is rather unbalanced and provocative. Unfortunately he also saw fit to make some remarks which on consideration, he will probably regret.

Motion lost 107:140.

12 November 1925

House would welcome introduction of compulsory vaccination.

Mr Nye *There can be no certainty that germs from other diseases were not put into the body at the same time as the cowpox germ.*

Mr Leslie Parker (New College) *The vast majority of the medical profession favours vaccination. So does a Royal Commission. So it is presumptuous and stupid for amateurs to suppose that their spare time studies will disprove the accepted view.*

Mr R. D. Davies (Magd.) *We are weary of statistics, and compulsory vaccine has never been fairly tried.*

Mr F. Bicknell (New College) *By compulsory vaccination, the state will save the weakly, the dirty and the unintelligent. Without compulsion only the best stocks will survive precisely because they have the intelligence to be vaccinated.*

Mr P. Parker (St John's) *There are always fads which frequently go together. They are to be found in members of the Liberal Party: Anti-vivisection, anti-alcohol, vegetarianism and anti-vaccination.*

Mr R. M. Wilson *It will be necessary for anti-vaccinationists to conduct propaganda, preferably through the medium of old ladies if they want to beat the vaccinationists.*

Sir Edward Hulton *People who refuse to be vaccinated should be incarcerated like conscientious objectors during the war.*

Motion carried 139: 70.

———⊶⊷———

19 November 1925

House is of opinion that the future does not lie with the Indo-European race.

Mr P. T. Robinson (Lincoln) *The idea of progress itself is something belonging to Western civilisation and it is a rare thing among human beings generally.*

Mr I. Treiman (Balliol) *We dispute among ourselves, and this is surely a good thing about the Aryan race. All that chaos and disunity is a sign of vitality, much more so than the philosophic detachment found among Orientals.*

Mr A. A. Thompson *I question whether the yellow races have achieved anything comparable to what stands to the credit of the Aryan race.*

Lord Ennismore (Balliol) *If a race has an advantage, it will have come less from military skill or economic vitality. What really matters is far-sightedness. The East is learning from the West, but only such things as will enable it to overthrow the present hegemony of the West.*

Mr P. M. Skinner (Magd.) *The East may be an excellent imitator, but that is always limited by its pattern. Only the negro race has been more barren of achievement than the oriental.*

Mr R. C. Wilson (Queens) *Western civilisation has concentrated too much on science at the expense of broader subjects. Morally, the West has ceased to care about the soul and so must become barren in all things moral.*

Mr V. P. David *Dominion passed from Persia westward. So it will pass to America, a land flowing with milk and money, and thence to Japan and China.*

Mr C. D. Smith (St Edmund Hall) *I believe that racial trouble arises from the doctrines of equality taught to the coloured races by missionaries when such equality was given politically.*

Mr W. J. K Diplock[27] *'Mid-European' is an adjective applying to language only and there is therefore no Mid-European race.*

Mr W. S. Adams (BNC) *So far as the oriental races are concerned, they have a past rather than a future.*

Mr Thackrah (Wadham) *The East has great artistic past and will have a great scientific future.*

Motion lost 103:106.

———— ✼ ————

3 December 1925

House condemns the Government's policy of building cruisers.

Mr Isham *I want to question their effectiveness as a means of defence. Much greater progress has been made by Krupps in Germany in beating swords into plough shares. The reason given is that our government has not told companies that there will no longer be a steady demand for instruments of war. A recent American experiment has shown that an aeroplane can sink a battleship, yet here we are ready to spend untold* millions on cruisers which do not dare attack a battleship. Mr Baldwin has talked about the will to disarm. Is this evidence of it?

Mr M. A Thompson *Whether or not we took the right decision three hundred years ago, we are now definitely committed to an Imperial policy, and we are in honour bound to accept the burdens…Our greatness came from the sea, and on the sea it depends today. I am amused to hear Labour and Liberal supporters giving their opinions upon technical naval matters and flattering themselves that they are more likely to be right than the experts at the Admiralty.*

Mr J. H. Hudson MP (Visitor)[28] *I take as text the official War Office statement. 'As war can only be prosecuted by the will of a united people, the aim of war is to put such pressure upon the people as to compel them to demand peace.' Are these cruisers likely to protect our civilian population? General Seeley says that the only safeguard for the population of London on the first dark night after a declaration of war is to run like rabbits into the open night. General Swinton has said that it would soon be possible to exterminate the population of an entire city by means of germs, even if ordinary gas was not used. What likelihood is there of there being any independent occupants of this island, left to eat the food when it arrived?*

Mr J. C. C. Davidson MP, Financial secretary Admiralty (Visitor)[29] *The Hon. Gentleman paid great attention to the next war. The Admiralty was devoting all attention to the next war, and it was to avoid the dangers of that, that it was building cruisers. The question is often put 'Which enemy do you have in mind?' You might as well ask a policeman which thief he has in view. As to danger from the air, there is little that I can allow myself to say, but those in office are not blind to the danger. If, as Mr Hudson says, we are in danger from the air, we should find ourselves in the unfortunate position of facing ruthlessness from the sea. I would remind the House of what damage one small light squadron of the German navy did to Scarborough in twenty minutes—more than the German Air force had done to towns just behind the lines in France over several days. The average number of ships built for the navies of the four other great naval powers is 65. We have so far, built eleven. Peace depends upon the effectiveness of the League of Nations. It is essential that we have the means to enforce the League's decisions.*

Motion lost 123:171.

12

Imperial Fatigue and
New Clouds

21 January 1926–20 November 1930

No confidence/national barriers breaking down/Mussolini/Humanitarianism/
Education policy damaging/MAGAZINE HIATUS/American threat/Blackpool v
Cardiff/No more Liberals/More disarmament?/Land crisis/Welsh and Scottish
parliaments?/No confidence/Lib–Lab pact/India as a Dominion?/Budget/Al
Smith/Second chamber?/Athletes or aesthetes/Censorship/Tired of the Empire/
Nationalise the pits?/weary of the Commons/Birth control/Capital Punishment/
Labour Party/League disappoints/Fancying Fascism/US/Rejecting Indian self-
government/Three dislikes/Majority always wrong/Deploring Tory success

The music of the 1920s may have been lively, its mood 'madly gay', and
accompanying a vivid social life, good for circulation. The chief chron-
icler of that high life was Evelyn Waugh, the 'significant and relevant'
writers—the names to be dropped—James Joyce and T. S. Eliot. By contrast,
the political figures were dispirited trade unionists, like J. H. Thomas and
Herbert Smith, the leading politicians, underpowered regulars, Baldwin
and MacDonald, with depressingly reactionary figures like Joynson-Hicks
and Leopold Amery in important places. Churchill was off-stage at the
moment, but his recent return of sterling to the gold standard at pre-war
parity, which is to say over-valued and clogging exports, was quite enough
to be going on with. Investment, also madly gay, was certainly too speculative and everything was open to worst effects if anything should,
unthinkably, go wrong in the United States.

329

It was ironical that a campaign for so much economic semi-paralysis had been lit when the means to a better-read, more thoughtful country had recently been created. Oxford had admitted women way ahead of customarily more radical Cambridge; and, altogether more daring, had abolished compulsory Greek! Education was widening and improving on the back of a great Education Act in 1918, the doing of H. A. L. Fisher, also responsible at about this time for compulsory education for all children and superannuation for teachers. This was in no way the 'Land fit for Heroes', promised by wartime rhetoric; but foundations for better times had been dug.

The General Strike which spread out of the miners' strike in the spring of 1926, did not altogether fit. The Labour Party was in moderate, perhaps too moderate, hands. The union leaders, whatever the *Daily Mail* might say, were not Soviet sympathizers inspired by sinister alien forces. Arthur Cook of the Miners, a man depicted by a very right-wing press as Lenin shading into Beelzebub, was a son of rural Somerset, earnest local preacher, much loved in the pits, and 'in it' for anything but himself. The root of the miners' quarrel was a raising of expectations smartly followed by their bleak withdrawal. The occupation of the coal-mining Ruhr, initiated by Poincaré in 1921, had continued, doing its bit for German embitterment, until 1924, producing demand for the home product for two and a half years and bringing higher earnings. However when it abruptly stopped just after a new, and again better, settlement, early in 1925, the mine-owners abruptly cancelled that settlement.

They were not good at explaining the perfectly good reasons—falling exports and rising losses, and unable to communicate beyond a peremptory bark in letter form. They required surrender of the seven-hour day which had very lately been conceded. The unions understandably saw only the major retreat from most of what had been gained. Solidarity being a great trade union asset and liability, the TUC General Council committed itself to support. The efforts of a good mediator, the Lord of Appeal, Lord Macmillan, still left the offer at a minimum wage, varying sharply by district, often very low, and a supposedly temporary return to the eight-hour shift. The government retreated, set up an enquiry under the Liberal Herbert Samuel, but looked to emergency powers, while private stirrers, including the (Pre-Mosley) Fascist groups, strove to fight the Red Menace.

Meanwhile the miners seemed secure in wages, hours, and a national agreement as against the harshest for the weakest regional ones. The terms suggested by Samuel indicated the nationalization which would come in 1946—extensive amalgamation within the coalfields, plus farsighted things for the future: housing, pit-head baths, and annual paid holidays. The owners talked about Communism and suspended flexibility for the duration—and long after. The same owners obdurately required specifically local settlements, meaning lots of bad ones, lower wages where possible, and specifically, a revision downwards of the lowest point defining a subsistence wage.

The outcome was the deeper involvement of the TUC and the prospect, uneasily contemplated by its leaders, of a General Strike of unions at large. However in this intense period, it seemed at one point that something might be achieved working with a statement drafted by a conciliatory Lord Birkenhead including the phrase '… we accept the [Samuel] Report as a basis of settlement and we approach it with the knowledge that it may involve some reduction in wages …' This, with TUC involvement, looked like the formula which could have produced a settlement. Suddenly, Baldwin who had talked conciliation throughout, would, after a meeting with his Ministers, pull the rug sharply away, talking about 'overt acts' and demanding 'an immediate and unconditional withdrawal of the instructions for a General Strike'.

The Overt Acts were *one* act, the refusal of union printers at the *Daily Mail* to set an inflammatory piece talking of 'a revolutionary movement…not to be tolerated by any civilised Government' and calling on people 'to hold themselves at the service of King and Country'. The piece was the sort of fraught fascist squeak natural to the newspaper which in the next decade would offer the headline 'Hooray for the Blackshirts'. Baldwin and his rational line appear to have lost authority over the right wing of the Cabinet, hard but slightly hysterical spirits exploiting/fearing every sort of Jacobin vision—the likes, not only of Douglas Hogg and Amery, but Neville Chamberlain and unsurprisingly Churchill.

As a result, Baldwin would be presented with a great, but discreditable triumph. The TUC, though solidly bent on not getting into a General Strike, got in deeper than they wanted by way of this embittering conflict between miners and mine-owners and would, hours after promising talks with the Prime Minister, find themselves issuing instructions for precisely a General Strike.

It lasted for nine days. John Simon, busiest political lawyer of this era, former Liberal Minister, and future long-term member of the Baldwin and Chamberlain national governments, floated the notion, quickly refuted, that a General Strike was an unlawful act, making every trade union leader advising it 'liable in damages to the uttermost farthing of his personal possessions'. Neville Chamberlain, deploring appeasement, would write that '…the kindest thing now is to strike hard and quickly'.[1] There were also rumours of arrests. Churchill, shrilling from the *British Gazette* government sheet, breathed patriotic menace. Oxbridge students, only seven years before the King and Country debate, signed up as strike breakers.

Herbert Samuel would come to a sort of rescue by again talking sense. He reconvened his commission unofficially, and, in what became known as the 'Samuel Memorandum', called for resumed negotiations, creation of a National Wages board, but with immediate wage rates held out for the doing of everything else. For the General Council of the TUC, which had never wanted a General Strike, and with the politic J. H. Thomas in the van, this was a working, or at any rate, a talking base. For the miners, it might mean something if the lock-out notices were withdrawn. Unfortunately at the same time, Ministers were looking for a bill to define and make illegal whatever acts they might draft as 'intimidatory, illegal and subject to harsh penalties'. King George, to his great credit, intervened at this point, warning the Home Secretary and Attorney General against fining people getting by on strike pay, and noting, amid the scare talk, that the strikers had 'until now been very quiet'.[2]

On 12 May the TUC, after two days' discussion with the miners, pulled back. Thomas and the other TUC figures came to Number Ten with acceptance of the available terms. The miners did not. Nor, in a brief re-conjuring of a sort of general strike, did a number of workers in other trades, notably railwaymen. They had been bidden by one company, on returning, to sign self-menacing admissions of culpability. There was a good deal of vindictive enjoyment among the likes of those railway directors in having the upper hand and abusing it. The moderation in which Baldwin believed he believed, was not in evidence. The miners' strike went self-impoverishingly along until the start of July. Districts resolved wages—very unequally, with the Samuel recommendations making little effect on the variety of cuts which followed. It had been a class war and people who did hard work with their hands had lost it.

In purely political terms, the second half of the 1920s saw a Conservative government broadly benefiting, but despite its victory in the class war, oddly depressed and under-purposed. There were advocates of something altogether nicer, perhaps the use of public money and state intervention even by way of representation on company boards to bring working-class voices within hearing distance. It didn't happen and the words lacked impact, though such things would have a future in the 1950s under two men who, not very discreetly, detested each other, Harold Macmillan and R. A. Butler. Otherwise, at this time and for the most part, Baldwin, shrewd man though he had proved in a crisis, had elevated laziness into a virtue. The sons of driving industrialists commonly made off for the life of longer-rooted equestrian gentry. Baldwin, by temperament a pessimist, and a lazy pessimist at that, could at times come dangerously close to being, in the monarchical sense, a constitutional Prime Minister.

More life was showing among the Liberals. Their fall from the power of politics, except where, as with Samuel, they were asked to solve a problem, was the product of more than a decade back. Lloyd George, Baldwin's foot-tapping, hyperactive antithesis, having judged himself the better man, had conspired against Asquith in the middle of the First War, to make a government of the ablest people—as he saw it. When the Liberal

Party had consequently split itself, its vote divided into two factions of able men—it was that sort of party—loyal by choice to Asquith or Lloyd George, both of them cleverer and harder working than 'Honest Stan' as one puff, instantly suggesting a bookmaker, had identified him.

As election time approached, they applied their minds and especially Lloyd George's. His position papers, put out well ahead of the election, were worth attention. He had taken Keynes's writings into account before the *General Theory*, and Keynes would back him. The title *We Can Conquer Unemployment* may have an ironical ring at the brink of the Great Crash, except that in the lucky 1920s, there was already quite enough unemployment to be getting on with. LG was ready to have the state put money into major roads, badly needed in a country now viewing the car with the popping eyes of Mr Toad. He wanted ring-roads, and to go with the cars, he wanted serious house building, telephones installed—all this plus land drainage. Whatever Lloyd George's deserved reputation for quick-talking deviousness, there was nothing wrong with his thinking. The country's earliest modernizer had worked to deserve that reputation.

Science and engineering had changed the actual needs of the landscape and the city. Baldwin's lethargic ruralism stood in the way like a farm cart stuck fast in February. The things proposed wanted doing; they would unquestionably throw up great numbers of entirely useful jobs. Party apart, anyone could have voted for it. On 30 May, quite a lot did, but only enough in a clumping, skewed system (5.1 million votes) to make 59 seats in the Commons. The Tories fell back to 260 (8.25 million votes) while Labour, weakly led, had 287 (8.04 million) with 300,000 fewer votes than the Tories, above their 260, but still minority status producing minority government.

This was at the end of a period of some relative, if meagre economic performance. The New York Stock Exchange stood trembling and ready to set a harder challenge than any election, one of ideas and nerve, neither of which was evident in the two large parties.

21 January 1926

House has no confidence in Mr Baldwin's government.

Mr E. H. P. Brown (Wadham) [3] *If 1925 was Locarno year, 1926 will have the name, Coal Mine year. The coal mines and the gold standard are the two issues on which government policy shows not mere slips, but cardinal errors. As for their anti-strike plans, they are the first blow of the class war.*

Mr Nye *Naval expansion is justified by the Italian battleships I have seen on a summer vacation in the Mediterranean.*

Mr Foot *The new tariffs have worried Conservatives. The apparent reduction of unemployment is more like a transfer from the dole to parish relief. I hope that in the next struggle between the Lords of the Admiralty and the Treasury, the government will accept the resignations of the former.*

Mr Lennox-Boyd *Of course no government can do everything at once. However, the spirit of Locarno has been introduced into industry and the Coal and Fuel Commission stands a good chance of settling two great problems.*

Mr Murthwaite-How still a little nervous (possibly because radicals have rather frequently 'barracked' his speeches). *Industries are being disabled by working class leaders. However I hope the Government will maintain the tradition of social reform dating from Disraeli.*

Mr A. A. Mocatta (New College) [4] *This is no time for experiment, but the one positive thing is a rising exchange rate showing confidence in the government.*

Mr J. D. Price (New College) *Let's be clear about the Locarno Treaty.* [5] *It is a disaster and will deal a death-blow to the League of Nations.*

Sir Edward Hulton *A government with this size of majority should be more Conservative.*

Mr Buck *The government behaves like a drunken man and we wonder where it will stagger to next.*

Mr S. S. Brooke *The Conservatives have done nothing to improve the relations between labour and capital and that is the great issue.*

Motion carried 127: 102.

⸿⸿⸿

28 January 1926

House views with alarm the breaking down of national barriers.

Mr H. A. Rumbold[6] *Nationalism is a better safeguard against war than supranational theories which have done so much to make war in the past. The safety of the world depends upon an aristocracy of nations. It is humiliating that a Great Power should have to submit its cause to an international court, and anyway, arbitration always fails.*

Mr Fraser (Librarian) *Where is nationalism strongest? Surely in the Balkans where there are most wars, though patriotism is not incompatible with ideals. Look at Scotland.*

Mr Acland *There is no shortage of national conflict. We have tariffs raised, anti-foreign feeling in China and America's general attitude. There are no signs of barriers breaking down!*

Lord Ennismore[7] *You can't look nationally at a problem if it is an international problem. Bad conditions and sweated labour are international evils and need world treatment.*

Mr Bicknell *War is a better check on population than birth control.*

Mr R. C. Wilson *A world consisting only of British elements would merely be dull. Composed of any other nation, it would be intolerable.*

Motion lost by 35 votes.

⸿⸿⸿

18 February 1926

House considers the continued activities of the Italian Premier, disastrous to the true interests of his own country and a menace to the peace of Europe.

Mr L. H. Scot (Ch.Ch.) *'A thing done has an end' is a principle set out by Lamberti.*[8] *Mussolini has advanced the true welfare of the Italian people. His is the only government.*

Mr C. S. M. Brereton (Balliol) *England is not Italy. Conditions in Italy were terrible and Mussolini has improved them.*

Major Hon. Henry Lygon *Mussolini has offended two classes in Italy, the professional politician and the Press, both classes responsible for the deplorable condition of Italy before the war. I dislike the inveterate habit of Englishmen in telling foreigners their business.*

Mr Moccata *I think of Mussolini as a second Peter Pan.*

Mr D. H. Dawson (Ch.Ch.) said that Mussolini was not the logical consequence of Italian History.—Why do these people always begin Italian history at Mazzini?

Mr D. V. Steere (Oriel) made an excellent speech in favour of Mussolini, justifying him with great ability.

Mr Brooke *Democracy has no chance in Italy. As for Italian fascism, English people can judge it by its English disciples.*

No vote recorded.

25 February 1926 Cambridge Visit

House deplores the current vogue of 'humanitarianism'.

Mr Durbin *It is wrong when it assumes a wrong state of society. Mere charity is futile.*

Mr M. A. Thompson disposed of the 'equality' of mankind.

It is a curious thing how few people see the solid thought on which Mr Thompson's wit and fancy are based.

Mr Rumbold dealt in the tiresome product of eugenics.

Motion lost 115:117.

Early 1926

House condemns Government's education policy as calculated to lower the standard of education and arrest its development.

Mr Bernays *Expenditure has been cut from 44 million to 40. The Minister has talked of 'a sham battle.' Is it a sham battle to have produced such protest from Miss Grier and Sir Michael Sadler? Lord Eustace Percy,*[9] *himself an educationalist, has been forced to abandon his ideals at the bidding of an incompetent Chancellor of the Exchequer [Winston Churchill].*[10]

Mr M. A. Thompson *On broad principles, economy is essential. I don't suppose anyone cares very much for economy. But if there is to be economy, it should be economy all round.*

Mr L. M. Fraser (Balliol) *The Unionist party in their election manifesto, promised to raise the standard of teachers and deal with under-equipped schools. They had actually decided that there was to be no provision for new capital expenditure.*

Mr Hill *As always, quality is not dependent on quantity and it is no argument against the government's policy to say that it is spending less money.*

Evidently speaking earlier, but listed here.

Miss Grier (Principal of Lady Margaret Hall) *The argument of the other side is that the new policy involved no serious threat to education. But it is not enough to say that no step backward is being taken. We need a great step forward. Reform and education have always gone hand in hand, and unless the 1918 act can be made a living fact, it will be a disaster for reform as it is for education. It is important to make the education structure so strong that it can resist all the efforts of those who do not love education.*

Lord Eustace Percy President of the Board of Education *I agree with all the principles laid down by Miss Grier. Education truly is a non-party issue and I welcome this motion for the interest in education provision for new capital expenditure.*

Motion lost, no figures given.

A complete hiatus occurs in the *Oxford Magazine* after this debate. The first renewed reports are cursory and concerned about style and manner, devoid of any account of the motion. Debates would once more be served by proper reporting at the start of Michaelmas term 1927.

---

20 October 1927

House believes England to be in greater danger from America than from Russia.

Mr Acland *We are the little, inefficient shopkeeper next to Woolworth's. More people are killed by Fords than by bombs. The only danger from Russia is that we shall be threatened with a Conservative government for the next fifty years. Russia puts in mind the example of what a terrible thing a revolution is.*

Mr B. J. McKenna (New College) *The Americans are always marching under someone else's triumphal arch. We can adopt their motto 'Dieu et mon Detroit,' but anyway the wealthier America is, the more she can buy from us. I am on the side of Los Angeles.*

Mr G. C. D. S. Dunbar (New College) *Russia stinks in the nostrils of the human race. But China has shown her military weakness. She has missed her chance. America's hostility is natural; what do we expect from expelled workmen, Irishmen and Germans? America, having built the largest amphitheatre in the world, then built the biggest navy. America is in the fullest sense indecent. And England's greatest danger is the vulgar acquisitiveness of America.*

Mr Shackleton Bailey (Worcester—Secretary) *I expect vitriolic attacks from people who have recently enjoyed our hospitality. But one should not ascribe Britain's get rich quick acquisitiveness to us. I am reminded of the South Sea Bubble. If America were off the map, do not expect to have the position you held in the Nineteenth century. We are a commercial, not an industrial country. Dumping is the purpose of England.*

Mr Hollis *Russia is naturally hostile toward us . . . we made them fight for us for four years and starve for eight. But she is very remote and militarily weak. But America is a worry. A millionaire there has given his son a sky-scraper to give him high ideals. I protest against allowing machinery to use me. America is a country without conversation, a country of competing monologues. Of course there are hundreds of thousands of sane men in America, but it is not the sane things we are asked to adopt.*

Mr Q. M. Hogg[11] *We all hate our rich relations and quite right too. Russia is a hostile, powerful and completely savage nation. Sacco and Vanzetti had more than a fair trial.*[12]

Mr A. Lincoln (Exeter) *In the interests of peace, the army must be called the Defence Force. The danger from Russia is that we owe her an apology.*

Mr S. M. Krusin (Balliol) *Parity begins at home.*

Motion carried 216:142.

27 October 1927

House believes Blackpool is more ridiculous than Cardiff.*

---

* An allusion to that year's party conferences: Labour's at Blackpool, that of the Conservatives at Cardiff.

Mr Julian Hall (Balliol) *While the Communists remained in the Trade Unions, it [Conference] was used to expel them from the Labour Party. I accuse the Labour Party, not of stupidity but dishonesty.*

Mr Durbin *The policy of Blackpool and Labour is international disarmament. As for Cardiff, it is House of Lords reform, something which creates an irrelevant controversy.*

Mr Brooke started gaily but relaxed into a drone. The Labour and Liberal party leaders attacked each other in the capitalist press. The Conservatives do, at any rate, unite to preserve the status quo.

Mr Aubrey Herbert *Mr Baldwin has declared, naively, that nobody is helped by the recognition of difficulties. Widows' and orphans' pensions he has declared delayed— delayed by whom? The Conservatives never discuss anything, but come to all sorts of conclusions; Labour discusses everything but never comes to any conclusion at all.*

Mr Diplock *Blackpool was divided; that is democracy. Cardiff was unanimous; that is parliamentary government.*

Motion lost 134:139.

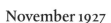

November 1927

House does not wish to hear from the Liberal Party again.

Mr Stewart *I have seen a newspaper advertisement—for the Morning Post: 'How Lloyd George bought the Liberals. One penny.'*

Mr Steere *The Liberals are a national party. Labour is a class party. Foreign policy divides Liberals from Conservatives. How have the Conservatives used these precious years since the war? They rejected the protocols of the League of Nations. They sold themselves to the military party. The most striking evidence of what they have done has been the resignation of Lord Robert Cecil.*[13]

Mr Hogg *American steel magnates are the true enemies of peace. The Liberals are a flock of rather quarrelsome shepherds without a sheep. If the Liberal Party were abolished, it would improve the public morals.*

Mr W. O. Bell (Worcester) *Isn't the Baldwin legend wearing a little thin?*

Motion lost 98:152.

---

2 February 1928

House regrets that the government has not pursued a more drastic policy of disarmament.

Mr Steere *I cannot defend the action by this government contrary to the Geneva Convention, on the question of ten thousand-ton cruisers. We are not exempt from a share of the blame for failure to reach an agreement.*

Mr Hogg *Labour began building the cruisers.* Mr Wheatley[14] *has said that he was ready to apply force to keep the Empire together. Both the great parties were agreed on this.*

Mr Wilson *Peace is something constructive and progressive and does not consist merely in the absence of war. I believe in people more than in governments.* Mr Wilson reminded me of Lord Grey*—while there was nothing strikingly original in what he had to say, he made a profound impression.

Mr Shackleton Bailey *Look at America. A navy is a complete luxury to her unless she proposes to attack the Philippines. If she were in a position to coerce us, she would try to dominate the whole world. If we were to disarm, what chance is there that others would follow the example. Would Mussolini go to hear the Bishop of Lichfield[15] and get converted? Hadn't all liberal statesman declared before 1914 that war with Germany was impossible?*

---

* Sir Edward Grey.

342

Mr G. W. Brown (Magd.) *The Tory party doesn't care tuppence about the League of Nations.*

Motion carried 157:78.

9 February 1928

The problems of the land can only be solved by state intervention.

Mr Stewart *I have heard tell of a squire who boasted that he had cleared every Liberal off his estate. (Cheers) State intervention has, in fact, been the long term policy of the Conservative Party.*

Mr S. S. Brooke *The landowning system is breaking down. The other side can only offer protection. Fantastic! Land is a monopoly and the state is quite justified in interfering. At present, two million pounds are being spent annually on the salaries of officials.*

Mr Acland *If a tenant farmer improved his farm and afterwards it were sold, he would have to pay a higher price as the consequence of his own improvements.*

Mr Shackleton Bailey *I object to the idea of centralised milking stations. How far would the poor cows have to walk?*

Mr Boyd-Carpenter (Balliol) *There are enormous spaces of fertile land in our Empire with no one to cultivate them. I wish Liberals would face facts. Think big! Think Imperially!*

Mr D. L. Orr (Balliol) *I admire Mr Lloyd George and at the same time, I distrust him. I am for the self-reliance of the yeoman.*

Mr C. G. Clark (BNC) *Farmers around Tiverton want the wartime committees again.*

Mr F. Ashe Lincoln[16] *Mr Baldwin is too much involved with votes for young women voters to give farmers credits.* Stanley Baldwin would in 1928 lower the age level for women voters from 30 to 21—pursuing, said cynics, 'The Flapper Vote.'

Vote not given.

———— ∞ ————

23 February 1928

House looks forward to the establishment of separate parliaments in Edinburgh and Cardiff. Cambridge Visit.

Mr G. Crowther (Clare Cantab.)[17] *We Saxons have a divine mission to fulfil. Let us root out exotic passion flowers from England's green and pleasant land. I speak for the Home Rule for England party. An English House of Commons would be all to the good.*

Mr E. M. Lustgarten (St John's)[18] *There is no such thing as the English point of view. The mother of parliaments should not have any more children.*

Mr W. H. Green (St Catherine's) *I am neither Scot nor Welshman, but a Yorkshireman, and I look forward to a return to Border warfare.*

No vote given.

———— ∞ ————

1 March 1928

House has no confidence in His Majesty's Government.

Mr Aubrey Herbert[19] *Being a visitor myself, I cannot help recalling the events of 1908. Mr Churchill was also a visitor, speaking in defence of the Liberal*

Government, of which he was a member, against the attack of the then Mr F. E. Smith, now his Cabinet colleague. I shall not let any of that obstruct my condemnation of the government's failure to deal with unemployment or the depression in our industries.

Mr Winston Churchill (Visitor) *I am a little disappointed in the moderation of my opponents. There are times when great reforms are imperative. This is not one of them. What is needed at present is tranquillity. For three and a half years, England has enjoyed the blessings of stable government.*

Motion lost 355: 454.

8 March 1928

House calls on Liberal and Labour parties to form a working alliance before the next General Election.

Mr G. W. Brown treated us to a highly-coloured account of the Socialist State and attacked the elements which make up the Labour party, adding 'And this is the conglomeration into which we are asked to congeal!'

Mr R. G. Cooke *a vote cast for the Liberal party always has the opposite effect from the intended one. The Liberals are all head and Labour is all rank and file.*

Mr Stewart *the Liberals are abusive, patronising, treacherous and disunited. I am against the motion.*

Mr J. M. Foot had some nasty things to say about Mr MacDonald.

Mr E. M. Reid (Ch.Ch.) *I refuse to allow myself to be swayed by sentiment or emotion.*

Motion lost 66:67.

3 May 1928

House believes that India should forthwith rank as a Dominion.

Mr Chettur Diarchy *has been tried and has failed. Unless England moves to allow real self-government, then she will have a revolution on her hands.*

Mr J. M. Foot was not very convincing.

Mr Stopford Brooke *I do not believe that India wants self-government; and she would be invaded at once if British troops were withdrawn.*

The Hon. Q. McGarel Hogg really must stop swaying about, but asked three pertinent questions which never received an answer.

Mr F. Correia Alfonso *I propose self-government first and democracy after.*

Motion carried 126:99.

———— ✦ ————

31 May 1928

The House likes the Budget.

Mr Stewart *The Budget is the last word of capitalism.*

Mr J. E. MacColl *The Conservatives are hiding behind red herrings.*

Mr S. G Sopote *talked about reactionaries, stagnatories, abstractionaries and progressives.*

The Reverend E. G. Drummond, summing up for the ayes, commended cricket to the house.

Motion carried 50:43.

25 October 1928

House believes that the only hope for America is the election of Governor Al Smith.

Mr J. Lawrie *There is too much efficiency in America and Mr Hoover personifies it. Mr Smith opposes big combines and Prohibition.*

Mr G. F. Wagstaffe (Exeter) *Hoover is a capable and honest man, widely travelled and well educated. Smith[20] is an illiterate politician who consorts with bootleggers, bandits, ward-heelers and sluggards. If he is elected, the negroes will run wild. Prohibition keeps aliens quiet.*

Mr A. D. C. Peterson (Balliol) *The Hoover administration is devoted to petty economy. If its industry is prospering, its farms are bankrupt.*

Mr Alan Tory (St John's) *America is two hundred years behind the times. As for Al Smith, he is corrupt and an intriguer.*

Mr George Ross *Hoover is no honest man. He changed his stance on the League of Nations to gain office. He represents isolation in foreign affairs and aggression in South America.*

Mr Craig (Pembroke) *Mr Hoover is fighting for an ideal. Mr Smith is fighting for himself.*

Mr G. C. Merrill (Ch.Ch.) *Smith is neither a statesman nor a gentleman.*

Mr J. E. F. Wood *Hoover has no principles. He gave up his religious convictions for the sake of political advantage.*

Mr R. J. N. Macleod (Trinity) *We ought to support Mr Hoover because he is pro-British.*

Mr W. L. Smith (Ch.Ch.) *A great deal has been said against Al Smith's character. I'm not impressed. There may be advantage in his failings. He has been charged with driving his car while drunk through Broadway. A man who can do that ought to be capable of governing America.*

Motion carried 231:150.

1 November 1928

House considers second chamber government to be necessary.

Hon. Q. M. Hogg *Elections are often fought on scare cries so that a government may carry out a policy, not in the interests of the nation. A second chamber should contain non-party members nominated by the Crown. The function of a second chamber is that of jury rather than legislative assembly. It should decide when the government was giving the country the right policy. It should have powers to submit issues to referendum.*

Mr Stewart *I think that theory originated with the Earl of Selborne. Nomination by the crown means nomination by the government of the day. It would thus always be a general election behind the times. On the other hand, if the second chamber were elected, it would always be at odds with the Commons. The remedy for hasty legislation is the next general election. The real remedy lies in a well-educated democracy and the extension of democracy to business and industry.*

Mr S. W. Brown (Magd.) *It is always in accordance with Socialist precedent to criticise the House of Lords. With the increase in legislation, the Lords are usefully employed dealing with it. Such a House of Lords should be reformed so as to make it more representative.*

Mr J. E. MacColl *A second chamber is no use to a Socialist party.*

Mr Wilson *The Civil Service should take the place of the Lords and become the most constructive part of the Government. It is easier to create a disinterested Civil Service than an honest second chamber.*

Mr Boyd-Carpenter *The other side are a hundred and sixty years behind the times. The House of Lords is stable and the most democratic chamber any country could have.*

Motion carried 176:120.

---

15 November 1928

House prefers athletic to aesthetic education. Visit of King George of Greece.

Mr B. J. M. McKenna (New College) *James 1 condemned football, saying that it was played by large, inflated men with brutal faces, obviously harbouring homicidal thoughts. Aesthetic education in English schools is limited to a plaster-cast of half a Greek and a lantern-slide of the Parthenon.*

King George I *was partly educated in an English school headed by a follower of muscular Christianity who was not particularly muscular and not particularly Christian. The English boys had learnt restraint and discipline while foreign boys were learning French and arithmetic.*

Mr Lustgarten *Bad education leads to boredom, boredom to immorality. It turns everything it touches cold—like a Midas who just mislaid his way.*

Professor de Madriaga[21] *The Englishman thinks with his body, especially with his elbows. If the instinct of the British race is to be kept strong, it must be kept free from education.*

Motion lost 237:286.

---

29 November 1928

House believes that all forms of censorship should be abolished.

Mr B. M. Alexander (McGill University) *There should be more individualism. Every young person should be encouraged to read the News of the World. The way to stop a young boy from smoking is to give him a big cigar.*

Mr Elletson (St John's) *Censorship of obscene books and films is the only kind that exists today. Just as it is the duty of a gardener to keep a garden free of weeds, so it is the duty of the government to keep literature clean.*

Mr R. M. Kenny (University of Toronto) *Rather than remove censorship, we want more of it. The removal of censorship in art cannot be tolerated. Since there are laws restricting a man's actions, it is only logical that the law should prevent anyone from injuring another's sensibility.*

Mr Diplock *Nothing is more conducive to cynicism than a knowledge of the facts of life.*

Mr G. F. Wagstaff *I stand for 'decency and morality' and 'liberty with respectability.'*

Motion carried 88:85.

---

24 January 1929

House is tired of the British Empire

Mr J. E. MacColl *At home, we produce a Devonshire White paper—on Scotland. But if African natives read it and say 'Africa for the Africans,' we send out thirty five policemen with machine-guns. Meanwhile a newspaper headline is 'Bolshevism among the Zulus'.*

Mr Boyd-Carpenter *Socialists simply damn the British Empire and talk of it as the pure jingoism of after-dinner speeches. Really it is a great, if complicated experiment which is not yet finished.*

Mr F. R. Moraes *I'm a cynic who thinks of the League of Nations as an organisation which touches nothing it does not adjourn. Even so the British Empire does not help the League as it might. The happenings in Egypt do not make for peace and everywhere the empire means muddle and confusion.*

Mr Hogg Here are three separate empires, the sentimental and commercial one, an immense power for constructive peace and good in the world; the Indian Empire, for which England is striving desperately to do the right thing in all honesty, and the crown colonies. There is a civilised man's burden.

Mr Correia Afonso—Secretary The Empire has conquered England. For of all its statesmen, Mr Baldwin alone may not say what he likes. Imperialism is political polygamy.

Mr J. H. Parker The Empire just means slavery which we call something else.

Mr R. E Marleyn The Empire is the source of all sorts of mistaken commitments.

Motion lost 121:171.

31 January 1929

House believes Nationalisation is essential to a solution of the mining problem.

Mr G. M. Reid The Coal industry has been treated with criminal negligence. Past history has shown the mine-owners to be incapable of co-operation with anybody. So if there is to be efficient organisation, nationalisation has to be the only way.

Mr Elletson Look at the Samuel Report.[22] It laid the blame for the present situation at the feet of the miners' leaders who are the kind of men to make trouble. The Labour Party can buy the mines or steal them, the latter being more probable.

Mr A. J. Lush was satirical about the mine owners. Speaking as a miner, he made a much appreciated speech.

Mr Hogg *The coal industry cannot be nationalised by itself. And doing so would cause more disorganisation than it would solve.*

Mr H. D'Avigdor Goldsmid *We have been arguing for two and a half hours on a false premise. There are the foreign markets and you have to sell in them.*

Motion lost 92:117.

---

14 February 1929

Cambridge visit: House is weary of the House of Commons.

Mr Correia Afonso—Secretary *Party loyalty is an insult to the electorate. Witness the outcry against 'stolen principles.'*

Mr McKenna—Librarian *Although Mr Gladstone did not live his life in vain, politics are not what they were. The best men do not go into politics, with the result that the House of Commons does not represent the people.*

Mr H. M. Foot—Vice President of the Cambridge Union[23] *The people opposite are disgruntled. Democracy is only nominally achieved, so it is stupid to be bored yet awhile.*

Mr Tory *The existence of the Home Secretary[24] shows that something is wrong. People like that should not be allowed to bother with politics. Also the supremacy of the executive has made the Commons worthless as a democratic institution.*

Mr N. G. Pearson *The House of Commons does not govern the country, but it sees that it is governed.*

Mr M. P. Pai *Members of the Commons do not have even the rights of members of a debating society.*

Motion lost 135:169.

14 February 1929

House is in favour of birth control as a national policy.

This was effectively a debate on Eugenics, the programme of the same Francis Galton, frequently cited here—more ruthless cousin of Charles Darwin. It involved the elimination of human beings of lower intelligence and/or physical defects by selective breeding and the ready use of contraception. Taken up by Germany over the instructive period 1933–45, it rather lost caste, though careful, temperate arguments in favour of (voluntary) contraception were now advanced, which, in that form, has since the 1960s been general practice. The guest at this debate, Dr Crichton-Miller, argued for the real thing.

Mr H. J. H. Parker *Those who object to contraception because it is contrary to nature should realize that all improvements are contrary to nature. We must not take the medieval view that celibacy is an ideal. Birth control is a way of getting rid of illegitimacy, reason enough in itself. And in general, children who will not have a decent chance in life should not be born at all.*

Mr Diplock *We must beware of taking the cowardly course. The courageous path is to refuse to rest until we have changed our social conditions. The remedy for Bethnal Green is to make it fit for children.*

Mr P. M. Lustgarten [sic] *Economic circumstances are creating immorality because it is impossible to square them with morality. At present, official reticence leads to the inaccuracy and uncleanness which comes from underhand dissemination of knowledge.*

Dr H. Crichton-Miller *Birth control is no solution to our health problem; and that is the possibility of realising a eugenic ideal. The only important aspect of the question is the qualitative aspect, and what must be found are practical men for breeding from above-par standard. In an ideal community, those who are not up to par should not be allowed to have children, but they should at least have the other joys of family life. There rests with everybody the responsibility for 'The august stewardship of the clean blood of the race' which means that only those with a fine background should come into the world at all. This is no question of legislation but of bold idealism.*

Motion carried 290:129.

---

28 February 1929

This House is in favour of the abolition of capital punishment.

Mr Phelps Brown *Retention is due to the fact that capital punishment is traditional and easy and that society is too lazy to think it worthwhile to change. The execution is degrading to all concerned except the criminal who is invested with the dignity of great suffering.*

Mr Hogg *I oppose, but the penalty should only be imposed for two types of murder, deliberate murder and an act done in furtherance of another crime.*[25] *The value of human life is so high that it must be protected by the hardest means. The possible reform of the murderer is too great a risk for society to take. And death is better than life imprisonment.*

Mr Stewart *The division of murder into kinds and types start a long road to leading to the cruellest and stupidest illogicalities. The revolting side of the death penalty is the fact that prison officers live with the condemned man for three week as human beings and then have to hang him.* Mr Stewart is the best debater and clearest speaker in the Union at present.

Mr Laurence Housman (Visitor) *We ought not to give too much weight to expert opinion. Cases are only re-opened when they concern somebody alive, so we do not know if someone has been wrongly hanged. Why do we look down on the hangman?*

Because we delegate work to him. We should recognise the indignity and beastliness in which society indulges.

Captain Gilbert Frankau *I speak for all those who deplore the sloppiness and sentimentality of the present age. Useless members of society ought to be dealt with ruthlessly; and therefore capital punishment has a function to perform. Looked at in this light, there is nothing revolting or illogical about it.*

Motion carried 204:111.

17 October 1929

Labour in the General election of 21 November 1929 had moved from 151 seats in the Commons to 287 and the Conservatives had fallen from 412 to 260 whilst the Liberals had pulled back from 40 seats to 57. Labour had only a simple majority, not the essential overall one. No actual coalition was formed with the Liberals, though early reasonable cooperation was observed.

House believes that the events of the last four months do not encourage this house to support the Labour Party.

Mr Elletson wisely made unemployment the centre of his attack, but mentioned also the costly pensions schemes in preparation.

Mr Lustgarten claimed for the Conservatives the credit for the Hague[26] and renewed the attack on unemployment.

Mr O. C. Papineau spoke from reasoned principles. *I dislike the politician's mentality, unintelligent democracy, and the delays of parliamentarianism. In the Labour party I find cultural enlightenment, The Hague, and the decision on the school-leaving age.*

Mr P. G. Hamilton (Trinity) *I find the raising of the school-leaving age premature.*

Mr J. M. Foot With the weighty manner of his brother, he echoed the Liberal war cry, pleaded for Trotsky and sneered at Sir O. Mosley.[27] He pointed to the Licensing commission and the death penalty as instances of Labour's desertion of pledges.

Mr J. F. F. Platts-Mills[28] rambled on pleasantly but irrelevantly.

Motion carried 151:143.

<hr>

14 November 1929

House believes the League of Nations to be an over-rated institution.

Mr C. L Harrison (St John's) *I believe that the League is at fault in paying too much attention to externals and too little to the spirit of international friendship.*

Mr G. M. Wilson (Oriel) *What has the League done? It has worked for the prevention of war and suffers from not too much, but too little publicity.* This was a good and interesting speech, but Mr Wilson should beware of such expressions as 'come to grief' and 'dirty work.'

Mr P. G. Hamilton (Trinity) *The source of the League is the Versailles Treaty, an evil source. The Germans are dissatisfied; the French put their trust in forts; Mussolini has bombarded Corfu. The United States has deserted and may yet wage war on Japan. The principle of one nation, one vote is wrong and the League is unprogressive.*

Mr J. A. Wiedermayer (Exeter) *Looking back at the League's performance, I am struck by its ability to be too visionary and too commonplace at the same time.*

Mr L. S. McLintock (Corpus) *Peace is the natural state of man.*

Mr A. J. Ayer (Ch.Ch.)[29] *I find the League in outlook, too economic and not sufficiently cultural.* The subject for debate merited a less flippant manner than Mr Ayer's.

Mr S. G. Gould *I consider the League a living thing whose mere existence is a cause for joy.*

Mr F. H. Phillips (Queen's) *Western nations should set a pacific example.* As soon as he stops using the adverb 'pretty,' he will be admirable.

Motion lost 83:134.

———— ✖ ————

13 February 1930

Cambridge Visit—House believes that Fascism is necessary.

Mr J. D. F. Green (Peterhouse Cantab.) He has the best and most of the worst qualities of the old-fashioned die-hard, always able to denounce democracy and bolster up vested interests. He argued that no one is interested in politics any longer, so they should be left to Mussolini. Also he used his powers of oratory to descant on the glories of the good old days of Pitt.

Mr H. Z. A. Kahir (Exeter) *Fascism has its place and works very well in early civilisations, but becomes a check on development. Only by getting into the water, can a man learn how to swim.*

Mr Papineau *Do we really think that a man who works for fifty weeks in the year gets very much satisfaction from the thought that he has the privilege of using the vote once in three years?*

Mr C. W. Jenks *A thing can only be a necessity if it is to achieve a desirable object. The break-up of democracy is not a desirable object.*

Mr Brian Davidson (New College) *The Fascist argument is that all great nations have been carnivorous. So by order of Mussolini all Italians must eat a given quantity of meat, slightly underdone.*

Mr D. C. Walker-Smith[30] *It is much better for men to live lives of individuality rather than they should be bludgeoned into sheep-like efficiency.*

Mr D. L. Renton[31] *supported the Liberals who found themselves supporting the motion.*

Mr G. E .O. Walker *spoke about his childhood. Apparently a disgraceful affair was put in order by the strong hand of his nurse. Evidently Mussolini is to do the same for Italy.*

Vote not given.

———— ∞∞ ————

8 May 1930

House holds that one can be happier in America than in England—visit of Californian debating team.

Mr McClintock (Stanford University) *The Pilgrim Fathers found a place where they could do unto others as others had been doing unto them. The English do have a happiness of sorts, but it is essentially vegetable.*

Mr E. G. Bantzer (University of California) *An Englishman is content to wait three days if he misses a train. An American lets out a squawk if he misses one section of a revolving door.*

Mr A. J. Ayer was the one person in the debate who asked 'What is happiness'.[32]

Motion lost by 47 votes.

———— ∞∞ ————

15 May 1930

House does not support India's claim to immediate self-government.

Mr Hogg (ex-President) *I move an amendment that this matter should not be discussed until the report of the Simon commission has been published.* He was supported by a number of people who had cajoled themselves into believing that debates in the Union are actually of first class importance and by a large number of people who enjoy shouting and are not members of the Society.

The adjournment produced several good speeches and one that was quite excellent, from Mr MacColl—ex-Librarian. The motion was rejected by 27 votes, whereupon over a hundred members, headed by Mr Hogg, who is of course the son of the late Lord Chancellor,[33] left the House as a protest. Otherwise huff.

Debate proper Mr Randolph Churchill (Ch.Ch.)[34] *was rather out of his class. He is content to repeat what he has read, but not digested, instead of producing some signs of the original thought of which we had thought him capable. Nor does his delivery improve because he insists on reading the greater part of his speech. Finally, though the Union is not noted for its manners, Mr Churchill should remember that it is customary for the mover to wait until his opponent has finished speaking, before he leaves the House.*

Mr Moraes (St Catherine's) *His matter was well thought out and it was delivered, in spite of provocation, with great moderation. Having of course, great knowledge of his subject, he was easily able to tear up the previous speech.*

Mr L. G. H. Holiday *spoke as a citizen of the world, so he said. We should have thought him an arch-imperialist.*

<hr />

30 October 1930

House dislikes Miss Amy Johnson, Hitler and University journalism.

Mr L. E. Lieven[35] (St Edmund Hall) *His peroration, an impassioned plea for Hitler, was the more effective because of its contrast with the earlier part of his speech.*

Mr W. R. L. Fraser (Balliol) *defended Herr Hitler on the grounds of his hostility to the reparation agreements.*

Mr J. Adenauer (Balliol) mentioned the economic condition of Germany.

Motion carried 227:132.

———ⱺ⊗ⱺ———

13 November 1930

House believes that the majority is always wrong.

Mr D. L. M. Renton (Univ.) With a voice suitable to the Albert Hall, great vitality and a power of profoundly believing in whatever he happens to be saying, Mr Renton has an obvious future as a Liberal leader.

Mr R. G. Cant quoted Lenin on the grounds that Trotsky was no longer persona grata.

No vote given.

———ⱺ⊗ⱺ———

20 November 1930

House would deplore a Conservative victory at the polls.

Mr John Foot (Balliol) It is probable that if he had made the worst speech of the evening, he would have been elected President. *Mr Baldwin does not have the courage of Lord Beaverbrook's convictions.*[36] *Attempts at the furtherance of Imperial trade are futile. Sir Austen Chamberlain's foreign policy is wrong.*

Sir Austen Chamberlain *I do not accept responsibility for the occupation of the Ruhr by reason of not having been in office at the time.* He is one of the few speakers who can deal with the future of the Empire without compelling one to feel that it essential to go out and buy a Union Jack.

No vote given.

13

The Old Familiar Faces

27 November 1930–31 October 1935

Trades Disputes Act/School military training/BBC/British imperialism/Nationalism—evil/Social Services/Pacifism/No Confidence/Indian Self-government/Only Russia has a future/Tory fiscal policy/mass production/Congresses: Indian and American/A new progressive party?/Class war/Tory Indian policy/No confidence/Russian experiment/No confidence/Russia succeeding?/Let's replace democracy/Socialism only solution/Censorship of the press/Liberal Party/British Empire threatening peace/King and Country/Undying faith in politicians/Expunging K&C motion?/Party system and poverty/Giving up the League/Fascism preferred to Socialism/Views nothing with concern/Toryism no solution/India white paper condemned/Roosevelt's experiment/Hitler's first moves/Western civilisation doomed/Arms industry/Politics and undergraduates/House of Lords/No economic recovery/Irish Republic for the Six Counties/Franco-Russian Alliance?/Hereditary principle/BBC as menace/Cult of the state/Failing the unemployed/No Confidence: Attlee guest speaker/British rule and native peoples/Collective security and re-armament.

There are all sorts of melodramatic terms for the 1930s. Auden spoke of a 'low, dishonest decade', authorial glibness from a pre-emptive US exile, about a nightmare unsurprisingly too much for ordinary people (and politicians). Though it is worth reflecting on the outburst of rapture towards the Nazis and their bright-eyed, marching youth indulged in by Winston Churchill in his overreaction to the King and Country debate (see below). That debate and its fervently negative verdict, looked at in the context of the First World War and the talk of 'honour' with which it had been garlanded, comes like a natural reaction to all the patriotic schoolmasters pointing sixth-formers toward the Somme. The war which supporters of the 1933 motion readily entered in 1939, was not for King and Country nor any of Churchill's bulbous rhetoric. Among the most politically alert, it was and would continue to be, a war *against* something—Fascism, Hitler, the self-evident horror building up in Central Europe.

At the start of the decade though, the mood was not quite Panglossian—that would patronize a great many good purposes and reasonable assumptions—but it was optimistic, and optimism was about to be sliced fine by a slashing and murderous version of the familiar stupid nationalism of pre-1914. The 1920s, if wrong about economics, had been internationally good-purposed. A symbolic figure is Lord Robert Cecil, familiar to the Union, moving from the uncritical pessimism and doctrinaire inactivity of the third Marquess to a belief in unselfish international action, cooperation, problem-settling, every kind of positive work, by way of the League of Nations. He wasn't wrong to want it; and Oxford undergraduates were a more attractive, decent, and humane bunch than the ones of a few years earlier, snarling at 'the scum of Europe, making their ways to these shores'. *These* young men were wrong, only in the abstraction of their good purpose.

There is a lot to be said for naive idealism. The First World War of fifty-two months' continuous shooting to kill other men also shooting to kill, was produced in various Foreign Offices and newspapers by believers in short, cleansing wars. It succeeded in making most people fear its recurrence like the long parade of death it was. The text of Union debates has so far been kept separate but equal from these commentaries on them. However this observation in January 1931, by a man from Christ Church, Derek Walker-Smith, catches very well indeed the shift of mood from 1911 when the House applauded the vision of the 'entire university—with rifles—parading down the High'. Incidentally, when the editor wrote about parliamentary debates for a living, Sir Derek, former Minister of Health, and still then present in the Commons, when observed in the

1980s was, though never unpleasant, a crusty backbencher *in excelsis*. However in January 1931, Mr D. C.Walker-Smith (Christ Church) said:

'The OTC stands for everything I hate in our educational system, one based on the assumption that anything sufficiently unpleasant is sure to be good for a boy, a system with Dr Arnold at its head and the doctrine of original sin as its justification.'

That stands as an irony at the head of the year in which Oswald Mosley's New Party became the British Union of Fascists, putting on black shirts and marching military fashion through unoffending High Streets. Stanley Baldwin's lazy but effective catchphrase 'Wait and see' was good politics for a bemused public hit by massive unemployment, and with so many of them cast onto the thin mercies of the Dole, at whose extravagance one or two unreconstructed young gentlemen can be found snapping.

The virtuous Mosley, member of a Labour Cabinet, asked to find something that might be done against all this, had been active. He was full of basically Keynesian ideas, keen to spend money on projects which would generate jobs circulating money and demand. In the United States, Franklin Roosevelt would do pretty much this despite screams at improvidence from banks and investors whose immoderation on a bull market had dug the hole. On just this improvident policy, Roosevelt had been elected and would next time, 3 November 1936, get himself elected again in forty-six states (to two against). The old dictum 'As Maine goes, so goes the Nation,' became 'As Maine goes, so goes Vermont.'

Mosley made his case for schemes to make jobs to the Labour government, in power since 1929, in other words hit on the head by crisis as soon as chairs had been organized around the Cabinet table. Philip Snowden was Chancellor, an altogether more coherent and competent figure than MacDonald, but of his generation, a clear-minded Free Trader, a Cobdenite of Cobdenites, who in 1930, baulked at Keynesian measures. Ironically though, after the event, out of office in 1935, Snowden would endorse proposals from Lloyd George for precisely those undertakings: pump-priming, major public works, and all the benefits of induced demand.

There are times for Keynes and times not for him. An example of the latter was Edward Heath's well-meant, but mistaken expenditure programmes calculated to reorganize local government and actually bloating it, all this at a time of extensive social welfare which made unemployment something very different from the stacked-up misery recorded in *The Road to Wigan Pier*. Heath's reflation came during a modest recession, best left to right itself and the pumps left unprimed. The demand induced was inflationary, the unions (of employed men), responded by demands which were conceded, and union power became for the first time seriously injurious.

Putting inflation into the high 20 per cents gave destructive fantasy leftism a la Arthur Scargill its chance, and Mrs Thatcher hers: 1931 wasn't remotely like 1972/3. Attempts to deny the need for demand stimulation miss the simple laws of situations altering cases. At the end of December 1930, unemployment touched 2.5 million and rose. By May 1931, it stood at 2.8 million men out of work. Money put into the economy then would have been readily repayable debt as the wages for schemes proved directly useful to what we have learned to call the infrastructure: roads, harbours, and for that matter hospitals. These are capital and social assets through which money flowing in wages would not have sparked inflation.

As it was, worse things were happening in continental Europe, the collapse of the Kreditanstalt of Vienna particularly injurious, as it affected Germany where the Reichsbank lost 840 million marks in the first three weeks of June. And naturally, all of Germany's ills spilt eastward to Hungary and Romania. On top of everything else, France reverted to Poincaré mode. The Germans had been saddled since Versailles with vengeful and punitive repayments. French Ministers of the cruder sort, like Tardieu, associate of Poincaré, cherished them. Faced with international crisis, they feared default and, where postponement or readier forgiveness of debt would have raised expectations, application of unrelenting immediate compliance, unsurprisingly in a market hoping for relief, began a run on the mark and the whole German economy. These are circumstances which delight extremists and Hitler moved nearer to power, in elections among fearful disoriented voters.

The British Labour government feared developments and appointed a committee under a Sir George May. It is reliably said that the only thing that can usefully be done with a public committee is to appoint the right chairman. May came from insurance and on 26 August 1931 reported accordingly—accordingly and clumpingly, with atrociously unconsidered timing for politics, business, and finance, with old hat prejudice generally dispersed. His committee's remedies were literally punitive, of a kind by which a Marxist could shock, teach, and not unreasonably, convert. The workers were to blame and must be punished. Foreign investors and bankers thought us prodigal and distrusted the soundness of this most moderate of Labour governments. What left-wing speakers call 'Clubbing the workers' was a pre-eminent requirement. The Labour government was to blame because foreign investors had no confidence in it; unemployment pay was too high and must be cut. Otherwise, foreign, especially American, investors would flee. *They* required the dole cuts as a condition of supporting the pound which was in danger and should be saved by a balanced (i.e. deficit-free) Budget. The idea of saying 'Let the pound fall or float down and let industry take advantage and confidence from the upward export consequence of selling cheap' was not contemplated.

There is an interesting parallel here. The political effect on the Major government (not, to any dispassionate reading, by any means a bad one) of withdrawal from shadowing the Euro in 1992 was never recovered from. Yet the pound had simply been pitched too high on entry, so members of that Cabinet assure us, at Mrs Thatcher's insistence, before withdrawing from politics. This was done, not out of foolish patriotism, but sensibly enough in theory, to restrain inflation. Inflation, however, was the grief of the mid-1970s. It wasn't a great threat in 1990. But a pound *artificially* high is a currency which shrewd men will sell down in order to buy cheap…and then profitably repeat the exercise.

If the sellers of currency had no confidence in Philip Snowden's Exchequer because it provided modest unemployment payments, it was a convenient alibi for a competitive selling which made other men sell more. All this was done in the hope of appreciation when the right wrong decisions should be taken and announced. It was not quite the conspiracy, alleged quite reasonably, by Marxists, rather the triumph of class prejudice in punitive mood looking for someone to blame and contriving to find a base to buy at. *Pace* Auden. It was, at any rate, a *sanctimonious* decade.

The terms of the May Committee were orthodox and wrong. They also represented a cruelty to the general working public, at which somewhere along the line of bitter compliance, the Labour Cabinet would break. A series of their meetings amassed a body of cuts, all of them deflationary and directed toward further unemployment and straight misery. They were pursued reluctantly and unhappily to a figure of £56 million against a set figure in banking demands of £78 million. In particular, the Cabinet had resisted the itemized cuts in unemployment provision. Interestingly, Lloyd George, who in due course would vigorously proclaim public expenditure as an aid to recovery, spoke pure economy, advising MacDonald on the phone to cut deeper.

The government would be heckled by the right-wing press, notably the same *Times* under Garvin and Barrington Ward (familiar here in earlier Union debates, as a right-wing undergraduate), which would later preach appeasement of Hitler. But no appeasers of the British public themselves, writers of *Times* leaders charged the MacDonald Cabinet with cowardice. Perfectly aware of the panic selling which wild-mouthed journalism can create—the peculiar unpatriotism of the raging Right—*The Times* worked hard to get it. Ultimately the Cabinet, having swallowed a succession of alien moves, all of them deepening the economic damage, reached the moment when men snap.

Counter-suggestions had been made: higher taxes on the rich, getting off Churchill's gold standard, and a revenue tariff, all of them things actually to be done later. At this moment, though, Snowden's perfect instance of sincere social democratic purpose caught up in classical economics and an over-schooled personality, together with MacDonald candidly at sea, broke with a majority of Cabinet colleagues over the proposed saving of £12.25 million by cutting unemployment pay. The great majority of the Cabinet, whatever their perplexity, knew what, as representatives of working people, they could not do. They were now directed by May to doing that which, by reducing purchasing power, they should not, on any account, do.

The government split at 50:50, agreed to resign on Monday 24 August; and the formation of a National Government under a bemused Ramsay MacDonald, dismally followed. It was not dirty or dishonest. It was uncomprehending: Minsters bullied into playing by rules which made things very much worse. The Cabinet split was a majority refusing the cut at issue; a National Government, with MacDonald as passive, dignified head, swallowed them, joined up with Baldwin and a section of the Liberal Party, led, naturally, by Simon, called an election and won it. With Labour demoralized, victim charged with a responsibility actually owing to a bankers' panic to which its leaders had deferred, it entered the contest without hopes and finished with 46 seats. Liberals standing outside the National Government had 33. By contrast, the Conservatives held 470 seats in the Commons, the National Liberals under Simon 35, and MacDonald's little group of National Labour 13.

Unemployment (with a cut in employment benefit) would rise to 15 per cent against the maximum of 5 per cent in France which had done a brisk devaluation at the start of the decade. Real interest rates would rise to 8 per cent. In September 1931, Britain would gratefully leave the gold standard. The 1930s would be a decade of immiseration for a great tranche of the innocent population, especially in the north, the base of British heavy industry. The unequal recovery showing in the mid-1930s, mostly new industry in the south, would itself be badly set back by a second recession in 1936 and only recover with rearmament.

Politically, the 1930s would be as vivid as the economy was drab. Mosley would become an imitation Mussolini, then picking up on anti-Semitism, an imitation Hitler. Street violence occurred, though the extent has been exaggerated by Mosley opponents for whom the 'Battle of Cable Street' resonates. A culture of innocent Marxism grew up among writers, increasing numbers of academics, and of course undergraduates. Foreign affairs were remote and only such minorities cared about them. Mosley, and indeed Hitler, might march, but the first half of this decade was one of making do at home under a secure and inactive government and hearing of unpleasant things happening in remote and impossible places like Manchuria and Ethiopia. In the worst sense of that two-edged word, it would get more interesting.

---

27 November 1930

House would deplore the repeal of the Trades Disputes Act.[1]

Mr R. G. Cant (Oriel) took a moderate—may one say a 'liberal' view of the General Strike. *The Conservatives have generally been 'the party of the landlords and the landladies'. Is it not time now to exclude all vested interests from politics?*

Mr J. W. Farnsworth (Balliol) *we have lacked for over a year a really embittered revolutionary. But Mr Farnsworth would class all the moderates with the present government as 'bourgeois reactionaries.' He revelled in strikes; talked about 'class', produced, accidentally, one of the best jokes we have heard for some time and, after the laughter, appealed to the Chair for order.*

Mr A. Dowdell (Queen's) *A member of the Durham Miners' Association, he introduced an atmosphere of reality into the debate. We were grateful to Mr Dowdell for giving us the benefit of his experience, and the ovation he received was well deserved.*

Mr Lieven *mentioned 'that rascal, Cook'[2] and referred to the illegality of the General Strike.*

Motion carried 84:39.

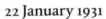

22 January 1931

House, believing the party system to have failed, would welcome the formation of a National Government.

Mr E. D. O'Brien[3] *His important matter was to preserve from adulteration the pure milk of Conservative orthodoxy ... His sallies were often too bitter—[describing] the Prime Minister[4] as 'a little dog squirming on its stomach.'*

Motion lost 105:165.

29 January 1931

House views with alarm the campaign for the abolition of military training in schools.

Mr D. Walker-Smith (Ch.Ch.) opposing *The OTC stands for everything I hate in our educational system, one based on the assumption that anything sufficiently unpleasant is sure to be good for a boy, a system with Dr Arnold at its head and the doctrine of original sin as its justification.*

Mr A. J. Irvine (Oriel)[5] *I would not be surprised if the chests of the mover and seconder of the motion were painted with woad.*

Mr Lieven [whose comments are not printed—presumably one of the woad-wearers] is a Tory of the old school. Mr Boyd-Carpenter's views [also omitted] *beside his, are almost seditious.*

Vote lost 85:131.

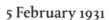

5 February 1931

House regards the BBC with mistrust and its policy and prejudice with disapproval.

Mr O. C. Papineau (Hertford) *I have given the matter some little thought...The BBC is ignorant when it is not deliberately partisan. I want to see intellectual anarchy.*

Mr H. Z. A. Kabir (Exeter) *It is ridiculous to think of denying to civilisation the immense advantage of wireless just because small criticisms can be made of its application.*

Sir John Reith (DG of BBC—Visitor)[6] Somewhat overawed the house by his magnificent presence. *This institution has all the advantages and none of the disadvantages of a state-owned concern. It is giving democracy a chance never enjoyed before. The idea of 'Giving the public what it wants' should be rejected because 'if you set out to do that, you will not succeed even in that.'*

Motion lost 56:148.

12 February 1931

House believes that British imperialism operates to the detriment of native races.

Mr J. Lewin (Cape Town University) *There exist in Kenya conditions of forced labour as disgraceful as anything in Soviet Russia. Imperialism is the adventures of capitalists abroad.*

Mr W. G. Murray (Witwatersrand University) *made an excellent speech notable for an attack upon British India and attacked the Liberal party* Under Mr Lloyd George, it is a flock of sheep led, not by a shepherd but a crook.

Mr E. L. Lieven *defended imperialism with superb ferocity.*

Mr S. G. Gould (Magd.) *is so depressing that one fails to appreciate what he says.*

Mr S. J. Pinto *made a magnificent attack upon British rule in India.*

Mr H. A. Fountain *thought well of the Empire.*

Motion carried 95:81.

---

30 April 1931

House regards the principle of Nationalism as an evil in the modern world.

Mr Papineau *Nationalism is a vague, warm, sentimental, emotional welter in which the intellect plays no part. He delivered an apology for the Mosley policy[7] and dismissed ordinary nationalism as a set of tribal myths.*

Mr Lieven *Italy and Germany have survived crises only by means of violent nationalism, whereas the policy of a small oligarchy of criminals in Russia essentially is Communism and essentially international.*

Mr J. M. O'Connor *created some surprise by saying that the secession of the American colonies was a great catastrophe.*

Mr O'Brien *was the first of those who spoke against the motion to refine nationalism into something so perfect that it could not possibly be evil.*

Mr L. M. Gelber (Balliol) *Nationalism is loyalty to what is close and familiar. It works as a cohesive force.*

Mr M. L. White *admitted that nationalism can go wrong.*

Motion carried 129: 90.

7 May 1931

House believes that any further increase in the Social Services is financially undesirable.

Mr Smuts *Reductions in the fighting services cannot pay for increases in the social services. Rigid economy is a vital necessity.*

Mr A. W. J. Greenwood[8] *Raising the school leaving age will pay for itself. Further, money not taken by the state is not guaranteed to be used for industrial investment.*

Mr Brian Davidson *has made a full return to the Conservative fold, but he painted a singularly black picture of England's future bankruptcy if she continued on her present high rate of taxation. His peroration was not treated with the seriousness which its unrelieved gloom deserved.*

Mr Kabir *Money not spent by the state is not merely wasted. Capital is found for luxury industries, but people are unwilling to lend it without a high rate of interest.*

Mr Papineau *Taxation falls chiefly on profits and serves the Chancellor whose fiscal views are obsolete.*

Mr D. R. Barker (Oriel) *made a passionate defence of the lower middle-classes and deplored extensions of the social services as they would destroy that element.*

Mr G. E. Whitrow (Ch.Ch.) *The social services may not be a cure for society, but they are a necessary palliative.*

Mr T. N. Fox *Conservatives always say that the country is about to go bankrupt, but there is no more evidence of it now than there has ever been. Mr Fox should speak more often.*

Mr A. B. Rae (Oriel) *confined himself to remarks about the dole. He thought it was bad and its retention mere bribery.*

Mr K. H. Digby (St John's) *asked why the officers of the Society sport expensive tail coats if there is no money for social services.*

Motion carried 84:52.

---

28 May 1931

House believes pacifism the only true form of patriotism.

Mr P. Heiman (Exeter) *From an economic point of view, pacifism is by far the better course. In such a complex world, international control is absolutely necessary.*

Mr E. F. F. White (Corpus) *described all pacifists as reactionary and made a scathing attack upon all conscientious objectors whose position was untenable, judged either as morality or courage.*

Mr Smuts *In time of war all must rally to the state.*

Mr Papineau *Ordinary people would have been just as well-off if the Germans had gone right through to Paris in 1914 without opposition and there would have been fewer horrors than there were.*

Mr P. G. Turpin (Exeter) *Pacifism has nothing to do with patriotism; and the doctrine of internationalism is pernicious.*

Mr Barker *was such an extreme pacifist that he thought patriotism just horrible.*

Mr S. S. De Chuie (Balliol) *The value of a revolver is its moral force.*

Mr S. Long (Merton) *described patriotism as a desire to further the interests of one's own country and thought Napoleon was a splendid man.*

Mr D. W. B. Maughan (Balliol) *wound up the debate by maintaining that wars don't pay.*

Motion carried 79:47.

---

4 June 1931

House has confidence in His Majesty's Government.

Mr Davidson *Labour's handling of India and its foreign policy has been satisfactory, but they have 'fiddled while Rome burned' by bringing in totally unnecessary legislation.*

Mr Kabir (Librarian) *The Conservatives would rather see good left undone than have it done by others. He passed on to an attack on Mr Winston Churchill and Lord Lloyd,*[9] *also making an eloquent defence of the government's Indian policy.*

Mr Papineau *The Government may only be questioned on its economic policy where there are two main difficulties—lack of capital and unfair competition. The Conservatives have only two remedies, lower taxation and tariffs, both of which will fail in their object. Even a ten per cent cut in Social Services will save a mere £20.5 million. So control of investments must be introduced. Mr Papineau then defended the New Party*[10] *insulation policy and argued that Labour had hooked the larger and more important part of the Liberal fish.*

Rt. Hon. Herbert Morrison MP[11] *did the previous speakers the honour of debating with them and made one of the best speeches that has been heard in this house for a long time. The Labour government has done more to relieve unemployment than any past government and the circumstances are more difficult. We have introduced a road Transport Bill and another to promote agriculture. The Land Drainage bill will absorb labour, as will plans for slum clearance.*

Motion carried 121: 115.

---

29 October 1931

House demands complete self-government for India.

Mr Smuts—Treasurer[12] seemed to feel himself on unsafe ground throughout. *There is a parallel between India and South Africa which has become wholly independent. If we were able to do that, then India should be given her freedom, in response to which, she would remain loyal to the Empire. If the prodigal son is given the latch key, he will stay at home in the evening.*

Mr Heimann (Exeter) *I am a simple member of the British Empire, a South African; and I object to the comparison made with India. India is a geographical term and no more a nation than the equator. Britain has also sunk a great deal of capital into India to which she has just claims given any morality.*

Mr W. L. R. Fraser (Balliol) *An irresponsible executive and a Central government which is frankly despotic, mean that we are giving India the shadow of self-government without the substance. I detest the horrible ebullitions of the British Press. There is nothing fine or dignified in attempting to govern a country against its will.*

Mr E. J. Thomson M.A. (Oriel) *Congress propaganda is as ceaseless as it is widespread and though the loyalty of the police has been magnificent, I am doubtful that it will stand up to another test of civil disobedience. No one race in India is fit at the moment to entrust with complete government. What is wanted is a ten year plan on both sides.*

Mr Papineau *Ideals are played out; we must start thinking in terms of interests—and thinking hard! The crisis is too grave for altruism.*

Motion lost 121:141.

5 November 1931

House believes that where other countries have pasts, only Russia has a future.

Mr A. E. U. Maude (Oriel)[13] *How do Communists reconcile the ultra-nationalism of the five year plan with the cry of 'Workers of the World Unite?'*

Mr F. M. Hardie (Ch.Ch.) *Russia is not a godless country. There is a religion in Russia, and rather a fine one at that: the religion of freeing one's fellow men from poverty. British anti-Russian propaganda is quite a virulent as Russian anti-British propaganda.*

Mr M. D. R. Meiklejohn *The Five year plan is about to collapse through incompetence and lack of transport.*

Mr Papineau *The Americans, the best judges, are confident that Russia will not collapse. I would rather live in Russia; for liberty in the capitalist world is, in Bertrand Russell's term, the liberty of the fortunate to take advantage of the unfortunate.*

---

21 January 1932

House believes the fiscal policy of the Conservative Party best meets the present situation.

Mr White (Corpus) *Talk of debt repudiation means one thing only, the imposition of tariffs. Protection brings, as its inevitable gifts, corruption and price rises.*

Mr Davidson (whose resemblance to Disraeli gets daily less remote) *The time for tariffs has arrived—they are the weapon for bargaining with foreign nations. The message must be 'Save England before saving the World'.*

Mr Wilson (ex-President) *I can imagine that policy causing the cessation of world trade in six months. The tariff policy is madness.*

Mr Boyd-Carpenter (ex-President) *Free Trade carried to its logical conclusion means sheer folly. Free Trade is fiscal Free Love.*

Mr Maude *looked angrily at Mr Hardie when interrupted by him…When Mr Maude is vehement, he is a first-rate speaker.*

Mr Heimann *I hope that, at this Lausanne conference, the British representatives will 'threaten the foreigners with something.'*

Mr M. M. Foot (Wadham)[14] *deplored the government's crooked policy and pious fraud, and very properly defended Mr Lloyd George.*

Mr Fountain *accused the Liberals of economic nationalism and called Free Trade 'a Bankers' Ramp.' These astonishing statements coming from Mr Fountain, do not astonish the House.*

Mr F. S. Meyer (Balliol) *spoke frantically for the Dictatorship of the Proletariat.*

Mr C. F. Wegg-Prosser (Oriel) *spoke unexpectedly against the motion and dislikes Sir Henry Page-Croft.*[15]

Mr J. D. Crichton (Balliol) *said there was a crisis and was vigorous.*

Motion lost 114:128.

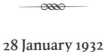

28 January 1932

House believes that mass production is a menace to culture.

Mr Maude *Mass production stunts the incentive to creation and reward. Contrast it with the days when a skilled workman could look upon the creation of his own craftsmanship. A civilisation giving ever more scope to mass production is in danger of losing its soul.*

Mr Hardie *Mass production makes leisure possible. It is something which allows culture to reach the poorest homes.*

Mr Giles Playfair *I have never yet met a Tory who knew what culture meant.*

Mr C. O. Rhodes (St Peter's Hall) *was argumentative.*

Mr A. von Trott zu Solz (Balliol)[16] *in an attractive maiden speech, likened members on the other side to 'paradise-birds'.*

Motion lost 75:111.

4 February 1932

House prefers the Indian to the American Congress

Mr H. Minza (Queen's) *I think of George III's Conservatism as one of the symptoms of his madness.*

Mr Foot[17] *was in tremendous form. He savagely declared that India had no more sincere friends than himself, but he denied that Congress had contributed anything of value to the situation. He closed with a dramatic peroration.*

Mr Greenwood *The central truth about India is that any imperialist system necessitates oppression.*

Mr Kabir (ex-Librarian) *rebuked the Viceroy for unwillingness even to discuss the situation with Mr Gandhi. Mr Kabir is always exciting.*

Mr Maude *Congress is guilty of organised blackmail.*

Mr D. M. Graham (Balliol) *Congress is deliberately choosing chaos. He is very fluent and sincere.*

Mr E. J. S. Clarke (Magd.) *Congress does not indulge in politics as a game. The American Congress had by this time vanished from the thoughts of members.*

Mr E. Rigby *defended anarchy very capably.*

Motion tied 132:132 The President, overcome with emotion, gave his casting vote in favour.

---

28 April 1932

House would welcome the formation of a new progressive party of the Left. Cambridge visit.

Mr T. R. Leatham (St John's, Cantab) *There is no time to form a new party. Speed is essential, a five year plan necessary. The idea of a new party was just an attempt to bolster up the capitalist system, merely an excuse to preserve the failed National Government.*

Mr S. S. Darhan *made an attack on the leisured classes which was magnificent.*

Mr A. E. Holdsworth (Gonville and Caius—President Cambridge Union) *I am not much given to violent language, but to deliver a rebuke to my officers is in order for the immature drivel they have been talking.*

Mr Irvine (Immediate Past-President) *ended with a tremendous appeal for the leadership of men of the calibre of Gladstone, not the inoffensive incapacity of the Lansburys[18] of this world.*

Mr W. D. Ross-Taylor (Trinity) *was a little too fluent.*

Mr W. Gordon Murray (Trinity) *is a polished speaker, but the Thames is not 'liquid history'.*

Mr D. F. Karaka (Trinity) *made a stirring defence of Mr Lloyd George.*

Mr E. Barton (Merton) *wound up for the Ayes in an attractive speech. Like many others, he was sympathetic to Socialism, but disdained the Class War.*

Motion carried 150:148. The result of the division was greeted with prolonged cheering.

---

5 May 1932

House thinks the idea of a class war preposterous and utterly declines to countenance it.

Mr Foot [Still a Liberal] proceeded joyfully to the attack. With a gesture of loathing, Mr Foot dismissed 'these barrel-organ politics'. *The way to cure past class legislation is not to introduce fresh class legislation. To some of us, justice seemed a nobler principle than hatred—the principle of Liberalism which had in the past done so much to better social conditions... Are we with Marx, to sweep away law, religion, morality, all in the name of class hatred?* A great speech.

Mr Farnsworth The class war is a fact. He condemned in turn the Mover, the Labour Party and the Class War. *Everybody desires a peaceful solution [Cries of 'Question?] Improvements in social conditions are not brought about by any decency on the part of the rich. The struggle between the few and the many is, and is bound to be, real: for myself, I am on the side of the big battalions.* Mr Farnsworth has a conversational style of oratory which makes him easy to listen to; this was a capable speech.

Mr F. S. Meyer *is one of the few speakers who should never be moderate. It was a joy to see how he turned and rent the wolves in sheep's clothing behind him for their pusillanimous advocacy of a policy which few of them understood and none of them believed in.* Mr Meyer was a happy class-warrior.

Mr T. W. Pillifant (Keble) *To give power to a class-conscious proletariat would be to exchange one bureaucracy for another.*

Mr Maude *The class war is not logical, hardly decent and possibly not wholly moral.*

Mr J. E. Winocour (Magd.) *commented unfavourably on the Librarian's button-hole as a sign that he had abandoned the workers. He thought that class was an evil, but hoped that out of evil would come forth good.*

Motion carried 105:75.

12 May 1932

House condemns the Indian policy of the present government.

Mr F. M. Hardie Treasurer[19]

Mr Hardie *has always seemed to me to be more fitted for the courts than for parliament. He took the refusal of Lord Willingdon[20] to interview Ghandi as the typical instance of the unhelpful and unsympathetic attitude of England, and built a very substantial case. We should not ourselves wish to be prosecuted by Mr Hardie.*

Mr Heimann walks about with his hands in his pockets while he speaks, but in spite of it contrives to impress the House. *The Irwin[21] administration in India is ineffective. There is, in any conflict, always a point where tolerance becomes weakness; and if law and order are to be maintained there must be no weakness.*

Mr Greenwood (Librarian) *The Mover will undoubtedly go forth to take up the white man's burden and lay it on the shoulders of the nearest black man. The proper policy is to leave India because it would be in our interests to do so.* It was a pity that his emotions led him to envisage Indians 'at the wheel of the caravan.'

Mr M. J. L. White (Hertford) *dismissed his Socialist opponents on the grounds that they, like him, had never been to India. It was no use saying that there were tens of thousands of political prisoners in India. Did Congress have any constructive proposals? If Indians could really govern themselves, it was odd that they had to come to England to learn the principles of democracy.*

Mr Kabir *It was a joy to hear Mr Kabir pouring scorn on the Opposer who had suggested that Indians were illiterate; the flood of oratory swept it aside and passed onto a passionate attack on the nation which by way of showing its solicitude for Indian welfare, had permitted only a thousand air raids in the past year. Mr Kabir goes home; and the Union loses one who has done more than any other to influence its opinions on India.*

Mr W. St John Tayleur (Queen's) *talked of traitors, snakes and tempered steel.*

Mr P. Proby *commented (a little unjustly) on the veneer of civilisation possessed by Indians.*

Motion carried 110:48.

⸺⚇⚇⚇⸺

13 October 1932

House has no confidence in H.M. Government.

Mr Foot *entered the debate with the fire and spark we have come to expect from him. He destroyed the case for tariffs, condemned the Tariff Board and laughed at the protection of Peter Pan industries which never grew up. He went on to show the evil effects of Ottawa on the Empire and on this, I did not think him so good.*

Mr Maude *ridiculed the idea of Socialist ministers ever being able to run nationalised banks. His claim for the National Government was that it had done better under the circumstances than any other government could have done.*

Mr Greenwood *opened by attacking Mr Foot and the Samuelites[22] who had said they would support the government in all but its fiscal policy. That meant supporting the government over the Means Test, Social Services, Disarmament, India and Ireland, all of which was disastrous.*

Mr W. M. Citrine General Secretary of the T.U.C.[23] gave the House one of the most balanced and statesmanlike speeches it has had the privilege to hear for some time. *The government was formed in a panic; it was given to the falsification of issues; it failed to carry out the things for which it was elected. The only way out is a policy of public control and international co-operation…The present government has refused even an enquiry into a convention for a forty hour week. At home, the government—no more than a handful of ex-Labour members and a dense mass of Conservatives—is simply aiming at stamping out education and reducing wages.*

Mr Gordon Murray *said that Free Trade was dead and defended Ottawa as a yoking together of logic and sentiment.*

Mr S. R. Finn (Exeter) *defended the Victorians who, he said, when they bought houses, paid for them.*

Mr Farnsworth *claimed that under present conditions of unemployment, bitterness in political affairs was justified and he hoped for riots. Mr Farnsworth is sincere and always worth hearing.*

Mr J. M. Buckland (Keble) *smacked less of the pulpit than last term.*

Mr H. Johnson (New College) *rolled out a great peroration.*

Motion carried 215:207.

---

20 October 1932

House believes that the Russian experiment is succeeding and welcomes the success.

Mr J. S. Cripps (Balliol) *The Russian experiment was not to be judged on the social injustice it had so far caused. The birth of capitalism had brought similar pains. The Russian experiment, he claimed, had solved the problem of democracy in the political and industrial aspects.*

Mr Murray *had once supported 'the aristocracy of the proletariat' which was the most pernicious thing in the world today. Russia was failing in the economic sphere; and in support, he quoted Stalin's promises and the figures of present achievements. The Communists regarded the rest of the world as ravening wolves 'including the British Socialist party.' He opposed Communism as a tyranny of ideas and doubted if Russians would tolerate it very long.*

Mr Hardie (Librarian) *Russian success was mainly agricultural. Comparison should not be with Britain but with the Russia of the Czars. Indeed Russia was militarist, but that flowed from fear of the designs of capitalist countries. In Russia there was no unemployment, though he had to admit that all labour was in the nature of forced labour. One cannot help being impressed by the honesty of the Librarian's speeches and the clarity of his thought.*

Mr K. H. Digby *was effective in claiming that we should compare the repression in Russia with the repression of Belfast, Liverpool and Birkenhead.*

Mr J. E. C. Quinn *was fluent in comparing Communism to the South Sea Bubble.*

Mr Farnsworth *rose amid cheers and declared that Communism stood for the solution of the economic problems of the community.*

Motion carried 197:135.

---

27 October 1932

House believes that Democracy has failed and should be replaced by some other form of government.

Mr Digby *Democracy had stirred the waters of politics so much as to bring all the mud to the surface. Attacking the press and the BBC, he suggested that today, democracy was only the tool of capitalism. But the greatest arguments against it were the hunger marchers and the insult of the last election.*

Mr M. L. I. White *said as Opposer, that Anarchy was the only possible ideal, the executive was unnecessary and government should be a matter of majority and logic.*

Mr E. W. Walker (Magd.) *Democracy had failed to cope with today's economic problems and had failed to give us any decent system of private law. More and more things were falling into the hands of the specialist. Government would have to go in that direction. Though we should keep an eye on the specialist.*

Mr D. F. F. Karkara (Lincoln) *Democracy means something to India. There is no democracy in India. There was no democracy in this country. If there had been, there would have been no Ottawa[24] and no Disarmament fiasco.* Mr Karaka got a great reception which he deserved.

Mr Maude *I think that today, Italy has the only good government; and that as Italy is virtually a Dictatorship, the case for the proposers is proven.*

Mr B. A. Faugh *attacked Fascism and spoke of donkeys driving shepherds. An able speech.*

Mr W. R. B. Foster (Corpus) *demanded a return to aristocracy.*

Mr R. J. M. Amphlett *whipped himself into fury. He must speak again.*

Mr P. L. B. Chamier (Ch.Ch.) *stood up for the constitution of the Greek city state, but modern states were too large for such institutions.*

Sir John Pritchard-Jones Bart *said that he could find no alternative to democracy.*

Motion lost 135:171.

---

17 November 1932

House believes that Socialism is the only solution to the problems facing the country.

Mr Hardie *I would define socialism as equality within the community. It is nauseating to live in a country where immense wealth and abject poverty exist side by side. The fundamental cause is technological. To deal with it, you need planning and in order to plan, you will need socialisation of the banks and of investment.*

Mr Giles Playfair—Treasurer *If you support socialism in the abstract, then in reality you are supporting communism. This socialism will get us out of the present problem, but will only get us into another one. We are facing a crisis and the crisis can only be solved by putting aside all party prejudice.*

Mr Duff-Cooper[25] *It is all very well to talk about the state, but what does 'the state' mean? In practice it means the government, twenty-three black-coated gentlemen sitting to the right of the Speaker. How can we hand over the control of industry to such men? Where does Mr Lansbury (the other guest of the night) intend to recruit the men to run the Bank of England and the Cotton Trade? They would be the same people who run them today, but with less incentive. Under capitalism, great advances have been made and they will be made again.*

Mr George Lansbury (Guest) was in marked contrast with the last speaker. He dealt in good humour with interruptions. *Capitalism brings poverty with it. Capitalism admits that it is unable to better the position of the unemployed. Look at the mismanagement of the mining industry and of our financial policy. Then, let us pull the veil off the banks and have a good look at them!'* The House was carried away by his speech—its obvious sincerity, the force of its delivery and its joviality left the House no other course.

Motion carried 316:247.

---∞∞∞---

24 November 1932

House would welcome a censorship of the daily press.

Mr J. A. Gibson (New College) *The idea is not new. Ancient Rome had its censors, though to the best of my knowledge, it didn't have a daily press to censor. The chief function of the press should be to give news, so I would like a censorship to see that it gave news—in the proper sense of the term. If this step were taken, I would not object to having editorial comment as well.*

Mr G. J. Grieve (St. Catherine's) *Any censorship would have to be in the hands of the government which means an increase in state domination and a restriction of the rights of the individual. Anyway the press isn't free today—because of the law of libel. What we want today is an increase in intelligence in the community.*

Mr Donald Mills (Keble) *What we have today is a post-publication censorship, one cause of that is the sheer cost of litigation. The real menace lies with Press Lords. The question is one of realism and practice; that circumstance today demands a control of public opinion.*

Mr L. M. Gelber (Balliol) *The proposer has not realised the function of the press which is to inform opinion. Democracy will be impossible without it. I don't deny the abuses of the press, but those abuses should not make us put power into the hands of a bureaucracy and leave us without independent opinion in times of crisis.* The best paper speech of the evening.

Mr Greenwood *suggested that the press should be run along co-operative lines.*

Mr Hardie *suggested that every daily newspaper should be compelled to print a bulletin after the style of the one given by the BBC.*

Mr P. R. Pain (Ch.Ch.)[26] *said that he had heard that the Times had falsified the views of hunger marchers at Stratford.*

Mr Giles Playfair[27] *said that theatre censorship had led to the production of bad plays and bad films; he anticipated the same results from censorship of the press.*

Mr Chamier *demanded the censorship as protection of the individual.*

Mr Dudley Barker (Oriel) *demanded the repeal of the libel laws.*

Mr Amphlett (Oriel) *said that he read the Daily Telegraph to see how the world was getting on, The Times, Herald and Mail for amusement.*

Mr S. R. Prince (Exeter) *attacked the press for its views on Peace and Disarmament.*

Mr R. W. F. Wooton (Corpus) *said that he put truth and purity above freedom.*

Motion defeated 41:137.

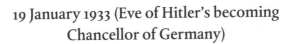

19 January 1933 (Eve of Hitler's becoming Chancellor of Germany)

House believes that British Liberalism has before it a great future.

Mr Playfair *began by congratulating Mr D. R. Jardine*[28] *on the English success in the Third Test Match.*

Rest of minimal report omitted.

Vote not given.

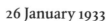

26 January 1933

House believes that the British Empire is a menace to international goodwill.

Mr Pain *spoke of the flagrant injustice of the policy of the present government toward Kenya and the loathsome hypocrisy of Mr Bennett*[29] *on the question of trade with Russia and said that he was heartened by that evening's news of the results of the Irish elections. His main claim was that the Empire was based on force.*

Mr Murray *In respect of Kenya, it is the Imperial factor in the form of the Colonial Office, which checks undue exploitation of natives by the white settlers. His main claim was that the British Empire was the finest example of international goodwill in existence and that its object was to serve men and nations.*

Mr D. F. Karaka (Lincoln—Secretary) *made the speech he was expected to make. He offered the House a clear-cut choice between British Imperialism and Indian goodwill and asserted that they could no longer co-exist.*

Mr Crichton *is a very difficult subject for criticism. He began with an imitation of one of last term's guests and referred to 'the short term of chaos' expected by the Socialists, and to the Mohammedans, Hindus and Moslems who compose the Indian population. 'The old Crichton' then did the vanishing trick and a new, sternly serious Crichton continued the speech. Mr Crichton is now the House's licensed buffoon and naturally, the House tends to be disappointed when its jester declines to jest. But pure buffoonery does not carry one to all the best places in the House, and Mr Crichton is quite right to try to develop a new manner.*

Mr Walker-Smith *said that he would have liked to invert the motion and look back to Queen Elizabeth when the Armada was defeated in twenty four hours and not four and a half years. He thought that Colonials were given to 'didactic sadness' and that internationalism was a product of post-war hysteria.*

Mr M. Beloff (Corpus)[30] *disliked the Empire because it was large.*

Mr R. F. K. Steel-Maitland (Balliol) *appeared to argue that all speeches at all international conferences should be given in English.*

Motion lost 85:122.

9 February 1933

House will in no circumstances fight for its King and Country.

Mr Digby *was perhaps at his best when he was making such serious points as that the peoples of the world were far ahead of the statesmen in their desire for peace. When he was making such points, he was undoubtedly holding the House; when he was not, he was as undoubtedly, amusing it.*

Mr Steel-Maitland *agreeing that pacifist arguments had been carried to their logical conclusion that evening, denied that Socialists who preached class war had any real right to call themselves pacifists. He might be criticised with regard to the substance, on the ground that his remarks about the King were not really relevant to the spirit of the motion.*

Mr Graham—Librarian *his argument was that war was likely, that force was no remedy and that therefore resistance to war should be organised. He dealt with the argument from police forces by pointing out that policemen were not even armed with pistols, let alone 16 inch guns.*

Professor C. E. M. Joad (Balliol) *made a magnificent speech and so caused the motion to be carried by an overwhelming majority in a very large House. He put*

the motion in what, in his view, were realistic terms and then did indeed carry the argu-
ments for pacifism to their logical conclusion, by saying that in the event of actual war,
an unarmed England or at most, a policy of passive resistance should be adopted.

Rt. Hon. Quintin Hogg (Ch.Ch. and All Souls) *claimed that he and his sup-*
porters were genuinely desirous of preventing another conflict and that the unilateral
disarmament of Britain would render us impotent to prevent war in other parts of the
world—for example in Manchuria.

Mr Greenwood *found in the speeches from the other side a suggestion that those on his*
side did not love their country, and asserted that such suspicion was without foundation.

Mr Murray *asked us what we would do if Southern Irish armies invaded Ulster.*

Mr Beloff (Teller for the Ayes) *made a speech which was an admirable combin-*
ation of good humour and sound sense.

Mr E. Da Costa (St John's)[31] *said that in his country, this particular slogan 'King*
and Country' had passed out of fashion.

Mr A. F. Schleppergrell *was very interesting indeed on the subject of passive resist-*
ance to the French invasion of the Ruhr.

Mr J. A. Gibson (New College) *was in favour of the method of persuasion and*
personal example.

Motion carried 275:123.

---

16 February 1933—Cambridge visit

House proclaims its undying faith in politicians.

Mr Cripps *His programme was economic democracy to be secured by the machinery*
of political democracy, though he gave a clear warning that coercion would have to be
applied to any recalcitrant minority which opposed the will of the majority.

Mr Michael Barkway (Queen's Cambridge) *took the two great problems of the hour, the problems of peace and unemployment and showed that in neither case, had the efforts of the politicians to deal with them met with any success.*

Mr Gibson *saw no reason after recent events*[32] *to withdraw his recent motion welcoming a censorship of the daily press.*

Motion lost 161:168.

Motion in names of Mr Randolph Churchill and Lord Stanley of Alderley[33] to expunge the motion of 9th February.

Mr Hardie, the President, *took the chair and asked Lord Stanley to move his motion. There was little doubt that the mood was on balance hostile, but there was a very strong element vociferous in his support. Lord Stanley explained that he did not come as a militarist, but as one who believed in and worked for peace. He particularly objected to the words 'in no circumstances'. This was pure pacifism and as such objectionable and futile. Lord Stanley faced his audience with great good humour and pluck. But his speech was peculiarly maladroit and gave many openings for the derisive humour of one of the World's most difficult audiences. He sat down amid cheers and counter cheers. The President then asked the Librarian (K. R. F. Steel-Maitland) to take the chair and come to the despatch box to oppose the motion. This move made a great impression on the House, many members regarding him as the guardian of their corporate dignity. On returning to the Chair, he received a very remarkable ovation.*

It was therefore a very antipathetic and even angry house that Mr Randolph Churchill had to face... he was unfortunate in his manner and phrasing. Innocent appeals to 'all loyal Oxford men' were greeted with delighted jeers. His words fell for the most part on deaf ears. A body, usually prone to flattery, derided the suggestion that after the House of Lords and House of Commons, the Union Society's opinions commanded most interest in the country. Mr Churchill then implored the House not to vote through resentment of himself, but at all costs, to clear the name of Oxford. But just when he was expected to perorate and retire, he announced that he and his associates had decided to ask the President to withdraw the resolution.

A loud cry of mingled triumph and dismay greeted this statement. By now, the blood of the House was up. The President announced that he gave permission, but was greeted with loud protests. An ex-president explained that a motion could only be withdrawn if the House assented. Mr Hardie put the question that permission be given to withdraw and it was negatived by acclamation. He then put the original question, 'That the Secretary be directed to expunge from the minutes of the Society, the motion which was carried on February 9th'. The House then divided and there voted:

For the Motion 138: Against 750.

One furious response among many came from Winston Churchill[34] and has, unsurprisingly, received little publicity. Addressing the twenty-fifth anniversary meeting of the *Anti-Socialist and Anti-Communist Union* on 17 February 1933, he observed: 'My mind turns across the narrow waters of the Channel and the North Sea, where great nations stand determined to defend their national glories or national existence with their lives. I think of Germany, with its splendid, clear-eyed youths marching forward on all the roads of the Reich, singing their ancient songs, demanding to be conscripted into an army; eagerly seeking the most terrible weapons of war; burning to suffer and die for their fatherland. I think of Italy, with her ardent Fascisti, her renowned Chief, and stern sense of national duty...' He would also, says the same source, be 'much too friendly to Mussolini and to the Japanese invaders of Manchuria'.

---

27 April 1933

House believes the problem of poverty can be solved through the medium of the present party system.

Mr Murray Slavery was abolished under the Party System. Why should not poverty? If Labour abandons democracy, it will mean the end of that party, but if it takes office pledged to observe democratic methods, I believe the Conservatives would be willing to help them.

Mr Digby *After remarking that he was not one to pour oil on the Officers, launched into a fiery attack on Mr Murray whose speech was full of 'amateur economics and unsound political theory'. The general Election had been 'a manifestation of the class struggle in its foulest aspects'—and thence by easy stages to Moscow and Broadcasting House where 'Jingoism and blasphemy mingle in approximately equal quantities'.*

Mr Karaka *Democracy gave as much chance to the Labour Party as any other, and if that party abandoned democratic methods, it would be the Right and not the Left which would triumph, as in Germany. In a sincere and emotional peroration, he called for loyalty to democratic ideals.*

Mr Graham parodied Shakespeare to show the wickedness of the Russians who would say 'What a piece of work is man! How bitter in class consciousness! How finite in faculty! In action how like a tractor. In apprehension, how like a sod'.

Mr Dingle Foot MP (Balliol) *Cannot he realise that the Labour Party is an integral part of the party system and that the only alternatives to that system were Mosleyism and 'the World combination of the ILP and the Communist Party?' Other classes than the workers are suffering and the Means Test is being applied even in Russia. Poverty is not inevitable under capitalism, but only arose during spells of maladjustment.*

Mr G. D. H. Cole M.A. (University) *I agree with the ex-Librarian about the need for a spiritual drive. I believe that a socialist government when returned, should stay in office long enough to make return to non-socialism impossible. Parliament however is useless for economic change, and the conventions of the present day parliament (like the wearing of white waistcoats), must be destroyed. We must not believe that socialism is merely a matter of party politics, it is something infinitely greater than that.*

Mr H. C. Wallich (Oriel) *In a maiden speech expressed the belief that capitalism would learn by its mistakes.*

Mr J. Starikoff (Exeter) *attacked the money magnates.*

Mr J. O. Griffiths (Exeter) *concentrated on class antagonism.*

Mr R. S. Rutherford (Wadham) *believed that socialism could not be achieved quickly enough under the party system.*

Mr M. Addison *showed real wit and ability in an appeal to the House to frighten Mr Baldwin. The House is always pleased to hear Mr Angus Maude who summed up for the noes with a bitter attack on wage cuts.*

Motion lost: 158:106.

---

4 May 1933 Kansas and Texas Universities visit

House believes that the League of Nations should be abandoned.

Mr W. C. Morris (Kansas) *I am quite as much of a pacifist as my colleagues and for that reason I am proposing the abandonment of the League of Nations. It has indeed done good work on social and labour problems, but it has also preserved the Versailles fiasco. The World problem isn't political; it is economic.*

Mr L. M. Gelber (Balliol) *Let me congratulate the Americans on abandoning their traditional national policy of 'ignominious and selfish isolation' which has been so largely responsible for the failure of the League of Nations. If we abandon it, there will be everywhere the sort of bloodstained nationalism evident in Germany—cutting off the Jewish nose to spite the German face. Nor do we realise just how much of humanity and civilisation has been inhaled through it.*

Mr F. S. Anderson (Texas) *I signed the pledge not to fight for King and Country years ago. My objection to the League is a socialist one. Peace is impossible in a world of imperialistic nationalism. At the root of the trouble lie attempts to gain economic advantage over other countries. They must be removed from people's consciences before we could have peace. The Society is grateful for the visit of so effective and delightful a pair of speakers.*

Mr Steel-Maitland *attacked America for its refusal to co-operate which had rendered sanctions nugatory.*

Mr Schlepergell *contended that the League was merely the instrument of the Quai D'Orsay. An excellent speech.*

Mr J. G. Cox *did not like the Pope and said we were hamstrung.*

Mr R. S. Rutherford *concluding for the Ayes, said that wars arose from religious differences and economic rivalries, neither of which was the League was able to settle.*

Motion lost 67: 179.

11 May 1933

House would prefer Fascism to Socialism.

Mr M. L. White *who began rather inappropriately by giving the President the Fascist salute, criticised both Fascism and Socialism as regarding the state as sacrosanct. Fascism though was less objectionable because it was 'an all-embracing tide.' Free Trade was a bad idea too.*

Mr Pain was superb—*The basis of the Fascist idea is that Right is Right. The Nazis are cracking the whip over the connubial couch of the faithful. It is a creed of beastly nationalism and the most unenlightened capitalism.*

Mr Schlepegrell (Univ.)[35] *I am neither a Nazi nor Fascist, but I want to defend my country from the indignities which it suffered between 1918 and 1933. It is the fault of the whole world, not just of Germany that Hitler is now Chancellor. Fascism and socialism have each the idea; but in an ignorant world, Fascism takes the better route.* Mr Schlepegrell's speech was one of the best and most dignified speeches the Union has heard, and fully deserved the applause it received.

Mr J. S. Cripps contrasted the respect for human nature implied in socialism with the beastliness of Hitlerism and its persecutions. *We must abandon capitalism if we wish to have equality and give human nature a chance to develop. The ways of the Fascists 'are not our ways and their gods are not our gods.'*

Mr Michael Foot *made a delightful speech which had nothing at all to do with the motion.*

Mr Murray *said that the Labour Party must be kept off the rocks of Marxism.*

Herr von Offen (Queen's) *made an excellent maiden speech in which he said that as a Nazi, he opposed Fascism.*

Mr M. Charles (St Catherine's) *was very good in suggesting that in England socialism would be the socialism of the middle classes.*

Motion lost 100:180.

18 May 1933

House flatly declines to view anything with concern, apprehension or alarm.

Mr Angus Maude *The government has been so successful in its efforts to obtain the world's long distance crisis record that soon even the meek will refuse to inherit the earth.*

Motion lost 203:353.

1 June 1933

House believes that Toryism offers no solution to the Nation's economic and social problems.

Mr Graham (Balliol) *I am uncertain whether the Toryism I am supposed to be attacking is that of Sir Henry Page-Croft, Lady Houston, Mr MacDonald or Mr Baldwin. It is anyway the creed of the slum landlord, and the stock exchange profiteer.*

St James told us that wars were occasioned by the lusts which war in ourselves, so the condition of the working class is the result of the lusts of the capital-controlling class for material gain.

Mr Alan Lennox-Boyd MP (Visitor) *Toryism may sound a little absurd, but nevertheless I suggest that we should go back to that old, historic Toryism. We must go back to feudalism and we must go back to service. It is a faith that asks that every class should justify the privileges it enjoys. No one should have a position in the country unless he is willing to fulfil them.*

Mr Michael Foot *Mr Foot's speeches are always full of bright remarks which delight the House, but he would do well to pay a little more attention to the serious parts of them. At present, he seldom really deals with the subject. But it was a great oratorical effort and fully justified the result of the polling.**

Motion carried 144:129 after a rather poorly attended debate.

---

8 June 1933

House condemns the India policy of HMG as contained in the White Paper.

Mr Michael Addison (Balliol) *India has been cheated. The Prime Minster has promised Dominion status, but the words which had come so glibly off his tongue are not to be found in the White Paper. The White Paper acted on the principle that India must have prosperity before she has independence and really, it was quite the reverse.*

Mr R. A. Lazard *I am a Socialist, but yet a supporter of the White Paper. Not enough is known about India. The Congress Party is much too extreme in its demands and would fail in them just as the Chartist Movement failed. Unless this is accepted, the only alternatives were those of Mr Winston Churchill and Mr Fenner Brockway.*[36]

* He was elected as President for next term.

Mr S. N. Wijeyekoon (Hertford) *The White Paper is a mockery, a futile attempt at die-hard bigotry and denial of the legitimate aspirations of the Indian people. India is to have no say in finance because, after a century and a half of British rule, only five per cent of the people are literate—and that was used as an argument against the Indians. The paper, if carried through, would disintegrate the country; and it was in the interests of humanity that he appealed for the rejection of the paper.*

Oxford Magazine: Reviewer's note.

If as I believe, Mr Quinn of Christ Church is the gentleman who presumes to criticise other members in the columns of Cherwell, *he should give himself better advice of which he is badly in need. That 'It was better to have a country quiet than educated' was one of the gems of his kindly wit which should do much to promote Anglo-Indian friendship.*

Motion carried by a two-to-one majority.

---

19 October 1933

House believes HMG should follow President Roosevelt's example.[37]

Mr David Lewis (Lincoln) opposing *Are we to follow Mr Roosevelt's lead over leaving the gold standard or show recognition of trade unions for having done those long since? For all his fine radio voice and charming smile, President Roosevelt remains a believer in the Capitalist System and whatever mitigation he might bring about, is likely to prove only temporary. His ideas are anyway inapplicable to Britain owing to the economic self-sufficiency which they implied.*

Mr Mills *That is a quibble. Several of them have been applied here. I ask the House to support this motion on the grounds that the President's proposals offer a sane alternative to Socialism in this country.* This gave Mr Mills the opportunity for a devastating attack on the Socialist Party.

Mr B. A. Farrell (Balliol) *turned with ferocity on the last speaker and argued with reason that it was irrelevant. If the President achieves anything at all, it will be purely temporary. Even if it should be successful, it cannot be applied in this country. Finally, the President is bolstering up a society which I believe to be rotten and which I cannot support.*

Mr Schlepegrell *argued lucidly in favour of the motion.*

Mr L. Larson (Pembroke) *spoke as an American.*

Motion lost 95:141.

---

9 November 1933

House strongly disapproves of Hitler's action in withdrawing from the League of Nations and the Disarmament Conference.

Mr Addison *I do not believe the German leader's claims that all he wants is work, peace and happiness; the military training going on in Germany and the education of youth in the arts of war are bound to make other nations suspicious. Germany is pugnacious, defeatist and surfeited. It will be held responsible for the break-up of Collective Security in Europe.*

Mr P. B. Glenville (Ch.Ch.) *Only a discussion of Germany's foreign policy is relevant; and recognition of her demands is essential to world peace. Germany has been held down since 1918 and the question now is whether she has a right to leave the ring. France, by her rigid insistence on the worst clauses of Versailles, and to a lesser extent, Great Britain, are responsible for the break-up of the League.*

Mr Schlepegrell *drove home Mr Glenville's arguments. Germany's withdrawal is the inevitable result of the humiliation imposed by the powers and the failure of those powers to give her equality of status. The whole German nation supported Hitler's action. Rathenau[38] and Stresemann[39] would have acted in exactly the same manner if they had been in power. After fourteen years of vacillation by the great powers, it is useless to say that the moment chosen for withdrawal is inopportune. The*

League exists to maintain the Treaty of Versailles; no attempt has been made at revision. Peace is impossible while the gulf still remains between the victor and the vanquished. Hitler has therefore contributed to the cause of peace by his withdrawal. Mr Schlepegrell combined great sincerity of feeling with lucidity of expression and it was undoubtedly this speech which was responsible for the defeat of the motion.

Mr Steel-Maitland *answered many points raised by the opposition. Nobody denied that Germany has a good case, but she has not acted in the right way to get that case heard. Her untimely withdrawal has led to the fall of M. Daladier[40] in France, the most friendly Premier of France we have had in years. The Treaty of Versailles was indeed an infamous document—the main obstacle to peace in Europe. But Germany would have a better chance of getting it revised as a friendly power within the League than as an enemy power, suspected and hated outside the League.*

Mr J. N. Jones (St John's) *said that any nation worth the name would have behaved as Germany has done in the face of such provocation.*

Mr David Lewis *dealt unmercifully with the Fascists in the House who were unwise enough to interrupt him.*

Mr Graham *said that Germany wanted results, not generous gestures. He was disgusted by the flood of abuse which had proceeded from the British press against Germany.*

Mr Favell *forsook his Socialist colleagues and spoke against the motion. The League was a futile institution in the present capitalist world.*

Mr P. E. Lewis (Univ.) *said with great justification that Germany's internal policy was relevant to the motion.*

Mr H. L. Gordon (Balliol) *made out a good case against Hitler.*

Mr H. E. Peacock (St Edmund Hall) *expressed the commendable hope that Hitler would be drowned in his bath.*

Mr A. du Porter (St John's) *defended fascism in spite of constant interruptions.*

Motion lost 187:190.

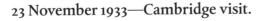

23 November 1933—Cambridge visit.

House believes that Western Civilisation is decadent and doomed.

Mr G. A. Forrest (St Edmund Hall) *To me 'Civilisation' means going up for the fortunate few, but for most others, it is going down and going down. Liberalism was what Gladstone said in 18—unless subsequently contradicted by Lloyd George. The decadence of Western Civilisation was caused by its raising fear and mistrust where trust and confidence were needed.*

Mr A. Spender (Selwyn Cambridge) *This is the age of Churchills, Beaverbrooks and other members of the criminal classes. The League of Nations is composed of vagabonds and senile defectives. But socialists should not regard this civilisation, with its slum clearance schemes and the work of the TUC, as decadent and doomed.*

Motion lost 53:110.

1 February 1934

House favours the complete nationalisation of the armaments industry.

Mr I. D. Harvey (Ch.Ch.) *I was once a Boy Scout, so my motto is 'Be Prepared.' Every factory is a potential armaments factory, and ninety per cent of all explosive works are for industrial purposes. The method of controlling armaments is not to nationalise the means of production, but by way of a heavy export duty.*

Mr Steel-Maitland *It would be impossible to nationalise armament production without also nationalising iron and steel production. Instead there should be control of the trade by the League.*

Motion carried 184:85.

1 March 1934

House believes that politics should be the main interest of undergraduates in a university.

Mr Solomon (Univ.) *The present race of politicians has no place in politics. The true function of politics is to make reason and the word of God prevail. Is it mere chance that politics is common to the dramatist, the philosopher and the mathematician? I believe that politics is the kernel of all social life. The influence of government is all-pervading. It is salutary to reflect that a study of politics neither implies, nor incurs, participation in the strife of the arena.*

Mr Beloff *began by denouncing by word and gesture, the memory of Mr Gladstone. While pointing to the bust of the late Lord Oxford (H. H. Asquith), he suggested that the intellectual eminence of Germany was endangered by enforced preoccupation with political affairs. Students anywhere will always remain a class within the state, and nothing but harm could come of their having real political power.*

Mr W. G. Shebbeare (Ch.Ch.) *Those who reach positions of power require enlightened views on political opinions. Comment and opinion based upon information is more desirable than sectional experience.*

Mr J. R. Hickerton (St Catherine's) *harped as only Mr Hickerton can harp, upon the political immaturity of the younger generation.*

Mr R. H. Croft (Lincoln) *in a good maiden speech, stated that a good degree and an absorption in politics were incompatible.*

Mr D. A. Young (BNC) *pleaded for fewer political motions. He suggested that the House might prefer more Elgar and less Eddington.*

Motion lost 60:70.

25 May 1934

House believes that the continued existence of the House of Lords is essential to preserve the balance of the Constitution.

Mr J. S. O'Callaghan *The Lords might well act effectively as a break upon a government near the end of its term in office and clearly unrepresentative. It is for the Opposition to prove that the Lords are superfluous. They are needed, precisely because the Commons can never be perfectly representative.*

Mr W. H. James (Worcester) carefully examined the obstruction by the Lords of the Asquith ministry. *The usefulness of the Lords has vanished and their Lordships' power has rightly been limited by the Parliament Act. Indeed, limitation could usefully be greater. If the Lords agree with the Commons, they are superfluous and if they disagree, they are obnoxious.*

Mr Forrest objected to the record of non-attendance in the Lords. *Many peers have no idea of their House's position or their functions in it. We should object to anybody whose only function was to perpetuate Conservative predominance in Parliament.*

Mr Shebbeare *objected to the Lords as being comprised of members of one economic class.*

Motion lost 50:54.

31 May 1934

House believes ministers have forfeited its confidence by their failure to promote economic recovery.

Mr Geoffrey Morris (Oriel) *There has been, it must be admitted, a great fall in unemployment over the past year. This though, is not the result of anything ministers have done. Fluctuations in the trade cycle are not likely to cure the country's permanent ills.*

Mr Murray (Librarian) *The 1929 Labour government had piled up sixty millions of debt on the Unemployment Fund. The recovery cannot be explained by trade cycle theories. The government's tariff policy has promoted trade recovery. As for the Unemployment Bill, it had been framed in order to help working class interests.*

Mr David Lewis (Lincoln) *asked what was the meaning of the Disaffection Bill? Is there a rebellion in the army or a mutiny in the Navy? There are three tests for the National Government: Has it raised the standard of living? Can it offer security of employment? Can it absorb the unemployed into the industrial structure?*

Mr Donald Somerville (Solicitor-General—Visitor) *I quite agree that it is wrong to lay all the blame on the 1929 Labour government for the World Depression. But by contrast, the administrative measures of this government have succeeded in restoring a measure of prosperity in the country. It is upon the movement of wholesale prices that industry depends. The Labour Party never remembers that the worker is a consumer as well as a producer.*

———— ∞∞∞ ————

8 November 1934

House would deplore the establishment of an Irish republic including the six counties.

Mr T. A. Brown (Balliol) *Ulster has always voted on is convictions and this has given a remarkable stability to its form of government. So a vote against the motion is a vote in favour of the coercion of Ulster by the Irish Free State.*

Mr Rutherford *Only Irish independence can free Ireland from nationalism. Only in Ireland, are the Catholics revolutionaries and the Protestants reactionary. I do object to the way southern Ireland has been refused the right, belonging to a Dominion, to establish a republic if it wishes to do so.*

Mr W. V. Emmanuel (Trinity) *The Protestant religion and independence are regarded in Ulster as synonymous. Ulster's people hold with tenacious loyalty to the imperial connection. Ulster is more intensely loyal than anyone, not from this country, could realise.*

Mr F. A. Pakenham (Ch.Ch.)[41] *had the distinction of speaking as a neutral because he thought that that Ireland's right to secede should be granted even though he hoped it would not be exercised.*

Motion carried 101:67.

29 November 1934

House would deplore a Franco-Russian alliance.

Mr H. G. Gilmour (Univ.) *Such an association would be unthinkable because it would be one between a nation under tyranny and a free country. I hope that the real nobility behind the League of Nations idea would prevent it falling into bad hands.*

Mr F. G. Barnes (Balliol) *A defensive alliance between the two would be a salutary contribution to the peace of Europe. Both countries possess a spirit of scientific research and have benevolent governments.* The opposers might have disputed the latter statement. *By contrast, the German–Polish agreement was nothing more than a time-controlled truce.*

Mr R. McM. Bell (Magd.)[42] *I oppose all alliances, but particularly one which can only be interpreted as anti-German. I agree with the German attitude of regarding the USSR as the enemy of European civilisation. The Third International is not the vanguard of the proletariat, but the Guards' band of the Russian Army.*

Mr C. L. Miller (St. Catherine's) *Just because France and Russia are so far apart, there is little danger of any alliance between them becoming aggressive; and if the movers of the motion do not condemn Germans for leaving the League, they cannot blame the French for seeking to strengthen themselves apart from the League.*

The reappearance of Mr Adolf Schleppegrell (ex-Secretary, Univ.) *was greatly appreciated by members. It is the personality behind what he says which is so successful in winning the confidence of the House. In this case, the sympathy of everyone was with the speaker when he told the House that he should not be suspect for he was one of those whom the present Germany would not have back. It was no wonder that the ex-Secretary's moving conclusion caused so many to vote on his side.*

The ex-President from Balliol (Probably Brian Farrell) *is at his best in Foreign Affairs. It is a compliment to the Visitor that his support was given in full measure, pressed down and running over. France was responsible for beginning the policy of alliances; and this alliance was one more attempt to encircle Germany, a Germany which from 1919 to 1926 had been denied access to international tribunals. Members will always be well-informed after a speech by the ex-President.*

Professor Mendelssohn Bartholdy, *one of the Society's few honorary members, could conceive of no greater danger to peace than agreements between the general staffs of two countries against a third one. If the alternative were between a Franco-Russian and a Franco-Polish one, then he would prefer the former. But much though he deplored the present condition of Germany, it was worse than useless to form alliances against her.*

Mr C. P. Issawi (Magd.) *said that no one would have deplored an Anglo-American alliance as it would have been one between peace-makers.*

Mr C. L. Hauser (Balliol) *had doubts that Hitler and the Nazis meant war.*

Mr G. S. Cox (Oriel) *spoke from first-hand knowledge of German labour camps. He must speak again.*

Mr P. J. Anderson (Worcester) *thought that Great Britain was always interfering in Foreign affairs.*

Motion carried by 64 votes.

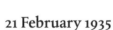

21 February 1935

House approves the hereditary principle in government.

Mr Bell *I appreciate that the motion relates to the principle of aristocracy and is not concerned with individual aristocrats. I object to primogeniture as there is no reason to assume that the eldest must have all the virtues of his particular family. But this hereditary principle is as applicable in Whitechapel as in Mayfair. For it is based on the biological truth that good breeds good. A society without an aristocracy would involve the institutionalizing of the family.* Mr Bell closed with a not very relevant quotation from Mill.

Mr G. G. Thomson *This motion is a defence of lost causes. The best in a nation is not necessarily found in an aristocracy. Bad breeds bad. The aristocracy is respected by some, not for virtues but because it is the aristocracy; and it is an evil principle to respect the mere aristocracy. The hereditary principle relates to the division of property. But is it expedient now? The answer is No. Selection of the rulers of a country should have nothing to do with family selection. The basis of democracy is that the best should rise to the top.*

Mr A. W. Kean (Queen's Cambridge—Secretary of the Cambridge Union) is difficult to report because a good deal of what he said was quite unfit for publication. *I did not come here to defend the House of Lords, even though it is a check on the Socialism which makes me shudder, but the principle is too important to throw aside. I simply object to the present perpetuity principle in the aristocracy.*

Mr M. S. Sundarnam (Balliol) *From Indian experience he attacked the Rajahs.*

Count D. M. Tolstoy-Miloslavsky (President of CUU) *How many members of the House of the Commons are put there because of their ability? The obstructive nature of the Lords is, in my opinion, much exaggerated. We do have a body free from vote-catching desires to co-operate in the government of the country. Continuity in government is very important, especially in such matters as foreign affairs. I have no objection to the creation of Labour peers or even an upper house of the extreme Left. To all this must be added the magnificent tradition of service in the monarchy and the aristocracy.*

Mr Murray *In a very good, and considering his party affiliation, brave, speech, said that the hereditary principle was incompatible with Conservatism.*

Mr R. J. Miller (St. Catherine's) *made the novel point that the presence of the monarchy prevents idolization of politicians as in Germany.*

Mr A. M. Neave (Merton)[43] *said that a figurehead was needed to retain the Empire.*

Mr D. S. O'Callaghan *is a heavy speaker.*

Motion lost 78:92.

---

9 May 1935

House believes the BBC to be a greater menace to freedom of thought and economic expansion than the popular press. United States Universities visit.

Mr A. M. Morgan (Magd.) *The BBC monopoly constitutes a threat to Newspapers. It can be converted into a political party. And because it is run in secret fashion, it constitutes a greater menace to the country than the popular press. Newspapers attack each other, but the BBC is a monopoly. Those newspapers are a joke and have ceased to be a threat.*

Mr J. A. Brown *Let me welcome the visitors from a land, exclusively governed, controlled and robbed—by Irishmen. The BBC is more conducive to economic emancipation than the press. The BBC stands for better and brighter culture. Fascism increased enormously when the Daily Mail embraced it.*

Mr J. R. Elliott (Emory University USA) *As to being governed and robbed etc. by Irishmen, the US is actually governed by College Professors, not policed by anyone and robbed by those nations who refused to pay their debts. As for the BBC, it tries to educate people which is not its real function. It is there to provide entertainment, not disseminate culture.*

Mr Shebbeare—Treasurer *Many charges might wisely be made. A large part of the staff consists of ex-Army and ex-Navy men. But there is no comparison with the real menace of the popular press. That is in the hands of advertisers. Freedom of thought is not necessary to liberty. The Daily Herald started out with altruistic motives but has become a party rag.*

Mr Douglas Woodruff ex-president (St John's)[44] *The BBC has brought Uncle*[45] *into children's homes. The only valid point made against it was that the BBC had done so well in the past, that it might become a menace in the future. Advertisers govern the British press and the American Broadcasting system. The strict censorship exercised by the BBC exists because it speaks to the whole family, and it is amazing just what people object to their daughters hearing. The mind of the public is debased by headlines, but the BBC has no headlines.*

Mr David Lewis *made a violent attack on the honeyed words of Mr Woodruff, whose speech, he said, invoked unscrupulous use of unscrupulous methods to disguise a monopoly.*

Mr Farrell—(Librarian) *It is hard to say which was the greater menace, but wireless has great political significance at this particular time. German Nazism could not have attained its present position without it. It is interesting that in their attempt to seize power in Austria, the Nazis had tried to seize the broadcasting station in Vienna.*

Mr C. P. Chenevix-Trench (Magd.) *There is no freedom of thought. Everyone follows the ideas of great men.*

Mr P. J. Anderson *I fail to understand what is actually meant by freedom of thought. Thought is governed by the endocrine glands.*

Vote not given.

16 May 1935

House finds that at the present time, the conception of everything for the state, nothing outside the state, nothing against the state, is the sole adequate basis for the self-realisation of the individual.

Mr L. Wilkes (Balliol) *The Social Democrats who tried to achieve socialism by parliamentary methods notoriously failed. The coercive state is the only way to achieve socialism. The Social Democrats had failed in Germany and Austria. There is no alternative to extreme socialism.*

The Liberal party had once believed in Free Trade, Honesty and the Ten Commandments. They are left with the Commandments. The Labour Party knows when to stop, but never gets there. The Fascist Party is led by Mosley, a well-groomed rodent. The Conservatives claim to be a constitutional party. Yet in 1914, Carson defied parliament over the Home Rule Bill. The proletarian state is the only alternative to capitalist democracy and in this country, capitalist democracy is two-chamber obstruction. The real slavery at the present time is wage-slavery, and only the Proletarian state can abolish it.

Mr Ian Harvey (Ch.Ch.)[46] *Consider two dogmas: Dogma A is that the individual is more important than the state. Dogma B is that the state interference is necessary, but that the state may not interfere in matters which concern the individual alone. The state is cold and impersonal and alienates where individual help creates good will.*

Miss M. P. Moxon (St Hilda's) (Visitor) *Hitler is the late night final, of which Ramsay MacDonald had been the midday sporting edition. The vote in England means nothing, but in Russia, it means everything.*

Miss Ruth McKee (St. Hugh's) (Visitor) *Under a rigid system of state, control over discontent is battened down, but under the English system, discontent can come to the surface, and be healed. Heathen Russia and anti-Semitic Germany would make this university impossible. Man can live alone and create his moral being. Fascism and Communism are forms of retrogression.*

Mr John McMurray (Visitor) *The end of the Fascist state is power in itself, and power for itself is a criminal principle. We are passing through what most people would call a crisis. The post-war world has contracted economically; the doctrine of state paramountcy is an attempt by nations to maintain their pre-war position on a narrower basis. Since the war, patriotism has become far more intense and bitter. People who believe in the supremacy of the state are either congenital idiots or knaves. A noted political thinker had once said 'That as Christianity was the final truth in religion, so Democracy is the final word in political institutions.' That thinker was Karl Marx.*

Mr H. C. Budden (Merton) *declared that the state would be found as necessary under a classless society as under one determined by class. The state is restrictive and not coercive. The state does not restrict those activities enough which limit the activities of others.*

No vote given.

---

30 May 1935

House considers the government's measures for the unemployed and the distressed areas to be totally inadequate.

Mr J. A. Brown (Balliol—President of the Liberal Club) *Government policy has been all tariffs and quotas. But how can unemployment be decreased by diminishing export trade? The Chancellor claims that 80 per cent of prosperity has now been recovered. The discrepancy with the facts is obvious. The state of the unemployed is gradually worsening. The government's record over the distressed areas has also grown worse. Commissioners had been appointed, but their task is merely to enlist local effort. There is idle money in the banks and idle men in the streets. They should be brought together by an extensive scheme of public works.*

Mr D. Maitland-Makgill-Crichton (Worcester) had lost his notes and was forced to improvise his speech. *The government's measures are experimental, so I could not deliver judgment upon the attitude toward the unemployed and the distressed areas.*

Mr P. R. Anderson (Worcester) *If a Socialist government were returned to office, they would turn a nation of shopkeepers into a nation of shoplifters. The Socialist party had turned a sectional need to the service of party propaganda. The unemployed have been the Socialist party's great stroke of luck. The National Government is Democracy's response to the crisis.*

Mr R. H. S. Crossman (New College)[47] *I regret that the government has been allowed to go on with its policy. The only event which could possibly intervene between the present temporary boom and another depression is war. Ministers should put men into conscription and then we would be able to look the Germans in the face and call them brothers.*

The government has adopted the principle of Vocational Training by means of which workmen have been hired for 1s 10d less to build jerry-built houses on new building estates. Democracy means the rule of the people for the people and it rejects every system which sacrifices the welfare of the people to the system itself.

No vote given.

<hr />

17 October 1935

House believes that the Foreign policy and Home Record of the National Government do not warrant its return at the General Election.

Mr W. A. Nield (St Edmund's Hall) *Nothing compares with the fundamental split in the Conservative ranks.*

On the principle of collective security. There is a dual Policy: lip service to collective security and, at the same time, a reversion to the pre-war power politics: as seen in the Manchurian dispute, the Stresa and other Disarmament Conferences. Labour is prepared to support collective security provided that it can be shown that re-armament is necessary and provided that the armament firms are nationalised.

Mr Bell *The Government is quite right to refuse to spend money on non-permanent schemes for the depressed areas. As for the present crisis … to have tried to apply sanctions against Germany would have broken the League, particularly as it was felt that the treaty was doomed. And to have tried to coerce Japan would have meant Great Britain policing the seas.*

Mr Shebbeare *The government has picked and chosen when to support the League of Nations—and when to revert to the methods of secret diplomacy. Witness Mr Eden's travels round Europe and the Stresa conference.*[48] *The objection to its Manchurian policy is that it has not even tried to get sanctions applied.*

Mr Walker-Smith *It is stupid to attack the government because it has not given us Utopia. As to sanctions, since they have the capacity of leading to war, we must be fully equipped. Only by Great Britain being strongly armed, can we have peace. Future rearmament will be decided at the polls soon.*

Mr C. R. Attlee MP (Univ.)[49]—Deputy-leader of the Opposition. *The means test is not only bad ethics, but bad economics; for mass consumption is essential to a system of mass-production. The Government, by means of tariffs and doles to industry, is pursuing a policy of scarcity which, though demanded by the old rules by which the government is playing, is sheer lunacy. There is no such thing today as National Defence. This demands a new concept of patriotism. Labour will stand by them provided they stand by the League. A very effective speech delivered in a crisp parliamentary style, interspersed with caustic humour. The House received it very well.*

Mr J. A. de G. Elles (Ch.Ch.) *We must meet the primeval with the primeval.' Mr Elles should concentrate on 'filling the House.'*

Mr R. S. Wicks[50] *The government are providing for the defence of the country from air attack, a precaution not thought of by Socialists.*

Mr R. H. Walton (Balliol) *The National Government is unsupportable because it is trying to put Socialism into practice.*

Motion carried by 11 votes.

24 October 1935

House believes that British rule operates to the detriment of native races.

Mr N. S. Jununkar (St Catherine's) *There is a minority which thinks British rule beneficial to natives since it upholds liberty and racial equality and furthers the economic position of those natives. The Government builds railways and other public works, not for philanthropic purposes, but so that countries may be exploited. It develops the police—not the social service-state.*

Mr O'Callaghan *The Government is quite ready to give self-government, but it has to come slowly. Let us compare the present position of Liberia to that of Uganda where British rule stepped in. It is obvious that native races benefited from Roman rule. Similarly, the much better British rule has been similarly beneficial.*

Mr C. P. Mayhew (Ch.Ch.)[51] supported the motion in a sober and informed speech. *We have treated the native races as means and not ends. Consider the words of Lord Brentwood:[52] 'By the sword we have conquered, by the sword, we should hold it.' Our impact has been to make self-sufficient natives dependent on a world market. Official figures show how negligent the Government has been over education, illiteracy and the general standard of life. Surely, it is the Indians who have the moral right to decide how they are to be governed. How is it that Indians are behind Congress and united on one thing that the English have to get out? We must bring forward the facts to dispel the ignorance of English people about the real position.*

Mr J. A. Brown (Balliol—Secretary) *We have no business forcing our own culture down other people's throats. The Irish opposition was always about the insufferable intolerance of the English. Bernard Shaw says that the good of foreign governments can never be proved to natives. It is high time we heard no more of the White Man's Burden. There is a grave danger of modern Germany following our example.*

Mr J. M. Gwyer (Ch.Ch.) *in quite a good speech, tried to refute the secretary by quotations supporting Italy's moral right to civilise Abyssinia.*

Mr P. J. Anderson *We simply must believe in our own country if we want to survive and we must find better ways for spreading our doctrine.*

Mr C. V. Narasimihan (St Catherine's) *The alleged English Civil Service in India are not English, not civil nor servants. They are the masters.*

Mr N. P. MacDonald (St Peter's Hall) *Surely we must feel sympathy for the Italians in view of the barbarism of Abyssinia.*[53] *Mr MacDonald was quite at home at the despatch box for his maiden.*

Mr B. J. Stubbings *British policy has had a great effect on the present very bad South African native policy.*

Mr E. A. Bramall (Magd.) *Consider the effect if the British Empire had never arisen. Clear and quite incisive.*

Mr R. N. Rayne (BNC) *Surely British rule encouraged rather than suppressed national individuality.*

Mr R. J. Gould Adams (New College)[54] *There has been too much talk about India. A conversational speech.*

Mr V. H. Ruse (Queen's) *The situation in Germany is far worse than in India.*

Mr S. G. Collier (Magd.) *Who are we to civilise other people?*

Mr S. O. Olson (Balliol) *However bad British government may be, there is none better.*

Motion carried 126:103.

———⌖———

31 October 1935

House thinks the Government's acceptance of Collective Security does not justify its claim to re-arm.

Mr Walton *The Tory party are exploiting the desire for peace for rearmament. It is false to say that our forces are inadequate. To re-arm now would imply lack of faith in Collective Security. It is also false to say that we have to be strong for the League to succeed, since collective security is collective. National rearmament means general insecurity.*

Mr Anderson *The only practical policy at the present time is rearmament. Would Italy have taken so firm a line if England's navy had not been so weak? It is our duty to rearm the League, the only institution in Europe upholding liberty against Fascism. This means that we have to be strong.*

Mr L. Wilkes *The Tory Party has always been concerned about national rearmament. The figures show that the alleged inferiority of British forces is false. The first essential of a co-operative peace system is to put armaments in the hands of a central authority.*

Mr Harvey—Librarian *We cannot defend our neighbours if we cannot defend ourselves. If we were to disarm, the Empire would be seized by other countries. And at present, we have been opposing Fascism with its 'Heroism of war.' The movers have not shown us what we should do about it. We have to rely on force at present though it will be a defensive, not an aggressive force.*

No vote given.

14

We Go into the Dark

6 November 1935 to 9 May 1940

Collective security or Isolation?/No confidence/Palestine/'War between nations can be justified'/No confidence/Back to religion/compulsory national service/ Chamberlain must go/the Press/Palestine/Statement of war aims/Soviet policy not in accordance with Socialist principles/Indian independence/No neutrality/ preferring Mussolini to Stalin?

Foreign policy in the years clear of the Versailles peace treaty, with its punitive French revenge on Germany, high-minded American nation-making and boundary shifting, became by contrast, on all sides, internationalist in rhetoric and decent good purpose. Given economic stability, there was political stability, but it remained utterly insecure against the realities of a grudge nationalism which would rise up snarling when economic depression descended.

The League of Nations was proclaimed as if it were the abolition of war. Though no one should deride in knowing retrospect the ardour with which the very idea was embraced. In Britain, witness the devoted commitment to its service of Lord Robert Cecil, a younger son of Salisbury, ideal-proof third Marquess and Prime Minister. This Cecil spoke the impulse of thoughtful people on all sides. And in early days, the spirit of the League would make it possible for sensible Foreign Ministers from Britain, Germany, France, and the new construction, Czechoslovakia— Austen Chamberlain, Stresemann, Briand, and Benes—to spend autumn days pleasantly in neutral Switzerland, seemingly underwriting the

417

definitive, open-ended guarantee of collectively protecting peace. The Locarno Pact, announced on 16 October 1925, defining Germany's western frontier and demilitarizing the Rhineland, also proclaimed international arbitration as the way to settle differences, promised all-round commitment to non-aggression, and had seemingly underwritten such promises. Undertakings by Britain and Italy, advocating active intervention against any breaker of those promises evidently confirmed it.

None of this should be mocked. As long as trade, and with it, the national economies and job markets held, idealism would be rational by reason of not having been tested. However on the New York Stock Exchange, four years and one week later, 23 October 1929, they were tested to what felt like destruction. More precisely, the crash, product of orthodox economics, uncomprehending restoration of the gold standard, backed by received standard opinion, equally wrong, started the descent. The ways for climbing out, providential improvidence, spending hard to drive money round, were left for retrospective regret.

The *political* consequence would be unemployment with another consequence. As the old poker-work text put it, *Satan finds some evil yet for idle hands to do*. It had been possible for Mussolini, in power since 1922, to attend Locarno on his best pacific behaviour and join Britain in promising redress against breakers of undertakings. Hitler was something else, and Hitler's rise derived vertically from an unemployment, uncontested by elected government, and huge. In Britain, the National Government existed to sustain sound finance, avoid debt, and leave the Trade Cycle to return uphill un-pedalled. The reaction here was one of a threadbare making-do, the phlegmatic instinct of victims, and a measure of radical talk and, in universities, a minority of undergraduates talking Marxism.

One of the ways out of depression is rearmament. It can, in the right, wrong hands, be acceptable, particularly to the Right, despite that end of the spectrum being usually against large expenditure. Patriotism is called into service to justify the absorption of unemployment in building warships and planes. In Britain, the idea of large expenditure on, say, railway renewal *and* road building or public housing schemes was perceived by the Baldwins of especially England, the temperate, flair-free, temperate Right, as ruinous. It was certain only to debase the currency and bring in the broker's men. There was another factor at play in this country, an unacknowledged, not altogether understood change.

The heroism of contesting empires including 'The greatest empire the world has ever seen,' a term droningly familiar in pre-1914 Oxford debates, had created a mood, keyed-up for, or resigned to, war, for embracing a great, cleansing conflict. Edward Grey had cited 'Honour' in August 1914, as he persuaded the Cabinet to fulfil promises better not made and failing that, better not kept. The Oxford Union had given a large majority in favour of compulsory military training, Prussian style. It was responding to that OTC half-colonel urging it, who had longed to see 'the whole University, carrying rifles, marching down the High'. The great vote in favour of *not* wanting in 1933 to fight for King and Country is eloquent here and should be seen entirely in that crazy context.

The assumption in the Union and the street, back in 1911, was innocent, in the sense that they didn't know what war was like. It had always been fought by professionals, the two military castes—of footloose gentry and trade-less proletarians. In 1933 and long before, the knowledge was general that in Europe, such a war would be fought by conscripted men between 18 and 42. We knew better now. Horror at the running blood, a narrow generation back, of people like themselves, had instructed more men than undergraduates in the general hell of it. The debates of 1935 and after, are long and earnest about the 'League', 'Locarno', and at home the 'Peace Pledge Union', and, embracing them all like a religious doctrine, 'Collective Security'. Liberal minds and bruised recollections had brought to the post-war generation and survivors of the previous one a deep, grateful trust in the talk and treaty-crafting which should stop 1914 from walking again.

Meanwhile Hitler, perfectly ignorant of classical economics, was spending money and more money—building autobahns and fighter-planes—a perfect Keynesian, creating employment for a grateful population. His country stood ready to re-elect him on a vote supervised by the

Heavenly Host, as all the while he assembled the means to make war or, quite as usefully, to threaten it. Hitler would find the neighbours, under all the collective self-persuasion of peace, in perfect abjection. Accordingly, he announced his intention to re-militarize the Rhineland.

French Ministers begged for British backing, though at this date they might have been able alone to rebuff a German army in its first year of rearmament. Meanwhile, Britain, whose Conservative press, led by *The Times* and Beaverbrook's *Express*, was promoting overt appeasement, offered nothing. The inadequacy of Baldwin and his Ministers was part of the recollection of the last war—how it had started with heroics and gone murderously on. Inertia *now* was quite wrong and entirely natural. Events would then proceed by way of successive failures of judgement. An unrelenting, negative response to each succeeding pitch by Hitler would be most unlikely to have sparked a war. He made the first one—that march into the demilitarized Rhineland—in order to re-militarize it. Failure to respond arm in arm with France in pointing the direction by which German troops should go back was failure itself, 1914 in reverse, but also by a circular route, creating war.

The march into that territory came on 7 March 1936, early in the long and complex process of German rearmament. Physical action would have been unnecessary. Hitler was bluffing; the extent of his military *equipe* could not, so early in the four-year process of rearmament, have been remotely adequate. An old-fashioned démarche which, in the best Palmerstonese, had said 'Stop that or we'll invade you' would have directed German troops and weaponry clean out of the Rhineland. Ironically, the German High Command, expecting at least *French* opposition, had opposed the move. For the old Prussian corps from whom the tragic assassins of 1944 would be drawn lacked all round regard for the Leader.

However Hitler's instinct told him that he would *not* be opposed. France's immobility followed, ironically, an attempt by Paris to organize Anglo-French military cooperation. It had been only a fortnight before the Rhineland adventure that the Sarraut Ministry had sought a formal British alliance. The National Government, now led by Baldwin, had wanted none of it. An alternative British response to the Rhineland remilitarization, that the case was altered and that an alliance should now be discussed at once, would have told Hitler that he must gamble, not only on success with quite inadequate military strength, but on a highly sceptical High Command not removing him at once.

Brisk British commitment would have shown Hitler as a Grand Old Duke of York marching his troops across a great territory and marching them back again. It would have needed nerve, but not a lot of it. France understood the menace next door, had done so since Hitler came to power. France might indeed have acted alone, but the British rebuff sent an implied message of indifference to Berlin and weakened every French instinct for action. Against all of which failure must be set the battles of the Somme and the Marne and the battalions of the dead. We made the mistakes of pre-1939 in fearful reflection upon the mistakes of pre-1914.

Not that nothing was being done. The National Government under MacDonald, Baldwin, and Chamberlain set rolling a programme which vitally included the Spitfires and Hurricanes which would defeat German invasion in 1940, a point made forcefully by Nigel Knight in his impressive assault on the Churchill legend.[1] But doing nothing over the Rhineland had added to Hitler's assurance in all future moves, including Poland when in 1939, at the worst imaginable time, Britain finally made the stand, apt and easy in 1936.

In parallel with Hitler's advance came in that year—in July 1936, the Spanish Civil War. As noted earlier, Oxford, which, for the next three years, would make a great show of left-wing militancy over Spain, had been pre-empted from the Right by a Union debater present here, Douglas Jerrold, who would personally fly General Franco from the Canary Islands. Franco commanded forces serving the coalition of clerical, military, and Ultra-Rightists attempting to seize power in a period of violent disturbance, after a Left and Centre coalition had come to office.

What mattered in the context of a response to Hitler was that he, like Mussolini, sent men and materiel to support the gallant Christian gentleman who would later kill prisoners of war on a generous scale. He would receive open-handed support from Hitler and Mussolini in terms of men and weapons. Stalin also engaged, though as Orwell related in his memoir of the war,[2] gaining control of the coalition against right-wing dictatorship in a struggle against all rivals, especially Trotskyists, a line of 'No friends on the Left' seemed to be the preoccupation of Soviet representatives. As an issue, Spain doesn't quite fit with the Rhineland or the Sudetenland. Fear of Communism which pulled right-wing and Catholic opinion into sympathy with gallant Christian gentlemen played a full part. Spain wasn't on the map of European contention and ultimately, except for the Spaniards, didn't matter. An interesting footnote is found in reports of conversations in 1940 between Franco and Marshal Pétain, contemplating collaborationist glory as head of the Vichy Republic. Franco advised strongly against[3] and would reject Hitler's later attempts to exact wartime gratitude. Member of a naval family of El Ferrol, he had too high an opinion of the British Navy.

Similarly, Hitler's takeover of the Austrian Republic, product of Versailles, was observed and disregarded. He had been there before in 1934 with a street putsch which the Austrian premier, Schuschnigg, himself standard issue twentieth-century Christian anti-democrat, briskly put down. As this had been, at least officially, a local affair, Hitler suffered very little loss of face and would in due course (11 March 1938)—swiftly ahead of Schuschnigg's snap referendum on Austrian independence—get it done. It would be conducted, as commonly with Hitler, suddenly, a *fait* briskly *accompli*, troops over the border and through the streets, leaving other governments in the wrong tense.

Chamberlain, caught by the news at lunch with, among others, the German ambassador and Churchill, said something which gathers together the bright, international assumptions of Locarno and the trucks, troops, crossed borders, and feet-through-the-door of the so many similar occasions. Austria, protested Chamberlain, was, like Britain, a member of the League of Nations; and Britain had a concern in central Europe and the peace of Europe. The Austrian putsch would be a working demonstration of the unarmed futility of all such dreams, maintained by legal proclamation on the assumption that the forces of such law existed.

Looking at the unpreparedness of this country ahead of September 1939, it is unfair to put all blame on the idleness of Baldwin or the delusive presumption of Neville Chamberlain. Left and Liberal opinion, themselves buried in being 'anti-fascist' and 'anti-war' at the same time, did nothing. Even realists like Attlee (Major Attlee actually, with a notable First War record in several theatres) all talked 'Collective security'. Yet there was some grasp of the fearful state of things. Symbolically, the Labour Party, in conference and tears, would in 1935 remove sweet, good George Lansbury as leader—for being too much of an on-principle pacifist. However, this was accomplished only after a hard shove from the trade union *realpolitik* of Ernest Bevin; and Labour would continue talking international generalities without edge or deterrence. The Labour Party's hard-bitten line against the post-war USSR was being learnt here—and Bevin, who would seek the Treasury in 1945, would in that year become, at Attlee's insistence, a formidable, surely great, Foreign Secretary.

Accordingly, the case for rearmament against Hitler as a monstrous threat to civilization, never mind peace, was never made. Government and opposition colluded in trembling irresolution. A swift pre-emption to strip Hitler naked if the re-militarization of the Rhineland had been challenged by a three-day ultimatum would have succeeded. The French had some sense of this. Overt appeasement began with the non-response to his sending of troops into this territory, single-handedly and without challenge, effecting its militarization. It was a far more threatening act than Habsburg Austria's invasion of Serbia which could and should have been ignored beyond an admonitory finger. Against Locarno and all the peace proclamations, German men and weaponry now stood in that territory, a harrow ready for the soil of France. But as Kipling put it, 'The butterfly upon the road | Preaches contentment to the toad.'

Everything now became a mirror image of the years immediately preceding the First War. The pre-1914 built-in and twitchy anti-Germanism of the FO war faction, Crowe, Nicholson, Bertie, and Edward Grey, was replaced by deluded fairness. Chamberlain, his advisers, and most of the press showed a readiness, conscious of past excess, to see Germany's point of view when it was Hitler's point of view. The old, self-fulfilling belief that as great contesting powers, Germany and Britain were destined to make war, no longer obtained. Such rationality and readiness to slow down and talk about things would have been perfect wisdom before August 1914.[4] There was then no single aggressor but in many countries many misapprehensions.

The late 1930s crises were rather different—assured, chance-taking aggression by one power, making calculated steps and displaying plain nerve against clear targets. Hitler walked with both eyes open, his route determined by his identity. He was a provincial Austrian, who would never be fulfilled merely by annexing the Versailles-defined small state. He had come as a young man to Vienna from an *echt Deutsch* hill town and found it full, not only of Jews, but of Slavs, especially Czechs. He had witnessed the street hatreds between Czechs and Germans divided into clubs and associations in conflict and sporadic fighting.[5] Now after German defeat, President Wilson had created a state linking Czechs and Slovaks, and had presented it with the preponderantly German-speaking Sudetenland.

A moderate German politician, heading an elected government and peacefully seeking a boundary revision, twenty years on, would have made slow or no progress. This would have been unfair, so when Hitler demanded it with threats of another European war, the impossible became a workable option. We had, in 1914, entered a hideous war over Austria's obscure problems with Serbia. We wouldn't do anything so rash and disproportionate again. In this light, with these facts set out, Neville Chamberlain can be seen as perfectly rational, but rational in a fatally narrow perspective. Leaving the Austrian Empire in 1914 to make a short, punitive war against a serious trouble-maker like Serbia, and telling France and Russia flatly that we were not coming into their crusade would probably have left the 1914 crisis dangling, but not exploding. In 1938, Chamberlain was being led by a historical analogy badly skewed by Hitler not being Berchtold, Bethmann-Hollweg, or even Kaiser Wilhelm.

The arrivals in international affairs of Chamberlain in 1937 and Lord Halifax in 1938, brought with them a style of command and confidence where Baldwin had embodied inactivity. They would approach the great crisis of October 1938 with misconceived confidence. Chamberlain used the word *appeasement* positively as if he were giving baby his bottle. This was his considered bold policy. The Sudetenland had been a territory of the Habsburg Empire since the middle ages with a majority German-speaking population, but had become the western curve of Czechoslovakia, granted to that new state at Versailles. The moderate German statesman mentioned above, arguing unsuccessfully for the province's inclusion into either Germany or the new, shrunken Austrian Republic, would have had a decent case. The decent case plus demands with menaces, having been made by a street-ranter turned dictator, should have altered the case. Equity was no longer at the centre of the argument. This would now be one of power, more exactly the impetus of power, the prospect of it going so very much further. The central failure of Neville Chamberlain, apart from a self-confidence, very much ill advised, was to concentrate on the equity and ignore the power politics.

Hitler had operated so far by a succession of sudden, assured acts which could have been stopped in their tracks by the resolute direction of Britain and/or France, never mind the dream constellation of the League. Over Austria, a forty-eight-hour ultimatum and troops sent to the Rhine *instanter*, for which an interim French government wanted British backing, would have turned Hitler out of power in Berlin at the hands of the Prussian officer corps, never mind sending his troops back. The case for repatriating the Sudetenland would never have been raised. However, where Baldwin had been inert, Chamberlain through the meetings at Godesberg and Munich was pro-active. The French Premier, Daladier, a far more alert and intelligent judge of the situation, came, with a certain briskness, to London as the crisis opened and argued for a joint commitment to war if Czechoslovakia were attacked. Chamberlain refused, putting unlikely possibilities of action into a different tense, the future indifferent! If this and then later, that... we could not guarantee to remain aloof.

To the Czechs themselves, people of a democratic country threatened with invasion by the Nazi state, Chamberlain was dismissive and downright hostile. If the thought crossed his mind that session of the Sudetenland which contained all of Czechoslovakia's quite formidable defences might be followed by German invasion of the rest of the country, there is no evidence of it. In France, itself unstable, Daladier's clear view of what should be done would be undermined by his coalition partner, the Foreign Minister, Georges Bonnet. Significantly Daladier was a former Minister of War and of Defence, Bonnet a Finance Minister who had been obliged to devalue the franc. He would also be a collaborator during the war while Daladier would survive Buchenwald.

The French Premier could claim total scepticism about any deal with Hitler at the expense of the Czechs achieving anything worth having and made this clear to Chamberlain. Yet he did not assert himself anything like as much in the negotiations as he should have, leaving his disastrous Foreign Minister with extensive scope. Bonnet was up for a position beyond Chamberlain's readiness to compel the Czechs to surrender the Sudetenland and those defences. Where Chamberlain was cocksure, Daladier tended to despair. When the French Cabinet voted against going to war to support Czechoslovakia if Germany attacked her, Chamberlain had *carte blanche* for candid full-dress appeasement. An option offered by Russia that she should intervene in defence of Czechoslovakia was understandably mistrusted.

The outcome of that policy, noisily transmitted by *The Times*, would be the final crunch—Munich. Hitler's diplomacy, threats which were maintained, backed by an utterly convincing intent of action, continued to work. He made demands on the Czechs, backed by local street violence from Sudeten Germans, which demands Chamberlain and Bonnet existed to exact, precisely from the Czechs! The Anglo-French illusion was that demands met, would stop; reliably they transferred somewhere else. The sellers of the pass began by a belief in some international authority, a sort of bureaucratic Holy Ghost, whose messengers they were. They learned that the only available success was conclusion of the claim, and that the only way of getting it was to underwrite Hitler's threats with their own desertion and cajolery. It would be, from the Rhineland to Munich, a superlative course of seminars in something older than Machiavelli and in contradiction to the Gospels—that power is to the strong. That was why fighter planes were being built for the RAF.

What followed immediately by way of a meeting with Hitler at Godesberg, then in the final abasement of Munich, was the total abandonment of the Czechs, with Chamberlain at one stage in Godesberg, actually running in his requirements of them ahead of Hitler. It was settled that the Sudetenland should be allowed to vote for union with Germany. An attempt by Daladier to have the two western countries guarantee that country's reduced boundaries was stymied by Chamberlain dissolving it in a meaningless guarantee of all boundaries including Germany's. The proposal then defined itself to impose the incorporation into Germany of all districts of the former Czechoslovakia which had a German population of over 50 per cent.

Benes refused and spoke of arbitration based on the Czech–German treaty of civilized days—1925, until he was brow-beaten by the British and French, and told 'to take a hold of realities'. Hitler, finding the Surrender Party ahead of him, muddling his schedule, made new demands: German troops to immediately occupy the identified German-speaking areas (taking plenty of Czech-speakers clean under Nazi rule). It took the Prime Minister a night to resume his abjection, asking that the transfer might be done 'in an orderly fashion and free from the threat of force'. Hitler essentially disliked being given what he had meant to march into. Chamberlain wanted whatever surrender was necessary, but signed off in polite form.

However surrender seemed to be evading the Prime Minister when Daladier came to Downing St. and declared France ready to go to war if Czechoslovakia were attacked. In an atmosphere of war expectation, Chamberlain broadcast, as they used to say, 'To the nation' with a touch-ing little whimper about 'How horrible, fantastic, incredible' it all was, to be putting on gas masks 'because of a quarrel in a far-away country of which we know nothing'. He followed this up by a piece of bad theatre, interrupting a debate in the Commons and provoking cheers as he picked up and read out a letter, passed to him at the dispatch box, and announcing an invitation from Hitler to go to Munich for further talks.

The pass had effectively been sold *before* Munich. Indeed Munich itself emerged rather like a house-purchase haggle, a slightly differently phrased version of the final agreement at Godesberg, with Czechoslovakia now required to begin surrendering a Sudetenland which would contain 800,000 Czechs, on 1 October and be done by the 7th—and piously, the new Czech frontiers to be guaranteed by *all* the parties. It was to be peace in our time.

It was also the getting of Hitler, against whom those senior soldiers were planning a putsch, out of any risk of that. It was instruction in the absurdity of keeping peace by international committee rather than by the credible fear of war instruction in every bright illusion about which more people than the members of the Oxford Union had talked nonsense for twenty years.

---

6 November 1935

The Government's acceptance of collective security does not justify its claim to re-arm.

Mr R. H. Walton (Balliol) *The Tories are exploiting the desire for peace for re-armament. It is false to say that our forces are inadequate. Re-arming implies lack of faith in Collective Security. It is wrong too, to say that we have to be strong for the League to succeed. Collective Security is collective!*

Mr P. J. M. Anderson (Worcester) *We face the alternatives of isolation or acceptance of Collective Security which means strengthening our forces to increase the power of a weakened League. Would Italy have taken such a strong line if our Navy had not been so weak?*

Mr L. Wilkes (Balliol) *The Tory Party has always been concerned with national rearmament. The only way to test the honesty of our government is to look at its bad record at Geneva… The first essential of a co-operative peace system is to put armaments in the hands of a central authority. This the National Government is opposed to doing.*

Motion lost 106 : 112.

The General Election of 1935 was the sort of defeat to delight any Party.[6] The Conservatives, losing 83 seats, still had 366. Labour, gaining 102, had 154. With characteristic melancholy pluck, the Liberals lost 12 and went down to 21. As to their leaders Baldwin, a civilized, fatalistic, and distinctly lazy man, represented low-octane politics. Labour had George Lansbury,[7] an accidental leader, landing there because his majority survived the firestorm of 1931 and going because his sweet pacifism couldn't survive Hitler. It went against the run of the party's luck that Clement Attlee, another 1931 survivor, would be an ideal leader who would shortly see off a more senior and far higher-profile figure, Herbert Morrison. Returning at the 1935 election, confident of his perfect right to the post, Morrison would claim it in a leadership election; and because loyalty (as against coherence) is Labour's secret weapon, Morrison, a man of inveterate tendencies, would stay that way, steadily sustaining a lifelong hatred toward a reciprocating Attlee.

Inside the movement, Lansbury was loved, the only word for it, but his fortuitous leadership, thrust upon him as the only Minister to survive the 1931 catastrophe, was skewed by that total pacifism, something confounded by the existence of Hitler. He would eventually be removed after defeat at party conference, this at the prime instance of Ernest Bevin, unsubtly set upon resisting the Nazis by rearmament.

---

28 November 1935

House regrets the return of the National Government at the General Election.

Mr W. G. C. Shebbeare (Ch.Ch.) *The government was returned to restore the credit of capitalism. But there is presently no such crisis; and the government has not given us a constructive policy. What does it have to offer the depressed areas? Socialism stands for the expression of democracy in industry, the planning of the country's economic life in the interest of all instead of the chaos of capitalist planning. Socialism also means the abolition of the distinction between rich and poor.*

Mr Harvey (Librarian) *On the depressed areas, the government has a different way of approaching the issue. They have not held up the disarmament conference; it has been frustrated by France and Germany. The Government upholds the capitalist system—the system which brings up industries A1.*

Mr Harold Macmillan MP[8] *I object to the rigidity of party dogmas. The election has been rather a vote of censure against the Opposition than one of confidence in the government. I look forward to the years before us with hope and confidence. They will be important years, if the government is true to the trust that has been given it. And there is undoubtedly the possibility that they will be.*

Mr Michael Foot supported the motion in a magnificent speech. *Yet the government should remember 'in the midnight of its intoxication' that there would be an awakening of the people. And that would occur because the government has done nothing about unemployment. They stand for Empire. I want a government that stands for peace first. Are we likely to get peace from a government of Londonderrys and Hailshams?* An excellent speech. The ex-president was applauded to the echo.

Motion carried 193:184.

The *Oxford Magazine* offers no reports of union debates long enough to be worth reproducing from this date until 10 November 1938.

---

10 November 1938

House deplores the indecision of HMG in its policy towards Palestine.

Mr L. S. Schulze (Corpus) *I do not believe that the government took over Palestine for love of the Holy Places, but for its strategic and economic value. Although Labour sympathises with the genuine Zionists, it is bound to support the national aspirations of the Arabs. The real struggle is not between Jew and Arab, but between the united interest of Jewish and Arab working classes and a government which exploits their racial differences on the old principles of 'Divide and Rule.'*

Mr A. F. Giles (Balliol) *Britain accepts the Palestine Mandate of 1922 in no spirit of imperialist vainglory, but soberly, as a trust. It is impossible to solve the problems of centuries over a few years. We need a more high-minded approach; and being a Conservative, I'm not ashamed to quote Burke.* Happily, he was not reported.

Colonel Josiah Wedgwood MP (Visitor) *As a Zionist, I have been calling for a Jewish Palestine since 1917 within the Empire. Much of the trouble flows from the insidious anti-semitism now being spread all over the Middle East. The Jewish influx has actually raised the local Arab standard of living. Arab states were transformed after the war: Syria, Iraq, Transjordan; surely one little corner could be left for Jewry.*

Hon. Hugh Fraser (Balliol) *The Jewish national home has been put in the wrong place. Palestine is too small to absorb all the immigrants. Its constitution is fatuous enough to have been drawn up by Common Room dons. A stern, authoritative government is needed. I hope the Woodhead report*[9] *will reject partition and recommend creation of a Crown Colony.*

Mr George Mansur (Visitor—former Secretary of the Arab Labour Foundation in Palestine) *The Arabs are not terrorists and murderers, but patriots fighting for freedom. Britain is attempting what France has achieved in Syria. Zionism is the unconscious tool of Imperialism. Jewish immigration has been encouraged in order to stifle the Arab cry for Home Rule. Immigration continues despite the unemployment, even among Palestinian Jews. Is it surprising that Arabs are alarmed?*

Motion carried 152:91.

The long grief of British and French having post-1918 intruded arms-length imperially in the Middle East, continues here as it has ever since.

———❦———

17 November 1938

House believes that war between nations can sometimes be justified.

This debate was a straight fight between the Pacifists and the Rest. The motion was commendably unambiguous, and replacing, rather than reversing, the decision of 1933 that the House would not fight for King and Country. That decision was not for Pacifism but against blind nationalism. This one was a clear rejection in a left-wing House of the Pacifist case in a context commanded by Adolf Hitler.

———❦———

Mr J. N. Henderson (Hertford) *In the King and Country debate of* 1933, *Mr Quintin Hogg*[10] *was prepared to fight for George V, but not, in* 1938, *for George VI! He ought to be prepared as we, on this side are, to fight for democracy, for freedom, for a way of life! It is as much in our interest to help China as it has been to intervene in any previous war.* Mr Henderson is developing a style of his own, but we should have welcomed more denunciation.

Mr J. R. Sykes (Corpus) *The first casualties of war are truth, sensitivity and imagination.*

Mr S. D. Kalelkar (Hertford) *If I am to be called an immoral warmonger, I want to know what is moral about handing over the economic resources of one country in order to avoid war in your own. I believe that the time will yet come which shows war bringing good.*

Miss Anne Harrison (Guest) Now as ever, the embodiment of arguments for admitting women as debating members. *I would ask non-pacifists to justify democracy before they try to justify war. Our C3 nation, our distressed areas and our corrupt government can show to the dictator states only an example of decadence. If we resist their unpleasant practices only with war, that will be the most decadent act of all. We must prepare at home for peace before it is too late.*

Mr C. M. Cadogan (Magd.—Treasurer) *Pacifism has been effective for peace against the Red Indians*[11] *and for Gandhi against Lord Irwin, but this is no analogy for international affairs. I agree with the mover about the calamity of submission to Germany and I foresee an end of International law and morality.*

Professor Joad, speaker at the King and Country debate of 1933 *Autocracies are worse after a war than before it; strength brings only insecurity. Britain armed has more to fear than Denmark armed. The enemy is nationalism and while it controls the world, war can never be justified.*

Motion carried 176:145.

---

24 November 1938

House has no confidence in the National Government.

Mr E. R. G. Heath (Balliol)[12] put his accusations clearly and reasonably. *The re-armament measures and the ARP undertaking have been inefficient. We are to guarantee new Czechoslovakian frontiers still unknown. The National Register is an unwelcome prospect and will be unworthy of this country. We suffer the insults of Herr Hitler while we have a government which in Disraeli's phrase, is an Organised hypocrisy.*[13]

All this was very well done, and if the speech fell short of brilliance, it was because invective is just not Mr Heath's forte; you cannot bite off more than you can chew and go on biting. He is pre-eminent in analysing situations, but in denouncing untruth, he is in a lower rank altogether. His is the guiding hand, but fire and brimstone are outside his province.

Mr J. R. J. Kerruish (Magd.) *The government rightly believe that a lasting peace can be won by co-operating with the dictatorships. Democracy can thus be pre-*

served at home, the re-armament programme accelerated and trade and employment promoted.

Mr John Foot (Balliol—ex-President) *The government's sympathies are with Fascism. We have lost the friendship of Russia; and the future holds only dark prospects. We must in Britain, recapture the old spirit and build a collective security system.*

Mr Wickham Steed (New College—Visitor)[14] *Just what has Mr Chamberlain been doing lately—intrigue with Germany, with German Generals, with Russian generals? I have actually read Mein Kampf in the original; and having done so, I trust the promises currently being made not an inch. Russia will be the next conquest; while the demand for colonies is a device to keep Britain and France engaged elsewhere and give Hitler a free hand in the East.*

Motion carried 203:163.

February 1939

House believes that a return to religion is the only solution to our present discontents.

Mr H. G. Head (Balliol) *Our root trouble is the instinctive selfishness of man, and if religion is discarded, the best we can hope for is an enlightened self-interest. Greece and Rome declined as self-indulgence increased. To change human nature is not enough. We must turn to God.*

Mr Schulze *Everything is undefined; to what religion, for what strength, are we to turn? Even religions could do useful things and do them with without religious reference; witness the sound, progressive social programme put forward by the Oxford conference on Church and State.*

Mr R. S. Mathai (Hertford) *By returning to religion, I mean to grant a pre-eminent place to spiritual values in the world, an appreciation of the impotence of man in relation to God, the rule of the Universe. You cannot feed the masses from within a concentration camp. Mutual confidence among men as sons of God is essential.*

Mr Stephen Spender (Univ.)[15] The evils of our time are threefold, a failure, especially on the Left, to recognise man's weaknesses, secondly a lack of charity or love—though this is done, not by Socialists and psycho-analysts, nor by Christians—and thirdly a lack of belief in external authority. The institutions of religion have failed or worse: insignificant and spiritual matters and a Pope willing to bless bombs for Spain! Religion is vague, a form of escape.

Dr W. R. Matthews (Dean of St Paul's) *Those who stood up most firmly to Fascism and Communism are those who admit God's authority and not man's…What is man? If he is not to be regarded as something more than a being with a limited span of life and incidental animal needs; and if it is not to be admitted that he has infinity in his soul, then we cannot hope for happiness, vigour and progress.*

Vote not given.

---

2 March 1939

House would welcome the introduction of a scheme of compulsory national service.

Mr Fraser—Treasurer *The present situation is so desperate as to make essential the fullest measures for immediate preparation for war. It will be necessary for young men to go through four months training in one service: ARP, Agriculture, Industry or the Army. The present voluntary system lessens efficiency, puts the responsibility on employers who cannot be expected to throw away profits unless all their competitors also allow their workers time for training, and are detrimental to democracy. Instead of a united country working for a common end, we have accentuated inequality of opportunity, and service to the community, something much too comfortable and profitable for some.*

No vote given.

11 May 1939

House demands that Chamberlain should go.

Mr Satish D. Kalekar (Hertford) *I assume that the House thinks Fascism a bad thing. Accordingly, a leader who retreats before Fascism must be considered either fool or a knave. But an English leader is not likely to be a fool; therefore…The Prime Minister fears Communism in Britain more than disintegration and is therefore prepared to support Hitler against Communism at the expense of Imperial security. Having brought us to the brink of disaster, Chamberlain is attempting to stave it off by robbing us of our liberties one by one: and conscription will not be the last step in this process. What we must realise is that co-operation with Russia is essential if we wish to emerge from our present predicament.*

Mr T. W. Peyton (Trinity) Heavily interrupted and needing the support of the Chair. *The Labour Party has done nothing to raise itself either in the esteem of either the country or its own rank-and-file. As it offers no alternative to this government, Mr Chamberlain must stay. He is a man of peace, but his Birmingham speech has made him the rallying point of all countries who are determined to protect themselves.*

Mr E. P. Street (Exeter—Treasurer) *To me as a Liberal, the question is not whether Chamberlain should go, but why he should stay. Though he goes down well with the women of England, though he has gained time by retreating, though he is advocating collective security, to support him now is to turn our backs on truth and honesty. Force and fear will dominate international negotiations until we have restored the balance of power; but we can only do this by widening the basis of our government.*

Mr Giles (Librarian) *Chamberlain has steered the boat onto the rocks for sure, but all Labour can do is gurgle and splutter 'I told you so.' And since we are all in the same boat—or rather water—we ought to be rallying round the captain, not driving him out. The only hope for the country—and perhaps civilisation—is to have a really national Government.*

Miss Ellen Wilkinson MP (Visitor) *I have heard brilliant but inconsequential arguments this evening. It is difficult to for us to realise how near we are to war; and yet at the head of affairs, we have a leader guided by party prejudices, a man who happily went fishing when he knew that aggression was taking place in Albania. Chamberlain, though claiming to uphold the Empire, is actually throwing it away. Germany, with her submarine bases along the Spanish coast, is in a much stronger position to harry our trade roots than in the last war. Nor is Danzig likely to have a better fate. And yet Chamberlain is doing nothing about an alliance with Russia, though he knows that the only way to hold Germany is to occupy her on two fronts.*

Mr Christopher Hollis Ex-President *Why are we so eager for an alliance with Russia? Russia is not innocent of past aggression and it is doubtful if Litvinov[16] did not try to manufacture a World War for the sake of Communism. Chamberlain is justified in hesitating about an alliance with the Reds. And if he were to go, who would take his place? The Labour Party will never succeed until it ceases to oppose the very measures it really wants to see passed. It will be time then to talk about Chamberlain going when a real Labour leader is born.*

Motion carried 139: 110.

———— ✦ ————

18 May 1939 Eights Week

House congratulates the Press on keeping the home fires burning.

Mr T. R. T. Kerruish (Magd.) Concealed the obvious fact that he had no knowledge of the press, except possibly the 'Diocesan Quarterly', by spending most of his time on the visitors. This he did with the unique poise and eloquence which made his reputation for wit at the end of last term. Mgr. Knox qv was introduced as 'A type of Papal Bull' sent to enliven the cows' faces which peered down on him from the gallery[17]…the British

Press Lords would keep the Bolshevist Wolf from the Door and the Empire together…The Government might be Danzig with Tears in its Eyes.[18]

Mr E. D. O'Brien—(Ex-President) *People believe everything they read in the papers. They even believed the Evening Standard when it claimed 'Hitler Swims the Channel'.*

Mr Evelyn Waugh had a delightfully subtle wit.[19] *It is the Criminal, who keeps the press alive. The surest way to get into the papers nowadays is not to be a Cabinet Minister but a Criminal. Just strangle a child and throw it over a hedge and you are sure to be in the papers next day.*

Monsignor Knox (Balliol and Trinity) *I want to stress the value of the newspaper for the average man heckled at breakfast…It cuts the householder off from the grim reality of life—his wife. In the train too, it is indispensable. Talking in trains is something that every Englishman abhors, but every Englishman feels it is his duty to do.*[20] *The newspaper opened up a new life to the disillusioned reader. He reads that Latvia will guarantee Great Britain on the condition that Britain doesn't guarantee her. Next day, Germans are pouring into Latvia. He reads that Franco is borrowing millions from Britain to storm Gibraltar. Jugoslavia is prepared to make an offensive, defensive or sit-on-the-fence pact with anyone who will give her Bulgaria, or a bit of it. Next day, Germans and Italians are pouring into each other!* This was a delightful speech and Mgr. Knox certainly had the House at his fingertips—a marvellous end to a series of Eights Week speeches covering more than a decade of Union history.

Motion carried 224:130.

---

1 June 1939

House condemns any settlement imposed on Palestine contrary to the wishes of its inhabitants—Presidential debate.

Mr Kalelkar (Hertford) *Palestine is of strategical (sic) significance to Britain. So Britain is using Palestine as a tool merely to establish her control there. In 1917, when it had been essential to curry favour, to win the war, Britain has made obviously incompatible promises to both sides and is now feeling the consequences. Instead of governing properly, Britain is effectively waging war there. If that country were left alone, the Jews and the Arabs would be perfectly capable of reaching an amicable solution. But the British and American capitalists will never leave Palestine alone while their capital is invested there. Every race has a right to self-determination* (Opposition cheers) *so Britain has no right to impose her own settlement.*

Mr Giles—Librarian *Self-determination is an excellent principle, but it mustn't be allowed to blur the other issues; and it isn't always infallible. Can the Danzigers be allowed to decide what should become of them? Naturally not! Even with the Sudeten Germans, self-determination has been far from an undiluted success. Is it not then dangerous to allow the Arabs alone to decide their destiny?*

The Balfour declaration when it was made, was a perfectly solemn and imaginative promise. But who would have foreseen that barbarism and racialism would spring up so soon in Europe? And who would have seen the violent opposition to Jewish immigration which Arabs are now putting up? Circumstances are quite different from what they were when promises were made.

Mr Musa Husseini—nephew of the Grand Mufti *The Arabs will on no account permit the establishment of a Jewish state in Palestine—their determination on this is unshakeable. Palestine is now full and cannot take or support more people— Arab or Jew. Why does England not send the emigrants to Australia which is now almost empty? Self-determination must be allowed. The Palestinians will be quite prepared to grant freedom to all three religions existing there—Judaism, Christianity and Islam. The Britons must see that they are injuring their Empire by antagonising the whole of the Arab world; the Jews must see that Zionism is damaging the interests of the great masses of the Jews. The Arabs want to be friends, not slaves, but Britain was terrorising Palestine long before even Hitler had emerged.*

Mr Alan Fyfe (Balliol)—Ex-President *Every attempt at settlement has failed because either the Jews or the Arabs had chosen to oppose it. Britain does not oppose any particular interest, but desires sincerely to promote peace and prosperity in Palestine and give it the opportunity to be independent.*

Motion carried 49:39.

---

19 October 1939

House considers HMG should make a detailed statement of its war aims without delay.

The Union discouraged extra-university publicity for its debate and this may be the reason (we hope not) for the absence of brilliance in the speeches.

Mr John Biggs-Davison (Magd.)[21] *He and his seconder, Mr Nicholas Henderson,[22] thought the destruction of Hitlerism a negative and insufficient cause. The proposers distrusted the government and its undeclared aims, but neither stated how these would be improved by their declarations.*

Mr P. A. O'Donovan (Ch.Ch.)[23] *I find no disagreement with the proposers of our cause; the one essential feature of the peace must be that it is negotiated, by and with the enemy, on equal terms.*

Mr E. P. Street *I can see aims that might with advantage be detailed now; the people have at last, forced the government to make a stand. It is for the people to drive on until the task is completed. We must have hope that a sound world may be constructed again, but we cannot see the shape of its foundation.*

No vote given.

---

16 November 1939

House considers that recent Soviet policy has not been in accordance with Socialist principles.

Mr R. H. Jenkins (Balliol)[24] *I am a socialist, but I do not think that a country's policy should necessarily be guided by what Marx would have thought or Lenin would have done. I am not prepared to accept the dictates of Moscow as infallible reason. Socialist principles will never be served by the forceful annexation of a country or part of a country.*

Mr C. A. R. Crosland (Trinity)[25] *The odd thing is that Russia negotiated with the British government for so long. The German–Soviet pact has been made in self-defence after the Poles had refused to allow Russian troops on their soil.* This was the best speech Mr Crosland has made in the Union. His sang-froid was very useful against interruptions.

Mr R. H. G. Edmonds (BNC) *If the German–Soviet treaty had not been signed, we would not now be at war. This sudden and cynical change in Soviet policy was supported by neither Blum[26] nor the French people.*

Mr W. J. Halse (Wadham) was severely interrupted. *The principles of Socialism are those of Lenin, not those of Blum which involve the support of non-intervention in Spain. The broadcasts from Moscow show that the Soviet Government was very anxious to overthrow Hitler. The German Soviet pact is second-best, but an Anglo-Soviet pact has been sabotaged by the British and Polish governments.* The House greatly appreciated Mr Halse's genuine and knowledgeable speech.

Mr H. R. Clifford in the best speech from the floor said that socialism is an international and not a national doctrine. Mr P. M. Williams[27] pointed out that Russia had given back Vilna to Lithuania; Mr P. E. Heffer had been reading a history of Russia which quietly shocked him. Mr T. W. H. Roche hated both Russia and Socialism. Mr Hull spoke of contradictions, Mr Shackleton of the sanctity of treaties.

Motion carried 93:40.

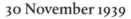

30 November 1939

House supports the demand of the Indian National Congress for the Independence of India.

Mr I. J. Bahadorsigh (St Catherine's) *India will always be divided as long as the English are there.*

Mr G. W. Rolls *Congress does not represent India. Independence will bring civil war, the confiscation of all British interests, an increase in taxation and a lowering of the Indian standard of living.*

Mr J. P. Comyn[28] *Let us not grieve for the Viceroy's garden party. British rule in India has produced very bad slums and worse railways.*

Mr R. I Gray (Queen's) *The British Commonwealth is the result of an evolution of sovereignty within sovereignty. What would happen to India if our troops should be withdrawn? India is very pleased today to see the British Navy in harbour at Singapore.*

Mr P. W Hodgens (Balliol) *When I hear a Socialist speak, I am reminded of a rag and bone man. British India is only a small part of India; what we going to do about the Princes?*

Mr R. F. Sanderson expressed the attitude of the die-hard, pointing his finger at Russia. Mr Chesham delivered his customary attack on talkers, intellectuals, socialists, conservatives and liberals.

Motion carried 82:47.

25 April 1940

House believes that the German aggression has left no room for neutrality.

Mr R. H. Jenkins—Librarian *The neutrals today are suffering from the same pathetic fallacy as the British Government had in its betrayal of Collective Security. England had then been the greatest neutral in Europe; but that is an explanation, not an excuse for the neutrals' attitude today. The neutrals' cause is the cause of the allies.*

Mr A. Beverley Baxter MP *We should see the parallel between Europe today and Chicago under the terror of the gangsters. Here as there, to remain neutral is simply to increase the criminals' power and to court disaster. The neutrals must unite against Hitler or fall his victims.*

Mr K. W. Riddle (St Catherine's) *A strong united body of neutral opinion is essential to prevent the war from spreading and to secure a just peace.*

The Hon. Harold Nicholson MP CMG[29] *Neutrality worked in 1914, but the League covenant has outmoded it juridically, while the inability of the neutrals to defend themselves made it unworkable in practice today. America, to whom so many appeals have been directed, is an Ophelia not a Pallas Athene. Real neutrality is now a fantasy.*

Motion carried 237:221.

9 May 1940

House dislikes Signor Mussolini less than it does M. Stalin.

Mr A. Bunting *Stalin is the greatest statesman of the Twentieth Century, the Five Year Plan is achieved.*

Mr S. J. Whitwell (Ch.Ch.) *I prefer the charade-esque antics of Mussolini to the drabness of Stalin, the hero of a slum novel. Russia is Germany's friend; Italy can only lose by following Russia's example.*

Mr D. Ginsberg[30] *I believe Russian foreign policy to be the best in Europe. A reconciliation with Russia is essential.*

Mr J. A. T. Douglas (New College) *Nobody but a Jesuit or an economist can believe there is anything in Russia; there is no liberty; even license is no more. The state should exist for man not man for the state.*

The Secretary thought Russia the only hope; The Librarian desired at least a pact of non-aggression with Russia. Mr L. G. Williams thought Stalin sadistic and unstable; Mr Telling pleaded for objectivity.

No vote recorded.

Debates continued and were recorded throughout the war, but in similar or even more heavily reduced numbers with very low involvement. The contributions quoted immediately above were included to give an idea of reactions to the opening weeks of a great historic war.

15

The Sunlit Uplands—almost

18 October 1945–26 May 1949

Welcoming Labour/UN German policy/shocking newspapers/UN to fail/Coal
nationalization/Spain/Lords/Fulton speech/Feeding Germany/Imperial obligations/
Domestic policy/Trade union tyranny?/Conservative policy/Palestine/Imperial
affairs/No confidence/Dangerous science/Truman doctrine/Liberal education?/
India —Scuttle?/No confidence/British civilization/Sharp's New Oxford/Hague
conference—Europe?/Emigration/Arts patronage/Home policy/WEU/Socialism
as barrier to totalitarianism/The Stuarts/BBC abused/Liberal Party/Spain—barred
from NATO/Women members/Conscription.

The contrast between the Labour government of 1945–51 and its predecessor of 1929–31 is vast. In place of the vain and incurious MacDonald stood
Attlee, crisp, competent, the best sort of military temperament, informed
and strengthened by five years as deputy Prime Minister. For Philip
Snowden, intelligent man calcified into doctrinaire Free Trader, there
stood high in the Labour Party a number of economists alert to Keynes,
serving at a time when reconstruction after war, plus the needs of a continuing anxiety over defence, underlined the need for a government to
spend strategically.

The second man in this government was Ernest Bevin, someone unique
in British politics. Ahead of his teens, he had driven a mineral-water dray
in Bristol, and by force of personality and self-education had surmounted
that hard, early life to create the biggest and strongest British trade union,
the Transport and General Workers' Union. Illegitimate, leaving school at

445

11 and, not long afterwards, driving that dray, he would, over forty years, do more than any other individual to make British trade unionism effective through all its tests of strength, legal standing, and public judgement.

He had earned the nickname of 'The Dockers' KC' when at a Wage Tribunal, with the press alerted, he bought the cheapest food available on the statistical/theoretical definition, just given by a nutritionist as a fit meal for a man in taxing heavy work. He then had his secretary cook it before presenting the meagre result dramatically to the court (and newspapers), his case unforgettably made. Long a power inside the Labour Party, imaginatively brought into the war coalition in 1940, Bevin had served very effectively as Minister of Labour throughout hostilities.

On top of which, the bond between Attlee (Haileybury and University College, Oxford) and his closest colleague, out working at 11, was absolute. And beyond them, it was a strong government: Aneurin Bevan at Heath, Dalton and Cripps, successive able Chancellors, sensible, experienced men like A. V. Alexander of the Co-operative Society and wartime First Lord, at Defence, and beyond them, young and just elected Hugh Gaitskell, later Chancellor and future leader, and his successor, Harold Wilson, academically brilliant and soon, at 31, promoted to President of the Board of Trade.

Bevin, who had seen the point of demand theory in plain practice where his members had work or didn't, had looked forward to the Treasury. Instead, Attlee, on a hunch, asked him to be Foreign Secretary. It was a long way from Lord Halifax, more like a Palmerston switched from laying down lines abroad, to resolute defence. In the circumstances of a Russia stopping her advance at the Oder-Neisse Line, taking former German (Prussian) territory, there was an essential job to be done—in semi-permanent crisis. Unlike so many men of goodwill, Bevin saw no gilding on the tops of the Urals. He had run the union he created autocratically and saw, in the super-activist Communists among the membership, power-players against whom he would reliably play power. He was a temperamental non-appeaser—of anybody. Bevin at Godesberg 1938 is a fascinating thought.

More generally, the government had been elected with a great majority. It had spent the Opposition years in reflection, supported by its own experts and any available good social research. From William Beveridge, there had come a costed vision. His report, commissioned by the wartime Coalition, proposed new unthought-of standards of life reaching out to the whole population, inclusive of the poor, however defined. There had existed in the past a right-wing version of the health argument. An imperial race giving orders to lesser breeds could not afford such unfit, undersized, puny creatures as many of the early century poor (including military recruits) had shown themselves to be. Labour's mentors had better-motivated sources; people like Eleanor Rathbone, a Liberal, preaching earlier in the century that people should have longer and better lives for the plain sake of longer, better lives. Just how important was that shift from fitness for national greatness, to health for a better life, is a measure not often enough stressed. But the NHS has been its expression, a pulling together of the bits and pieces of earlier legislation plus much more, everything consolidated into a castellation of free public health.

As to health insurance, which is to say the National Health Service, still today reckoned the major political resource for a Labour opposition, it had to get past the spiked ditches of the profession's trade association, turning a bland, unrelenting face on the merely abstract notion of such an outrage. Not this time: credit for that belongs to Aneurin Bevan for employing the considerable charm of a man often identified with public anger. He went to work on, ironically, Churchill's much tried physician, Lord Moran, usefully Chairman of the Royal College of Physicians, and made it clear that in low, financial terms, doctors would not be losers. Charm and expenditure worked, both of them, and Bevan did bring the Royal College round, but behind the acceptance lay an unacknowledged nod to democracy. The government had a huge majority. What it wanted, the public manifestly also wanted. Resistance to it à l'outrance would have been terrible politics with consequences.

In the middle of its programme of nationalization and creating the welfare state, Labour would do something momentous in a faraway country about which we knew a great deal—India. An authority going back to Robert Clive's snap victories of 1757, and under different precise commands since the Mutiny of 1857, had been the subject of slow-moving argument, lit up by steady agitation, since the 1920s. However it isn't necessary to accept the sentimental adulation of Gandhi in Richard Attenborough's prize-winning and essentially silly film. Gandhi had been naive enough to look for release from British abomination at the hands of an enlightened Japan.

In fact, the notion of loosening imperial authority had been serious business in 1935 when the Lord Halifax of Munich had been the Lord Irwin of 'Serious Conversations About Imperial Concessions' and the India Bill of 1935. Most Conservative ministers had approached the problem of the subcontinent in a reasonable way, however stiffly expressed, getting ready to contemplate greater or less retreat. Winston Churchill, for whom it was all so much 'Scuttle', was exceptional. 'I hate Indians,'[1] he had said. 'They are a beastly people with a beastly religion.' Adding that 'Gandhiism and all it stands for will, sooner or later, have to be grappled with and finally crushed.'

He had not changed in 1947 when Labour brought in its own India Bill. Neither had Attlee. He had been a member of the Simon commission, set up by Ramsey MacDonald in 1930, which had recommended the policy taken up by the National Government in the 1930s—running consultation, talk of Dominion status, and local self-government with nothing ruled out. Attlee's own India Bill broke away from drawn-out talk. He flatly accepted Indian independence. The jewel would be taken out of an imperial crown which, by the hands of Harold Macmillan, a few years later, would be set aside altogether.

The defect, offsetting this clear purpose in Attlee's immediate 1947 approach, was an excessive desire to get things done on a tight timetable. In the talks arranging matters, the hostility between Hindu and Muslim shone bright. Symbolically but substantially, Pandit Nehru and Mohamed Ali Jinnah led the respective communities and loathed one another. Asked ten years on, during a TV interview, whom among adversaries he had most disliked, Attlee said without drawing breath, 'Mr Jinnah.' On top of which tension, Mountbatten, showman and serial bungler, bad choice for last Viceroy, should have been able, on the ground in India, to have seen the risks of bloody conflict. Characteristically, he was ingratiating himself with a government he should have alerted.

A handover, needing gradual movement under alerted military super-vision, was rushed. Massive inter-communal riot and two-way slaughter ensued with bland viceregal excuses following. Yet even with this tragic mishandling, coupled with too brisk a main directive, the creation of the State of India, now a major nation with a thriving economy, had been the right, inevitable thing to do. The sensible exploratory approach of Conser-vative Ministers in the 1930s had been brave and provocative—it drove Churchill to make from the back benches speeches embarrassing to quote. Though a Churchill in power across 1945–8 is, in respect of India, some-thing better not contemplated, Labour had done the right thing in the wrong peremptory way.

Fortunately for everyone, the same Churchill, not always, but too often, a reactionary, was a reliable absentee for much of the immediate post-war political timetable. He wrote the war memoirs which would cancel losses made twenty years earlier in the New York Stock Market crash and gran-diose extravagance, putting his wartime Foreign Secretary Anthony Eden in his place. Eden was, on social matters, no enemy of the public good, and he turned for expert judgement to an amiably sly lieutenant, R. A. Butler. Butler both understood the detail and saw outraged hostility to reforms benefiting the public as precisely the resentful negativity which had given the Tory Party a bad name. The idea would now grow up more generally that the Tory Party must drop the officer-to-man style of address to the public, and with it, the social unconcern which invited people to 'snap out of it'. Bow Group Conservatism responsive to the welfare state was emerging.

Nationalization, a central objective of the government, was easier to argue against, though hardly in the case of the pits. The record of the coalmine-owners across living memory, not least in the 1920s and

1930s, had usually affronted into disbelief, neutral-minded chairs of commissions of inquiry and indeed soldiers like Sir Nevil Macready, trying to police strikes. Miners worked where nobody else worked, walls collapsed, numbers of men were reliably killed at work. Goodwill was general. Coal was a clear case; and as long as the miners, unionized in a federated regional diaspora, had leaders able to talk across a table to Ministers of either party, they would be gainers as most *other people* wanted them to be. The class antagonism of Scargill and Thatcher were thirty-odd years away.

The railways were a case of much the same order. Despite post-First War federation of a sort as a recommendation for 'Free Enterprise', the phrase the Conservatives would soon be propounding, those four under-capitalized and regionally based monopolies did it no favours. Nothing about the more recent doctrinaire act of de-nationalizing railways suggests great improvement. Otherwise, only iron and steel, a late stop on the itinerary, would be reversed by the succeeding Conservative governments of 1951–64. Much of what Labour had done stayed done until the great too-muchness of the later 1980s.

The true problem of the 1945–51 government would be a fearful one of national finance. It was a mixture of specific ministerial mistakes, notably by the over-confident Chancellor, Hugh Dalton, with an issue of low-return government stock—2.5 per cent, which was not taken up. The object was to establish a lower average rate for government finance and though that price was lower by the standards of later decades until the 2008 crisis, this venture flopped and the jaunty Dalton would be replaced by Stafford Cripps, crankish person, but sensible Chancellor. Though in ardent, severe style of utterance, he was rather too much of a Fifth Monarchy Man for the fallen electorate, Cripps in practice was practical and competent.

Beyond Dalton's error, there lay in the British economy a central flaw covered over by other people's money. For six years of the Second World War, we had lived hideously far beyond our means. It hadn't been an accident that the keenest appeaser, Neville Chamberlain, had been Chancellor of the Exchequer, mindful rightly of the open-ended cost of a continental war. As Hitler had been dead set, in tune with purposes set out in *Mein Kampf*, on making war in Eastern Europe, maybe he shouldn't *after* the folly of appeasement, have made new commitments. Certainly we hadn't been able to pay for it. The war was reckoned to have disposed of more than a quarter of our national wealth. Great stretches of productive industry had been wiped out, and the unacknowledged truth was that we had got through it on Lend-lease, an American payment in the good cause of resisting Hitler.

Otherwise 'An Act to further Promote the Defense of the United States', it was a gift, a gift in kind, a gift of food and goods worth around $400 billion, granted on 11 March 1941 and near-terminated by oversight in September 1945. The gift was enlightened and creditably rational, its proposed snap, unfortunate. The Labour government was making vast, necessary and expensive social reforms on no money at all. The cutting-off having been recognized as a mistake, John Maynard Keynes performed his last great service to the state before dying, when he scrambled together two loans of £3,750 million from the USA and £1,250 million from Canada. Crippsian austerity was what necessarily followed.

At the same time, after we had fought a second ruinous great war, circumstances indicated a need among the current scurrying notes of hand, to prepare now for another one. Our Soviet allies had had their great day of victory in May 1945 when they celebrated it in Berlin and cities west of it. The Potsdam conferences, at which East–West friendship was hailed naively, notably by Churchill, had ended in total two-way distrust; and the hanging-on and holding-tight of whatever hand was at that moment available became orthodox statesmanship for decades after. This may be something which, given recent unpleasantness in the Eastern Ukraine, has not lost its charm. In the 1940s, to all the burdens upon government and citizen was added the need to rearm. Stalin was paranoid of course. He could hardly have become all-powerful without being. People like the Trotskys, Kamenevs, and Zinovievs, who might conceivably have argued and amended like French and British Ministers, had been neither accommodated, nor sacked, but importunately stabbed or shot.

Fear of the USSR may have been overdone since we underestimated Stalin's conservatism and caution, but it was the safest mistake available. Rearmament, however, costs money and it had the additional quality of making politics easier for the Conservatives. Ironically, few people had been, or would be again, more naive and trusting toward Stalin than Churchill. On his half-cock return to office in 1951, he was still talking about the possibilities of a personal meeting with the Vozhd as the way to a solution.

18 October 1945

House welcomes the prospect of five years of Labour government in this country.

Mr J. Cameron Tudor (Keble) Ex-President *Five years of Labour Government lie before us whether we like it or not. Personally, I view it with relish. The Labour Party has a mandate for Socialist measures.*

Mr R. F. Brown (BNC) *The Conservative Party has received a defeat comparable with those of 1906 and 1910, but this government, unlike those of the dates mentioned, is not a strong one. It includes little ministerial experience and its approach to problems is doctrinaire. There is an increasing Marxist element in the party since it has gained power. The intentions may well be good, but nationalisation is an irrevocable step. It offers material prosperity, but only at the cost of personal liberty.*

Mr C. W. Sewell (Jesus) *Nationalisation of the Bank of England has not proved the bogey the Opposition used to maintain.*

Mr B. T. Wigoder ex-Treasurer[2] *I cannot welcome this Labour government because although it will bring some social legislation I welcome, it will take us far along the road to Socialism. It is sinister that both Labour and Conservatives are congratulating themselves on the continuity in our Foreign policy, Labour's election slogan was 'Vote for plan, not man.'[3] Man is incomparably the more important.*

Mr Hugh Gaitskell (New College—Visitor)[4] *Labour does not believe in controls for their own sake, but their premature relaxation will be followed by inflation. The Conservatives have left an awful legacy. It is a party of company directors, whereas Labour can claim to be a representative cross-section of the electorate. It is pink rather than red, with democratic ideals based on social and economic equality and industrial efficiency.*

Mr Ian Harvey Visitor (Returned from war service as Lt. Colonel, currently Kensington Councillor, later MP for Harrow East 1950.) *The Tory regime[5] he speaks of lasted for six weeks. Socialists had shared in the coalition policy. The Labour machine is excessively rigid and its pacifist record undermines confidence in its ability to preserve peace.*

Mr H. B. Lewin thought Labour was not elected because it was Socialist but because it stood for planning against chaos. Mr Holloway denounced political apathy; Mr Hyams said the government was grossly out of touch with feelings in the country; Mr A. C. Davies wanted to see a united socialist states of Europe.

---

8 November 1945

House considers disastrous the United Nations policy concerning the future of Germany.

Mr J. Pickles (Ch.Ch.—Treasurer) *The nations are very far from united and have little in common. Russian policy has dissipated the good will the country fostered during the war. Vindictiveness is natural, but brutality never pays dividends and the whole of Europe would suffer from any attempt to reduce Germany to penury.*

Mr N. Labovitch *The Potsdam declaration[6] is sensible. It is better that German government should be de-centralised than have a minority central government kept in power by allied arms. Reparations should be exacted from the equipment of German cartels; and Germany should take its rightful place at the end of the queue of European nations awaiting rehabilitation.*

Mr C. Schlesinger (BNC) *The present policy is disastrous because it departs from the Potsdam principles. After the last war, the defeated countries produced revolutions. New systems of government are being imposed from without by the victorious nations; and Europe is being divided into rival camps again.*

Miss Barbara Ward (Somerville—Guest) [7] *the Potsdam provisions are defeatist, retrograde and reactionary. They deny the possibility of eventual reconciliation which should be our aim. They do not touch the causes of war which are nationalism and the inequalities, insensibility and irrationality of the economic system. We should look to a federation of Europe on the basis of a socialist economy.*

So great was the number of speakers from the floor that the debate, adjourned at 11.45, was resumed and the vote taken on Friday evening November 9th. Outstanding among the many able speeches delivered to the House were those of:

Mr J. C. Tudor *Potsdam is not a policy but a concession to facts while the world is suffering from Delirium tremens.*

Mr P. M. Wise *The death of millions which the winter will bring, will be disaster on a grand scale.*

Mr A. A. Whitaker *The war has dulled our sense of human tragedy.*

Mr H. P. Palmer *It is not Germany, but seventy million people who are suffering.*

Mr J. F. Blitz *Politicians considering frontier problems are out of touch with reality in an age of atomic energy.*

Mr P. W. Winfield *Democracy is being judged by the conditions in the British-occupied zone of Germany.*

Mr A. F. Kirk *Disease recognises no frontiers and a stricken Germany will bring Europe down in ruins with it.*

Motion carried 354:120.

29 November 1945

House believes the modern newspaper is a degenerative influence.

Mr G. C. Daukes (Trinity) *The modern newspaper in Germany, Italy and Russia has stood in the way of international understanding and has helped to establish authoritarian regimes. Newspapers pander to their public.*

Mr A. M. Pilch (Balliol) *Their views are dictated by their readers; and it is they who are the degenerative influence.*

Mr A. P. F. James *The larger the circulation, the less the influence. Look at the Daily Express in the recent election. And wherever there is legitimate grievance, it receives attention from one other section of the Press. That does not make it a public watchdog.*

Motion carried 164:124.

---

31 January 1946

House believes that the United Nations are unlikely to succeed where the League of Nations failed.

Amended as 'unsuitable' to 'Any world organisation in order to succeed, must achieve a considerable curtailment of sovereignty.'

Mr A. Gibson (Queen's ex-President) *Not enough to have machinery for peace depends on the people who operate it.*

Mr R. F. Sanderson (Ch.Ch.) *We should be gracious and have confidence in the United Nations, for there is no other practical alternative.*

Mr A. A. Whitaker let loose a diatribe against a certain foreign power which asked for and received great many interruptions, dealt with extremely competently and livening-up the proceedings.

Mr Pliatzky[8] thought half a loaf better than no bread and Mr Henriques (BNC) tried to define sovereignty. Mr Idelson (New College) disliked the veto provisions. Mr Carnall (Magd.) raised the moral issue. Mr Connor (Exeter) had faith. Mr Campbell (New College) wanted culture on an international basis. Mr Sampson (Trinity) was historical, Mr W. Rees-Mogg (Balliol)[9] was philosophical and Mr Butterworth (BNC) thought there was no cannibalism in Timbuctoo. Mr F. W. Mulley (Ch.Ch.)[10] took a dim view of the motion.

So many members wished to speak that the House resumed on Friday for an hour and a half. (Delayed) Vote not available.

---

7 February 1946

House welcomes the Coal mines nationalisation Bill.

Mr Crosland[11] argued that as the government would have to supply the necessary finance, there was no solution but nationalisation.

Mr D. Bell (St Edmund Hall) made an earnest and passionate plea for state ownership as the only remedy for the intolerable conditions of the miners. His sustained an emotional appeal made this an effective and outstanding speech.

The Rt. Hon. Harold Macmillan MP (Balliol) launched into a logical and careful attack on the Bill, criticising it not so much for the principle involved, as for the details which would lead to inefficiency and would work against the interest of both consumer and mine worker.

Sir Edward Boyle (Ch.Ch.) attacked the compensation proposals. Mr W. Rees-Mogg was anti-Liberal, Mr E. Sniders (Magd.) denied he was a vested interest. Mr Crosland took advantage of his right to reply. The House resumed on Friday evening for longer than ever.

Motion carried 208:157.

---

28 February 1946

House supports the present policy of the British Government toward Spain.

Mr N. Labovich (BNC) *There is general opposition to Franco, but intervention would only strengthen his position. Did the other side think we should try to abolish every dictatorship in the World?*

Mr M. J. Pickles (Ch.Ch.) *There was in fact still civil war in Spain. The Franco regime was the rallying ground of World Fascism; and the problem should be dealt with by the United Nations.*

Mr M. Nadin (Pembroke) *The position was not yet clear and it was impossible for us to intervene so long as the situation remained fluid.*

Mr A. N. Wedgwood-Benn[12] showed that the restlessness of the House could be overcome with confidence and vigour. *A moral principle is at stake and final victory has still to be won in the war against Fascism. Franco was put in power by foreign intervention; he can be removed in the same way.* Among supporters of the motion, Mr Gibson (BNC) defended the interests of the Spanish people; Mr Southgate (Ch Ch.) trusted the Royalists; Mr Kroyer (Ch.Ch.) believed in the balance of power. For the opposition, Mr Entwisted (Wadham) was willing to take risks; Mr F. W. Mulley (Ch.Ch.) disowned Mr Bevin;[13] Mr Levius (Jesus) logically demanded it, atom bombs and all, and Mr P. Connor (Exeter) wanted to put back the Spanish monarchy by force.

It was noteworthy and deplorable that this issue, which would certainly split both Conservatives and Socialists in the House of Commons, produced in the Union an absolutely solid line-up according to party.

Motion defeated 116:122.

7 March 1946

The House of Lords in its present form is a menace to democracy.

Mr D. R. J. Jewell (Wadham) *That House is now only a symbol of defunct aristocracy. The only reason it has not been a menace over the last twenty years is that it had been supporting Conservative governments.*

Mr P. E. Kroyer (Ch.Ch.) *I see the House of Lords rather as an annexe to democracy. There is a great deal to be said for a second Chamber, particularly in its role as brake upon the chariot of the Left.*

Mr A. C. Davies (St Catherine's) *The Upper House represents the evils of wealth, privilege, property and hereditary rights and gives the lie to man's democratic and equalitarian strivings.*

Mr F. R. Boardman (Queen's) *Let us look at this realistically. The House of Lords has not shown any signs of ever being active again.*

From the floor for the motion, Mr Wedgwood Benn gave a historical and Gilbertian survey; Mr J. A. Baker entered a pathetic plea on behalf of the Bishop of Sodor and Man;[14] among the opposition, Mr Southgate favoured the representation of land, money, and commerce; Mr G. C Daulkes (Trinity) thought of progress and tradition as synonymous and the Hon. E. R. Palmer delivered inappropriate extracts from the Conservative Candidates' hand book.

Motion lost 57:117.

---

2 May 1946

This House supports the policy of the Anglo-American alliance as advocated by Mr Churchill in his Fulton Speech.[15]

Mr Southgate Mr Churchill has been vindicated against his critics by later events. An Anglo-American alliance, so far from being incompatible with the UN Charter, is essential to the success of UNO.

Mr Pickles—Librarian Such an alliance would be a premature confession of failure and will inevitably be destructive of unity among the Big Three. I acknowledge that Russia is being troublesome, but I haven't lost hope of an eventual partnership with her.

Mr Kroyer I do not care for the Soviet regime. The only question is whether I dislike them more than the Nazis.

Mr Pliatzky American opinion is predominantly against the Fulton proposal. It would make Britain merely the European outpost of a new Anti-Comintern Pact with disastrous effects on our relations with the rest of Europe. From the floor, supporters included Mr Palmer—menace of The Anglo-American alliance. Mr Jur-Chuven Communism is quite sufficient justification for an Anglo-American alliance.—I have experience of the Russians and like them less than ever. Mr Gibson was unnecessarily virulent toward opponents.

Mr M. E. Howard (Ch.Ch.) Such an alliance will signal a drift away from global co-operation toward a world of blocs and unilateral pacts; Mr C. E. Monteith[16] made a quiet and thoughtful maiden speech.

Motion defeated 145:167.

---

16 May 1946

House would support a further reduction in British food consumption in the interests of feeding the German people.

Before the main debate, the House enjoyed its annual interlude of discussion on the admission of women undergraduates. Mr Weisweiller prophesied that the only women who would join would be those inelegant creatures who read 'The Economist' in Hall.

Motion rejected 176:39.

Main Motion.

Mr P. M. Wise (Wadham) *painted a sombre picture of the food situation in Germany and bitterly attacked the notion that Britain could do no more to help.*

Mr N. Orgel (Queen's) *with great intensity protested against the squeamish sentimentality of those who were more concerned with our enemies than our friends. India and China were in a far worse plight than Germany and had a far stronger claim on any British resources.*

Mr D. R. Jewell (Wadham) *argued that the amounts that Britain could make available were too slight to make much difference and that in any case, there were stronger claimants than Germany.*

Mr R. Shackleton *strongly upbraided those who said that we had tightened our belts to the full and pointed to the fact that our calorie consumption even now was 95 per cent of pre-war.*

Mr E. M. Belfield (Pembroke) *just back from Germany, maintained that Germans had lived for too long on the fat of Europe's land to be starving now.*

Mr R. F. Brown (BNC—ex-Librarian) *speaking with the authority of a medico, said the German people, though not starving, were too ill-fed either to administer their country or produce the coal which Europe so badly needed.*

Mr H. J. C. Cotter *was haunted by the thought of five hundred Soviet divisions.*

Motion carried 105:50.

---

6 June 1946

House approves the way in which HMG is fulfilling its imperial obligations.

Mr Pickles *The present government has to take over a heritage of ill-will in India; and they are making an admirable effort to overcome it by an act of Justice, too long delayed. There is similar heritage in Egypt, but we have no right to treat that country as though it were still a dependent one.*

Mr R. F. Brown (Brasenose) *The government has bungled the Egyptian treaty revision. As for India, the main fault lies with Congress back in 1942; and, in Malaya, the government has infringed its sovereign rights.*

Mr J. D. M. Bell (St Edmund Hall) *The legacy is appalling. The Tory policy of too little, too late is responsible for the present hostility of the Indians and Egyptians. But the government are making superhuman efforts to reach final settlements and doing more by way of any previous government for economic development.*

Mr M. E. Howard (Christ Church) *Ministers are ignoring the urgent advice of the resident Minister in the Middle East that Cairo and Alexandria should be evacuated as soon as the Japanese war is over; consequently they lost the goodwill of the Arab peoples and had only themselves to blame for their present hostility.*

Mr Adrian (Aidan) Crawley MP (Trinity)[17] *The Left are in a dilemma given their past views on Empire; now they are saddled with the responsibility of governing it. Given our limited resources, we can no longer defend the Empire ourselves. We need local alliances and above all, positive co-operation from the local people themselves.*

Mr Hugh Molson[18] *The government has been very uncertain and hesitant in handling Imperial problems. We are moving into an age of great powers where small nations cannot defend themselves. We have ourselves a credible record, especially in India, to look back upon.*

Motion carried 130:94.

17 October 1946

House applauds the Government's domestic policy.

Mr A. A. Whitaker *Look at the overall picture of Government policy, not day-to-day irritations and inconveniences. The government has succeeded in dealing with the aftermath of war and restoring our prosperity.*

Mr R. I. Gray (Queen's—ex-Treasurer) *The failure of the Government has been actual and potential.*

Mr Blitz *The real wages of the worker have improved over pre-war figures and see how removal of controls would hurt.*

Mr Gibson *If the government wants co-operation from industry, it should announce policy changes on wages, the closed shop and the exact scope of future nationalisation plans.*

Dr Edith Summerskill MP[19] *We have put seventy Acts on the statute book, which, in the near future, will promote the health and well-being of the people. The National Health Bill will make medical services available to all, according to need, not to pocket. There will also be a wider distribution of essential foods.*

Mr Boyd-Carpenter MP (Balliol)[20] *Instead of fulfilling their election promises, they are building up a Socialist Commonwealth of a dull, dumb, dim, tourist-third equality, regimented and controlled from the municipal pre-natal clinic to the county crematorium.*

Motion lost 375:424.

———⊛———

31 October 1946

House deplores the growing menace of Trade Union tyranny.

Mr A. Hever (Queen's) *Trade unionists hold twelve out of twenty-five seats on the Labour Party Executive, provide 76 per cent of party funds and 56 per cent of voting strength. Will the government be strong enough to resist increased wage demand inside nationalised industries if such increases can only be at the expense of the taxpayer?*[21]

Mr A. N. Wedgwood Benn (New College) *The Trade unions do not tyrannise the worker. They are associations of working men with common interests. These associations facilitate wage bargaining; they do not trouble the Labour Party which is a workers' party with socialist aims.*

Mr Southgate *The tendency in unions today is over-centralisation creating 'octopus unions' to include men with little in common. This leads to the separation of Union Executive from the Rank and File and to waves of unofficial strikes.*

Mr H. B. Lewin (St John's) *The argument for the Closed Shop is the demand for it among workers. TUC policy is one hundred per cent membership if it can be got by democratic means, but it requires compulsion for its maintenance.*

From the floor Mr Kirk Social pressure against opting out is tyranny. Mr Furnell: It is not in Trade Union leaders' interest to achieve industrial peace. Mr Fridman: There should be no Trade Union exemption from the law of tort.

Mr H. R. Thomas *Trade Unions are strong independent organisations capable of protecting the community from State Totalitarianism.*

Motion carried 251:121.

———— ∞ ————

21 November 1946

House believes that the Conservative Party has no constructive alternative to Socialism to offer the electorate.

Mr Whitaker *Not only isn't there one, there is no conversation about one. The Conservative attitude to industry is directed solely by business interests, while efficiency and the public interest are ignored. As for a 'Property-owning democracy,' more detail will have to be provided before this could be called a policy.*

Mr Gray *We did not go to the polls with nothing but a blind adulation for Mr Churchill. We are committed to many bills and white papers for improving social conditions. We wish to improve industrial output, not by changing ownership, but by schemes of industrial welfare. We also want to do something for the joie de vivre of the public. The choice is between a nation-wide property-owning democracy and a tea-drinking bureaucracy.*

Mr A. Hever (Queen's—ex-Librarian) *Conservatives harp on about policy, but have no intention of carrying one out. They are a party with the blackest record, with no spiritual values, but adept at all forms of electoral trickery.*

Mr Labovitch (ex-Treasurer) *This is the only alternative to Socialism. Conservatism is no panacea and its policy no magical incantation to substitute for practical government. When theory overrides facts, the results are farcical.*

Mr Pickles *Liberty is not definable or static, but must be defended from abuse, anachronism and tyranny. Why wasn't co-partnership proposed earlier? It is the last resort of a Party desperately in need of a policy.*

Rt. Hon. Anthony Eden MP (Ch. Ch.) *A sane handling of foreign affairs and defence arrangements is an essential pre-requisite of a stable domestic policy. In domestic policy, how conditions have altered in the last decade and how mechanisation has reduced the worker to a mere cog! These conditions are not to be remedied by a change of ownership, but co-partnership and profit-sharing schemes are both useful to examine for answers to this as yet unsolved problem.*

I wondered how Mr Gladstone would have voted in the House today: surely in the other lobby with Colonel Byers[22] and those other Liberals who, with Tory support, opposed the tyranny of the Closed Shop.

Motion carried 615:397. The largest anti-Conservative majority in the history of the Union.

⧈

28 November 1946

House approves the present Government's handling of the Palestine problem.

Mr Mulley *We must reject either a purely Jewish or purely Arab state—partitioned. The Government's Federal plan should provide a suitable basis for discussion. Appealing to UNO will only embarrass it and would be simple evasion.*

Mr P. Furnell (Trinity) *The government has engaged in unnecessary delay which, in large measure, is the cause of the civil strife in that unhappy country.*

Mr H. Nelson Williams (BNC) *The delay has a purpose. It is essential to bring the Americans in and get their co-operation. The objective is eventual reconciliation so that Arab and Jew may live amicably side by side.*

Mr D. Broome (Oriel) provoked the House to numerous interruptions with which he dealt well. *Zionism is encouraged by official pre-election Labour Party policy, and this has created a subsequent disillusionment causing the present strife. Apart from which, Ministers have never faced the problem of displaced persons, lying at the root of the Palestine crisis.*

Mr J. L. Stobbs *Immigration into Palestine has rightly been restricted. The over-emphasis, here and in America, on the Jewish case at the expense of the Arab has done serious harm.*

Mr B. C. Roberts *We must continue to garrison Palestine in order simply to prevent incredible bloodshed.*

Mr Burton *The government must commit itself to a single course of action. This fire will not go out and the pot will soon boil over.*[23]

Mr R. B. Cantle *I have only recently returned from Palestine and I can tell the House that anti-Jewish feelings are growing in the Army as a result of daily outrages by the Zionists.*

Mr G. H. Fridman *It is useless to offer other homes to the Jews. They only feel safe in Palestine.*

Motion defeated 111:97.

23 January 1947

HMG is displaying dangerous incompetence and foolish indifference in the handling of Imperial and Commonwealth affairs.

Hon. Gerard Noel (Exeter—Librarian) *The government is making a withdrawal from India without attempting to provide any substitute for British rule. It appears to have ignored the importance of the Army in the administration of India and made no provision to prevent anarchy and bloodshed. It is carting away the benefits of 200 years of British administration without reason or foresight, and is leaving the future in the hands of the Hindus.*

Mr Wedgwood Benn—Treasurer *The government is entirely sincere and determined to raise the standard of living throughout the Empire, with final Dominion status for all. In India, every assistance is being given to the Indian leaders; no more can be done. There may have been mistakes, but the general lines of policy have been consonant with the time.*

Mr Clive Wigram (Oriel)[24] *In Ministers' haste I see both incompetence and indifference. The plan for India is ingenious, but forms of government do not make a nation. Problems are not being tackled so as to ensure the future stability of the Commonwealth.*

Mr Kroyer *The objects of imperial policy should be renunciation of sovereignty and administration by force, with adequate safeguards for minorities. The crux is HMG recognition of the Constituent Assembly? If parts of the empire want complete freedom, we should not and cannot prevent it.*

Mr A. A. Chappell *The motion is childish and I can't understand why anybody should support it. Conservative moves toward Liberal policies are always too late and too little.*

Mr J. M. King *Pandit Nehru is not a democrat.*

Mr S. C. Allonby *I am surprised to see the concern shown by Conservatives for oppressed peoples.*

Mr G. M. Layborn *The government is trying to get through as much as possible since its stay in office may be short.*

Motion carried 205: 178.

---

27 February 1947

House has confidence in the domestic policy of Mr Attlee's administration.

Mr Wedgwood Benn must be congratulated upon facing a predominantly Conservative House in a fearless and admirable manner. *The Tories cannot have it both ways. Either they should decry planning or support it. The aim of the government is more plans and better plans. Nationalisation is essential. The government is the friend of good men. It is planning in the long-term interests of the country; and that is the criterion on which it should be judged.*

Hon. G. E. Noel (Exeter—Librarian) *attacked Mr Shinwell's handling of the coal crisis with most effective satire. The Librarian made good use of damaging quotations from the past statements of Socialist ministers.*

Mr Pickles *I am not here to defend Mr Shinwell or his Gandar-Dower[25] determination to remain in office. However the effect of the government's policy is that houses are going to the people who need them and that the majority of people are better fed than ever before.*

Mr R. Gibson (BNC) *The latest White paper comes twelve months too late. As to Industry, Ministers show a lack of understanding, confidence and leadership and they are carrying on an intolerable class warfare.*

Sir Hartley Shawcross KC MP Attorney General[26] faced an extremely hostile House. For the first thirty five minutes, he was subjected to continuous cries of dissent and interruptions. Sir Hartley carried on with great forbearance. There were two regrettable incidents born with great forbearance, an outburst of booing from the gallery and an incipient refusal of the Attorney General to obey the Chair. He denied the charge of class warfare and stated that the fuel crisis[27] was weather produced.

Motion lost 261:418.

1 May 1947

House considers the safety of states and the world necessitates the supervision and control of the scientist by the politician.

Mr H. J. Nelson-Williams (BNC) *There must always be scope for unfettered scientific investigation. However since the world does not yet have confidence in the success of UNO to meet the problems raised by the discovery of atomic energy, a safeguard through political control is essential.*

Mr Baker *Nationalism lies at the root of all our difficulties while scientific truth is international, with its spread leading to international co-operation. The government concentrates on military research, and I distrust it. What lie behind this motion are restriction and control of man's creative urge.*

Mr Kroyer *I have no faith in international plans to outlaw war and would like to see control of the scientist at home combined with international control under UNO of scientific development.*

Sir Edward Boyle[28] *The sharp division of politician and scientist into separate categories is absurd when our aim should be team-work. Given that scientific progress has so outstripped our powers of political organisation, it would be wrong to increase the politician's control in the field of science.*

From the floor Mr S. C Allonby stressed the necessity of enlisting world public opinion in the cause of peace; Mr J. Poels compared Al Capone and his gang to the TUC; Mr A. Bogie impersonated Dr Joad. The outstanding speech of the evening came from Mr U. Kitzinger[29] who argued that Hiroshima was our collective responsibility. Mr H. Palmer hated secrecy and Mr H. L. Cohen hated the Communists, claiming thereby to be unbiased.

Motion lost 112:150.

15 May 1947

House considers the Truman Doctrine[30] to be the one-way road to war.

Mr Furnell *Unilateral action will make a mockery of UNO. Whatever may lie behind the Russian attitude, this is no way to modify it.*

Mr M. B. Abram (Pembroke) *The Truman doctrine is based on consent. It is designed to assist and protect nations threatened externally or internally. But it is in no sense directed against Socialism. America is naturally concerned with her own security; and she believes that in the short run, just where she stands is the best place.* This was quite the best speech the house has heard for many terms.

Mr Palmer *This is simply a policy directed against Communism which makes it something contrary to the United Nations Charter; and anyway, I don't believe that Communism can be stopped by dollars.*

Mr Gibson *Let's be realistic. The Americans have made themselves absolutely clear. Civil order must precede financial assistance. Restating objectives as Wallace[31] does, will get us nowhere.*

Mr Levins *The Truman Doctrine has produced failure in diplomacy at a time when the Russians are ready to conciliate. We may have to consider the effect of an American slump on the world economy.*

The clearest and best presentation of the Wallace argument which the House heard.

From the floor Mr J. Timms disliked American coercion, Mr C. Allonby had no faith in 'the Big Stick', Mr J. Goldstein said we should accept American help as necessary, however undesirable.

Motion defeated 79:142.

12 June 1947

The workings of a modern democracy require a liberal rather than vocational education.

Mr A. J. D. McCowan (BNC) *Liberal education prepares men for citizenship in a democracy whereas a vocational education makes for narrow-mindedness.*

Mr A. Bogie (Balliol) *Beware the theorists of today. What we need are short-term plans such as only practical men can devise and not the long-term schemes of the amateurs.*

Mr R. S. Faber (Ch.Ch.) *Specialists are of course needed, but without a liberal education, the ready-made prejudices adopted nowadays in lieu of informed opinion, may threaten the democratic system.*

Mr R. C. S. Donald (Ch.Ch.) *what is called Liberal education is a snobbish hangover from the Eighteenth Century. The electorate and MPs both need more practical knowledge.* From the Floor: Mr N. Coleridge analysed the electorate's function as critic, judge and thinker. Mr Abram emphasised in an impressive speech the need for more thought about what should be done and not just how things should be done. Mr Beaumont was rather uninteresting on Navel training. Mr J. L. N. Stobbs stated baldly that all politicians were rogues.

Motion carried 87:29.

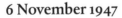

6 November 1947

This House condemns HMG's Imperial policy of 'Scuttle.'

Mr M. Chandler (Hertford) *Conservative policy had aimed at handing over power to the Indians in an orderly fashion as soon as they were ready for self-government. Labour has abandoned India to chaos; and many in India would welcome the return of British officials and the restoration of order.*

Mr J. L. Stobbs (Pembroke) *The government did what it said it would do. The British Empire has been the greatest force for peace in the world. How much wiser to let unwilling members of the Empire go rather than keep them there by force. British policy after the Boer War provides ample justification for the government's Imperial policy.*

Motion carried 247:206.

22 January 1948

House would welcome the return of a Conservative government.

Mr L. Price (Keble) *Our history, even that of Social Welfare, was already a proud history before 1945. The Labour party has been too cocksure after the election. It is cocksure still, even though it has proved itself thoroughly incompetent. Let the Socialists take their traps and their baggage into Opposition where they belong.*

Mr Nelson-Williams—Librarian *Public confidence is far higher in January than it was in the summer. We carried out Coalition policy, and where there had been disagreement, the Tories have been proved wrong. India and Burma have been freed and our prestige raised in the Empire. A Conservative government means social insecurity and unemployment; the future lies with Social Democracy.*[32]

Mr Kirk (Trinity)[33] *The government is a collection of fly-blown hacks exalting dogma in place of policy: iron and steel nationalisation being example enough. The Tories would remove all unnecessary controls like those on petrol, newsprint and employment. Co-partnership will bring new life to industry.*

Mr Stobbs *The Tories will put an end to the new towns and ruin any attempt to plan the countryside. Before the war they suppressed patents; what reason is there to think they will turn expansionist now? Full employment in a free society must replace the tyranny of the profit system.*

Sir David Maxwell-Fyfe[34] rising among loud and deferential cheers *The Government's lack of efficiency and courage are producing a succession of ever-growing calamities; the American loan has been spent. The Conservative programme would end this stultifying process, giving advice at the centre while allowing individual decision at the circumference. Today freedom is endangered. I fear nothing so much as the blindness which hides the fact that we are losing what our forefathers took for granted.*

Mr G. R. Strauss Minister of Supply[35] spoke with a suave sincerity which made a great impression on a hostile House, and must have had its effect on the subsequent division. *Private interests should come second; especially in times of uncertainty; public control is eminently desirable. The Conservative attitude over the last two years, has been one of constant opposition to controls. They talk of 'setting the people free.' Were the people free between the wars? Capitalism, and with it Conservatism, had once been necessary, even desirable; at the present time, they are neither. Social Democracy is in tune with our history and our traditions of orderly progress. I call on the House to reject reaction.*

Motion carried 392:278.

---

5 February 1948

House believes that British Civilisation is on the wane.

Mr R. S. Faber (Ch.Ch.) *I cannot believe that the promised Utopia of the Common Man will be either brave or happy. Civilisation is supported by uncommon acts. The modern yearning after primitive art, combined though it is, with a dislike of primitive taboos, seems to show dissatisfaction with our complex form of society.*

Mr S. Hills (St Catherine's—Secretary) *Every society has its pessimists who see nothing in change but decay. Social democracy, plus the political and economic institutions of the day, are enabling the average man to become more civilised than ever before. There is too, a 'cultural dynamic,' the urge which has recently driven hundreds to queue on Mill Bank for the Van Gogh exhibition. The challenge of uniformity is being met.*

Mr Donald *It is impossible to live in Oxford without realising that our civilisation is on the wane; our Dons are reduced to reading their most eccentric lectures on the Third Programme. The decline can be seen beyond Oxford: advertisements imported from America, the jargon of the newspapers. Over it all, I can hear the tick of Dr Joad, the death-watch beetle of our civilisation. The marsh gas of centuries is swirling around us.* [No floor-report.]

Motion carried 131:123.

4 March 1948

This House Welcomes Mr Sharp's[36] proposals for the re-planning of Oxford.

Mr R. Pitman (Worcester)[37] *Jericho calls aloud for a latter-day Joshua. There are good enough reasons for moving the Cowley works, provided light industries are available for the workers who do not want to go with them. The plan involves the destruction mainly of buildings already condemned as slums. It is a turning point for City and University.*

Mr J. C. Stacpoole (Magd.) *This plan will destroy the peculiar life of Oxford. It is too extravagant. Britain will never again be able to afford it.*

Mr P. W. Lowell (Magd.) *Either there must be twin cities or satellite towns or else the works must move. If industry cannot be confined, let it go.*

Mr A. L. Mildon *The plan defeats its own object which is to provide a University city of a very special kind. In his plans to divert industry, Mr Sharpe has succeeded in doing away with the gardens and parks. The (proposed) Merton Mall, with its constant streams of traffic, would destroy a great asset and the University city would be destroyed.*

Mr Thomas Sharp (Planner) *Continuous industrialisation is destroying the character of Oxford. In a year or two, we may become a minor Detroit. We cannot allow this. There are thousands of Cowleys and only one Oxford. The works must go, though our economic position will need consideration. In any case, the centre of the city though our economic situation will also have to be considered.*

Motion carried 153:50.

---

29 April 1948

House regrets that the Labour Party NEC should have discouraged members from attending the Hague conference.[38]

Mr Kirk *Mr Churchill has made it clear that the United European Movement was non-party. So why are Labour members being discouraged from going to The Hague? Did Labour want an International Socialist Eastern union? We should follow Churchill's lead now. We did during the war.*

Mr Hills—Librarian *We suffered between the wars through our simultaneous support of the League of Nations and of policies which subverted it. Today Labour must support Bevin and look on other queer agglomerations with suspicion.*

Mr Robin Day (St Edmund Hall)[39] *The Hague conference is there and available.* *Mr Shinwell[40] has been much too concerned about its composition. As it is, more Labour delegates will be going than Conservatives.*

Mr Colin Jackson *Essentially, this is a Tory affair. We should not build up the Union only out of dislike of Communism and Fascism. It is unlikely that the conference will stress the economic side sufficiently. Socialist parties must appeal to the under-privileged. Monetary and trade policies are all important.*

Major C. E. Mott-Radclyffe[41] *Is it perhaps the case that the government is afraid of offending Russia? Or is it a case of petty jealousy? The policy of pursuing a middle way between Communism and capitalism breaks down as the government finds itself asking the USA for dollars.*

Mr William Warbey MP[42] *Mr Churchill has made a stir here. Mr Churchill believes in the divine right of kings and thinks that he is in the succession. Since he can no longer be Prime Minister of Great Britain, he wants to be Prime Minister of Western Europe. This conference was inspired by United Europe Committee which had been inspired by the Fulton Speech. That speech has done more to increase international tension than any other delivered since the war.*

Motion carried 239:80.

---

21 October 1948

House believes that a policy of emigration would be an inadequate solution of Great Britain's population problem.

Mr Goldstein *There is no such thing as an optimum population in Britain. The strategic advantages to be gained by a smaller population are offset by the economic disadvantages. Congestion is due to mal-distribution. The case for emigration is founded on pessimism about the future.*

Mr Fridman *The motion is sombre, topically significant, and sober. Britain does not need to preserve her present numbers to preserve her usefulness. Though our civilisation has reached its zenith, there are still many experiments to be made.*

Mr C. E. Ross (St Edmund Hall) *Between 1814 and 1915, seventeen million people had left the country. 'It can't be done' is unEnglish.*

Mr J. R. Lucas (Balliol) *The difficulty is to get the Dominions to share Britain's burden of old age pensions.*

Mr J. C. Miller Bakewell *We need to raise the birth rate and increase the death rate.*

Motion carried 192:144.

⚬⚬⚬

4 November 1948

House believes that patronage is essential to a full development of the Arts.

Mr A. L. Price (Keble—ex-Treasurer) *Patronage can be an insult to artistic genius. But it is often necessary to save artistic genius from commercial prostitution. While it appears that in Britain, the day of the private patron is over, future patronage may lie in the hands of the municipal authorities.*

Mr Kitzinger *A transport café and the Carnegie Trust can both be patrons. But there is a difference. Dostoyevsky could never have been produced by an All Souls for Artists.*

Mr Faber *There are two heresies: One that the artist must be prepared to starve in a garret, and the other which sees the artist as a state parasite. Bad patronage is better than none if activity is to be kept alive. The fatal thing is indifference.*

Mr Geoffrey Johnson-Smith[43] *For the artist, not all patronage can be good. The patronage of Queen Christina was fatal for Descartes, left waiting in the Swedish cold. And just look at the Oxford Theatre proposals.*

Mr Nevill Coghill (Dean of Exeter)[44] *As all modern art derives from art sup-*
ported by patrons, the motion appears to be proved. The BBC gave a chance to artists
to express themselves in a new medium.

Dr B. Roniger *It is better to support prophets and charlatans than neither.*

Motion carried 187:151.

---

11 November 1948

House thinks the conduct of Home affairs by HMG gives us no cause for
confidence.

Mr Kirk *The government has failed over national defence, particularly in respect of*
the term of service for conscripted men. As for housing, the government has achieved
only half the coalition target. As for redistribution of parliamentary seats, it has been
a dirty piece of business.[45]

Mr Jackson *That statement matches well with Mr Churchill's charge that the Labour*
government had broken the mainspring of production when the country had made a
remarkable recovery.

Mr Price *The Socialists have an organic theory of society. We do not. Given this flow*
of cliché, perhaps Sir William Harcourt's remark 'We are all socialists now' should be
amended to 'We are all criminals now.'

Mr Douglas Jay MP (New College and All Souls)[46] Economic Secretary to
the Treasury. *Consider the record of the present government and that of the govern-*
ment in power in 1935. This government has the support of working people; second,
it has shown the ability to deal with a post-war crisis; thirdly it has kept the
Commonwealth together and even recruited new members; fourthly it has carried out
its election promises. He ended his speech with an analysis of the Conservative
Party's policy which further excited an already restless House.

Motion carried by 158 votes.

———⧟∞⧟———

20 January 1949. Visit of McGill University Montreal.

House believes that British participation in a Western European Union[47] would strengthen rather than weaken the bonds of the Commonwealth.

Mr Jackson—ex-Treasurer *Economic union with Western Europe must benefit the Commonwealth to an overwhelming extent. For we would not be able to buy raw materials from the Commonwealth unless we were in that Union. Several of those European states have colonial interests of their own and would sympathise with our difficulties over the Commonwealth.*

Mr E. H. Knatchbull (McGill) *The bonds within the Commonwealth vary from country to country, but they are never entirely spiritual and the military ones are in danger of being shattered. Britain has not been able to supply Canada with capital goods for many years and Canada has had to sign a standardisation of arms treaty with the US. The Commonwealth recognises the fact that Britain must join WEU for her own salvation, but that doesn't alter the fact that the bonds would be loosened.*

Mr Sydney Philips (McGill) *Why, because Britain is supplying capital goods to Western Europe, must the Commonwealth turn away from her? Disruption of Britain's economy would be the chief cause of weakening Commonwealth bonds; and this will certainly happen if Britain does not go into Western Union. Empire preference need not go if she did, and she will still need to trade with the Commonwealth to secure certain goods.*

Mr Kitzinger *If Britain joined such a union, she could no longer speak as Britain, but as part of a larger whole. WEU would take the place of Britain in Commonwealth affairs and we must remember that Britain would control only a fifth of the votes in Western Europe.*

Motion carried 220:197.

———⧟∞⧟———

27 January 1949

House believes that Socialism forms the only effective barrier to totalitarianism.

Mr Rodney Donald (Christ Church) *The main totalitarian threat comes from Communism and it has conquered a quarter of the World's population. If we dispose of the Communists, we shall get rid of most of the Fascists as well. It is significant that the countries which turned to Communism were those which had returned to free enterprise. The Conservatives had been a first rate target for the Communists as they were the party of privilege. Socialism was a much more coherent creed to set against Communism, for democratic socialism cuts the ground from under the Communists' feet.*

Mr Day—Secretary *Socialism itself is directly conducive to the totalitarian state for it is ideologically linked with Communism. The Communist Manifesto is the foundation of present day Socialism. Democratic Socialism is a contradiction in terms as is progressive Conservatism. Liberalism is the only way out.* The Secretary's best speech to date.

Mr Hills *Socialism has other inspirations besides Marxism, notably the Christian ethic. Conservatives and Liberals didn't realise that political democracy must be accompanied by economic democracy. Another ten years of Toryism and there would have been a strong move to totalitarianism. Liberalism is no use because it believes in ultra-free trade. Since Labour came to power there has been a marked decline in totalitarianism.*

Sir Edward Boyle (Ch.Ch.) *I agree with him about the causes coming from the economic consequences of deciding to have political democracy. There is a human right that all ought to claim the right to criticise; all parties have a duty to encourage people to choose between them. Totalitarianism has two causes: people being prepared to sacrifice political liberty for economic security and one party believing that it, and it alone, had discovered the absolute truth. Socialists are apt to believe that they alone were right; and for that reason, there would always be totalitarian tendencies.*

Mr R. H. S. Crossman (New College) *Mr Churchill has said that socialism in Israel is the only way of preventing Communism in the Middle East. I don't repudiate the Marxist origins of Socialism, but it is only possible to oppose Socialism if you understand it. Judge the supposed totalitarian tendencies of the Labour Party by its record. They have often sacrificed economic advantage for political liberty; and planning isn't centrally imposed, but accepted by both sides. This is additional proof that they are not communistically inclined. Atom bombs cannot prevent Communism; only those bombs can win the next war and Socialists want to win without another war.*

Sir John Maude KC MP (Ch.Ch.)[48] *It is impossible under a Labour government to save enough to retire on. Socialists cannot take credit for full employment when it is the result of aid from a capitalist country which itself is the main bulwark against Communism. Measures are not enough. Men are wanted as well and the Labour Party doesn't have them. Socialism is something indefinable, largely built up on hatred and which has caused a great deal of suffering.*

Motion lost 200:279.

---

3 February 1949

House deplores the fall of the House of Stuart.

Mr Faber *The Scots are a romantic race with their hearts in the Highlands and their salaries in the English Midlands. I am a plain Englishman, flooded all my life with legitimist propaganda. The Stuart kings touched the hearts of their subjects in a way not again equalled until the days of Queen Victoria. And they were far more cultivated than the Hanoverians.*[49]

Mr Johnson-Smith *The 1688 revolution was a triumph for Law and Order and the Scots don't know what Law and Order means. Further more, the restoration of the Stuarts would have a disastrous effect on the balance of payments.*

Mr J. J. Thorpe (Trinity)[50] *James I insulted parliament, Charles I was unfaithful, ungrateful, haughty, and ambitious. Charles II kept his mistresses at public expense and James II was indescribable. The Stuarts who once took refuge in Oxford, were romantic because they were failures.*

Mr Michael Maclagan Dean of Trinity, himself descended from Charles II[51] *The Stuarts and the Hanoverians were about equally immoral and the question was which were immoral in the more agreeable way. The Stuarts had variety in their Christian names and didn't all look the same. We cannot sympathise with their opponents; Hampden was the first tax evader on a grand scale.*

Carried 235:210.

⤞⤝

17 February 1949

House believes the BBC is a disgrace to the country.

Mr R. S. Arthur (Keble) *The Bastille of Portland Place will soon be swept away by the infuriated people. It is only prepared to defend its reputation on its own programmes and will not be examined before a disinterested audience. The BBC is built with a rubble of culture and though its purpose is to amuse, insists on trying to influence people. The alternative is not commercial broadcasting, but restricted broadcasting, for broadcasting standardises humanity. It is better than the American corporations, but the issue is whether we are to allow the existence of large opinion-forming bodies without any form of control.*

Mr P. W. Lowell (Magd.) *The BBC must be good because Radio Moscow says it is bad. The Corporation won a tremendous reputation during the war; and in particular, for the broadcasts of Mr Churchill and Tommy Handley. The BBC is an objective forum, catering for all and giving instruction to some.*

Mr G. N. Dalzell-Payne *The BBC has been gutless in the face of attack from America. We need something like Radio Eirene which rations broadcasting. The BBC just provides a sedative. And its pronunciation is simply shocking. There is no firm hand in the direction of the Corporation.*

Mr Godfrey Smith (Worcester) *The BBC is like a prima donna, half way between the British Council and a fate worse than death—a ponderous body run by people like Louis MacNeice,[52] that stale old Chelsea bun in the post-war patisserie. It is a fallible institution, but not a disgrace and one of the few finishing schools we have left.*

Mr D. F. Hudson (Trinity) *Look at the BBC in the light of the average intelligence and you cannot listen consistently. I think the 1950 election will be fought on the broadcasting issue; and the Party that wins will be the one promising to dissolve the BBC.*

Mr Mark Barrington-Ward[53] *What is the alternative? The sole purpose of commercial broadcasting is to reach as large an audience as possible, so their programmes are too soothing. The quality of the BBC is higher than anywhere in the world and gives the best kind of entertainment. Over a million and a half Frenchmen listen to the BBC broadcasts in French every week.*

Motion lost 126:188.

---

28 April 1949

The Time has come for all good Liberals to leave the Liberal Party.

Mr Arthur—Treasurer *Members may fear hearing far too much about what happened forty years ago. The Liberal party is as capable as the Communists of gross intellectual dishonesty; and it has no respect for the individual. Liberals should discard their diseased respectability, but I say all this in no disrespect for actual Liberals.*

Mr Day—Librarian *Labour Party Members should remember how that party was built up when it was said that there was no room for Labour in the two-party system. The reply to socialism will not be given by the present Opposition. Liberalism alone has a coherent basis of principle for a similar base of principle, I look vainly at the Tory party.*

Mr Faber *The Liberals are over-optimistic in thinking that people are Liberal at heart; and the parallel with the Labour Party is misleading. Those people can do better by liberalising one of the main parties rather than maintaining chaste, but unproductive isolationism. They should liberalise the Labour Party which is most in need of it.*

Mr A. L. Mildon (Wadham)—Secretary *Liberals will find satisfaction in neither of the other two parties. Both are undermining parliamentary authority: one in unemployment, the other in the closed shop while Liberals believe in co-partnership.*

Mr A. J. Irvine MP (Oriel)—Ex-President *The things for which Liberalism once stood are now safely protected by the Labour Party. The Liberal Party had made itself look foolish by accusing the Government of seeking to curb the press. It has failed to recognise the need to distribute economic power among the masses of the People. Co-partnership can only be worked out in the Nationalised industries. A party cannot exist merely on the right to survive and the right to complain; and Labour has a firm grip on economic and political liberty.*

Mr Frank Byers MP *Labour has no respect for the individual in matters of conscience. The strength of this party is increasing and a Liberal Party is essential for the preservation of democratic freedom. We have been right on the veto, the Atlantic Pact and trade policy. The Closed Shop shows Labour's disrespect for political liberty.*

Vote not given.

---

12 May 1949

House believes that Spain should be excluded by the Atlantic Pact.

Mr D. Taverne (Balliol)[54] *Consider first mere expediency. Spain is strategically useless, and a Fascist alliance would greatly assist Communist propaganda. The Spanish regime has made a mockery of justice and is notorious for imprisonment and execution without trial. The inclusion of Spain will imply an abandonment of morality by the signatories of the Atlantic Pact,*

Mr Peter Emery (Oriel) *The House should not become morally excited. The withdrawal of ambassadors has only strengthened the Franco regime. Spain must be met half way. It is illogical to argue that a military agreement is not possible. Spain introduced a good health service long before Britain. As for defence, the Pyrenees are a barrier for the protection of the Mediterranean. Inclusion would create a united defensive bloc in Western Europe.*

Mr D. J. W. Benn[55] *The idea of division of the world into East and West is fatal to world peace, and it is essential that a settlement be reached with the Communist powers; the foreign policy of the West has brought us into contact with people whom four years ago they would have been ashamed to have as allies.*

Mr Paul Dean (Exeter) *the Franco regimes methods are indefensible, but ostracising Spain is the best way to reinforce the government there. Excluding Spain from a pact to defend Western Europe is ridiculous. She might remain neutral in the event of a war between East and West; whilst on moral grounds, the only way to help the Spanish people is to enable them to work their passage.*

Mr Oleg Kerensky (Ch.Ch.)[56] *An alliance with Franco would be a disastrous step in either a hot or a cold war against Communism. Spain, like Nazi Germany, might conceivably ally with Russia as Hitler did, or avert internal trouble by foreign aggression. On top of which, Spain would be of no strategic use in a war against Communism.*

Mr N. A. Dromgoole (St Edmund Hall)[57] *Spain has immense strategic advantages. It is much better to add Spain to the Western Alliance before a Russian onslaught rather than during it. Taking all the advantages available from an alliance with Spain is the only realistic attitude; and on grounds of principle, it is right to leave a nation to choose its own government.[58] A dictator can always get out of difficulties at home by uniting his nation against foreign hostilities. For that reason Spain should not be ostracised.*

Motion lost 104:124.

26 May 1949

The evening opened with the perennial question whether women should be admitted to debating membership which was moved by Mr Michael Summerskill (Merton). The House was in a boisterous mood, but managed to work off its feelings in half an hour, the motion being lost by 311 votes to 98.

Main motion House believes that conscription is no longer necessary.

Carried 235:210.

16

All Sorts of Dangerous Modern Ideas

20 October 1949–31 May 1951

Social equality/Third Force?/Modern art/House of Lords/Apartheid/Social record of churches/German recovery/Free birth control/Depending on US/New German nationalism/Divorce reform/Labour out of date.

The last eighteen plus months of the 1945 Labour government were burdened by the monstrous costs of the nation having fought a second world war and in the process, used up all its money and the much more it had borrowed. Britain might have done things differently. We could have left Hitler marching east to be eventually defeated by the USSR, perhaps aided by a strategic British stab in the back some time in 1943–4. An alternative, dimly passed up, had been the pre-emptive option, a decade earlier, of declaring the sweetly available knock-out ultimatum over Nazi reoccupation of the Rhineland. Either piece of immoral good politics would have kept the British Empire intact, and expenditure delightfully confined.

Instead, the servant of events, we were, economically speaking, technically dead. We were a pauper nation on life support. We owed, we were granted credit and fed; and yet in 1949, we were still in debt. It was not the fault of nationalization which, for such a great undertaking, had been done without burdensome costs. These debts were cumulative, and continuing. In the middle of so much tribulation, we had, early in 1947, suffered a fuel crisis induced by the worst winter on historical record. It had

486

been handled very badly by an inept Minister, Emanuel Shinwell, soon after replaced by the economic grasp and strong confidence of Hugh Gaitskell. The energy suspension had shut down production and, with it, exports and earnings, something inevitably followed by a flight from sterling to dollars.

That, humiliatingly but vitally, would produce straight American subvention. General George Marshall, the serious man in charge of the State Department for a Democratic administration alert to the rest of the world, had come up with straight emergency money—Marshall Aid. It went far enough, and the economy worked with it. But that economy remained frail. A wage-freeze was imposed (rightly) by the workers' party. Things began to go right, surpluses appeared in budgets and exports flourished, but the balance against the USA remained in deficit. Stafford Cripps, who had been at the Treasury since 1947, listened to advice, murmuring bad words, one of them particularly immoral, the national equivalent of cheating debtors with bankruptcy—'Devaluation'.

This was the rational end conclusion of Keynesian thinking. National economies, hanging upon each other's gloves, can recover. Normal trade remains possible. So, in 1949, the pound was moved down against the dollar from four-to-a-pound to 2.78. There continued to be austerity including rationing, but as with any competently handled devaluation, we now traded effectively and widely. We were equipped to trade ourselves out of the worst tribulations and inhibited from spending lightly.

The hypothesis above about dodging the World War column could never have been charged to Labour's (and especially Bevin's and Attlee's) account. Three million soldiers' worth of early demobilization had been moved sharply forward from mid-1945. But we would, in 1947, quickly settle for little less than 'the whole University marching down the High' in the form of compulsory Military (aka 'National') Service. We turned from being occupiers into resident defenders of the British zone of Germany, later the Federal Republic, with a million men still under arms. In that year, the bill for the military would take 18 per cent of GNP. It would be down by 1951, but still 6 per cent. Every lesson of the 1930s was read, marked, and inwardly digested. What was not learned was that we had *not* won the war. It had been decided and won in Eastern and Central Europe by the Soviet Union with some help from the United States and Britain. Indeed a good deal of *our* war had been spent in expensive and difficult marginalities—the campaigns in North Africa and Italy: long, wasteful excursions rather than rational routes toward the central conflict.

A military competence so carefully kept up would soon acquire a new pertinence. In 1950, North Korea (today recognized everywhere as a one-off world loon nation), had declared war upon South Korea, at that time a very nasty, but Washington-loyal regime, whose monstrous dictator, Syngman Rhee, had ordered a massacre of opposition supporters. (Think of South Korea as Franco Spain a little worse.) Unfortunately in 1950, anti-communism, working like repentance for the naive *pro*-Communist views of a few years back, saw here an imperative cause. The political class of 1936, which might have gone like John Cornford and Eric Blair to fight in Spain, now sent aircraft and troops. (For Britain, always good for a *Daily Mail* slogan, it was 'the Glorious Gloucesters'.) Did we know it was a testing ground, *the* testing ground?' We, with the Americans, were spinning the 1930s disc in a different way. Hitler should have been stopped at the Rhineland. Very well. Kim Il Sung should be stopped at the 38th parallel.

Now the Soviet Union *was* involved in North Korea's attack and it was rightly met. The League of Nations had never cohered to answer aggression with a military response. A desire, especially among Labour politicians, to avoid repeating this mistake with the UN, was creditable. The questions were: would British financial limits let the aggression succeed and, crudely, how much were we, the British, needed? There was a single answer. For reasons of a strong motive and ready funds, the USA would pick up almost any bill, making a large response from an exhausted six-year participant in the Second World War .

It would have been wisdom for a country as strapped for reserves as Britain, a country recently devaluing its currency, to have made a tightly measured and modest involvement against the aggressive parties. Stalin was notoriously careful. He had picked up Poland and the other nearby East European countries because he had won them in the war. He picked up Czechoslovakia because that country's own Communist Party was strong enough over 1945–8 to be encouraged in using the methods of the Right—another putsch. In Korea, Stalin was helping the Communist north try something harder. A historical lesson was learnt too well, pride was too strong. Broke we might be, but we had a tough army corps and lots of conscripts. Modest subvention it was not to be.

Importantly, we were not officially going to war as ourselves or as an ally of the United States. With uncharacteristic carelessness, Stalin had removed his delegation from the United Nations Assembly in New York where it had put in steady shifts of vetoing all calls for any imaginable collective international action. Instead *this* call for intervention was passed and the UN acquired, not altogether deservedly, the reputation of being quite different from the abstracted Holy Ghost of the League in the business of international resistance to plain aggression.

Conflict with the USSR was going to obsess us for a very long time. Hugh Gaitskell, very able and very obsessive, would, as Chancellor, respond to the Korean War with an act unique in Treasury history. In the course of his contribution to electoral defeat in October 1951, Gaitskell would do, against gravity and nature, what no Chancellor should: tell armed service Ministers that they might/must spend more money than planned—more than the useful sums already being diverted from everything else. We had lost an Empire and obtained a rather good Labour government, but the call of that Empire in public schools long before was still being heard and responded to.

What was *not* heard inside the Labour government, beyond certain valiant individuals, was a call to note the new constructive goings-on in Europe *about* Europe. Britain, or 'England', had been a major single power for so long, holder of an empire and, as the cliché reliably put it, a far-flung one. In Europe had been found either our enemies—Louis XIV, Napoleon (at a pinch, Kruger), Kaiser Wilhelm, and Hitler—or allies, useful perhaps, but needful of our pressed sailors, and Wellington's 'Scum of the Earth' infantry. If there were good people out there, we subsidized them as the Americans now subsidized us against the overmighty threat of the day.

With the West German de facto state established, British troops encamped themselves there and it became an ally for real, Lord Beaverbrook assured *Daily Express* readers that nothing had changed. Our boys were still occupying Germany. Anyway, reconstituted (and doubtfully grateful), it didn't really count as a nation. In which case and new state of play, we didn't take Germany or anybody in Europe very seriously—except for the very palpable USSR. Tentative gettings-together like West European Union or the Council of Europe might be attended by delegations of British politicians and civil servants, bringing sincere but surely eccentric goodwill, or enjoyed as jollies worth the attendant speechifying of earnest foreigners. But when the talking and goodwill-making turned into hard, useful business, British politicians and civil servants back home would respond with dismal negativity.

Witness the Coal and Steel plan proclaimed in a speech of 9 May 1950 and then brought to substance by an outstanding French Foreign Minister, Robert Schuman. The purpose was open-and-shut good sense: equalizing trade and pricing in those vital industries to avoid international disputes (and price wars) between signatories of the eventual treaty. Warmly invited to join, the Labour Cabinet responded with a flat, unanimous No—failure of imagination mingling with delusional notions of high and aloof world purpose—in company of course, like nobody else, with the United States—our role as the Hero's best friend. The actual foundation document was signed on 18 April 1951 by six countries, France, Germany, Italy, the Netherlands, Belgium, and Luxembourg, hereinafter *Les Six*.

The unpleasantness of 1939–45 would be cherished as a guiding light for a long time, like English footballing success in 1966—with a message not very different from the 'We won the Cup' still heard at England–Germany internationals in the late 1980s. So, together with the United States, we had liberated the Europeans. Russia, now hostile and potentially an aggressor, had done unimaginably more fighting and come in arms, driving Hitler back from Stalingrad to Prussia. But imperial assumptions and a quiet national conceit had turned legitimate pride in having hung on after 1940 into a not-too-quietly voiced self-esteem. It was a view of being separate and unequal when set against the countries conquered across land frontiers with Germany in 1940. Germany was still Germany to be watched for its next hostile move.

The rest were a sort of honorary Belgians. We were different. We were better. *Labour* thought that in 1950. And in 1959, Hugh Gaitskell, as party leader, made a Conference speech on prospective membership of what had become the European Economic Community by invoking Vimy Ridge! This was a First World War battle involving heavy losses by New Zealand troops. Gaitskell employed it to offset talk of a federal Europe which would mean 'the ending of a thousand years of history'.

Labour had worse enemies in 1950–1 than the conspiring Belgians—itself! The party had been remarkably united and stable in this term of creative office through both achievements and serious problems. A great deal about which politicians and voters could agree had been done at a remarkably quick, efficient pace. The arguments were either abstract—how much (and how one defined) Socialism, or personal—Aneurin Bevan and his moral authority. This finally, was the one which mattered.

Bevan had been an outstanding presence, a masterful Health Minister, size of a great scheme and its obstacles overcome. Into the bargain, he was a brilliant, moving, and funny debater. He had instituted the National Health Service by charm and the making of concessions, together with great firmness where something at issue, like nationalizing the hospitals, really mattered. He knew, like Robert Walpole, that every man has his price—in this case, letting consultants bring private practice and payment into those nationalized hospitals, along with their NHS work. The mansion had been built. The breaking point in Nye Bevan, when it occurred, would be personal.

Notorious to a couple of generations were three words, trumpeted or snarled. 'Teeth and spectacles.' Upon the free provision of which, Hugh Gaitskell as Chancellor, facing his Budget in 1951 and tight for money needed for military purposes in Korean Wartime, had imposed taxes. Most of them were ideologically sound Labour items—income tax up to nine shillings and sixpence, surtax imposed, leaving plutocrats with sixpence in every pound: no grief to Labour voters or MPs. But spreading the pain a little, he put a shilling surcharge on the erstwhile entirely free medical goods like, indeed, glasses and false teeth! It wasn't tactful, but would generally be thought equitable. Notwithstanding which, the balloon went up—the balloon of Aneurin Bevan's protection of his achievement and fear that this was a base for further incursions.

The argument turned into a quarrel. Bevan made it an issue of principle and resigned. It was suggested that the cut was deliberate, a conscious picking of a fight with the rival future leader. The party candidly split—split into Bevanites and Gaitskellites. It would take on other elements involving several kinds of Left, candid pacifists, a small group accused of 'fellow-travelling' with the Soviet Union, and, in due course, a career Left looking to please selection committees where the factionalism often favoured 'Bevanism' whatever it precisely was. The element in the Labour Party for whom, honourably enough, peace is the supreme principle objected all the more strongly because this money was needed to help finance the rather dubitable Korean War.

There would have been a very good case for keeping that involvement to a token force and candidly recognizing that in the West versus East conflict, the active Western champion must and could only be the United States. Such a rational cutting of cloth to fit our modest coat was not thought right. It was thought demeaning, unworthy of our perception of us. Gaitskell looked back to 'a thousand years of Britain'—most of it in the hands of a marauding upper class in plate armour. Less splendidly, Labour supporters agreed. Most voters thought like football supporters. Of *course* we were a great nation. Meanwhile the nations of continental Europe, with the partial exception of France—imperial hang-ups of her own, about to become mired in a colonial war in Algeria—wanted to stay at home, turning all together into a ghastly, ignoble trading bloc without pride or nationhood. We were different. Even, perhaps especially, among working-class voters, the curse of this country was that of Hilaire Belloc's Godolphin Horne:

Godolphin Horne was nobly born
And held the human race in scorn
He never shook your hand or smiled
But merely smirked and nodded.

It would show over Europe. 'If federalism were the issue, why not join Europe—up to a point?' The editor once asked this of a senior civil servant. Why hadn't we applied for *Associate* membership of institutional Europe, getting the trade and avoiding the small print requirements? He was stricken. It was an utterly unthinkable thing that a nation such as the United Kingdom could settle for being only a miserable trading partner. The Godolphin Horne complex ran deep. 'He never smiled or took your hand | But merely smirked and nodded.'

The immediate 'Labour Party Split' would descend into something deeper across the decade, though in 1958, the quarrel between the two men would be mended. At almost that moment, the split on principle between honest believers was given fizz and new point by nuclear weapons which we had developed and the large, ardent marching lobby against them, the Campaign for Nuclear Disarmament. This would happen *in opposition*, two years before Bevan's death, five before Gaitskell's.

Again, were British sovereign nuclear weapons something needed for defending ourselves if the United States should geo-politically cut and run—an unlikely notion given the USA's own more rational pride of actual strength? Or did believers in them echo the *vaunting* quality of Sir Edward Grey, talking round the Cabinet in August 1914, with 'honour'? There seems to have been, over all such issues, a fearful want of low tradesman's thinking. 'What do we get? What do we risk? Let's not do anything silly.'

Back in harassed 1950, the Labour Party, having conducted a peaceful social revolution, created free health care, made India a nation, and for thirty years brought the Conservative Party into quiet and essential liberal-minded assent, went to the polls and lost a great many seats. They did so rather freakishly with more votes and a higher percentage of the poll than the Conservatives. In 1951, tribulated by that small majority and to oblige George VI, who did not want to go on his planned tour leaving a government with such a vulnerable majority, they went to the polls again. (The King would in fact, die on 6 February 1952.) But the Labour government, again ahead on all relevant numbers (13,948,385 and 48.8 per cent to 13,717,850 and 48.00 per cent), except, this time, seats fell and it would be out of government for the next thirteen years.

They had operated in exceptionally difficult circumstances—the vast debt of war, the threat of another conflict forcing extensive military expenditure, and the quarrels which, late in term, they had inflicted on themselves. It was still, to the objective or, at any rate, non-partisan observer, an outstandingly constructive and useful government. Across parliamentary history, the 1945–51 government stood with the great reforming Liberal ministry of 1905–14 and Peel's Cabinet, embracing Free Trade. In terms of social policy, as well as over-commitment abroad, it would be followed—surprisingly respectfully—by a Conservative government not caring to make enemies.

---

20 October 1949

House considers social equality a mistaken ideal.

Mr Rees-Mogg *I would define social equality as equality of social status; and looking at social relationships individually, I come to the conclusion that it means 'Equality of social status' and the further conclusion that people do not want social equality. It isn't in human nature. What they want is to be better!*

Mr Taverne—Secretary *You will only obtain social equality when you have first achieved a society with proper scope for individual responsibility. There should be no stigma of inferiority attaching to any occupation.*

Mr J. Lemkin (Merton) *As Marx would certainly have agreed, society requires order and rights. But rights depend upon organisation—who is suited to do what.*

I do not suggest the attendance of a Camel at a University. In any society there must be rulers and ruled with due respect paid to the actual qualities of citizens.

Mr Conrad Dehn (Ch.Ch.) *Inequalities there are and will be expressed, notably by inequality of income. What we must not have is anything resembling a caste system; and to be fair, since the war and because of it, we have moved at last to seeing that it need not be inevitable.*

Mr Barrington-Ward *'Equality before God' is my notion of an equality to be accepted. However, social equality is simply not attainable practically. The administrators of society simply build up power and privilege for themselves. The standards of society must always be created and preserved by a minority. Opponents of the motion do not aspire so far. What we want is simply a rational standard of inequality.*

Mr Kerensky *Public school education is valuable in itself, but confined. It should be extended by the state. Equal opportunity is a proper thing and is essential to develop abilities, but hereditary wealth has no virtue to justify it and the state should abolish it. Social equality is an ideal, difficult to live up to, but all worthwhile things are difficult.*

From the Floor Mr Miller thought the idea amorphous; Mr Hopkinson thought that there could be no society without a hierarchy; Mr Thorpe was trenchant against the motion; Mr Summerskill supported equality, but stressed its difficulties.

Motion lost 243:251.

———— ❦ ————

3 November 1949

House thinks the creation of a third force, rather than an Anglo-American bloc, should be the immediate aim of British Foreign policy.

The motion led to strange groupings on either side. Strong Europeans, extreme socialists, and the supporters of Lord Beaverbrook united to propose it; while it was attacked by supporters of both the Left and the Right.

Mr Peter Emery (Oriel) *What I want to see is an amalgamation of Europe and the Empire. We must have economic independence and greater trade; and production within the Empire is the way to do so. We can't count on undercutting American goods in America. This Third Force should not be anti-American, but should hold the balance of power between Russia and the USA.* Listened to with rather more affection than respect.

Mr Summerskill *It is very difficult for the Foreign Secretary. Britain alone doesn't have the means to become Third Force. So we must look to Europe, but for that to work, the governing classes of Europe must stop putting class before country. Something else, we should be alert to the very possible emergence of a Germany economically superior to Britain.*

Mr D. Wedgwood Benn *What evidence is there of actual military aggression by the Soviet Union? That should be separated in our minds from the advance of Communism. As it is, any incident occurring may lead to an explosion of conflict. Meanwhile no war will get rid of Communist influence. I look toward harmony between the great powers at the highest level.*

Mr Thorpe *We must never again make the mistakes of Neville Chamberlain at Munich. We must realise that there is a Russian threat; as for breaking away from America, it would be sheer suicide.*

Mr John Gilbert (St John's)[1] *Mr Bevin's Foreign policy simply doesn't differ enough from Conservative foreign policy. Without holding a brief for the Soviet Government, some of their claims are justified; and I think the idea of essential conflict between capitalism and communism should be rejected. I look toward Universal Socialism and Universal Peace.*

Mr N. Dromgoole *As a Conservative, I consider these proposals for union with Europe impracticable and undesirable. They would cause a drop in our standard of living which public opinion will not accept; not least because of the Socialist refusal to co-operate with European countries.* From the floor; three of the best speeches here came from foreigners: Mr V de Pange made an excellent speech in praise of Franco-British union; Mr H. Shuman was a genial and impressive ambassador for America; and Mr A. Mitra made a moving maiden speech for the motion as a neutral Indian.

Motion carried 229:185.

10 November 1949

House deplores the modern movements in poetry and the fine arts.

Mr P. Lowell (Magd.) *Art must not be confined by the limits of either a sophisticated circle or a lunatic fringe. Modern poets are too eager to produce new effects. They simply have not reached the ordinary man.*

Mr P. Weitzman (Ch.Ch.) *The modern movement is already part of history, even what is called the 'sensationalism.'*

Mr J. Lucas *What we have in modern poetry today are an emptiness of content, an obscurity and tricks of style. Modern culture shows a disintegration. It must be esoteric, something most apparent in the works of Joyce and Eliot.*

Mr Peter Parker (Lincoln)[2] *The proposers have nothing to offer us but a blighting deliberation as they pass judgment. More feeling please. Artists at present feel isolated from the community. We should not blame them, but make the effort to co-operate in understanding and it doesn't happen.*

Mr Rees-Mogg *I detect a lack of self-confidence in modern art.*

From the floor Mr M. Hall was amusing; the Secretary was logical; Mr Hodson was very competent.

Motion lost 148:270.

24 November 1949

House believes that the House of Lords should be strengthened, not weakened.

Mr Hall *As a mere Brasenose man, I can still appreciate the value of their Lordships. For a start, they are free to start legislation if it is not controversial. And at a time when government likes to set up new extra-parliamentary sources of authority they can be very useful.*

Mr P. Hutber[3] has a pleasant vein of kindly sarcasm used to good effect. *The House of Lords performs no essential function; it is merely an ingenious device for enabling Conservatives to retain power over the legislature.*

Mr Miller *No institution can perfectly represent the will of the people, but the House of Lords is, in a sense, representative. Conservatism needs to be an element in parliament as in the human mind. As to deadlock: when that occurs, the question should be settled by referendum.*

Mr P. Blaker (New College)[4] *In whatever form the Upper House might be retained, it would be a mistake to increase their powers of delay. Public opinion doesn't take long to form. In the 19th Century, the Lords did great harm. If they re-emerge as a strong, reformed chamber, they will give political parties alibis to escape responsibility.*

Mr M. Essayan *Ill-considered legislation needs someone to keep an eye on it. The Lords is apt for doing that precisely because its members are not subject to party discipline.*

Mr D. Jarrett (Keble) *The potential irresponsibility of the House of Commons is subject only to five yearly elections. It is not enough. The Upper House must be restored to esteem in the eyes of the nation. It must be reformed then strengthened.*

Mr R. Vaughan-Williams (Wadham) *Their Lordships have been debased by commerce. They are no longer aristocratic and extraordinary. They are ordinary and they are intolerably bourgeois.*

Motion carried 197:156.

———— ∞ ————

26 January 1950

House considers the Union of South Africa under its present administration not worthy of the Commonwealth.

Mr Thorpe *South Africa has refused to subscribe to the Charter of Human Liberties. She has refused to hand back South West Africa to the UN. Everywhere she has sabotaged the new organs of international co-operation. I'm not asking her to leave the Commonwealth; but if no change of policy emerges in the future, the question of her membership must be very seriously reconsidered.*

Mr Gilbert *Actually Britain's own treatment of her colonial problems is not much better. Anyway, only by keeping South Africa within the Commonwealth can we bring any pressure on the Malan government.*[5]

Mr B. J. Krikler (University of Capetown) *Although natives are represented in a parliament of 153 by three white men, no constitutional reform can be hoped for. If you argue against apartheid, back comes the answer 'Do you want your daughter to marry a coloured man?'*

Mr P. J. Fraenkel (University of Witwatersrand) *History has split South Africa through the Bantu Wars, then through fear of African labour which is becoming ever more skilled. Apartheid is a positive way of dealing with this tension. In a generation, it will bear fruit in the form of self-respecting independent native communities.*

Mr Ajai K. Mitra (Allahabad University and Univ.) *I do ask you to recall how hesitantly South Africa joined us in the last war. I have spent time in British jails in India, but British justice never sank to the levels of this South Africa mockery. The House cheered Mr Mitra wildly.*

Mr Howard Shuman (Illinois U. and New College) *The point is what acts for the Blacks of South Africa, available outside, are actually useful? And expelling South Africa from the Commonwealth isn't one of them. It won't help a single native labourer.*

Mr S. N. Maira (BNC) *just let us remember that the Apartheid people don't only want to keep down the Native African. They aim at White domination over the coloured races and Afrikaner domination among the whites.*

Mr J. M. Mohapaloa (New College) *Please do not let us forget, in our concern for South African conditions, that the same discrimination against coloured races is to be found all over the Commonwealth, not least in Britain. In the abstract, British people are friendly toward the coloured races, but when it comes to practice, Africans find it difficult to secure accommodation. As for social relations between white and black, they are still frowned upon.*

Mr J. N. Docker (Queen's) *Only while South Africa is kept within the Commonwealth, will such criticism help to establish Christian principles in the Union.*

Mr A. N. Binder (Magd.) *Race prejudice is bred by intermingling. Apartheid teaches each one his own social station and keeps him in it, and Dr Malan's is therefore the only sensible policy.*

Mr Morland (Ch.Ch.) *South Africa gives nothing to the Commonwealth; and what she should give to the natives is self-respect, not 'reservations.'*

Mr G. H. France (Jesus) *The races of South Africa would resent amalgamation as much as the Welsh resent absorption in the United Kingdom.*

Motion carried 298:131,

---

9 February 1950

House condemns the Social record of the Churches.

Mr Dehn *The churches have been callous in concerning themselves only with men and not their condition of life. They have obstructed the prevention of pain. The Roman Catholic Church still stands out against the freedom of the press and of conscience; and the Church of England was blind until this century about savage penal laws, slavery and slums.*

Mr Ivan Yates (Pembroke) [6] *The Church's duty in social matters is not its overriding one; and people asking 'Why don't they do something about it?' would be the first to tell them to mind their own business.*

Mr Rees-Mogg *The Priests of God must be the tribunes of the people; yet in Spain 60,000 clergy depend for their protection on a fascist gangster from their own congregation; and everywhere national Churches have blessed national wars. Too often in history the priest and the Levite have passed by on the other side.*

Mr John Lucas (Balliol) *The churches made compromises and are blamed for them. What would have happened if those compromises had not been made? The Church has done its work so well that one cannot imagine a world in which it had not succeeded. No one can build a* Civitas Dei *without God.*

Mr Day—ex-Librarian *I look upon the rise of Communism as a judgment on Christian failure during the industrial revolution. The quarrel of the sects has retarded education.* Mr Day has become so good a master of technique that one would like to point to a few remaining imperfections. In spite of his superb mastery of the House, it rejected some of his antitheses and quotations as too glib for a debate of such intellectual seriousness. For the rest, he was given well merited applause.

Professor J. B. S. Haldane[7] *The record of Monsignor Tiso[8] had shown the priest in power. The Papal message,* Quadragessima anno[9] *declared Catholicism and Socialism contradictory terms and had reserved praise only for the Fascist corporate state. The Church of England, with its contradictory promises, is corrupting the morals of the country, the Nonconformists have not shed their intolerance and no Church is taking seriously the command 'Thou shalt not kill.'*

Dr Nathaniel Micklam *Christianity imposed Christian mythology for the old pagan version; the Virgin Mother of Gods for the lascivious mother of the gods. Christianity has imposed order on the chaos of barbaric Europe; civilisation had come to us only through the monasteries. Also the whole new situation in a resurgent Far East is the result of the creative efforts of Christian missionaries in education and in the care of the sick.*

Mr David Howell *The standards of sexual morality set by official Christianity have been impossibly high.*

Mr A. M. Allchin (Ch.Ch.) *Either the proposers are talking about the work of church organisation in which case, all the words about dissolute bishops are irrelevant, or they give the Church credit for the works of individual members, in which case, most of the social progress of the last hundred years would be found to have been inspired by Christians.*

Motion lost 183:315.

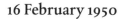

16 February 1950

House regards an economically strong Germany as essential to world peace.

Mr J. K. Kyle (Magd.) *To meet the Communist anger, Europe must build up the standard of living all over the globe; and Europe cannot do so without harnessing the German economy to the task. Again, Germany will not be able to deal with her own refugee and unemployment problems unless she once again becomes economically strong.*

Mr Barrington-Ward *This motion is a direct attack on present British policy. An economically strong Germany must include both the Ruhr and the Saar. Sheffield will then be facing the competition of cheap German labour. With economic power will come military and political power. A Germany in charge of her destinies will fight for her eastern provinces and indeed perhaps involve all Europe in the struggle as well.*

Mr G. N. Dalzell Pyne *weathered a difficult passage bravely in an intelligent debating speech. To restrict the total wealth in the world and be frightened of healthy competition is, in the long run, politically and economically wrong. There has been a great change of heart in the ordinary German in the street.*

Mr J. Lemkin (Merton) *A strong Germany is not good for peace, but only for winning the next war. Whether German Steel competes with ours in a buyer's market, or is absorbed in armaments, she gains power at British expense; and wars are not made by the Hon. Gentleman's German in the street.*

Mr Oscar Newton (University of Alabama) *If Germany is not restored to economic strength, Europe will inevitably collapse just as the Soviet Union hopes. If she recovers, there will be risk, but that risk must be taken; for the alternative is suicidal.*

Mr Benn *A partitioned state is above all, interested in unity, and this desire is stronger than any economic bribe. Only after re-unification can we let Germany become strong again. The solution of German problems and all the others in Europe is impossible without agreement between Russia and the West. So any hint of willingness to discuss these problems at the highest level is of the utmost importance.*

Mr Charles Radciffe (Bates College Maine) *You can only keep a man in a ditch by staying down there with him. Democracy travels on its stomach and, as Churchill said, German industry and German genius must help to bring back prosperity to the continent and to the world.*

Mr Kerensky *Sixty per cent of Bavarians in power are still Nazi. Russia might, by a bribe, secure a German alliance. No ally could be more doubtful than Germany. This motion is fodder for Communist propaganda and encouragement to the German right wing.*

Mr Hutber *What this motion says is that encouragement to the very worst elements in Germany is advantageous to peace.*

Mr Victor de Pauge (Wadham) *As a Frenchman from Lorraine, I still support this motion and ask for an act of faith in the German people. Only this will end an enmity which has been disastrous to Europe.*

Mr K. D. Stern *Militarism is an ineradicable part of the German character.*

Mr Dromgoole *The House should remember its genetics.*

Mr Wright (Lincoln) *But there has actually taken place in Germany a great change of heart.*

Motion carried 240:147.

2 March 1950

House would welcome establishment of free birth control clinics under the National Health Service.

Mr Hutber *It is a pleasure to be meeting not only Oxford's First Lady (Miss Florence Elliott), but to be encountering a Roman Catholic dignitary somewhere other than in Dante's Inferno. Birth control clinics are essential to safeguard health generally and to banish fear. Every child that is born should be a child that is wanted.*

Mr J. H. Edwards (Merton) *Motherhood should be given all honour by the state. The cost is no handicap to any family and a large minority of the population should not be asked to pay for what they regard as morally wrong.*

Mr Blaker *Pacifists, vegetarians, and osteopaths are contributing to the maintenance of services which they regard as wrong. Yet the Roman Catholic hierarchy is asking us to subsidise the teaching of doctrines which the majority regard as false. So how can Catholics dare use such arguments against supporting something which the majority thinks right?*

Mr C. K. Davidson (BNC) *The Empire is crying out for immigrants, and these clinics will reduce the birth-rate. It is all a vote of no confidence in the British race.*

Miss Florence Elliott (St Hilda's) First woman undergraduate to address the house for some years. *Unlike men, women need advice on this subject. The gynaecological out-wards are quite inadequate and the consequent lack of instruction for women discriminates in favour of men. Tens of thousands of women are forced into illegal abortions every year. The state gives free services to venereal victims and to unmarried mothers.*

The Rt. Rev. George Andrew Beck RC Bishop of Brentford[10] *Lack of self-control lies at the root of most of the evils in the modern world. The rising rate of crime, of pre-marital intercourse and of divorce, all point to a disrespect for the rational part of the soul which should act as philosopher king over the appetites. Man is a creature, subject to a creator, and the modern world refuses to obey the Maker's instructions. Contraception frustrates the purpose of the sexual act. Man is condemned to live in twilight, but what matters is the direction in which he moves.* The house greatly appreciated this good-humoured and highly intellectual speech.

Mr Kerensky *As a result of modern science which separates intercourse from conception at will, it is now time that the social stigma of extra-marital intercourse is rooted out.*

Motion passed 196:172.

27 April 1950

House believes Mr Attlee's administration is unworthy of the confidence of the country.*

Mr Rees-Mogg *Every branch of the Armed services is in disorder and our national security has been damaged by this neglect.*

Mr Taverne—Librarian *Political decisions are the basis of economics. Meanwhile the Tory party wants the electoral benefits of the Welfare state without any of the burdens. The government deserves confidence because its economic means have succeeded and its political ends have been just.*

Mr Kyle *The best way to achieve Mr Morrison's[11] desire that the Welfare State should be above controversy, is to let the Tories prove their sincerity in office.*

Mr Kerensky *Mr Attlee's administration is one of the greatest reforming governments in history. The dollar gap is closing. Communism has been routed at the polls. Lord Keynes was right—Labour's belief in redistribution of income is based on hatred—hatred of social injustice.*

Marquess of Reading[12] *Labour is no heir to the Liberal tradition. There is no peace, retrenchment is scorned and great reforms are being mishandled. The administration is a menace to the prosperity of the country and the liberty of the individual citizen.*

Lord Alexander[13] *What greater efforts could have been made for peace? Devaluation was forced on us by the wicked propaganda of the newspapers and people who abused their country abroad. It has been absurd of the Conservatives to praise the magnificent*

---

* The formula follows that designed on 11 November 1830 by the then Secretary of the Union, William Gladstone, about the ministry of the Duke of Wellington.

output of the steel industry and at the same time, complain that Socialist controls are frustrating the economy.

Motion lost 220:267.

⸺ ⛭ ⸺

11 May 1950

The head of a Southern African tribe had become engaged to a white woman to the displeasure of Apartheid Ministers in Pretoria and the embarrassment of the Labour government, stuck with Commonwealth responsibilities bringing grief specifically to the ever luckless Patrick Gordon Walker. It should be said in fairness that a black man marrying a white woman would have raised fists as often as eyebrows in the Britain of 1950.

House calls for the immediate recognition by HMG of Seretse Khama as Chief of the Bamangwato tribe.

Mr Dudley Thompson (Merton) *The government has toadied to South Africa whose racial policy is the cancer of the Commonwealth. His treatment is not the true expression of the British outlook. Where is the tradition of fair play between man and man, black and white?*

Mr Gilbert came well-briefed to the despatch box. *Seretse is unsuitable for the Chieftainship. We could not have risked the turmoil and the building-up of factions by Tshekedi and Seretse.*[14] *The long-term objective of the government is the establishment of democratic institutions. Five out of six newspapers in the protectorate have condemned Seretse. The Evidence shows that this policy is not merely a concession to white South African Fascism.*

Mr Benn *The Union in discussing this case, has been granted a privilege not extended to the House of Commons. The policy has created a wide sense of injustice hardly calculated to promote a peaceful atmosphere. By the government's own test of expediency, its policy will fail. It should declare and apply a clear and positive policy toward all the coloured races.*

Mr P. Mayhew (Balliol)[15] *I see no alternative to the government's decision. If Seretse were put on two years probation as Chieftain, he would have no authority. Far from appeasing Dr Malan, we are forestalling inevitable intervention by South Africa by preventing tribal disorder. The validity of tribal decisions about Seretse is open to question and incidentally, there is no democracy in the Bamangwato tribe.*

Mr Shuman *The goal of democracy is not likely to be reached any more quickly by a decision overruling an almost unanimous opinion of the tribe.*

Mr Dromgoole *The movers wish to perpetuate an undemocratic, corrupt and hereditary system. The movers, Liberals and Socialists, are the real reactionaries trying to prevent progress.*

Mr Ajai Mitra *I moved a motion last term that South Africa was unworthy of the Commonwealth. I could not say that now of a Commonwealth whose standards could sink as low as the Seretse Khama white paper. It is well known that Dr Malan had urged the banning of Seretse. The Socialist government's consistent policy of racial discrimination is disgusting.*

Mr Lowell *A king or chief is not a free agent in marriage. Seretse was wrong to have married a white woman. We have no right to endanger a whole tribe by pursuing principles unrelated to circumstances.* A forthright and incisive speech.

Motion carried 202:154.

A further motion calling for a minute's silence in protest against the banning of the Communist Party in South Africa and Australia was carried 128:70.

---

9 November 1950

House deplores the decline of the middle classes.

Mr Mayhew *Although we are all being levelled down, the class system is making converts of its conquerors, witness the ennobled mobsters now going to the Lords. The substitution of a new middle class for the old one is turning out to be a poor transaction. A multiplicity of talents is needed to run a country, but our present rulers have an apparent contempt for all but manual labour.*

Mr Maurice Shock[16] *Middle class virtues and standards tend to spread out among communities. Nowadays ladies from North Oxford and women from Cowley look exactly the same in Marks and Spencer's.*

Mr J. R. G. Owen (Oriel) *Middle class incomes have remained steady whilst those of others have soared. This reflected a general impoverishment of the nation, brought about by international forces far more powerful than a Labour Government. The rising tide of nationalism in Asia cannot be without repercussions on living conditions in metropolitan countries.*

Mr Kaufman[17] *The middle class has lost confidence in itself because the Middle Class International has faded out of existence.*

Motion carried 332:127.

Monday 21 November 1950

House regards the immediate re-arming of Germany as essential to ensure the defence of the West.

Mr George Carman (Balliol)[18] *There are terrifying gaps in our defences. To meet them we need Germany to create an autonomous army with the ultimate end of becoming a federal German Army. It is essential that the Franco-German feud should die. The real answer to German nationalism is social reform and economic progress. Such an army is needed to fight not against Communism but Russian divisions.*

Mr Fred Jarvis (St Catherine's) *the real threat to peace lies in the militant Communist parties of France and Italy. Would the proposer arm General Franco? What notice is he taking of the deep and passionate opposition to this idea among the French? Instead let us put the Schuman plan[19] into operation. Britain, the US and France all oppose the revival of the German armaments industry? How can you have an army without an armaments industry? There is potential for Nazism to revive. To re-arm Germany is to accentuate and accelerate an already dangerous arms race.*

Mr John Stewart (Balliol) *The Germans are not irrevocably opposed to rearmament. But they are suspicious of being used as cover for our 'glorious retreat to the Pyrenees'. Our policies in the last five years: protracted war trials, dismantling, procrastination and vacillation, have failed abysmally to win the confidence of the German people. The Germans ask to be equal partners in Western Europe. They are very tired of war. If Germany re-arms we will be able to face that Germany with a steady nerve.*

Mr Geoffrey Smith (Pembroke) *It is useless to draw up a plan like this which is received with fear and distrust, not only in Europe, but by democratic elements in Germany itself. Please note the sinister request by discharged German officers for arrears of pay dating back to 1945.*

Baron W. R. von Pachelbel-Gehag (Hamburg U. and St Edmund Hall). *German rearmament will not go unchecked since it is under the rigorous scrutiny of the occupying powers. We all prefer butter to guns. How else can the disillusioned youth of Germany be brought to play a willing and constructive part in the defence of the West?*

Mr Bryan Magee (Keble) *So exiguous are our defences that no re-armament will make any difference.*

Mr Binder *I think the Germans are pathological.*

Motion carried 90:79.

Thursday 1 January 1951

House thinks the foreign policy of HMG in the Far East, as elsewhere, displays too great a dependence upon that of the United States.

Mr Yates *The places where we are dependent are Japan, Korea, Western Germany and the atom bomb. It is not enough to disagree with the US about these four places. We must speak out.*

Mr Dalzell-Payne—Librarian *In three spheres we do differ from the US. In China, we recognised Mao Tse-tung's government. In Spain, where the Americans were alone in carrying out a realistic policy,[20] and the Soviet Union itself. We have shipped strategic materials behind the Iron Curtain. He knew about all this. His brother was in the cavalry, and he knew all about Centurion tanks.*

Mr David Wedgwood Benn[21] *Britain gives too little thought to how she may influence the trend of world affairs. Achievement of a settlement in the Far East should be our greatest objective. Second, increased armaments are no alternative to Soviet friendship. Finally, we should not regard the atom bomb as a Maginot Line. As for the Far East, that is the biggest problem. We are too dependent on the US, not to be dependent on General MacArthur.[22] We must fight war psychosis—armaments only aggravate international tension.*

Mr St John Stevas[23] *Those who ask for tolerance of Asians are usually the ones most bigoted in their attitude to the United States. There has been no dependence. Only in Palestine, has it been a case of where you zig, we zag. There have been differences with the US over China and Formosa. What more is wanted here to show that differences exist?*

Viscount Stansgate[24] *The Commonwealth conference had been proof of the great moral part we have to play. The Americans are wrong to look upon the USSR as an evil force emanating from the Kremlin. They thought that everything could be settled by the metric stone. So many things may happen. What of a German–Polish conflict? In Korea the US blundered in not knowing when to stop. The doctrine of bargaining from strength is one of the most dangerous heresies. Is the Chinese republic to be deprived of Formosa which is its rightful property? I do not want to create a split between Britain and the USA, but we must take the lead. We must revise our pacific policy. The Chinaman is a man of a thousand years of culture who looks upon a Russian as a gorilla. Before a ceasefire in Korea, let us see China in the UNO and rid Formosa of its nest of rebels.*

Mr Anthony Wedgwood Benn[25] *I agree with an immense amount of my father's speech. American dollars are not making us dependent on the USA. We are equal partners with America.*

Vote not given.

---

1 March 1951

Leave of notice motion 'To condemn the commission of anti-Semitic outrages, the liberation of high-ranking Nazi Prisoners and the rise of Nationalistic parties in Germany.' Moved by Mr David Lutyens (Wadham) Carried 96:32.

Main Motion House thinks the Government's defence policy is more likely to provoke than deter aggression.

Mr Bryan Magee[26] *In the teeth of all past experience, we are engaging in yet a third arms race, in spite of the fact that history has shown that it can lead only to disaster—to war—in fact, to aggression. According to the figures given by the Government, there is a smaller percentage of Russians under arms than Englishmen. Russia has the largest land frontier in the world. England has no land frontier at all. Intensive rearmament by the West will only be interpreted by Russia as a sign of aggressive intentions.*

Mr Guy Barnett (St Edmund Hall)[27] *Russia isn't just armed, she has armed satellites in Eastern Europe. She also has the largest submarine fleet in the world for which she has no justification. As to our Defence policy, the Russians have no right to feel provoked because we are prepared to defend ourselves. The answer to the problem is a defence policy coupled with negotiations.*

Sir Andrew Cunninghame Bt. (Worcester) *The Russians have been guilty of every sort of mischief short of war. They have sponsored a policy of aggression by proxy. In the face of it, the government has failed miserably. German armament is irresponsible. The Government has cold-shouldered the Schuman and Pleven*[28] *plans. We must have a Western European Defence policy if we can be led by men of repute. The past histories of many of our ministers are hardly likely to inspire confidence in Europe.*

Mr Geoffrey Samuel (Pembroke) *A third force is impracticable as no European country has the power to build up an effective bloc. We have to rely on the US. The present policy is adequate for safety, yet not so large that it would inevitably launch us into a third world war. Policy is based on Collective Security and from positions of strength. The Berlin airlift, for example, is not more liable to provoke than deter aggression.*

Mr Richard Blackmore (Wadham) *The prime need today is not to be found in an arc of air bases, but in a prosperous community. Our policy had taken away those who are making our wealth which they can no longer defend.*

Mr Norman St John Stevas (Ch.Ch.) *The best contribution the government can make to Defence policy would be to resign which would result in the return of a Conservative government. This government is the one least suited to carry out a re-armament policy. Their heart is not in it. For thirty years they had had two principles, friendship with Russia and a higher standard of living. They are still prisoners of the past. They are weakened by fellow travellers in their ranks. There is no good sitting behind barricades. We must foster unrest within Russia's vast Empire.*

Motion carried 116:99.

———— ❦ ————

3 May 1951

House views with apprehension any reform of the divorce laws which would endanger the sovereignty of the marriage tie.

Mr T. J. Brooke (Balliol) *Most Christian thinkers agree that it is right for the state to legislate for the non-Christian majority. We are not moralising apes and do not want to see rows of semi-detached houses containing semi-detached couples, but a divorce-conscious society is a great evil and the existence of divorce makes marriage more difficult.*

Mr Hutber *Under the present rules where a marriage breaks down, the husband is supposed to do 'the gentlemanly thing.' This quaint phrase means that he has to perjure himself. He has to take a co-respondent to a seaside hotel and spend a night on a sofa in the bedroom. This is called 'upholding the sanctity of the marriage bond.' The whole business is an ignoble and degrading sham. Something has to be done for those who suffer in silence tied to vindictive wives. It will be alleged that this will introduce a whole new principle into English law. Of course it will—and why not?*

Mr Neely *Marriage claimed to be no more than a business contract, but that contract is signed in the blood of the created child. Divorce is inevitably a renunciation of the parents' responsibility to the child and if through divorce, re-marriage were possible, then irresponsible people could commit the same crime all over again. Divorce has its roots in selfishness.*

Mr Simon Carey *No law should be so harsh as to lead to common disregard, nor a divorce law so lax as to undermine the sanctity of marriage. The danger at the moment is of the law itself being brought into disrepute. By encouraging collusive adultery, the law breeds the evil it exists to prevent.*

Mr Carman *Marriage is the problem, not divorce. Divorce appeals to weakness. Marriage needs strength. Marriages break down because of bad housing, inadequate family allowances and an aloof clergy. People should go into it meaning to make it work. Divorce by consent will do away with marriage.*

Mr Richard Blackman (Pembroke) *Marriages are not made in heaven and we are not in heaven anyway. But on the old earth which contains the American President[29] and Rita Hayworth,[30] I would oppose any legislation which tended to recognise the transitory nature of the vital institution of marriage.*

Mr Kaufman (Queen's) *They should be seen as life-long voluntary associations. The Churches cannot legislate beyond their own jurisdiction. The answer to the problem of divorce is to make marriage more difficult. The churches cannot legislate beyond their own jurisdiction. The answer is to make marriage more difficult. Divorce is of course very hard on children, but is having a bad home going to change it?*

Motion carried 135:124. The last time this issue was debated was in 1919 when the same motion was lost by one vote out of 400.

---

31 May 1951

House believes that the philosophy of the Labour Party is out of date.

Mr Shuman—Librarian *There are irreconcilable differences typified by individuals, by men like Laski, Cole, Crossman and Gordon-Walker. Everything is done after the terms of the axiom: that is good which does not work—that which works should be nationalised. The approach to people is embodied in decentralisation and dehumanising in Industry. This has met with protest from no less a body than the National Union of Railwaymen.*

Then what about Labour's attitude to peace? Is Social Democracy the answer to Communism? Can one impose democracy on a country as primitive as Korea? Does Mr Bevin have a socialist foreign policy?

Mr Yates *You can say that we are all socialists now. Professor Hayek has even dedicated a book to 'Socialists of all Parties.'*[31] *All parties are dedicated to full employment; and to this objective, state control is necessary. The Labour Party is criticised for holding this debate, but debate is a sign of strength. The tenets running through Labour are not out of touch. The party has deep roots in Nonconformity and in idealism. And paradoxically, idealism is the only realistic policy for the future.*

Sir David Maxwell Fyfe *How can a state be more selfless than its constituents? The system today comprises non-competent complacency at the centre, frustration at the perimeter and unparalleled patronage throughout. The Party which had stood for international brotherhood has become protectionist at heart and National Socialist in action! We are the heirs of Castlereagh and Canning who gave us a hundred years of peace.*[32]

Sir Richard Acland[33] *What is the dominant fact of our time? The breakdown of individualist philosophy. Consider the trouble we would have had today in India, Pakistan, Ceylon and Burma if we had behaved as the French behave in Indo-China. It beggars the imagination. How can the Tories talk about 'streamlining the machinery of government,' when they had been palpably incapable of streamlining the depressed areas out of existence before the war?*

Motion lost 142: 147.

17

The Old Order Not Changing
Very Much

15 November 1951–19 May 1955

UK staying Middle East/Capital punishment/Trust Churchill/Vatican influence/
China into UN?/Trade Union issues/Commercial broadcasting/No co-operation
with Franco/Rules of War/Irish partition/No Women/Rhodesian Federation/Korean
War/Social Service cuts/Parliamentary reform/European Union/Commonwealth
declining/curbing Press/Party government/Moral fibre/Enough to be English/
Europe losing influence/Better red than dead/Horror of 19/The conservative government returned 3/Arts censorship/British imperialism/Trades Union privi-
leges/Catholics/Republican Britain?/Churchill must go/Approving of Apartheid/
Billy Graham.

Not changing very much but cannily changing just enough, the Conservative
government, returned to office in October 1951, was markedly unBourbon. It
had learned rather a lot and had forgotten much, though not all, of that presumptuous defeatism: 'We are the only ones fit to govern, but in the case of an
economy in slump, there is nothing we can do about it.' It was less incurious.
'Keynes has tried and has worked—Got that! Labour, with all their faults,
have managed full-employment and set up a working and hugely popular
NHS. Without quite saying so, we will do nothing to contradict it. Me-tooism
if you like. We prefer to say me-betterism.' In fact, Keynes works, as he kept
telling people, in specific circumstances—in a cold economy where the
conjuring of demand creates employment but not dangerous inflation.

Happily, Churchill kept away from the direct involvement with the
economy which he had mishandled with such panache in respect of the

gold standard and its concomitant deflation. The Chancellor from October 1951 would be R. A. Butler, academically outstanding, but politically suspect. He had been a Foreign Office Minister of State before the war, unreservedly supporting appeasement. Against that, he would, in opposition (1947), produce the *Industrial Charter* which, though it deplored bureaucracy and the growth of the Civil Service, also spoke vaguely of workers' rights and, more credibly, the mixed economy. Following what this implied, he would advise retaining many of Labour's nationalizations which, given the state of, say, the current more recently resurrected independent railway companies, seems sensible.

Finally, the *Charter* gave the congé to whatever might be left of ancestral Tory protectionism. Butler had luck on his side when the terms of trade turned abruptly in Britain's favour. On top of which, the end of the Korean War and its costs allowed him to get rid of the food-rationing which Labour, responsibly fearful of popular extravagance, had carried deep and unloved into peacetime. Suddenly, all sorts of rationed nice things— sugar, butter, eggs, and the sins of our childhood, sweets, 'would,' as we said in those days, 'come off the ration'. It might be possible to see the Tories as the party of injustice and inequality, but, at that moment, they became the party of maltesers and hedonism all round. Long afterwards, Butler's delightful second wife/widow, Mollie, would tell the story of Rab's stopping his car one Friday, on his way back to home and constituency in Saffron Walden, getting out, and, privately, all by himself, tearing up copies of all the restrictions.

Butler's picture of the Conservative Party of 1951, put early into efficient circulation in 1947, was reckoned to have done them great service in the elections of 1950 and 1951. The new Chancellor was a cerebral and emollient man, given to saying deadly things under, but not quite completely under, his breath. Witness his comment in 1955 on Anthony Eden after the tired heir had finally limped up to the throne. 'He's the best Prime Minister we've got.' Butler was, despite two starred firsts (French and German then History), economically literate enough to be tempted by the super-sophistication (for those days) of a floating currency in the form of the *Robot* scheme (devised by the Treasury in 1952, but never actually implemented). Because the currency might float *down*, this would be another of those things rejected by the British consensus, Left and Right, as derogating from our national greatness. It would have involved accepting the consequences of overspending in the form of a falling pound. This might be resisted through buying it back or acknowledged as an adverse vote from the money market, offset by generating more competitive exports.

With Churchill marking time and making futile attempts to obtain a summit with Stalin and a close relationship with the new US President, Eisenhower, neither of whom were having any, Anthony Eden, fretful and suspicious back at the Foreign Office, was the scheduled successor. Eden, however, was both seriously unwell and, if not precisely vulnerable, widely thought of as promisingly so. He had been appointed Foreign Secretary long ago, in 1935, to replace Samuel Hoare, co-respondent with Pierre Laval, Premier of France (later shot for collaboration), in assigning a large part of Abyssinia to Mussolini who had invaded that country.

The new Prime Minister's credit was good, his public standing high, his profile worthy of any West End leading man, but his health, at 57, was poor. And politically, being a specialist expert, he was reckoned very little of a politician. Once nodded through as Prime Minister, he at once called an election and, with an improved majority, won it. It doesn't get better than that and in Eden's case it didn't. A succession race to the succession was already evolving, a two-man affair involving Butler, the serious thinker about the economy but candid former appeaser, and Harold Macmillan, downright opponent of Chamberlain,[1] high on the list of 'rats and disloyalists' logged by Chamberlain's unsubtle Chief Whip.

His pre-war parliamentary insubordination was now a mark of political edge, of creditable and rather glamorous delinquency. Butler's political style was donnish and rather muted. Macmillan affected the flaneur and hinted the assassin. (He had had an adventurous contact and intelligence post in Africa during the war.) As PM after 1957, he would seem to measure unfashionable Ministers for their ermine or, at a lower level, according to Bill Deedes, would consolingly offer the dear departing 'a little something to wear under your tie'. In 1951 and practical peacetime politics, he had recognized a good idea; and straight away, in his first Cabinet job, had taken hard hold of it. Here and now, at the start of a steep climb, he needed impact. The lacuna among all Labour's social achievements was Housing. There had been good reasons for this—resources, stretched on Health, Welfare, and, more disputably, the Korean War. Very well, there should be houses. As an officer of the Union he had been a Liberal, admirer of Campbell-Bannerman and Asquith, and would show warmth toward the emerging Labour Party. For the leader of the Tory Party, he wasn't much of a Tory. He would of course live to snub Margaret Thatcher and all she stood for.

Macmillan as Minister of Housing (a new, attention-concentrating Ministry) set a target clearly too high—300,000 new builds by 1955—got the money, and achieved it. The standard build was a little reduced in quality, but saying so sounded like a cavil. They were decent houses, and lots of them. They were too, as Labour's new houses had been, largely Local Authority business. Macmillan had done something which Labour, busy in office with so many things, just hadn't reached. For the 1955 election under Eden's recently assumed leadership, it was the perfect calling card.

There was however one mighty flaw in the moderation of the 1951 government, a determination on the part of Churchill that his government would not open up a second front with the trade unions. The great distinction long-term post-war, between Britain, economically laggard and West, later Federal, Germany, way ahead, lay in trade union and business relations. The Germans, perhaps from the desperation of their initial situation, did not engage in conflict at the workplace. There would indeed be Mitbestimmung—talking together, which sounds anodyne and wasn't.

German workers pretty generally understood that a rising standard of living, judged by real wages, depended upon competitive prices. So, accordingly, wages should only rise within the performance of the trade. Strikes were looked upon as failures by union leaderships as, conversely, success in profits created an entitlement to be met, given its effect upon future sales and, especially, exports and increased employment. In Britain, by small degrees, the unions asked for, and too readily got, uneconomic settlements. By degrees, wages rose by pre-emption. Could a company get away with paying only moderately over the economic rate?

Doubting it, Churchill had appointed Sir Walter Monckton, intelligent man, highly successful legal counsel, who believed that unions would behave with most wisdom when not provoked. The Ministry of Labour developed a pro-union basis, or at the very least, an expectation of successive defeats which must be seen and portrayed as reasonable compromises. The line taken by this Conservative government was altogether weaker and less prudential than that of Labour Ministers. The notion of requiring ballots to validate strike calls was rejected as provocative. In the way of retreat, uneconomic settlements began across the 1950s, to be granted pre-emptively for fear of official hearings granting even more.

Labour, immediately post-war, had been able to get reasonable conclusions from the union leadership and enjoyed high growth. But what Macmillan had started, the weak Wilson government (small initial majority and carrying the uncomprehending Michael Foot in the relevant department) would expand. Commonly, a senior judge like Lord Wilberforce—with no economics background but the clear understanding that a settlement, good or bad, was required—would be sent in to award it—terrible government. The unions, with a complacency of their own, would bid up and not be disappointed. If ever a benign intention turned into a vicious circle, this was it.

The Conservative government was full of the privilege, public school grandeur, social caste, and the languid accents of men feeling guilty. It was short of men who had worn overalls or met a wage bill. The union command—Vincent Tewson at the TUC, Arthur Deakin, General Secretary of the Transport Workers' Union, and like moderate leaders—would try to temper shop floor militancy. However, in the absence of legal requirement for strike-ballots, strikes readily took place as demands were met as less trouble, short term, than the seeing-out of an issue. By degree, shop floor extremists, including all sorts of far-leftists and rogue egos, rose to official status and power. The Electrical Trades Union would, in the early 1950s, become the territory of the British Communist Party, only got rid of by the efforts of other members of that union, led by Jock Byrne and Frank Chapple, through the legal action which commenced in 1961.

A fair comment in 1955, with Churchill finally and unwillingly gone from office, would be that the country had, over the previous ten years, benefited from two fallible but, at core, good governments, with Labour proving the more professional and harder working, the Conservatives more politically astute. Both had a guiding personality, something underlined by the *Economist's* naughty confection of Butler and Gaitskell into 'Mr Butskell'. Although oddly, both of them were the sons of the Indian Civil Service, the two personalities were perfect antitheses. Gaitskell's was adjusted to good fighting—against a raid on Abadan, overly in favour of pursuing the Korean War. When faced with the apparent high tide of CND and, while others winced, temporized—or admired—Gaitskell made the speech of his life defending, probably wrongly, British nuclear weapons, something best seen from here as more empty swank than essential defence. Butler would in far away 1963, out of an apathy unbecoming a twelve-year Cabinet Minister, pass up the Tory leadership he wanted to Macmillan's candidate, the archaic and TV-fatal Lord Home. It was a failure of both of them.

Even so, back with the unions and the Churchill government, Butler, not many people's idea of a hardliner, would argue the necessary stronger line—proposing resistance to a threatened rail strike for a 15 per cent increase, saying that 'We should not pay what we cannot afford.' Churchill is then quoted as saying, 'We cannot have a railway strike, it would be so disturbing to all of us. You will never get home. Nobody will be able to see their wives.'[2] To the original award was soon after added a second one, two months later. Butler would be told by Churchill in a midnight phone call that 'Walter and I have settled it,' and asking, 'On whose terms?', he was told, 'Theirs, old cock.' Intimating the cost of such flights from hard sums, Butler would say, in his pre-Budget statement of April 1955, that across 1953–4, wages and salaries had risen by three times output. The retreat from simple arithmetic which produced such consequences was, for the long term, quietly and not much noticed, catastrophic.

Churchill's Ministry had been overall, at least in the short term, uneven government and clear political success. As politics, it had turned upon individuals. It was too, in its achievements, something made possible by families. Those two conflated names would not just cover a political hominid, but establish a defining abstract principle. *Butskellism*, in a way unhelpful to the ambitions of both men, proclaimed a wise, if rather water-colourist quality to their political good sense. Yet the quick-minded Butler was emollient and, in the way of many clever men, rather lazy; while Gaitskell, working too hard for his long-term health—he would die at 56—was fighter and sticker, right and wrong, also accordingly disliked and ultimately admired—and grievously missed.

Labour realized that the snapping division between Bevanites and Gaitskellites was better theatre than politics. Hugh Gaitskell would be elected Labour leader in 1955, the third post-war election having been lost by an actual majority of voters, something new. Attlee retired; he had stayed on, not out of Churchill's near addiction to down-stage centre, but as symbol of a lost and desired unity. The contenders kissed and made up, just about credibly. And by two to one, Hugh Gaitskell would defeat Aneurin Bevan (now deputy in the shadow Cabinet) to become leader of the Labour Party and HM Opposition.

Against all this constructive moderation, the parties of government were facing problems which, being ex-imperial, followed the injunction of the tacky anthem which the imperializing Conservative Party had cherished: 'Wider spread and wider may thy bounds be set...' The term 'Empire' had been dropped for 'Commonwealth' (unofficially divided into white and non-white), but large stretches of it were imperial enough. Post-war British history would be pocked by 'emergencies'—Kenya, Malaya, Cyprus, and the Rhodesian Federation among them. Malaya involved inter-racial/political conflict: top-dog, British-backed Muslim Malays against underdog, Communist-led Chinese; dominant and rebel-ling Kikuyu sustaining Mau Mau rebels against British-dependent Luo and smaller tribes. The killings done by Mau Mau were echoed by a lot of nasty retaliation by way of emergency law and lots of hangings in this fag-end of empire.

Back in very late Labour days, there had been Abadan in Iran where British-owned oil assets (BP) had been nationalized in March 1951 by Mohammed Mosaddegh, uppity populist doing anti-imperialism. Over which problem, Hugh Gaitskell had, as noted, sensibly stopped Herbert Morrison, by then, *faute de mieux*, Foreign Secretary, from doing the impe-rial thing. The dispute lasted through to 1954 when we would eventually get them back after the American-dependent Shah of Iran had been helped to his own coup by US and British intelligence. This created a res-pite, lasting until, three decades later, Muslim militancy took back oil, by then not only Iranian, but sacred.

Cyprus would enjoy, if that is the word, an emergency lasting four years. Government during the emergency was begun under a field mar-shal (Sir John Harding) and ended under a Foot, Sir Hugh (of the three sibling Presidents of our Union, the elder one). Soft line would follow hard in the experimental way of mid-century British governments. Archbishop Makarios, spokesman/guiding figure of the revolt/terrorist outbreak, would first be exiled to house arrest (in the horror of the Seychelles), then recalled and, after much saving of British face, emerge as President of Cyprus. An unofficial State of North Cyprus also emerged, with the Turks of the north-eastern region enjoying security and lots of tourist euros, from which currency it is officially excluded. This sensible solution has been condemned, denied recognition, UN status, and entry to the Eurovision song contest, but thrives as a delightful/illegal holiday resort, all the more popular for the token illegality.

Assumptions about our Empire/Commonwealth beyond the old white dominions rolled more or less with the punches landed by nationalist movements and bogeyman native leaders. Such assumptions of conti-nuity had been the key barrier to our ever taking seriously the urgings of the absurd Europeans, anxious for our commitment to this unsound integrationist caper of theirs. The problem might just possibly be the soundness of those assumptions.

⚮

15 November 1951

House holds that British rights and possessions in the Middle East should in no circumstances be abandoned.

Mr Simon Carey (Ch.Ch.) *We must distinguish between the genuine nationalism which is to be found in India and the bogus variety prevalent in the Middle East. Abandoning these places will solve nothing.*

Mr Hutber *Labour policy in Palestine is simply wrong. In Persia the only party wanting to raise an appalling standard of life is Tudeh.*[3] *Abadan is a privileged enclave in a land of poverty. Even the most simple men can grasp a few political ideas. They may turn to Communism; our troops and cruisers will assist this movement. In the Middle East, we need to follow the course we followed in India. We must throw off our Welfare State imperialism. It is better for nations to make their own mistakes than have them made on their behalf by other people.*

Sir Andrew Cunninghame Bt. *British possession does more to alleviate bad conditions than the independent governments in the Middle East. Charges of exploitation are gullibly used by callow Leftists. By abandoning our rights, we gain nothing and leave a vacuum. Why indeed should we have rights in order to abandon them?*

Mr Raghavan Iyer (Magd.) *Treaties remain valid only so long as no material change takes place after their signature. Egypt is not fit and Britain has no business to run the Suez Canal. Both duties and rights must go; it is time for international action and control to be upheld.*

Mr Oliver Crawford *UNO provides no prospect of an answer to the problems of the middle east. It failed completely in Palestine. Furthermore, it is simple cowardice to say that Britain has no place in the Middle East. We alone have a constructive policy for dealing with soil-erosion and poverty. We should not bow to nationalism which is a symptom, not a disease.*

Mr Samuel[4] *Imperialism dies hard. We keep hearing the question—'Why should we deprive the Middle East of the benefits of British rule?' The fact that we are now making a new treaty with Persia is a tacit admission of exploitation. Withdrawal is not only morally right, but politically expedient.*

From the floor Mr Patrick Mayhew denied the virtue of withdrawing from Burma and India; Mr Gerald Kaufmann believed in altruism; Mr Norman Short suggested that fanaticism was part of the natural process of politics in Egypt. Mr Peter Tapsell[5] has a common-sensible determined manner. 'To do right is usually the right thing to do.'

Vote not given.

⊛⊛⊛

Monday 3 December 1951

House would abolish capital punishment.

Mr Magee *Capital punishment has been abolished in 36 countries. The evidence showed no increase in the murder rate. An execution in private is only slightly less barbarous than a hanging at Tyburn.*

Mr Brooke *To end capital punishment is to destroy an invitation to adventure. The judges like it. Murderers like it. Anyway there is no alternative.*

Mr Kaufman *Public revenge is as immoral as private revenge.*

Mr Short *To take life in defence of the community is as justifiable as self-defence in war. As a deterrent, it has a noticeable effect on armed gangs.*

Mr Tapsell *The death penalty is so morbid that it provokes as much as it deters. The judges are against abolition and events have generally proved them wrong.*

Mr George Steiner[6] *I would like to see death given back a certain solemnity which could best be provided by a public execution. Many of the greatest speeches have been made from scaffolds.*

From the floor, Mr Guy Lorimer *The death penalty is drastic only if one regards death as the end of everything. I do not. Judges do not condemn to death. They only fix the date.*

No vote given.

—∞∞∞—

24 January 1952

House is confident of the ability of Mr Churchill's administration to meet the country's domestic needs.

Mr St John Stevas[7] *The first need is to save the Pound and the government is following the only course which could save us from financial ruin.* (He) lacked variety of tone and tempo. Without them the Debating Hall can make even fluency a handicap.

Mr Hutber *I do sympathise with the disappointment of his high hopes. Mr Butler is just a kind of non-vegetarian Stafford Cripps, but one with unique capacity for combining inflation with a slump.*

Mr Shuman *Charges of inconsistency miss the point that we must distinguish inconsistency from a vigorous independence of mind. Neglect, as the government does not, the supreme need to meet the danger of inflation and the balance of payments crisis. Neglect these and all talk of preserving the Welfare State is futile.*

Mr Kerensky[8] *What actually has the government done? Perhaps they have adopted Labour policy, something which turns their election promises into wilful deceit. I was taken in by their assurance that they had not seen the books. If they hadn't, that was criminal negligence. If they follow a policy of deflation they will bring with it the risk of serious unemployment. The right policy would involve a vigorous drive against monopoly and state driven competition with inefficient wholesalers and retailers.*

Lord Swinton (Visitor)[9] *Mr Attlee says we are creating a scare. No, we are talking common honesty. Everything depends now upon our all being in this together and the Commonwealth understanding.*

When Mr Attlee stepped briskly to the despatch box, he was greeted with one of the longest and loudest ovations the union has given for many years. *This galaxy of co-ordinators whom the Tories have created, is no more than a cloak by which they seek to conceal their distaste for the Welfare State. You cannot have confidence in a government which, in spite of all this 'Me-tooism,' has the same philosophy it had before the War.* It was easy to see, though he lacks the qualities of voice and gesture that make an orator, how he has acquired the reputation of one of the most effective speakers in parliamentary debate.

---

31 January 1952

House deplores the social and political influence of the Vatican in the modern world.

Mr Crawford *The Roman Catholic Church stands at variance with democracy because it believes that it alone has the right to be right. Witness the blocking by the Church of the proposed health service in the Republic of Ireland.*[10]

Mr George Carman (Balliol) *How can you say that the Church encourages illiberality, corruption and social backwardness when 400 million people cling to that faith? The Church is maligned for the evils of the Franco regime, but those evils are equally characteristic of the republic! The Church in Europe is vigorously opposing Communism without leaping into the arms of American Imperialism. And it is one of the few institutions genuinely working toward racial equality.*

Mr Barnett *The ambiguity of the language in Papal pronouncements can be used to justify the co-existence of the poverty of the Italian peasant with the rich splendour of the Vatican. Absolution was denied to Communists and Socialists during the Italian General election of 1948, but Hitler was never excommunicated. The Vatican believes that education is not good for the poor.*

Mr Neely *It is no good for supporters of the motion to go round the garbage cans to find filth to throw at the Vatican.*

Mr Simon Carey (Ch.Ch.) *Consider the Syllabus of Errors.*[11] *Consider the doctrine of Papal Infallibility. There is nothing in this motion to prevent Roman Catholics from voting for it.*

Father Mark Brocklehurst O.P. *There are some things to be regretted, but the Vatican tends to look at things in a round way as the international unit which it is, many of the things it says are liable to offend someone. We are blamed for intervening on social and political affairs. But they are the most important concerns of the world. How should we not have a view?*

Motion lost 155: 227.

———— ∞ ————

21 February 1952

House believes that Communist China should be admitted to the United Nations.

Mr Mayhew[12] *There is one central question: 'Will the peace be better kept with China in or out of the United Nations? It will be said that in Korea, she was an aggressor and should not be rewarded. The evidence that she went in with aggressive intentions is not conclusive. The first principle of the UN is that no nation should be excluded on the grounds of un-American activities. Look at the results of not recognising Russia after 1917. American policy makes the mistake of assuming that there can be such a thing as 'The right war at the right time, at the right place.'*

Sir Andrew Cunninghame *The arguments in favour will be that admission will provide opportunity for discussion, that it will help the West gain the friendship of Asia and that the chance of preserving peace will be improved. All three are unfounded or fallacious. What advantage lies in offering opportunities for discussion when China is not willing to discuss. She has proved that by rejecting Mr Nehru's overtures.*

Mr Iyer *Formosa, not China, not being one of the great powers of the UN, is something which no argument can persuade me to believe. If you keep China out of the UN, then the UN doesn't represent Asia. A military assault on China simply won't succeed. The Communists have done more for the Chinese people than Chiang Kai Shek has ever done. This is likely to remain the effective government of China.*

Mr Rodney Elton (New College) *People talk about gaining credit with China by admitting her. Well, you can gain credit with a burglar by opening your safe. Admit China and you tell the people of Malaya and Indonesia that they can go Communist too.*

Mr Stewart *The true criterion for admission to the UN is whether the government truly represents the people. The Communists satisfy the test; Chiang Kai Shek doesn't. We must avoid letting the UN become an American weapon or drifting into a fixed state of mind. The opposers here are prepared to make no concessions.*

Mr Ben Crane (University of Iowa) *My opposition to the motion doesn't stem from dislike of the regime, but from the necessity of preventing another Korea. China's intervention there was offensive, not defensive, and showed that she would not be a good member of the UN.*

Mr Magee[13] *The American White Paper of 1949 set out the lines of an option it described as disastrous. Current American policy follows them. Look at the illogic of simultaneously proclaiming Formosa[14] to be the best representative of China and, at the same time, saying that Formosa is not part of China.*

Mr Joe Barse (North-Western University) *We must contain Communism, but not suppress it where it exists. The UN in reality is now a non-Communist league. Moral and legal arguments are irrelevant. So are comparisons with Tito. Admitting China prevents us from negotiating from strength. And it would be an invitation to Asia to go ahead and become Communist.*

Motion carried 274: 131.

---

3 March 1952

House regrets the influence, attitude and practices of the British Trade Unions.

Mr Loriman *I speak as a Conservative, but Central Office refused to send me material to support such a motion.[15] However the Unions are the prop of one political party. They are no longer the protectors of the weak, but the oppressors of the individual, and advocates of the closed shop.*

Mr David Gorsky (Trinity) *The Unions are entitled to support the Labour Party as they founded it. Having trade union MPs, has the good effect of restraining Mr Bevan.[16] Let us not condemn the Unions because they contain some Communists.*

Mr M. P. Elliott (Keble) has self-assurance and a good voice but the Central office line. *The trouble with the unions is that they demand immediate perfection in working conditions.*

Mr David Steel (Wadham)[17] *True the unions are large, but the proportion of active members is small. But the same is true about elections to Municipal Councils. They were involved in politics long before the founding of the Labour Party and their present political activities are admirably responsible. As a medium for ventilation of grievances, they form a bulwark of the constitution.*

Mr Maxwell-Hyslop *Their role should be economic only, not political. They are abusing the potential they have for good.*

Motion carried 86:80.

Mr Hutber moved a rider adding the words 'and the brewers and the F.B.I,' carried 28:15 amid scenes of spontaneous enthusiasm accompanied by the singing of 'The Red Flag'.

---

8 May 1952

In no circumstances would the House welcome any form of commercial broadcasting in this country.

Mr Stewart *The Conservatives have made a god of competition. Competition will not extend variety, but will contract it. The BBC is now a national institution and part of the British heritage which should remain intact.*

Mr Loriman *The BBC is self-satisfied, stuck in the groove, and has made little progress technically or in new ideas for programmes. I am not advocating free enterprise, but a certain amount of commercial broadcasting controlled by an unbiased authority and ultimately responsible to parliament.*

Mr Tapsell *The present system is opposed by selfish interests—a curious collection of cranks and capitalists. In the absence of fresh wave lengths, a new system can only come at the expense of existing programmes.*

Mr Thomas Ponsonby[18] His speech was a cataract of explosive mutterings about evil campaigns, political exploitation and 'the thin end of the wedge.'

Mr Maxwell-Hyslop *The BBC is notorious for its payment of small fees. Colour television and other technical innovations are now feasible improvements which were kept from the public because of financial difficulties.*

Mr David Worthy (Balliol) *The social purpose of broadcasting will be destroyed by the commercial principle.*

Mr David Lutyens *Great artists have always been inspired by the patronage of inspired individuals. The Third Programme is too intellectual and alienates the masses. When the many set the standard, as in the age of Shakespeare, then a new and vivid art form will arise from what is now a comatose culture.*

Motion carried 183:128.

⧉

12 June 1952

House would deplore any further co-operation of HMG with the Franco regime.

Mr Allen Deyermond (Pembroke) *The regime is rotten and disgusting and there is too much co-operation in trade and in de facto recognition. It is impossible to contemplate such steps as admission to NATO, the Council of Europe or the UN.*

Mr E. D. D. Money (Oriel) *I stand on two points: expediency—the strategic importance of the Iberian peninsula and morality—Christianity against Communism. Franco, like the Germans, should pay part of the cost of defence. How is it that the West supports Yugoslavia and not Franco?*

Mr Michael Elliott (Keble) *A liberal government is impossible in Spain while outside opposition strengthens Franco's hold on the people. The picture has been painted too black anyway. It is ridiculous to say that a country should not be recognised because of our likes and dislikes. The people protesting are not consistent as they asked for recognition of China on grounds of expediency.*

Mr David Gorsky *Further co-operation will be a further drain on the resources of the West and would antagonise countries not yet committed in the Cold War. Even the strategic arguments are dubious as we may gain Spain and lose France.*

Mr David Lutyens *I have to say that I am changing my mind. Early hopes of a Christian and Catholic Society have been lost and many supporters of Franco have been turned away by the harsh treatment suffered by individuals. We must not deal with him as we must not deal with any undemocratic forces—for fear of being corrupted.*

Motion lost 110:116.

---

23 October 1952

House considers that in modern conditions, rules of war are obsolete and illogical

Mr Crawford *It is crying for the moon to expect agreed limitations of violence in modern war, when the prize is nothing less than survival. To survive is a nation's first duty; and to this end, I can see no essential difference between the use of bacteria and other weapons. I object to war as an absolute evil; if rules should be applied, it will be admitted as a legitimate alternative policy.*

Mr Tapsell *May it not be that the rules of law are too logical for an illogical age? It is the counsel of despair to advocate the genocide of total war. Today the hand that rocks the world rules the cradle—all the more reason to dispute the 20th Century Adam Smiths with their cry of* Laissez mourir.

Mr Colin Mackenzie *War is encouraged by those rules. The danger lies in the popular attitude 'The next war won't be so bad—we can take it.' Witness the hysterical relief at the Munich betrayal, replaced twelve months later by whole-hearted endorsement of war. Rules confuse the issue; it is rather like fighting fire with a flamethrower.*

Mr Steele *The value of rules is seen when troops are told they will be murdered if taken prisoner; resistance increases as it does when populations are subjected to indiscriminate air attack.*

Mr Carey *Rules of war are bound to be based on expediency; and it is therefore logical that they should be illogical. A belligerent country starved by blockade might have no alternative but to starve its prisoners; rules will always break down before expediency.*

Motion lost 163:187.

---

30 October 1952

House considers partition to be another injustice to Ireland.

Mr Geoffrey Samuel *The boundaries of Ulster are artificial. There were originally nine, not six, counties in Ulster. Three have been sacrificed to unity in England and disunity in Ireland.*

Mr Stewart *Ireland is no more one country than the sub-continent of India. I don't think the other side are calling for reunification with Pakistan. Ulster has always been ready to fight rather than join with the Catholic-dominated south.*

Mr Bloom *A temporary measure, partition, has been artificially maintained, creating a false economy. As a result, Ulster between the wars had a higher rate of unemployment than anywhere in the UK.*

Mr Maxwell-Hyslop *Since 67 per cent of Ulster has voted Unionist, the joining of the North could create only one thing, an uneconomic state. I regret the influence of the Church which has forced the resignation of Dr Noel Browne.*

Dr Sean McBride (Visitor)[19] *All in Ireland are of the same race and the religious differences are politically significant only as the result of secular exploitation. Nine Ulster Unionists can ensure a Conservative government in England.*

Colonel Montgomery Hyde (Magd.) MP—North Belfast[20] *Why, when England recognises the right of Eire to withdraw from the UK, should not the same recognition be given to Ulster to remain within it.*

Mr Ian Josephs (Pembroke) *No Irishman has ever desired partition and there can be no moral grounds for maintaining it.*

Mr Michael Heseltine (Pembroke)[21] *Mr MacBride speaks with feeling about the wartime defence of democracy. Yet Ireland didn't take part.*

Mr Brian Hutton (Balliol)[22] *Why have the Catholics of Ulster not only remained there, but actually increased in number if conditions are so bad? They had only 70 miles to go south.*

Mr Critchley (Pembroke) *There are two Irelands; and in the South, the standard of living is lower than in Western Europe.*

Mr Bruce Barton (Jesus) *Ireland to the UK is as the negroes are to the United States—both give the lie to those who speak of democratic government.*

Mr W. D. Rutter (Ch.Ch.) *Partition was imposed to prevent a civil war and the same reasons hold good today.*

Motion lost 245:284.

6 November 1952

House regrets the exclusion of Women.*

Mr Money *Women are everywhere advancing on what had been a male preserve...*

Mr John Collins (Queen's) *I believe in the principle 'One man, one vote. One married and two votes.'*

Motion lost 288:185.

—⊗⊗⊗—

13 November 1952

House believes time is now ripe for a federation of Central Africa.

Mr Neeley *All the territories involved in this proposal need resources, especially the resources of the great Zambesi which, at present, is only a boundary. The answer to their economic difficulties lies in Federation, which alone will attract sufficient capital.*

Mr Barnett *To the Conservatives it is now respectable to grant self-government; so far have they moved since Gold Coast days,[23] that they cannot be restrained. Sir Godfrey Huggins[24] has described the 200,000 whites, who will rule five million blacks, as a 'benevolent aristocracy'. I suspect their motives, but if they are honest, there is no reason to hurry and if not honest, every reason for delay.*

---

* Regretting for neither the first time nor the last.

536

Mr Elliott *In the next 25 years the population will double and the resulting conditions of the people will be worse than ever before. Clearly the Africans do not understand the proposal. Their language made no distinction between amalgamation and federation. And their newspapers made the Daily Worker look like a non-political publication.*

Mr Gorsky *No reasons had been given why federation was necessary to the setting-up of a customs union. The one works well without the other in East Africa.*

Mr Short *Without the confidence which federation brings, it won't be possible to attract capital so the individual territories will inevitably turn toward South Africa. The whites are not fools; to put it at its lowest, they know that a policy of repression can only drive them from this country.*

Mr James Griffiths[25] *There is in the draft no sufficient protection of the interests of the Africans themselves; HMG is surrendering responsibilities for the protectorates and there is no general agreement in Africa to Federation. It is true that I argued with African leaders and tried to get them to agree, but they were afraid. My advice to the government is 'Take time'.*

Motion lost 207:236.

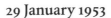

29 January 1953

House believes the Korean situation has been mismanaged.

Mr Gorsky *The military part of the team has been dislocated from the political direction of this war. Syngman Rhee[26] has been an obstacle. On top of which, it was necessary to dismiss an American general, Douglas MacArthur, because he got above himself and above the US Government's purposes.*

Mr Bloom *The Indian peace proposals were supported 53:5 at the UN, but were roundly condemned by Russia and China. They, by refusing a peaceful settlement, become responsible for the war continuing.*

Mr Julian Critchley[27] *We are, in Korea, still stuck in the position we occupied two years ago. MacArthur's refusal to stop at either the parallel or the waist,[28] has cost the UN 200,000 casualties—and for what? All we have achieved in two years of war is the corruption of our cause; we went into Korea to defend liberty and we are now defending Syngman Rhee.*

Mr Steel *What are the alternatives? It is laughable to talk of stopping at a parallel which cannot be defended. It is useless to complain about prolongation of truce negotiations, for the Chinese obviously don't want a truce.* Mr Steel is one of the few speakers in the House who can make orthodoxy sound interesting.

Mr Fred Floyd St Joseph's Philadelphia. *We went into South Korea to drive the Northern invaders back behind their own frontier. We have achieved that and so should withdraw our troops. Never before has there been a war without a political objective. MacArthur didn't know where to stop because he had been fighting without a specific objective.*

Motion carried 168:100.

---

12 February 1953

House believes that cuts in the social services should play no part in any solution to our economic problems.

Mr Tapsell *Those services are necessary and because they are, they should be preserved. Conservatives are always a generation behind in their political beliefs. Social services might now seem a dangerous and new-fangled luxury. In thirty years they will be seen as part of the national heritage.*

Mr Crawford *The Social Services stand third in order of the three great tasks before us. Solvency, achieved and preserved, is first, national defence second. The Social Services come last.*

Mr Stewart *No other political service is worth the sacrifice of this. Conservatives speak about them as of a luxury. Comedians made jokes about free teeth and spectacles. Getting such things to people who cannot afford them is more important than all the income tax concessions in the world.*

Mr Heseltine *There was a resolution at Morecambe Labour Conference to promise return to the former level of food subsidies; and the NEC asked for it to be withdrawn as committing a future Labour Government in unforeseeable circumstances. This was an admission that cuts in the Social Services might be necessary in the future.* Mr Heseltine should guard against artificial mannerisms of voice and calculated flashes of self-conscious histrionics; this is only worth saying because he has the makings of a first class speaker, and it would be a great loss to himself and the Union if it were to develop in the wrong direction.

Mrs Barbara Castle MP (St Hugh's)[29] spoke a very pretty fifth.[30] *Our problems are those of trade and productivity, not government expenditure. Anyway the Welfare State redistributes wealth, it doesn't destroy it.*

Mr Angus Maude MP (Visitor) *I don't call for a reduction in the aggregate welfare budget, rather a more carefully planned use of those resources which would mean cuts in some of them. All we are doing is to put a ceiling on welfare expenditure.* He gave an account of the loving care with which the Welfare State had been built up by Conservative hands and lamented the damage done to it by Labour governments between 1945 and 1951.

Motion lost 121: 152.

5 March 1953

House believes the time is now ripe for Parliamentary Reform.

Mr Jonathan Boswell (New College) *All malcontents must support this, though they may well contradict each other: the man content with the Commons, but wanting reform of the Lords; the man favouring Proportional Representation, but ardent in defence of the Lords. Opponents must show that not a single reform is needed in either chamber.*

Mr Pattinson (Trinity) *Proportional Representation is absurd; and increasing their lordships' unelected power is reactionary, but decreasing it means single chamber government I like the idea floated by Lord Simon,[31] of life peerages, but this is only an extension of what we already do about Lords legal and spiritual.*

Mr Anthony Bartlett (Balliol) *Forms and procedures today haven't changed over the last hundred years; and frankly, they can't cope with modern business. Drafting is sloppy, bills are often constructed without sufficient knowledge. I watched the passage of a Transport bill through the Commons; and it was nothing more than a tired farce. We should set up a much expanded committee system and devolve the local affairs of Scotland and Wales to those countries.*

Mr Raymond Robinson (St John's) *We can dismiss systems other than our own as being at best foreign and, at worst, barbarous. Look at Proportional Representation. France has it and France suffers enormous political troubles because of it.*

Mr Anthony Howard (Ch.Ch.)[32] *Frankly, I am not interested in either PR or Lords reform. We should though consider the University Vote[33] which is simply a business vote and as such, under the counter and distinctly undesirable.*

Motion carried 69:63.

30 April 1953

House would welcome the establishment of a Western European Union in which Britain played her full part.

Mr Bloom *The US has shown how a union can produce prosperity and power; and the British Commonwealth stand to gain a great deal from a similar union in Europe.*

Mr Kaufman *The Union idea is bad because it is an artificial and Utopian idea. The world needs more effective remedies than this.*

Mr Tapsell *Let us go for the full thing, a federal, supra-national affair. It would be the only thing able both to save us in a slump and keep Germany in check.*

Mr Michael Heseltine *I am rather against this, partly because of the difficulties which anything so complex would create over Defence. And we are seeing a change of attitude in the Russian government which we wouldn't want to snub.*

Sir Andrew Cunninghame *The more we have to co-operate with Western Europe, the nearer we move politically. Our proper task is to integrate ourselves in it within NATO. Meanwhile other obligations to the US and the Commonwealth are compatible.*

Mr Denis Healey MBE (Balliol)[34] *I have no objection to close co-operation with Western Europe, but I do have one against the sort of Union which can only work if dominated by political federation. That will simply allow Germany to dominate her neighbours. Any Commonwealth–European bloc will give colonialism an unwelcome fillip and America a good excuse for reverting to isolationism.*

Mr Robert Boothby MP (Magd.) *The model for any union should be the Commonwealth which has the supreme merit that it works in a crisis. The tragedy is that after the war, we let slip the chance offered by our huge prestige to create another Commonwealth in Europe.*

Vote not given.

∞∞

4 June 1953

House believes the British Commonwealth is falling.

Mr Heseltine *The Commonwealth is the only possible third force in the world; yet its actions are not those of a co-ordinated unit. We must come to grips with the problem of South Africa. Equally, we should prevent anomalies like the Argentine meat and the Cuban sugar deals. Finally we, and not the United States, must produce whatever capital is needed. We must spend less on rearmament and more on development or we will be out-bidden by the Communists.*

Sir Andrew Cunninghame *I don't want to say that the Commonwealth is perfect. However the obvious imperfections—the Irish business or the situation in South Africa, are the result of a liking for independent action and devolution. It is only by fostering nationalism, however dangerous, that we can forestall Communism. In fact, the only worthwhile multi-racial unit in today's world.*

Mr Sydney Silverman MP (Visitor) [35] *All this nationalistic talk puts me in mind of G. K. Chesterton's variant of 'My Country, right or wrong'—'My mother, drunk or sober.' The Commonwealth falls short of its ideals in three ways. There is no equality of citizenship; no economic self-sufficiency and no seizing the opportunity to guide and befriend the new revolutionary movements around the world.*

Rt. Hon Leopold Amery C.H. (Visitor) [36] *It is European economic development which is making it possible to improve the standards of living and education for African peoples. The Commonwealth system is the only answer to the problems of a world which compared with fifty years before, is too small to allow us the luxury of non-co-operation with our neighbours.*

Motion, 'in a House decimated by Schools' (Oxford for final exams), lost 77:121.

———— ∞∞∞ ————

11 June 1953

House would welcome legislation to curb the license of the press.

Mr Jeremy Isaacs (Merton)[37] *The press is more sensitive to criticism than any other body. Yet it is guilty of worse crimes than mere distortion—wholesale allegations, never confirmed or withdrawn, and interference with people's private affairs. There should be a Press Council with real disciplinary powers.*

Mr Martin Morton (New College) *A Press Council is being set up.[38] Anyway the license of the press is not such a tragic thing as it is made out to be. The newspapers themselves are damaged by mis-reporting. Trying to limit their freedom will create greater evils.*

Mr Howard Apin (Ch.Ch.) *Any such Press Council will be made up of Owners and Editors.*

Mr Richard Hoskin (Ch.Ch.) *We can never be sure that we are doing right when we stifle any sort of freedom at all. In the case of the Press, such action will actually be more dangerous because less justified.*

Mr Peter Stein (Balliol) *I doubt whether the press has a divine right to be forgiven anything it might choose to print. Its standing derives from a supposed ability to form intelligent public opinion. And democracy, itself, depends upon that.*

Mr Robert Day (Trinity) *We should accept the basic tenet of freedom of the press. Legislation, even if necessary, would be impossible to introduce or administer and would produce something worse, propaganda.*

Motion carried 81:66.

———— ∞∞∞ ————

12 November 1953

House holds that Party government today is detrimental to the liberties of the subject and the wellbeing of the Country.

Mr John King-Farlow (Ch.Ch.) *Our aim should not be a classless society, but a fair one. Party government creates tensions between the Haves and the Have-nots, in which social prejudice defeats material and moral aims. Portmanteau party manifestoes mean frustration rather than stimulation of the individual.*

Mr David Worthy (Balliol) *The motion is either anarchist or totalitarian. Parties are no more than organised bodies of opinion in other words, the basis of the Constitution and a guarantee of stable government. Party government is what it has always been, the guarantee of parliamentary government.*

Mr Malcolm Weisman (St Catherine's) *Parliament has become a fulltime job, with the MP losing his independent status. The executive has more power backed by a stern, unbending majority, excessively influenced by the TUC or the City of London, and no longer representing opinion, but concerned chiefly with attacks upon each other.*

Mr Robinson *The proposers make up a heterogeneous mass of political abnormalities. They think themselves unique, righteous and intellectually superior. Party government is useful, for the powers of party grow with the growth of population.*

Mr R. D. Kernohan (Balliol) *Parliament must be an Eternal Vigilance Society. For Government, stable government, functioning rather like a monarchy, is a fundamental threat to the dignity and purpose of parliament.*

Mr Bloom *Consider France which operates multi-party government in a multi-party parliament. The result is not encouraging. In Britain there is no demand for extra-parliamentary devices like the referendum, something which is actually a tribute to the system. Party government works, not perfectly, but well.*

Motion lost 113:146.

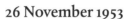

26 November 1953

House thinks the present generation in Britain lacks the moral courage and initiative to deal adequately with the problems which face it.

Mr Ian Josephs (Pembroke) *The record of this century has not been good and has left us with war, poverty and illiteracy problems which need solving and will only be coped with if financial generosity, education and a drastic revision of moral standards can save the Twentieth Century.*

Mr Desmond Watkins (Keble) *We are always told that religion is dying out and that the problems of the present are much greater than those of the past.*

Mr Roy Dickson *We need productivity and sales. But the British worker is lazy and in his present frame of mind, cannot hope to compete with those of America, Germany and Japan. But this is partly due to the lack of reward. We set up the NHS, did the Berlin airlift, fought the Korean War, courage and initiative enough, surely?*

Mr Robin Grieg (Ch.Ch.) *The older generation managed to understand the meaning of Communism, but had never met it with Christianity which is the only true safeguard.* On the whole this was a mainly ironical speech…

Mr Oscar Macrae-Gibson (St Catherine's) *Let me give examples of such virtues from the past and present: the border raids, say—or the conquest of Everest. But there is still a great need for national and personal initiatives to be correlated; and Scottish nationalism is a perfect example of this union.*

Motion lost 58:148.

18 February 1954

House believes that it is enough that we are English.

Mr Robert Day *We should accept our responsibilities as citizens of the leading nation of the Commonwealth; and firm in our tradition and heritage, should take the foremost place among the nations of Europe. This is the very reverse of mere isolationism and has nothing to do with selfish nationalism. We should not ignore nor be ashamed of our Englishry.*

Hon Edward Northcote (Trinity) [39] *I speak as a member of the middle class of the aristocracy. The English aristocrat goes though a sort of fall: Eton, Christ Church, the Season, and the House of Commons to the House of Lords, where one ceases to be a gentleman and becomes a nobleman. At last he retires to his club.*

Mr Weisman *In a world where other nations are discovering their nationality and taking their place, often a very important one, mere nationalism is neither enough nor really desirable. Patriotism and pride go hand in hand with intolerance.*

Mr Laurence French (New College) *The enemy is the self-styled, self-righteous Englishmen who believe in Force, God and Money or a combination off all three. The logical outcome of this proposal is the setting up of an UnEnglish Activities Committee.*

Mr Siegler (St Catherine's) *As an American, I have greatly enjoyed this debate. You might call it 'The British Lion coming out of his shell.'*

Motion carried 115:95.

4 March 1954

Western Europe can have no real influence in the modern world.

Mr Clovis Maksoud (St Catherine's) *Europe has committed itself to one of the power blocs; it is vulnerable to existentialist philosophies like Communism; it has joined in the dehumanisation of man. Unlike Asia, it showed no willingness to learn, no sign that out of its sufferings would grow, not despair but a capacity to love.*

Mr Bryan Ellis (St John's) *Crisis is the occupational disease of Western Europe, the depressed area between the Iron Curtain and the dollar gap—Spain, the buffer-state between the Pentagon and the Vatican. All we have to offer is parliamentary government, freedom of expression, uncorrupt administration and the Rule of Law.*

Mr Frank Wells (BNC)[40] *Europe is bankrupt of influence whether cultural, political or religious. It has become and will remain a gaming ground for the concepts of power it had healed to foster. It has become a walking shadow of itself. The real influence in the western world is America. Western Europe is nothing but a tourist attraction to the few and a gaming ground for the many.*

Mr Bill McCarthy (Ruskin)[41] *This is all irrelevant. The greatest thing Europe has to offer is ideas. The tragedy is that when other people get hold of these ideas, they tend to corrupt them into a dogma—Communism, capitalism or the American political system. Our greatest failure is in not managing to export our greatest quality, doubt. We must question all assumptions, not least counter trans-Atlantic evangelists who to popularise religion, are willing to vulgarise the Day of Judgment.*

Mr Cornelius O'Leary (St Catherine's and Nuffield)[42] *While European culture lasted, it could have nothing but influence, but about 400 years ago the real decline set in. There has been no smooth, unimpeded progress over the last 2,000 years, but we have survived in the past and will do so again.*

Motion lost 43:80.

———— ∞∞ ————

20 May 1954

House would prefer even a Communist regime to a Third World War.

Mr Deyermond *Communism is an evil system of misgovernment. I am ready to lose my life to prevent it. But to avoid a politically abhorrent political system, we have no right to inflict anarchy, disease and death on millions of people who have no part in our decision.*

Mr Maxwell-Hyslop *We cannot really make a decision or choose on what here is a hypothesis until such a decision is upon us.*

Mr Patrick Bourke (Wadham) *For mankind there will be no victory in a third world war. It would be a crime for us to sacrifice the accumulated inheritance of earlier civilisations. A new weapon should give new values and we should dare to live.*

Mr Patrick Finn (St Catherine's) *Peace without liberty is too great a price to pay for one's life. We must fight for the right to educate our children as we wish. If we should not give away the lives of others, we should be even less prepared to give away our own souls.*

Mr Christopher Hall (New College) *Life without liberty is a living death. If life is sacred, cowardice is a crime.*

From the floor Mr Ralph Samuel (Balliol)[43] put the Communist cause with fine irony.

Motion lost 92:94.

3 June 1954

This House refuses to be alarmed and despondent at the thought of 1983.

Mr Boswell *The intellectuals conspire to set a grim and gloomy stage. They foresee the smiling monolith, the test-tube baby and the electronic brain. Like all dogmatisers and soothsayers, they are wrong. It isn't for us to quail at an imaginary future, but to get on with the task of making it tolerable. Today we have greater choices than ever we had before.*

Mr Bruce Burton (Jesus) *I do not advocate Stoic fatalism nor, like Louis XV, say 'Let us amuse ourselves by making ourselves miserable.'*[44] *Everywhere Western civilisation seems to have left behind legacies of bitterness. In its supreme crisis hour, the World needs a moment of vision, a flash of self-discovery if it is to re-assert its moral power and survive. Without the honesty to be alarmed and the humility to be despondent at our present inadequacies, we cannot find a common source of hope for the future!*

Mr Roger Booth (Jesus) held the House by the sheer intensity and simplicity of his convictions which he quaveringly conveyed through well chosen words. *When the first whispers of panic have grown to shouts of despair, it is the part of prudence and common humanity to exercise the hope which lies not in the temperament which is founded in faith. Christianity alone can counter fatalism. We need to change from believing that religion is a good thing to finding a reserve of spiritual power overcoming fear, renewing courage, directing conscience, dedicating life. We must have the courage to put aside alarm and despondency and say 'The Lord is my light and my salvation.—of whom shall I be afraid.'*

Mr Heseltine *The greatest terror in the world today is totalitarianism. In its struggle for freedom, the West is in very great danger. Parliaments were increasingly dominated by the parliamentary machine. In America, the cult of Senator McCarthy has become the curse of democracy. Can anyone not be alarmed at what the future holds for South Africa? We need a new humility and new sanity born of a bitter experience that lies in the future.*

Mr Victor Gollancz[45] *To recognise the tragic quality of life is different from being made despondent by it. There will always be at least a few believers in spiritual freedom through whom deliverance will come. To doubt this is inconsistent, a faith in the power of the human spirit. To calculate in terms of consequences is not the way of the true Christian. The motion re-affirms an essential element in the heritage of western civilisation—the importance of freedom of choice.*

Mr Malcolm Muggeridge[46] *The motion has been transcendentalised out of existence. The greatest cause or alarm is the degeneration of the democracies under universal suffrage. A largely ignorant, greedy and short-sighted electorate is being continuously bribed by rival political machines, avid for power and supporting mostly indistinguishable policies. The old panacea of mass education has failed to produce a flock of Socratic sages. The English in their own inimitable way, are steadily turning into members of a servile society, without almost anyone noticing it. The outlook for the future fills me with a deep and increasing pessimism.*

Motion carried 211:126.

---

21 October 1954

House thinks censorship of the arts an unwarranted interference with personal liberty.

Mr Michael Brown (Wadham) *Time is the only censor for values, and standards change. In the integrity of Art, there is no place for external censorship and we should not be censors where there is no absolute standard.*

Mr Tom Bedham (St Edmund Hall) *I read Miss Lejeune's column. It is comforting of a Sunday when one can't go to the pictures, to read every Sunday that there were no pictures worth going to see.*

Mr Anthony Thwaite (Ch.Ch.)[47] *The Art of today was censored yesterday.*

Mr Fred Siegler *To imagine a form of Art is to imagine a form of life; and some forms of life are better undisplayed.*

Miss C. A. Lejeune (Visitor)[48] *Censorship goes back to the days when it was thought necessary to protect the government from attack. It was like that as recently as the publication of Bernard Shaw's Mrs Warren's Profession,[49] that his first attack on dramatic censorship appeared.*

The Reverend Keith de Berry[50] *The proposition is starry eyed. Not everyone has read the Kinsey report from a scientific point of view. The censor is a necessary evil used to protect man from his inherent evil. Two things: It is necessary to spread the moral code of Christianity; but, at the same time, to prevent moral degradation, it is essential to preserve the form of art censorship existing in this country.*

Vote not given.

———— ✦✦✦ ————

28 October 1954

House welcomes the decline of British imperialism.

Mr Anthony Howard *I suggest that we should be ashamed of our colonial record. We have no need of Captain Waterhouse[51] or the Bygadsby Tories who believe in the godhead of the Anglo-Saxon race. By trying to prop up the decaying structure of imperialism, we are playing into the hands of Mr Palme Dutt[52] and the extension of the Communist Party throughout the world.*

Mr George Macbeth (New College)[53] *It is impossible to prove logically that people have a right to self-government. The result of the debate must be determined by values, not by fact. Imperialism is not force condemned by definition; and attempts to unite the Commonwealth are offset by the blemishes on the British colonial record.*

Mr Edmund Ions (Merton)[54] *We should try to separate the new concept of a constitutional Commonwealth from the older economic concept of Empire.*

Mr Magee *Imperial successes in recent years far outweigh the failures. The Statute of Westminster has changed the nature of imperialism. Today colonial people are governed only until they can govern themselves. We must face our responsibilities, for it is only within the framework of the Empire that the people can advance outside the Communist world.*

Mr Julian Amery (Balliol)[55] *There is an irony today in our having our hearts wrung over British imperialism by an agent of the greatest imperial power in the world. The choice today is not between imperialism and no imperialism, but one of 'Which imperialism is to triumph?' Wherever Britain ignores her responsibility and leaves her possessions, then war and bloodshed follow. The conjunction of West Europe with the Commonwealth is emerging into a new constellation of force and power based on voluntary co-operation.*

Motion lost 281:381.

———— ✕✕✕ ————

11 November 1954

House would welcome changes in the privileges and practices of the British Trade Unions.

Mr King-Farlow *The unions must be subjected to continuous criticism and improvement, especially so when every dispute reduced our competitiveness abroad. The TGWU is the most prominent monopoly since Noah's Ark, while Union affiliation of the Labour Party is a millstone round the neck of a demo-cratically elected Labour Government.*

Mr James Clark (Ruskin) *We are not debating refinements of the Trade unions. It is an attack on the very roots of unionism itself. This motion concerns wages, hours, living standards as freedom for the working man depends on the power of the unions.*

Lady Violet Bonham Carter (Visitor) [56] *The Liberal Party laid the foundations of the Union movement and it is a voluntary association to advance freedom. But the power is mis-used, and the victimisation cases negate the old standards. The neces-sary reforms are the prevention of unofficial strikes, election of shop-stewards by secret ballot, the banning of restrictive practices limiting production and the replace-ment of contracting-out by contracting-in.*

Mr Arthur Horner (Visitor) [57] *This country depends upon coal; and at present, the relationship of employer and worker is that of buyer and seller. The Depression of the inter-war years was brought about by the ravages of uninhibited demand and supply. The petty illustrations given by Lady Violet are as nothing compared to the good achieved by the unions. The social consciences of the unions can be relied upon to prevent excesses.*

Motion carried 338:200.

———⊗⊗⊗———

27 January 1955

The world would be a better place without the political power and influence of the Roman Catholic Church.

Mr Robert Kenohan (Balliol) *It is odd, given Roman Catholic claims to be better armed by their faith against Communism, that Catholic Italy has the largest voluntary Communist Party membership in the World. If we count liberty a good, we must deplore the power and influence of the Roman Catholic Church.*

Mr Northcote[58] *Before the Reformation, caused by a dissolute monarch's desire for a divorce, the ordinary people of England, though poor and ignorant, were happy and not suppressed. After it, when the monasteries ceased to be a stabilising factor in the economy, the country went into a decline in which social evils prevailed as Protestantism rose, and were only now being alleviated as Protestantism fell. Members wouldn't understand this because of their Anglican bias.*

Mr Siegler *There is plenty of evidence about the way the Catholic Church works, its unscrupulous way in the schools and the unions. What is the price we pay to have the Vatican as our ally? And remember that the enemies of our enemies are not necessarily our friends.*

Mr O'Leary *If Catholics know they are right, they are entitled to take stern measures to propagate and defend what they feel to be the truth. The end justifies the means, but the means would always be subject to the most searching of all scrutinies, that of the individual Catholic conscience.*

Dr Marie Stopes[59] *Let me tell you how the Catholic Church has treated me. Three times they attempted arson on my clinics. They kept our advertisements out of the Times. In Britain, we have to pay for their schools, yet figures show that the number of Roman Catholics in our prisons are disproportionately high. That Church has sought, from the Inquisition to this day, to destroy other churches. The methods it used in the past, it uses today when it gets the chance. It would be better for the free soul of man for the Catholic Church not to exist.*

Father Joseph Christie SJ *No government can afford to be absolutely tolerant. The Catholic record is no worse than most; and no Christian country, with the exception of South Africa, is preparing to persecute anyone. I do assure Dr Stopes that I will use my personal influence to see that there is no more arson.*

Motion carried 339:313.

---

17 February 1955

This House looks forward to a Republican Britain. Some wore red ties others clutched 'Almanachs de Gotha', but that was all.

Mr Robert Cook (Exeter) *The monarchy is being vulgarised beyond belief. True we have not yet gone to the Caliguline depths of knighting a Derby winner, but the day cannot be far off. The keel of a lavish royal yacht was laid on the day when President Eisenhower had scrapped his as an unnecessary extravagance. Modern genetics have made it plain that heredity is the worst means of transmitting power and privilege. We should cut the vulgar expenditure which the monarchy entails and introduce new equity and dignity into our national institutions.*

Mr Keith Thompson (New College) *The proposers will not sleep easily at nights until the last crowned head rolls. Better to suppress the popular press for vulgarising the monarchy than having the monarchy vulgarised. We have evolved the ideal compromise, one more than justified by the royal example in the last war.*

Mr Alec Grant *The Queen's birthday comes but twice a year. The Crown is supposed to be above class distinction. Yet nobody below the rank of Bishop or Baron came to the Coronation service excepting Mr Richard Dimbleby and the Moderator of the Church of Scotland. The monarchy contains a daily reproach to our democratic faith and a standing insult to the dignity of man.*

Mr Denis Orde (St Catherine's) *Blood is thicker than water and the monarchy at least keeps the weather out.*

Mr Bill McCarthy is perhaps the best debater in the Society. *Monarchy fosters the illusion that birth rather than brains is a criterion of ability. It exploits the worst traits of the English Character—snobbery, hypocrisy and love of show. I look forward to the day when the people of this country have enough colour in their own lives. They would then be their own nobility.*

Mr Jeremy Lever (University) *If we had a president, he would be a successful soldier or an unsuccessful politician. To chose him by election would cost more than the Civil List.*

Motion lost 109:193.

---

3 March 1955

House believes that Sir Winston Churchill must go.

Mr David Galloway (Lincoln) *I offer this as a non-party motion commanding the support of almost all politicians. One looks at his heir, Sir Anthony Eden, yesterday's man of tomorrow, and senses a feeling in parliament of 'Be off or I'll kick you upstairs.' Sir Winston has latterly been so wrong so often. In 1945 he compared Socialism with Fascism. He was wrong about India; he was wrong in entering the arms race instead of negotiating. As has been said 'He has outlived his colleagues, his policies and his powers.'*

Mr Peter Stott (St John's) *Sir Winston's influence is as great as ever. His experience of government is unrivalled, as is his dedication to the cause of World peace.*

Mr Brian Walden (Queen's)[60] *Mr Churchill has moved between parties from the Liberals to the Conservatives—from the unmanageable to the untouchable. A man of over eighty does not have the physical stamina to rule and this is not the man anyway.* Mr Walden, whose style is so reminiscent of Mr Michael Foot, gave nothing away, conceded no favourable point to the man or the government. His speech became a blood sport, in which he, too faithfully, followed the newshounds of the leftwing press. It was hard to tell if it was intolerance or indoctrination.

Mr George Gregg (Merton) *Anthony Eden is politically, a young man—howls of laughter. The proposition has not proved that Churchill is incompetent, it just said so. His being an old man doesn't matter. He is a friend of the Anglo-American alliance and an enemy of Bolshevism. It needs two sides to negotiate successfully and the Russians show no signs of weakening.*

Mr James Dickens[61] *I am not attacking the man. I am concerned with the government and the class he represents. Churchill is a great man—the enemy of social progress and the focal point of reaction. Men like Attlee, Morrison, Gaitskell and Churchill are basically of the same political ilk. Look at his 'Get Tough' stand. We spent seven billion in four years and stand secure in the knowledge that we will be wiped out in thirty hours.*

Mr John Heyman (St Edmund Hall)[62] *I am a socialist, but I can see the merits of Winston Churchill. He saw as early as anyone, the implications of the hydrogen bomb. We need the American alliance; and to it Churchill brings experience and versatility.*

Motion defeated 97:100.

28 April 1955

House believes that in the absence of any other constructive policy for South Africa, House approves of Apartheid.

Mr Northcote *I hold no brief for what is being done in South Africa, but in the abstract, Apartheid is a rare and sensible policy. It is still possible for a black bishop to preside above white clergy. Native art has its place and is respected.*

Mr Kernohan *People in Oxford really do talk too much about subjects of which they know nothing. It is all very well to call South Africa 'a living hell,' but Africans are pouring into it from all points of the continent. We must be very vigilant to see that we do not drive South Africa from the Commonwealth. But of course, any racial policy must consist of levelling up rather than down.*

Mr Walden delivering himself straight at the South African Director of Information, was vitriolic. *South Africa is a police state in which the methods of fascism are employed.* This is a point which has not been made in the House for three years.

Mr A. W. Steward S.A. (Visitor—Director of Information) *there is no identifiable alternative to Apartheid. Government is the art of the possible and parliamentary government just isn't possible with the Bantu. The Government plans for harmony, there are affairs crucial to the White Man in which African interference will never be permitted. History—I repeat history—has shown this. Apartheid is the only answer. You may deplore this, but we cannot alter it.*

Mr Peter Abrahams (Visitor—South African journalist and novelist) *There is tyranny in South Africa. I know all about it. I grew up under it. One sixth of male Africans in the Union are currently prisoners. If Mr Steward wants an alternative, here it is. Let there be an educational qualification for the franchise, one which would take out a lot of Europeans and bring in a number of Africans.*

Motion lost 61: 322.

———— ✇ ————

19 May 1955

House regrets the approval given to the Billy Graham crusade.

Mr Thompson *The churches have decided, albeit a little hesitantly, that God believes in Billy Graham—at any rate as a working hypothesis. It is now being suggested that such support should be withdrawn. If one thing is clear, it is what the churches should not do, that is to leave people high and dry at the peak of an emotional experience. Do they want churches to pass all Graham converts by on the other side? To do that they must prove that Graham is a totally false prophet, that his theology is antagonistic to all the other churches.*

Mr A. W. Cook *I went to Wembley and was wholly converted—to a conviction that the message Graham had brought was harmful to many of those who accepted it, at variance with the teaching of the churches and repugnant to the reasoning facilities of all reasonable men. Graham is a fundamentalist. He believes that the first chapter of Genesis is an exact account of what happened in the beginning. Is there a single reputable Christian theologian in the country who believes this? Why then did they all stand aside and allow multitudes of people, bewildered, seething with the consciousness of guilt, palpitating with fear of Hell, to be brow-beaten into believing what is not true. I ask the Bishop of Barking to tell me whether, if he were killed tonight he would go to Hell.*

The Bishop intervening *Unless I repented, I would, in the punishment of hell, be humbled into dross.*

Mr Trevor Lloyd *Billy Graham's theology is out of date. His preaching lacks a social message; we may not like his methods. But he succeeds and the churches do not. To the man who brought back so many prodigal sons, the churches are not to be allowed to show so intangible a thing as approval.*

Dr George Macleod of the Iona Community *I have no quarrel with Mr Graham personally. However every night at Wembley stadium, Graham claimed that he had exclusive knowledge of when the Father called to individual Christians. And what about his claim that once you made your decision, you were safe for life?—That is not what the Bible says! Evidently the Bible was dictated to a series of hypnotised secretaries. It is this kind of rubbish which raises again the profitless conflict of which we are all weary, between religion and science. People like William Temple, Father Grosser and Trevor Huddlestone have dedicated their lives to destroying the vicious myth that politics and religion are separate.*

Motion carried 232:231.

18

Invading Countries is Wrong

13 October 1955–8 November 1956

No confidence already/Pestilent equality/Disestablish the C of E/National service futility/Russia doesn't change/too many humanities/Emotion before reason/Still no confidence/Morality above religion/British invasion of the Suez canal zone.

This period marked the learning of a lesson, the core of which had been apparent for some time to cynics, realists, and the politically alert. Britain having fought two world wars and set up her imperial status as a cosmic prefectoral duty, had simply as a nation, dwindled. Her economy was vulnerable to market hostility or want of confidence. The Robot proposals of 1952 had been a good, forward-looking scheme, damned and stopped because it would have exposed the pound to market judgement. Post-imperial pride, the shabby-genteel aspect of the post war decade required endless skimpings and evasions to sustain the delusive four dollar rate. Today we float in acknowledgement of the market's sovereignty.

What came without *Robot* was pressure on the pound anyway, for which Butler was blamed and shifted to the Home Office. The move was sharp enough to constitute temporary crisis. The intellectually overbold, too far-sighted Butler had had to make way at the Treasury for Macmillan. The concern would be to sustain old, tried and untrustworthy protection of the pound and its extended family, the sterling area, both subject to recurring assault and to be held off by recurring purchase of our own currency.

What went for economics, would go for international standing. We still had an empire, but the strutting language about the Transvaal of 1896, present in this record, was underwritten by nothing strong enough to validate it. The overseas property portfolio called Empire still underwrote British assumptions, but we would stand by uneasily, watching all the stages by which Robert Schuman's public memorandum, which we had spurned down the decade, turned it into the thing to get into, though on worse, more federal terms than could have been had earlier. After 1958, *Mon Général*—President Charles de Gaulle, patronized long since when down—would stand at the door of this once spurned EEC thing which we now required, remarking our unEuropeanness and exercising his veto.

We had assets of course, some of them toxic. To reprise a little, the bases in Cyprus chiefly meant that we had a problem. The call of the Greek majority for *Enosis*, union with mainland Greece, simply could not be granted. The base and the status of the handsome gratuity Disraeli had organized for us eighty years before, at the Treaty of Berlin, gave us a military/naval presence in the Mediterranean, and we were into presences, evidence of supposed reach and an unquantified importance mattering emotionally more and more. Cyprus, island or not, was the Balkans, and our role there was just a little reminiscent of Austria's in Bosnia-Herzegovina; something underlined by a remnant of Ottoman ownership with 20 or so per cent of the population being Turks living in the north and the pan-handle of the island. Its real merit was utilitarian. For a major power which might need to demonstrate authority given any conflict on the north coast of Africa, it suited very well.

However what conflict would that be? Churchill's word for the total good sense of abandoning the Indian Empire had been 'scuttle'. We had never actually owned Egypt imperially, just enjoyed commercial control of it and employed Egyptian servants, the sort of non-imperial state in which a British ambassador could and did drive through the closed gates of the Royal Palace. All had been in the good cause of wartime, all of it humiliating to those Egyptians who, in 1952, without asking our ambassador, would, a decade later, remove the King and put themselves, a regime of colonels, ordinary Egyptian nobodies, risen through the army, in his place.

The British government, ironically still that of Winston Churchill, born in 1874, could not and did not do anything about it. This had been real power but never proclaimed as *de jure*; and besides, the colonels were in no way Commie bastards. The United States, oddly censorious of *British* imperialism, would never have permitted anything like that. What was important internationally was the Suez Canal, built by de Lesseps in the 1870s to make north-west/south-east trade quicker and easier. It was a sort of public company owned by a foreign government. Any dispute over it might, over an age, have been won by Britain through international law. However the dispute, when it came, would be American-made.

Gamal Abdul Nassser, the top Egyptian nobody, wanted to construct a dam, the Aswan High Dam, to gather Nile waters and create energy for the country's economy. The American Secretary of State, John Foster Dulles, having approved a loan to build the dam, would, without proper notice, withdraw it, leaving Nasser humiliated and unable to build the proclaimed and promised economic asset. The Egyptian president, functioning on his country's territory, if not among its shareholders, nationalized the canal and proclaimed Egypt's right as owner, to find the High Dam money from the tolls upon commercial ships.

Eden and his Ministers were humiliated; not least they found the Tory press demanding action and ready to abuse the Premier, always too liberal for them, for not doing the immediate decent, violent, British thing. Time dragged.The British legal case about the status of Disraeli's shares in what was anyway a declining asset, was far from assured. A revolt among dispossessed owners instructing feral leader-writers, it shouldn't have mattered. Unfortunately, Eden, vulnerable to serious illness, also vain and sensitive, was being pushed toward military action, legal or not. He was encouraged in this by his Chancellor, Harold Macmillan.

Some of that was war hero's reflex. Having killed those Germans in a Loos trench in 1915, he had instincts perfectly inappropriate for a dispute in international civil law. He also had a broad streak of Machiavelli. The poorly Eden, encouraged to do the decisive thing and win, with Macmillan jumping in behind him, was sure to have a triumph. The man beside him, fitter though older, would in due course have succeeded. Butler, the Foreign Office junior-appeaser of the 1930s, and alternative next leader, was, for far better reasons, against this adventure. He had a cautious man's regard for law, international and moral. The pessimist wasn't at all sure that we would be allowed to keep anything we won. Like Lord Hartington in the 1880s, his reliable response to bold initiatives in Cabinet was 'Better Not.'

The international processes were gone through, but in accompaniment to heavily dropped hints about possible action. The American reaction was negative. Submitting to American direction over a conflict which the peremptory crassness of Dulles had flung up was intolerable. Yet a clinging deference to the USA, as Great Power whose best friend we rather tragically tried to be, had already programmed our foreign policy. To break from it, and assert entitlements rooted in our triumphal days, was temptation flecked with resentment, and a fearful risk.

Butler, the careful man, barred from First War heroism by a crippled hand, was far too sensible, had he been Premier, ever to have tried. The same caution ironically held him back from revolt, from the threat or act of resignation. Sir Edward Boyle's departure from a Treasury post when the invasion began would be announced in the Oxford Union to fervent applause. Butler would have been lectured by The Times which would support the eventual invasion and damned for cowardice and treason by Mail and Express.

What particularly stuck in the gullet was the matter of the actual invasion being undertaken on a stupefyingly false pretext. France and Israel, who resented Egyptian support for, respectively, Algerians, and the Palestinians, with our denied and palpable knowledge, would do their own assault, something which for weeks ahead would make 'Collusion' the commonest abstract noun in print. 'We had,' Eden would say, 'intervened to separate the combatants.'

To tell a lie is deplorable. No spokesman of Israel or France tried to levitate this leaden fiction. To tell a lie is not creditable. To tell a palpable lie breaks all the rules about successful untruth—at the very least, interim credibility with all the liars lying together. Incompetence is not necessarily worse than untruth, but incompetent untruth is fulldress failure. The United States, whose authority over us had been ignored, would moralise and watch the pound fall indifferently. The Suez invasion was the triumph over national interest of national pique. A total and unamended failure and essentially his policy, it would make Harold Macmillan Prime Minister.

Usefully, both cunning and impetuous, he had argued throughout for strong, decisive action and boys' story heroics for this undertaking. Less than a week into invasion, with the money market falling downstairs in its rush to be rid of sterling, he would, as Chancellor, inform the Prime Minister that a pound, whose fixed rate could only be sustained by buying it ruinously back, flatly required Britain's rightful defence of her sovereign property to stop dead.

Back in domestic politics, the Labour Party under Gaitskell had behaved well and sensibly, condemning the Egyptian snatch of the canal, but going into Trafalgar Square and onto television to condemn illegality from us. Individual Labour figures, like the long-ago Chancellor Hugh Dalton still spoke imperial certainty. Tony Benn's first volume of memoirs records him in the lobbies late in the day shouting about 'bloody wogs'. But *Eheu*, Imperial glory was departed.

Hugh Gaitskell showed judgement and authority. After supporting every legal step in the early days, he was genuinely outraged and spoke with earnest intensity in the Commons chamber and to an overflowing Trafalgar Square. Labour had contemplated action over that other asset, Abadan. It had though listened and gained a slightly singed sophistication from that case. The clear reality early on was that candid assault, what the law recognizes as self-help, wasn't on. This was now being demonstrated in the case of 'Separating the warring parties'.

Meanwhile, the pound was being sold beyond the Treasury's ability to buy it back, the immediate concern of the Chancellor, Mr Macmillan. The United States, regular intervener in other people's countries, dissociated itself. The thought may have occurred that a floating pound would have been a better bet than the battered castellation of the day. If we were to make war on Egypt and get back the canal, it had to be by subterfuge, pretext, and deceit. A little war involving an alley, halfway up which Great Britain would seek to separate the combatants and, accidentally-on-purpose, take and keep the Canal Zone, had always been an absurd fraudulence. It was certain of calamitous consequences. The Suez invasion had been as spurious as the Jameson Raid which, sixty years on, it echoed. That raid had been undertaken from strength; as stupid as this, also injurious, it was not fatal. This version lit up something which had already happened. It was our lost authority made plain.

The chief irony would be Conservative success in the 1959 election; total failure more than offset by longer-term soft money from a low bank rate, showing up in nice time for a spring boom. In Imperial days, in 1896, just ahead of advance in the Transvaal, a great consensus agreed that beyond question we commanded the greatest empire the world had ever known. The year 1956 would be concluded with recognition that if it had mattered then, it certainly didn't matter now. We weren't quite either Nineveh or Tyre, but in a phrase which would rattle through the next decade, we were an off-shore island. Macmillan didn't have the cards which allowed Disraeli simply to buy key Canal shares in 1875 (foundation of ownership a few years later), as, in 1878, he would pick up Cyprus at the Congress of Berlin. He was, though, near enough to Disraeli in showmanship and style, fit in fact to follow the apostle of Empire as its soothing winder-up.

As Eden collapsed across the New Year, destroyed by the adventure, he would be succeeded by this man, its most vivid advocate. Macmillan knew the script of 1896 and its assumptions and dabbled in belief, but he also had the qualities with which to change the subject and commence (too briskly for its good) the getting rid of empire as irrelevance and overhead cost—not glorious at all. Territories not ready for either self-government or abandonment to settler command would in the next very few years be sharply directed to both. Junior members of the royal family arrived in countries of 10 per cent literacy, each bearing a parliamentary mace, swiftly put away as local dictatorships were established.

A responsible Conservative might have argued that while empire, old style, with all its pride and show, was no longer an option, a duty to govern, educate, and prepare, and to prevent future excess, clearly followed. It was a duty never observed. Dare one even say that a government, its Ministers bred up to imperial duty and pride, incontinently *scuttled*?

---

13 October 1955

House holds the administration of Sir Anthony Eden is undeserving of the confidence of the Country.

Mr Alec Grant (Merton) had a beautifully constructed speech which deserved an even better reception than it got. True Love, the Ministry of Supply, the Board of Trade, the Hawker Siddeley group, 'secret agreements, monopolies, big business and financial restriction': all came into the Librarian's catalogue of criticism...Some of his irony was excellent and some of his shots stuck, but his manner was disappointing and the gait of his speech seemed too conscious of a tail coat and dignity.

Mr Keith Thompson (New College)—Secretary *began to try infusing life into the debate, by ridiculing first, the guests, then the Labour Party...There were flashes of real wit 'They must face the fact that when a man's trousers are falling down, it is at best, a temporary expedient to roll up the bottoms.'*

Mr Walden *The outstanding political issue in the world today is whether or not the free world can meet the ideological challenge of the Communists.* No one laughs when Mr Walden is serious. *The present government is blatantly materialistic, wanting in the equal moral distinctions of government and does not touch the potentials of reason and humanism in Man.*

Mr Jeremy Lever (Univ.) *Socialists have scorned us for not having, as they said, a principle, and by that, they mean a catchword.* Mr Lever was however the only person on the paper to try to defend the Government...

The Rt. Hon. J. Chuter Ede[1] delighted the house with his humour and seemed to enjoy it himself, for he laughed like a friendly elephant at the end of each joke…and concluded to something like an ovation, with an appeal for a moral outlook and fervour in moments of crisis.

The Rt. Hon. Reginald Maudling,[2] Minister of Supply was a little bit annoyed with the Labour party's assumption that they had a monopoly of morals. He improved greatly when he began to debate. In particular, his defence of the Government's economic policy was convincing, and his argument for the retention of a two year period of National Service, lucid and helpful.

Motion lost 278:315.

---

17 November 1955

House thinks that equality is in theory, a pestilential heresy and, in practice, a pitiful illusion. For three quarters of an hour, the lights were out of action—to the delight of everyone in the Union—then the man from the electricity board put the main fuse right…

Mr Michael Brown (Wadham)—Treasurer *Men are not born equal, nor do they live as such. Who treats the college porter as he treats his College Principle? Society needs leaders, and it needs individualists, and these are incompatible with equality.*

Mr Grant *Lets consider that exercise in high-powered Pelmanism known as the Examination Schools. The only thing in favour of finals is that they are final. I'm not saying that men are similar, only that as human beings, they are equally entitled to consideration and respect. All inequalities are absurd, whether of social status— Nancy Mitfordism[3]—wage discrimination based on colour, and those fatuous tokens of fossilised social status, dukedoms and OBEs. The differences which divide men are less important than the common humanity which unites them.*

Mr Neil Creighton Miller *I want not just to discuss the equality of men, but the matter of women—the only opposite sex we've got. Can I persuade Hon. Members that they don't want all women to be alike?* Mr Creighton Miller is a member of the Cambridge Footlights and there were times when his gangling, tortured gestures, foot hovering near mouth, made us think of Jonathan Miller rather than Macaulay.

Mr Dennis Wheatley (Visitor) [4] *No two men are created alike physically and mentally; and this is shown in races. Africans are happier people and Asian philosophers more advanced. In the French and Russian revolutions, equality means in practice, murder and wholesale loss of life, at the end of which there is no real equality. The commissars have country houses, butlers and champagne.*

Mr Victor Gollancz *The basis of Christianity is equality and Jesus Christ, the only person who has achieved perfect equality. 'Love your neighbours' is the supreme expression of equality. Equality is not a pestilential heresy, but a divine world in which we should be perfect as our father in heaven is perfect—who makes the sun to shine on the evil and the good.*

Motion lost 222: 524.

---

19 January 1956

House considers that the Church of England should be disestablished.

The House stood in silence in memory of the ex-President from Keble, the late Archbishop of York,[5] and then disestablished the Church of England by a majority of 102 votes.

Mr Thompson *Because it is so closely tied in with the state, the Church of England is forced to compromise between what Jesus taught and laws made by a secular authority. The New Testament differs in its views on marriage from those held by the courts of the Probate, Divorce and Admiralty Division. In fairness, I don't pretend that Dis-establishment will go very far to promote Church unity, but it would be a step in the right direction.*

Mr Trevor Lloyd (Merton) *The proposers seem to be united largely upon slogans: 'The Church should be strong and free,' or 'Look at what parliament did in 1928.'*[6] *But the troubles of the Church don't have much to do with Establishment. There is a shortage of men, a shortage of money and a shortage of ideas. Disestablishment will not bring the Church up to date. Another slogan one hears is 'The Church is bad…Disestablish it.' No one can show how being disestablished would make it better. Modern states seem to need a faith, but the Russian and American ideologies don't seem very relevant to this country. I want to see a faith directed from the middle at the ordinary men who make up the majority and who are not fanatical or fervent, or even very well educated. If Church and State can keep together, the Church of England might just provide that faith.*

Mr Walden *The weakness of Neville Chamberlain is that he looked at great issues of state through the wrong end of a municipal drainpipe.*[7] *There are three arguments for an established Church of England: association with the country's development, its numerical superiority, and its claim to represent the spiritual side of the State. As arguments, they are respectively tautological, wrong and incomprehensible. We have lately been told by Mr Wolfenden*[8] *to beware 'minds bound fast against new ideas, hidebound, prejudiced and conventional.' An established church claiming to represent a sacred English way of life encourages this mentality.*

The Rev. J. R. Kerruish (Magd)—ex-Librarian *Establishment still has something of precious value to contribute. It provides continuity and stability and is protection against extremes and passing fashions. If the country were to overthrow its Christian inheritance now, the result would be a setback to Christian morale throughout the world.*

The Rev. G. A. Lewis Lloyd *The opposers of the motion have argued that Establishment worked in practice. But in religion, if something is wrong in principle, then it should be rejected, however well it works. A religious society should be free to order its own affairs. Establishment is bad for the Church because it is rooted in power, something that risks being confused with the government.*

The Bishop of Rochester Dr Christopher Chavasse The first twenty minutes of his speech received close attention, but later the house became a little

restless. *National self-consciousness demands an established church; the newly cre-*
ated states of India and Pakistan are examples of this emotional need. If the Church
is to represent the religious consciousness of the people, then the people must be able
to instruct the Church through parliament. The Church of England is so deeply
rooted in the national mind that it has played a great part in the making of the
English character.

Motion carried 238:136.

---

9 February 1956

House thinks that National Service is a waste of time and money.

Exactly three years ago, the House had refused to welcome a reduction in
the period of the National Service and had done so by 106 votes to 90. But
at that time, conscription was still an accepted institution. Last Thursday's
debate was altogether a more serious affair.

Mr McCarthy *I offer three reasons for supporting the motion. There is no longer an*
atmosphere of potential world conflict. As the ex-Treasurer from Balliol[9] remarked
recently 'There ain't gonna be no war.' The last two years have seen a reduction in the
number of military commitments overseas and there has even been a revolution in
strategy so widespread that it has reached the Cabinet.

Mr Stuart Griffiths (Magd.) *We must be clear about the distinctions between*
strategic and tactical atomic weapons, and between global and local wars. What the
proposer suggests is an abolition of conventional weapons. That would leave us with
Mr Dulles[10] on the brink of thermo-nuclear disaster.

Mr Neville Brown (New College) *By employing authoritarian measures like conscrip-*
tion, the West abandons its moral case. Economic aid matters more and is more effective.

Mr Bill Evans (Wadham) *Army food is so bad that pygmies come from darkest*
Africa to dip their darts in it.

Mr Ian Mikado MP[11] *If NATO fights a war at all, it will be a war to annihilation. The US has realised the impossibility of maintaining both atomic and conventional force. And having a conscript army is grossly inefficient; the overheads are out of all proportion to the value obtained.*

Mr Airey Neave MP (Merton)[12] was too much on the defensive to score heavily. *The government cannot take the responsibility for abolishing conscription when the success of future recruiting is still so uncertain.*

Motion carried 223:117.

———— ∞∞∞ ————

26 April 1956

House refuses to believe that there has been any change in the Russian policy of world domination.

The undergraduates had greeted B and K[13] with an apparent mixture of curiosity, cynicism and deflationary ragging. Thursday night's debate showed that ragging extends to other personalities as well.

Mr Robert Maxwell (Visitor)[14] *There has always been a Russian policy of world domination and such a policy is still in operation. 'Who will conquer whom'[15] is the crude problem presented to the late Josef Stalin. In the Middle and Far East, the Russian policy is still. 'Divide and fool' for as long as it suits her, while anti-Western propaganda continues unabated on the extended tours and within the Soviet Union. I would ask the audience not to make itself ridiculous, whatever might be the delusions of that strong, silent man of British diplomacy.[16]*

Mr Brown Mr Zilliacus (Visitor)[17] *has achieved the triple distinction of being expelled from the Labour party, denounced by the Cominform and denied access to the USA. I regret to say that time has not allowed me to organise a protest meeting at the visit of Mr Malcolm Muggeridge. Look, Russian policy has changed fundamentally since Stalin's death. He had always played great Power politics; his inspiration seems to have been not so much Karl Marx, but Tsar Nicholas 1st. Russian leaders now seem bent on winning the war for minds, precisely what Harold Stassen[18] and Ex-President Truman seek to do on behalf of capitalism. The West should snap out of what is now an archaic attitude, or lose the ideological competition.*

Mr Griffiths *The creed of Mr Muggeridge (Visitor) can best be called political nihilism. His idea of freedom would be the strangling of the last shop steward with the guts of the last managing director. B and K condemn the cult of personality. So did Lenin, and he became a god? So did Stalin who became a super-god. Only through concrete proposals, like free elections in East Germany, can there be any thought of a radical change in Russian foreign policy. Poland remains a country with its parliament in Warsaw, its capital in Moscow and its population in Siberia.*

Mr Michael Bird *The great change in Russian policy came in 1923 when the theory of world domination was abandoned. The policy of buffer states on Russia's borders is an old one, a policy of protection. We must stop being political puritans. It is too early to condemn the new Russian mood.*

Mr Muggeridge *There is no new leadership in Russia. The people in power there now are people who have been in power for a very long time. The British people seem to be particularly gullible. Our enemies announce what they are going to do; they never deviate from it, and we never believe them until they do it.*

Motion carried 237:173.

---

17 May 1956

House believes that the humanities play far too great a part in the British Educational system.

Mr Patrick Chambers (Univ.) *Science and technology are Britain's livelihood, but she is taking a long time to realise it. The British educational system has not yet recognised the Industrial Revolution and is still in the backwoods of the Nineteenth*

Century. Germany offers a vivid contrast. In Britain, everything has been either revolutionised or nationalised except education which is based on an unholy alliance of Kipling, Dr Arnold and Sir David Eccles.[19]

Mr Rudolf D'Mello (Pembroke) *The Workers Education Association stated in a report, that the best technologists were those with a liberal education, for they were more adaptable. If Russian education suffers from an overdose of technology, then it is time Russian education was humanised. There is an international issue here. If the scientist is not willing to shoulder responsibility for the use or misuse of his inventions, then it becomes all the more urgent to give a liberal education to all men bearing responsibility.*

Mr Robert Cook (Exeter) *What oppress me are the awful sense of superiority and almost pitiful delusions of grandeur characterising the people reading those subjects so oddly termed 'The Humanities'. So much time is wasted on philology and textual criticism which, in turn, leads to students missing the real substance of the classical authors. My alpha in the Mods general paper owed not a little to someone's Pelican History of Greek Literature. As for the Humanities, what could be more humane than medical studies? The world is faced with semi-starvation. The possibilities of Science meeting this are infinite. Men must choose between devoting their energies to academic piffle and relieving the abject and soul-destroying poverty of so much of mankind.*

Mr Martin Henry (Pembroke) *To concentrate on too many facts without a sense of purpose is absurd. That has been the pattern in Central and Eastern Europe. Consider the curricula of East Prussia, Poland, Galicia, Silesia and Bohemia: so many facts, so much intellectual indigestion. Here at Oxford back in the days of Roger Bacon,*[20] *the Trivium (Arts Course), had to be taken before the Quadrivium (Science Course). It was felt that the mind should be trained first. Facts could come later.*

Mr Ritchie Calder[21] *There was a serious struggle before UNESCO got an 'S'—for 'Scientific'. Science is part of the Humanities, but the traditional humanities keep on rejecting it. As for the ignorance of science among politicians charged with making decisions about its consequences, well, one famous politician remarked 'I know nothing about science.' The next morning he flew to New York to negotiate about the atom* bomb. In their ignorance of science, people become afraid of it and adopt a kind of fatalism. Here in Oxford, I'm told, the faculties are hardly on speaking terms.

Mr Harold Loukes (Department of Education) [22] Mr Calder is right, a knowledge of science is necessary for all men. But here and now in the 1950s, I think we have the balance about right. There is too much hue and cry about the three per cent upon whom a little Latin and Greek is wasted. The aim of a good education is to produce a good all-rounder. What is the use of exchanging gravel-grinding and hair-splitting for chisel-grinding and atom-splitting. Technology may be the means to a livelihood, but is it more important? Consider the ends.

What I abhor is the 'Let me be your guardian' attitude of the scientific pundits. What I value most is the thought that in spite of all the scientific inventions, in spite of all the destruction that their mistakes might bring, two young people might still get a thrill from holding each other's hands.

Mr Bill Ensor (Catholic Workers' College) Man must first learn to think for himself. Every invention must be watched lest it diminishes the physical or mental power of man.

Motion lost 89:102.

———— ∞∞ ————

31 May 1956

House prefers the appeal of the emotions to that of reason.

Mr Tom Bendhem (St Edmund Hall)—Secretary Emotion is not the prime source of action and reason, merely its servant. Emotion tells a man that he dislikes being called irrational. Much mental illness today derives from the notion 'Listen to reason before you do anything else.' Reason is neutral, utilisable for good or bad.

Mr Edmund Ions (Merton) I listened intently to the Secretary as he held the House spellbound in the hollow of his head. Emotions are first of all, dangerous. Apartheid is enforced because of the emotion of fear felt by white South Africans. Fear of Communism has lately produced Senator McCarthy. Look at Germany not very long *ago and observe the emotional reaction of people there to militarism and see what happens when you think with the blood.*

Mr Rubin (President of Debates, London University) *Emotion is man, reason is automation. Soon we shall need push-buttons to push the buttons. If Columbus had listened to the sages, America would have gone undiscovered. There is little reason for trying to climb Everest.*

Mr Ronald Peierls (President of Cambridge Union)[23] *The advocates of emotion have been admirably rational. The Champions of reason have indulged in emotional outpourings. I am puzzled by the appeal for obedience to illogical orders exemplified by the Charge of the Light Brigade. A little emotion is a dangerous thing and a great deal of it is fatal.*

Mr John Cranko (Visitor) [24] *Reason is like a tape measure, but emotion can reach the real essence of things by a process of emotional intuition. Reason and emotion are like a pair of Siamese twins. Luther was on the record as saying that God is stupid. Goethe had ideas without knowing where they came from. Emotion is the boss, reason the office-boy.*

Professor MacMurray *Reason is not to be restricted to the intellect. A Bach fugue is very much a creation of reason, for there is imaginative and creative reason. For Plato, reason was a passion for wisdom. Emotion on its own can be destructive and must be socialised. Otherwise people would turn from reason to authority which in turn, would mean the triumph of totalitarianism.*

Motion lost 83:17.

18 October 1956

A motion of general censure against the government—not specified by the report.

Mr Walden *Tory principles have never been more evident than in their conduct of the Suez dispute. Labour compelled the government to refer the matter to the United*

Nations. The Tory party has been for force and only Mr Gaitskell's compulsion had extracted the Prime Minister's promise at the end of the Suez debate at Westminster. He should now resign.

Mr Peter Brooke MP (Balliol) [25] *Let us look at everything: that the Commons debates, the subsequent negotiations and the Times correspondence. I conclude that Egypt has abrogated the 1888 convention; her attitude was unilateral. HMG had always intended to take the matter to the United Nations—but it was for the Prime Minister to choose the right time for this.*

Mr Michael Bird *To consider economic affairs, a 'free' economy is today producing unemployment, short-time, and a failure to deliver the goods. Britain is falling behind competitors. Tory freedom does not work. As for abroad, Sir Anthony Eden's handling of the Suez problem has strengthened Nasser and shown Tory threats of force to be empty utterances.*

Mr David Morgan (Univ.) *Opposing the motion's condemnation of the Government, I would point to Cyprus. There, historical fact proves that Greece cannot claim ethnic or historical links with the Cypriots. That island's position in the Eastern Mediterranean makes it a vital base for geopolitical conflicts. Our British interest is not selfish imperialism. It is recognition of a vital link in the Middle East defence chain. Finally let us not forget Russian ambitions in the East.*

Mr Patrick Gordon Walker MP (Ch.Ch.) [26] *Donnish quips on the Chancellor's ineptitude gave way to searching criticism of our low gold and dollar reserves. They are now 22 per cent lower than when the government took office. Bank rate is an Edwardian blunderbuss of a weapon. Mr Gordon Walker made sharp criticism of the Conservative Llandudno conference. It was disgusting, particularly its handling of capital punishment; and he wished to stress that Labour does not seek to divide the nation over the Suez issue; Labour has in fact truly represented the nation's case, as subsequent action has shown.*

Sir Edward Boyle MP (Ch.Ch.) [27] *We do indeed need planning for any economy, witness electricity and coal-and-steel. But piecemeal planning is dangerous and can only work in wartime when people would tolerate direction of labour. I dislike statistics and they prove nothing, but let me prove my case by quoting you some…* It was an appeal to the intelligence and did more than all the other speeches together to rescue the government in the division later.

From the floor Mr John Cohn stated the Liberal case and welcomed the end of bulk-buying; Mr Narindra Corea spoke lucidly against the motion and Mr Anthony Quainton[28] brought American criticism against the government. The division of 270 for, 273 against, showed a very narrow majority of three in favour of the present government.

---

1 November 1956

On 28 October British forces in collusion with France and Israel, making a separate attack upon Egypt on another front, invaded the Canal Zone of Egypt in an attempt to reclaim the canal, a commercial property which had been nationalized, an act contestable in international law, though with no judgement likely to be enforced. It was the start of a shooting war, generally denounced around the world, including clear and certain expression of United States displeasure. There was also a fearful run on sterling. In just over a week, the British would be instructed to halt so as to withdraw, over a short notice period, from the greatest national humiliation of the century. Vast flight from sterling, anchored at an unsustainable fixed rate, also helped. The officers of the Oxford Union out of a fearful responsibility unbecoming in anyone under thirty, chose the following subject of debate.

In the opinion of this House, the modern man does not require religious belief in order to be moral.

It was obvious that many hon. members hoped for, and the majority expected, an emergency resolution on the situation in the Middle East. At a meeting of the Standing Committee that same afternoon, it was unanimously and abjectly agreed that a motion on the adjournment would be injudicious at that stage of the international situation. A full debate was promised to the House within the next two weeks when speakers on both sides would have time to prepare a case.

The motion announced for debate on 1 November proceeded.

Mr Bryan Ellis (St John's) *Opponents must produce evidence of an after-life and establish that the universe was divinely controlled. This they cannot do! Believers in a moral god-head are shelving their own moral responsibilities. In the claim that God ordains all justice, belief in an afterlife has for centuries caused the Church to shirk social duties in this life. Only man can solve current problems for 'the proper study of mankind is man.'*

Mr Bob Evans (Wadham) *Lets not have a war between the godly and the godless. Lets look for the basis of morals. And I would remind the proposers that just as I cannot prove the existence of God, no more can they prove his non-existence. The humanist asks the religious believer to give those beliefs up and substitute his own particular moral code. Yet all moral codes have proved unstable and inconsistent. Religion and God did at any rate make up a stable belief.*

Mrs Margaret Knight (Girton, Cambridge)[29] *A belief in the Christian God is not necessary. The other side expect all moral statements to contain a reference to God. That is no more necessary than a similar reference to God in a statement about aesthetics. Religion requires intellectual dishonesty and double-think for the enquiring mind, particularly for the child. It also encourages emotional insincerity by ordering the child to love God. Human altruism can be the basis for a moral code as much as any religion and it is something just as present in man as selfish and evil instincts.*

The Lord Bishop of Rochester (Dr Chavasse) *Evil is always present and Christianity provides a working solution to this. The Humanist is involved in the Kantian dilemma of providing a categorical imperative[30] for his actions. At which point, religion comes in to provide a standard of morality. Human nature is so unstable that it requires the strength of the Christian ethic to oppose those forces.*

Thursday 8 November 1956

On Monday November 5th Standing Committee voted for a debate on the Suez situation to replace the debate arranged for Thursday. Ex-officers of the Society were contacted and at very short notice, agreed to prepare speeches for and against the Government's action.

House opposes Great Britain's military action in Egypt.

Mr Bryan Magee (Keble)—ex-President *This is a national issue rather than a party one. I can think of six consequences capable of flowing from this action, none of them welcome.*

Mr Peter Tapsell *Israel has made her move, but she is not to be treated as an aggressor. Rather she has decided to join arms with Egypt now rather than await certain destruction later. The UN has failed to take action in the Middle-East to prevent an arms build-up such that Israel and then Great Britain, have been forced to act swiftly.* He faced and dealt ably with persistent heckling during a powerful speech.

Mr Jeremy Thorpe *This assault should be opposed on moral grounds. I believe that the Prime Minister misled the House of Commons and the nation when he gave them both assurance that there had been full consultation with the Commonwealth and with America. In fact, political morality has been subordinated to political expediency.* There followed undoubtedly the House's most dramatic moment in recent years. The announcement came from Mr Thorpe who was handed a note at the despatch box and then announced Sir Edward Boyle's resignation. The supporters of the motion came to their feet and gave a long ovation in favour of Sir Edward Boyle's resignation. It must be said that Mr Rees-Mogg who followed Mr Thorpe showed great courage in accepting the news, yet resolutely adhering to his views on the government's action.

Mr Rees-Mogg *Our intervention in the Middle East has prevented a trap of Russian arms in Egypt. The crisis in Egypt, like the crisis in Hungary, owes its origin to the Russian policy in the Middle East. Our prompt action may have contained a war in Egypt that could have become World War III.*

Motion lost.

ENVOI

This account has dealt with Oxford debates across the plateau of what Marxists delight to call 'Late Imperialism', hence the period chosen: Boer War to Suez. It is also an era of world struggle, of great powers and *blocs*. In narrowly British terms, it has meant the Grab for Africa, the descent into the War to End All Wars, the delusion of escaping the next one, but also a period of much greater governmental concern with the no-account people of this medium-sized country. Government would broadly push on with the social transformation of post-war humanity and show full regard for the generality of people. However after a number of colonial conflicts of varying legitimacy, Malaya, Kenya, Cyprus, it would briefly, in 1956, essay the great throw-back, the miscalculation that we had not lost the eye of cold command.

The Suez expedition—the putting back in his place of the cheeky canal-nationalizing President Nasser—was undertaken with France and Israel in a stunning piece of duplicity—'Putting out a Forest Fire' it was called: something done in the belief that our writ still ran and our truth still stretched. World opinion was, of course, against it, as if that mattered. This was a war undertaken without the confidence of the currency markets. Everything else since, in Oxford as in Britain, has been post-imperial. The Prime Minister, Anthony Eden, resigned. His Chancellor, Harold Macmillan, who had urged him to take the valiant course, now took over. The consequence was what Churchill had called 'Scuttle' when we withdrew from India. It was hasty, careless, and a blatant piece of cutting losses on all sides. Something rightly done for sure, but better done carefully, was now carried out to a new, accelerated timetable.

As we got out of overseas dominion, there would be renewal at home in the form of adjusted priorities. Politics had for a long time grown milder, with the Conservatives accepting Labour outlines of social policy, despite occasional reversals to harder values, like the ever regretted destruction of far too much of the railway network masterminded by a Transport Minister from the construction trade. Basically, however, the catchword was Bow Group Conservatism and general moderation. In terms of the Oxford Union, this brought economic and social debate closer to the centre and enhanced issues, political but not party-political.

Yet from time to time, good old party politics would rear its fascinating head. Labour, out of power from 1951 to 1964, would grow more disputatious and personalized. Given Bevanites against Gaitskellites, with abstract Marxists and class warriors set against Social Democrats, a term not yet borrowed from the admired West Germans, the real, enjoyable animus of Oxford debate was within the Labour Party. The Labour Right, as mentioned elsewhere, was formidable—people like Brian Walden and the drily brilliant mature student Ron Owen. The far Left didn't blossom until the 1960s when it was growing everywhere else like Begonias.

The most impressive Tory, from personal recall, was Tony Newton, admired and very much liked across party, someone who would live to keep the Department of Health pretty much intact and busy inside Mrs Thatcher's hard-eyed government. Equally notable would be a young Michael Heseltine developing a self-satirical platform manner, suggesting an address from a South American balcony. But in ministerial practice, he would be ready to rescue Liverpool from serious talk of letting that difficult city slide into the Mersey.

Aristos, with rare delightful exceptions, like the deft and graceful Lord James Douglas-Hamilton (Balliol), President in Trinity term 1964, were not a notable force. Had equivalents of the nineteenth-century figures who walk in these pages—a Lord Wolmer (later Earl of Selborne), an Honourable Henry Lygon, or any of those characters from Victorian farce—manifested themselves, they would have been…cherished!

One technical development post-war was that the old innovation of having guest speakers became a requirement. It could have been seen as earnest concern to hold major political figures (and they were mostly political) to account. More realistically, it was, for the seriously political Union members, a desire to touch fingers with the current generation of government and Opposition, whom they planned, in due course, to join, as a prelude to replacing them. The Church does not have the laying-on-of-hands all to itself!

The Union signalled its general internationalism in the recurring words and phrases of so many speeches in the 1890s. 'The Greatest Empire the World has ever seen' became 'Colonial Freedom now'. Ironically, it would dislike the Afrikaners as much as had Cecil Rhodes. It had never been 'No coloureds need aspire' at the Union—too many Asian noblemen for that. But now, any number of former children of the Empire would make big names in the Union: Lalith Athulathmudali (Jesus) and Lakshman Kadigamer (Balliol) both served as President. Both played a serious role in their country Ceylon/Sri Lanka and both would be assassinated—as had been S. W. Bandaranaike (Christ Church, and Prime Minister of Ceylon, 1956–9). The deaths were an irony, an Oxford irony, good purpose confounded. Another leading figure indicating an abrupt direction being taken away from Empire was Uwe Kitzinger, one of the earliest advocates of Britain in a united Europe and author of the key best-selling book, who lives yet.

As the Union gave more attention to humanitarian issues, so it would, on some of them, put itself at last on the winning side nationally. The Union had debated the death penalty since mid-Victorian times and had been early in supporting abolition. This had now become a full-dress parliamentary issue, put in abeyance for the period of debate when nearly ended by parliament in 1948. By the late 1950s, it was clear that the next Labour government would—on a free vote with a respectable Conservative contribution—get rid of the thing.

Then there would be a wonderful, but ambiguous, moment in 1958 during the state visit of Mr Macmillan, when the adjournment was sought against the detention without trial of Dr Hastings Banda, black leader of

White Rhodesian-administered Nyasaland. Macmillan killed the bid dead by telling the Union President, an amiably laconic American, Joe Tratner, that if it were put, the Prime Minister would walk out. This episode is a measure of the long-term naivety of so much undergraduate mid-century anti-imperialism. Dr Banda would indeed be released—by Mr Macmillan; would become President of Nyasaland (later Malawi), in 1971 make himself president for life, would *not* be assassinated, but, according to the lowest estimate, would kill 6,000 of that country's citizens.

In the early 1960s, the Union was particularly political. Indeed Michaelmas 1960 under the deft and gentle presidency of Robert Rowland, future major BBC apparatchik, gives a good idea of the mood. It attracted the better class of controversy from Lord Salisbury (Bobbety, sixth Marquess, keen friend of the Rhodesians), Fenner Brockway, ancestral pacifist, charming the Union sideways, Enoch Powell, then a ready-spending Health Minister, mildly controversial only as advocate of shading interest rates higher than Mr Macmillan, Konni Zilliacus—ubiquitous Finnish Marxist, and, setting a pattern for the decade, a Peace (which is to say a 'Lets leave NATO') Debate, roundly declined at the voting door.

The outcomes were Social Democratic: against the (Conservative) government 2:1 and approving African self-government by 50 votes out of 650, after an outstanding speech by David Prior-Palmer. We denied the Old Hat nature of the unions 3:2. We were willing to fight for Berlin 5:1, rejected capital punishment by better than 2:1, and came heavily down in favour of the space travel impending.

That was benign, good stuff for all the optimism, but the latter 1960s would abandon restraint and argument for rage, and self-righteous rage at that. The debate in 1968 on the Vietnam War struck the high point of a puerile development. The authorities across the universities had cringed before an adolescent tantrum of students pretending to be workers or peasants, higher education as play-school. Read the *Letters of Hugh Trevor-Roper* and the altogether cheekier ones of Mercurius! In the Union, a shrill assault was made on the Wilson government, not for participating in that ultimately futile war, which they were not, but for failing to *denounce* it.

His Foreign Secretary, the humane and rational Michael Stewart, was drowned out of all argument in a chant of 'Ho, Ho, Ho Chi Minh'. It was a disgrace, not for being unseemly, often an interesting option, but as regressive self-importance dispensing with argument.

Five years earlier, internally, there had been delicate business to do on the margins of comedy. It had become a vivid priority to admit to full membership what were almost compulsorily called 'Women', as Ladies never had been. A rule of the Union since pre-Victorian times required, if demanded by a quota of members, the endorsement of 'Life Members'. This, until long after the Second War, meant a body of elders—mostly, according to legend, rectors of Wolds villages or prebends of Trollopian cathedrals, all fatally prejudiced against the irredeemable Daughters of Eve—thought insufficiently intelligent for politics. As remarked above, in a pre-war debate, one graceless young flaneur had referred to the women spectators, confined to the gallery, as 'cattle'.

The fix the Union regularly found itself in was funny of course—also humiliating. Here would be Oxford being progressive and enlightened. A motion would be passed by the people who belonged here and who, here and now, attended debates... and their vote could be nullified from, if not the grave, then the Cathedral Close. Finally, in 1963, the vote went through that parish barrier with a squeak of sufficient assent. Women guests had spoken in the Union in the past, all of them surely Ladies, but the first speech by a woman *member* would come from Lydia Howard, grand-daughter of Professor Harold Laski, well known here. An ironical and regressive footnote to the laborious achievement of this good cause is that one of the moving spirits behind it, Garth Pratt of Corpus (President, Hilary 1964), would, not long after, seek the Liberal candidacy in a Liberal-promising Lancashire seat only to be rejected, the Rochdale Liberal Committee preferring a certain Cyril Smith!

The Union survives—flourishes, has a quite evidently benign business connection. The queues to the Debating Hall on Thursday evenings can reach down St Michael Street. Other universities, led by Cambridge, do their honest best and, if it has all been fun, it has been fun taken terribly seriously.

NOTES

Introduction: Early Days

1. In the main text of debates, the House will much later be found giving tumultuous applause for the speech of Mr Jack Lawson of Ruskin College, future leader of the Durham Miners.
2. A fourteenth-century foundation, now incorporated into Oriel College.
3. Christopher Hollis, *The Oxford Union* (Evans Bros., 1965), 96–9.
4. *The Oxford Union*, 125–6, a source to which I am much more generally indebted here.
5. A. N. Wilson, *Hilaire Belloc* (Mandarin, 1984), 372–3.

Our Empire: Pride Before Fall

1. That of Henri Queuille (thirteen and a half months), record for the Fourth Republic of 11 September 1948–28 October 1949.
2. Kenneth Rose, *The Later Cecils* (Weidenfeld and Nicholson, 1975), 25.
3. Joseph Chamberlain, 'Foreign and Colonial Speeches', quoted Bernard Porter, *The Lion's Share* (Longman, 2004), 145–6.
4. Porter, *The Lion's Share*, 177.
5. All at Richard Shannon, *The Crisis of Imperialism* (Hart-Davis/MacGibbon and Kee, 1975), 325.
6. Marquess of Crewe, *Lord Rosebery*, Vol. II (John Murray, 1931), 575, quoted in Porter, *The Lion's Share*, 130.
7. B. Semmel, *Imperialism and Social Reform* (George Allen and Unwin, 1960), 16, quoted Porter, *The Lion's Share*, 132.
8. *Milner Papers*, Vol. II (Cassell & Co., 1933), 291, quoted in Porter, *The Lion's Share*, 131.
9. Hilaire Belloc of Balliol, d. 1953, part-French and self-conscious about it, was a virulent controversialist, open-mindedly anti-German and anti-Semitic, also unrelentingly Roman Catholic and an uninstructable Anti-Dreyfusard. In his writing, brilliant light verses and much enjoyed accounts of travel and sailing contrast with ranting, careless histories written for money in a hurry. Considered

a brilliant debater at the Union, though it isn't shown here, he was President (Hilary term 1895), rejected for All Souls and a number of other college fellowships, for, his biographer A. N. Wilson thinks, his unamiable qualities. Liberal MP (1906–10) for Salford, after a long, pugnacious life, including a friendly view of Mussolini, he would be saved from support for Hitler only by anti-German prejudice.

10. The South Africa Company of Cecil Rhodes, grand territorial holder of what would become the Rhodesias (Northern and Southern).

11. An 'Oxford Character', generally known about Oxford, where he returned after London parish service, as 'Canon Claude'; President in Hilary 1893 and a nebulous revenant long after.

12. The Rt Revd Cyril Forster Garbett (Keble)—1875–1955, successively Bishop of Southwark and Winchester (1932), one of the major clerics of the century, liberal in politics and, from 1942 until his death on the last day of 1955, an outstanding Archbishop of York (ODNB).

13. Frederick Soddy 1877–1956. Major scientist who identified, in parallel with Kazimierz Fajans, the decaying nature of matter which created radio activity, coining the word 'Isotope' meaning 'the same place'—the matter as it rotted. He specifically anticipated atomic weapons. He had a separate distinction as an unofficial economist in parallel with J. M. Keynes, proposing in the 1920s things which have since been done: abandonment of the gold standard, use of deficits and surpluses as economic tools, letting exchange rates float, establishment of a consumer price index and other assemblages of changing economic information. (Entry in *Oxford Dictionary of National Biography*.)

14. Courtesy title—Richard Walter Hely-Hutchinson, later sixth Earl of Donoughmore, d. 1948 (*Debrett's Peerage and Baronetage*, 1990).

15. Matthew White Ridley, second Viscount Ridley from 1904; d. 1916. Earlier MP for Northumberland and, in spite of being a Protectionist (President of the Tariff Reform League), PPS to the resolutely Free Trade Chancellor Charles Ritchie (Complete Privilege)—Ancestor to Rt Hon. Nicholas Ridley and his daughter, the distinguished historian Jane Ridley.

16. George Canning, d. 1828, Tory politician with untypical flair; for which, together with being the son of an Irish actress, he was, witness Mr M.W. Ridley, in 1896 never quite forgiven by sound Tories.

17. The US President at that date, approaching the November 1896 election which would re-elect him, was William McKinley, a par-for-the-course conservative Republican who devoted a great part of his campaign against the Democrat, William Jennings Bryan, to opposing bi-metallism. This was a theory that silver should be counted at a specific value as backing for the currency, increasing the dollar's volume and economic demand. The idea was Keynesian before Keynes

and by quite other means. See the long, satirical, but sympathetic poem 'Bryan, Bryan, Bryan, Bryan' by Nicholas Vachel Lindsay. Bryan had spoken with genuine eloquence: 'You shall not press down upon the brow of labour this crown of thorns. You shall not crucify mankind upon a cross of gold.' He would, though, stand twice more and again miss the White House. Far more orthodox in his Christianity, he would, long after, be counsel at the famous Dayton trial of Thomas Scopes for contravening the state legislation of Ohio by teaching evolution in high school class, and be played in the film about *that* by Fredric March.

18. Leopold Amery, right-wing Conservative, as a young man, member of Milner's 'Kindergarten', ally of Churchill against Appeasement, and maker, in 1940, of a devastating speech credited with precipitating the departure of Neville Chamberlain. It invoked Cromwell's words to the Long Parliament. 'You have sat here too long for any good you have done. Be gone I say. Let us have done with you. In the name of God, go!'

19. Francis Hirst, Editor of *the Economist* 1907–16, *Common Sense* 1916–21. A Liberal purist and prolific author and pamphleteer, he was devoted to Free Trade, against most taxation and state expenditure—on the Welfare State *and* armaments—and wept at the outbreak of the First World War. *ODNB*.

20. Later first Lord Desborough, comprehensive sportsman: Oxford Oar twice, (including the dead-heat of 1878), shot, golfer, fisherman, fencer, and more; President of MCC *and* British Lawn Tennis Association also Captain of the Yeomen of the Guard. Less spectacularly, Member of Parliament in two constituencies, Salisbury, then Hereford, for two parties: first as Liberal, then, as inveterate opponent of Irish Home Rule, amongst the Tories who would make him a peer—father of the emblematic dead war poet Julian Grenfell. *ODNB*.

21. C. Valarius Flaccus, unrevered poet, contemporary with Vespasian, wrote the *Argonautica*, described as 'an unfinished epic of learned mediocrity'. *Chambers' Biographical Dictionary*.

22. Roy Jenkins, *Gladstone* (Macmillan, 1995), 619, 627. This was Gladstone's last outcrying against atrocity—in this case, against the Hamidan massacres by the Turks of something under 300,000 Armenians and other Christians. His speech, when aged 85, of an hour and twenty minutes at Hengler's Circus, Liverpool on 24 September 1896, was an echo of the crimes and denunciation of 1876. Rosebery, affronted at the implied criticism, would call it 'The last straw on my back', and, twelve days later, resign as Leader of the Opposition. Jenkins speaks of him as 'looking for a chance to flounce'.

23. Jobbing learned pamphleteer who published *The Aldermen of the City of London* (2 vols.) and on such topics as 'Errata in Official Returns of Irish House of Commons'.

24. See excellent biography by David Gilmour (John Murray, 1994). The 'Simple Dutch farmer' was Paul Kruger, leader of the Boers—not all that simple.

25. Porter, *The Lion's Share*, 177 quoting J. A. S. Grenville, *Lord Salisbury and Foreign Policy* (Athlone Press, 1964), 122. Milner had candidly wanted war.

26. Conservative MP in various offices just outside the Cabinet, e.g. Solicitor General, Financial Secretary to the India Office, in Tory governments between 1885 and 1902. However, before entering parliament, he was seriously important, as the reorganizer of that party's structure for the successful election of 1874 and would later be associated with Randolph Churchill in the larkish, trouble-making, *soi-disant* Fourth Party in the mid-1880s. Gradually, as a Free Trader, alienated by the rise of Chamberlain and Imperial Protection, and calling the Tories 'no longer the party of Disraeli', he joined the Liberals, but failed in his Liberal candidacy at Preston in 1910 (*Encyclopaedia Britannica*).

27. 1872–1930. Hard, charming, cynical, witty, and self-made, also a provincial without connections (Birkenhead!), his patriotic/dramatic Conservative raptures hardly disguised the absence of serious conviction. A natural ally of Lloyd George as fellow brilliant amoralist, he lived and (unlike LG), drank hard, dying of it under 60, but as Earl of Birkenhead and Baldwin's Lord Chancellor, managed, in his Land legislation of 1925, to organize into coherence what Cromwell had called 'this ungodly jumble'. See Second Lord Birkenhead, *F.E.: The Life of F. E. Smith First Earl of Birkenhead* (Eyre and Spottiswoode, 1960).

28. George S. G. Douglas-Pennant, second baron, inherited from his father a system at the Penrhyn quarries, by which a committee of workers held extensive authority. He withdrew recognition of it, brought in a financial adviser, instituted direct control and increased annual profits by £150,000 p.a. and became unpopular. The reaction led, at this time, 1901, to a strike which, with wider union support and national interest, lasted until 1903. Pennant, having won it, instituted the blacklisting of former strikers, though also making *ex gratia* payments to workers kept from work by exceptional weather, and became hero or villain according to taste.

29. Edmund Clerihew Bentley, irretrievably humorous writer who produced 'Trent's Last Case' and invented the clerihew, two rhyming couplets with lines of unequal length verse, sometimes wonderfully funny—*vide*: 'John Stuart Mill, by a tremendous effort of will | Suppressed his natural bonhomie | and wrote "Principles of Political Economy".'

30. The vote at Cambridge University that year on admitting women to study courses at roughly first degree level (see above) had shown massive resistance. A college for women (Somerville) studying to that level had been created at Oxford in 1879.

31. Later Sir John, later still Lord Simon, a busy future multiple Minister in Liberal, War Coalition, and National governments over thirty years, finally, in the Second War National Government, Lord Chancellor; also in this university term, reviver as President of two-way visits with Cambridge Union Society.

32. Frederick Soddy: see n. 13.
33. From Union Office listings, this open-minded fellow must have been E. C. Bentley, professional humourist.
34. Frederick Temple, whose son William would also become Archbishop of Canterbury.
35. 2 September 1898, Major Jean-Baptiste Marchand's French military expedition (see above) across the watershed of the Congo and Nile basins, an area of expansionist competition, found him facing Kitchener at Fashoda. The crisis was avoided when the French government, toiling at the high point in the Dreyfus Affair, which carried the material for a possible putsch, ordered their man to retreat, landing Britain, in the view of Richard Shannon (*The Crisis of Imperialism*, 318), with nothing but further expenditure for its Egyptian budget.
36. Historian specializing in Scandinavia but best known for his account of the post-war Versailles Treaty.
37. A cousin of the Salisburys, violently abusive toward the unquartered and venomously eccentric where his cousin, Hugh Cecil, was often likeably so. In his various roles as Roman Catholic convert, professional aristocrat, and forgettable writer, the Honourable Algernon Cecil was a mannerist on steady call.
38. Journalist and Socialist as well as Oxford historian, wrote the admired (and best-selling) volume (1870–1914) of the entire first series of Oxford Histories of England, though he was himself, originally and by continuing interest, a classicist. Barred from any of the fellowships expectable after a brilliant degree and major prizes, but not helped by his candid, unthinkable political stance, he fell back on journalism at the *Guardian* through friendship with Laurence Scott, its future chairman. There and later, at the *Sunday Times*, he would flourish in a first (and continuing) career as political commentator. He also functioned as a working barrister. A Balliol man with friendships in the Asquith Circle (notably Raymond Asquith), he shaded reasonably enough through events and Fabian acquaintance into a Labour position (P. J. Waller, *History Today* (January 1987)).
39. John Buchan, the future best-selling novelist (*Thirty-Nine Steps* etc.). Also politically active: as a young man he was a junior imperialist and one of Milner's kindergarten of advisers in South Africa. Later, and uncontentiously, made Governor General of Canada, he would be ennobled as Lord Tweedsmuir. (Apart from the well-crafted, but rather dated adventure novels, try the later *Midwinter* which ironically envisages an earlier date where Samuel Johnson is present at the edge of the '45 rising.)
40. Raymond Asquith, eldest son of the future Prime Minister: admired and loved in his circle and, when killed in the war, becoming something of a symbol—one of several former presidents of the Society to die in the conflict.
41. Rosebery, misaligned Tory that he was, had retained the Liberal principle of Free Trade.

42. Likewise, the Duke, breaking with Gladstone over Home Rule (and Land reform), had, like him, also remained a Free Trader.

43. Later President, later yet (by advantageous marriage) Sir Arthur Steel-Maitland— son of a colonel marrying the daughter of a general. Chairman of the Conservative Party 1911, successive seats in and about Birmingham, successive minor office under Lloyd George in the wartime coalition, later, 1917, a baronet, entered the Cabinet under Baldwin 1924–9 as Minister of Labour.

44. Studied at Queen's College, one of the richest; became, for two years at its inception, Chairman of the Executive of Ruskin College. An academic, he taught public administration at Bristol University and the LSE. In parliament with breaks from 1910 until his death in 1941 and originally Liberal, he had moved in 1919, to the Labour Party of which he would eventually become Chairman.

45. Founded at this time, later known as Ruskin College, providing courses for working-class students with possibility of access to a university degree.

46. This was a recurring theme in the press and political circles for four or five years. It indicated a fissure among official Liberals not reflected in the party in the country. After Gladstone's departure came a hiatus and Rosebery was part of it. An Imperialist with good links to the Transvaal conspirators, he followed the pectoral-rippling language of Milner and thought the British Empire 'the greatest secular agency for good that the world has seen' (J. G. Garvin, *The Life of Joseph Chamberlain* (Macmillan, 1932), quoted Porter, *The Lion's Share*, 135).

47. Andrew Lang, littérateur, and more usefully, collector of legends and fairy tales.

48. Most liberal and socially welcoming college in Oxford, and Ensor's own.

49. Captain Alfred Dreyfus, innocent, but satisfyingly Jewish; victim of a historic miscarriage of justice and prolonged demission to a blazing equatorial island, was at this time in the late stages of total exoneration. Belloc, in the last days of his life, July 1953, would snarlingly proclaim obsessive, necessary faith on a question first raised in 1892 and its answer by then settled for over half a century. Speaking to a visiting Roman Catholic cleric, he asked, 'And what is the news, Father? Do they still think Dreyfus was innocent? Poor darling, he was as guilty as sin.'— Wilson, *Hilaire Belloc*, 372–3.

50. The retrial in Rennes by a military tribunal of Dreyfus, cleared already in a civilian court of the treason alleged against him, had temporarily reversed that verdict under direction from senior officers 'protecting the honour of the Army'.

South Africa—Last Late Prize

1. 'Mr Gladstone and our Empire', *The Nineteenth Century*, September issue 1877.

2. Dicey in the *Spectator*, quoted Shannon, *Crisis of Imperialism*, 105.

3. Shannon, *Crisis of Imperialism*, 326.

4. Shannon, *Crisis of Imperialism*, 334.
5. Shannon, *Crisis of Imperialism*, 336.
6. Shannon, *Crisis of Imperialism*, 337.
7. Alfred Beit 1853–1906. Maker of vast profits from gold, diamonds, and other good things in South Africa; also, in fairness, an open-handed supporter of causes, especially education. Ultimate demon capitalist in some eyes. Lucky not to be called 'Diamond Alf', he had started business with Cecil Rhodes, as co-founder of the British South Africa Company; profitably active in Kimberley, then Witwatersrand, he financed many good causes and the Jameson Raid.
8. Almost certainly from the dismal partisanship, Algernon Cecil.
9. Hardinge Giffard, later Second Earl of Halsbury (known as Viscount Tiverton), who would die in an internment camp in France during the Second World War. His father had been a Conservative Lord Chancellor and an extravagant upholder, during the 1911 Lords crisis, of that House's powers of veto over finance bills, something buried over 200 years. See the editor's *Lines of Most Resistance* (Little Brown, 1999), 340–66 *passim*.
10. Weird and depression-inducing late-middle Ibsen though it is.
11. On 13 January 1900 Balfour, in Manchester, excused lack of preparedness for a war, essentially provoked by the Rhodes faction, implying that such early, idly incurred defeats derived from a high-minded belief that the Boers were as pacific as the British government—brass neck of a high calibre.
12. The term 'Little Englander', now used unhistorically and confusingly about UKIP, a party of gargoyle nationalists, was directed in 1900 at the likes of Campbell-Bannerman, Lloyd George, and the radical journalist Edmund Morel, all unfashionable opponents of rabid nationalism in the form of the Second South African War. Morel had also campaigned earlier against the atrocities of King Leopold II's private mining interests in the Belgian Colonies and would be a dedicated opponent of the First World War.
13. Subsequently a great and creditably controversial Master of Balliol who took over a medium sized niche in history by standing in the Oxford by-election against the ever egregious Quintin Hogg whose candidacy as a supporter of appeasement would provoke the future White's Professor of Moral Philosophy (J. L. Austen 1911–1960: an austere pure philosopher if ever there was one) to proclaim that 'A vote for Hogg is a vote for Hitler.' Sandy Lindsay's welcoming approach to non-European students caused the rugby-minded part of an audience at an Oxford cinema to greet a newsreel of tribesmen paddling dug-out canoes with cries 'Come on Balliol'—causing a small riot. See Denis Healey's splendid autobiography *The Time of my Life* for a Balliol man's affectionate account of Lindsay and his Balliol.
14. Herbert du Parcq, Lord Justice of Appeal 1938.

15. James Keir Hardie d. 1915, Leader of the Labour Party, sincerely revered then and since, opposed the First World War, dying profoundly distressed, 1915.

16. Arthur Cecil Pigou 1877–1959, one of the outstanding economists of his day, his thought chiefly directed to Welfare Economics and the distortions created by *Externalities*—costs or benefits not accounted for by those creating them.

17. The Rhodesian Press supported Cecil Rhodes or was owned by him—nothing to do with the much later states of that name.

18. President, Easter 1896, Archibald Boyd-Carpenter, future Conservative MP, son of the Bishop of Ripon and father of the better-known Conservative MP Sir John Boyd-Carpenter (MP—in Cabinet under Eden and Macmillan—later a life peer).

19. Back in the mid-seventies Rhodes had extravagantly left business in the hands of his partner and commenced *in statu* at that happy college, staying for a single term, before returning to do less sympathetic things.

20. Almost certainly Auberon Herbert. Otherwise Lord Lucas, war correspondent who lost a leg in the Boer War. A Liberal who rose through junior office to enter the cabinet as Minister of Agriculture, but enlisted in the Royal Flying Corps in 1915 and was killed, presumed shot down flying over enemy lines in 1916.

21. Edward Grigg, subsequently MC DSO, *Times* Journalist—Colonial editor, later Private Secretary to Lloyd George as Prime Minister, Governor of (Kenya) after his fall, Conservative MP from 1922 for Oldham and Minister Resident Middle East 1944–5, retiring in 1945 as Baron Altrincham.

Chamberlain and Milner Go to War

1. L. O'Broin, *The Chief Secretary* (Chatto and Windus, 1969), 31.

2. R. J. Q. Adams, *Balfour: The Last Grandee* (John Murray, 2007), 147.

3. Edward Grigg—Conservative politician later serving in wartime coalition, later first Lord Altrincham.

4. Fashoda, a village in the South Sudan, now called Kodok, was the point at which two forces, British under Kitchener and French under Marchand, encountered one another. It related to the competition between French and British imperialism, with their respective railway-driven, enforced, colony-linking ambitions, and east–west and north–south strategic appetites. At Fashoda, the French had numbers, the British, artillery. Happily both commanders had sense. They behaved unlike imperial orators and agreed to a stand-off so that diplomacy could work. It did, much of the credit owing to Delcassé, French Foreign Minister, and indeed to Rosebery at his best, both perhaps looking ahead to Anglo-French need of each other against Germany. Accordingly, a solution with an agreed line of demarcation based on the source of Nile and Congo rivers was worked out.

5. Future Archbishop: York, then Canterbury; one of the outstanding English churchmen, very widely admired—especially by Liberals.

6. In 1886 Joseph Chamberlain, then thought of as a radical Liberal, had split the Liberal Party, slighted by Gladstone's proposal of all-Ireland Home Rule when he had ready a scheme for, as it were, Home Local Government. The Liberal Unionist Party which emerged behind him had long since effectively merged with the Conservatives—Chamberlain featuring as second voice even in the era of Lord Salisbury.

7. This relates to the filibustering by which relays of Irishmen on five-hour individual digressions had immobilized legislation in the recent past.

8. Later a distinguished judge.

9. Not the real thing, the second son of H. H. Asquith and known as 'Beb.' His comments may though reflect the imperfect liberalism of his father at this time when closest to Rosebery and Grey.

10. This is Sandy Arbuthnot, John Buchan's hero, a Carnarvon Herbert and genuinely astonishing person: virtually blind, smuggling himself into the army, shifted to intelligence, not least because of a fistful of languages, including Turkish and Albanian. Despite the short way with press comment here, he played a benign and constructive part generally, involved in the creation of the Albanian state. After the war, he became a Conservative MP of an unlikely, generous-minded sort, opposing the generational stupidity of that party over Ireland; dying at 43 through the ignorant error of a doctor.

11. Something seen by modern historians of the First World War, like Sir Christopher Clark, as the involvement which brought this country into that dark defile.

12. Elder figure among Liberals and reliably in the Gladstone tradition.

13. Kipling had expressed contempt for 'The flannelled fool at the wicket, the muddied oaf at the goal'—neither of whom have let it worry them.

14. Later headmaster of Rydal School and, all too probably, the author of *Lord Roberts, his Story Told for Boys* (1915).

15. Serfs emancipated by order of Tsar Alexander II, well-intentioned liberal of well-intentioned liberals, later assassinated.

16. This debate is essentially, in an uninformed and generalizing way, about rival economies. But hostility to France recurred more irrationally and enjoyably during this period. France at this time, was undergoing a radical shake-up, a consequence of resolving *L'Affaire Dreyfus*. That long incarceration in tropical duress of a young artillery officer, blameless but Jewish, accused of espionage actually committed by a disreputable cousin of the imperial Esterhazy family, had gone into political orbit. Senior officers, Catholic and Royalist, not quite but nearly, to a man, had formed a circle of wagons, like any bad Western, before disappearing

into cataleptic commitment to a clearly wrong verdict, so much more easily defused by any variant of 'Sorry, we got it wrong.'

As it dragged through the Chamber, the Military Courts, and the street, ordinary citizens became Dreyfusard or Anti-Dreyfusard accordingly as they were Radical/Socialist/Secular or Royalist/Catholic/anti-democratic. The governments of Rene Waldeck-Rousseau and Émile Combes, a man of relentless scientific cast of mind (and two doctorates), set about the full secularization of France, not least by way of state and secular education. The Church having been fiercely anti-Dreyfus, lost caste and influence. It was the continuation of an argument from the Revolution, indeed from Voltaire. See debate of 17 May.

17. The Liberal League, involving the likes of Haldane, Asquith, and Gray, had been the Liberal Imperialists, gleefully called 'Limps', supporters initially of Chamberlain and Milner's South African adventure and the war it created. This being a discredited cause, they stopped talking about it, but still represented on a personal basis, the Liberal right wing willing to wound the radical leader, since 1899, Sir Henry Campbell-Bannerman, at this time universally underrated, not least by these three.

18. The Hon. Neil Primrose, son and heir of Lord Rosebery (five houses in the UK, two villas in Italy, and a yacht). After serving as joint Chief Whip to the Coalition formed 1916, he would volunteer and die of wounds in Palestine 1917.

19. The point of this amusement is not apparent. Hamilton at this time was in the middle of an eight-year stint as India Secretary, had a couple of honorary degrees, and much later became Chairman of the London Underground. Possibly the office of Captain of Deal Castle accounts for the hilarity.

20. The government of Ireland Act introduced by Arthur Balfour and his brother, Gerald, was, as remarked, of a liberal and thoughtful sort, certainly the best done by any Conservative government.

21. Probably the future criminal lawyer and author of a biographical essay on the Old Pretender.

22. Notable bare-knuckle prize fighters of the early nineteenth century.

23. In 1896 Irish Members and Conservatives became involved in a sixty-strong physical fight around the chair of the Clerk of the Commons. The Speaker, William Gully, was widely and irrationally criticized for failing to maintain order.

Ironically, Gully, later made Viscount Selby, was the grandson of a champion bare-knuckle fighter in the days of the Game Chicken and the Lancashire Giant, and who, according to the Greville diaries, 'then took to the turf, was successful, established himself at Newmarket where he kept a Hell and began a system of corruption of trainers, jockeys and boys...and which in a few years, made him rich'. *The Diaries of Charles Greville*, abridged and edited by the present editor (Pimlico, 2005), 110.

24. The Anti-Clerical government of Emile Combes 1902–5 (see above) lasting thirty months and exceptionally long-lived by the standard of Third and Fourth

Republic Ministries, was a reaction to the abuse of power by the Catholic Church in France, allied in practice with the extreme Right and an officer class grazing at the border of treason, heavily involved in the Anti-Dreyfusard cause, reliably royalist, and no friend of constitutional democracy. Effectively, Combes separated Church and state in France. Despite excesses like the prejudice against Catholic officers shown by the Minister of War, the reforms of Combes very reasonably removed a meddlesome Church from politics.

25. To owners of public houses closed under recent legislation

26. No need for H. Thorpe (Wadham) to sound so contemptuous of Sir Thomas who made an honest fortune selling cheaper food to less well-to-do people; who enjoyed yachting, but devoted great sums during the war to emergency hospital services in Serbia and later left the bulk of his fortune to the City of Glasgow.

27. Followers of Chamberlain and his Imperial Preference scheme with its federated empire, here 'Colonial consolidation', disliked such entanglements and may have been right.

28. Edward VII's public-personal initiative in a state visit to France was judged, at the time and by historians later, to have been, in reaching its objectives, a total success. Whether or not an alliance with France who was developing contingent and adhesive commitments elsewhere, notably with an expansionist, slavophile Russia at potential odds with the Austrian empire, was such a good idea is another question altogether. It has been impressively disputed by Christopher Clarke in his account, *op. cit.* of the pre-1914 crisis *The Sleepwalkers* (Allen Lane, 2012).

29. The Berlin Conference after a Balkan war of 1878 which propped up the Ottoman state.

30. 'I have brought you back peace, but peace, I hope, with honour.' Disraeli on return from that Congress.

31. On the conduct of the Second South African War.

32. Lansdowne had been at all material times, 1895–1900, Secretary of State for War and as such blamed, justly or otherwise, for the manifold deficiencies of material and conduct during that misconceived and wonderfully ill-run adventure. The notion of the horses and Sir Henry Campbell-Bannerman having brought about ministerial and military failure carries partisanship to new and charming heights.

33. The point of the Japanese alliance was that it was naval, had in fact been something urged by the alert and perceptive Admiral Fisher whose navy of four capital ships in that region faced six Russian and French and with three more Russian ones under construction. The alliance had effectively been made with the admired and substantial Japanese navy. See Shannon, *Crisis of Imperialism*, 339–40.

34. These were taxes called for by the Chamberlainite front, the Tariff Reform League, to protect British manufacturers from 'unfair competition', something they had never objected to practising.

35. Put, simply but accurately, the Tory party, especially in its Cecilian days, was Anglican triumphalist. Nonconformists voted Liberal often because of the fact. In terms of state money, the Church of England had been a kept virgin of Conservative governments, especially since Forster's Act of 1870. It was also the case that despite such favour, Church of England schools were doing too much not very efficiently and could truthfully plead desperate need. Bringing them into the state system at the non-denominational public expense, with most of their autonomy intact made (sectional) sense.

36. Famously imposing duties upon tea and losing the American colonies.

37. Term, originally Arabic, meaning non-Muslims; applied later, contemptuously, for black Africans: not advised.

38. Salisbury had conceded the American case based on the Monroe Doctrine, in a dispute over the Venezuela/British Guiana border, part of a general policy of ingratiation with the USA at the expense of other people in the middle.

39. The town council of Gothenburg, Sweden, had responded in the mid-1860s to thirty-four litres of spirit consumed annually per person, with a trust system. There were to be no individual licensees. Instead trusts were appointed enjoying a local monopoly, but with a 5 per cent maximum profit, the rest of the takings channelled into amenities, sports grounds, parks, libraries, and the like. There was some take-up in Scotland where a common feature was the banning of both hard spirits and attractive decoration or entertainment. The Scottish impulse to lower found expression in the absence of décor and enjoyment. Known understandably as 'Goths', they flourished to a degree, but found that, even in Scotland, grimness was bad for business.

40. *Taff Vale Railway Company v Amalgamated Society of Railway Servants* 1901 held unions to be liable for loss of profits deriving from strike action—a judgment later reversed by legislation.

41. Any worker in a cotton mill, like my grandmother or Bolton-born Bill Naughton, who made the point in one of his plays, could have enlightened Mr Swallow to the fact that, challenged only by the small-quantity Sea-Island product, Egyptian cotton has the finest, longest thread anywhere!

42. Royalists, ci-devant nobility, clericalists, and those with faith in the treason of Captain Dreyfus to defy all evidence.

43. 1884–1962 MC and Croix de Guerre, founder and first Master of St Peter's Hall (now College) 1928, Bishop of Rochester 1940–60.

44. Legislation in response to this fearful sort of thing was passed in 1905, officially and sensitively called The Aliens Act. The influx was overwhelmingly Jewish, the product of Russian Christian persecution and overwhelmingly positive in its impact. The discernment and sensibility live on.

45. This, since 1903, had been Alfred Lyttleton whose wife, Olivia Tennant, was a member of a notable theatre family.

46. *That* Keynes.

47. That House would be carried away, kicking and screaming in August 1911 by its own exertions against a 200-year-old precedent forbidding amendment of finance bills.

48. The First Russian Revolution began in mid-January 1905, sparked by the humiliation of defeat by the Japanese and the fall of Port Arthur. However, burning on all sorts of spare wood, the fire was to run the length of the year, achieving cinematic effect with the march on the Winter Palace. But taking in pogroms, naval mutiny, or wide-scale similar diversions—street violence, rural risings (the consequences of earlier land bankruptcies), and with Lenin and the Mensheviks alerted, they juddered on very widely before eventually a government, under the harsh but rational Stolypin, began the last period of pre-revolutionary, richer-peasant creating sort of stability. Which advance made the direct 1914 involvement in a Slavophile Balkan adventure provoking a subsequent European war, all the more fearfully incredible.

49. Delayed response in 1903 to the earlier discovery of recruits for the South African adventure extensively under-sized, unfit, and ill-nourished. The Physical Deterioration Committee made three central recommendations: free school meals for very poor children, health inspection of schools, and training in mothering.

50. Party of non-violent but emphatic Irishmen seeking Home Rule, led from 1900, until his death in 1918, by John Redmond.

51. Early leader of the party, Protestant, founder 1870 of the overly reasonable and thus discounted Home Government Association. Home Rule MP for Limerick 1871–9 and thereafter Youghal, succeeded as leader of Irish nationalism by Charles Parnell.

52. Thibet/Tibet was in revolutionary turmoil throughout 1905, due to the revolt of a sect of Lamas against the presence of Christian missionaries given access by the ruling Chinese dynasty. Bloody murder would be followed by bloody execution. As usual, and not necessarily wrongly, the British government expected Russian moves. Curzon, ruling in Delhi, had responded with the mission of Sir Francis Younghusband in 1904. This is probably the policy objected to by Mr du Parcq.

53. The government of Émile Combes had completed the work of Waldeck-Rousseau in removing the privileges and formal status of the Roman Catholic Church.

54. A distinguished servant: Mayo man, Liberal, Roman Catholic (and thus burdened), also a supreme meritocrat, MacDonnell had risen through a pre-university status Irish college to academic distinction and the upper British Civil Service. Able precisely as an Irishman, to understand India and its small peasant society,

he had done a great body of admired work in India, notably in legislation friendly to Indian small farmers and fighting famine.

He had finally been brought in, by Wyndham, Conservative Irish Secretary, against all Conservative prejudice, to be Under-Secretary for Ireland on the recommendation of Lord Curzon, remotely grand, but able to set prejudice aside. Consultations ensued with a group of liberal landowners about a form of devolution with a Council in Dublin which did not infringe Pitt's Act of Union. It leaked and Ulster Unionist rage would lead to MacDonnell's censure, but left him in office to pursue, when the Liberals came in, a version of his Council of Ireland Idea.

Enter the Liberals

1. Oscar Wilde, *The Importance of Being Earnest.*
2. Duncan Sandys—'Dear Duncan—so *cassant!'*
3. *National Union Gleanings*, 24 (1905), 463–7, quoted in Adams, *Balfour*, 176.
4. Adams, *Balfour*, 177–8, quoting Austen Chamberlain.
5. John Wilson, A *Life of Sir Henry Campbell-Bannerman* (Constable & St Martin's Press, 1973).
6. Wilson, *Life of Campbell-Bannerman*, 552.
7. Almost certainly a son by second marriage of the sixth Earl Beauchamp.The Lygons were patrons of Edward Elgar; and his aunt, Lady Mary, appears in *The Enigma Variations*, represented in a movement entitled 'Romanza'. The seventh Earl, (half-brother) fell victim to the malignant Duke of Westminster who denounced his homosexuality, also of the good intentions of Evelyn Waugh who in his largely embarrassing novel, *Brideshead Revisited*, vested the Earl's fictional persona, 'Lord Marchmain' with many paragraphs of soupy deathbed glorification of the chivalric classes.
8. For the rest of his speech, Mr Lygon pointed out that Efficiency was the real justification of the motion and attacked the Irish obstructionists with tremendous vigour. Mr Lygon was obviously not quite himself and this produced a certain lack of grip on the subject.
9. In 1801—after a campaign of festive and open-handed bribery.
10. Witness the press gang.
11. Later 1930s Editor of *The Times* and prideless appeaser.
12. Killed in the First World War.
13. Leader of the Irish Nationalist Party.
14. Augustine Birrell. Noted above, but at this point, Minister responsible for Education attempting to offset the Anglican bias in the most recent Tory legislation. His bill would be thrown out by the House of Lords, an early intimation of the coming gunfight at the Treasury Corral. Later he would be a thoughtful Irish

Secretary, actually sympathetic to Ireland and in the process, irritating leading Sinn Feiners [see Study by Leon O'Broin], but unlucky enough to be in office when the Easter Rising began. In the immediate Bill, his mild attempt to provide schooling less weighted to the Anglican interest would be killed in the unelected Upper House, the first of a run of ultimately suicidal legislation-blockings by their Lordships.

15. Clause added by Liberal Peer to the 1870 Education Bill, one permitting parents to withdraw children from (Anglican) religious education in schools.

16. William Temple, as noted above subsequently Archbishop of York and Canterbury—also politically leftish and personally, an unprelatical bishop, widely loved. Here he stands remote from the sectarian interest group mentality of his own, established, Church.

17. Heir to Lord Selborne—Despite this sympathetic intervention, an irremediable blue sky ultra; later during the Second World War, Deputy-Controller of Cement.

18. More to the point in restoring Transvaal self-government, the Liberals failed to do anything for the black population whose share in anything remained nil.

19. Later a leading figure in the Baptist Church.

20. At this time, Oxford and Cambridge and the combined Scottish universities had constituency status, returning their own MPs. In 1829, Sir Robert Peel had felt obliged, after undertaking Catholic Emancipation, to resign and re-contest his seat of Oxford University, losing it to an inept Ultra Tory, Sir Robert Inglis. In rather different circumstances, after heading the 1931 'National Government', Ramsay MacDonald, unelectable in his old seat, would be rescued in 1935 by the Scottish universities.

21. Disraeli, in the unexpected bill of that year, effectively admitted urban working men to the vote, but although he lost the next election, he won the one after that. And the Conservative Party, despite recurring palpitations at most electoral reforms, have not, over all, been losers by them.

22. A headmaster and country walker, he would be the prime mover in the creation of National Parks.

23. This annual boating rally has generally been the occasion for the more imaginatively irrational union motions, to which this party-political moan was an exception.

24. [Reporter note:] *Speaking against. The proposal—by a Mr Byles—is not recorded here.*

25. Edward Saunderson, landowner in County Cavan (a Catholic region of historic Ulster and now part of the Republic) joined the Orange Order in 1882 and favoured arming and training its members. Pearce, *Lines of Most Resistance*, 82. Not without a curious charm, he was furiously active against all concession to Catholic Ireland.

26. A moderate Conservative politician (opponent of Protection), sharing a title connection with William Cecil, Lord Burleigh d. 1598 (Elizabeth's long-term chief Minister), provoked this now obscure and always undeserving pun.

27. Killed in First World War.
28. Later a fashionable Roman Catholic priest, minor wit, and literateur, admired in his day, also a socialite, making converts among susceptible members of the upper classes—beaten away from the nearly predated Harold Macmillan by the latter's strong-minded American mother.
29. Who, as noted above, had recently defected to the Liberals.
30. Leader of the Irish Nationalist Party, a political moderate who would die in 1918, his purposes to be superseded by the consequences of the 1916 coalition, under Conservative influence, not listening to the message of this motion.
31. Returning from Canada where he had briefly been Governor General, the Earl of Durham, a political radical central to drafting and obtaining the Reform Act of 1832, proposed that, essentially, Canada should be self-governing, a radical principle, wonderfully accepted, and the foundation of level, friendly relations with what at this time were called 'The Colonies'.
32. A decent left-liberal at this time, subsequently, after conversion to Roman Catholicism by Ronald Knox (see n. 29), he would follow a familiar pattern, becoming an admirer of Mussolini, campaigner for General Franco, and devotee of the charmless American cause of 'Moral Rearmament'.
33. Third son of the Prime Minister, third Marquess. Ablest and best of all the later Cecils, Free Trader in a protectionist party, internationalist working through the League of Nations for all the decencies, headed by peace; an open mind in a family whose members, gifted and not, had inclined to reverent and ice-bound faction.
34. At this time, Liberal MP, later dogged by electoral mishaps, partly technical, a late victim of the 'Re-election on taking office' rule. During the war, head of wartime propaganda—revealing the Turkish massacres of Armenians—*not* propaganda.
35. Tsarist Russia was playing an active aggressive role in Persia [contemporary Iran] and doing so with British connivance. This would follow the wishes of Grey, now lamentably Foreign Secretary, pursuing entente with France, itself also involved or involving with a brutal and fragile Tsardom, to do its bit to precipitate war in 1914. The twitchy Raj lobby was also complicit, hence a number of the interventions here.
36. A word earnestly avoided by Muslims.
37. The hanging jury of remote graduates found in some hundreds of country parsonages. From which, notoriously, incumbents made their way to Oxford to stop anything sensible.
38. It got one—Hamar Greenwood, last, disastrous Chief Secretary of Ireland for thirty months 1920–2, responsible with Winston Churchill for creation of a counter-terror, the Auxiliaries, Black and Tans, and the burning down of much of Cork.
39. 'The two imperial conferences, 1907 and 1911, finally ended any lingering hopes of economic integration and defence and political integration.' Shannon, *Crisis of*

Imperialism, 403. A year before Chamberlain, Tariff Reform, aka Imperial Protection, quietly died.

40. Both stood on the extreme right of their respective parties.

41. On 24 July 1911, Hugh Cecil, disregarding Mr MacFadyan's 'confidence in decency and good order', would stand screaming 'Traitor, Traitor' at the Prime Minister while leading an orchestrated Conservative nervous breakdown. According to *Toby* of *Punch* who was there, 'For a full forty minutes the struggle lasted'—finally causing the Speaker to suspend the Commons chamber.

42. Concern late in the day for the physical well-being of poor people only came when they were examined for recruitment and very frequently proved undersized, physically weak, and malnourished. The dismissive, ugly contempt of the word 'degenerate' was ubiquitous at this time.

43. Killed in the First World War.

44. Jack Lawson would become leader of the Durham Miners, key but politically moderate part of the Miners' Federation (Later NUM), also a key figure at the top of Labour politics. Often called 'the uncrowned King of County Durham', he was held in very wide general respect.

45. Patrick Leigh-Fermor's posthumous (and delightful) third volume, *The Broken Road*, recording the final stage of his travels on foot through Europe, contains an account of ferocious celebratory riots in a Bulgarian town—tables and benches flung from a café veranda onto equally delighted people in the street after receiving news of the assassination of King Alexander of Serbia in October 1934. Christianity in the Balkans seems to have been primarily doctrinal.

46. Winston Churchill, tediously obliged under the rules of the day to seek re-election on accepting ministerial office, was defeated with a 6.6 per cent swing, only slightly above the current by-election norm. The consequences were not onerous; though he was forced to become MP for a Scottish seat (Dundee).

47. Asquith's surprisingly liberal Budget of earlier that year.

48. This major contemporary legislation for Ireland, in harmony with the work done by Gerald Balfour as Secretary, while leaving Trinity College Dublin intact and autonomous, created the Queen's University of Belfast and the National University of Ireland.

'The Whole University Marching Down the High'

1. Lord Willoughby de Broke, *The Passing Years* (Constable, 1924).
2. Roy Jenkins, *Asquith* (Harper Collins, 1988), 197.
3. Rose, *The Later Cecils*, 76.
4. Parliamentary Debates Lords, 22 November 1909, PD cols 731–50.
5. Parliamentary Debates, 22 November 1909, cols 750–60.

6. Parliamentary Debates, 22 November, cols 775–85.
7. Parliamentary Debates, cols 942–54.
8. Parliamentary Debates, cols 966–78.
9. Parliamentary Debates, 1031–43.
10. Parliamentary Debates, 1011–16.
11. Parliamentary Debates, 1023–31.
12. The present purposes to which land was devoted put a fine on enterprise and a premium on waste; shutting in land meant shutting out men.
13. In Mr A. D. C. Russell's speech.
14. Reverting to direct speech for its subject.
15. A reference to the Dreadnought-demanding slogan of Admiral Fisher's truculent Navy Lobby: 'We want eight and we won't wait.' In the actual war they mostly functioned as spectators.
16. Lightweight, not very funny, professional humorist, eventually knighted in the way of leading jockeys.
17. Supreme far-right and overflowingly virulent publication, edited by Leo Maxse—son of an equally reactionary admiral.
18. This Budget is now judged rather moderate. It taxed luxury goods—motor cars and petrol, though also alcohol and tobacco—put a shilling in the pound duty on mining royalties, and most famously set a duty on land—undeveloped land—of a halfpenny in the 240-pence pound of the day, also modest death duties. It was the work, together with an attentive Prime Minister Asquith, of David Lloyd George, near abstainer and steady adulterer described by the charmless Charles Whibley as 'the cad in politics', also known rather later as 'the man who won the war'.
19. Not Lord Robert Cecil.
20. The London home of the marquess of Lansdowne, at which peers organizing votes against major government legislation, notably the Lloyd George Budget and the Parliament Bill its rejection provoked, would assemble. L. J. Stein's point was more than a cool quip, it represented a sort of *soto governo* operating against the elected House. Ironically Lansdowne himself was uneasy at the degree to which peers were overreaching themselves.
21. The Liberal government, as shown above, had lately been passing licensing Acts in an attempt to bring the free-range Edwardian brewer under restraint.
22. Leading Liberal newspaper, brilliantly edited by A. G. Gardiner, dedicated enemy of Joseph Chamberlain.
23. Palmerston—Commons speech on the combination in 1857 of Gladstone and Disraeli against a Chinese war.
24. Odd figure, wit, writer of quirkish detective stories, eccentric—'I am in Crewe. Where should I be?' Not helped by his Catholic-influenced closeness to the feral

Belloc who brought the French Right and its anti-Dreyfusardism to the fringe of British politics, but much nicer.

25. Osborne Judgment: Legal direction that barred Union funds being directed for a political purpose—as in funding the new Labour Party.

26. Later Sir Walter Monckton, divorce lawyer engaged for Edward VIII in his difficulties, and as Conservative Minister of Labour in the 1950s, notable for a decidedly conciliatory approach toward the union interest. See essay by Andrew Roberts 'Sir Walter Monckton and the Retreat from Reality', 243–87 in his *Eminent Churchillians* (Simon & Schuster, 1994).

27. In Ireland.

28. Former Viceroy of India who had recently said that 'the principles upon which it [the Budget] stands must lead to a social demoralisation among the people'.

29. Boutros Ghali (grandfather of a subsequent General Secretary of the UN, Boutros Boutros-Ghali), was assassinated on 1 February 1910 as a protest against the Denshawi incident, and in the belief that he, a Coptic Christian, owed first loyalty to the occupying British. The shooting took place in the aftermath to the Denshawi, a piece of British insensible high-handedness, in response, with public whippings and hangings, to a disturbance.

30. Shot with his heir, Luis Filip, in Commerce Square, Lisbon, February 1908.

31. Theophil Braga, for ten months after the 1910 revolution, Prime Minister, subsequently President, of Portugal.

32. The general historical view.

33. Norman Birkett (1883–1962), distinguished barrister—entering late, after time as a Methodist minister, famous beyond the bar, knighted then raised to the Lords with a hereditary title; twice briefly Liberal MP, Criminal Counsel, usually for Defence, alternate judge at the Nuremburg trials. A man from the north-west (Barrow in Furness), his last act was a vastly popular and successful speech in the Lords, fending off an attempt to turn Lake Ullswater into a reservoir.

Mourning their Lordships, Worrying about Women

1. *Lord Lansdowne: A Biography* (Macmillan, 1929).
2. *Punch*, 2 July 1911.
3. *The Times*, 10 August 1911.
4. Ibid.
5. *Punch*, 2 July 1911.
6. *National Review*, 57: 928–9.
7. *The Times*, 27 July 1911.
8. Ibid.
9. Ibid.

10. Ibid.

11. Ibid.

12. Ibid.

13. Ibid.

14. Quoted in Roy Jenkins, *Mr Balfour's Poodle* (HarperColllins, 1954), 267.

15. Ironically, it would be the same Walter Long who, in the 1922 negotiations with the Irish winning side after the war which the brutal misgovernment of H. C. Duke and Harmer Greenwood, Birrell's successors, had brought about, would beg them to settle for Home Rule—something politely declined.

16. The Nine County Ulster was 43 per cent Catholic at this time. Today's Six County Ulster is almost as close.

17. By which, at this date, was meant Jewish immigration.

18. The Siege of Sydney Street of December 1910, never properly worked out, but involving Latvians and other East Europeans, included the irresistibly named Peter the Painter otherwise Peter Piatkov.

19. Given Russia's role in 1914 and our obligations to it and France, something to regret. (E.P.)

20. This is the British naval doctrine of the desired measure of superiority over rival military shipping. It was drum-rolled incessantly by Fisher, oblivious to the foreseeable supremacy of air power, able to bomb places naval guns couldn't reach, which would be the desperate preoccupation twenty five years later, of sensible Ministers like Philip Cunliffe-Lister. Meanwhile the Army which would fight the war saw its share of the services budget decline between 1905 and 1914, from 48 to 36 per cent.

21. Sir Norman Angell, whose pamphlet/later book, *The Great Illusion* (G. P. Putnam's Sons, 1913), argued that, economically, victory in war and acquisition of territory never translated into gain for the citizen. Such reasonableness, very widely taken on from a best-selling work, did not in 1914 influence the high contracting parties.

22. Birrell in those numbers was referring to pre-Treaty nine-county Ulster, not the six-county version of today.

23. Gladstone's second attempt at legislation, rejected by the Lords in 1893, modified the original Bill of 1886.

24. Under a free trade Liberal government, Conservatives still yearned for Tariff Reform/Imperial Protection, with the people they called 'the Colonials', participating behind a wall built against unfair, cheaper goods from unfairly competitive European economies.

25. It is worth mentioning that the future Sir Walter Moncton, described above as a nice man and liberal Tory and, as acknowledged, rather too conciliatory a Minister of Labour, would make a pleasant fortune as a divorce lawyer. He would be adviser to the Prince of Wales/King Edward VIII.

26. Tory legislation involving compensation (mostly to brewers). Smith-Gordon was quite wrong. The 1910 Act continued the compensation (how divided is not apparent).

27. As explained above, this meant that there should be no decision in a private huddle by Tory peers (as celebrated by Lord Willoughby de Broke in his memoir) to kill Liberal legislation in their Lordships' no longer very effective house.

28. Chairman of the Liberal Daily News, member of one of the great cocoa and chocolate making families—devoted to Lloyd George, something which much later led to rupture with his editor, Alfred Gardiner, who, reasonably enough, thought him corrupt.

29. Denis Robertson—Distinguished economist, working with J. M. Keynes and as such, a major contributor to the General Theory, though they would fall out—over the savings–investment relationship.

30. Alfred Harmsworth erratic, intermittently insane, and ludicrously influential owner of the *Daily Mail*.

31. Puzzling, but if he means John Wilkes, contester of General Warrants and useful tormenter of George III, he is presumably referring to the *Essay on Woman*, a tepid piece of small-time smut, most of it thought to have been written by the son of an archbishop.

32. R. B. Haldane, Liberal Minister responsible for Britain's reasonably adequate military readiness—driven from office in 1914 by press/Tory hysteria, discovering in his wide German culture clear treasonable intent—the tell-tale stain of Goethe.

33. Some other Wilson—too early and the late Prime Minister thought the Union a waste of time.

34. With the prelude that theft was the only common factor, enumerated the enormities of the Triplice [*sic*—for Triple Alliance: Germany, Austria, and Italy]. Events in Bosnia, Agadir, and Tripoli, morality, international law, and England's interests were weighed against the policy of the Allies.

35. Bosnia, which would return to crisis in the mid-1990s, had been an Ottoman *vilayet* or province; and had a population, Serbs (Orthodox), Croatians (Roman Catholic), and Muslim—all tending to call themselves Bosnian, and all of whom would, in the twentieth century, murderously persecute each other. Aehrenthal, Austrian Foreign Minister, had annexed Bosnia, previously a protectorate, in October 1908. Not a good idea, it enraged the Serbs and helped set the scene for the 1914 murder (in a Bosnian town—Sarajevo) of an archduke who planned a liberal confederation for much Habsburg territory (probably including Bosnia)—and the outbreak of the First World War.

36. Already noted above as an over-emollient Minister of Labour in the Macmillan government, Walter Moncton would, aptly enough for a debate on Northern Ireland's irreconcilable relation with the future republic, be an eminent divorce silk and adviser to Mrs Simpson and Edward VIII.

37. Holder of many Cabinet offices in Liberal and National governments, later Viscount Samuel, followed Asquith in the great split: later leader of the declining parliamentary Liberal Party, but kept very busy: Home Secretary, High Commissioner in Palestine, also heading Enquiry into Mining Industry recommending many reforms and certain mistaken economies.

38. The Representation of the People Act 1918, abolishing all meaningful property qualifications, something done out of respect for the sacrifice of life during the war and reinforced by admitting women over 30 to the vote, went beyond anything contemplated here.

Unions, Women, and Unionists

1. Wilson, *Life of Henry Campbell-Bannerman*, 511.
2. Ibid.
3. Leon O'Broin, *The Chief Secretary: Augustine Birrell in Ireland* (Chattto and Windus, 1965), 84. (Quoted in Pearce, *Lines of Most Resistance*, 388.)
4. Parliamentary Debates 1912, vol. 36, col. 1468. Speech entire cols 1466–74 (quoted in Pearce, *Lines of Most Resistance*, 410).
5. Albert Venn Dicey, Vinerian Professor of Jurisprudence at Oxford who in 1886 compared the granting of Home Rule to Ireland to stepping off a cliff into a bottomless ravine. Cousin of James Stephen, exalted civil servant, another British triumphalist who spoke of Britain as 'a belligerent civilisation … founded on conquest, implying at every point the superiority of the conquering race …'
6. Not two-keel ships, though for yachts at least these are prized—simply two British ships to every German one.
7. Famous as an undergraduate debater (see also 'Our Empire', n. 9), Belloc (1870–1953) made a reputation as an independent radical and undermined it in several ways. He wrote too much with too little care. The charming travel books and delightful *Comic and Curious Verse* were offset by unchecked, dashed-off history embarrassingly discounted by professional historians and vitiated by the crude truculence of their Roman Catholic slant. Belloc himself, briefly (1906–10) an MP, lost credit by a reliable abuse of the Jews (present, if unproclaimed, in this diatribe), a reliably snarling aggression, and the increasing effects of heavy drinking. His career was darkened at the start, despite his First, by the unwillingness of all the Oxford colleges, starting with All Souls, essayed for a fellowship, to grant him one. His biographer, A. N. Wilson, speaks of interviews and dinners at which his arrogance persuaded examining dons that this was not something they wanted to endure on a permanent basis.
8. A sordid case of French overreaction to the arrival of a German warship the *Panther* in that Moroccan port. It was a chance of war narrowly missed followed by finalizing the annexation by France of Morocco.

9. Kurt Hahn, later headmaster of the unnerving Gordonstoun School.

10. Interestingly, the principal advocate of this had been Joseph Chamberlain. It would certainly have been less dangerous than the entanglement with an increasingly adventurist Russia brought about by Gray's Foreign Office team. See Clark, *The Sleepwalkers, passim* but esp. 279–81.

11. A national strike of just over a month, expanding from a local one in the Derbyshire field to the National Federation of Mineworkers, and one which challenged the random coalfield-to-coalfield terms and conditions, and sought a national minimum wage which the Liberal government accepted and established by statute.

12. Conservative politician, raised on Merseyside, very intelligent, hard drinker, soon to be galloper to General Roberts in an intimidatory demonstration of military strength by Ulstermen arming against Home Rule. He was too a future Lord Chancellor and reformer in 1925, of Land Law—also an occasional affecter of a serviceable piety for which he was famously sent up by Chesterton in verses ending 'Chuck it, Smith'.

13. Successful extremist. A southern Irishman, Church of Ireland (Disestablished), Trinity Dublin, southern accent, who would be called the uncrowned King of Ulster, lawyer and Law Officer who had urged and got a widespread provincial arming against parliamentary legislation, this same Home Rule Bill of 1912. In all of which successful exertion, Carson became probably the single most responsible bringer about of an Irish Republic wholly independent of the UK and the indefinite continuation of extreme violence in the six counties—historically and in character, a pernicious man.

14. An invitation sweetened by unexampled bribery of Members of the Irish Parliament to disestablish themselves

15. At about this time students from countries in the then Empire and other British-controlled countries begin to be a serious presence in Union debates and a running contradiction of its assumptions.

16. The parliamentary timetable limiting debate.

17. The First Balkan War begun in October 1912 leagued Serbia, Bulgaria, Montenegro, and Greece against the Ottoman Empire aka Turkey, lasted five months, effectively ended Ottoman territorial holdings in Europe, and caused major ethnic Turkish flight into residual Turkey proper. The second, begun in June 1913, expressed Bulgarian disgruntlement at a low share of the receipts and ended in defeat at the hands of her recent allies.

18. Contemporary English form for Serbia, Serbian form being Srpska.

19. Montenegro [Crna Gora].

20. The future Professor Harold Laski—learned, voluble, and widely loved, but famously requested by Clement Attlee for 'a period of silence'. He enjoyed fame

and controversy the way a certain kind of don does, but made the mistake of taking an official part—Chairman of the Labour Party's National Executive without the common sense to recognize its limits. Sadly the public slap-down given him by a real politician is the thing most commonly remembered about him.

21. Founder of an outstanding publishing house of the same name, notable for a special 1930s list—the Left Book Club—which, *inter alia*, published George Orwell's *The Road to Wigan Pier*; later an over-ardent public Christian to less effect.

On the Eve

1. The Home Rule Bill, made necessary after Lords' resistance to the Budget and Irish support in the Commons, was under way with Conservatives crying after an election to stop it.
2. Professional humorist—admired in his day.
3. Back to *Oxford Magazine* italics and profuse present-tense running commentary.
4. Future public intellectual and pronouncer in undergraduate embryo.
5. Future very useful and unlucky Minister.
6. Despite this sentiment, Jerrold would be a fascist of the Catholic sort, falling out with the Conservatives through his hostility to business. Founder of the *English Review*, he argued in favour of dictatorship and was directly involved in flying General Franco from the Canaries back to mainland Spain, the fearful Civil War, and logically enough, Catholic, Fascist dictatorship, thirty-six years of it.
7. Son of Joseph Chamberlain and someone who, according to one contemporary, 'always played the game and always lost'. A. G. Gardiner, Editor of the *Daily News*, said that Austen 'suffered not from filial piety, but filial servitude'.
8. Idea of the mystically inclined Tsar Alexander 1 after the Napoleonic Wars and taken up by Metternich, director of Austrian foreign policy, as one of pan-European reaction and suppression of argument.
9. A perceptive remark, if one ignores the 'true Liberal' aspect. Lloyd George was, even at this time, showing a hubristic taste for joining up with 'the first rate men of other parties', closest in this with F. E. Smith, who also made fierce partisan speeches and stood ready for cross-floor advancement.

The Threshold of the New

1. Translates as 'majority', something which that group had only briefly been.
2. Directly in charge of the actual explosion, it is widely stated, was a 17-year-old called Sean Lemass. In the early 1960s, the editor recalls hearing a moderate and conciliatory speech, very well received by the Union, delivered by the Taoiseach of the Republic of Ireland, the Honourable Sean Lemass.

3. C. E. Calwell, *Wilson* (Cassell and Co. 1927), 263, quoted in Charles Loch Mowat, *Britain Between the Wars* (Methuen, 1976), 76.

4. Annual report of Chief Medical Officer 1919–28.

5. OM italics/reported speech continue.

6. Returning with the rank of major after service in Flanders and Salonika. Naturally a Liberal, he would be obliged by the circumstances of the 1931 crisis to join the Coalition. After a brilliant reforming performance at Transport he was appointed Minister of Defence. Hostility came from the brusque way in which he did the urgent work of military reform offending the brass en route and a strong suggestion of the stupidest sort of anti-Semitism to which Chamberlain caved in. He was an able man not used when there was most need for all the able men in reach.

7. Ranting voice here of classical middle-class resentment and scorn for industrial workers. John Stewart Collis would emerge more amiably as a celebrant of rural life and an early ecologist. He would write fourteen books, notably *The Worm Forgives the Plough*, after a second war spent, ironically, as a farm labourer in Dorset and Sussex.

8. At this time and until October 1922, Lloyd George.

9. Conductor, like Lenin, of massacres.

10. Edward Marjoribanks, born 1900, heir to Lord Tweedmouth, also half-brother to Quintin Hogg (heir to the hereditary title of Lord Hailsham, later extensively amended), elected as Conservative MP for Eastbourne, had written a great part of his biography of Sir Edward Carson when, in 1932, and disappointed in love, he shot himself.

11. 'Uncle Arthur', by own choice, universal second man in Labour Party.

12. (1857–1940), exemplary leader in their hardest days of Scottish and British miners, engaged in creation of the TUC, very close to Keir Hardie, only late in life a Labour MP.

13. (1856–1941), leading trade unionist in the engineering trade, ILP man, President of the AEU, sincere as Christian and Communist, but a restless wanderer between organizations.

14. John Beverley Nichols (1898–1983), amiable de luxe hack with own manservant: writing sixty light books: on gardening, historic house restoration, biography, cats, para-psychology, and, briefly, pacifism—plus novels and children's stories. The journalism which also increased a charming income included a twenty-one-year column in *Women's Own*.

15. Ferociously right-wing paper far beyond Conservative Party, the post became defunct 1937; notably around 1920, it was an enthusiastic buyer into the (forged) 'Protocols of the Elders of Zion'.

16. Later Sir Edward: notable economist and business man, deeply involved with the League of Nations, KCMG for his work there. Later Chairman of the Britain in Europe Committee.

17. Sir Charles Petrie (1895–1977): more or less respectable far-rightist, an ultra-Conservative historian showing an early sympathy for Fascism, including Mosley, and cautiously supporting General Franco's regime, but disliking and distrusting Hitler. A phenomenally active writer, producing sixty books. A romantic admirer of the Stuarts, he wrote an alternative account of life after 1689 supposing the survival of James II.

18. G. K. Chesterton, associate of the pro-Mussolini Hilaire Belloc (see above), enjoyed a large reputation in his day, as humorist, Roman Catholic convert, and propagandist, highly tolerant of the right-wing politics seizing power in southern Europe. His eloquence as here, on the importance of marriage, rather tempered by the wide suspicion that he was conducting a *marriage blanc* through impotence.

19. Edwin Montague served as Under-Secretary for India 1910–14 and as Secretary of State for India 1917–22. He knew a lot about it. He had cooperated with Lord Chelmsford, a liberal Governor General, to create the India Act, the first deliberate granting of powers to Indians (members of regional assemblies elected by Indian voters), something furiously resented by the India lobby. He was also, as a Jew, opposed to Zionism as unfair to the Muslim inhabitants of Palestine whose relegation and neglect he correctly anticipated! He saw official facilitation as a way of decanting Jewish citizenship out of European countries into a receptacle state. He was also the husband of Venetia Stanley, object of Asquith's obsessive but interesting correspondence.

20. He also said to his friend Leopold Amery: 'I hate Indians. They are a beastly people with a beastly religion.' Amery diary, 9 September 1942.

21. Returned captain MC, later Conservative MP: pro-Franco, anti-Hitler, Christian Scientist, killed with Polish General Sikorski in speculated-about plane crash 1943.

22. (1894–1958), late entrant after naval service, including the defence of Amsterdam and German captivity, which inspired one of his best-known novels *The Fountain*. His play, *The Flashing Stream*, had its moment, a moment which passed. Morgan became an author out of the fashion, his intense earnest not helping. (The passage he quotes in this speech gets the sententious drift.) Only his association with the modish Tolkien and inescapable C. S. Lewis in sessions at the Eagle and Child gatherings gave him a thread of reference in his assured margin.

23. In many ways, the political equivalent of Charles Morgan, John Strachey enjoyed a good deal of unwelcome but deserved attention as an Etonian Socialist who joined Oswald Mosley's first draft *New Party* for creditable but dim reasons, surprised to find that it was turning Fascist, rejoined the Labour Party to be naive about Russia; and as member of the 1945 Labour government during post-war shortages, was given the short bread-stick of the Ministry of Food.

24. Greenwood, as noted in narrative above, was a Canadian lawyer turned Liberal MP (later Tory). A former Minister at the War Office with a reputation for taking

hard lines and backed by the likes of Carson, F. E. Smith, the Churchill of that moment, and indeed Lloyd George, he was made Chief Secretary in 1920—the last person to hold the office, perhaps too, the last one who should have been!

25. Leading Liberal politician from Wales rather than Welsh Liberal politician. Familiar from the Liberal government, he entered as Law Officer; subsumed into 1931 National Government: one of its better members; always in high office, never popular, Asquith loyalist, but would chiefly flourish in coalition, later Lord Chancellor.

The Consequences of the Peace

1. Public speech at Cambridge 9 December 1918.
2. *Third Winter of Unemployment*, Private Report produced in 1922 by the economist A. L. Bowley and others, 333. Quoted Mowat, *Britain Between the Wars*, 125.
3. Son of Ramsay MacDonald who, out of loyalty, would follow his father into the National Government in 1931, but would make an independent reputation as a very capable Minister, especially in what were then called 'Colonial and Dominion' matters, his ministerial period being followed by commissionerships in successive Commonwealth countries.
4. R. H Tawney, author of *Religion and the Rise of Capitalism* (G. Bell and Sons, 1926), History Chair at LSE. Much loved Christian Socialist who fought through the war as an NCO, refusing a commission and badly wounded. Altogether symbolically he would be married to William Beveridge's sister by William Temple. He had an enormous influence, historical and moral, down to recent times. There has however been a regretful conclusion reached that the evidence supporting his ideas has been offset by leading contemporary research in a different direction.
5. Having been *twice*, in a double-fit of Vice-Chancellor's power-mania, sent down did not prevent Gerald Gardiner enjoying an outstanding career at the bar, nor the record of a distinguished and reforming Lord Chancellor throughout Harold Wilson's first governments 1964–70.
6. Soloman Bandaranaike (1899–1959), with a Christian background, adopted Buddhism politically, Prime Minister of Ceylon from 1956, moderate leftist, moderately irksome to British, was assassinated by Buddhist monk, and, after an interval, succeeded by his wife.
7. (1902–77), Conservative MP of a liberal, humane sort 1945–55 (against the death penalty), equally temperate Roman Catholic convert. Latterly a publisher, also cricket-loving, wide-ranging journalist and author, not least of one of the best books about the Oxford Union, very useful here.
8. See 'The Threshold of the New', n. 16.

9. Editor of that Ultra-right-wing daily, in concert with its ultra-rightwing owner, Lady Bathurst.

10. Edwin Montague, Secretary of State for India since July 1917, responsible for the India Act which looked forward to India achieving Dominion status, making him a hate figure to the far right, something not diminished by his being a Jew. Such opinion is represented here by Howell Arthur Gwynne. Montague would in fact go very shortly, but over Chanak and its aftermath where he had opposed further dismemberment of Turkey. Allegedly, in India, he was trying to reconcile Muslims, anxious about his necessary democratizing reforms embodied in the Government of India Act. Gwynne's hatred was for the joint creator of that liberalizing legislation.

11. An error, there being no such earldom—probably the tenth Baron Middleton of Birdsall near Malton, North Yorks.

12. Rapallo Agreement made during the Russo-German flit along the Italian Riviera. This is the conference of April–May 1922 at which Lloyd George spoke with real vision about reconciliation of European nations and a combined drive on shared economic recovery, only for the blindly vengeful Raymond Poincaré, in that parallel speech at Bar-le-Duc, to insist upon the last grinding-down letter of Versailles. It was also from the Genoa gathering that German and Russian delegations quietly slipped along the coast to delightful Rapallo and a private treaty of their own. This played its contributory part in the coming fall of Lloyd George, for whom a triumph at Genoa was embarrassingly denied.

13. Richard Pares (1902–1958), later the outstanding and assumption-upsetting historian of the mid-eighteenth century—*George III and the Politicians* (Oxford University Press, 1953). Chair at Edinburgh; joint editor of the *English Historical Review* until his early death in 1958.

14. Poet and literary editor—won the Newdigate Prize (poetry).

15. Horatio Bottomley, alcoholic/charlatan editor of the trashblat *John O'London's Weekly*, involved in raucous and notorious recruitment rallies, bullying fitter, younger, and better men than himself into war graves—later imprisoned for embezzlement.

16. An earlier, obscurer earl, Edward Pakenham (1902–61), neither the present one —historian of the 1798 Rising, Thomas Pakenham—nor his earnest and political father, Frank.

17. Later a Republican Congressman dispassionately opposing both Prohibition and the Tennessee Valley Authority.

18. The familiar F. E. Smith *resartus*, famous as a Union debater thirty years earlier, now Lord Chancellor, notable in 1925 for legal reforms, for a sparkling, alcoholic cynicism, and for dropping-by-and-joining-in at the Union Debating Hall as a life member.

19. Minor politician, Liberal Conservative, of great charm and decent sympathies, but imperfect rectitude and worse judgement of company, who declined into radio celebrity.

20. Most ruthless and most pious of Irish Republican leaders, very nigh perpetual ruler of the country for forty years, deferential to the views of his next-door neighbour, the Archbishop of Dublin, dedicating the nation in its constitution to 'The Most Holy Trinity', and retarding its economy.

21. A gathering in 1919 in Amritsar, Sikh holy city, protesting against extended repressive measures which was met by an order to fire from General Reginald Dyer which killed nearly 400 people and wounded thousands. Followed by public floggings and the exoneration of Dyer, doing British authority in the sub-continent or anywhere else, no sort of good. Moplah gives its name to a violent Muslim rising violently put down—casualties at a higher rate put at 10,000.

A Rather Circumspect New World

1. Mowat, *Britain between the Wars*, 179–80.
2. Ibid. 182.
3. As in Nicholson's gin.
4. Charles Vane Tempest Stewart seventh Marquess (1878–1949); after an exceptionally brave and horrific war at the front including the Somme, forgivably though not everywhere forgiven, he became an active supporter of appeasement. His many visits to Germany and contacts with the Nazi leadership led to mistaken notions of sympathy. He conveyed to a sleeping government Hitler's 1936 observation that he would make war on Czechoslovakia and Poland (N. C. Fleming, *The Marquess of Londonderry: Aristocracy, Power and Politics in Britain and Ireland* (I. B. Taurus, 2005), 189). Wrongheaded for reasons created across 1914–18, and naive with it, this descendant of Lord Castlereagh followed purposes decent enough.
5. Later Master of Pembroke, historian, Liberal, and particular admirer of the Campbell-Bannerman government.
6. Outstanding, but desolating novelist and supreme stylist, also deeply oppressed and socially savage, professed supporter of all die-hards; and, as elegantly recorded in his late novel *The Ordeal of Gilbert Pinfold*, lifelong super-tippler (gin-and-liqueur mixes favoured), with vivid, apparitional delusions intruding to join the steady jobbing rage and tightly clutched religion.
7. Still Edward Pakenham sixth Earl, died 1961.
8. A strange question asked with wonderful insensibility after the recent experience of ferocious unemployment rising from 691,000 in December 1920 to 2,171,917 (17.8 per cent) in June 1921 before falling to 1,431,929 (12.2 per cent) in December 1922; the government reacted by effectively bypassing its own limitations and

conditions on benefit to avoid the feared consequences. In parts of the north—Barrow, Hartlepool, Stockton—the percentage unemployed rose well above 40 per cent.

9. Liberal MP for Penistone. A Liberal politician of some calibre, bitter opponent of Lloyd George, and opponent of cooperation with Labour. He lost the seat in 1924 and died in his mid-fifties in 1928.

10. Australian journalist, later diplomat. Critical of Chamberlain and appeasement, editor of *Sydney Morning Herald* and, after conflict with owners, transferred to Diplomacy: Australian ambassador to the Netherlands, then Italy where he died 1961.

11. Italics resumed.

12. Later a distinguished research chemist.

13. Shrewd and true. Baldwin despite, or perhaps partly *because*, of a steady inertia, also an un-Tory good nature, was essentially liberal.

14. Translator of virtually the whole corpus of Greek Classical drama, an Oxford figure, holder of the Greek Chair, married into the Carlisle Howards, and ancestor to the Toynbees. Essentially a Liberal figure, he would nevertheless in 1956 head the list of eminent persons supporting the Suez invasion as against the hostile list headed by Bertrand Russell.

15. Actually *Sir* Gyles, eleventh Baronet, film actor, also ten seasons at the Old Vic.

16. Roger Fulford, *Times* journalist and historian, joint editor of Greville's Diaries, also biographer, *Royal Dukes* (HarperCollins, 1933) of the sons of George III; finally in a busy life, Liberal Party activist and candidate.

17. Anthony (Puffin) Asquith, youngest son of H. H., later a well-respected film director. *Tell England, The Way to the Stars, Pygmalion, The Importance of Being Earnest.*

18. Headquarters of the League of Nations.

19. Future Conservative MP and Minister. As Colonial Secretary in the 1950s, he assembled the Central African Federation to help secure the command of a 200,000 plus white population. It fell succinctly apart.

20. Sir Dingle Foot, one of the four political sons of Isaac Foot. Liberal MP (1931–45) later turned to Labour. Solicitor General 1964–7, resigned over Wilson government's realistic inactivity in Rhodesia and wrote a book about the party divisions of his lifetime. At this time, and certainly on this issue, well to the right of Lennox-Boyd, his views on divorce reflected his family's strong Nonconformist beliefs.

21. Before his death aged 42, rescuing his daughter and another girl from drowning, Evan Durbin had become the chief intellectual influence on Labour's serious-minded right wing, stressing Keynes and rejecting Marx. Close friend and ally of Hugh Gaitskell.

22. (Lance), Legal silk and Liberal MP pre-war, later Labour. Not to be confused with his better-known, left-wing, journalizing brother, J.P.W. (Bill).

23. Taxation of land value as circumstances, like appearance of major roads, increased that value.

24. First in Philosophy, later a much and unjustly abused Foreign Secretary in the Wilson government, victim in the late 1960s of a self-righteous adolescent tantrum in this House.

25. Second Baronet 1906–88, later press proprietor, notably of *Picture Post*, and reliable rightist.

26. Parody-patriotic journal, noted elsewhere, a widely read publication, edited by Leopold Maxse, q.v. (son of its owner, a similarly paranoid admiral), who believed during the First War that 'a circle of evil men were conspiring to betray Britain to Germany'.

27. Kenneth Diplock, leading lawyer, Lord of Appeal, headed the semi-secret Diplock Courts for the fearful circumstances of Northern Ireland.

28. Chairman from 1921 of the National Peace Council.

29. Pre-eminent insider. Conservative Member for Hemel Hempstead 1920–37 with eight-month gap of Labour government. Essential confidant and backstage lieutenant (usually as Chancellor of the Duchy) to Stanley Baldwin, after whose retirement, Davidson left front-of-stage politics. Viscount Davidson 1938. Succeeded at Hemel by his wife.

Imperial Fatigue and New Clouds

1. Keith Feiling, *The Life of Neville Chamberlain* (Macmillan, 1946), 157–8.

2. Harold Nicholson, *George V* (Constable, 1984), 418–19.

3. Sir Henry Phelps Brown (1906–94). After a Second World War, engaged fighting in North Africa, then Italy, including horrific Monte Casino, would return to Economics with a chair at LSE. Deeply concerned at the practicalities of development economics.

4. Later High Court judge and president of the Restrictive Practices Court—also presided at Carmarthen Assizes over the 55-day-long *Black Mountain Lime Fraud* case, the longest ever British criminal trial.

5. Attempt to fix internationally binding boundaries with East and Central European largely new nations, but only reached on the western side.

6. Sir Anthony Rumbold, senior diplomat, son of Sir Horace Rumbold, altogether more distinguished Ambassador, later Minister to Paris and Ambassador to Thailand, then Austria. A man talking like successive generations of British Foreign Office figures, asserting, against all and any evidence, our (and by discreet extension their) importance.

7. Courtesy title of William Hare (1906–97) later fifth Earl of Listowel, otherwise Billy Listowel, active Labour politician: London County Council, last Secretary of State for India and other Cabinet/ministerial posts in the Attlee government.

8. Not found!

9. Younger son of the Duke of Northumberland, a distinctly Liberal Conservative with proper knowledge of education, having been Principal of Armstrong College, the incipient University of Newcastle. Served in his ministerial post for the duration of Baldwin's 1924–9 government, later Minister without Portfolio.

10. Churchill, calamitously incompetent in this post, mindful of show, and ignorant of economics, had returned sterling to the gold standard making for domestic deflation and the unemployment which followed. This revaluation upwards also intensified the effect on Britain of the US stock market crash.

11. Future Lord Hailsham (hereditary), future Mr Quentin Hogg (peerage discarded for unsuccessful attempt on the Conservative leadership), again future Lord Hailsham (life peerage), a highly intelligent man but political absurdist.

12. Italian Anarchists accused of two armed bank robberies in Massachusetts. The case became highly contentious because of the alleged prejudice, not least against foreign immigrants, of the presiding judge, something intensified by the powerful and moving speech in fervent denial made from the dock by Bartolomeo Vanzetti. Both were executed by electric chair.

13. By this time a devoted servant of the League of Nations.

14. John Wheatley: major Labour figure, best known for half million council houses, commitment of 1924, accepted and honoured by Stanley Baldwin as Prime Minister.

15. At this time, John Augustine Kempthorne—occupancy 1913–37; relevance of comment unclear.

16. Queen's Counsel, later Master of Inner Temple Bench, distinguished naval record, in both Sicilian and Salerno landings, first British officer to the Rhine bridge at Remagen, reliably mentioned in dispatches; active in many Jewish causes, twice denied Conservative constituency nominations amid charges of anti-Semitism and sympathetic resignations.

17. Geoffrey Crowther, editor of, and masterful influence upon, the *Economist*, 1938–56.

18. Edgar Lustgarten, broadcaster and minimal writer, best known for stagey broadcast accounts of criminal cases.

19. Not clear which Aubrey Herbert this is. The famous one, offered the Throne of Albania, had died in 1923!

20. A grotesque description like most of the others. Al Smith made his mistakes, particularly falling out with Roosevelt and drifting to the business right, but though he had to work with Tammany Hall, he emerged from his creditable government of New York State, free of any credible charge of corruption. As for the 'giving up his religious convictions', Smith didn't. He gained and lost votes as a Catholic, the first to seriously seek the presidency.

21. Don Salvador de Madriaga, Spanish academic and Liberal—future exile in this country from Franco.

22. This was wrong. Samuel made proposals critical of both sides: against Nationalisation, rejecting extra hour demanded by owners, telling the same owners to stop their charges against workers, recommending nationalisation of coal royalties like the earlier Sankey report and while favouring private reorganisation, eliminating smaller pits, he also recommended production incentives for miners.

23. Later Sir Hugh Foot from a Devon family with radical Nonconformist traditions—brother of John and Michael. Diplomat with major postings in Jamaica and Nigeria, but best remembered as conciliatory governor of Cyprus 1957–60, briefed Macmillan government to bring the emergency to an end. Later made a peer, Lord Caradon, serving as Minister of State at the Foreign Office under Harold Wilson, father of the radical and impactive journalist, Paul Foot.

24. Sir William Joynson-Hicks.

25. Pretty much the terms of the Homicde Act, the compromise legislation introduced by the Conservative government in 1957.

26. The periodic Hague conferences, the first in 1899, widely extending the scope and recognition of private international law. The speaker here must be referring to the one of 1930 concerned with the codification of League of Nations rules.

27. At this time a blameless member of the new Cabinet, an energetic, intelligent man charged with ideas to combat unemployment, at which he earnestly engaged without useful response; later an emulator of Mussolini and Hitler.

28. Later leading counsel and Labour MP, later yet, in late forties, expelled from party for the 'Nenni telegram' supporting the leading Italian Socialist, Pietro Nenni, his party at that time, in temporary alliance with the Italian Communist Party, itself later a model—over its sustained control of regional government in central Italy—of constructive Social Democracy and standards of honesty above the Italian political norm. His expulsion from the Labour Party looks in retrospect excessive and unjust to an un-sinister idealist.

29. Logical positivist philosopher and, notably on the *Brains Trust*, a mannerist television personality.

30. Sir Derek Colclough Walker-Smith (1910–92) Conservative MP (1945–83), Junior posts (1955–7), Minister of Health (1957–9), thereafter long-term senior backbencher. Before life peerage of 1983, he became in 1960 one of the very last baronets.

31. Long-term, very conservative Conservative, MP for Huntingdon preceding John Major.

32. Variant of the same enquiry about almost anything, for which Professor Ayer became painfully famous.

33. Douglas Hogg, later as LC, first Baron Hailsham.

34. Embarrassing, brutish son of Winston and minor national embarrassment.

35. Otherwise Eugene Lieven of the Baltic aristocracy, apparently Prince Lieven, and none the nicer for it.
36. For Imperial preference.

The Old Familiar Faces

1. Anti-union legislation passed in aftermath of the General Strike.
2. Arthur Cook, leading figure among the miners' leaders, no sort of rascal, but intense, emotional, and a poor tactician, essentially a tragic hero.
3. Otherwise Toby O'Brien, future advertising man and, in the 1950s, onlie [correct] begetter of commercial television!
4. Ramsay MacDonald—the comment instructive about its maker.
5. Sir Arthur Irvine QC MP (Labour) for Edgehill, Liverpool 1947 until his death in 1978. Solicitor General 1967–70.
6. Imperious and over-godly Chairman of first British Broadcasting Company (later Corporation). Earnestly Scottish, favouring higher cultural standards than are now thought advisable—good thing damaged by posthumous publication of diaries, all wonderfully preoccupied with the shared concerns of God and Sir John.
7. Not at this time, remotely Fascist, but rather Keynesian and favouring economic expansion.
8. Anthony Greenwood, anticlimactic son of key Labour figure and Cabinet Minister Arthur Greenwood. He had fleeting ambitions of party leadership c.1960, offering to stand against Hugh Gaitskell and embarrassing Harold Wilson into announcing his candidacy.
9. Ultra right-wing colonial administrator (Bombay and Egypt) and like Churchill rabidly hostile to Indian independence. Lobbied for declaration of war in August 1914, believer in special virtue of English upper classes, fervent opponent of Indian independence, but struggled through his own intense anti-Semitism to worry about Hitler.
10. The still not-yet-Fascist party of Oswald Mosley picking up on Keynes, before he ordered it into black shirts.
11. Exceptionally able municipalist, rising through success while heading London County Council, to expectations of Labour leadership, baulked by loss of his seat in the Labour calamity of 1931. Stood against Clement Attlee (lucky in his seat in that election) who had been chosen deputy leader of the temporarily shrunken party. On re-election in 1935, Morrison immediately stood against someone he now cordially hated. Attlee's understandable return of pique was backed threefold by Ernest Bevin's concentrated loathing. Both would periodically rejoice in what they called 'Doing down Herbert'. Much valuable service during wartime and post-war Labour governments, dimmed by a brief spell as Foreign Secretary,

seven months in 1951, approving in principle the putsch restoring the Shah of Iran to full (and abused) powers. This was carried out after his departure by the Americans with the British Conservatives, against a democratically elected government of Iran wickedly nationalizing its own oil resources.

12. Not a visiting Jan Christiaan, but his nephew.

13. Angus Maude, Conservative MP twice, returning after spell editing an Australian newspaper to act managerially in Margaret Thatcher's leadership campaign, then Paymaster General/chief henchman. Able, unemollient, commonly as below (see next debate) 'looking hard' at people; departure from Thatcher ministry characteristically leaving, not 'let go'.

14. Another brother Foot, at this time a Liberal, later Labour, deeply sincere and widely loved in the movement and beyond, but irksomely obsessive and certain of being right. Personal experience of editor is of explaining to him that William Wood's early 1720s Irish coinage, object of Swift's *Drapier's Letters*, had been certified as excellent and full value by Isaac Newton, also that Wood owned copper mines in Wales—and receiving the reply, 'No, No. Swift was right.' His calamitous leadership of the Labour Party 1980–3 showed the same regard for reality.

15. Parodic nationalist right-winger and Herefordshire squire, with a virulent style, briefly involved in creating the National Party. Winston Churchill in his unpleasant, 'I hate Indians, they are beastly people with a beastly religion' early thirties phase, was warned against association with him in opposition to Indian independence. Under-secretary at War Office, chiefly concerned with 'Home Front' 1940–45, later peer. (Nigel Knight, *Churchill: The Greatest Briton Unmasked* (David & Charles, 2008), 55.)

16. Hanged August 1944 as member of the Kreisauer Kreis (the main anti-Nazi grouping) in Hitler's little massacre after the 20 July 1944 bomb plot.

17. This must be Michael.

18. George Lansbury, Labour leader 1931–5, much loved in the party, but ousted 1935 by the attack of Ernest Bevin for his pacifism in the face of Hitler.

19. Author of an interesting article in the *New Statesman* 'Oxford Goes Left', quoted below; later historian and journalist.

20. At that time, Governor General of India, as he had been of Canada.

21. Courtesy title of the future Lord Halifax, future and ill-advised Foreign Secretary, engaged at this time in sympathetic dialogue over Indian moves toward Independence, his conduct more appropriate with the Indian Congress than the Nazis. His Polish Guarantees, instituted after the failure of Munich, involved Britain going to war at the most under-armed and dangerous possible moment. The war started and going badly, he would then favour accommodation with Hitler.

22. Main body of the shrunken Liberal Party—the group participating in the National Government and led by Herbert Samuel who took the Home Office.

23. An outstanding figure chairing and guiding the TUC at the hardest period of its history, closely allied with Ernest Bevin, the creator of the T&GWU. Also author of the ubiquitous *Citrine on Chairmanship* (*ABC of Chairmanship* (Fabian Society, 1939)).

24. July–August 1932 Commonwealth Conference in Ottawa giving up on the gold standard and embracing high tariffs for the rest of the world, lighter ones inside the imperial ring.

25. Intelligent Churchillian Tory, Alfred Duff-Cooper, later Lord Norwich, married to the better-known and shimmering Lady Diana: DSO for bravery 1918, anti-appeaser, good and readable biographer, *inter alia*, of Talleyrand. Close to Churchill, various offices, resigned in protest the day after Munich, later a popular and welcome Ambassador to France.

26. Later Sir Peter Pain QC, distinguished and popular judge with left-wing views—influenced by walking tour in Germany 1937 which convinced him of the certainty of war.

27. Playwright and biographer, notably of Edmund Kean, also broadcaster.

28. Agreed by all sources to have instigated Leg Theory, or Bodyline fast bowling, to physically intimidate batsmen, Douglas Jardine was known for intense, contemptuous hatred of Australians generally, ironically creating a long-service provocation for later Australian equivalents. He exploited Harold Larwood, a very fast bowler of Notts, telling him in the seigneurial way of Gentlemen's cricket, to bowl short so as to threaten the batsman's face. The injuries created an international breach with Australia which had loyally sent troops to fight in a British quarrel and defined a Pommie bastard worthy of the name.

29. R. B. Bennett, Canadian Premier, was less hard on Russia than authoritarian and repressive in dealing with the not very frightening Canadian Communist Party, to which cause he devoted the suppression of a number of legal and constitutional safeguards. Prime Minister from 1930, he would, despite late gestures toward New Deal economics, be swept out of power in the 1935 elections.

    In the context of an ultimately unsuccessful attempt at the Ottawa conference to achieve a measure of imperial protection, Bennett had offered Britain a preference in her market based on the addition of 10 per cent in present and future tariffs in return for Britain swapping the same preference with Canada and other Dominions. Unwillingness by the British government to embrace what ministers saw as a cynical bad deal led to a press campaign and backbench revolt against Baldwin's leadership seen off 4:1 in a vote.

30. Sir Max Beloff, distinguished political historian and full dress Oxford Great One.

31. His country was Portugal which, by means of assassination, had rid itself of monarch and monarchy before the First World War.

32. Overwrought and extensive response of patriotic opinion led by the *Daily Mail* soon to produce that headline 'Hoorah for the Blackshirts' and to treat that debate

as a species of treason and national degeneracy rather than a wrongheaded lark wonderfully timed for Hitler's first weeks in the Chancellery.

33. Evidently an amiable man, Lord Stanley would marry and be divorced four times with economic consequences.

34. Roy Jenkins, *Churchill* (Macmillan, 2001), 469.

35. Adolf Schlepegrell of University College, later Secretary, was indeed no Nazi. Neither was he shot, as stated by Christopher Hollis in his generally accepted account, *The Oxford Union* (1965), but by the end of the 1930s had made his way to Canada.

36. Archibald Fenner Brockway (1888–1988), ultimate English idealist in politics, held in dungeons—Tower, Chester Castle, Lincoln (where he met De Valera), as First War militant conscientious objector; born India, lifelong advocate of its independence. MP, latterly and ironically for Eton and Slough, where he was very well received, speaking to the young gentlemen, helped create both the Movement for Colonial Freedom and War on Want and finally, sweetly and ironically, be himself created a member of the House of Lords.

37. The broadly Keynesian measures of the New Deal with public works and ready expenditure, limited though it was!

38. Walter Rathenau, industrialist, liberal Minister and man of high, thoughtful culture. Responsible for keeping the German economy functioning during the First World War, he worked with the Social Democrats as an earnest of his belief in the constraining of capitalism. He achieved an important further piece of state-craft with the 1922 Rapallo agreement which brought Russia back into trading relations. Two months later he was murdered by two young nationalists who paradoxically admired him.

39. Gustav Stresemann, benignly tortuous German politician, Prussian nationalist, equipped as Foreign Minister, for the compromise, achieved at Locarno, in restoring normal relations with France. His death at 52 removed the man most likely to have kept Germany at peace.

40. Edouard Daladier, twice Prime Minister of France, provider of elements of a welfare state in his first ministry, later unwilling and unbelieving participant in the 1938 Munich agreement and projecting the essentials of what would happen. He had made that journey conscious of France's unpreparedness, especially in the air, and sought desperately to buy great quantities of US aircraft only to be stymied by French debt and American legalism.

41. Later seventh Earl of Longford, benign but interminable member of Labour governments, father of the popular historical writer, Lady Antonia Fraser.

42. Ronald Bell, Conservative QC, MP 1950–82, Libertarian and multi-racial sceptic.

43. Airey Neave, future war hero, successful Colditz escaper, Conservative MP, immediate adviser to Margaret Thatcher on her election victory, made Shadow

Northern Ireland Secretary, murdered by 'INLA', offshoot group of IRA 1979—both legs blown off, died in hospital.

44. Roman Catholic advocate, editor of the *Catholic Herald* at a time when Rome was close to Franco and under the Pontificate of Pius XII, generally authoritarian and right wing.

45. Derek McCulloch,'Uncle Mac'. BBC figure, chiefly on the 5 p.m. Children's Hour programme, alleged by responsible sources to have been a pederast preying on children visiting the studios.

46. Later President: after a war in which he saw action and left with the rank of Lt-Colonel, Harvey (1914–87) entered Parliament for Harrow East. In 1958 he was charged with gross indecency—found in park bushes with consenting guardsman; acquitted but convicted of breach of regulations, fined £5, resigned, though happily resuming successful career in Public Relations.

47. Oxford academic (New College), b. 1907, already a don at this time (author of *Plato Today*). MP 1945, denied junior office by Attlee who met his complaint by saying, 'Nothing to do with your ability Dick, strictly character,' which indeed, it was. Gentile Zionist, urging heavier Jewish immigration to Palestine, reliable intriguer in the Labour Party, helping found Keep Left, an internal faction, seeking out Harold Wilson early morning on the northern sleeper in 1960, to stand for leadership against Hugh Gaitskell. Housing Minister responsible for 1960s high-rise council domestic building, including high-alumina cement causing collapse, not strictly his fault, but wonderfully symbolic. Had joined successful libel action against the *Spectator* for an article truthfully describing drunken party involving Aneurin Bevan, Morgan Phillips (Labour Party Secretary), and himself in 1957, £7,500 awarded to each; career of the (truthful) young woman journalist ruined, something followed by her early death. In his autobiography, always a candid scoundrel, Crossman admitted perjury. He concluded his career as editor of the *New Statesman*.

48. An agreement at the lakeside resort of Stresa by which Ramsay MacDonald, Pierre Laval, and Mussolini guaranteed Austria against its difficult son, something rendered pointless when Mussolini invaded Ethiopia.

49. Active service at ironically Gallipoli, Churchill's First War disaster—second-last man out of Suvla Bay, also in Mesopotamia. Wounded twice—at Battle of Hanna and Western Front. Prime Minister 1945–51.

50. This is, as they say, 'a bit previous'. The appointment of Philip Cunliffe-Lister (later Lord Swinton), who would indeed make serious and effective efforts over aircraft production, only occurred in this same year.

51. Christopher Mayhew, later an intelligent and independent-minded Labour MP, with a highly sceptical view of the Israeli–Palestine issue putting him at odds with Harold Wilson and away from office.

52. Title taken by Sir William Joynson-Hicks (known as Jix—originally William Hicks—once perhaps Bill Hicks?)(1866–1932), Conservative Home Secretary, notable for moralistic comments and conflict with High Church revisers of the Prayer Book, though a conscientious and moderately reforming Minister.

53. Mussolini's son, a bomber pilot, described the effects of a bomb dropped on Abyssinians as 'Beautiful like the opening-up of a rose'.

54. Richard Gould Adams, journalist, author of 'Middle East Journey' and biographer of J. F. Dulles, more importantly a Pentagon-friendly journalist at the *Economist* and a founder of the Institute for Strategic studies, reliable defender of Washington right and wrong.

We Go into the Dark

1. Nigel Knight, *Churchill: The Greatest Briton Unmasked* (David and Charles, 2008), 58–62.

2. *Homage to Catalonia* (Frederic Warburg, 1938), *passim*.

3. Charles Williams, *Pétain* (Palgrave Macmillan, 2005), 295–6.

4. Clark, *The Sleepwalkers*, 555–62. It was all done by cumulative mistakes and failures of information in several countries. It was a sophisticated catastrophe.

5. Brigitte Hamann, *Hitler's Vienna: A Dictator's Apprenticeship* (Oxford University Press, 1999), *passim*.

6. This was hardly a second coming, but it trebled Labour's share of the vote to 38 per cent against Conservatives at 47 per cent, but badly understated with only 154 Members.

7. Born 1859, founded *Daily Herald*. Pacifist on principle throughout First War; sent to prison for part in the rates strike in Poplar, elected MP for Bromley and Bow, First Commissioner of Works. At the time of post-1931 cuts in health care, he referred to the Ministry (under Neville Chamberlain), as 'The Ministry of Death'.

8. Having been assured of the Union presidency in Michaelmas 1914, Harold Macmillan was now MP for Stockton-on-Tees, one of a number of north-eastern towns put out of work and impoverished by the slump. Notable among these was Jarrow, memorialized by its devoted Woman Member (not a lot of these in the 1930s), Ellen Wilkinson, in *The Town that was Murdered* (Victor Gollancz, 1939). Though the Prime Minister of 1957–63 would make later play with memories of his constituency at this time, Stockton-on-Tees, his sincerity should not be questioned. He had also served, an overlooked VC, with Durham miners at the front and remembered them warmly. See Simon Ball, *The Guardsmen* (Harper Collins, 2004), *passim*.

9. The Woodhead Commission Report (9 November 1938) proposed a projected partition of the territory, something rejected by the government as impractical.

10. Quintin Hogg, as Tory candidate loyal to Neville Chamberlain's appeasement, would, in the Oxford by-election of 27 October 1937, after Labour and Liberal withdrawals, be opposed by an 'Anti-Munich' candidate, the Master of Balliol, Sandy Lindsay, and get back with only a halved majority. A blow even to that brass-bound ego was reinforced by the crisp slogan coined by J. L. Austin, a philosopher normally abstracted out of sight: 'A vote for Hogg is a vote for Hitler.'

11. When might this have been?

12. Leading (liberal) Conservative and dedicated European, unlucky in a heavy style and poor tactics, but a decent, humane man and, uncommonly among politicians, a dedicated music-lover (Balliol Music Scholar). He was, at Oxford, at one with the Left in opposition to the Nazis and Munich.

13. Disraeli's definition of a *Conservative* government.

14. Journalist with good central European contacts, briefly editor of *The Times*, believed in Jewish conspiracies, especially in Vienna, which made him anti-Austrian, and who attacked moves to avoid the First World War as 'a dirty German-Jewish attempt to bully us into neutrality', but he did ultimately begin to worry about Hitler.

15. Well-meaning man, showered with attention in his time, but ultimately not the major poet he sought to be—doomed in a knighthood.

16. Maxim Litvinov, People's Commissar for Foreign Affairs 1930–9, closely identified with Collective Security and rapprochement with Western nations: removed and replaced in 1939, just ahead of a shift to the Hitler–Stalin pact, by V. M. Molotov who was not. Had British connections, an English wife, and a number of English friends, including H. G. Wells. Not quite certainly, but probably, Litvinov managed to survive violent death at the hands of Stalin's diligent servants.

17. Women, as gracefully designated here, were until 1963, confined to the gallery.

18. About to be annexed by Hitler.

19. Often but not here.

20. Not necessarily the most asinine speech in the history of the Society, but a decent contender.

21. Amiable Leftist then, later as an MP, amiable High Tory, as which he became popular knighthood material.

22. Sir Nicholas or 'Nico'—Superior Foreign Office eminence maintaining the Office's mystique over four decades.

23. Journalist on the *Observer*, primarily a war correspondent—China, Korea, etc., balanced, useful, and decently written.

24. Roy Jenkins, a leading Labour figure. From 1945 with Anthony Crosland (see n. 25) and Denis Healey (leader of the CP cell and general ignorer of Union debates), on the moderate wing of the Parliamentary Labour Party from 1945. Great reforming Home Secretary, then Chancellor in first Wilson government.

Would leave Labour after the Far Left *excelsis* of 1979–82, then helped form and lead the SDP, also author of sound and very readable historical studies—too kind to Churchill.

25. With Jenkins (see n. 24) an advocate, not least in a widely read book, of a non-Marxist Social Democracy; as Minister of Education in first Wilson government abolished grammar schools; later engaged with the *Guardian* journalist, Peter Jenkins, in a happily unsuccessful campaign in the late 1970s to remove Denis Healey from the Treasury, where he was imposing essential austerities, and, as his proposed successor, institute the ancient Tory nostrum, Protection; died 1979 when Foreign Secretary in the Callaghan government.

26. Leon Blum, formidable French intellectual, friend of Proust, leader of French SFIO (Socialist Party), much hated by Catholic/anti-Semitic element in France. The phrase 'Mieux Hitler que Blum' speaks an acreage of French rightwingery: Premier of Popular Front government formed 1936.

27. Philip Williams, friendly don, sensible right-wing Labour; specialist, based at Nuffield, in modern French political history, author of *Politics in Post-War France* (1957).

28. Future High Court Judge, also author of several entertaining books, notably *Irish at Law* (Secker and Warburg, 1981).

29. Best known as husband of Victoria Sackville-West (a marriage mixed in every sense), and owner with her of Sissinghurst Castle—well-meaning but naive figure, ill-advisedly engaged at the edge of politics, victim of his own self-injurious diary-keeping—also son of Sir Arthur Nicholson, one of the Foreign Office clique advising Grey behind the backs of Cabinet colleagues along the course which ended in the First War.

30. Later the moderate (and creditable) Labour MP for Dewsbury.

The Sunlit Uplands—almost

1. Knight, *Churchill: The Greatest Briton Unmasked*, 55.

2. Back from service in the Artillery, subsequently legal silk, often defending celebrity cases: Lord Snowdon for speeding, Francis Bacon for carrying cannabis. Continued active as Liberal, including candidacies, later going to the Lords.

3. The phrase responded to a Conservative attempt to ride on the reputation of Winston Churchill with the election slogan 'Let him finish the job.'

4. Not a Union type in his undergraduate days—future and embattled, loved and hated leader of the Labour Party in opposition from 1955 to his early death in 1963—valiant above the political norm, but something of a Manichee.

5. The interim Conservative government which looked after the democratic shop for the period after the war and before the 1945 General Election.

6. The Potsdam commitments were an unreal and potentially calamitous attempt to reduce Germany to a nation confined to agriculture and light industry (notably toys and beer), by dismantling or redistributing its heavy industry, thus guaranteeing its political virtue. In the light of Germany's present economic status and general virtue, this was one of the great irrelevancies of history.

7. Economist, best known and, as a campaigner, influential about development and conservation. Especially concerned with un- or underdeveloped countries.

8. Leo Pliatzky, exceptional Treasury civil servant, heavily and creditably involved during Denis Healey's Chancellorship with its early inflation, brief IMF episode, and final reduction of that inflation to 10 per cent. See the editor's biography of Lord Healey—*Denis Healey: A Life in our Times* (Little, Brown, 2002) and the excellent, enjoyable autobiography.

9. Too familiar pronouncer from a high place, *The Times*, for at least thirty years.

10. Sensible, intelligent, but unfashionable Minister or Secretary of State at Transport, Education, and Defence in the Wilson era.

11. At this time, a temporary don at, probably, his old college, Trinity, before being returned for South Gloucestershire in 1950.

12. Tony Benn—name demotically contracted *c.*1970 in an impulse of Identification with The People, since when, by gradual degrees, most politicians have shed the fearful elitism of their full, given names.

13. Foreign Secretary, as remarked above, resolutely anti-Soviet and hostile to Zionism, the General Secretary of the Transport Workers' Union who had dished George Lansbury's otherworldly pacifism as Labour policy before the war, a genuinely great man.

14. He didn't have a cathedral—and wouldn't get one, a done-over chapel, until 1980.

15. The one which defined the Cold War as an 'Iron Curtain' which had 'descended from Stettin on the Baltic to Trieste on the Adriatic'.

16. Charles Monteith, always quiet and thoughtful, later a quite outstanding publisher's editor at Faber, cherished by writers.

17. Television journalist/editor, early defector, unsurprisingly given the tone of this, to the Conservatives, in 1957. Later 1962, elected as such.

18. Conservative MP (with brief break) 1931–61. High point, Minister of Works, later ennobled.

19. Sincere and hard-working specialist in health and welfare, but given to remarks which right-wing newspapers enjoyed quoting.

20. Dynastic Tory MP and Minister, reminiscent of his father (see above *passim*)—jocose, patronizing and ever, incrementally, more intolerable.

21. Ironically, the Conservative governments of 1951–64 would, via Walter Monckton and Winston Churchill, concede substantially more to union wage demands than did that of Clement Attlee.

22. Frank Byers, then an MP, but during a long post-parliamentary afterlife, the leading Liberal and universal media stand-in for the party well into its recovery. (After the war military titles were all the fashion until the mid-1950s, especially on election posters.)

23. It did.

24. Almost certainly son of the baronet, soldier, and courtier (secretary to King in the 1930s), Sir Clive Wigram.

25. Kenneth Gandar-Dower (1908–44), tennis player, general athlete, fivefold Cambridge Blue, aviator, and polymath of every kind of adventure; a boyhood hero lost with 1,300 others, by Japanese sinking of the SS *Khedive Ismail*.

26. Recurring butt of Conservative ill-humour after the early, ill-advised comment, 'We are the Masters now,' though later nicknamed 'Sir Shortly Floorcross', he left party politics, generally sitting in the Lords as a cross-bencher.

27. The winter of 1946–7 was indeed one of historic ice and snow-bound ferocity such as no planning could mend, one which naturally created unprecedented demand for fuel. The mean maximum day temperature for February 1947 was below freezing point at 31.7 F; the night figure was 24.1 F: all lower than next highest yearly figures—of 1995.

28. Later one of the best-liked of politicians, a mild and thoughtful liberal Tory.

29. An inspirational Oxford figure who, here and in a highly successful book, provided a strong and impressive case for what would become the European Union and for Britain's taking part in it.

30. An undertaking was made by President Harry Truman in March 1947 to intervene indirectly, but effectively, in the Greek civil conflict and, if necessary, in Turkey. It was apt and cost-effective at the immediate time, but led to an unselective intensification, caught in President Kennedy's inaugural address of 1961 to 'Go anywhere ...' much of it demonstrated, in Vietnam, Afghanistan, and Iraq, to be too far.

31. Henry Wallace—idealistic and rather naive agrarian, owner of *Wallace's Farmer*, a premature peacenik who would be a third candidate in the 1948 US presidential election, ironically making Republican victory over the subsequently victorious Democrat President, Harry Truman, a supposed, if unfulfilled, certainty. Wallace was widely and unfairly characterized as a 'Fellow Traveller' with the Soviet Union.

32. First use of this invaluable refinement spotted here so far.

33. Peter Kirk, a typical new liberal Tory, pro-European and accepting mixed economy, probably a Bow Grouper, followed Rab Butler at Saffron Walden in 1965 and would be advanced to office by Alec Douglas-Home then Edward Heath, after which his career would be cut short in 1977 by early death at 49 with over-application to work blamed.

34. Heavy Scottish lawyer and future Home Secretary, eloquently despised by R. A. Butler—'... living proof that Carlyle was wrong to define genius as a transcendent capacity for taking trouble'.

35. MP for variously named and adjustable parts of South London—Lambeth North, and Vauxhall, with a break in the 1930s, until 1979, retiring as Father of the House. Founder with Stafford Crips of the left-wing non-Labour Party-line weekly, *Tribune*. Responsible for the last and later reversed act of nationalization—Iron and Steel in 1951.

36. The Sharp plan was not proceeded with; and a future piece of brilliant, imaginative unpleasantness, the later high-calibre road through Port Meadow of the early 1960s, was also unaccountably resisted.

37. Robert Pitman (1925–69), journalist with column on the *Sunday Express*, moved from Labour supporter to an idiosyncratic Right, largely in exasperation at the mood of the 1960s—died, stoically, of leukaemia.

38. Gathering with attendance of major European figures Adenauer, Spinelli, and Churchill, to discuss prospects of European Union first by creation of the council of Europe.

39. Big Oxford personality, who became big television personality—a formidable man and a likeable one for all that.

40. Briefly mentioned in 'The Threshold of the New', commentary, but worth more: long time old-timer, 1920s Clydesider, Scottish-Jewish, virulent style; temperamentally and personally, rather than ideologically, bitter—hated *most* people.

41. Conventional Tory MP: Windsor 1942–70, unhappy about Rhodesia, a busy whip at Suez. Later and inevitably, 'Sir Charles'.

42. Uncritical Soviet loyalist, useful chiefly to the Conservatives.

43. Well-liked TV journalist who became a well-liked and moderate Tory MP.

44. Eng. Lit. don, Merton Professor 1957–66, translator, up-dater, and, it sometimes seemed, proprietor of Chaucer and Langland.

45. Contradicted by the election results of 1950 and a refusal on principle by Sir Stafford Cripps to advance legitimately favourable redistribution, reducing Labour to an overall majority of six with a clear lead in votes.

46. Ally of Hugh Gaitskell, influencing him to resist entry into Europe.

47. A West European Union as preliminary organizing, then consolidating body 1954–2011, has to be distinguished from the actual accomplished European Union to which, at the time of writing, we belong.

48. Conservative MP for Exeter 1945–51 resigning mysteriously *after* re-election: later a judge, enthusiastic for capital punishment.

49. Charles I loved art; the first two Georges were devoted to music; George IV, with educated knowledge and love of architecture, was also an intelligent admirer of the novels of Jane Austen which he kept always to hand.

50. Future brilliant, amusing, dodgy leader of flourishing Liberal Party. Later yet, in the days of homosexuality's criminal status, tried for attempted incitement to murder.

51. In the early 1960s, a dour and offputting presence as Senior Member.
52. Major twentieth-century poet, also thoughtful producer on the former Third Programme.
53. Son of the editor of the 1930s *Times* (see above *passim*), he had a quieter life editing papers in Darlington and Oxford.
54. Labour MP for Lincoln from 1964, Minister of State at the Home Office then Financial Secretary at the Treasury. His de-selection at Lincoln in 1972 marked the beginning of not only Far Left hostility to the broad Labour tradition, but the exploitation of local parties to organize zealot groups to control or depose MPs. Taverne made a stand, resigning his seat and re-contesting it, winning then, but narrowly defeated at the subsequent 1974 election. He continued active alongside a serious and reputable business career, on the Pro-European liberal Left. Close to Roy Jenkins and Shirley Williams, he was a force within the SDP, but not an enthusiast for Mr Blair.
55. Tony's more reasonable brother, if not evidently so here.
56. Distinguished civil engineer: built Dome of Discovery at the 1951 Festival of Britain, involved in construction of Sydney Harbour Bridge; son of Alexander Kerensky, the liberal democratic Prime Minister of Russia in 1917, replaced by the Lenin admired by so many of these young gentlemen.
57. Ballet critic.
58. *Choose?*—which until 1975, it didn't.

All Sorts of Dangerous Modern Ideas

1. Long-term Labour MP and latterly, ultra-rightwinger, harder bitten than many Tories.
2. Sir Peter Parker, d. 2002, businessman, active with many companies, but best known as an embattled Chairman of British Rail, Labour appointment, most of it—1979–84—stuck with Thatcher; Oxford friend of Shirley Brittain (Williams), and himself a Labour candidate, later supporter of the SDP. His interest in the arts, lifelong—Sir Peter, an indisputable good thing.
3. Later an amusing and combative financial editor of the *Sunday Telegraph* and author of a defence of the middle classes, his life cut short by a motor accident.
4. Foreign Office man eliding into politics as MP for Blackpool South, Junior Minister in two departments, Defence and the Foreign Office.
5. Daniel Malan elected premier of Nationalist government in 1948, retiring in 1954; Reformed Church minister, founder of Purified National Party, later merging with the National Party, opposed South African involvement in Second World War; instituted the whole system of statutory, organized black inferiority known as Apartheid.

6. *Observer* journalist, not to be confused with Irish pol and racing tipster.

7. Eton and New College, aristocrat, nephew of the Liberal War Minister, Cambridge geneticist of the highest order whose ideas partly anticipate the 'Selfish Gene' thinking of Richard Dawkins; politically something of a fool. Admirer of the Soviet Union through the purges, camps, and Nazi–Soviet pact. Retreated from Communism, *c.*1960, but remained an admirer of Stalin. Author of at least one, captivating children's story.

8. Monsignor Joseph Tiso (1888–1947), Roman Catholic priest, headed a collaborationist government in Slovakia under Nazi tutelage. On two occasions he approved the sending of some thousands of Jews to the camps and, on one other, avoided doing so. He was also seen by Czechs as a busy mover in the break-up of the Czechoslovak state in collaboration with the Nazis. Tried before the establishment of the Communist regime, and refused a reprieve by President Benes, he was hanged in 1947. The Vatican *apparat* of Pius XII, which, creditably, had tried to stop his deportations, now treated him as something of a martyr.

9. The slightly squashy but welcome encyclical of Pius XI 1931 which acknowledges all sorts of mutual obligations in society, using the language of all-round restraint and mutual concern. It spoke most unThatcherly about doctrinaire support of the markets, attempted unwisely to define the fair wage, and leant further to the liberal Left than anyone would have expected from a papal encyclical. On the other hand, it talks in the old Pio Nono style about the Vatican being an island in the middle of Italy and takes great care not to offend the Fascism prevailing in that sea. Even so, the advent in 1939 of Pius XII would put Pius XI into a comparative and shining light.

10. Later Roman Catholic Bishop of Leeds.

11. Herbert Morrison—when he was about to succeed a dying Ernest Bevin as an unlucky Foreign Secretary who he would do the wrong thing, badly, during the Persian (Iranian) Oil Crisis.

12. Gerald Rufus Isaacs, second Marquess (d. 1960), would hold subordinate positions at the Foreign Office until 1957.

13. A. V. Alexander, a Somerset man, long representing Hillsborough, Sheffield, leader of the Co-operative Party element in the Labour Party, someone who, in Cabinet, judged right on certain important specifics: supporting Philip Snowden in defence of Free Trade—and opposed there the proposed cuts which split Labour and fatally defined the National Government for Labour supporters. A capable Minister, usually of Defence (though overshadowed and overreached by Churchill in the War coalition), and again in the Attlee government.

14. Close relative of Seretse—and rival.

15. Later Conservative MP (Tunbridge Wells), Solicitor General then, and across 1983–92, the two law offices: Solicitor General, then Attorney General, before

becoming Northern Ireland Secretary 1992–7. Finally raised to the Lords—dry, cool, proficient. and very much Lord High Everything else.

16. *Sir Maurice*—Professional academic administrator—Leicester University, Lincoln College; another elder presence as a Senior Member of the Union Society—his observation here surely a prized entry in any anthology of insensibility.

17. Gerald Kaufmann divider of opinion: long-term Labour MP till late, then peer, but forever denied shadow-minister, capable of pettiness and point-scoring, scored heavily expenses-wise, but made valiant efforts for constituents and a brave contrarian as steady Jewish critic of the General Sharon/Settler-mentality aspect of Israel—a proper MP.

18. Trained for Roman Catholic priesthood, hence the stern views ahead of a busy marital record; turned to better money and more fun as demon Defence brief, getting Jeremy Thorpe off on serious charges. His status and a talent for bullying is alleged, when he was retained by Jimmy Saville, to have persuaded the *Sunday Mirror* that with 'a watertight case' against the brute for molestation of two girls, they dared not print it.

19. One 'n'—spelling correct: this is the *French* Minister, M. Robert Schuman.

20. Recognizing Franco.

21. Younger brother of Anthony, son of Viscount Stansgate—minor voice-off in politics.

22. Near-megalomaniac US general therapeutically sacked by President Truman.

23. Gifted Conservative MP, academic, and useful person: edited Bagehot, influential in reforming and liberalizing law on obscenity; career as Cabinet Minister spoiled by delusion that Margaret Thatcher had a sense of humour.

24. William Wedgwood Benn, Viscount Stansgate—father of David and Tony. Naive upper-middle-class Left lost in aspiration.

25. Son of William Wedgewood Benn, aspirant and foiled Labour leader: eldest and successfully reluctant heir to Stansgate title, monstered by Tory press, by which his opinions and ambitions were cherished. Charming to meet, but the ultimate tiring idealist in politics.

26. Labour, later SDP, MP after late entry at Leyton, but better known as interpreter and facilitator of philosophy—also Inspector Morse-like, an excessive Wagnerist, but very nice man.

27. Initially unlucky though blameless Labour candidate, later MP, given bad time but saw off local zealots, published specialist in Kenyan folk culture.

28. Named for the French Premier at the time of its proposal, Rene Pleven, but largely the work of the eternal Jean Monnet—it called for a supra-national European army and was furiously demonstrated against by the large Communist Party of France.

29. Harry Truman.

30. Headline Queen of the 1950s.

31. Also wrote, 1945, *The Road to Serfdom*, intelligent but over-the-top denunciation of Socialism.

32. As to the giving and the peace, a recurring Conservative illusion.

33. A fourteenth baronet helping to found CND and to teach maths in a South London grammar school, Sir Richard disarmed standard Tory abuse by a shining and not-to-be-argued-with disinterest.

The Old Order Not Changing Very Much

1. We now know something relevant to this defiance, something about the man, from *The Guardsmen*, Simon Ball's magnificent and fiercely readable account of a group of First War officers, later in Parliament—that he had been well worth the VC he didn't get at Loos.

2. Andrew Roberts, *Eminent Churchillians* (Weidenfeld and Nicolson, 1994), 267.

3. Post-1918 Marxist/Nationalist party.

4. Ralph (later Raphael) Samuel, historian of working-class life: most likeable member of the new left group about to emerge at this time.

5. Future City man and notably good-humoured Tory MP.

6. Much garlanded and rather oppressive public intellectual.

7. Norman St John Stevas: serious scholar, slightly absurd politician, tried to ingratiate Mrs Thatcher with jokes—fatally!

8. Met by me as undergraduate, now distinguished architect.

9. The former Philip Cunliffe-Lister whose pre-war exertions, building fighter planes for the coming war, may have been the most important thing done by a British Minister across the century.

10. Noel Browne, Minister of Health in a Fine Gael/Labour coalition, who in 1947 introduced his 'Mother and Child Scheme' in a Health Bill, a version of an NHS for Ireland, only to be driven out of office when the hierarchy, headed by the far too powerful Archbishop of Dublin, John Charles McQuaid, perceived this to be incipient Communism and forbade the service. Irish people still talk about it.

11. This papal statement was issued by Pius IX in 1864, condemning a great acreage of free thought, opinion, and study. Something done in the aftermath of Garibaldi and the Italian state taking away the papacy's swathe of secular territories in Central Italy, the *Syllabus* looked like an offsetting and imperious claim on moral and intellectual command. Notably appalled were people of the highest moral and intellectual calibre outside and within the Roman Church, like respectively Gladstone and Newman.

12. Labour MP, naval Minister, pioneer of televised political journalism, sympathetic to Palestinian Arabs—typically of his independent, unfashionable politics.

13. MP and long-service well-regarded junior in several departments 1979–86, thereafter permanent academic, author, and public intellect.

14. What the Americans used to call Taiwan when they were not calling it China.

15. Sending such materials to speakers was standard CCO practice. It also had a minimal publication, setting out the party line.

16. Aneurin Bevan (1897–1960). See above in commentary. Outstanding radical Minister of Health responsible for creation of the National Health Service, but at this time, falling out with the Labour leadership and specifically with the other contestant for the Labour Party leadership, Hugh Gaitskell.

17. Not the former Liberal Democrat leader and graduate of Edinburgh University, some other David Steel.

18. 'Hon. Tom Pon', later the well-liked Labour Chief Whip in the Lords.

19. IRA man, son of John McBride (one of the sixteen shot for taking part in the 1916 rising). Sean, after acquittal on charge of murder, followed an unsuccessful career, attempting to float a left-wing nationalist party, Clann na Poblachta, took a late law degree, and became, via Europe and the UN, something of an international code writer, notably on codifying human rights—something also of an international bore.

20. Later disowned by the Ulster Unionists as too moderate and liberal, also a very readable popular historian.

21. Sensible politician with unnerving style of address. Holder of major office under Mrs Thatcher and John Major, having played a meritorious part in removing the Lady.

22. Law Lord, author of the Hutton Report on the death of Dr David Kelly, speaking of whom, Alastair Campbell has been quoted as having told Mr Blair, 'I've found you the right judge.'

23. There had been reluctance in dealings with local nationalists in the Gold Coast, like J. B. Danquah, and leaders had been detained. But the territory would become a sovereign nation in 1957.

24. Surgeon with distinguished medical record during First War, later leader of the c.200,000 white settlers of Southern Rhodesia and Prime Minister for twenty-three years. He instituted the federation of Northern and Southern Rhodesia and Nyasaland. Retired as Viscount Malvern.

25. Rose through Miners' Federation as leader of Welsh miners. As Minister for National Insurance from 1945, introduced a key part of the welfare state, the benefits system. He would later be Colonial Secretary, giving authority in this debate. In 1956, as Hugh Gaitskell's deputy, he was an angry opponent of the Suez venture.

26. Corrupt, imperious, and impossible Premier of South Korea given to extensive arrests and massacres of opponents, ultimately overthrown 1960 after crowds had been fired on. Fled to, unsurprisingly, the United States.

27. Amusing and stylish Liberal Tory, unappreciative of Margaret Thatcher, close to Michael Heseltine.

28. Narrowest area of the Korean peninsula.

29. Long-time Labour pillar, essentially of the party's Left, but finally, though honourably, defeated through the machinations of her enemy, James Callaghan, in response to her brave attempt to bring trade unions within some legal restraint. The manoeuvre reinforced Callaghan's prospects of becoming leader and as Prime Minister 1976–9, inheriting two years of trade union excess.

30. Not something you could say today.

31. The former Sir John; see 'The Threshold of the New', n. 27.

32. The widely liked and very readable political journalist and broadcaster, editor of the *New Statesman* and deputy editor of the *Observer*.

33. Entitlement of graduates of certain universities to vote both in their domicile and in contest for a university seat—abolished by the Representation of the People Act of 1948.

34. The outstanding Labour figure not to have held the leadership—ultimately successful as Chancellor over five painful years, 1974–9, in tempering, by personal intervention and persuasion of reluctant union figures, the disastrous inflationary consequences of union strength and thus stabilizing the economy at 10 per cent inflation after it had touched 28 per cent. See the editor's full and authorized, with private papers, biography *Denis Healey: A Life in our Times* (2003).

35. A strange, interesting man who combined disgust at the death penalty which made him the driving force behind ultimate abolition, with uncomplicated reverence for the Soviet Union and Stalin, practitioners of execution on a stupendous scale.

36. Old style Imperialist, a member of Alfred Milner's 'Kindergarten'. *The Times* correspondent 1899–1900 on the South African War, but also ardent advocate, close to Churchill, of rearmament to resist Hitler. His words in the 1940 Confidence debate resonated. He called out to the Labour spokesman, Arthur Greenwood, as he stood up, 'Speak for England.' His own quotation in the same debate, from Cromwell's dismissal of the Long Parliament, 'You have sat here too long for any good you have been doing. Be gone, I say and let us have done with you. In the name of God, go!' fitted better and has resonated.

37. Early mandarin of independent and later BBC TV, indelibly associated with high standards and good programmes.

38. One which, over fifty subsequent years, proved a model of futility and has been replaced by something else…

39. A younger son of, probably, the *third* Earl of Iddesleigh, a title granted to Sir Stafford Northcote, holder of a 200-year-old baronetcy, and, rather more important, Disraeli's Chancellor—a recurring family in these pages.

40. Rhodes Scholar and film executive, ending as President of the Walt Disney corporation; unsurprisingly perhaps, given his opinions here, a close friend of Clint Eastwood.

41. Ruskin man turned Nuffield man, encyclopedic student of political ideas, practice, and everything—very good thing, later peer. Worked in close cooperation with Barbara Castle on her white paper, *In Place of Strife*, 1969—proposing the union reform legislation scuppered by a fearful James Callaghan.

42. Irish historian noted for valiant hostility, while teaching in Belfast, toward IRA violence.

43. Later reverting to given name 'Raphael': Marxist cultural/social historian of the sympathetic, interesting, actually likeable, sort. Concerned with the human aspect, the faces of the people in the statistics, he left a body of respected work.

44. Whatever Louis actually said, it wasn't that.

45. Astute and effective publisher of Orwell, A. J. Ayer, Kingsley Amis, and a number of light bestsellers who found religion and lost impetus.

46. Journalist of every sort, *Guardian* reporter for one, though his account of Soviet Russia in the 1930s, almost alone in its recognition of terror and starvation, proved un-reprintable after the war, because of its marked anti-Semitism. Wartime undercover operative, he shrewdly admired De Gaulle above Churchill—later, in the early 1950s, a very good editor of *Punch*. An in-law of the Webbs, he defected from the Left, assumed, as here, a facile despair, and became a tiring Roman Catholic convert. His lip on auto-curl, the astringency soured into undifferentiated all-round scorn, he became, via television, what in mid-century was called a 'personality' and now a 'celebrity'.

47. Poet, critic, anthologist, literary editor (of *Encounter*), biographer, working man of letters with an Edmund Gosse-like scope, mingily rewarded for vast and meritorious activity with an OBE.

48. Swiss-extracted decliner of Oxford University for Manchester who became a leading film critic of the day (*Manchester Guardian* later *Observer*).

49. A play, much denounced, dealing, very chastely, with prostitution.

50. Vicar of St Aldates, author, 1959, of *The Making of a Christian*.

51. Tory MP who resigned in disgust at the failure of the Suez adventure. A high and low Tory both (and relentless with it), military/patriotic and reactionary; also a director of Union Miniere, urging upon ministers a friendly attitude to Moise Tsombe, that Company's creature, later ruler of the breakaway company state of Katanga.

52. The British CP's intellectual and guardian of its correct line, one as hard and implacable as lines come.

53. Poet of some standing.

54. Former President of the Union, biographer of at least two presidents of the United States.

55. Son of Leopold, long-term Tory MP, old-fashioned Empire man, not the most effective speaker, but courteous, honest, and decent, way above Waterhouse.

56. Tutelary demi-goddess of Liberalism, daughter of Asquith, grander in manner than she quite intended to be, the steel-penetrating voice contributing, but resister of Tory advances and not a bad old thing.

57. Trade unionist whose detailed grasp and command of a case achieved major advances for the miners as leader of the Welsh section of the old Federation. A Communist, on the back of an intended Nonconformist ministerial career and pretty much respected beyond the CP. Disinterested and rational in every way, a superior article to some successors.

58. Another of the Iddesleigh Northcotes, reliable convert descendants of Disraeli's quite sensible Chancellor.

59. Queen of contraception, valiant and successful battler, especially against the idea of the child's life mattering above the mother's and her soul above an everlastingly pregnant body—a liberator/liberatrice!

60. Labour MP 1964–75. He had seemed, to younger university contemporaries like the editor, the most brilliant debater imaginable, something of the elder Pitt's 'diamond eye', as he argued for a rational, moderate Labour position. In actual politics, the House of Commons, he had very little effect and, a victim of bad timing, in the grim 1970s period of Stupid-Left ascendancy and union command, never seemed to try. A willingness, legally but unimpressively, to take payment as the bookmakers' lobbyist in the Commons left him self-sold very short. He turned to TV and was very effective as an interviewer, though his thin journalism at the *Sunday Times* was best noted for adulation of Mrs Thatcher—'The choice and master spirit of the age.' He chose to minimize taxation by living in the Channel Islands.

61. Briefly 1966–70, an ardent left-wing MP for the marginal seat of Lewisham West, later holding managerial posts in nationalized industries—resigned creditably 2001 from the Labour Party in protest at the invasion of Iraq.

62. Brought as babe-in-arms from Leipzig, 1933. Film producer of high quality work—*The Go-Between, The Hireling*, and *Edward Scissorhands*.

Invading Countries is Wrong

1. Semi-invisible politician, Attlee's Home Secretary—came out against the death penalty after five or so years of signing death warrants.

2. Humane, very clever and pleasant, but ethically careless, liberal Tory who, when sicked with the job of governing the place, defined Northern Ireland to the flight waiter for all time: 'God, what a bloody awful country. Can I have a large whiskey?'

3. A great and tiring fuss was being made at this time by the novelist/journalist/gentlewoman, Nancy Mitford and her concepts of 'U' and 'non-U'—in speech, usage, deportment, little-finger crooking in the nice conduct of a cup of tea, boiled-egg-opening and anything handy—as Upper class or Not-Upper class.

4. Vastly prolific and high selling novelist, of such genres as crime and the occult, also involved with Home Security at a high level during the Second World War; a man of bitter and extravagant political views, mightily contemptuous of the working classes generally—rather nasty.

5. Dr Cyril Garbett heard above as gently wise undergraduate, a good and sensible man worth mourning.

6. Under the influence of two Low-Church Conservative politicians, Sir Thomas Inskip and Sir William Joynson-Hicks, Parliament threw out a revised prayer book alleged to betray 'Romish tendencies', more accurately, Keble-ish tendencies.

7. With all Neville Chamberlain's resolute error, the recurring, smart-alec trick of deriding him for having been Lord Mayor of Birmingham is so much smugly one-up Oxbridge.

8. Don turned headmaster, turned report writer to governments who, in 1957, would notably lead a commission recommending legalization of homosexuality.

9. Ex-Librarian actually, at this time Chancellor, soon, after the failure of the invasion he had advocated in Cabinet, to become Prime Minister.

10. US Secretary of State from 1953 until a month before his death in 1959: a dull, dispiriting Republican lawyer in rimless glasses, given to unnerving bellicose language, driving an inspired onlooker to invent the term Brinkmanship.

11. Untrusted and faux bonhomous Labour MP making reliable money from business dealings with East Germany, something kept up even after Ulbricht's establishment of the Berlin Wall.

12. As noted above, soldier, Colditz escaper, later Conservative MP, close adviser to Margaret Thatcher, murdered by IRA.

13. Bulganin and Khrushchev, lately on a trip to Britain, on which they had visited Oxford.

14. Dishonest, sinister/comic newspaper owner and publisher with Oxford business base (where editor, as undergraduate, was warned by his tutor not even to think of getting a job). Too close to Labour Party for its good. At its conferences, he would stalk the hall, a black mac cloakwise over his shoulders, looking oddly like Dracula: ultimately a suicide.

15. The aphorism was not coined by Stalin, but by the more stylish Lenin—and more briskly—'Who whom?'

16. Anthony Eden.

17. Konni Zilliacus, Finnish-American born in Japan, unsurprisingly a linguist, also League of Nations man, apologetic for Soviets, but deviationist over Yugoslav defection, somehow occupying Labour seat, tolerated—probably rightly.

18. Two-term Liberal Republican from a Democratic state and delegate to the San Francisco gathering which proclaimed the United Nations, thereafter an ill-advised, obsessive seeker of his party's presidential nomination.

19. At this time, Minister of Education, a foppish man who as a foppish Minister of Works, managing the 1953 Coronation, had referred to the Queen as 'My perfect leading lady'.

20. The Friar Bacon to whom is attributed the invention of gunpowder, something not pursued in the Humanities.

21. Better class of journalist, with wide scientific interests and understanding—had scoop on DNA; also ardent unilateralist and what used to be called a 'peacenik'.

22. It is a fearful thought that, even in 1934, the maker of this hapless speech won, here in Oxford, a First in English.

23. Reasonably presumed as family connection of *Rudolf Peierls* distinguished Nuclear scientist.

24. Ballet dancer and choreographer, gaining notable distinction at Sadler's Wells, created the ballet *Cranks*.

25. In due later course, reputable but flair-free Conservative Minister: Chief Whip, Paymaster, Northern Ireland Secretary, but missing speakership: dynastic figure—son of the unlucky Henry.

26. A heavy, unlucky, honest, donnish, and flair-free politician, his understandably unpublished diary is instructive but flat. Himself once a great theoretical Marxist, he was also, as Secretary of State for Commonwealth Relations, caught up in the late 1940s in the racial snarl-up of Seretese Khama's unspeakable marriage to a white woman which he was required to oppose. Later, in the 1964 general election, narrowly won by Labour, he would lose his Smethwick seat to a West Indian-bashing Conservative candidate, not much fancied by the Conservatives; then, in the by-election organized for this Foreign Secretary-outside-Parliament to return, he lost there as well. A man, at all times lugubrious (and with reason), he characteristically chose on such a night to talk about several other subjects, majoring on dollar reserves, before coming last and perfunctorily, to the Suez Crisis, up since the beginning of August, still running, and now a fortnight from stupendous explosion.

27. Most Labour people's favourite Tory before Kenneth Clarke. See next debate for one of the many reasons why. Would give up politics for administering a good, unsmart university—Leeds.

28. Would conclude long career of postings in the Far East, Africa, Central and South America, as Director-General of the US Foreign Service on the nomination of President Clinton: at this time a Marshal Scholar—and evidently getting it right.

29. Early (and valiant) modern atheist before it was fashionable. Lecturer in Psychology, Aberdeen University who, as it were, 'came out', arguing for atheism, as here, quietly and persuasively.

30. Surely this is to cite the categorical requirement of a categorical imperative without giving reason why the imperative should be categorical. Vote not given.

INDEX

Near East 94, 194
Neave, Airey 408, 570, 621
Neely, Mr 513, 528, 536
Nehru, Pandit 448, 467, 529
Nelson, E. T. 34, 50, 53, 59
Nelson-Williams, H. J. 465, 468, 471
Netherlands 490, 614
New Deal 620, 621
New York Stock Exchange 334, 418
New York Stock Market crash 449
New Zealand 121, 235, 282, 491
Newnham, H. A. 287
newspapers/press 20, 25, 30, 44, 56, 63,
    66, 71, 76, 84, 119, 121, 145, 173, 185,
    205, 220, 222, 228, 253, 256, 264,
    275–6, 282, 286, 301, 330, 331, 337,
    341, 350, 361–2, 366, 375, 384, 386–7,
    391, 400, 408–9, 417, 420, 424,
    437–8, 445–6, 455, 463, 473, 500,
    505–6, 516, 537, 543, 554, 556, 561,
    587–8, 590, 592–3, 602, 605, 612,
    615, 619–20, 626, 631, 637
Catholic Herald 622
Clarion 28
Daily Express 455, 490
Daily Herald 255, 262, 387, 409, 623
Daily Mail 1, 151, 298, 330–1, 387, 408,
    488, 562, 605, 620
Daily News 122, 175, 178, 605, 608
Daily Telegraph 387
Daily Worker 537
Economist 521, 616
Guardian 635
Globe 186
John Bull 1
John O'London's Weekly 612
Morning Post 124, 186, 289, 341
National Review 186
Nineteenth Century 203
Picture Post 615
Punch 124, 186, 601

Spectator 41
Standard 186
Sydney Morning Herald 614
Times 7, 64, 262, 300, 366, 387, 562,
    598, 614
Workers' Weekly 300
Newton, Isaac 619
Newton, Lord 185
Newton, Oscar 502
Newton, Tony 580
Nichols, J. Beverley 263, 270–1, 609
Nichols, P. R. S. 223, 225, 232
Nicholson, Godfrey 301–2, 304–6
Nicholson, Harold 443
Nicholson, Sir Arthur 240, 625
Nield, O. 228
Nield, W. A. 413
Nietzsche, Friedrich 306
Nigeria 617
Nightingale, L. 18
Nihill, J. H. B. 240, 252
Nobbs, Mr 323
Noble, R. H. S., 82, 86, 92, 94, 103, 111,
    115, 119
Noel, Hon Gerard 466–7
Nonconformists 48, 67, 82–3, 99, 103,
    108, 123, 125, 133, 138, 163, 501, 596,
    614, 617, 636
North Africa 488, 615
Northampton 186
Northcliffe, Lord 206
Northcote, Hon Edward 546, 553, 557
Northcote, Sir Stafford 634
Northumberland, Duke of 189, 616
Northwestern University 530
Nyasaland 582, 633
Nye, L. H. 311, 320, 325, 335

O'Brien, E. D. 369, 438
O'Brien, William 220
O'Broin, Leon 599